THE LEGISLATIVE BRANCH

THE
LEGISLATIVE
BRANCH

Paul J. Quirk
Sarah A. Binder

EDITORS

THE ANNENBERG FOUNDATION TRUST AT SUNNYLANDS

OXFORD
UNIVERSITY PRESS

OXFORD

UNIVERSITY PRESS

Oxford University Press, Inc., publishes works that further
Oxford University's objective of excellence
in research, scholarship, and education.

Oxford   New York
Auckland   Cape Town   Dar es Salaam   Hong Kong   Karachi
Kuala Lumpur   Madrid   Melbourne   Mexico City   Nairobi
New Delhi   Shanghai   Taipei   Toronto

With offices in
Argentina   Austria   Brazil   Chile   Czech Republic   France   Greece
Guatemala   Hungary   Italy   Japan   Poland   Portugal   Singapore
South Korea   Switzerland   Thailand   Turkey   Ukraine   Vietnam

Copyright © 2005 by Oxford University Press, Inc.

Published by Oxford University Press, Inc.
198 Madison Avenue, New York, New York, 10016
http://www.oup.com/us

Library of Congress Cataloging-in-Publication Data

The legislative branch / Paul J. Quirk, Sarah A. Binder, editors.
p. cm — (Institutions of American democracy series)
Includes bibliographical references and index.
ISBN-13: 978-0-19-517285-0 (alk. paper)
ISBN-10: 0-19-517285-X (alk. paper)
1. United States. Congress.   I. Quirk, Paul J., 1949–.   II. Binder, Sarah A.
III. Annenberg Foundation Trust at Sunnylands.   IV. Series.
JK1021.L44   2004
328.73—dc22   2005020891

Book design by Joan Greenfield
Copyedited by Melissa A. Dobson and Jonathan G. Aretakis

Printed in the United States of America on acid-free paper

CONTENTS

DIRECTORY OF CONTRIBUTORS

Paul J. Quirk (Editor)

Phil Lind Chair in U.S. Politics and Representation, The University of British Columbia

Dr. Quirk has written on a wide range of topics in American politics, including Congress, the presidency, presidential elections, public opinion, regulatory politics, and public policymaking. He has published in the *American Political Science Review*, the *American Journal of Political Science*, and the *Journal of Politics,* and served on the editorial boards of several major journals. His books are *Industry Influence in Federal Regulatory Agencies*, *The Politics of Deregulation*, and *Deliberative Choices: Debating Public Policy in Congress*. His awards include the Louis Brownlow Book Award of the National Academy of Public Administration and the Aaron Wildavsky Enduring Achievement Award of the Public Policy Section of the American Political Science Association.

Sarah A. Binder (Editor)

Professor, Political Science, George Washington University;
Senior Fellow, The Brookings Institution

Dr. Binder received her Ph.D. from the University of Minnesota in 1995. Her research focuses on the historical development of Congress and contemporary legislative politics. She is the author of *Minority Rights, Majority Rule: Partisanship and the Development of Congress, Politics or Principle: Filibustering in the United States Senate* (with Steven S. Smith), and *Stalemate: Causes and Consequences of Legislative Gridlock*. She is also a coeditor of the forthcoming *Handbook of Political Institutions*. Supported by the Carnegie Corporation, she is currently writing (with Forrest Maltzman) a book on the process and politics of federal judicial selection.

David T. Canon

Professor, Political Science, University of Wisconsin-Madison

Dr. Canon received his Ph.D. from the University of Minnesota in 1987. His teaching and research interests are in American political institutions, especially Congress. He is author of *Race, Redistricting, and Representation, The Dysfunctional Congress: The Individual Roots of an Institutional Dilemma* (with Ken Mayer), *Actors, Athletes, and Astronauts: Political Amateurs in the U.S. Congress*, several edited books, and various articles and book chapters.

Christopher J. Deering
Professor and Chair of Political Science, George Washington University

Dr. Deering is coauthor of *Committees in Congress*, editor of *Congressional Politics*, and has written a number of articles and chapters on congressional leadership, committees, and careers and on Congress's role in foreign and national security policymaking. He served as Director of Academic Planning and Development for the American Political Science Association's Congressional Fellowship Program and on the Robert Wood Johnson Health Policy Fellowships Advisory Board. He has served on the editorial boards for *Legislative Studies Quarterly* and *Congress & the Presidency*. As an APSA Congressional Fellow he served as a legislative aide to Senator George J. Mitchell. He also served as a Brookings Institution Research Fellow in Governmental Studies.

C. Lawrence Evans
Professor of Government, The College of William & Mary;
Coeditor, Legislative Studies Quarterly

A former Brookings Institution research fellow and APSA congressional fellow, Dr. Evans has authored two books, *Leadership in Committee* and *Congress Under Fire: Reform Politics and the Republican Majority*, as well as numerous articles about congressional decision making. With support from the National Science Foundation, he is currently conducting an historical study of party coalition building and the congressional whip system. In 1992–1993, he served as the staff associate for Chairman Lee H. Hamilton on the Joint Committee on the Organization of Congress. He received his Ph.D. from the University of Rochester in 1988.

John R. Hibbing
Foundation Regents University Professor of Political Science, University of Nebraska

John Hibbing has been editor of the *Legislative Studies Quarterly*, and president of the American Political Science Association's Legislative Studies Section. With Elizabeth Theiss-Morse he coauthored *Congress as Public Enemy: Public Attitudes toward American Political Institutions*, which won the APSA's Fenno Prize for the best book on Congress, and *Stealth Democracy: Americans' Beliefs about How Government Should Work*. His recent interests involve biology and the social sciences, especially the extent to which genes influence political attitudes and behaviors.

Gary C. Jacobson
Professor, Political Science, University of California, San Diego

Dr. Jacobson was a fellow at the Center for Advanced Study in the Behavioral Sciences. He is the author of *Money in Congressional Elections, The Politics of Congressional Elections*, and *The Electoral Origins of Divided Government*. He has served on the Board of Overseers of National Election Studies, the Council of the American Political Science Association, and the APSA's Committee on Research Support. Dr. Jacobson is a fellow of the American Academy of Arts and Sciences.

Frances E. Lee

Associate Professor, Political Science, University of Maryland

Dr. Lee received the American Political Science Association's E. E. Schattschneider Award for her dissertation. She was a research fellow at the Brookings Institution and an American Political Science Association Congressional Fellow. She has contributed articles to the *American Political Science Review, American Journal of Political Science, Journal of Politics,* and *Legislative Studies Quarterly,* and is coauthor of *Sizing Up the Senate: The Unequal Consequences of Equal State Representation,* which received the D. B. Hardeman Prize for the best book published on a congressional topic in 1998.

Forrest Maltzman

Professor, Political Science, George Washington University

Dr. Maltzman is the author of *Competing Principals: Committees, Parties, and the Organization of Congress, Crafting Law on the Supreme Court: The Collegial Game,* and numerous articles that look at decision making within Congress and the Supreme Court. He is currently working on a book with Sarah Binder that explores the dynamics of federal judicial confirmation and nomination politics and a project with Michael Bailey that explores the relationship between the president and the Supreme Court.

David R. Mayhew

Sterling Professor of Political Science, Yale University

Dr. Mayhew is Sterling Professor of Political Science at Yale University, where he's taught since 1968. He has held APSA Congressional, Guggenheim, Hoover National, and Sherman Fairchild fellowships, and is also a fellow of the American Academy of Arts and Sciences. He has won book prizes for *Congress: The Electoral Connection* and *Divided We Govern* as well as the Samuel J. Eldersveld Award for career work on political parties and the James Madison Award for career achievement in political science.

Eric Patashnik

Associate Professor, Politics, University of Virginia

Dr. Patashnik is the author of *Putting Trust in the U.S. Budget: Federal Trust Funds and the Politics of Commitment* and of essays in edited volumes and in journals such as *Political Science Quarterly, Governance,* and *Policy Sciences.* Dr. Patashnik has been a Research Fellow at the Brookings Institution and previously held faculty positions at Yale University and UCLA. He also served as a legislative analyst for the U.S. House Subcommittee on Elections.

David W. Rohde

Professor of Political Science, Duke University

Dr. Rohde has served as chair of the Michigan State University Political Science Department, editor of the *American Journal of Political Science,* and chair of the Legislative Studies Section of the American Political Science Association. He is an elected member of the American Academy of Arts and Sciences. He is the author of books and articles on various aspects of American national politics, including a series of twelve books (coauthored with Paul Abramson and John Aldrich) on national elections since 1980.

Eric Schickler

Professor, Government, Harvard University

Dr. Schickler is the author of *Disjointed Pluralism: Institutional Innovation and the Development of the US Congress*, which received APSA's Richard F. Fenno Award, and *Partisan Hearts and Minds* (coauthored with Donald Green and Bradley Palmquist). He has authored or coauthored articles in the *American Political Science Review, American Journal of Political Science, Legislative Studies Quarterly, Comparative Political Studies, Polity, Public Opinion Quarterly*, and *Social Science History*. He received his Ph.D. from Yale University in 1997.

Charles R. Shipan

Professor, Political Science, University of Iowa

Dr. Shipan is the author of *Designing Judicial Review: Congress, Interest Groups, and Communications Policy* and *Deliberate Discretion? The Institutional Foundations of Bureaucratic Autonomy* (coauthored with John D. Huber), which received the Richard F. Fenno Prize, the William Riker Award, and the Gregory Luebbert Award from the American Political Science Association. He has published widely on legislatures, agencies, and courts. Dr. Shipan was a research fellow at The Brookings Institution, a Robert Wood Johnson Scholar at the University of Michigan, and a visiting research fellow at Trinity College in Dublin.

Barbara Sinclair

Marvin Hoffenberg Professor of American Politics, UCLA

Dr. Sinclair's publications on the U.S. Congress include articles in the *American Political Science Review*, the *American Journal of Political Science*, and the *Journal of Politics* and five books. Among the latter are: *The Transformation of the U.S. Senate*, winner of the Richard F. Fenno Prize and the D.B. Hardeman Prize, and *Unorthodox Lawmaking: New Legislative Processes in the U. S. Congress*. Dr. Sinclair was an American Political Science congressional fellow in the office of the House Majority Leader in 1978–1979 and a participant observer in the office of the Speaker in 1978–1988.

Steven S. Smith

Director, Weidenbaum Center on the Economy, Government, and Public Policy, Washington University in St. Louis;
Kate M. Gregg Professor of Social Sciences and Professor of Political Science, Washington University in St. Louis

Dr. Smith has worked on Capitol Hill in several capacities and has served as a senior fellow at the Brookings Institution. He has authored or coauthored several books on congressional politics including *The Politics of Institutional Choice* and *Call to Order: Floor Politics in the House and Senate*, and most recently is working on books on party leadership in the U.S. Senate, the nature of party effects on congressional voting, and presidential-parliamentary relations in Russia.

Charles Stewart III

Department Head, Political Science, Massachusetts Institute of Technology

Dr. Stewart has been teaching at MIT since he received his Ph.D. in political science in 1985. His areas of expertise are congressional politics, electoral politics, and American political history. Dr. Stewart's most recent books are *Analyzing Congress* and *Committees in the U.S. Congress, 1789–1946* (4 vols., coauthored with David Canon and Garrison Nelson).

GENERAL INTRODUCTION:

THE LEGISLATIVE BRANCH AS AN

INSTITUTION OF AMERICAN

CONSTITUTIONAL DEMOCRACY

Jaroslav Pelikan

O F THE FIVE SUBJECTS BEING TREATED IN THE VOLUMES of this set as "institutions of American democracy"—the press, the schools, and the three branches of government—the topic of the present volume, the legislative branch, has the most obvious claim to that honorific title. The Congress, and in particular the House of Representatives before the Seventeenth Amendment of the Constitution, ratified in 1913, allowing direct election of senators, is known as "the people's branch." Etymologically, "democracy" means "governance by the people," or, in Abraham Lincoln's definitional phrase, "of the people, by the people, for the people"; and it is preeminently through the legislature that this governance is most directly exercised.

And yet there is in fact nothing essentially democratic, much less distinctively American, about "legislating." In all three of the ancient literary sources of American democratic ideology—the Hebrew, the Greek, and the Roman—the concept and the term can appear without any democratic point of reference. When Moses came down from Mount Sinai with the tablets of the Law, that made him preeminently *Moses legislator*, which is the technical term that Thomas Aquinas applies to him as a title.[1] But the narrative of the Book of Exodus makes it clear that nothing was further from the mind of this *legislator* than submitting the God-given legislation of the Ten Commandments to a plebiscite by the people of Israel, who indeed, when his absence had given them an opportunity to voice their own preferences, voted to make the golden calf "your gods, who brought you up out of the land of Egypt"; "as for this Moses," they could even say dismissively, "we do not know what has become of him" (Exodus 32:2–4 RSV). That particular expression of the *vox populi*, at any rate, was certainly the furthest thing possible from being the *vox Dei*.

More relevant than the biblical precedents are the classical ones, where the dual translation we give in English for the Latin *legislator* or the Greek *nomothetēs*, as "lawgiver" or as "lawmaker," encapsulates the problem: a "lawmaker" may function democratically, as ours do, but a "lawgiver" like Moses or Solon does not. In Book 3 of the *Politics* Aristotle does indeed argue that "legislation is necessarily concerned only with those who are equal in birth and in capacity." But famously (or notoriously) he is doing so in the course of considering the problem raised for the state by "some one person, or more than one . . . whose virtue is so preeminent that the virtues or the political capacity of all the rest admit of no comparison with his or theirs." For such extraordinary persons, he is forced to conclude, "there is no law—they are themselves a law," and justice requires that they be monarchs or go elsewhere.[2] Above all, it was the Roman experience of "legislation" to which the framers of the American Constitution looked for guidance as having, in the words of "Publius" (Alexander Hamilton) in *Federalist* 34, "attained to the utmost height of human greatness."[3] For as this and other repeated allusions to Rome in various essays of *The Federalist* make clear, Rome as example—and, even more in some respects, the history of Rome as cautionary tale—loomed before the eyes of the framers as they designed the United States of America and sought to formulate a constitution for it. There would seem to be more than chronological coincidence in the fact the year 1776 should have been the date both for the issuance of the Declaration of Independence and for the publication of the first volume of Edward Gibbon's *The History of the Decline and Fall of the Roman Empire*. It is noteworthy for the intention of the framers, therefore, that in addition to their use of the designation "republic" as their common name for the new political entity, which they were at pains to distinguish from a "democracy,"[4] they should have chosen the name Senate and Senator for the upper house of its legislature. For, as James Madison averred in *Federalist* 63, "history informs us of no long lived republic which had not a senate."[5] The acronym SPQR, *Senatus Populusque Romanus*, "the [Roman] Senate and the Roman people," which can still be seen today all over the modern city of Rome (even on its sewer covers), symbolized the power and prestige of the Roman Senate, as well as its identification with the common weal of the Roman people. Conversely, when those who, after what Erich S. Gruen has called "the last generation of the Roman republic,"[6] created the Roman empire as, in Gibbon's brilliant phrase, "an absolute monarchy disguised by the forms of a commonwealth," fastened upon the Senate as the venue for this farce, they "concealed their irresistible strength and humbly professed themselves the accountable ministers of the Senate, whose supreme decrees they dictated and obeyed."[7] History had taught the framers that if the American experiment was to work and if the Constitution was to help make it work, that kind of manipulation of the legislative branch by the executive branch had to be avoided at all costs—which was why, before so much as mentioning the executive, the Constitution gave the legislative branch pride of place when it opened with an Article I that reads: "All legislative Powers herein granted shall be vested in a Congress of the United States, which shall consist of a Senate and House of Representatives."

At the opening of the fifth chapter of this volume Sarah A. Binder raises this question of what we are doing "when we call Congress an institution of democracy." The answer on which she concentrates there is, quite properly, the decisive role of "elections—free, regular, and competitive—[as] the lifeblood of the institution"; and she marshals both historical materials and scholarly literature to back it up. The recurrence throughout this volume of the phrase "the electoral connection" from the title of David Mayhew's by now classic monograph of 1974[8] proves her point. Allowing for the controversial idiosyncracies of the electoral college system, the same answer—elections—could also be given to the question of what we are doing "when we call [the presidency] an institution of democracy": the president is chosen by the vote of the people, even though there can be a discrepancy between the popular vote and the electoral vote. It would not, however, apply to "the judiciary as an institution of American Constitutional democracy"; and, as the volume of this set on the judiciary indicates, the repeated effort to use elections as a device for making the court system an institution of democracy through the direct election of judges have often been superficial and, at best, ambiguous in their results. But pressed to its consequences, the question of Congress as "an institution of American Constitutional democracy" does go beyond elections, campaigns, and parties to entail the full range of practices, laws, and institutions that have come to characterize the legislative branch after two centuries of evolution. Some of the most important of these, interestingly, are not subject to election or to any other clearly "democratic" control.

That is true most notably of the congressional staff, in its relation both to congressional committees and to individual members of Congress. This volume does not include a separate chapter on the subject of staff, though it might well have done so, but the subject comes up repeatedly in one chapter after another. As Eric Schickler points out in Chapter 2, the size of congressional staffs nearly doubled after the Legislative Reorganization Act of 1946, which made the mission of each committee more precise. The steadily increasing specialization of the information needed to make workable laws has become evident above all in science and technology. No individual legislator, nor even all of them together, could reasonably be expected to keep up with the implications of new research and with the scholarly literature in the physical sciences and the biomedical sciences, which nevertheless continue to demand new and constantly changing legislation to address the practical and budgetary, and perhaps above all the ethical, issues being raised. Modern warfare, especially in the nuclear age, calls for a level of scientific expertise not only in the military itself (with all the problems this raises for recruitment and training), but in those who are called upon to make appropriations for the military and its governance. It would be absurd to extend the case by arguing that "elections" are "the lifeblood" also of the congressional staff as an "institution of American Constitutional democracy," and yet the modern Congress itself cannot function as such an institution without the support of skillful and dedicated staff. Such staff are needed also in relation to their counterparts in the executive branch. Much of the activity analyzed by Charles Shipan in Chapter 15 on the relation between the Congress and the executive branch as represented by the federal bureaucracy goes on at the level of staff members—none of whom, in either branch, attain and keep their positions through "elections—free, regular, and competitive." Only when, as in the Army-McCarthy hearings, staff are perceived as having flagrantly gone beyond the bounds of propriety do the media or the public pay attention to them. But the paradox is that, appointed by the authority of an individual legislator or an individual chairman, they do make a major contribution to the working of Congress as an institution of American Constitutional democracy.

As several of these chapters suggest, a similar contribution has come from those agencies that are charged with serving the Congress as a whole. The most venerable of these is the Congressional Research Service (CRS) in the Library of Congress, which is also the most visible mark of the Library *of Congress* as part of the legislative branch rather than an agency of the executive branch. Charged with providing research services for Congress and its members, the Congressional Research Service must not only respond to requests, many of them quite urgent, for the most reliable research data on a bewildering variety of issues as legislation comes under consideration, but perforce must also anticipate such requests long before they are actually made in order to have the material available when it is needed. These requests cover a vast range of subjects, far exceeding, as has been pointed out, the range of the curriculum of most universities. It is a tribute to the intellectual integrity of the Congressional Research Service that even in periods of intense partisanship it has been praised on both sides of the aisle for its objectivity and thoroughness. Similarly, as Eric Patashnik explains in Chapter 13, the Congressional Budget Office (CBO) "has maintained a strong reputation for neutrality and competence under periods of both Democratic and Republican legislative control," providing lawmakers for the first time with "independent, credible sources of budget information." If, in the persuasive case argued by Paul Quirk in Chapter 11, the business of the Congress is "deliberation," and if deliberation is to be based on something more substantive and more verifiable than opinion and ideology, such agencies for information as CRS and CBO, together with the congressional staffs, must be seen as essential "institutions of American Constitutional democracy" regardless of their being selected by other than democratic means such as elections.

The internal governance of the Congress raises a second cluster of issues involved in describing it as an institution of American Constitutional democracy. One of the unintended by-products of letting C-SPAN with its cameras into the chambers of Congress is the discovery, apparently for the first time by a considerable portion of the viewing public, that those chambers are largely empty much of the time. This does not look like the national town meeting as perpetuated in the mythology of high school civics classes. Where *are* the members of Congress, and what are they doing when they should be attending to the work of Congress? The short answer is that they are doing the work of Congress as an institution of American Constitutional democracy, much of which consists either of committee work or of representing the interests of their constituents.

It is certainly an exaggeration, probably an intentional one, to say, as Frances Lee in Chapter 10 quotes George B. Galloway, that "the typical Congressman is primarily a Washington representative for his district, not a national legislator." It was soon discovered that one of the deficiencies of the Articles of Confederation of 1777 was that they made the legislature, in Charles Stewart's apt phrase in Chapter 1, "an assembly of ambassadors." It nevertheless remains true also under the Constitution of 1787 that articulating the needs of one's congressional district and acting in Washington on behalf of constituents when they are aggrieved or when they are unable to find their way through the Washington maze is not only an essential component of the congressman's job description but an important part of how Congress functions as a democra*tizing* institution. Charles Shipan's delineation in Chapter 15 of the complex relation between Congress and the Washington bureaucracy, of which his discussion of the Federal Communications Commission (FCC) is an especially helpful clarification, documents some of the lines of communication and influence that help to give the Congress and its members this unique function. Members of Congress, therefore, are representing their constituents not only when they vote on the floor, but when they act as the voice of those who need to be heard.

Several chapters raise, in one form or another, a troubling question is relation to such representation. Frances Lee puts it perhaps the most directly in suggesting in Chapter 10 that "exclusive use of geographic representation seems increasingly anachronistic." And David Canon in Chapter 6 calls attention to the most dramatic contemporary exception to "geographic representation," which is the special connection between members of Congress, individually or in groups, and "racial and ethnic minorities," the Congressional Black Caucus (CBC) being the most prominent (but by no means the only) instance of that connection. For there are certain issues on which a member of the CBC will be acting—and should be acting—not only, perhaps even not primarily, on behalf of a geographically defined congressional district that elected them, but of a distinct segment of the broader American society. In response to the specter of "Balkanization" that this issue somehow always seems to summon up, it should perhaps be pointed out that in the Balkans, under the Austro-Hungarian Empire and especially since its breakup, it has traditionally been difficult or impossible to draw political lines corresponding to ethnic lines, so that even the atrocities associated with "ethnic cleansing" must be seen as misguided attempts to deal with a genuine problem.

More subtle and even more controversial than "the role of racial and ethnic minorities" is the role that "special interests" play, or should play, in identifying whom or what members of Congress represent, especially if we include as one such special interest the force of "ideology."

In the tradition of "umbrella parties," members may on some issues have greater ideological affinities with certain colleagues on the other side of the aisle and yet vote and be asked to act with their own party. As Barbara Sinclair puts it in Chapter 8, "certainly in the American context, ideological homogeneity never means identical legislative preferences." The limits of party discipline, in relation not only to the demands of "ideology" but ultimately to the dictates of conscience, have been responsible for some of the most wrenching moral and political dilemmas that members have faced, as their autobiographies sometimes attest.[9] When the position or "ideology" involved is not only a philosophical (or theological) doctrine, but a recognizable political entity or lobby, the dilemmas are compounded. Yet, as David Rohde reminds us in Chapter 7, on balance "most bills the Congress considers are neither partisan nor controversial"; therefore, as several of the chapters argue, it is rarer than the polemics would suggest for there to be a simple one-to-one correlation between any particular "special interest" and the voting record of a member or group of members, and this warning applies across the several states and across the political spectrum.

Often lost in the clashes between interests or ideologies is a force that, at its best, has served to make the Congress a "democratic institution" in the most profound sense: what Paul Quirk calls "bipartisan cooperation," or Christopher Deering "comity," or David Rohde "consensualist democracy." Significantly (and ominously), each these terms appears in the repeated discussions here of what has been lost when, in Forrest Maltzman's description, "the two parties are more ideologically opposed today than they have been for the past few decades," the eventual result of which he quotes Senator Patrick Leahy as labeling a "breach of trust." It is useful to be reminded again, in the very first chapter, of "the framers' distrust of factions . . . best expressed in *Federalist* 10 and Washington's Farewell Address." Faction was defined in *Federalist* 10 as "a number of citizens, whether amounting to a majority or minority of the whole, who are united and actuated by some common impulse of passion, or of interest, adverse to the rights of other citizens, or to the permanent and aggregate interests of the community."[10] By hindsight it does sometimes seem naive for them to have supposed that the republic would be able to get by without developing groups and ultimately parties "who are united and actuated by some common impulse of passion, or of interest," even though these parties would all insist that these are not "adverse to the rights of other citizens, or to the permanent and aggregate interests of the community" but supportive of them. The traditional "distrust of factions" continues to echo in the consistency with which members of both parties use "partisan" as a pejorative term—even when they are being stridently partisan.

But when Gary Jacobson describes a "remarkable increase in national party involvement in congressional campaigns" or when Sarah Binder speaks about a "decline in trust between the parties," this does assume what the Constitution does not assume, the existence of parties, and yet asserts at the same time that there are, and must be, limits to partisanship. Partly because of the difference in length of term and more profoundly because of its own internal rules and organization, the Senate has traditionally been thought of as promoting a spirit of "comity" and courtesy more easily than the House of Representatives. But the sheer passage of time together, enhanced by incumbency, has often helped create such a spirit also in the House. One of the implications, unspoken and yet "loud and clear," of these chapters is that if there would be chaos in the Congress without defined parties, there is also a line—difficult to draw, but far too easy to cross—beyond which party spirit must not be permitted to go without seriously damaging the very conception of Congress as an "institution of American Constitutional democracy." It is to be hoped that the wealth of material collected here and the seriousness of the analyses and arguments presented here will serve to advance and deepen "the people's branch."

Notes

1. Thomas Aquinas *Summa Theologica*, Part III, Question 22, Article 1 ad 3. See this and other references in *A Lexicon of Thomas Aquinas, edited by* Roy J. Deferrari and Mary Inviolata Barry (Washington, D.C.: Catholic University of America Press, 1948), 630, s.v. "legislator."
2. Aristotle *Politics* 111.131284a, translated by Benjamin Jowett (New York: Modern Library, 1943).
3. *The Federalist* 34, edited by Jacob E. Cooke (Middletown, Conn.: Wesleyan University Press, 1961), 210.
4. *The Federalist* 14, 83–89.
5. *The Federalist* 63, 426.
6. Erich S. Gruen, *The Last Generation of the Roman Republic* (Berkeley and Los Angeles: University of California Press, 1974).
7. Edward Gibbon, *The History of the Decline and Fall of the Roman Empire*, edited by J. B. Bury (7 vols.; London: Methuen and Company, 1896–1900), vol. 1, 68.
8. David R. Mayhew, *Congress: The Electoral Connection* (New Haven, Conn.: Yale University Press, 1974).

9. For a particularly thoughtful interpretation of such dilemmas by a U.S. senator of profound moral sensitivity, see Paul H. Douglas, *In the Fullness of Time: The Memoirs of Paul H. Douglas* (New York: Harcourt Brace Jovanovich, 1972), 35–37, 109–110.

10. *The Federalist* 10, 57.

INTRODUCTION:
CONGRESS AND AMERICAN DEMOCRACY:
INSTITUTIONS AND PERFORMANCE

Paul J. Quirk and Sarah A. Binder

T HE UNITED STATES CONGRESS IS THE MOST IMPORTANT
national legislature in the world. That is not because the United States
is the most powerful country. It is because, among the national legislatures of major countries, Congress is the only one that still plays a powerful,
independent role in public policymaking. In all other cases, the top political
executives—typically prime ministers and the cabinet—provide all the leadership. The legislature debates policies but ultimately, with rare exceptions,
enacts the executives' bills. Only Congress initiates legislation, makes decisions on major provisions, and says "no" to executive proposals. If the United
States was the modern world's first experiment with self-government, it is
now also the most enduring experiment with government by an elected
assembly.

The stakes are high on this legislative experiment succeeding. In view of
Congress's central role, its performance is obviously crucial to the health of the
American democracy. Yet Congress has long had severe critics. In the middle of
the twentieth century, Samuel P. Huntington argued that Congress had failed to
adapt to the modern world.[1] He suggested that Congress essentially step aside
and permit government by the executive branch. In a widely read book, Morris
P. Fiorina put forth the arresting proposition that Congress makes government
programs unworkable more-or-less intentionally—so that individual members
can get credit with their constituencies for fixing problems that result.[2] More
recently, many members and close observers have perceived that the health of
Congress has taken a turn for the worse, lamenting various pathologies of "the
broken branch."[3] Still, Congress has long had articulate defenders.[4] If nothing

else, such defenders can point to the fact that the American democracy is, broadly speaking, a manifest success.

This volume tackles basic questions about the performance of Congress as an institution of democracy. How well do Congress and its members serve democratic values and American constitutional principles? Which conceptions of those values does Congress implement, and which does it overlook or fail to realize? What are Congress's strengths and weaknesses in performing the tasks of democratic governance? What reforms, if any, are necessary to ensure the health and success of Congress as an institution of democracy in the future?

As the essays in this volume recognize, such questions are difficult to answer. Tradeoffs between conflicting values, differing and changing opinions about priorities, diverse policy issues and political circumstances, and varying accounts of why legislators behave as they do—among other difficulties—complicate efforts to make judgments about Congress's performance. The authors in this book do not offer absolute judgments. They implicitly take for granted widely held values and beliefs, for example that Congress should control budget deficits or that chronic gridlock is undesirable. The authors also make contingent judgments: for example, that *if* voters should hold the majority party accountable for national policies, then party leaders should have considerable leverage over rank-and-file members. Nevertheless, the essays embrace a common view of the signal importance of a healthy and independent Congress: The path to a healthy democracy, in the American context, leads through a robust Congress.

Judging Congress's Performance

Perhaps what is most remarkable about Congress in recent decades is how little has remained the same. From the mid-twentieth century to the present, among many other important developments, Congress essentially ceded war-making power to the president, attempted to reassert that authority with the War Powers Resolution in the aftermath of the Vietnam War, and then struck various bargains accepting half-way presidential compliance in particular conflicts. It has created elaborate new budget-making institutions to compete with the president in the making of fiscal policy, and experimented with a variety of rules to promote budgetary discipline. It has shifted policymaking power from seniority-entrenched standing committee chairs to rank-and-file members, and then to party caucuses and leadership. It has opened hearings and floor debate to more public scrutiny, especially through television coverage of debate. The Senate has reduced the number of votes required to invoke cloture, making it easier to end a filibuster, though senators have resorted to the filibuster with less provocation. The Senate has also exercised its authority under the Constitution to play a more assertive role in offering its "advise and consent," taking the opportunity to influence the policy orientations of the judicial and executive branches.

Elections have changed as well. Congress has twice legislated major new constraints on fund raising in congressional election campaigns, although declining both times to provide public funding. Incumbents have enjoyed increasing job security since the 1960s, squeezing out all but the most seasoned (and wealthy) challengers. Intervention by the courts and state legislators—as well as voting rights legislation passed by Congress—have brought ethnic and racial minorities to the House of Representatives in record numbers, though minorities and women remain vastly underrepresented in both chambers. Redistricting and other forces have eliminated all but a handful of truly competitive districts and have left most House seats safely in the hands of one party or the other. All together, these institutional and electoral forces have created a polarized partisan climate, one that pervades and molds nearly every task Congress is called on to perform.

These transformations are consequential for several reasons. First, they suggest that Congress's performance varies with the historical period, circumstances, and issues at stake. Political, social, and economic events shape the demands and desires of a diverse American polity, and thus create challenging and potentially conflicting expectations for Congress to meet. Second, they suggest that Congress's performance turns on the design and management of congressional institutions, matters that are decided mainly by its members and that are subject to considerable change. To evaluate Congress's strength as an institution of democracy, the chapters in this volume necessarily explore both the historical development of Congress's rules and practices and the contemporary implications of those institutional modes. Institutions shape Congress's performance, which in turn helps to reshape congressional institutions.

Critical Questions

Three questions are vital, therefore, to understanding how and how well Congress meets its responsibilities as an institution of democracy, and to discovering what conditions enable it to meet them most effectively. Although differing in their degrees of emphasis on the various questions, all of the authors in this volume address each of them.

How Do Congressional Institutions Develop?

First, the authors ask why senators and representatives choose the rules, structures, and practices they do. Scholars have given enormous attention to this question in recent years. They have stressed motives ranging from career advancement, to partisan advantage, to enhancing collective deliberation. Our understanding of the evolution of the House and Senate has developed considerably, but our knowledge of the dynamics of congressional change is uneven across the various formal and informal institutional structures and practices of

the two bodies. This understanding is important not only as a matter of historical interest. More important, deciphering the dynamics of institutional change
has direct bearing on prescriptions for future reform. If the design of Congress
helps to shape its governing capacities, then we must understand the political circumstances that make possible substantial reforms.

How Do Congressional Institutions Affect Performance?

Second, the authors ask how Congress's institutional arrangements affect its
performance as a democratic institution. They consider four aspects of this
performance:

1. *Constitutional stability.* How does the constitutional position of Congress
   today match the intentions of the framers of the Constitution and other
   conceptions of the constitutional system? Has Congress adopted expansive or restrictive views of its constitutional mandate and of its role in a
   separation-of-powers system? Does Congress effectively assert its constitutional authority, especially in relation to the president? Does it avoid
   encroaching on the other branches? Have its constitutional roles evolved
   constructively? Does it at least have reasonably definite roles, such that a
   constitutional system can be said to exist?
2. *Democratic values.* What balance does Congress strike between majoritarian and consensualist democracy? Between collective accountability of
   national parties and individual legislators' accountability to their states
   and districts? Are elections free, fair and competitive, with citizens able to
   make informed choices? Does Congress provide access to minorities and
   women? Does it conduct its affairs in a transparent, procedurally fair
   manner? Does it adopt and comply with measures that prevent corruption and the appearance of corruption? Does it explain itself effectively
   to the nation and the world?
3. *Policymaking.* Does Congress respond, and give reasonably proportionate
   weight, to public opinion, interest-group pressures, and other sources of
   policy demands? Does it work out cooperative arrangements to serve
   common or collective interests? Does it deliberate intelligently, taking
   account of relevant knowledge? Does it face up to the real effects of policy choices—or rather, for example, balance budgets through "smoke and
   mirrors?" Does it avoid gridlock?
4. *Adaptation and Reform.* Does Congress adapt effectively to long-term
   changes in American politics and society and the role of government?
   Does it respond to challenges to its success as a democratic institution—
   policy failure, severe internal conflict, scandal, and the like—by adopting
   institutional changes suited to deal with them? For example, does it
   devise effective methods for controlling budget deficits? Find ways to

subdue overly intense partisan conflict? Balance the opportunities for action by the majority and for participation by the minority?

Do Feasible Strategies for Reform Exist?

Third, the authors ask whether there are realistic opportunities for significant reform. The easier part of identifying potential reforms is identifying institutional changes that would probably improve performance, if adopted. The really hard part is matching up useful reforms with individuals or groups who might have both the capability and the incentive to get them adopted. For example, how could the Senate and the president cooperate to facilitate timely disposition of appointments? On what terms might Democratic senators consent to such measures during a conservative Republican administration? Similarly, are there ways to moderate partisan conflict over opportunities to debate and amend bills in the House, and why might majority party leaders offer the necessary accommodation? Of course no single dynamic of congressional reform applies to all aspects of the institution. Each author derives estimates of possibilities for reform from the record of prior reform efforts in the same area.

Plan of the Book

No single book can treat in detail the full range of institutional arrangements and political forces that shape Congress's performance. Each chapter in this book focuses broadly on a major topic about Congress. Three chapters treat the entire period of Congress's history. Most treat the period from the late 1960s to the early 2000s—almost four decades of sustained flux in congressional institutions—with particular attention to the most recent years. Taken together, the chapters offer—as much as any book of comparable length could offer—a comprehensive analysis of Congress. They do so with a view toward assessing and explaining how well Congress performs as a part of the U.S. constitutional system and, more broadly, as an institution of democracy.

To enhance the timeliness of the analysis, and bring to bear insiders' perspectives, several chapters draw on a pair of recent surveys conducted for the Institutions of Democracy Project. In late 2004 and early 2005, Princeton Survey Research Associates International conducted two surveys for use in this book (along with several other surveys undertaken for the larger project). Designed by Joel Aberbach, Kathleen Hall Jamieson, Mark Peterson, and Paul Quirk, one survey interviewed 247 staff employed in Congress members' offices; the other, 1,500 members of the general public. A summary of the findings and details of the methodology appear in the Appendix.

In Section I, the authors provide historical and constitutional perspectives on Congress's evolution as a democratic institution. Charles Stewart offers an original perspective on the age-old topic of Congress and the Constitution, exploring in what ways the framers' language and intentions remain central to the functioning of Congress, and in what ways they have been superseded or rendered irrelevant. Stewart identifies the institutional compromises at the heart of the constitutional compact, and explores how the resulting provisions have influenced—or not—the flow of congressional politics over the succeeding two hundred years. He shows how constitutional imperatives have been filtered through electoral and partisan trends that were unanticipated by the framers when they drafted the document in the late eighteenth century. Stewart's historical and constitutional perspectives set the stage for the volume's deep focus on the impact of institutions on Congress's democratic performance and potential.

Eric Schickler in Chapter 2 presents an analysis of the long-term development of Congress as an institution. The chapter explains the origins of Congress's formal rules of procedure and structural arrangements, including the committee and party systems in each chamber. Focusing on crucial junctures in Congress's history, Schickler pays special attention to the forces that have shaped the emergence of the modern House and Senate and their differences. Why have parties and committees evolved as two competing sources of policymaking, and with what consequence for the functioning of the institution? In Chapter 3, David Mayhew offers an innovative view of the changing roles of legislators. For Mayhew, Congress, in an important sense, is what individual members consequentially do—their "actions in the public sphere." In addition to legislating, members contribute to public discourse and political life by staging opposition to the executive, investigating, running for higher office, and undertaking other important actions. He traces the frequency of the various actions from the founding to the Bush Congress. He considers why and when members take on these activities and with what consequence for Congress's broader performance.

In Section II, the authors address the micro and macro politics of congressional elections. Gary Jacobson explores the rise in candidate-centered, media-based campaigns in recent decades—some of which are intensely contested by polarized political parties. Jacobson asks how congressional elections shape legislators' ambitions for and behavior in office, and how those very same ambitions and behaviors shape subsequent elections. Both candidates and parties matter in today's congressional elections, creating a tension between individual responsiveness by members to geographic constituencies and collective responsibility of the institution to the nation writ large. Jacobson evaluates the desirability and feasibility of reforms, offering a frank and realistic account of the hurdles faced by ambitious reformers.

Just as legislators' behavior is shaped by the electoral environment, Congress's legislative performance is shaped by broader trends in the electoral sphere. The rise and fall of the Conservative Coalition, the recurrence of divided government in the late twentieth century, the polarization of the political parties in recent decades—each of these electoral trends have affected Congress's internal organization and the dynamics of lawmaking. Sarah Binder explores in Chapter 5 how national electoral outcomes help to shape Congress's capacity for governance, with an eye to explaining the impact of electoral trends on Congress's policymaking performance over the past half-century.

In Chapter 6, David Canon turns to questions of representation, noting that the representation of racial minorities, especially African Americans, has increased multi-fold in recent decades. Still, the representation of ethnic and racial minorities continues to fall short of their demographic proportions. Canon explores the norms of racial representation that are prevalent in the United States today, and evaluates how well they are achieved. How have electoral reforms of past decades—created by Congress and interpreted by the federal courts—altered the functioning of and prospects for minority representation? What does the future hold for the faithful representation of black and Latino interests in Congress?

The rules, structures, and processes of the House and Senate take center stage in Section III. The structure of committees has been at the heart of the most prominent—including successful and failed—reform efforts over the past few decades. Today, some question whether committees are still able to play a meaningful role in the policy process, claiming the "crumbling" of congressional committees. Many point to the decline of authorizing activities, in favor of legislating by appropriations and the budget process. Others question whether policy bias emerges when committees formulate legislation. David Rohde tackles these and other concerns in Chapter 7, exploring the many complaints and challenges congressional committees in the House and Senate have faced in recent decades. How valid are these concerns? Are House and Senate committee systems adequately structured to ensure the incubation of policy and the formulation of solutions to public problems? Can an essentially decentralized committee system thrive in an era of polarized parties and an increasingly complex policy agenda?

Polarized parties come under scrutiny in Chapters 8 and 9, essays that explore the forces that shape the powers (and limits) of party leaders in the House and Senate. Barbara Sinclair focuses on the House, a chamber in which House party leaders in recent decades have augmented their powers and increased their reach into most aspects of legislative life. Sinclair details the activities of party leaders, explores why rank and file legislators tolerate centralized party control of the House agenda, and assesses the impact of strong party leadership on the performance of the House and Congress more broadly.

Steven Smith turns in Chapter 9 to party leadership in the Senate, exploring the ways in which the body's unique procedural rules and enduring history of individualism pose challenges for Senate parties and their leaders. Despite an era of polarized parties that has fueled the development of the two Senate parties, chamber leaders face enormous challenges in gaining control of the agenda and building winning coalitions. Why are the challenges of leadership so steep in the Senate and what costs to the chamber and to Congress are incurred by the limited powers granted to Senate leaders? Smith pays special attention to the prospects for Senate reform, showing how rules and practices inherited from the past constrain even the most ardent supporters of Senate change.

The chapters in Section IV pose numerous questions about Congress's performance in the formation of public policy. In Chapter 10, Frances Lee tackles the question of why legislators find it so difficult to put aside parochial interests in favor of the nation's general welfare. Under what conditions and by what means does Congress tame parochialism and group interests in the writing of national legislation? Can Congress legislate for the long-term, or is it doomed to enact short-term—often symbolic—fixes? Lee carefully explores the pressures that result from Congress's twin responsibilities of responding to diffuse constituencies and organizing itself for collective action. The balance between those chores has, of course, a strong bearing on our ultimate evaluations of Congress's governing capacity.

Acquiring information and deliberating intelligently is perhaps the most critical capacity of an independent legislature. Congress's difficulty in this regard is certainly not lack of information. Instead, the key challenges for Congress in achieving sound deliberation are the superabundance of information, the difficulties of assessing the validity and significance of the information it acquires, the obstacles to reflecting thoughtfully in a charged, competitive environment, and the temptation to employ facts and arguments as tools for manipulation. In Chapter 11, Paul Quirk explores the difficulties Congress faces in pursuing intelligent deliberation. Is Congress effectively organized and staffed to acquire and apply information and knowledge? Does it conduct debate in a manner conducive to learning? Could Congress deliberate better? These and other questions orient the chapter's evaluation of Congress's deliberative capacities.

Congress's performance in shaping public policy is also affected by its relationships with the executive and judicial branches. Any evaluation of Congress's performance in the realm of foreign affairs and war, for example, must necessarily examine how, when, why, and to what degree the Congress has shared its constitutional powers with the president, as shaped by the intervention of the federal courts. Christopher Deering takes up this challenge in Chapter 12, asking how well Congress discharges its role in foreign affairs (including security and trade policy) and in the making and ending of war. Exploring the historical trajectory of Congress's institutional capacities and political will for engagement in this area, Deering reminds us of the considerable variation across American history in Congress's perceived role in shaping decisions about foreign affairs and the conduct of war. He analyzes how congressional structures and partisan pressures today affect Congress's actions in this area, and assesses the viability of potential institutional reforms.

In Chapter 13, Eric Patashnik focuses on Congress's constitutionally-prescribed power of the purse—arguably one of body's most powerful weapons. Since the 1970s, that basic constitutional power has been augmented by a series of new budgeting rules that grant Congress a considerable role in checking the president's fiscal policy and in formulating the federal budget. Reforms since then have tinkered with budgeting rules, typically prompted by rising federal deficits. How has Congress's power of the purse weathered these statutory and economic changes of the past decades? Is Congress organized effectively to discharge its constitutional power of the purse? Do the rules of the game for budgeting and fiscal policy matter? What consequences do such rules and institutions have for the economic health of the nation now and in the years to come?

Congress's constitutional power to provide advice and consent for the president's appointments to the federal bench comes under scrutiny in Chapter 14. Many argue that increased partisanship and individualism in the Senate have transformed the process of picking new federal judges into a minefield. What are the stakes in advice and consent, and why and when did they become so high to senators and presidents? Forrest Maltzman explores both the causes of recent slowdowns and acrimony in the confirmation process for federal trial and appellate court judges, and evaluates the desirability and feasibility of potential process reforms.

Congress's relationships with the bureaucracy are scrutinized by Charles Shipan in Chapter 15. The growth of the administrative state poses enormous challenges for Congress's ability to oversee the actions of the unelected bureaucracy. Coupled with the expansion and centralization of presidential power and the assertiveness of federal courts, the bureaucracy exercises considerable discretion in its implementation of the business of government. To some, this poses little problem for legislators: they simply use their power of the purse to control the activities of the bureaucracy. To others, Congress's legislative capacities allow it to design the bureaucracy in such a way that Congress can secure the policy outcomes it desires. Still, others suggest that Congress lacks the ability to challenge the bureaucracy, constrained by its parochial focus or its informational disadvantages. Why and when is Congress significantly constrained in its effort to control the bureaucracy? What extent of delegation is appropriate and by whose standards and with what consequence?

The volume concludes in Section V with assessments of Congress's past, present, and future. John Hibbing looks in Chapter 16 outside the institution to probe the views and expectations of Congress held by the American public. By almost all accounts, the public chronically holds a dim view of the performance of Congress—even while strongly approving the constitutional design and often holding individual legislators in high regard. Indeed, recent scholarship concludes that Americans love democracy in theory, but often disdain it in practice. That paradox poses a critical problem of public legitimacy for Congress, an institution whose internal politics are highly permeable to the public. Why does the public generally distrust Congress, and what difference does it make that they do? What would it take to elevate public support for the institution, and would the potential benefits and costs of such reform be worth bearing?

C. Lawrence Evans in Chapter 17 takes on the central topic of explaining the dynamics of congressional reform. Close observers and leading participants in Congress often agree on the desirability, or even urgency, of significant institutional change. Yet efforts to promote such change encounter stiff resistance, from within and outside Congress, and usually fail. Evans explores the diversity of efforts to change Congress—ranging from campaign finance to committee and procedural reform. What are roots of reform in the historical and contemporary Congress? Why do political players inside and outside Congress often become engaged in promoting or fighting reform? Of most practical importance, under what conditions can reform succeed? And what are the consequences of Congress's success and failure in securing reform?

The volume concludes with a general assessment of Congress and its capacity for governance. Is Congress a healthy democratic and representative institution? What are the most important problems in its electoral and institutional worlds? What are the prospects for significant improvement? How do the politics of institutional design and reform constrain the opportunities for improving Congress's legislative and representative capacities? Evaluations of the health and welfare of Congress have implications for assessments of the strength of our representative democracy more broadly, raising the stakes for all who care or should care about Congress's present and future performance.

Acknowledgments

This book has benefited from extraordinary support from the Annenberg Foundation Trust at Sunnylands, the Annenberg Public Policy Center at the University of Pennsylvania, and Oxford University Press. One form this support took was the enlisting of an extraordinary cast of persons to provide assistance. Among the remarkably distinguished group of individuals on the National Advisory Board of the Institutions of American Democracy Project, former Representatives John Brademas and Lee Hamilton took special interest in this volume and gave us valuable advice at an early stage. A number of outstanding scholars, journalists, and practitioners attended one or more meetings at the Annenberg Center to discuss the larger project or to plan this volume and critique the chapters. These were: Stan Bach, Richard Cohen, Joseph Cooper, Kirk Victor, Tom Mann, Norman Ornstein, Elizabeth Rybicki, Don Wolfensberger, and Garry Young. Their assistance was invaluable. The project's Scholarly Director, Jaroslav Pelikan, provided remarkable insights. Kathleen Hall Jamieson conceived the entire project and offered guidance. The staff at the Annenberg

Center, especially Laura Kordiak and Annette Price, were remarkably helpful. Mary McIntosh and Princeton Survey Research Associates provided exceptional assistance with the survey of congressional staff, which Joel Aberbach, Mark Peterson, and Kathleen Hall Jamieson helped design. We received remarkably skilled and patient assistance from several individuals at Oxford University Press, Joe Clements, Anne Savarese, and Timothy DeWerff.

Notes

1. Samuel P. Huntington, "Congressional Responses to the Twentieth Century," in *The Congress and America's Future*, edited by David B. Truman (Englewood Cliffs, N.J.: Prentice-Hall, Inc., 1965).
2. Morris P. Fiorina, *Congress: Keystone of the Washington Establishment*, 2nd ed. (New Haven, Conn.: Yale University Press, 1989).
3. Richard Cohen, Kirk Victor, and David Baumann, "The State of Congress," *National Journal* (January 9, 2004). See also Thomas E. Mann and Norman J. Ornstein, *The Broken Branch* (New York: Oxford University Press, forthcoming).
4. Alfred DeGrazia, *Republic in Crisis: Congress Against the Executive Force* (New York: Federal Legal Publications, 1965); Arthur Maass, *Congress and the Common Good* (New York: Basic Books, 1983); Joseph Cooper, "Assessing Legislative Performance: A Reply to the Critics of Congress." *Congress & the Presidency* 13, no. 1 (Spring 1986): 21–40.

THE LEGISLATIVE BRANCH

IDEALS AND DEVELOPMENTS

1

CONGRESS AND
THE CONSTITUTIONAL SYSTEM

Charles Stewart III

THE AUTHORITY OF THE UNITED STATES CONGRESS springs from the Constitution. It is not an unbridled authority, but one that was hobbled by a dispersion of power, between the central government and the states, and among the several national institutions created by the Constitution itself. By design, Congress, and therefore national authority, should be effective only when these dispersed power centers happened to agree.

In assessing how the text of the Constitution continues to influence the contemporary Congress, it is important to understand that the underlying political reality that made this dispersion of power so easy for the framers to achieve came under attack once the founding generation had passed from the scene. The attack did not take the form of a bloody coup, but occurred gradually. Its form was the creation of a type of political institution that we now take for granted, the political party.[1]

The rise of political parties had a profound impact on how the Congress that was embodied in the "Framers' Constitution" acted on the political stage. Over time, individual members of Congress began to come to Washington predisposed to cooperate with their co-partisans and resist the opposition. Members of Congress increasingly had more reason to rely on the president for policy leadership—at least those members who shared his political party—and less reason to jealously guard the institutional prerogatives of their own institution. Political parties gathered up power and redistributed it from Congress to the president, and as a consequence political attention shifted from localities and states, toward the center. What the Constitution had dispersed, political parties collected back up in interesting and important ways.[2]

This chapter examines the important features of congressional politics and behavior that owe their origins to the text of the Constitution. The significance of the Constitution for understanding Congress is *not*, however, that it provides a set of detailed prescriptions. Even if this was the intent, the grand sweep of national politics has dashed those hopes. The significance of the Constitution for understanding Congress is that politicians and the people continue to take its words seriously, even in the foreign context of nationalized politics and robust political parties. This fact establishes a creative tension fully anticipated by the Framers, between the ambitions of politicians and the Constitution's unwillingness ever to allow power to be firmly rooted in one place.

The Centrality of the Constitution

The Constitution that was crafted in Philadelphia over the spring and summer of 1787 created an integrated system of government that was predicated on balancing power horizontally and vertically. The vertical balance was between a national government, with newly enhanced capacities, and state governments, which had operated under considerable latitude ever since independence. We now call this balance "federalism." The horizontal balance was between the various components of the new national government itself, which had hitherto been organized around a unitary structure. We now call this balance the "separation of powers."

There was a single fulcrum supporting both axes of balance, and that was the newly constituted United States Congress. Even knowing nothing about the actual deliberations of the Constitutional Convention, the centrality of Congress in balancing federalism and the separation of powers is immediately evident in the text of the Constitution itself—fully half of the Constitution was given over to Article I, which constructs Congress. Compared with the sparseness of details in the rest of the document, Article I provided a substantial blueprint for the body's electoral base and political authority. Reflecting the experience of nearly half a century of failed attempts to knit together the thirteen colonies (now states) along the Atlantic seaboard, Article I's provisions embodied a carefully crafted compromise that attempted to amass political authority sufficient to save the foundering experiment in independence from England.

Popular understandings of the Constitution often treat it as a seamless example of Enlightenment thinking applied to governing. It is true that the framers drew heavily on Enlightenment thinkers, especially Hume, Montesquieu, and Locke, who argued that the twin (but possibly conflicting) goals of effective government and individual liberty could best be achieved by dividing authority. Yet other governments around the world have also been established on the same Enlightenment principles, and almost all of them have come to different conclusions about how to balance power between the national and provincial governments, and between the various components of the national government itself. A tradition of ideas was important in guiding how Congress was initially placed within the American constitutional system, but ideas were not enough.

The additional ingredient was politics and a desire to fix a system whose failures were political, not intellectual. Yet to pull the national government away from absolute collapse, the framers had to face the facts as they found them. What did they face? For one thing, they faced a Congress that was failing to attract a quorum and incapable of enacting legislation that the states would voluntarily comply with. The result was increasing domestic instability and discredit among the great European powers, which were eager to forcefully reassert themselves along the eastern seaboard. Furthermore, they faced states that enjoyed the independence enshrined in the Articles of Confederation—large states, which were free to use their commercial power to exploit smaller ones, and small states, which valued the political equality that was enshrined in the Articles of Confederation.

In getting distrustful state governments to give up actual political power in return for a promise of greater stability and standing in the world, the Framers were helped by two things. First, public officials and other social elites understood the gravity of the situation and shared a vague sense about the new direction the national government needed to go in. They were open to a proposal. Second, the framers were deeply knowledgeable about the workings of popular governments on the North American continent and around the world. They were practical, informed, and moderate men. They inherited a tradition of popularly elected assemblies on the North American continent that stretched back a century and a half. Almost all of them had served in the Continental Congress or state legislatures in the preceding decade, and so had a working sense of how legislatures actually behaved in a wide variety of governing contexts. Some had served in unicameral legislatures, others in bicameral settings, and some in settings that could even be considered tricameral. Some came from states with an executive who had no check over legislative pronouncements, others from states whose governors enjoyed an absolute veto over legislative enactments, and yet others from states in between.

Using their knowledge and the political opening they enjoyed, the framers threaded the political needle they were given. The Constitution, and the Congress contained within it, was a significant departure from the past that was compelling enough to overcome the substantial doubts that were raised against it in the ratification debates.

And then life under the Constitution began. Although the text of the Constitution, especially Article I, was fairly prescriptive, it was not self-enforcing. It was tailored for a political system that was populated by economic and social elites whose ideas of a continental nation were only a dream. But politics migrated from elite to mass; the center of population wandered ever westward.

5

Some critical assumptions of the framers, about the role of political parties and the primacy of local governments in setting the agenda for national politics, turned out to be wrong. Viewed at a great distance from the Constitutional Convention, the influence of the Constitution on Congress has proven to be varied and not always obvious.

The purpose of this chapter is to examine how the Constitution has molded national politics, particularly the politics of Congress, from 1789 to the present. My attention is on the Constitution (particularly Article I) as a political document, in its conception and implementation. *In its conception*, the Constitution was political because its purpose was to address a political crisis; its ratification by the states was constrained by the stuff of normal politics. In the words of John Roche, the framers "were first and foremost superb democratic politicians."[3] Had the crisis been a different one or the constraints bearing down on ratification been different, the entire fabric of the Constitution would have been different.

The Constitution was political *in implementation* because the most important legacy of the document was in how it channeled political ambition. The most astute of the framers understood that over time their words would be reduced to mere ink on parchment. The most complete expression of this realization was provided by the author of *Federalist* no. 51:

> Ambition must be made to counteract ambition. The interest of the man must be connected with the constitutional rights of the place. It may be a reflection on human nature, that such devices should be necessary to control the abuses of government. But what is government itself, but the greatest of all reflections on human nature? If men were angels, no government would be necessary. If angels were to govern men, neither external nor internal controls on government would be necessary. In framing a government which is to be administered by men over men, the great difficulty lies in this: you must first enable the government to control the governed; and in the next place oblige it to control itself.

The text of the Constitution provided a set of initial conditions that attempted to connect the interests of politicians to the prerogatives of the institutions they inhabited. So long as the political interests of members of Congress were fundamentally at odds—against each other individually and against the president collectively—the framers believed that the federal government would be powerful enough, but not too powerful.

Yet this key assumption that undergirded so much of the framers' constitutional thinking became less and less relevant as the nineteenth century progressed. The political interests of individual members of Congress came to be less and less at odds; masses of members of Congress became the president's easy allies, not his great nemesis. What caused this change? A half century after the

Philadelphia convention, American national politics was transformed forever, by the rise of political parties that had explicit national ambitions, which in turn drew political attention toward the center. This transformation unleashed a direct assault on the fine details of the Constitution, which is most obviously manifest in the modern era by how presidential elections are conducted. The nationalization of politics brought forth by national political parties challenged the constitutional design by aligning the interests of disparate politicians so that ambitions were no longer neatly counterpoised.

Even so the neophyte observer on Capitol Hill ignores the written Constitution at his or her peril. As the world learned in 2000, just because the voters *act like* the presidential election is decided by the popular vote does not relegate the Electoral College to a nullity. Political parties have mitigated conflicting political ambitions, not eradicated them. The division of labor between the chambers and between Congress and the president has been breached but not destroyed. The fine details of the Constitution still have a material influence on how Congress legislates. Thus, a nuanced understanding of how the Constitution influences the role of Congress in today's politics requires us to be two-handed analysts. On the one hand there is the document that spells out important institutional details that continue to be relevant. On the other hand, some of these details have been contradicted with impunity or have fostered a style of national politics that was unanticipated by the framers.

The remainder of this chapter spells out this argument in more detail. We start by stepping back in time, to the Constitutional Convention and the years immediately preceding it. We then examine how various compromises at the Convention influenced subsequent congressional politics in four different realms—in representation, the institutional capacity of Congress, bicameralism, and political competition with the executive.

The Crisis of Governance and the Convention

The Constitutional Convention[4] created a new form of national government for the United States but, of course, it did not create the first form of national (or central) government, nor did it create the first legislature. Popular assemblies in Virginia and Massachusetts had their start more than a century before Philadelphia. Even the proprietary colonies, like Pennsylvania, had popular assemblies with real authority. Before the Revolution every colony had a functioning local legislature that bore major responsibilities for local governance.

Legislative Experience before the Constitutional Convention

At least a minimal colony-wide governmental infrastructure was in place before the Revolution—Benjamin Franklin's appointment as deputy postmaster

7

for the British colonies in the 1750s is the best known example of this, but there are others. Before relations between the colonists and the crown turned sour, several plans for a united assembly linking the colonies had been floated. Franklin enters the picture here again, as the prime architect of the so-called Albany Plan of Union, which proposed a unified "Grand Council" of all the colonies, apportioned by population and wealth, which would raise taxes and be responsible for common defense and the encouragement of trade. This idea was rejected by both the crown and colonial assemblies, all of whom recognized the Grand Council as a potential rival for power.

It was with this experience—effective local assemblies but distrust of the greater authority of a "national" assembly—that the colonies participated in the First and Second Continental Congresses. The Second Congress continued as the official national legislature under the Articles of Confederation and Perpetual Union, which were proposed on 15 November 1777 but not ratified until 1 March 1781. The Articles reflected the supremacy of local authority and suspicion of centralized power by declaring that the thirteen states had entered into a "firm league of friendship." Friends don't push each other around, and the formal structure of Congress embodied in the Articles reflected what the body truly was—an assembly of ambassadors.

In imagining what governing was like under the Articles, it is unfortunate that its national legislature shared the same name with the American national legislature under the Constitution—Congress—because the national legislature under the Articles was nothing like the national legislature we know under the Constitution. Under the Articles, members of Congress were effectively ambassadors. They were elected by state legislatures, paid by state legislatures, and could be recalled by state legislatures. State delegations ranged in size, but that did not matter for voting, since each state only had one vote, regardless of how large it was or how many delegates were in attendance. For any decision of consequence, the Congress depended on the state legislatures to voluntarily pass the implementing legislation. Congress could not directly lay and collect taxes, even when it had international obligations to discharge.

Although we now recognize that Congress was hamstrung under the Articles of Confederation, the early returns were not so bad. Congress was fairly successful in navigating the crisis of the Revolutionary War. The war was prosecuted, foreign countries were willing to extend credit, revenues were more-or-less raised, and legations were sent to foreign nations to conduct foreign policy. The generals and diplomats sent forth under the authority of Congress defeated the English and gained independence from the crown.

In the early days it appeared that the claims of the most radical Republicans would prove true. Great resources, men and money, could be gathered together by the central government *asking*, not *demanding*, that the states face up to their mutual obligations.

8

The sacrifices of local interests to the common good ceased with the peace, however, exposing the infirmities of a national government that was built solely on friendship and volunteerism. The Treaty of Paris, which formally ended the war with England, required the United States to compensate loyalists for economic losses inflicted during the Revolution. Congress had no means to implement this requirement directly; the states themselves refused to comply, giving entree to England to retaliate by refusing to decamp from forts it occupied in America's western frontier. State delegations to Congress regularly eviscerated the financial plans of the Superintendent of Finance, Robert Morris; only a small fraction of the taxes requested of states were ever forwarded to the national treasury. States risked trade and shooting wars—on the east as they passed predatory tariffs against each other's goods and on the west as they fought competing frontier land claims.

The Constitutional Convention Deliberates

The so-called Shays's Rebellion of 1786–1787 is usually viewed as the precipitating event of the Constitutional Convention of 1787. Had Shays's Rebellion not occurred, some other event would have taken its place, since men of affairs were already debating how to achieve a more coherent commercial and military presence on North America. Shays's Rebellion became the symbol for those who already believed that the existing governing arrangements for national affairs had failed to secure stable governments within and between the states.

The fifty-five delegates who convened in Philadelphia in the spring of 1787 were practiced politicians, unlike the more radical assembly that had met a decade before, in the same room, to declare independence from England. Of these, forty-six had served in a state legislature and forty-two had served in one of the Continental Congresses.

The Philadelphia debates were preoccupied with questions of power sharing along two dimensions of institutional design—power sharing among the states and between the branches. James Madison's "Virginia Plan," which was presented almost immediately upon the assembly of a quorum, was aimed at consolidating national political power in one institution, the Congress, and basing political power on population, rather than on state equality. The legislature was to be bicameral, but it was clear where political power ultimately lay—with the lower chamber. States would be represented in both chambers in proportion to their population. The people would elect the lower chamber; the lower chamber, in turn, would elect the upper chamber. Both chambers would then elect the executive. Compared with the national government under the Articles, this was about as different as one could get.

The Virginia Plan was unabashedly nationalist, moving commercial and foreign policy firmly within the orbit of the national government. There was no better sign of its strong nationalism than the proposal that Congress be given the right to veto acts of state legislatures.

Although most delegates had qualms about the particulars of Madison's plan, it was adopted as the working outline, with details to be hammered out over the course of the convention. This was not an enthusiastic endorsement, a fact that became clear as debate proceeded to perfect the plan. Majorities could never be mustered to scuttle Madison's blueprint, but the political limitations were obvious. A government apportioned by population would strip smaller states of their political power in national councils. While no one quite knew what the various state populations were, it was assumed that variation was substantial. (Eventually, the 1790 census would reveal that the largest state, Virginia, was more than ten times more populous than the smallest, Delaware. The four largest states held more than half the population.)

A proposal by a collection of small state delegations, termed the New Jersey Plan, essentially returned the national legislature to the status quo under the Articles. After long debate, it failed. A proposal by Roger Sherman to compromise on representation was ignored at first, as well. But, as debate proceeded, it became clear that the actual choice was between compromise on the one hand and adjournment and disunion on the other. Disunion would mean a fate worse than a return to dominance by England, since Spain and France were now eager to jump in and carve out spheres of influence for themselves as well. Compromise was the only way out.

To appreciate the hurdles the delegates faced in reaching a compromise, it is useful to remember that many delegates were simultaneously members of the Confederation Congress—the legislature whose structure faced radical surgery.[5] Others were leading members of the state legislatures that had elected the members and indirectly called the shots in the existing Congress. They were redistributing power among themselves. Even if they regarded this exercise more patriotically than typical mortals, they understood fully that they would have to leave Philadelphia and sell this redistribution to others who were not in the room and who would scrutinize the plan more skeptically.

The value of Sherman's "Connecticut Compromise" became apparent through the arduous and often unfocused debate of the summer. Importantly, it retained union, which in the long run favored the smaller states who would have suffered the most from the predatory practices of the larger states had disunion in fact occurred. The formula of the compromise was the familiar design that has been handed down through the ages: a lower house apportioned by population, an upper house of equal representation of the states, and an executive elected independently of both through a method that was a modification of weighted voting.

Deciding on a scheme to apportion voting power in Congress among the states was the major preoccupation of the delegates during the summer of 1787, but it was not the only topic of debate that pertained to the overall power and responsiveness of the new national government. The delegates were also concerned about how to control the newly empowered national government once it had been elected and had assembled in the nation's capital.

The delegates generally agreed that the national assembly needed to be more than a congress of friends. But the delegates also worried that a national assembly with real teeth would upset the system of checks and balances they all valued as children of the Enlightenment. The structure of the inter-branch compromise was also similar to the compromise on representation: slightly different institutions were laid on top of each other and required to function simultaneously. In this case those institutions were the two coequal legislative chambers and an executive elected independently by the states.

The complexity of the compromise that needed to be worked out caused the Constitutional Convention to deliberate for four months. Yet by focusing on the contentious issues of representation and institutional balance, we risk forgetting that some issues were never in dispute at the Convention. Included among these noncontroversial provisions were those that made the two chambers the regulators and judges of their own elections and the writers of their own rules. In other words, both chambers of the new Congress were given the authority to construct independent institutions. Because the Congress of the Confederation distinctly did not have this authority, and because so many of the convention delegates had direct experience with the existing Congress, it is doubtful that these provisions were snuck into succeeding drafts of the new constitution surreptitiously.

Across the range of opinion in Philadelphia about the relative strength of the central government and its legislature, no one doubted that the new legislature needed to be in a position to better protect itself organizationally. Being able to regulate and judge elections would allow the two chambers to guard against states using their Article I authority to prescribe how their members of Congress would be elected to sneak back in state legislative election of lower house members or the recall of senators. Being able to establish chamber rules would allow policy majorities in either the House or the Senate to shape the internal rules of the institution to their advantage, even if it meant running roughshod over the rights of chamber minorities.

The convention was the start. In a whirlwind of activity, within the next two years the Constitution was ratified by state conventions and congressional elections were held. The constitutional story begun in Philadelphia continued when the first Congress under the Constitution convened in New York in April 1789. As a comprehensive blueprint for amassing and using national power, the written document was a starting point, but only a starting point. In the move from Independence Hall to Federal Hall, the Constitution left the hands of the Framers and entered the hands of ambitious politicians for whom the document was both a means and an end. For the remainder of this chapter, we consider how the important details written into the Constitution in Philadelphia have affected congressional politics in the 217 years that have followed.

The System of Representation

The legitimacy of the Congress of the Confederation during the Revolution rested on how well it prosecuted the war. Any national legislature rises in the estimation of its citizens during times of foreign crisis, to the degree it manages the crisis to a successful conclusion. Sources of democratic legitimacy during peacetime are different, and the Congress of the Confederation lacked the most important of those sources—it was not popularly elected. The Constitution fixed that defect.[6]

But in fixing that defect, the framers unwittingly planted a seed that would, over time, lead to a transfer of power from states and localities to Washington. That seed was the reliance on state legislatures to structure the electoral environment for members of Congress, both the House and Senate. Simply said, the states legislatures passed the laws that determined things like whether House members would run in districts and when elections would be held. The framers assumed that this would allow the states, as sovereign entities, to maintain a major say in how they were represented in Congress, even if that say was not as direct as it had been under the Articles of Confederation. However, the state legislatures were subject to the same forces that gave rise to the national political party juggernaut that rolled during the Jackson years. As a consequence, the states, through their legislatures (and governors), became willing participants in the steady accretion of actions throughout the nineteenth century that allowed members of Congress to largely come out from under the collective thumbs of the state governments.

If we put out of our minds what we know about modern congressional elections and simply read the text of Article I that pertains to elections and representation, we notice a strong lingering role for the states in these elections, even as the locus of power was being pulled away from them. Most obviously, senators were elected by state legislatures. But the regulation of House elections also had a strong state-centered flavor. Seats in the House were apportioned to states in proportion to population, with very little prescribed about how states would structure House elections. Nothing required states, for instance, to divide themselves into districts.

One feature of the Constitution that has not held up as predicted has been this strong state-centered flavor of representation within Congress. Best known is how the Senate eventually evolved to embrace popular election, but the House as well has a story of how the state-centered scheme of representation was gradually eroded.

Throughout the nineteenth century, four trends conspired to transform House elections, moving them from local, state-centered affairs to more-or-less national events, tinged by local concerns. These trends were (1) the rise of political parties, (2) the expansion of the electorate, (3) the rise of districts, and (4) the coordination of the electoral calendar. In designing the form of representation in the Constitution, the framers failed to anticipate the two most important developments in mass electoral politics of the nineteenth century, the rise of political parties and the expansion of the electorate. The two developments were, of course, related.

Political Parties, the Expansion of the Electorate, and Congressional Representation

The framers' distrust of factions is well known, best expressed in *Federalist* no. 10 and Washington's Farewell Address. Still, this dislike of factions was most often understood within a framework of limited suffrage. Party sentiment first emerged in the conflict between followers of Jefferson and Hamilton; this conflict occurred mostly within the halls of government, at a time when the franchise was confined mostly to an elite level. This factional animosity spilled over into elections, but it did not fundamentally challenge the system of elite-based politics.[7] That challenge would come in the next political generation, as Andrew Jackson and his followers worked to push the doors of white male suffrage wide open.

The Jacksonian expansion of the electorate had a distinctly partisan purpose, to provide an electoral base for the Democratic Party as a national organization. As a *national* organization, the leadership of the Democratic Party worked hard to suppress divisive regional issues, particularly slavery.[8] The Democrats, and then the other parties that followed them, further worked to coordinate their electoral efforts. Critical to this coordination was the creation of political parties that muted their programmatic characters.

The Jackson–Van Buren system of office-seeking political parties also relied on a dramatic expansion of the electorate. The initial electorate was quite small, generally restricted to property owners. The early nineteenth century saw a gradual expansion of the franchise, abetted most importantly by the actions of Andrew Jackson and his supporters in the sequence of elections from 1824 to 1832. The immediate goal of this expansion was to sweep Jackson into office and keep him there. It was accompanied by the change in many state laws to require the popular election of presidential electors. This president-centered expansion also had immediate consequences for House elections.

The contours of this expansion are illustrated nicely in the congressional turnout in New York State throughout the nineteenth century. Between 1824 and 1828 alone, the size of the New York congressional electorate grew by 40 percent; from 1800 to 1852 it grew by tenfold over a period when its population grew sixfold.[9]

Over time, developments in the states that expanded the franchise and facilitated the rise of political parties undercut the electoral world on which the
framers had reached a compromise on representation.

The Decline in State Electoral Idiosyncrasy

When the framers met, state elections were idiosyncratic. They were held on
different days. Districting schemes spanned the waterfront, from at-large to single member districts. States even had majority election requirements that no
longer exist in the United States. Massachusetts, for instance, required candidates
for the House to win an absolute majority of all votes cast, leading to many cases
in which election after election would have to be held to fill a seat, because of the
failure of anyone to achieve a majority.

The earliest House elections were only local elections to a limited degree.
Three states, Connecticut, New Hampshire, and New Jersey, elected representatives through a general (at-large) ticket. At-large elections to the House persisted
until the 1840s, when the Apportionment Act of 1842 finally required single
member House districts.[10]

Another way in which local electoral heterogeneity gave way to national uniformity was in setting the Election Day. The current first-Tuesday-after-the-first-
Monday-in-November Election Day was set for president in 1845, but it was not
extended to the House until 1875.[11] Until a unified date was established, elections
could be held as early as twenty months before a Congress convened; occasionally
states did not hold their elections until Congress had already convened.

As congressional election days became synchronized to correspond with
the presidential election, the obvious happened—election outcomes became
synchronized. The electoral fates of rank-and-file members of Congress (MCs)
became linked with the fates of the presidential candidates and incumbent
presidents.[12]

The end result is House elections that are simultaneously *local* affairs and
national affairs, but not *state* affairs.

The Decline of State Legislative Responsibility for Senate Elections

The mediating role of states in the representation of the Senate eventually
disappeared, as well.[13] The Framers explicitly excluded from the Constitution a
mechanism for senators to be recalled by the states that elected them. Without
recall, state legislatures lacked the mechanism to instruct senators (another practice under the Articles of Confederation). Not that states did not try. Up until the
advent of popular election in 1913, state legislatures continued to address
Congress, beginning with the stereotyped phrase "Be it resolved that our
Senators in Congress are hereby instructed, and our Representatives are
requested, to vote for . . ." Legislatures did instruct, but senators were free to
ignore the instructions. They could rely on the long term of office before they

would be held accountable, and the hope that the next election would return a legislature controlled by a friendlier majority.

Failing to develop an effective instruction mechanism, some states attempted a different tactic, censure and attempted forced resignation. This mechanism was first used successfully against John Quincy Adams, whose vote for the Embargo Act became a campaign issue in the next Massachusetts state election. The new anti-Adams legislature boldly elected a successor to Adams six months ahead of time. Offended, Adams resigned. Others would follow a similar fate, but only those with tender enough sensibilities, or disgust with politics back home.

Forced resignations had sporadic success in the antebellum period, but gradually faded from the scene, disappearing after the 1840s. As William Riker argues, instructions failed "through lack of a dependable substitute for recall. Forced resignations, the only available sanction, required that elections turn on the issue of obedience and that senators love honor more than office. By mid-century, neither requirement could be met. Voters quite reasonably refused to consider form more than substance. . . ."[14]

Without a formal mechanism reliably subordinating senators to their state legislatures, they were free to build their own political bases. As national politics popularized in antebellum America, senators joined the fray.

The apotheosis of this trend gave rise to one of the great moments of popular politics in the antebellum period, the Lincoln–Douglas debates. What were Lincoln and Douglas running for? The Senate. But why would senatorial candidates be stumping the state of Illinois in 1858, if it was the state legislature that would do the electing?

The Lincoln–Douglas debates were occasioned by the first instance in which a state party convention endorsed a senatorial candidate and then sought out state legislative candidates who would serve as pledged electors. This practice caught on, leading many (but not all) states to adopt the *popular canvas* for Senate. As the nineteenth century came to a close, even when parties did not endorse senatorial candidate ahead of time, state legislative elections that corresponded with the election of a senator were approached as shadow senatorial contests. In the Gilded Age, the descriptive relationship between senators and state legislatures stood the normative relationship on its head. Party bosses like Matthew Quay, Nelson Aldrich, Roscoe Conkling, and Thomas Platt, if anything, controlled the state legislatures, not the other way around.

In the *Federalist* no. 63, James Madison predicted that the Senate would serve as an "instrument for preserving the residual sovereignty" of the individual states. Yet, eventually lacking subservient political ties to the state legislatures, the Senate failed to serve this role. Hence, it is not surprising that once pressures built in the late nineteenth century for the *de jure* popular election of senators, state legislatures were on the forefront of efforts to eliminate the federalist charade. When the U.S. Senate proved recalcitrant in moving the popular election amendment through the Congress, states acted to reinforce the popular tie of senators to the people—first through attempts to manipulate the nomination and election of senators, and then through petitions to call a constitutional convention, if necessary, to move the amendment along.[15]

Policy Consequences of Different Constituencies

Developments in the larger polity have conspired over the past two centuries to homogenize national politics, making the Senate and the House less distinct as representative bodies. Still, it would be a mistake to conclude that senators and representatives are identical, either as individual candidates or as collective members of two legislative chambers. Senators serve longer terms than House members and represent larger constituencies. Certainly these differences make a difference.

But the differences are subtle. Ironically enough, longer terms probably do not give senators a significantly longer time horizon than House members. The reason is that since the Seventeenth Amendment brought the popular election of senators in 1914, the longer term and greater prestige of being a senator draws more robust competition for Senate seats than for House seats. Senators are more likely to be defeated for reelection than House members, and they are more likely to retire at the end of their terms. The consequence is that over a six-year period, House members and Senate members have roughly the same survival rates. In addition, the greater electoral vulnerability of senators compared to House members has meant that by some measures, preferences represented in the Senate have been more volatile than in the House.[16]

On the other hand, there is ample evidence that the equal state apportionment of the Senate has led distributive coalitions in Congress to be more broadly dispersed geographically than if the Senate were apportioned by population.[17] But on the major issues that tend to split the political parties and hold the attention of national electorates, there is no correlation between state size and the ideologies of senators, nor has there ever been.

Therefore, the electoral system in the United States has evolved in such a way that the original representational compromise that made the Constitution possible is mostly irrelevant. There are no issues that divide small and large states, and individual state idiosyncrasies are not what they once were. This is not to say that the different electoral schemes in the two chambers are inconsequential, only that they are less consequential than they once were and, in some ways, may be consequential in ways diametrically opposed to the expectations of the framers.

The Flowering of Internal Legislative Capacity

A political institution will be powerful and effective to the degree it can match the speed and effectiveness of competing nodes of political authority in the polity. This effectiveness does not come automatically. The institution's members must be induced to put in long hours of tedious work to investigate policy alternatives, to narrow down the possibilities to those that are technologically feasible, and then to investigate the political considerations and find solutions that will actually garner majority support. A major goal of the framers was to invest the new Congress with the possibility that it would develop into an effective political institution that could channel its members' energies in productive ways.

The Continental Congress was ill-constructed for effective action. For all practical purposes it could act only if a consensus emerged among all the states. Therefore, Congress was reluctant to pass rules that would be considered "coercive" or in the least way perceived as favoring one perspective over another. Congressional rules were rather loose, befitting an institution that valued consensus. Measures introduced on the floor were considered in the order they were submitted, regardless of how important they were. They were referred to ad hoc committees for study that were newly constituted for each measure; a committee appointed to consider a matter one day was unlikely to be appointed again to consider a similar matter the next. Once the matter returned to the floor, neither the original proposal nor the committee's recommendation had any privileged position. Consequently, it was possible for floor proceedings to unravel. This, in turn, led to frustration on the part of members, as their hard work on committees and behind the scenes frequently came to naught. Frustration over the inability of Congress to productively focus the considerable talents of its members finally led to high levels of absenteeism, to the point that Congress had a difficult time even getting a quorum to legislate.[18]

Perhaps the best example of how floor proceedings could unravel in Congress under the Confederation is what happened when members reacted to being attacked by mutinous troops in the summer of 1783. Retreating from Philadelphia to Princeton, Congress turned its attention to where members would meet next, that is, where the capital would be relocated to. They first decided to vote for each state, starting with New Hampshire and moving south; the capital would be located in the state that got the most votes, provided it received at least seven votes.

No state received more than four votes to become the site of the new capital. A new voting scheme was called for.

A motion was introduced narrowing down the options to two sites, one on the Delaware River and one on the Potomac. An amendment was made to move the capital elsewhere; under the Congress's voting rules, the first vote was whether the original language would stand. Only four states voted to retain the original language, so a blank was inserted instead. But no actual location ever received the required seven-vote majority. The blank remained. Abandoning the idea of a single location, a motion was then made to have two capitals, in Trenton and Georgetown. This finally passed, but ended up being so unsatisfactory that

Congress eventually decided to move back to New York temporarily and start voting on a permanent location for the national capital again.

To the modern observer of Congress, the organizational state of the Confederation Congress must certainly be a puzzle. Capitol Hill now is a city-within-a-city, largely because of the committees that so dominate the legislative process. In the House, the rules are such that bare majorities can cut off debate and amendments from minorities; *in extremis*, the majority party can hold open roll call votes long enough to twist arms and carry the day.[19] Even the Senate's cloture procedure, which has regularly been considered the culprit in delaying Senate floor action, has more teeth in it than what was allowed in the Congress of the Confederation. How is this possible?

Article I, section 5, clause 2 makes this possible.[20] It states, "Clause 2: Each House may determine the Rules of its Proceedings, punish its Members for disorderly Behaviour, and, with the Concurrence of two thirds, expel a Member."

This provision appeared in the first report of the Committee on Detail and was never challenged. The framers had intimate experience with a Congress that could get tied in knots when majorities were unable to work their wills. They were set on ensuring that at least procedural barriers would not stand in the way of action.

It took a while for Congress to take full advantage of this provision. In the years immediately following the Founding, a "Jeffersonian ethos" emerged that opposed strong-armed parliamentary tactics. So, early procedures in Congress actually resembled practices in the Congress of the Confederation, especially the practice of relying on ad hoc committees that had little autonomy in considering legislative proposals. Still, the groundwork was laid for a more purposive set of rules. As majorities became receptive to a more structured set of rules, some of which might favor some legislators over others, no constitutional barrier stood in the way. Thomas Jefferson, in his copious free time as vice president, wrote a set of legislative procedures that were consistent with the principles of early public choice theorists such as the Marquis de Condorcet. *Jefferson's Manual*, written for the Senate, was rejected by that body, but embraced by the House. The House also was the first to embrace standing committees as a way to enhance its competency in battles with the executive branch, when it established the Ways and Means Committee in 1789.

The nineteenth century saw the steady accretion of formal and informal institutions within both chambers of Congress, moving the institution a long way from the egalitarian, purely democratic chamber of mutual friendship that was the Congress of the Confederation (see Schickler in this volume). The important constitutional point right now is this: As important as providing a direct electoral link between the people and Congress was in ensuring a robust political base for Congress, the Constitution also provided an institutional base for strength. In the modern age, the president enjoys an even greater electoral link with the people than does Congress. If the Constitution had *only* provided an electoral link between Congress and the electorate, it is doubtful that Congress would have remained a robust governing institution into the twenty-first century. It is Congress's institutional capacity, explicitly sanctioned by the Constitution, which gives congressional majorities a fighting chance when they disagree with the president.

Bicameralism

The framers inherited a legacy of bicameral legislatures, rooted in the English parliamentary practice of balancing popular representation (Commons) with the representation of wealth (Lords). In the heady days of the Revolution, some states, like Pennsylvania, experimented with unicameralism, abolishing the special place that the better class of people had in governing councils, relying instead on the popular will alone.

Two decades of experience with highly democratic state legislatures had cooled the ardor of the governing class toward unchecked democratic legislatures. At least among the delegates to the Constitutional Convention—who were admittedly a self-selected bunch uninterested in radical words or deeds—replacing the incumbent Continental Congress with a bicameral institution was taken for granted. The Virginia Plan called for a bicameral legislature, even though the upper chamber was electorally subservient to the lower. True, the New Jersey Plan proposed returning to a unicameral scheme, but it was rejected resoundingly. Significantly, it was the bicameralism of the Connecticut Compromise that swung small state delegations back in favor of making a more radical departure from the Articles than they had originally favored.

The bicameralism written into the Constitution was both expedient and functional. It was expedient because the creation of two coequal branches allowed a compromise over representation. It was functional by its divvying up of policymaking responsibilities in a way that mapped important elements of national politics onto the expected political tendencies of the chambers. The lower house was given the right of first movement on taxing, cementing a principle of "no taxation without representation"; the upper house was given special prerogatives in two executive-related areas, foreign policy (treaties) and agency administration (nominations). And, of course, neither chamber was constitutionally favored in regular legislation; both were allowed to move first, and both were required to agree.

Two questions emerge in assessing the consequences of the functional distribution of bicameralism in the Constitution. The first is simply whether the functional division has held and whether it has made any difference in policies that have been pursued. The second is whether bicameralism has been a brake on policymaking and, if it has been, what have been the consequences.

Has the Constitutional Division of Labor between the House and Senate Held?

The answer to the first question is "mostly yes." The constitutional division of labor between the House and Senate has fostered a specialization in the two chambers that persists to this day. This is most easily seen in the operations of congressional committees, which are the work horses of congressional activity. The most desirable committee in the House is Ways and Means, which has jurisdiction over all tax matters, plus spending programs like Social Security, which were designed as tax schemes.[21] Ways and Means's counterpart in the Senate, the Finance Committee, is certainly important, but Foreign Relations is nearly as desirable an assignment—much more desirable than the House International Relations Committee. The Senate Judiciary Committee handles judicial nominations, which makes Senate Judiciary also highly sought after, unlike in the House, where the House Judiciary Committee is just another committee. The chambers also allocate resources that are consistent with this specialization—the House Ways and Means staff is larger than the Senate Finance Committee staff and works with a larger budget; the Senate Judiciary Committee has a considerably larger staff than the House Judiciary Committee.

The division of labor has frayed around the edges in areas such as raising taxes and making treaties, however, bringing consternation to some constitutional scholars. One area where the division of labor has frayed is in the origination of tax measures in the House. The early 1980s represented the greatest challenge to the House's preeminence in making tax policy. The first challenge was political, not constitutional, as the norms of fiscal restraint that had enveloped the Ways and Means Committee were undermined by the leaders of both parties in the House.[22] The constitutional challenge followed on the heels of the political. The 1981 tax cuts, the largest in the nation's peacetime history (in percentage terms), were ushered through Congress in an institutional environment in which the House's ability to resist raids on the Treasury was momentarily weakened. The hemorrhaging of revenues spurred the tax writers in Congress to find ways to raise taxes. When the House proved unable to move a major tax increase forward, Senator Bob Dole (R-Kans.), chair of the Senate Finance Committee, took the lead by performing the legislative equivalent of a full body transplant. He crafted a tax increase, working out the details in a closed Senate Republican caucus. The House's right to originate tax legislation was acknowledged only in the barest of formalities. The Senate took a minor tariff bill that had already passed the House, voted to remove the entire text of the bill, substituting instead Dole's Tax Equity and Fiscal Responsibility Act (TEFRA). Although Dole's parliamentary maneuver amounted to a charade, the House passed the bill and the courts refused to intervene.[23]

The Senate's unique legislative responsibility, treaty making, has also come under attack, from two directions. The best known challenges have come from

20

the president, where executive agreements have replaced treaties.[24] Nowadays, executive agreements end wars; treaties set the price of postage stamps.

The new challenge to the Senate's role in guiding international alliances and agreements is that the House has begun sharing more of the responsibility. Consider the North American Free Trade Agreement. This is a treaty if there ever was one. Yet the resolution under which Congress approved the pact passed the Senate on a 61–38 vote, far short of the two-thirds agreement necessary to ratify treaties. Why is it law of the land? Because it was entered into as a congressional-executive agreement that received majority support in both chambers.

To anyone enamored of the plain meaning of the constitutional text, it must be perplexing that this clear violation of the treaty clause went unremarked at the time of the agreement's passage. Indeed, such agreements have become commonplace since World War II.[25] In fairness, the House had long entangled itself in the implementation of treaties, as the House controversy over implementing the Jay Treaty (1794) or the interminable politics over Texas annexation attest. Still, for most of American history entering into solemn agreements with foreign powers was considered something that the Senate did without the assistance of the House. The high hurdle of the two-third ratification requirement and the well-known ability of a small number of senators to delay made presidents cautious and treaties rare. The world America entered into after World War II changed all that.

The whittling away of the "origination clause" and the "treaty clause" illustrate the limitations of relying on political ambitions and institutional jealousies to guard the constitutional prerogatives of the congressional branches. The protection of these prerogatives is predicated on counteracting ambitions creating intra-branch jealousies that swing institutional loyalties into play whenever special prerogatives are challenged. Jealousies are feeble, and thus prerogatives unguarded, when ambitions are no longer in high tension. The nationalization of politics and the shared political fates of members of Congress in both chambers, plus their shared fate with presidential candidates, often undermine the axiom of having counterpoised ambitions in the first place.

The political implication of the erosion of the House's preeminence in fiscal policy and the Senate's preeminence in foreign policy is that both policy areas are now more prone to forum shopping among presidents and legislative policy entrepreneurs. International agreement too controversial to yield two-thirds agreement in the Senate? Craft a legislative-executive agreement. House unwilling to raise taxes? Try the Senate.

Bicameralism's Effects on the Pace and Quality of Legislation

The Constitution not only specified a functional division of labor between the two chambers, it also instituted a concurrent majority requirement for legislation in general. What are the consequences of this requirement?

Had the two chambers of Congress continued to be populated by members who were elected by autonomous constituencies that were not knit together by unifying devices like national political parties, one major consequence of bicameralism would have been delay in legislation, as policy majorities were knit together first in one chamber, then in the other. However, national political parties create ready-made policy coalitions that not only span geography, but span the two chambers. Thus, the judgment of history is that bicameralism, *per se,* has had very little effect on delay, especially delay of significant legislation. The loyalties of senators and representatives are to the same set of political parties and the same collection of ideological battles as in the nation as a whole. Bicameralism inserts itself most strongly when majorities in the two chambers are ideologically opposed. Operationally, this means that when the parties are both ideologically distinct and the chambers are controlled by different parties (as in the 107th Congress, 2001–2002), gridlock is to be expected. When they are less distinct (as in most of the cold war era) or control is unified, delay is less in the cards.[26]

American political history has witnessed three periods when bicameralism probably *did* make a difference in how quickly Congress responded to social problems with ameliorative legislation, and in the nature of the legislation that was finally forthcoming. The first was during the antebellum period, when national politicians consciously supported a "balance rule" in the admission of new states to the Union. For each slave state admitted, a free state balanced it. This institutionalized a southern veto over efforts to weaken slavery, in light of the fact that the population of the free states was growing much more rapidly. It is undoubtedly true that the balance rule, which could only have worked if the Senate was apportioned equally, prolonged slavery in the United States while forestalling civil war.

Bicameralism was also implicated during the Civil War and Reconstruction eras, when a series of Republican-dominated Congresses managed to admit a number of Republican-leaning, small-population states to counterbalance the numerical advantage that Democrats would have in the House once the Civil War was over and southern states returned to full participation in national politics.[27] For the decades of the 1880s and 1890s, the presence of these Republican "rotten boroughs" in the Senate had the effect of protecting many of the pro-commercial and pro-western settlement policies first enacted during the Civil War Congresses and augmented in the 1880s and 1890s; it also influenced the composition of the Supreme Court during the Lochner era, making it more pro-business than it might have otherwise been. The irony in this strategy of packing the Senate with Republican states came when an agriculture and mining depression hit late in the nineteenth century—states that had been admitted for their Republican proclivities became the hotbeds of agrarian radicalism, and thus the location of the Progressive and Populist revolts that eventually split the Republican party.

In more recent times, bicameralism retarded civil rights legislation that a majority of Americans supported. How much progress was delayed is still subject to debate. The House was willing to push forward when the Senate was not, but that could have been due more to the Senate's filibuster, not bicameralism per se. Had the House had the filibuster, not the Senate, progress would have been no swifter. Nonetheless, opponents of racial equality were willing to use any means at their disposal to halt the advance of equality. The fact that there were two sets of legislative hurdles, not one, no doubt worked to their advantage.

History's verdict on bicameralism in Congress's development is that the framers would have been surprised at its effects, which, if anything, have been subtle. The Senate has not become the staid, aristocratic chamber that "cools the legislative tea." The House has not become the Hall of Firebrands. Having two chambers, whose members possess slightly different perspectives due to their electoral origins, introduces subtle differences into the legislative product. And having two chambers with specialties—even specialties that are no longer as stark as they once were—has helped to bolster congressional influence over fiscal and foreign policy. A bicameral Congress *is* different from a unicameral one. Still, the national electoral context that is the common influence on members of both chambers brings together two chambers that the framers wished to push apart.

The President

The role of the president as a constitutional influence on Congress has been saved for last. To the modern student of American government this may seem like an odd choice, since the president looms so large over contemporary American politics. The president's preeminent place in American politics is comment enough about the disjuncture between the expectations of the framers and the evolution of American politics. To the framers, the legislature was the keystone of republican government, the executive being necessary only to effectuate legislative intentions and to act decisively in rare instances of imminent national peril.

Populist excesses in the state legislatures after independence led the framers to appreciate that the popular election of legislators could create an irresistible political force when they assembled in a legislature. Although the framers shared the popular distrust of strong executives, they also understood that the only hope of providing an effective ballast against populist legislative excesses was through an effective, yet constrained, executive. Throughout the Constitutional Convention, the delegates wrestled with the right mix of details—term lengths; methods of election; extent of veto prerogative; veto override hurdle, if any— that would allow for an effective executive to emerge and remain independent of Congress, especially the popularly elected lower House.

In considering the act of balancing political power between Congress and the president, it is important to remember that the framers did not consider that the president might gain a robust popular following. Thus the protections the Constitution gave the president in reining in Congress were largely institutional, mainly the veto power. The president might use other resources at his disposal to dominate Congress, but these were resources—money, troops, patronage—that Congress would have to give him. Therefore, within the worldview of the framers, the president was strong, but still subordinate to Congress.

What the framers did not anticipate was the Jacksonian revolution, coupled with an ever-growing reach of the national media, which together forged an even stronger link between the public and the president. If you ask citizens of the twenty-first century which branch of the national government is more closely attuned with the American people, Congress or the president, you will get a different answer than the one you would have gotten in the eighteenth century.

Therefore, the constitutional space that the presidency and Congress cohabit is one that has seen presidential institutional prerogatives remain unchanged, but exercised in a context in which the popular political advantage has migrated in the president's direction. Prefiguration of this dominance could be seen in the nineteenth century. From early on, the most eagerly awaited moment in a congressional session was the president's message, and in the earliest days House and Senate committees were organized around elements of that message. President James Polk's movement of American troops into Mexican territory in May 1846 precipitated the Mexican War, a conflict the sitting Congress would not have approved. President Lincoln's usurpation of Congress's role in suspending habeas corpus during the Civil War is well known. Yet these were halting steps toward occupying center stage in American national politics. Full strides were only taken once Congress became an active participant in expanding the role of the executive during the Great Depression and World War II, giving the president a seemingly endless set of responsibilities that fundamentally shifted the constitutional balance-of-powers.

The Constitution created an executive office that was to interact with Congress in two significant ways. First, the president was essentially made a third legislative branch, through the mechanism of the veto. Second, a long list of executive functions that the Continental Congress enjoyed—ranging from the general administration of the executive departments to conducting military and foreign policy—were taken away and given to the president. The exercise of all these powers would initially depend on Congress acting. But once a nascent administrative state was in place, the framers recognized that the president would have a potent set of tools at his disposal. These powers, over the far-flung executive branch and over the army and navy, yielded political resources that would grow in the president's favor over time.

Congress, the President, and the Veto

An earlier generation of legal scholars maintained that the Framers intended the veto to serve as a very limited check on legislative power, used only to scuttle constitutional encroachments or forestall the passage of laws that would be impossible to administer. Recent scholarship, relying on a close reading of Convention proceedings and contemporary practices in the states, suggests otherwise.[28] The more recent thinking starts with the fact that the framers lived in a world in which the states generally had given their governors at least a limited veto; the contemporary trend was to strengthen gubernatorial vetoes as state constitutions were revised. It continues to the sequence of deliberations in the Convention itself. The framers considered a number of veto formulations; the one that was finally approved imposed the fewest restrictions on the president of anything actually proposed. In short, the framers knew how to write a highly circumscribed veto into the Constitution if they wanted, and they did not.

Although the Constitution's text did not limit the use of the presidential veto to grand constitutional matters, in fact before Andrew Jackson's veto of the Maysville Road bill in 1830 and the re-charter of the Bank of the United States in 1832, vetoes were rare. This rarity, coupled with the firestorms these two vetoes prompted, led to a common view in most of the twentieth century that Jackson subverted the original intention and practice of the veto, inventing the policy-oriented veto. Yet this view simply does not comport with the facts. George Washington, who presided over the Constitutional Convention, issued his second veto on a bill that reduced the size of the army. His veto was not based on deep constitutional objections; he simply disagreed with Congress's military judgment. From Washington onward to Jackson, the rare veto messages were mixes of constitutional arguments and policy disagreements.

This leaves an important question: If presidents and members of Congress at least vaguely understood that the president could legitimately veto legislation in the early years of the Republic because of simple policy disagreements, why did it take until 1830 for them to become common? The first answer is simple: Until then, a majority in Congress and the president rarely disagreed over important policy matters. Divided government, which is common in our era and the most powerful predictor of when the president will issue a veto, was rare in the early days of the Republic.

The second answer requires us to notice which president first used the veto as a major policy weapon—Andrew Jackson. Jackson had larger electoral fish to fry, including establishing a clear policy identity for his party. Actions like his two highly visible vetoes pushed his policy leadership into the limelight, rallying his followers to support his electoral vision of building a Democratic party dedicated to states' rights and limited government.

Since that time, vetoes have helped to frame policy debates and set a stark contrast between the president and a Congress that is dominated by the opposite party. There are many examples one could cite. One was in 1992, when the Democratic-controlled Congress passed campaign finance reform knowing that the Republican President Bush would veto it. Had the Democratic majorities desired a feasible reform law at that point, they could have compromised with the president, but they did not. Bush's veto of the bill allowed Democrats to blame him for the failure of campaign finance reform in the 1992 general election. Further evidence that this was an example of "blame game" politics came after the election, when Democrat Bill Clinton, who had attacked Bush's veto of the original legislation, was elected president. The subsequent Congress, which if anything was even more favorably inclined toward campaign finance reform than the previous one, deadlocked and was unable even to re-pass the bill it had sent to the president just a few months before.[29]

It is certainly true that the veto can be used as a pure legislative tool, allowing Congress and the president to give and take over complicated legislation. Recent research by Charles Cameron has shown that roughly half the time when a veto is issued, the vetoed bill is stripped of the offending passage(s), passed again, and signed into law.[30] These are not typically the bills the public hears about, however, since these are bills in which both sides desire the outcome more than gaining political advantage. To attentive citizens of the twenty-first century, the most important thing to understand about the veto is that it has been transformed into a mechanism that is more broadly political than anything imagined by the first generation of American politicians, including the Framers.

The President as Chief Executive and Commander in Chief

The Constitution also set the president over the executive branch, civil and military. The framers were certainly aware that the secrecy and unity of leadership that characterized executives could lead to an ultimate usurpation of legislative power by the president. Still, in the nineteenth century, presidential usurpations were rare enough that even a brief survey of American history is likely to bring one into contact with all the significant instances.

The role of the president as chief executive, head of state, and commander-in-chief expanded significantly in the twentieth century. The most important point to make about that expansion is that it was almost entirely made with congressional support and encouragement.[31] Landmark legislation that led to executive aggrandizement—ranging from the Budget Act to the Employment Act to the creation of the "Alphabet Soup Agencies" during the New Deal—was popular in Congress at the time. The decline of Congress's power throughout most of the twentieth century was primarily of its own making.

It is hard to imagine how it could have been otherwise. By the time of the New Deal, the country had been living a century of gradually expanding and nationalizing politics. In the early days of the New Deal, to deny the president authority because of a republican (meaning the theory, not the party) aversion to executive authority would have meant electoral death to members of Congress. The disastrous faring of congressional Republicans (meaning the party, not the theory) in 1934 and 1936 was widely interpreted for the next generation as precisely such a verdict.

The forty-year period beginning with the election of Franklin Roosevelt in 1932 witnessed a dramatic expansion of the role of the federal government in the lives of individual citizens and a substantial shift of political authority from the states to the national government. Both shifts would have been unthinkable to the framers. Indeed, one suspects that they thought they had written a Constitution that would guard against precisely such a development.

Taking office at the depths of the Great Depression, Franklin Roosevelt outlined a bold agenda to get the country back to work. These plans and their consequences were enormously successful politically. Whole blocs of voters shifted partisan allegiances (urban dwellers and African Americans, particularly), with Democrats reaping electoral awards of historic proportion.

What is most of interest to us is the form these plans took, because they deeply affected the constitutional balance of power between Congress and the president. The regulatory state that was championed by FDR, leading to the so-called alphabet soup agencies, formally shifted oversight of the economy from Congress to the president. The largest social program, Social Security, created a permanent "entitlement," that is, a program that beneficiaries received payments from automatically, without an annual appropriation from Congress.

What the Great Depression did for the presidential-congressional balance of power in the domestic realm, World War II did in the foreign policy and military realms. The war itself spawned the greatest military mobilization in the history of the nation. The demobilization left the United States with one of the world's largest standing armies and foreign entanglements. Standing armies are by their nature instruments of national executive power, as is the conduct of foreign policy.

Clearly, the precipitating crises that led to these shifts in the locus of political power, war and depression, were out of Congress's power to control, but the responses were fully in its power to control. In these crises, huge majorities chose to give power to the president and the executive agencies that reported to him. Why?

The most direct answers are two. First, the crises were manifestly problems that demanded unified action, a characteristic of government that even the framers recognized was in more abundant supply within the executive. Second, the responses to the Depression and World War II were so manifestly successful that for many years few members of Congress dared run on a limited government platform. Even the Republican party adopted a stance that was accepting of much of the "welfare state" and the "national security state." In a dangerous world, members of Congress were happy to hitch their electoral wagons to the greater organizational capacity of the president.

The shift in authority from Congress to the president was not unambiguously benign—congressional passage of the Tonkin Gulf Resolution is a case study in how presidential aggrandizement could feed on itself, leading to a national tragedy. In that case, the Johnson administration went to Congress following an attack on American warships by North Vietnamese vessels. After being misled by Secretary of Defense Robert McNamara about prior American military operations in the region, Congress pass a resolution giving the president the authority to use any means at his disposal to help the South Vietnamese government. That, in turn, eventually led to the deployment of hundreds of thousands of American troops, tens of thousands of casualties, and deep political divisions in the United States that persist to this day. In the wake of the Vietnam experience the political tables turned, showing that the American electorate's tendency to trust the president more than Congress could be reversed.

The early 1970s, the so-called Watergate era, is known for the throttling back of presidential prerogatives, as Congress passed the War Powers Resolution, over a presidential veto, and laws such as the Congressional Budget and Impoundment Control Act. The internal capacity of Congress was strengthened. The war in Vietnam was put on a short leash through the use of the oldest legislative trick in the book, appropriations restrictions. In the words of James Sundquist, who wrote the definitive book on the subject, Congress had undergone a "decline and resurgence."[32]

Still, it would be a mistake to view congressional resurgence in the 1970s as representing a permanent roll-back of the most important constitutional dynamic of the past two centuries, which has been the tendency to intertwine constitutional developments with partisan and electoral politics. The greatest strides bolstering congressional capacities against the president were made when the Republican president Richard Nixon's popularity was on the decline and Democratic majorities in Congress were on the rise. It is hard to believe that the institutional resurgence of Congress in the 1970s would have been quite as vigorous had Hubert H. Humphrey won the 1968 election.

Thus, the Constitution designed two institutions, the Congress and the president, to be rivals. The rise of popular politics has complicated this rivalry enormously. On the one hand, members of Congress still have an electoral perspective that is different from the president's, and thus even the president's own co-partisans will occasionally challenge his nominees and oppose his policies. On the other hands, the profile of the president has been raised to the point that presidents by-and-large set the overall agenda and tone for most policy debate in Washington. For members of Congress of the president's party, a successful presidential program is a top legislative priority. For members of the opposition, opposing that program is the top order of the day. Any legislator would obviously prefer more power to less. Still, the sweep of history suggests that Congress as a body will usually trade a loss of autonomy or policy leadership in order to become more surely swept up in the president's protective electoral wings.

Conclusion

In understanding Congress's role in the American political system, it is important to start with the Constitution, but not to finish there. The framers sought not to change the natural impulses of the ambitious politicians who would compete for congressional office, but to channel those ambitions, producing a mix of policy results—effective action when a national consensus called for it, caution otherwise. What the framers failed to anticipate was how the most creative and ambitious politicians of the 1820s would stage an end-run around the Constitution by establishing organizations, the political parties, that were dedicated to bridging the divides that the Constitution had created. The consequence, after more than two hundreds years of national politics, is a polity that is more unified, centralized, and powerful than the framers anticipated, or even desired.

This state of affairs might seem like a failure of constitutional design, but that conclusion would be incorrect. It is incorrect because the dispersion of powers within the Constitution still legitimates the nurturance of competing policymaking voices within government itself. Because of the dispersion of power through the Constitution, a year does not go by without some serious movement within Congress that challenges a policy priority of the administration. Sometimes those challenges find the president's own partisans mortally wound his top policy priority, as the Democratic Congress did against President Bill Clinton's plans to reform the nation's health care system, and as the Republican Congress may currently be doing against President George W. Bush's plans to reform the Social Security system or restrict fetal stem cell research.

As these examples suggest, however, a major consequence of how the constitutional balance has actually played out is that Congress is now more often reactive than creative. Policy leadership in the early days of the Republic was often (though not exclusively) Congress-dominated; now it rarely is. This, in turn, has a major impact on how Congress is perceived by the electorate and how members of Congress play their role in the larger polity. The system as it has evolved rewards members who are reactive and cautious. It is also a system that may encourage irresponsibility among members of Congress, who may find greater electoral benefits in railing against bureaucratic ineptitude and assisting constituents through casework than in changing the policies that constituents find so burdensome in the first place.[33]

The American state is currently more powerful than the framers would have anticipated, given the Constitution they wrote, but it is less powerful than it might have been had power been centralized in the first place. The political backlash to the New Deal, which lurched to life with the Republican candidacy of Barry Goldwater in 1964 and came to full force with the election of Ronald Reagan in 1980, showed that the party-based, nationalized political system could also turn against centralized power. The conservative movements that have dominated the current era have demonstrated that the greatest brakes on the centralized power of the State are now more electoral than institutional.

A recurring theme of this chapter has been the way in which the initial expectations and assumptions of the framers have been superseded by subsequent political developments, particularly the rise of national political parties and the nationalization of politics. The cynic might come away from such an argument with the conclusion that the Constitution is simply an empty shell and irrelevant to the grand politics that occupy the Congress and the president. Such a cynical reading is possible only if one's view of the Constitution is that of detailed instruction manual.

I would argue that the more optimistic, and realistic, view is that the Constitution has successfully provided two features of national political life that seem unassailable. The first is a Congress that is institutionally robust and capable of gathering information and seeking opinions independently of the president. The second is that Congress is still linked directly to the people through elections. The president is a stronger popular rival than he once was, but he is not the only game in town. It is that unbreakable electoral link that provides its continuing legitimacy, ensuring real political power.

Notes

1. This chapter takes a position consistent with E. E. Schattschneider's famous thesis that "the political parties created democracy and that modern democracy is unthinkable save in term of the parties." *Party Government* (New York: Farrar and Rinehart, 1942), 1.

2. An important account of early political development that is consistent with this discussion is Stephen Skowronek, *Building a New American State: The Expansion of National Administrative Capacities, 1877–1920* (New York: Cambridge University Press, 1982).

3. John P. Roche, "The Founding Fathers: A Reform Caucus in Action," *American Political Science Review* 55, no. 4 (1961), 799.

4. The account in this section draws heavily on Calvin C. Jillson and Rick K. Wilson, *Congressional Dynamics: Structure, Coordination, and Choice in the First American Congress, 1774–1789* (Stanford, Calif.: Stanford University Press, 1994), Jillson, *Constitution Making*; Berkin, *A Brilliant Solution*; and Jack N. Rakove, *Original Meanings* (New York: Knopf, 1996). See also Lance Banning, "James Madison and the

Dynamics of the Constitutional Convention," *The Political Science Reviewer* 17 (Fall 1987), 5–48, and Max M. Edling, *A Revolution in Favor of Government* (New York: Oxford University Press, 2003). For a more extended discussion along these lines that relies on the theory of rational choice to discuss the unfolding politics of the Constitutional Convention, see Charles Stewart, III, *Analyzing Congress* (New York: Norton, 2001).

5. Although it is a commonplace to express the conflict between large and small states in substantive terms, there is no major substantive issue of the time that split the nation along state population lines. Small-population Georgia had similar border perils to large-population Virginia. Small-population Rhode Island had as vigorous a coastal and international trade as large-population Pennsylvania. Large-population New York could block small-population Connecticut in coastal trade, but small-population New Jersey could block New York; Delaware could block Pennsylvania. More systematically, an analysis of the correlation between state size and political preferences, using the DNOMINATE measure of Poole and Rosenthal, reveals that there never has been a Congress where state size and political preferences have been significantly correlated. For an explanation of Poole and Rosenthal's methodology see Keith T. Poole and Howard Rosenthal, *Congress: A Political-Economic History of Roll Call Voting* (New York: Oxford University Press, 1991).

6. Along with fixing the problem of having no direct tie to the electorate, the Constitution also mandated a degree of "transparency" of action that is still not always followed in other national legislatures. The transparency requirement comes in Article I, section 5, clause 3, which requires each chamber to publish a journal of its proceedings and publish roll call votes if only one-fifth of the chamber demands it. I thank David Mayhew for suggesting this point.

7. The close link between governmental partisans and the electoral process is seen in the life of the first Clerk of the House, John Beckley. On this linkage see Edmund Berkeley and Dorothy Smith Berkeley, *John Beckley: Zealous Partisan in a Nation Divided* (Philadelphia: American Philosophical Society, 1973).

8. On the strategies of Democratic party building see John Ashworth, *Slavery, Capitalism, and Politics in the Antebellum Republic*, 2 vols. (New York: Cambridge University Press, 1995), Aldrich, *Why Parties?*, and Robert Remini, *Martin Van Buren and the Making of the Democratic Party* (New York: Oxford University Press, 1959).

9. Michael J. Dubin, *United States Congressional Elections, 1788–1997: The Official Results* (Jefferson, N.C.: McFarland, 1998).

10. This requirement, which represented the first time Congress used its authority to "make or alter" state election laws pertaining to Congress, was in reaction to what was called the "Broad Seal War," the constitutional crisis the country was thrown into in 1839 resulting from New Jersey's continued insistence on using a general ticket to elect House members. In that instance, an electoral dispute involving just a few votes in a couple of New Jersey towns cast doubt on the rightful composition of the entire New Jersey House delegation. The resolution to this dispute would determine which party controlled the House. The dispute threw the House into such turmoil that it took more than two weeks to organize for business, John Quincy Adams seized the chair extra-legally to help facilitate organization, and the House seriously

considered adjourning and calling new elections. Laurence F. Schmeckebier, *Congressional Apportionment* (Washington, D.C.: Brookings Institution, 1941), is still the classic treatment of congressional apportionment, although he dismisses the importance of the Broad Seal War in forcing the issue of abolishing general ticket voting for representatives. See also Johanna Nicol Shields, "Whigs Reform the 'Bear Garden': Representation and the Apportionment Act of 1842," *Journal of the Early Republic* 5 (1985), 335–382.

11. A uniform law regulating senatorial elections was not passed until 1862. Under that law, state legislatures were required to vote to fill expiring Senate seats on the second Tuesday after convening. While most state legislatures met biennially in odd-year Januaries, not all did—some met annually or triennially, while others convened in other months. So, a truly uniform senatorial Election Day did not emerge until popular election was established in 1914. See Erik J. Engstrom and Samuel Kernell, "Manufactured Responsiveness: The Impact of State Electoral Laws on Unified Party Control of the Presidency and House of Representatives, 1840–1940," *American Journal of Political Science* 49, no. 3 (2005), 531–549.

12. Gerald H. Kramer, "Short-Term Fluctuations in U.S. Voting Behavior, 1896–1964," *American Political Science Review* 65, no. 1 (1971); Gary C. Jacobson and Samuel H. Kernell, *Strategy and Choice in Congressional Elections* (New Haven, Conn.: Yale University Press, 1981).

13. This discussion relies heavily on Riker's classic examination of the pre-1914 contribution of the Senate to the development of American federalism. William H. Riker, "The Senate and American Federalism," *American Political Science Review* 49, no. 2 (1955), 452–469.

14. Ibid., 462.

15. On the movement to institute the popular election of senators see George Henry Haynes, Election of Senators (New York: H. Holt, 1906), George Henry Haynes, *Senate of the United States* (Boston: Houghton Mifflin, 1938), and Kris W. Kobach, "Rethinking Article V: Term Limits and the Seventeenth and Nineteenth Amendments," *Yale Law Journal* 103 (1994), 1971–2007.

16. Charles Stewart, III, and Barry Weingast, "Stacking the Senate, Changing the Nation," *Studies in American Political Development* 103, no. 2 (1992), 223–271.

17. Frances E. Lee, "Representation and Public Policy: The Consequences of Senate Apportionment for the Geographic Distribution of Federal Funds," *Journal of Politics* 60 (1998); R. Douglas Arnold, *Congress and the Bureaucracy: A Theory of Influence* (New Haven, Conn.: Yale University Press, 1979).

18. My characterization of internal procedures in the Second Continental Congress relies on Jillson and Wilson, *Congressional Dynamics*.

19. Two recent examples illustrate this seemingly extreme parliamentary tactic. On 22 November 2003, the Republican-supported Medicare bill was going down to defeat on a roll call vote by a margin of 218–216. However, the House leadership decided not to gavel the roll call vote closed for almost three hours (the rules provide for roll call votes to last fifteen minutes), so that they could twist arms and change three votes, ensuring passage. David Broder, "Time Was GOP's Ally on the Vote," *Washington Post*, 23 November 2003. On 8 July 2004, an amendment to a spending

bill was added by Rep. Bernie Sanders (I–Vt.), prohibiting the Justice Department from accessing library or bookstore records under the USA Patriot Act. In a surprise to the Republican majority leadership, the amendment was on the way to passage, until the Republican majority leadership held the roll call vote open another thirty minutes, to induce enough Republicans to switch their votes to guarantee a tie, and a defeat for the amendment. Ben Pershing and Erin P. Billings, "Parties Gauge Fallout from Controversial Vote," *Roll Call*, 12 July 2004.

20. It is also possible to argue that the so-called incompatibility clause gave both chambers of Congress the institutional room to develop their own powerful internal institutions. This clause, in Article I, section 6, states that "no Person holding any Office under the United States, shall be a Member of either House during his Continuance in Office." In other words, no one in the executive branch may service in Congress. This cleanly cut off the possibility that the United States would evolve into a parliamentary system. With no formal links possible between Congress and the executive, it was only a matter of time before the two chambers began to create a sort of "shadow cabinet" system among the committees. See Steven G. Calabresi and Joan L. Larsen, "One Person, One Office: Separation of Powers or Separation of Personnel?" *Cornell Law Review* 79 (1994), 1045–1157.

21. Charles Stewart, III, and Timothy Groseclose, "The Value of Committee Seats in the United States Senate, 1946–91," *American Journal of Political Science* 43 (1999); Timothy Groseclose and Charles Stewart, III, "The Value of Committee Seats in the House, 1946–1991," *American Journal of Political Science* 42 (1998).

22. Charles Stewart III, "The Politics of Tax Reform in the 1980s," in *Politics and Economics in the Eighties*, edited by Alberto Alesina and Geoffrey Carliner (Chicago: University of Chicago Press, 1991).

23. John L. Hoffer, Jr., "The Origination Clause and Tax Legislation," *Boston University Journal of Tax Law* 2 (May 1984); Thomas L. Jipping, "TEFRA and the Origination Clause: Taking the Oath Seriously," *Buffalo Law Review* 35 (Spring 1986); James V. Saturno, *The Origination Clause of the U.S. Constitution: Interpretation and Enforcement* (Washington, D.C.: Congressional Research Service, 2002).

24. Sundquist, *Decline and Resurgence of Congress*; Louis Fisher, *Constitutional Conflicts between Congress and the President* (Princeton, N.J.: Princeton University Press, 1985).

25. Bruce Ackerman and David Golove, "Is NAFTA Constitutional?," *Harvard Law Review* 108 (February).

26. Sarah A. Binder, "The Dynamics of Legislative Gridlock, 1947-96," *American Political Science Review* 93 (1999); David R. Mayhew, *Divided We Govern* (New Haven, Conn.: Yale University Press, 1991).

27. Stewart and Weingast, "Stacking the Senate, Changing the Nation."

28. See also Wilfred E. Binkley, *President and Congress* (New York: Knopf, 1947), and Nolan McCarty, "Presidential Vetoes in the Early Republic: Changing Constitutional Norms or Electoral Reform?," in *History of Congress* (Stanford, Calif.: Stanford University Press, 2004).

29. Stewart, *Analyzing Congress*, 78–79.

30. Charles M. Cameron, *Veto Bargaining: Presidents and the Politics of Negative Power* (New York: Cambridge University Press, 2000).

31. Sundquist, *Decline and Resurgence of Congress*.
32. Ibid.
33. The classic statement of this point is Morris Fiorina, *Congress: Keystone of the Washington Establishment*, 2nd ed. (New Haven, Conn.: Yale University Press, 1989).

Bibliography

Aldrich, John H. *Why Parties? The Origins and Transformation of Political Parties in America.* Chicago: University of Chicago Press, 1995.

Berkin, Carol. *A Brilliant Solution: Inventing the American Constitution.* New York: Harcourt, 2002.

Cameron, Charles M. *Veto Bargaining: Presidents and the Politics of Negative Power.* New York: Cambridge University Press, 2000.

Jillson, Calvin C. *Constitution Making: Conflict and Consensus in the Federal Convention of 1787.* New York: Agathon Press, 1988.

Sundquist, James. *Decline and Resurgence of Congress.* Washington, D.C.: Brookings Institution, 1981.

2

INSTITUTIONAL DEVELOPMENT
OF CONGRESS

Eric Schickler

W HEN DISSATISFACTION WITH CONGRESSIONAL PER-
formance rises, demands are commonly made for major changes in
how Congress is organized. These recurrent calls for reform raise
questions about the origins and development of congressional institutions. The
Constitution offers little guidance: beyond providing that the House select a
Speaker to preside over its deliberations and that the vice president preside over
the Senate, the Constitution allows each chamber to make its own rules. But
what determines the choices made by members of Congress as they design key
features of institutional organization, such as the committee system and party
leadership instruments? What explains the politics of institutional change in
Congress?

While the basic constitutional framework governing Congress has changed
little over the past two hundred years, a member serving in the 1790s would have
considerable difficulty recognizing today's Congress. At the outset, the formal
structure of both chambers was quite limited. Deliberation occurred primarily
on the floor, where members would debate proposed topics for legislation before
a specific bill was introduced. The chamber would then authorize a temporary
select committee to frame a bill for the membership as a whole to consider,
amend, and possibly approve. Party leadership structures were also weak and
fluid. The House and Senate shared these original features, though the Senate
took a less active role in initiating legislation and also maintained a much lower
public profile than the House.

Over the past two centuries, both the House and the Senate have fundamentally changed their mode of organization. Each chamber has developed a special-

ized committee system, which processes most legislation before it reaches the floor. Both chambers now feature elaborate and formalized party structures in which majority-party leaders play a significant role in determining the floor agenda. Individual members in both chambers are now empowered to introduce legislation at will, and each member employs a large personal staff to assist in both legislative activity and constituent service.

Yet the two chambers have also diverged organizationally in important respects. Most notably, majority-party leaders in the House enjoy more prerogatives than their Senate counterparts: their control of the agenda is firmer and their ability to shape committee composition and committee deliberations is greater. The committee system has also traditionally been more powerful in the House than in the Senate. House committees have more extensive property rights over legislation and their proposals are better protected from floor amendments.[1] By contrast, individual members enjoy greater prerogatives in the Senate. In particular, the Senate's tradition of unlimited debate differentiates it from the House. While a determined floor majority can work its will in the House, the filibuster empowers senators to block action indefinitely. A sixty-vote supermajority is required to ensure action in the Senate, and the threat of filibusters leads to the reliance on elaborate unanimous-consent agreements to manage floor deliberations, which give substantial leverage to individual senators.

What were the sources of these major changes in the House and Senate? How did the United States end up with two chambers that differ so much from the original congressional blueprint and from one another? Furthermore, what factors have affected the relative influence of committees, party leaders, and individual members across time? To answer these questions, this chapter will focus on a series of junctures at which fundamental institutional changes were adopted in each chamber.

No single member interest has been the dominant force in explaining these institutional developments. Indeed, major institutional changes in both chambers typically were attributable to a confluence of multiple interests, rather than due to a single, simple logic. However, several factors have repeatedly proven critical and have, in conjunction, given rise to the contemporary Congress. Members have repeatedly sought to bolster congressional capacity and power in order to maintain their chamber's institutional position. These moves have generally come in response to a burgeoning workload and to threats of executive encroachment. But general concerns with institutional maintenance have rarely proven sufficient on their own to motivate major changes. Instead, partisan interests and members' more personal interest in reelection and exercising power as individuals have also proven critical. Personal power interests have played a more important role in the Senate, due to the chamber's smaller size, which allows greater latitude for individual members. By contrast, partisan calculations have more often proven significant in the House, giving rise to a chamber with tighter agenda control and more limited individual member prerogatives.

These House-Senate differences began to take shape early in the nineteenth century, and have been reinforced by the incentives created by inherited institutions.[2] The options available to decision makers today depend on prior choices. The House early on developed mechanisms for a floor majority, often acting through party leaders, to force a final vote on both policy changes and rules changes. From early in its history, by contrast, the Senate allowed greater latitude for individual members to block action. These inherited institutions have made it more difficult for a floor majority to force institutional changes, thus limiting the majority party's ability to consolidate its power in the upper chamber. As a result, understanding the role of parties, committees, and individual members in today's House and Senate requires attention to historical development.

Rise of the Standing Committee System, 1789–1830

One of the most enduring and consequential transformations in congressional history was the creation, in the early nineteenth century, of a system of specialized standing committees. For a legislature to have the capacity to initiate and shape legislation independent of the executive branch, it requires a division of labor that allows it to bring expertise to bear on policy problems. Indeed, one of the key distinctive features of legislatures that have retained such influence is an effective committee system.

Members of Congress were initially hostile to the creation of a specialized committee system. They distrusted concentrations of power over policy making, which they believed threatened the equality of the legislators.[3] As a result, members sought to ensure that the full chamber would make all important decisions about legislation. In the first several Congresses, legislative proposals were initially considered by the full membership, which would decide whether action was warranted and, if so, refer the proposal to an ad hoc select committee for detailed drafting. The proposed legislation would then return to the floor for further debate and approval. Select committees initially existed to handle only a single piece of legislation and thus did not develop substantial expertise or influence. The House created 220 select committees in the First Congress alone. In the first fourteen Congresses (1789–1817), the House and Senate each appointed over two thousand select committees.[4]

The early prominence of temporary committees gave way by the mid-1820s. As Figure 1 indicates, the transition occurred gradually in the House, with a total of five standing committees created by 1795 and nine by the end of the Tenth Congress (1807–1809), which coincided with the last years of Thomas Jefferson's administration. Another burst of standing committee creation occurred in 1816, with the formation of seven new standing committees, includ-

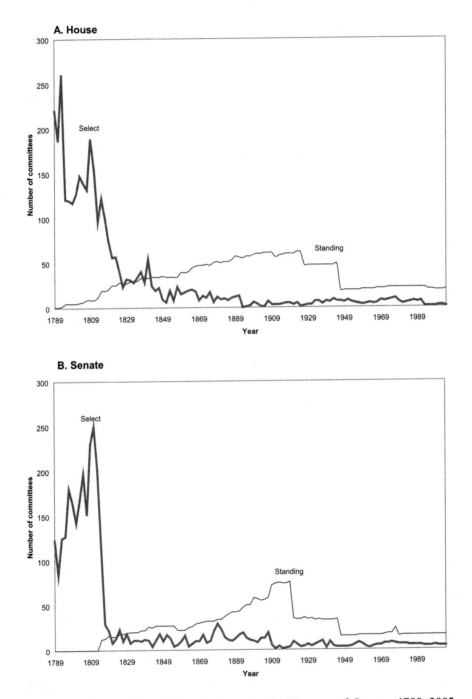

Figure 1 The Number of Committees in the House and Senate, 1789–2005

ing six committees charged with overseeing expenditures in the various executive departments. Finally, the transition culminated in 1822, with a series of rules changes that created three new standing committees and, more important, gave standing committees firmer property rights over legislation in their jurisdiction. Prior to 1822, even if a standing committee existed with jurisdiction over a specific problem area, bills covering that topic could still be referred to a select committee instead. After 1822, standing committees could generally expect that bills in their jurisdiction would be referred to them. The 1822 reforms also allowed committees to propose bills on their own initiative. Furthermore, the House adopted a strict germaneness rule that barred floor amendments that were unrelated to the text of the bill under consideration. These changes protected the jurisdictional claims of the standing committees. By the Eighteenth Congress (1823–1825), nearly 90 percent of all bills were referred to standing committees, as compared with fewer than half of the bills a decade earlier.[5]

Developments in the Senate followed a similar, though more abrupt, trajectory. The upper chamber did not establish its first standing committee until 1807, and that committee dealt with mere internal housekeeping tasks. But it caught up with the House in a single moment of innovation in 1816, when it created twelve new standing committees, including the Finance, Judiciary, and Foreign Relations Committees. After this change, the number of select committees fell dramatically and referral to the appropriate standing committee became the norm. But the Senate did not provide its committees the secure property rights accorded House standing committees. The Senate has never adopted a strict germaneness rule and even allows bills to be referred to the floor without going to committee, thus providing individual members with greater leverage in relation to the committees. For example, if a senator's pet proposal is bottled up in committee, he or she can seek to force floor action by proposing it as an unrelated amendment to another bill that has reached the floor. Such maneuvers have long characterized the Senate, making it a more open and unpredictable legislative body than the House.

Understanding the rise of the standing committee system is complicated by the dearth of discussion of most of the key changes—either on the floor, in newspapers of the time, or in members' personal papers.[6] However, the changes appear to have been rooted in two major forces: conflict with the executive branch, which generated incentives for members to enhance their institution's access to independent expertise, and a rising workload, which highlighted the costs of reliance on temporary committees.

The role of legislative-executive conflict in driving the creation of standing committees is evident from the timing of committee creation. The most important House committee, Ways and Means, was made a standing committee in the Fourth Congress (1795–1797) in order to provide the chamber with a source of financial advice independent of the powerful Treasury secretary Alexander

Hamilton. Members understood that the alternative to a standing committee would be continued reliance on Hamilton and his department for information about such issues as tariffs and economic development. The creation of six new committees to oversee expenditures by the executive departments in 1816 appears to have been a response to concerns about fiscal instability in the wake of the War of 1812 and failures to pay government suppliers in a timely fashion.[7] This is the first instance of what became a common pattern in congressional history: innovations to improve congressional capacity have repeatedly come in the wake of wars, the waging of which threatened congressional power and put new burdens on governmental machinery.[8]

Some have argued that the personal ambition of Henry Clay, the powerful early nineteenth-century House Speaker, also played a role in the expansion of the committee system.[9] While there is reason to suspect that Clay encouraged the creation of at least one committee—a committee on manufacturers that he expected (correctly) would be more favorably inclined toward his high-tariff policies—on the whole it appears that larger contextual forces predominated.[10] Indeed, it is worth emphasizing that the start of the rise of the standing committee system began before Clay's first term as Speaker (1811-13) and continued while he temporarily left the speakership in the Seventeenth Congress (1821-23). Furthermore, the Senate's sudden 1816 move to expand its committee system is at least circumstantial evidence that the response to a rising workload and to conflict with the executive branch in the postwar period played the more important role. Even in the absence of a domineering force similar to Clay, the Senate moved aggressively to create a standing committee system.

It is also worth emphasizing that several of the earliest standing committees created in the House dealt with the onslaught of constituent requests for government assistance in the new republic. These included the Claims Committee (created in the Third Congress), Public Lands (Ninth Congress), and Pensions (Thirteenth Congress). Congress was confronted with thousands of petitions requesting government benefits of various sorts, and these committees facilitated the processing of such requests. This suggests that workload concerns, perhaps combined with members' incentive to claim credit for providing efficient constituent services, motivated the development of the committee system.[11]

The House rules reforms of 1822, which constitute the final key moment in the transition to the standing committee system, appear to have been a response to the chaos engulfing the chamber as party lines gave way to nonpartisan factionalism. With parties essentially absent from the House, speakership elections turned into protracted battles among disparate factions. Jeffery Jenkins and Charles Stewart show that these battles at times were resolved through compromises involving the Speaker's use of committee assignments to cobble together a broad coalition.[12] Jenkins and Stewart hypothesize that the changes tightening committee jurisdictions were necessary to make these compromises "stick." That is, as long as standing committees could easily be bypassed, rewarding potential opponents with valuable committee assignments would not necessarily be a credible concession. But once the committee system became institutionalized, committee assignments became an effective coalition-building currency. The Jenkins-Stewart hypothesis is consistent with the Senate's failure to provide similar property rights protections for its committees. Since the Constitution specified that the vice president would be the Senate's presiding officer, the chamber did not have organizing battles analogous to speakership elections. Instead, the Senate continued to operate more on the basis of informal rules that left considerable latitude for individual members. The relatively small size of the Senate also likely contributed to its ability to rely upon informal constraints rather than formal rules to provide a modicum of order and organizational stability. Indeed, the contrast between the two chambers would continue to grow as the House relied heavily upon formal institutional rules and party leaders, while individual senators enjoyed far greater prerogatives that kept both committees and party leaders in check.

Party Leadership: Formalization and Expansion, 1860–1910

The most prominent institutional changes in the late nineteenth and early twentieth centuries concerned the expanded role of party leaders. Although party leaders gained strength in both chambers, the House once again delegated greater formal authority, while Senate leaders enjoyed more limited prerogatives vis-à-vis individual members. The majority party's policy goals were the primary impetus for the moves to strengthen party leaders, though broader concerns about congressional capacity and power also played a significant role in the House. Individual members' personal power interests were the primary constraint limiting the strength of party leaders; this interest proved particularly important in the Senate, thus furthering the distinctiveness of the two chambers.

The Speaker enjoyed the power of appointing committees from early in the House's history, and speakership elections became a focus of partisan organizing as early as the 1790s. However, the weakness of electoral parties through the 1820s and the deep regional split within both parties in the 1840s and 1850s limited the Speaker's ability to take on a consistent leadership role. Starting in the Civil War era, party lines became more firmly drawn and the House adopted a series of rules and precedents that enhanced the Speaker's influence over the agenda. For example, in the 1870s and 1880s, the Speaker gained firm control over recognizing members who wished to speak on the floor. This was followed by adoption of "Reed's Rules" in 1890. Adoption of the rules, named for their sponsor, the powerful Republican House speaker Thomas B. Reed (1889–1891; 1895–1899), is without question one of the most significant events in the institutional development of the Congress. No single change did more to secure majority rule in the House. The two most important features of Reed's Rules were the provisions instructing the Speaker not to entertain dilatory motions, and to put an end to the "disappearing quorum." The dilatory-motions ban empowered the Speaker to deny motions made solely to delay business. The disappearing quorum involved members' refusing to vote on a roll call even if they were actually present in the chamber, thereby depriving the House of the quorum needed to do business. Reed's Rules authorized the Speaker to establish a quorum by counting those members who were present but refused to vote. In the fifteen years after the end of Reconstruction, dilatory motions and the disappearing quorum had reached epidemic proportions, often bringing House business to a halt. The *Washington Post* observed in 1888 that "no other body in the world takes up so much time and spends so much money doing nothing. . . . The system of rules . . . is the prime cause of the wonderful inertia of this unwieldy and self-shackled body."[13] Reed's Rules eliminated the disappearing quorum and severely limited dilatory motions; no equally effective substitutes have since been devised.

Republicans' shared interest in passing their ambitious agenda was undoubtedly a major motivation for empowering the Speaker to eliminate obstruction.[14] Party members enjoyed unified party control of the government for the first time since the 1874 election, and did not want a recalcitrant Democratic minority to block their program of tariff and pension increases and voting rights protections for southern African Americans. Republicans thus backed Reed's Rules nearly unanimously, while Democrats fought the reforms vigorously.

Yet it is also the case that broader, institutional concerns contributed to the institutionalization of Reed's Rules. This is apparent from the battles over their repeal and reinstatement in 1892–1894. Democrats used Reed's allegedly tyrannical rules (the Speaker was popularly criticized as "Czar Reed") as one of their main campaign themes in the 1890 congressional elections. They argued that Reed's Rules exemplified Republicans' belief in excessive centralization, which was also manifested in such initiatives as high tariffs and national enforcement of voting rights. After the Democrats won an overwhelming majority in the election, the new Democratic House kept its promise to repeal most of Reed's Rules. But Reed soon launched a campaign of obstruction explicitly designed to force Democrats to admit that his procedural innovations had been necessary to allow the House to function. With considerable reluctance, Democrats eventually surrendered to Reed's filibustering in 1894 and adopted the quorum rule. Reed's own steadfast advocacy of reform—while in the minority as well as the majority—contributed to the slowly emerging consensus that majority rule would benefit all members. Illinois Democrat William Springer, echoing earlier statements by Republicans, expressed the newfound bipartisan sentiment: "We have tried the old system. We have been here a month without doing two days' actual business, and our constituents are tired of this delay. . . . If we shall adopt this rule, we will from this time forward have it in our power to discharge the duties which our constituents have confided to us."[15] By the early 1890s, the House had over 350 members and a much more extensive workload than in the antebellum period. As a result, the costs to the institution of unbridled minority obstruction became too great to tolerate. Although many Democrats were unhappy with the quorum rule, 1894 marked the end of their party's long-standing commitment to the "right" of the House minority to block legislation.

A similar confluence of partisan and broad institutional interests illuminates another major institutional development in this period: the House Rules Committee's acquisition of a series of prerogatives that allowed it to manage the legislative agenda. At this time, the Rules Committee was a small body, composed of five members and chaired by the Speaker. Its duties initially focused on proposing changes in the permanent rules governing the House, but its role expanded greatly toward the end of the nineteenth century. Starting in 1883, the committee began to use "special" (that is, temporary) rules to allow the House to bring matters to the floor out of their regular order by just a majority vote. This move was initiated by Reed, prior to becoming Speaker, in order to help Republicans pass a controversial tariff bill as adjournment loomed. In 1892, Democrats on the Rules Committee proposed a change granting the committee the privilege of immediate consideration of its reports, with no dilatory motions allowed. This protected bills carrying the Rules Committee's endorsement from many filibuster tactics, but not from the disappearing quorum. Most Democrats supported the new rule, believing that it would limit obstruction without requiring complete acceptance of Reed's Rules. It is noteworthy, however, that minority-party Republicans did not resist this change. Instead, Republicans argued that a degree of centralized agenda control was required for the House to function effectively amid a burgeoning workload. Indeed, Reed called the 1892 increase in the Rules Committee's powers a "very great advance . . . henceforth we shall have some governing and responsible power in the House."[16] This again suggests that broad concern about the House's capacity to legislate contributed to the development of centralized agenda control in the late nineteenth century, even as the majority party's more immediate legislative goals were likely the impetus for reform. By the close of the 1890s, the House was a remarkably centralized institution featuring a powerful Speaker who controlled committee assignments, regulated obstruction on the floor, and, through the Rules Committee, exerted considerable influence over the chamber's agenda.

While the House was empowering the speakership, the Senate also developed a more formalized, though limited, role for party leaders. The Constitution's provision of an outsider as presiding officer slowed the development of party leadership institutions in the upper chamber. The Senate experimented with selecting committees by ballot (that is, vote of the full membership) and by the vice president or president pro tem of the Senate,[17] up until the mid-

1840s, when party caucuses gained the dominant role in committee assignments and soon delegated this authority to a party committee on committees. Selection by ballot had proven cumbersome, and delegation to the vice president was highly problematic, since that officer did not owe his position to the Senate and could differ from most senators' partisan and policy allegiances.[18] After the shift to party control of assignments, the majority party enjoyed a majority on nearly all of the major committees, in contrast to the more uneven record when committees were selected by ballot or by the presiding officer.[19] Nonetheless, the party committees relied heavily upon seniority in doling out assignments, thereby limiting the extent to which this shift gave the majority party the ability to dictate outcomes to the committees. Reliance on seniority gave individual senators more independence in advancing their own personal agendas, since they did not owe their assignments to party leaders.

Indeed, even with committee assignments organized by party, the Senate still lacked a single leader analogous to the Speaker who could take primary responsibility for agenda setting. This meant that the Senate floor tended to be a chaotic place in the nineteenth century, as committee chairmen competed among themselves and with individual senators for priority for their bills.[20] Starting in 1892, the Senate parties began to rely upon steering committees to set the floor agenda. Gerald Gamm and Steven Smith argue that this experiment was rooted in each party's electoral goals: with the party balance in the Senate extremely tight, Democrats and Republicans alike realized that they needed to act as a team in order to promote legislation that would bolster their respective party's electoral prospects.[21] As the parties polarized on policy issues later in the decade, the majority party tightened its agenda control further. By the late 1890s, an interlocking directorate of senior Republicans—led by Steering Committee chairman and party caucus chairman William Allison of Iowa and Finance Committee chairman Nelson Aldrich of Rhode Island—had largely taken charge of the Senate's agenda. Aldrich, Allison, and their allies controlled the most important committee chairmanships, along with the Steering Committee and Committee on Committees. They used this influence to promote their shared conservative policy goals.

Nonetheless, although Aldrich and Allison provided a modicum of centralized leadership, their influence never approached that of House Speakers Reed and Joseph Cannon (1903–1911). The reliance upon seniority in doling out committee assignments meant that even the most important committees at times behaved contrary to the leadership's preferences. For example, during the heyday of Aldrich and Allison's tenure, the Finance Committee forced important changes in the party's top legislative priority, the Dingley Tariff Act of 1897.[22]

Perhaps more importantly, individual members continued to enjoy tremendous prerogatives to disrupt the leaders' plans. In particular, the tradition of unlimited debate meant that even a small group of senators could use the filibuster to delay or even block legislation completely. The House had begun the process of limiting debate in 1811 when it adopted the previous question rule, which allowed a floor majority to bring a matter to an immediate vote.[23] As noted above, over the course of the nineteenth century the House built upon this initial reform by adopting a series of innovations—culminating with Reed's Rules—that allowed the majority-party leadership to clamp down on obstruction. By contrast, the much smaller Senate, with its tradition of weaker party leaders, relied heavily upon individual self-restraint as the main limitation on debate. This worked reasonably well for much of the nineteenth century. The floor agenda was not terribly crowded, which meant that senators could employ their prerogatives to delay measures and test the majority's commitment to passage, but that in the end a committed majority could generally expect to triumph.[24] However, as the Senate's agenda became more crowded and as the chamber grew in size with the admission of new states, this informal system became more problematic. By the end of the nineteenth century, filibusters were increasing in frequency and undermined party leaders' ability to control the agenda. Yet individual senators continued to value their individual prerogatives, meaning that such leaders as Aldrich failed in their efforts to eliminate obstruction.[25] As a result, individual senators' personal power interests sharply limited the rise of party government in the upper chamber.

Revolt against Centralization, 1910–1930

The late nineteenth and early twentieth centuries represent the historical high-water mark for centralized party leadership in both the House and the Senate, even as the upper chamber was well behind the House in terms of the extent of party government. The first decades of the twentieth century, however, featured a move away from centralization as individual members sought to enhance their own prerogatives. Once again, the intersection of multiple interests proved necessary to gain adoption of major changes. Members' individual power interests aligned with the policy goals of an ideological faction to motivate reform. Just as the initial centralization occurred through more formal and dramatic changes in the House than the Senate, the moves to fragment power were based more in formal rules changes in the lower chamber, while changes in the Senate were more subtle and gradual.

The critical changes in the House occurred in the final years of Illinois Republican Cannon's speakership. A series of changes in 1909–1911 took away the Speaker's control over committee assignments, removed the Speaker from the Rules Committee, and created mechanisms for a floor majority to force matters to the floor over the Speaker's opposition. With the Speaker's authority diminished, seniority soon became the dominant consideration in determining committee leadership positions. This helped to launch the so-called textbook

Congress, in which specialized standing committees played an especially prominent role and party leaders receded in importance.[26]

Three forces fused to produce the revolt against Cannon. First, starting in 1905, progressives became more numerous within the Republican Party as President Theodore Roosevelt began to push for major policy change. These ideological divisions within the majority party fostered greater resistance to centralized party control, particularly since Cannon had used that control to push only for conservative policies. When a party is internally divided on policy, centralized leadership becomes more costly for its members.[27] Insurgent leader John Nelson, a Republican congressman from Wisconsin, illustrated progressives' mounting frustration in 1908 when he argued that "President Roosevelt has been trying to cultivate oranges for many years in the frigid climate of the Committee on Rules, but what has he gotten but the proverbial lemons?"[28] A second source of dissatisfaction with Cannon was the belief that his tight personal control deprived individual representatives of opportunities to exert influence. As members began to view Congress as a career in this era, they sought greater leeway to make a name for themselves without the Speaker's interference. The insurgents against Cannon included a handful of relatively senior and fairly conservative Republicans who had each seen Cannon commandeer legislation from their committees. Weakening the Speaker promised to safeguard committees from such incursions and thus to allow individual members more opportunities to pursue their own agendas. A third source of Cannon's downfall was the minority party's reaction to his aggressive leadership. After years of frustration in the minority, Democrats responded to being shut out of the policy process by attacking the House as an institution and turning Cannon into the symbol of an undemocratic and unresponsive legislative branch. The Democrats focused heavily on Cannon's leadership style in the 1908 campaign and planned to continue their attacks in the upcoming 1910 elections. They hoped to identify all Republicans with the increasingly unpopular Speaker and thereby improve the electoral chances of Democratic candidates. Cannon's mounting unpopularity eventually forced several vulnerable Midwestern Republicans with no history of progressivism to back the revolt.

In 1910, the House voted to remove Cannon from the Rules Committee and to make that committee subject to election by the floor. When Democrats took control of the House after the 1910 elections, they gave authority over the party's committee assignments to a Committee on Committees (made up of the party's members of the Ways and Means Committee). Although Democrats experimented with governing through their party caucus and a strong floor leader in 1911–1919, the long-term significance of the Cannon revolt was to weaken party leadership. By the 1920s, committee assignments came to be largely dominated by seniority, and the Rules Committee eventually became a much more independent agenda-setting body.

Even though the Senate had never delegated as much power to party leaders, it moved largely in tandem with the House toward greater decentralization. While Republicans had enjoyed a reasonable degree of unity on key policy issues in the 1890s and early 1900s, both parties featured major internal divisions by 1910, which persisted for the next several decades. This undermined member support for vigorous party leadership. The interlocking party and committee leadership of the late 1890s gave way to a clearer separation of party and committee leadership. By the 1920s, several key committees featured majorities of progressive Republicans and Democrats, notwithstanding the nominal Republican majority in the chamber as a whole. These committees pursued policies on issues such as agriculture prices that were out of step with conservative Republican party leaders.[29]

The Senate also emulated the House in providing more formalized floor and agenda management in this period. Prior to the turn of the century, the Senate did not feature formal floor leaders charged with managing the chamber's agenda.[30] But starting in 1911–1913, both parties moved to elect a single floor leader. This was a period of extremely narrow floor majorities, in which garnering every single vote was essential.[31] Not surprisingly, both parties also created the position of whip during these years in order to promote attendance on the floor. Under the Democratic majority in power from 1913 to 1919, the floor leader often worked closely with the White House to promote a common party agenda. But the majority leader lacked the ability to defeat minority obstruction and had only limited sway over the committee system. As such, the formal party leaders are better viewed as managers who facilitated the processing of legislation and the development of a common party position than as aggressive policymakers.

A further move toward formalization in the Senate occurred in 1917 with passage of the chamber's first cloture rule. Prior to 1917, the Senate lacked a mechanism for ending debate in the face of minority obstruction. But a series of high-profile filibusters in the early twentieth century brought increased pressure for reform. With World War I rising on the agenda, the Senate's inability to pass much-needed legislation at the end of the Sixty-fourth Congress (1915–1917) led to President Woodrow Wilson's famous attack on the "little group of willful men" who had stood in the way of the majority. The Senate responded in March 1917 with a rule that allowed two-thirds of senators present and voting to adopt a cloture resolution, which provided a timetable for ending debate. It is worth emphasizing that the cloture rule did not curtail the practice of filibustering. Instead, it provided a formal mechanism for ending obstruction, but only in the presence of supermajority support. The 1917 change thus reinforced the contrast with the majoritarian House. Indeed, as the Senate's workload continued to rise after 1917 and as individual senators became more assertive in attempting to make a name for themselves in the political system, filibusters would only become a more prominent feature of Senate lawmaking over time.

Still, although the Senate moved toward greater formalization in the early twentieth century, this shift did not stop the more potent trend toward decentralization. Party floor leaders and the cloture rule allowed for slightly greater predictability and more efficient management of the Senate's agenda, but the basic mode of operations in the upper chamber became ever more individualistic. The constitutional amendment providing for direct election of senators in 1913 likely reinforced the upper chamber's tendency toward individualism and its resistance to collective controls. The basic difference between the chambers can be seen in the contrasting methods used to set the terms of debate for controversial legislation on the floor. Even as parties weakened in the House, important bills generally reached the floor through special rules from the Rules Committee that set specific time limits for debate and on occasion limited the amendments that could be offered on the floor. It required a simple floor majority to adopt such a special rule. By contrast, Senate floor leaders came to rely upon complicated unanimous-consent agreements to maneuver items on the floor. A single senator could block such an agreement, and thus each senator had the leverage to greatly complicate the leader's task.

By the end of the 1920s, both the House and the Senate had developed elaborate committee systems and formalized party leadership structures. The power of party leaders had peaked at the turn of the century in both chambers amid sharp party polarization, but had subsequently given way as a result of deepening internal party divisions and the increased assertiveness of individual careerist members in the early twentieth century. Even after the revolt against Cannon, party leaders continued to play a greater role in the House than the Senate, where individual members enjoyed more extensive prerogatives. But even in the House, party leaders could no longer count on control of the key agenda-setting body, the Rules Committee. Indeed, in 1937, a coalition of conservative southern Democrats and Republicans took effective control of the committee. After 1937, the Democratic majority in the chamber faced a formidable obstacle to pursuit of a party program. Proposals favored by the party's northern majority would now have to be extracted from an often-hostile Rules Committee. With conservative southerners also in control of several key legislative committees, the separation of party and committee leadership was virtually complete.

Rise of the Modern Presidency and the Legislative Reorganization Act of 1946

The fragmented congressional system that existed in the first decades of the twentieth century came under tremendous challenge with the rise of a far more aggressive and powerful presidency in the 1930s and 1940s. The expansion of federal responsibility during the New Deal, President Franklin Roosevelt's domestic program for economic recovery and social reforms following the onset of the Great Depression, and the unprecedented mobilization effort for World War II combined to lavish immense influence upon Roosevelt and his successors. In the absence of equally strong leaders in the legislature, members of Congress began to worry about the future of their institution. Academic studies, congressional hearings, and journalistic accounts in the 1940s echoed the theme that Congress must reorganize in order to retain its coequal place in the constitutional system. Mike Monroney (a Democrat congressman from Oklahoma), one of the leading advocates of reform, stated the widely held view that "we simply cannot struggle along under this type of workload unless we equip ourselves to answer the challenge that the Constitution's framers intended the Congress to carry."[32] Many reformers called for a return to party government, but in the absence of an internally unified majority party, such calls found little resonance in Congress. The deep Democratic divisions between northern liberals and southern conservatives meant that members had to look elsewhere to create an institutional counterbalance to presidential power.

In response, members chose to streamline and strengthen the congressional committee system by adopting the Legislative Reorganization Act of 1946. The act bolstered the capacity and influence of standing committees in both chambers. It emerged in reaction to the rise of the modern presidency, and reflects how members of Congress sought to defend their institution in ways that were compatible with protecting their existing committee power bases. Members' interest in individual power and improved perquisites fused with their stake in congressional capacity to promote a major institutional renovation.

Prior to the Reorganization Act, there were forty-eight standing committees in the House and thirty-three in the Senate. These committees often had vague and overlapping jurisdictions, were poorly staffed, and had come to rely heavily upon the Roosevelt administration for legislative proposals. The Reorganization Act for the first time defined committee jurisdictions in specific terms and made these jurisdictions more systematic and comprehensive. It also combined committees with related responsibilities, creating a more streamlined set of nineteen standing committees in the House and fifteen in the Senate. The act provided committees with professional staff so that they would have the expertise to frame their own legislative initiatives independently of the executive branch. The committees nearly doubled their staffs in the first four years after the act took effect; in 1946, committees had employed 356 staffers—few of them professionals—while in 1950, they employed a total of 673 staffers, 286 of whom were professionals.[33] Finally, the Reorganization Act charged each committee with exercising "continuous watchfulness" over the agencies in its jurisdiction. This was in response to concern that lagging congressional oversight had allowed federal agencies to usurp the legislative branch's prerogatives during World War II. Congressional investigations expanded in frequency and aggressiveness during this period, challenging the executive branch on numerous fronts.

The primary motivation for the Reorganization Act was the perceived need to improve congressional operations and thereby resist presidential encroachments. The measure garnered substantial support from members of both parties and from across the ideological spectrum. A striking feature of the deliberations was that even liberal Democrats, who ostensibly stood to gain in policy terms by deferring to the liberal White House, sought to enhance congressional power vis-à-vis the executive. For example, the liberal House member Jerry Voorhis attacked Congress's recent failure to put "forward any alternative constructive program of its own." Voorhis's adversary in many policy fights, the conservative Democrat Eugene Cox, commended the California Democrat for his "magnificent statement" and added that "you have been classified as an ultra-progressive and I as a mossback reactionary, and still there is not the slightest difference between my views and the statement you make."[34] Republicans also emphasized the need to bolster congressional capacity in order to defend the institution's power. For example, Republican senator Owen Brewster of Maine observed that Congress must reorganize "if we are to retain any semblance of the ancient division of functions under our Constitution."[35] Republican representative Edward Rees of Kansas summed up the attitude of many members when he claimed that "the time has come when the Congress should no longer be satisfied with the role of a rubber stamp."[36] The consistent message from Democrats and Republicans, liberals and conservatives alike, was that Congress had become institutionally crippled and that reorganization was essential for its rehabilitation.

However, interest in congressional capacity and power was not sufficient to pass the Reorganization Act. The reform measure had to overcome the opposition of members who would lose their personal power bases because the act eliminated so many committees. Reformers worked before and after passage of the act to compensate these members with good assignments on the consolidated committees, thus tempering their opposition. Perhaps more importantly, the bill's authors also included a pay raise and a pension system in the act in order to elicit support from potential foes. Members understood that public reaction against the raise would be mitigated since it was part of a major bipartisan reorganization bill supported by the press and outside experts. Senator Robert La Follette of Wisconsin, the cochairman of the special committee that framed the act, noted that he had pushed to have the pay raise, pension system, and committee consolidation "wrapped up in one package" for just this reason: members would be more willing to sacrifice some committee power bases if doing so would lead to a better salary.[37] Thus reformers harnessed individual members' desire for increased pay and perquisites to enact a reorganization plan that primarily served broad institutional interests. Monroney claimed that the 1946 act had been approved partly because of its "ice cream" provisions, which made its "spinach" more palatable.[38]

Political observers have repeatedly asserted that Congress is generally unable to act collectively as an institution to defend its power, and that as a result it has steadily lost power to the White House.[39] However, an important lesson of the 1946 reorganization is that efforts to improve congressional capacity and defend congressional power can be enacted when these reforms are linked to individual members' electoral, personal power, or even financial, interests. Such efforts at institutional reform are particularly likely following major wars and crises that enhance executive power at the expense of Congress.[40]

The Reorganization Act profoundly affected the congressional authority structure by reinforcing the already strong system of standing committees and committee chairmen. By reducing the number of committees and expanding their jurisdictions, the Reorganization Act made each committee a more potent institutional power base for its members and chairman. Since many of these chairmen were conservative southerners, this posed significant problems both for Democratic administrations and for mainstream northern Democrats. Although some reformers attempted to include provisions empowering party leaders to counterbalance the fortified committees, these features were either eliminated before passage or not implemented in practice. The one centralizing provision included in the act—a mandate that a joint House-Senate budget committee frame a legislative budget that sets binding spending and revenue totals—was never implemented, due to the resistance of the turf-conscious House Appropriations Committee. As a result, members of Congress had provided themselves with greater capacity to initiate individual legislative proposals and to scrutinize particular executive actions. But they had not provided integrative mechanisms that would allow Congress to pursue a coordinated, coherent program of its own. The Reorganization Act thus bolstered Congress's power over the individual "pieces" of governmental policy, but the legislative branch remained dependent on the executive when broad, coordinated programs were required.

Reform Era of the 1970s

The committee-dominated system institutionalized by the Legislative Reorganization Act of 1946 persisted for several decades, but it gave way in the 1970s amid a wave of major reforms. In both the House and Senate, junior members' interest in increased access to institutional power and liberal Democrats' goal of undercutting the influence of conservative committee chairmen combined to propel reform. But where the House enacted a complex combination of changes that spread power from chairmen both downward to subcommittees and individual members and upward to party leaders, the Senate continued its long-term trend toward individualism and fragmentation.

By the early 1970s, the old textbook Congress confronted increasingly sharp challenges from several sources. Liberal Democrats, who augmented their numbers following Democratic sweeps in the 1958 and 1964 elections, were deeply dissatisfied with a committee system that empowered southern conservatives from safe districts, who rarely faced a serious electoral challenge. This dissatisfaction was exacerbated by the shift in the broader political context toward candidate-centered elections, which encouraged members to place a greater premium on gaining rapid access to their own power bases within Congress in order to make a name for themselves. Junior representatives and senators thus sought to undermine the seniority system, which placed disproportionate power in the hands of senior committee chairmen.

Both chambers responded to these pressures in the 1970s with a series of innovations that undercut the seniority system, spread greater resources to subcommittees and individual members, and, particularly in the House, granted new tools to party leaders. The first major reform was the Legislative Reorganization Act of 1970, which targeted chairmen's arbitrary exercise of power by requiring committees to adopt written rules and promoting open committee meetings. The most important legacy of the act was a provision for recorded votes on floor amendments in the House. Prior to 1970, it was relatively easy for a committee chairman to defeat floor amendments, because votes on amendments were generally not recorded, so that constituents would not know how individual representatives had voted. In the absence of constituent pressure, chairmen were well positioned to defend their bills against floor assaults. By allowing the public to know how individual members voted on amendments, the Reorganization Act fueled floor-amending activity and thereby weakened the position of the chairmen. A coalition of liberal Democrats and junior members of both parties pushed for the 1970 act.[41]

After 1970, the primary venue for institutional change in the House shifted to the Democratic Caucus, where all Democrats would meet to set party rules and procedures. The Caucus was revitalized as conservative southerners began to dwindle in number and liberals gained a clear majority within the party.[42] Liberals used the caucus to take power away from the standing committees and to spread it downward to subcommittees and individual members and upward to party leaders.

A "subcommittee bill of rights," adopted in January 1973 by the Democratic Caucus, transferred the power to appoint subcommittee chairmen from the full committee chair to the committee's majority-party members. This committee caucus would also set subcommittee jurisdictions. In addition, the bill of rights guaranteed subcommittees an adequate budget and staff, along with automatic referral of legislation. An earlier 1971 caucus reform had limited each member to a single subcommittee chairmanship, thereby spreading access to these influential positions more broadly. A 1975 change adopted by the House further bolstered subcommittee resources by authorizing each subcommittee chairman and ranking member to hire one full-time staff person to handle subcommittee work. Since there were over one hundred subcommittee chairmen and just twenty full committee chairmen, these reforms spread power to more members. Even the most junior Democrat could reasonably aspire to a subcommittee chairmanship within a few terms of entering the House. But the subcommittee reforms did not benefit all junior members equally. Liberals lobbied hardest for the reforms, in part because they believed that strengthening the subcommittees would not only empower them as individual entrepreneurs, but would also weaken conservative committee chairmen, who often blocked liberal legislation. Therefore, the subcommittee changes passed because liberal Democrats had policy reasons to undercut conservative committee chairmen and found that they could forge a broad coalition for doing so by simultaneously appealing to representatives' power-base interests.

A similar confluence of forces generated the revolt against the seniority system for selecting committee chairmen that occurred in 1971–1975. This movement started with liberal-sponsored initiatives to force secret-ballot votes on individual chairmen in the caucus. It culminated in 1975, when the huge freshman class of seventy-four "Watergate babies," elected in the wake of Richard Nixon's resignation, propelled a successful movement to overthrow three aging southern committee barons. Although only one of the southerners had generally used his position to support conservative policies—Edward Hebert of Louisiana, who chaired the Armed Services Committee—the overthrow symbolized that the Democratic Caucus expected all chairmen to be more responsive to party members. Interestingly, House Republicans also undermined seniority by changing party rules to provide for individual votes on the party's ranking committee members. This reinforces the hypothesis that the seniority changes were not simply a product of liberal policy interests. Instead, the common dynamics across parties indicates that the changes were in part spurred by junior members' restiveness with a system that advantaged long-serving members.[43]

The subcommittee and seniority changes contributed to a seismic power shift in the House. Committee chairmen were forced to share power with rank-and-file committee members and to look to the caucus for guidance on important policy issues. Each subcommittee chairman now had a power base that could be used to launch initiatives, claim credit, and gain press attention. Policy entrepreneurship became increasingly widespread, and subcommittees proved a valuable source of programmatic innovation. While subcommittee influence varied across issue areas, subcommittee chairmen now generally had disproportionate access to important resources, such as staff expertise and communication networks. Meanwhile, the roughly twenty committee chairmen who had in the past served as focal points for coalition building suffered greatly reduced stature.

The fragmentation brought about by the rise of subcommittees and the weakening of the chairmen was partially offset by changes that provided new powers to party leaders.[44] In 1974, the House authorized the Speaker to refer bills to multiple committees. This reform was in part intended to bolster the chamber's capacity to address issues that crosscut committee jurisdictions. As such, it enjoyed broad, bipartisan support. But the innovation also promised to enhance the Speaker's ability to structure the committee process. Although used sparingly at first, it eventually became an important leadership tool for encouraging committees to coordinate their efforts. The Democratic Caucus adopted additional changes that more directly strengthened party leaders. Most importantly, the caucus strengthened leadership influence over committee assignments. In 1974, Democrats took the power to make committee assignments from the party's members of the Ways and Means Committee and granted it to the recently created Steering and Policy Committee, on which the Speaker and majority leader controlled several votes. The caucus also granted the Speaker the power to select party members who serve on the Rules Committee. This change made the committee an effective arm of the leadership, essentially reversing one of the main elements of the revolt against Cannon.[45] Before long, the committee was developing complex special rules that allowed the leadership to restrict the amendments offered to bills in ways that often advantaged the majority party's preferred policies. By the mid-1980s, as Democrats became increasingly unified when confronted with Ronald Reagan's conservative agenda, party leaders began to use their new powers particularly aggressively. The Texas Democrat Jim Wright, who took over as Speaker in 1987, used multiple referrals, committee assignments, and the Rules Committee as instruments to pursue a far-reaching agenda that challenged the Republican White House and led observers to comment upon the "new centralization" on Capitol Hill.[46]

The Senate experienced a movement toward fragmentation in the 1970s that paralleled that of the House, but formal changes empowering party leaders were far more limited. As a result, the reform era deepened the distinctiveness of the chambers, as expanding Senate individualism contrasted with the partial revival of party leadership in the House. Although no Senate chairmen or ranking committee members were deposed, both Democrats and Republicans adopted new rules easing the way for votes on individual chairmen. The Senate also adopted a generous new staffing policy in 1975 that provided each senator on a committee with additional staff assistance independent of the chairmen. This made it easier for junior members to engage in policy entrepreneurship.

The most striking change in Senate operations was an informal one: the filibuster, which had been used relatively sparingly for much of American history, became a routine tool used by individual senators to extract concessions or to block bills entirely. While it is impossible to quantify the amount of obstruction precisely, Sarah Binder and Steven Smith document increasing filibusters in the 1970s and 1980s.[47] They count just 23 "manifest filibusters" in the entire nineteenth century and they report that the typical Congress in the 1940s through the 1960s had about 5 filibusters. By contrast, there were 191 filibusters from 1970 to 1994. In just the 102nd Congress of 1991–1992, there were a record 35 filibusters, and the prevalence of filibusters remained high throughout the remainder of the decade. The boom in obstruction, like the move toward improved staffing for junior senators, was partly rooted in the new, candidate-centered political context, which rewarded individual activism.[48] Heightened time pressures, however, added to the temptation to filibuster: as the Senate's schedule became more crowded, the mere threat of a filibuster was often sufficient to extract concessions.[49] As partisan polarization has increased in the chamber, filibusters have also been fueled by the minority party's interest in blocking policies that it opposes. Although partisan filibusters have been a recurrent feature of Senate politics, they have increased in frequency since the 1970s. Since the cloture rule now requires sixty votes to end debate, the routinization of the filibuster means that legislating typically requires supermajority support. Indeed, a 2002 study suggests that roughly half of all major bills encounter filibuster difficulties, often resulting in either defeat or substantial concessions.[50]

A final change adopted in the reform era of the 1970s featured somewhat different dynamics than the fragmenting and party-building changes described above. In 1974, Congress adopted the Congressional Budget and Impoundment Control Act (commonly referred to as the Budget Act). The legislation created budget committees in the House and Senate, charging them with proposing budget resolutions that set spending and revenue targets. These budget resolutions would not require the signature of the president. Annual reconciliation bills would then enact the specific tax and spending changes required to meet the budget resolution targets. The Budget Act also curtailed the power of the president to impound funds and created the Congressional Budget Office as a source of independent expertise for the House and Senate. The immediate impetus for the Budget Act was President Nixon's use of impoundments to attack domestic programs, along with more general concerns about declining congressional power in the wake of the Vietnam War. As such, the act reflected members' stake in defending their institution's power, and enjoyed broad, bipartisan support. Members understood that credibly responding to Nixon's encroachments required that Congress provide its own mechanisms for coordinating revenue and spending decisions. In addition, conservatives hoped to use the new process to force trade-offs that would result in lower spending.

The new budget process created a new set of committees and procedures that were superimposed on the existing structure of authorization, appropriations, and revenue committees. To avoid fierce opposition, the framers of the act respected existing committee power bases, adding a new framework to the existing decision-making structure. But the resulting need to gain the cooperation of these entrenched committees made the budget committees' task more difficult. The budget committees have fought recurrent battles with the appropriations and authorization committees over spending priorities, and with the revenue committees over tax policy and entitlements. Still, the long-term impact of the new budget process has been to increase centralization in both the House and Senate. In the House, the majority party has long dominated the Budget Committee, and with a few critical exceptions—such as Reagan's 1981 budget triumph, when a coalition of conservative Democrats and Republicans enacted a massive tax cut and defense build-up—has used the process to pursue its fiscal agenda. Although budgeting in the Senate has featured more bipartisan cooperation at times, the 1974 act shielded budget resolutions and reconciliation bills from filibusters. This allows the majority party to use the budget process to achieve its policy goals—such as big changes in tax policy—without the need to gain the minority-party support necessary to invoke cloture. Perhaps the most enduring impact of the budget process is that it has provided a mechanism for even a slim majority in each chamber to enact sweeping changes in the nation's fiscal policy. If a major concern in the wake of the Legislative Reorganization Act of 1946 was that Congress had the capacity to shape the individual elements of federal policy, but not to coordinate policy at a more general level, the Budget Act provided an important new tool for Congress to rectify this shortcoming.

Republican "Revolution" of 1995

The institutional development of Congress is ongoing. The most recent important changes occurred following Republicans' takeover of the House and Senate in the 1994 elections. Under the assertive leadership of Republican Speaker Newt Gingrich of Georgia, Republicans adopted an array of reforms intended to centralize party control. Although the most important changes occurred in the House, Senate Republicans also adopted a handful of innovations meant to strengthen party discipline in the notoriously unruly chamber. Nonetheless, the persistence of the right of unlimited debate has precluded the consolidation of effective party government in the upper chamber. The combination of the filibuster and intense partisan polarization has magnified the challenges facing Senate leaders.

The basic thrust of the GOP reforms in the House was to create a more hierarchical organization: party leaders enhanced their influence over committee chairmen, and the chairmen, in turn, were empowered vis-à-vis subcommittee leaders. Thus, party leaders intervened aggressively in the selection of committee chairmen. Under the Republican system as it has become institutionalized since the late 1990s, prospective chairmen are interviewed by the leadership-dominated Steering Committee, which relies on party loyalty in voting and fund-raising as criteria along with seniority.[51] The imposition of six-year term limits for the chairmen further weakened committee leaders' prospects for acquiring an independent power base.[52] At the same time, Republicans have not emulated the Democrats' subcommittee bill of rights. Instead, full committee chairmen now control the selection of subcommittee leaders and staff. Republicans have also expanded upon Democrats' practice of using partisan task forces to supplement, or at times displace, the standing committees' role in writing important legislation. Combined with reductions in committee staffing, these changes have led observers to worry about a "crack-up" of the committee system as a whole, which may be undermining Congress's capacity to bring to bear independent expertise on policy problems.[53] Although Gingrich's successor, Dennis Hastert, Republican of Illinois, took on a much lower public profile than his predecessor, the trend toward centralized party leadership and weakened committees appears to have been sustained.

If the 1910 revolt against centralization presaged the development of a more independent, specialized committee system, the institutional innovations that have occurred since the 1970s suggest a movement in the House back toward the model of leadership offered by Reed and Cannon. Nonetheless, it is an overstatement to claim that Congress has returned to "czar rule." Instead, Hastert and his leadership team showed a deep dependence on the ongoing support of rank-and-file Republicans, and they worked assiduously to involve these members in the party machinery. Indeed, the critical shift has been that members' participation now occurs more through party machinery and less through the committee system than in the past.[54]

The impact of the Republican takeover in the Senate has been more subtle. Republicans have challenged the seniority system, though more gingerly than in the House. The GOP adopted rules specifying that the party conference would vote on an official legislative agenda prior to selecting committee chairmen, providing a potential benchmark for evaluating their loyalty. Furthermore, the party adopted a term-limit rule of their own for committee chairmen in September 1995, which has forced a handful of longtime chairmen to surrender their posts. The declining independence of committee chairmen was underscored following the 2004 election when Republican senator Arlen Specter headed off a conservative-backed challenge to his ascension to the Judiciary Committee chairmanship by proclaiming that he would work to promote the confirmation of President George W. Bush's judicial nominees. This episode suggests that the majority party in the Senate has become more willing to demand loyalty from committee chairmen.

Nonetheless, Senate majority-party leaders still confront the task of building supermajority support before they can adopt most major new policies. Furthermore, individualism remains a potent force in the upper chamber. Republican Party mavericks such as John McCain and Chuck Hagel, along with moderates such as Olympia Snowe and Susan Collins, have exercised far more influence than like-minded House Republicans in challenging their party's leadership. Therefore, even as the Senate, by 2005, had come to look a bit more like the House in terms of partisan activity, the two chambers continued to differ markedly in the relative prerogatives of individual members and party leaders.

Lessons for Congressional Reform

Over the past 225 years, the House and Senate have developed an elaborate committee system and party leadership structure to enable members to better pursue their goals. The power of committees and of party leaders has waxed and waned over time, in response to external pressures, such as challenges from the executive branch, and internal dynamics, such as the level of party polarization and individual member careerism. Today's House has returned to a level of party strength not seen in nearly a century, while the Senate remains highly individualistic, notwithstanding its high level of partisan acrimony. Although developments in the two chambers have typically moved in tandem, the general pattern is for formal party leaders to enjoy greater prerogatives in the House, while the smaller Senate has featured greater individual prerogatives, looser rules, and weaker party leaders.

One reason to study the institutional development of Congress is the belief that institutions affect member behavior, and thus that the House-Senate differences described above help explain political outcomes. Yet a cursory examination of roll call voting data suggests that the seemingly sharp institutional differences between the House and Senate do not impact how members vote on the floor, and therefore would appear to have limited importance for policy outcomes. That is, levels of party voting are generally as high in the Senate as in the House, notwithstanding the much greater individualism and weaker party leaders in the upper chamber. For example, the percentage of votes that divided a majority of Democrats against a majority of Republicans reached two-thirds in the Senate in 2003, as compared with 52 percent in the House. In both chambers, approximately 90 percent of the members stuck with their party on these votes.[55] Nonetheless, inherited institutions—such as the filibuster—have had a profound impact on the meaning of this polarization. In the House, as Democrats and Republicans came to represent distinctive constituencies, their policy preferences polarized along party lines, giving members greater incentive to delegate power to party leaders. The majority party has come to dominate the legislative process in the chamber; in the 108th Congress (2003–2004), minority-party Democrats were generally shut out when it came to decision making on most important issues. In the Senate, by contrast, the need for supermajority support for most legislation means that the preference polarization that produces high levels of party voting has not translated into majority-party government. Instead, the minority increasingly uses party-based filibusters to block action. The cloture votes to defeat these filibusters produce numerous sharply partisan roll calls, but in the absence of support from several Democrats, they are doomed to failure. As a result, even perfect party-line votes in the Senate do not necessarily generate majority-party victories, in contrast to the majoritarian House.

In sum, the polarization of party members' preferences has fostered majority-party governance in the House, but has only made the challenges confronting Senate party leaders more daunting. The combination of immense individual prerogatives and polarized party-based teams fighting it out has at times seemed to make the Senate ungovernable, in sharp contrast to the disciplined House. Thus, the filibuster and related institutional differences between the chambers have an enormous impact on policy making, even as voting patterns are broadly similar in the House and Senate.

Notes

1. *Property rights* refers to each committee's right to have legislation in its jurisdiction referred to it before the bill reaches the floor.
2. See Binder, *Minority Rights, Majority Rule*; and Schickler, *Disjointed Pluralism*.
3. See Cooper, *The Origins of the Standing Committees,* for the definitive study of members' attitudes toward committees in this era.
4. See David T. Canon and Charles Stewart III, "The Evolution of the Committee System in Congress," in *Congress Reconsidered,* edited by Lawrence C. Dodd and Bruce Oppenheimer, 7th ed. (Washington, D.C.: CQ Press, 2001).
5. Canon and Stewart, "The Evolution of the Committee System." See also Joseph Cooper and Cheryl D. Young, "Bill Introduction in the Nineteenth Century: A Study of Institutional Change," *Legislative Studies Quarterly* 14, no. 1 (1989), 67–105; and Jeffery Jenkins and Charles Stewart, "Order from Chaos: The Transformation of the Committee System in the House, 1816–1822," in *Party, Process, and Political Change in Congress: New Perspectives on the History of Congress,* edited by David W. Brady and Mathew D. McCubbins (Stanford, Calif.: Stanford University Press, 2002).
6. See Charles Stewart III, *Analyzing Congress* (New York: Norton, 2001).
7. See Jenkins and Stewart, "Order from Chaos." For a more general discussion of legislative-executive relations and the early committee system, see Liam Schwartz, "Friend and Foe: Congressional Development in a System of Separated Power," Working paper, Harvard University.
8. See Schickler, *Disjointed Pluralism,* chapter 6, and discussion below.
9. See Gerald Gamm and Kenneth Shepsle, "Emergence of Legislative Institutions: Standing Committees in the House and Senate, 1810–1825," *Legislative Studies Quarterly* 14, no. 1 (1989), 39–66.
10. Randall Strahan, "Leadership and Institutional Change in the Nineteenth-Century House," in *Party, Process, and Political Change in Congress,* edited by Brady and McCubbins.
11. See Cooper, *Origins of Standing Committees,* on the importance of workload.
12. See Jenkins and Stewart, "Order from Chaos."
13. *Washington Post,* January 19, 1888.
14. For accounts emphasizing partisan dynamics, see Binder, *Minority Rights, Majority Rule*; and Douglas Dion, *Turning the Legislative Thumbscrew: Minority Rights and*

Procedural Changes in Legislative Politics (Ann Arbor: University of Michigan Press, 1997).

15. *Congressional Record,* April 17, 1894, 3790.

16. Ibid., January 26, 1892, 556.

17. The president pro tem is a senator selected to preside over the chamber when the vice president is absent.

18. Delegation to the president pro tem was also problematic because, in the nineteenth century, it was understood that the president pro tem's term would end abruptly whenever the vice president returned. See Steven S. Smith and Gerald Gamm, "The Dynamics of Party Government in Congress," in *Congress Reconsidered,* edited by Dodd and Oppenheimer, 254.

19. See David T. Canon and Charles Stewart III, "Parties and Hierarchies in Senate Committees," in *U.S. Senate Exceptionalism,* edited by Bruce Oppenheimer (Columbus: Ohio State University Press, 2002).

20. See Smith and Gamm, "The Dynamics of Party Government."

21. See Smith and Gamm, "The Dynamics of Party Government"; Gerald Gamm and Steven S. Smith, "Emergence of Senate Party Leadership," in *U.S. Senate Exceptionalism,* edited by Oppenheimer.

22. See Gamm and Smith, "The Dynamics of Party Government."

23. See Binder, *Minority Rights, Majority Rule,* on the previous question rule.

24. See Gregory J. Wawro and Eric Schickler, "Where's the Pivot? Obstruction and Lawmaking in the Pre-Cloture Senate," *American Journal of Political Science* 48 (October 2004), 758–774.

25. For example, Aldrich attempted to force cloture by majority vote during the filibuster of the federal elections bill of 1890–1891, but failed when a coalition of Democrats and dissident Republicans sidetracked the measure.

26. See Kenneth Shepsle, "The Changing Textbook Congress," in *Can the Government Govern?* edited by John E. Chubb and Paul E. Peterson (Washington, D.C.: Brookings Institution, 1989).

27. See David W. Rohde, *Parties and Leaders in the Postreform House* (Chicago and London: University of Chicago Press, 1991).

28. *Congressional Record,* February 5, 1908, 1652.

29. See Schickler, *Disjointed Pluralism,* chapter 3, and John Mark Hansen, *Gaining Access: Congress and the Farm Lobby, 1919–1981* (Chicago: University of Chicago Press, 1991).

30. The parties each had a caucus chairman, but this post was not generally considered to carry with it floor leadership responsibilities.

31. See Gamm and Smith, "Emergence of Senate Leadership."

32. *Congressional Record,* July 25, 1946, 10039.

33. George B. Galloway, *The Legislative Process in Congress* (New York: Crowell, 1953), 606.

34. U.S. Congress, Joint Committee on the Organization of Congress, *Organization of Congress: Hearings,* Seventy-ninth Congress, First session (Washington, D.C.: Government Printing Office, 1945), 41.

35. Ibid., 230.

36. Ibid., p. 237.

37. *Congressional Record,* June 8, 1946, p. 6533.

38. Ibid., July 25, 1946, 10045. See Roger H. Davidson "Legislative Reorganization Act of 1946 and the Advent of the Modern Congress." *Legislative Studies Quarterly* 15 (1990), 357–373, for an excellent review of the maneuvering that led to the adoption of the Reorganization Act.

39. See, e.g., Terry Moe, "The Presidency and the Bureaucracy: The Presidential Advantage," in *The Presidency and the Political System,* edited by Michael Nelson, 5th ed. (Washington, D.C.: CQ Press, 1998).

40. See Schickler, *Disjointed Pluralism,* chapter 6. This is consistent with the accelerated move toward a standing committee system following the War of 1812. In addition, Congress centralized its appropriations process in 1920–1922 following World War I. The appropriations centralization was at least partly rooted in the perceived need to improve Congress's scrutiny of budget requests. As discussed below, the new budget process adopted in 1974 reflected broadly similar dynamics.

41. See Rohde, *Parties and Leaders;* and Schickler, *Disjointed Pluralism,* chapter 5.

42. See Rohde, *Parties and Leaders;* and Nelson W. Polsby, *How Congress Evolves: Social Bases of Institutional Change* (Oxford: Oxford University Press, 2003).

43. Still, the GOP did not experience an actual purge, suggesting that though junior members' power base interests encouraged the challenge to seniority, ousting a specific committee leader likely required additional factors, such as the Democrats' ideological feud.

44. The attack on seniority had mixed effects for party leaders. On the one hand, the leaders benefited to the extent that the chairmen now had to be responsive to the party caucus. However, key party leaders such as Democratic Speaker Thomas (Tip) O'Neill generally opposed purging the chairmen. This suggests that party leaders believed that weakening the chairmen would make their job of building coalitions more difficult (see Schickler, *Disjointed Pluralism*).

45. See Bruce I. Oppenheimer, "The Rules Committee: New Arm of the Leadership in a Decentralized House," in *Congress Reconsidered,* edited by Lawrence C. Dodd and Bruce I. Oppenheimer, 1st ed. (New York: Praeger, 1977).

46. See Roger Davidson, "The New Centralization on Capitol Hill," *Review of Politics* 50 (summer 1988), 345–364.

47. Sarah A. Binder and Steven S. Smith, *Politics or Principle?: Filibustering in the United States Senate* (Washington, D.C.: Brookings Institution, 1997).

48. Barbara Sinclair, *The Transformation of the U.S. Senate* (Baltimore: Johns Hopkins University Press, 1989).

49. Bruce I. Oppenheimer, "Changing Time Constraints on Congress: Historical Perspectives on the Use of Cloture," in *Congress Reconsidered,* edited by Lawrence C. Dodd and Bruce I. Oppenheimer, 3rd ed. (Washington, D.C.: Congressional Quarterly, 1985).

50. Barbara Sinclair, "The '60-vote Senate,'" in *U.S. Senate Exceptionalism,* edited by Oppenheimer (Columbus: Ohio State University Press, 2002).

51. Kathryn Pearson, "Party Discipline in the Contemporary Congress: Rewarding Loyalty in Theory and in Practice." Ph.D. diss., University of California, Berkeley, 2004.

52. The GOP also set an eight-year term limit for the Speaker, but this change was repealed in January 2003.
53. Richard Cohen. "The Crack-Up of the Committees," *National Journal,* July 31, 1999.
54. Barbara Sinclair, *Legislators, Leaders, and Lawmaking: The U.S. House of Representatives in the Postreform Era* (Baltimore: Johns Hopkins University, 1998).
55. See *CQ Weekly,* January 3, 2004.

Bibliography

Binder, Sarah A. *Minority Rights, Majority Rule: Partisanship and the Development of Congress.* Cambridge, U.K., and New York: Cambridge University Press, 1997.

Cooper, Joseph. *The Origins of the Standing Committees and the Development of the Modern House.* Houston: Rice University Studies, 1971.

Deering, Christopher J., and Steven S. Smith. *Committees in Congress.* 3rd ed. Washington, D.C.: Congressional Quarterly, 1997.

Schickler, Eric. *Disjointed Pluralism: Institutional Innovation and the Development of the U.S. Congress.* Princeton, N.J.: Princeton University Press, 2001.

Sinclair, Barbara. *The Transformation of the U.S. Senate.* Baltimore and London: Johns Hopkins University Press, 1989.

3

ACTIONS IN THE PUBLIC SPHERE

David R. Mayhew

W HAT DO MEMBERS OF THE HOUSE AND SENATE DO that is particularly conspicuous—that is, what kinds of actions performed by members of Congress are particularly likely to be noticed by the American public? The role of Congress in the American system hinges to a significant degree on the highly visible actions of its members, since actions performed by members in the American public sphere at a high level of prominence ensure a continuing connection between politicians and public.

Members of Congress perform actions beyond just making laws. Yes, Congress is a lawmaking body, but its members take part in the public sphere in an impressive variety of other ways. They investigate. They impeach. They oppose presidential administrations. They run for president themselves. As important as anything, perhaps, they take stands. American political history amounts to, among other things, a more than two-centuries-long sequence of representatives taking highly public stands—from Congressman James Madison (DR-Va.) opposing Alexander Hamilton's banking and credit plans in the late eighteenth century to Senator Edward Kennedy (D-Mass.) opposing President George W. Bush's war in Iraq in 2003.

Tracing the conspicuous actions performed by members of Congress in the public sphere over the course of American history can provide a useful perspective on the development of Congress's role in the political system and its contribution to the political process.

Member Actions under George W. Bush

As a preface to a historical analysis of prominent actions by members of Congress, it may help to begin with the concrete and familiar—a brief selection of conspicuous moves by House and Senate members during the 2000 presidential election and the first three years of the George W. Bush administration. The recitation below is for illustrative purposes only, to offer a sense of the range and impact of members' actions. It is not intended as an exhaustive description of American national politics during those years.

- In January 2001, as television zeroed in on the Senate's official counting of electoral votes emanating from the 2000 presidential election, House members Alcee L. Hastings (D-Fla.), Jesse L. Jackson Jr. (D-Ill.), and other African American members of Congress appealed (unavailingly) to the upper chamber not to credit Florida's votes to Bush.[1]
- As the 107th Congress convened, Senate majority leader Trent Lott (R-Miss.), confronted by a new 50–50 party tie in the Senate, worked out what one analyst described as a "sweeping, bold—and risky—power-sharing arrangement" with his Democratic counterpart, Thomas Daschle (D-S.Dak.), for conducting Senate business.[2]
- In May 2001, President Bush's plan for a $1.6 trillion tax cut, assisted by an early endorsement from Democratic senator Zell Miller (D-Ga.), won passage courtesy of Senate Finance Committee leaders Charles Grassley (R-Iowa) and Max Baucus (D-Mont.), who struck a complicated deal for $1.35 trillion. "Rarely has a high-ranking senator provoked more displeasure from his own party colleagues," a commentator from the *Washington Post* observed with respect to Baucus. Daschle had told his fellow Democrat that he was not empowered to reach any deal with Grassley. "I don't have the authority to negotiate?" Baucus is said to have responded, stunned. "That's right," Daschle answered. After reportedly brooding during the night, Baucus struck a deal anyway.[3]
- In May 2001 Senator James Jeffords of Vermont defected from the Republican Party, thus giving control of the Senate to the Democrats for the next year and a half.[4]
- In 2001, Senator Edward Kennedy worked in harness with the White House to craft a major education enactment, the No Child Left Behind program—"a classic piece of horse-trading that provides the Republicans with testing and accountability in return for more federal money and more generous treatment of poor children." This endeavor continued the Massachusetts senator's record of reaching across party lines to generate new policy programs.[5]
- In the wake of the attack on the World Trade Center on September 11, 2001, Lott, Daschle, House Speaker Dennis Hastert (R-Ill.), and House minority leader Dick Gephardt (D-Mo.) rallied behind the White House and served as a kind of consultative council to Bush for a time.[6]

- At the cost of attracting death threats, Congresswoman Barbara Lee (D-Calif.) cast the only House or Senate vote against the use-of-force resolution enacted on September 18, 2001, to combat terrorism.[7]

- In 2002, campaign finance reform finally succeeded. Under President Bill Clinton, Senators John McCain (R-Ariz.) and Russell Feingold (D-Wis.) had advanced the idea of regulating "soft money"—that is, very large money contributions made by individuals and groups to the American parties during the 1990s in violation of the spirit, if not exactly the letter, of previous rigid ceilings on contributions. In the House, moderate Republican Christopher Shays (R-Conn.) and Democrat Martin Meehan (D-Mass.) had maneuvered a floor victory for that anti-soft-money cause in 1998 on the strength of an aroused C-SPAN audience and a principally Democratic coalition over the opposition of the chamber's Republican-majority leadership. McCain, after his prominent bid for the White House in 2000, had "capitalized on the momentum of his presidential campaign by threatening to tie the Senate in knots if Lott did not accede to his demand for an unfettered debate on campaign finance reform." McCain and Feingold staged "town halls" on the subject around the country. In March 2001 an "unaccustomed spectacle"—a "serious, substantive debate"—did indeed take place in the Republican-led Senate, and a McCain-Feingold bill cleared that body as it had in the House on the basis of largely Democratic votes. McCain's "adept stewardship of the bill surprised many colleagues." In February 2002 Shays and Meehan succeeded again in a Republican-controlled House, staving off a "near-17-hour barrage of rival bills and amendments that Republican leaders had hoped would derail the legislation."[8]

- In the wake of the Enron scandal Senator Paul Sarbanes (D-Md.) is said to have brought unusual knowledge and strategic skill to the crafting of a new bipartisan regulatory blueprint for the accounting industry.[9]

- Congressman Jim McDermott (D-Wash.), during a visit to Baghdad in September 2002 as war loomed, claimed that Saddam Hussein had more credibility than Bush.[10]

- In 2003, Speaker Hastert and House majority leader Tom DeLay won notice for their efficient Republican Party apparatus. The *Washington Post* reported that they had "systematically changed internal rules to seize greater authority over rank-and-file members," as in the awarding of committee chairmanships. Two years earlier, Hastert had found ways to "inoculate House Republicans against Democratic attacks on [embarrassingly framed] issues by scheduling House floor votes on GOP-flavored legislative remedies," in the words of Richard E. Cohen in the *National Journal*.[11]

- Senate majority leader Daschle, on the other hand, had drawn criticism for allegedly poor agenda planning as the 2002 midterm election approached. Couldn't the Democrats have positioned themselves more coherently on Bush's Iraq resolution in October 2002? Did the authorization of the new Homeland Security Department need to be held up during the last weeks before the election, offering an issue for the Republicans?[12]

- As the war in Iraq proceeded in 2003, Senator Robert Byrd (D-W.Va.), now in his mid-eighties, dean of the chamber, took on a role familiar from Roman times as a senatorial guardian against what a *Wall Street Journal* commentator described as "an increasingly arrogant, wartime White House." Byrd's speeches were posted on the Internet, where especially the younger generation, it is speculated, responded with some 3.7 million hits during March 2003 alone.[13]

- In the legislative realm in 2003, Senator Kennedy helped spark another cross-party enterprise, this time on the question of financing prescription drugs through Medicare: on June 16 the *Wall Street Journal* reported that "at a Democratic luncheon this past week, Mr. Kennedy set off a storm by loudly urging his colleagues to declare victory and embrace [a centrist proposal then being discussed, rather than a purely liberal one] as their own." The Democratic senators did that, more or less, to their and Kennedy's later regret as the agreement paved the way to a successful Republican-flavored enactment in November 2003 that they strongly opposed. This enactment, which is said to have called for the biggest changes in Medicare since its creation in 1965 cleared the House in a riveting 220–215 vote, for which Hastert's leadership team kept the count open for a record-setting three hours during the middle of the night in order to badger and inveigle the needed support.[14]

- In 2003, six Democratic members of Congress ran for the presidency— Senators Joseph Lieberman (D-Conn.), Bob Graham (D-Fla.), John Edwards (D-N.C.), and John Kerry (D-Mass.), and House members Gephardt and Dennis Kucinich (D-Ohio). On the Iraq resolution of October 2002 giving the White House authority to wage war, all of the six except Graham and Kucinich voted yes. On the later measure of October 2003 appropriating $87 billion to fund the war and its aftermath, all but Lieberman and Gephardt voted no.

- As the war ensued, Senator Kennedy took an unusually strong oppositional stance, accusing the White House of "fraud" in staging the intervention.[15]

- In 2003, House majority leader DeLay reached into the politics of his home state to maneuver a mid-decade gerrymander of Texas's congressional districts aimed at converting a Democratic majority of 17–15 into a Republican majority as large as 22–10.[16] (In fact, a Republican edge of 21–11 accrued from the subsequent election of November 2004.)

Aspects of High-Profile Member Actions

The various moves by House and Senate members listed above were all per-formed at a particularly high level of conspicuousness. At least four points can be made about them.

First, to dwell on the conspicuousness, on exhibit here is the public face of Congress and its members. Insofar as the American public watches, takes note of, monitors, audits, is influenced by, or is induced to react to the con-gressional realm, the odds are that it does so substantially because of high-profile activity by members. The moves cited above were probably noted by millions of people, many by tens of millions, some even possibly by more than a hundred million.

Second, these member actions were important. More specifically, to give that idea some empirical grounding, credible reason very likely existed among the relevant audiences taking note of these actions to size them up as consequential, potentially consequential, or otherwise in some fashion significant. Especially for the African American population, the appeal on the Florida vote dramatized an alleged injustice and spotlighted the absence of blacks at that time in the Senate (not one of the hundred senators took up the appeal).[17] It was a statement. Probably the Lott-Daschle power-sharing agreement made a difference. Possibly Zell Miller's early endorsement of the Bush tax cut made a difference. Many infuriated Democrats thought that Max Baucus's maneuvering on that measure made a difference. Senator Jeffords's defection made a difference (even if it stopped well short of radically switching control of the Senate for policy pur-poses from a typical conservative Republican stance to a typical liberal Democratic stance).[18] It was consequential for the American population that Senator Kennedy helped along both the education measure and, to his regret, the Medicare prescription drugs measure. For both domestic and foreign audiences, it was an important signal that the leaders of the congressional parties formed their consultative foursome after September 11. Barbara Lee's nay vote was a statement, a kind of footnote to the 9/11 crisis. In the cases of McCain, Feingold, Shays, and Meehan on campaign finance, recalling the role played by James Stewart in *Mr. Smith Goes to Washington,* here is a classic instance of members of Congress whipping up public support to enact a reform over the resistance of a congressional majority party. It was probably important that Speaker Hastert led the House the way he did, possibly important that Majority Leader Daschle led the Senate the way he did (trying to herd senators is no bargain for any leader). It would likely be a mistake to underrate Senator Byrd's speeches. The Texas redistricting plan engendered by Tom DeLay, it was speculated, could help keep the House in Republican hands for a decade or more. As usual, for the party not holding the White House, Congress supplied much of the talent for the presi-dential nominating season in 2003–2004. The roll call positions that Kerry,

Lieberman, Edwards, Gephardt, and Kucinich had taken on the key Iraq questions supplied much of the discussion material for that season.

Third, the members who undertook the actions highlighted above did so with an appreciable degree of personal autonomy. True, the actions were typically *influenced*, it is fair to say, by states of affairs or considerations outside their control. Typically, bands of political feasibility existed within which the politicians crafted their moves. It would be highly unlikely that a representative from Tom DeLay's conservative district in the Houston suburbs would have protested the Florida count or voted nay on the use-of-force resolution along with Barbara Lee. Montana, Max Baucus's home state, had scored a 25 percent edge for Bush in the election of November 2000. Lott, Daschle, Hastert, and Gephardt after September 11 were representing the public of the United States, not that of, say, Syria. On balance, Speaker Hastert's largely united Republican caucus was pleased to give him some leadership leeway. With the upcoming Democratic primaries and the November 2004 election in mind, those congressional representatives aiming for the White House had to think very carefully about these different contexts when positioning themselves on the Iraq questions.

All this is true. Yet it does not add up to anything like a case that external considerations *determined* these representatives' actions. Trent Lott would have surprised no one by organizing the Senate in its customary partisan fashion even with a wafer-thin 51–50 majority, relying on Vice President Dick Cheney to break ties. Senator Baucus could have brooded himself into a different decision on the tax cut (the Democratic senators from neighboring, even more decisively pro-Bush, North Dakota opposed the cut).[19] Senator Jeffords could have stayed put (as most senators who are miffed at their parties do). Senator Kennedy could have passed up his education and prescription-drugs endeavors (as most Democrats would have done). McCain and Feingold could have given up on campaign finance reform—consigning their cause to the historical dustbin alongside many other legislative drives of the past like those for a school-prayer amendment and a federal consumer-protection agency. Senator Byrd could have orated less. Absent Senator Sarbanes's efforts, the accounting reform could have ended up less effective (like some other regulatory reforms). Speaker Hastert could have run the House in a more relaxed way in the style of, perhaps, Speaker Tom Foley (D-Wash.) in the early 1990s. Senator Kerry could have joined his home-state partner Kennedy to vote nay on the joint resolution authorizing the use of force against Iraq in October 2002. Barbara Lee would have caused little surprise by joining her customary allies on the left such as Maxine Waters (D-Calif.), José Serrano (D-N.Y.), and Jan Schakowsky (D-Ill.) to vote yes on the use-of-force resolution in 2001. On Iraq, Kennedy could have looked for a term other than *fraud*. Certainly Tom DeLay could have refrained from the mid-decade Texas redistricting.

An additional consideration bears on member autonomy. During 2001–2003, what did the members *not* do that they might have done? What are the plausible counterfactuals? Where human autonomy is involved, it is a great mistake to accept whatever happened as an exhaustive universe of the possible. Why didn't the conservative Zell Miller, who later endorsed President Bush for reelection, defect to the Republicans in 2001 to counter Jeffords? While controlling the Senate during 2002, why didn't the Democratic leadership mount a harder-hitting investigation of pre–September 11 intelligence failures? (Consider the explosive investigations of the intelligence agencies in 1975–1976.) After September 11, why didn't some enterprising committee chair conduct a flashy probe of alleged domestic terrorist elements? Imagine Islamic fundamentalists appearing before cameras. Why didn't some Democrat market an appealing argument against the repeal of the estate tax (labeled shrewdly the "death tax" by Republicans)?[20] Where were the deficit hawks? Why didn't Senator Pete Domenici (R-N.M.), a power on budget questions, blanch at Bush's deficits the way he had blanched at Reagan's? Why didn't some Republican committee chair probe into allegations of dubious activities in Senator Daschle's very narrow reelection in South Dakota in 2002? Why wasn't any senator available to craft a deal with the White House on energy the way Kennedy did on education? Couldn't some innovative Democratic members of Congress have devised a more gripping domestic program for the party? Where were the Democratic equivalents of Newt Gingrich (R-Ga.) and Gingrich's Contract with America? Why didn't House minority leader Nancy Pelosi (D-Calif.) try to counter Tom DeLay by pressing for a mid-decade redistricting in, say, Illinois, where the Democratic Party came to control the entire state government as a consequence of the 2002 election? None of these moves would have been highly implausible during 2001–2003, but no one made the relevant moves.

The Realm of Public Affairs

The fourth point about the actions of members of Congress such as those highlighted above is that they do not enjoy much of a place in social science, even if they rate high with journalists, traditional historians, and alert citizens. As a theoretical matter, social scientists tend to see Congress as a place where externally determined views or interests—that is, those of the society's classes, interest groups, electorates, and the like—are *registered*. Causal arrows are aimed at Capitol Hill, and they hit. That is virtually all that happens.[21] Also, as a conceptual matter, the making of laws tends to be the only activity worth addressing. And as an empirical matter, roll call voting in the service of lawmaking is virtually the only evidence worth examining.

This is a caricature of contemporary congressional studies as undertaken by social scientists, but not by much. Certainly it leaves out too much and also gets certain essentials wrong. For one thing, "registering" preferences or interests on Capitol Hill, given that they can be said to exist, is more problematic than it might seem. Members of Congress actually have to *do* things in order to advance their various aims, and they might or might not perform. Talent and drive need to be applied.[22]

For another thing, on many kinds of matters it is a precarious assumption that preferences or interests really do exist out there in society in anything like a pristine form to be congressionally "registered." The content of public life is complicated. In politics as opposed to, say, personal tastes in ice-cream flavors or a desire to earn fifteen dollars an hour as opposed to ten dollars an hour, a high degree of influence external to individual human beings is often brought to bear in the crafting of personal preferences or self-perceived interests. It is a good bet that members of Congress, along with presidents and many other political actors in society, to be sure, figure significantly in the crafting. Political products can be invented and merchandised, hence such causes as the "Contract with America," "family leave," "unfunded mandates," "campaign finance reform," the "death tax," and the "patients' bill of rights," all of which have been shaped by elite actors and found appreciative audiences in recent times. Elite influence over individual preferences bears on congressional roll call studies, too. To array members of Congress from most liberal to most conservative on a summary roll call measure, a popular simplifying device, is to say little about the substantive content of that dimension. The ingredients of the content need to be invented day after day, year after year, generation after generation, by enterprising politicians and others. They do not exist "naturally."

There is much to be said for the intuitions of journalists, historians, and alert citizens. Legislators' "actions" can take on a major role, and the relations between the public and the government can take on a rich, complicated, and interesting form if one abandons—at least as anything like axiomatic or exhaustive—the idea that Capitol Hill life consists merely of carrying out or catering to preferences or interests that exist coherently outside the legislative realm, waiting to be carried out or catered to. Once past this notion, relations between the public and elective officials can be seen as interactive rather than just one-way. Members of Congress are not simply the targets of society's vectors. Opinion formation can be viewed as internal to political processes rather than somehow executed externally. Members of Congress and other elite actors can be hypothesized to *shape* opinion as well as to react to it. In their various undertakings, veteran representatives such as Kennedy, McCain, and DeLay can be seen as effective cue-givers to a nationwide audience, owing to their long built-up "policy reputations." In lawmaking and otherwise, members can take on a role familiar in the private market economy as "entrepreneurs."[23]

More generally, the realm of "public affairs" or the "public sphere" can supersede the registering of preferences or interests as a model of political reality. If members of Congress enjoy a significant degree of autonomy, the American realm of public affairs can be seen as a stream of collective consciousness in which certain actions by individuals, including members of Congress, come to be noticed and remembered. Individuals' actions seem to reach this standing if they are widely thought to be consequential, potentially consequential, or otherwise significant. They are observed by politically aware citizens trying to size up events in their environment. They afford a kind of connection. They are worth noticing. Baucus's support of the Bush tax cut signaled a nationwide audience that significant Democratic support existed for the measure, thus possibly helping to legitimize it. McCain's drive for campaign finance reform defined a problem and helped shape a nationwide constituency for that reform measure. Lee's negative vote on the use-of-force resolution post-9/11 signaled a nationwide audience, in particular African Americans, that misgivings were possible about that solidly backed move. Kennedy's cry of "fraud" on the Iraq War advised a nationwide liberal constituency what they should be thinking, or at least considering thinking. In the American system, public affairs is "a busy timestream of events featuring uncertainty, open deliberation and discussion, opinion formation, strutting and ambition, surprises, endless public moves and countermoves by politicians and other actors, rising and falling issues, and an attentive and sometimes participating audience of large numbers of citizens."[24]

Members of Congress are in the thick of this activity, which, given the country's constitutional contours, may entail members' actions of several varieties beyond lawmaking. With the member's job goes a license to persuade, connive, hatch ideas, propagandize, assail enemies, vote, build coalitions, shepherd coalitions, and in general cut a figure in public affairs. A legislature can be a decision machine, a forum, an arena, a stage, or a springboard.[25] Some members may craft bills—in the long reach of American history, consider Senator Robert F. Wagner (D-N.Y.), the author of the landmark National Labor Relations Act (the Wagner Act) of 1935. Some may conduct investigations—consider Senator Joseph McCarthy (R-Wis.), the anticommunist investigator of the 1950s. Some may undertake issue crusades—consider Senator Huey Long (D-La.) and his "Share Our Wealth" crusade of the 1930s. Some may run for president—consider Senators Barry Goldwater (R-Ariz.) and John F. Kennedy (D-Mass.) of the 1950s and 1960s.

Actions That Gain Public Notice

With public affairs or the public sphere as a conceptual template, one can analyze the *kinds* of activities that win members of Congress significant public notice. What kinds of things do legislators do that people actually pay attention to? In principle, this is an empirical question whose answers should feed back into a theoretical illumination of the public sphere. If a kind of activity is reasonably widely noticed, then the very noticing of it might say something about the connection between the elected officials and the public—or at least an alert sector of the public. In principle, this is a view of representative relations in which the public itself has a large role in choosing the sorts of things it sees fit to monitor. The following discussion will cover a selection of the more important categories. Categories covered in the study but *not* taken up here include member moves in regard to processing presidential nominations, taking appointments (as when a member of Congress moves to the cabinet), revising congressional rules, impeaching executive or judicial officials, censuring other members of Congress, running for president or vice president, or serving as party leaders.

Approached as a serious empirical enterprise, determining the kinds of member action that get "noticed" raises considerable problems of evidence. Rather than ransacking newspapers over many generations, a 2000 study conducted by the author resorted to a fallback data source.[26] The study covers American national history from the beginning. It utilizes a selection of thirty-eight works of "public affairs history"—a genre in which the historians, whatever else they do, try to gather and transmit a past collective understanding, at least among the politically aware public at relevant past times, of what was going on in the public sphere. "Noticing" by the public is in principle captured. These are standard, well-known books on such subjects as "the Jacksonian era" and "the New Deal era." They tell us that Henry Clay (W-Ky.) did this, George Norris (R,Ind.-Neb.) did this, and Robert A. Taft (R-Ohio) did that. Many difficulties arise in using a data source like this, not the least of which is that serious tracking of representatives' actions is not possible beyond 1988. That is because adequate history books do not yet exist that would allow it. The result is a data collection that covers exactly two centuries, 1789 through 1988. Recorded were the historians' mentions of actions of all kinds engaged in by individuals serving as members of Congress. The result was 2,304 member actions in all. Each one was sorted into a category or categories according to its *kind*. An action might be multiply coded, for example, as both "legislate" and "big speech." The issue area of "foreign policy" had its own category.

Patterns of member actions as they have accumulated across two centuries can serve as a useful window into the American regime. Presented below are the main data displays from the author's 2000 study, supplemented by suitable, albeit unsystematically collected, information for more recent years. The traditional roles of several kinds of congressional action in the American system are discussed, followed by a speculative analysis of how those roles may be upheld or attenuated during the twenty-first century, keeping in mind the following questions: What is the future of conspicuous action by members of Congress? What is necessary for its sustenance? Why should the citizenry care?

Legislating

The obvious story about legislatures is that they legislate. *Legislate* is coded here as any sort of rhetorical, coalition building, or formal parliamentary move by a member of Congress (whether or not it was successful) aimed at enacting, amending, or blocking a congressional measure.[27] At the least, member actions in the legislative process can tip off an alert sector of the public about the issue content, prospects, and coalitional underpinnings of lawmaking drives. Monitoring and appraisal by the public are assisted. At the most, member actions can help to shape those drives—as in Senator McCain's definition of the issue and mobilization of nationwide support in the cause of campaign finance reform.

In the 2000 study, the coding scheme for "legislate" picked up 1,079 items from 1789 through 1988. For their frequency by decade, see the vertical bars in Figure 1.[28] For the percentage of member actions of all kinds that they comprised during each decade, see the dotted line in that figure. Not surprisingly, the 1910s and the 1930s stand out. In the former era, many members of Congress figured prominently in the Democrats' New Freedom legislative drive under Woodrow Wilson, as did also Senator Henry Cabot Lodge (R–Mass.) and others in thwarting the president's campaign to ratify the Versailles Treaty with its League of Nations commitment a few years later. In the uniquely busy 1930s, Senator Wagner, perhaps the leading designer of the American welfare state, joined many other members in prominently advancing or impeding the many

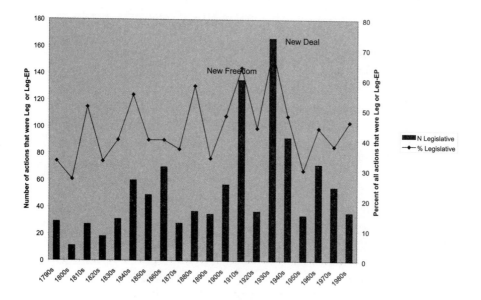

Figure 1   Legislative Actions

legislative enterprises of the New Deal era. In the decades after World War II, the main exhibits of congressional action were the historic drives to enact the Civil Rights Act of 1964—fifteen actions, including the orchestration by Senator Richard Russell (D-Ga.) of a seemingly endless although losing filibuster; and Reagan's tax and expenditure cuts in 1981—ten actions, including some adept maneuvering by Congressman Phil Gramm (D-Tex.), a key White House ally at that time although not yet a Republican.

An appropriate continuation of Figure 1 beyond 1988 might generate vertical bars about as high as those of the 1970s or 1980s. Legislating on a New Deal scale has not been seen in this period, although there have been moments. Likely among the highlights, for example, would be several member actions during President Clinton's unproductive drive for health care reform in 1993–1994— skillful though uphill committee work by Congressmen John Dingell (D-Mich.) and Daniel Rostenkowski (D-Ill.), critical comments dropped by Capitol Hill's unconvinced leading intellectual on the subject, Senator Daniel Patrick Moynihan (D-N.Y.), energetic leadership by Senate majority leader George Mitchell (D-Maine), temporizing but then tough opposition by Senate minority leader Bob Dole (R-Kans.). In the Congress of 1995–1996, Speaker Newt Gingrich (R-Ga.) certainly made a public mark as a legislative entrepreneur. His Contract with America foundered after winning passage in the House, as did the Gingrich-Dole budget that provoked a showdown with the Clinton White House over shutting down the government, yet the failure was not complete in either case—and it is true that American high politics was largely structured for a while by these endeavors. There were other promising items under George H. W. Bush and Clinton, such as the framing of banking reform by Senator Gramm (R-Tex.) in 1999. High-profile legislative actions under George W. Bush have already been discussed. In general, members' legislative actions since 1988 if suitably documented would probably approximate the two-century norm in volume as well as texture—nothing special.[29]

To go back to the main dataset, however, perhaps the most interesting aspect of the "legislate" realm of member action is that it constituted only 47 percent of the items during 1789 through 1988—1,079 of the total 2,304. Clearly, members of Congress do other kinds of things that win notice.

Investigating

One of the things members of Congress do to gain attention is *investigate,* a category that accommodated 114 member actions or 5 percent of the dataset from 1789 through 1988. That is, a member of Congress called for, took part in, or was otherwise associated with a congressional investigation or hearing on any subject for any purpose—and won the requisite notice for it.[30] Since seventeenth-century England, a basic prerogative of free legislative bodies has been the right to investigate—if necessary through use of the subpoena power.

Transparency in the conduct of executive branches has been one end often served; illumination of problems in society has been another. The investigative role is by nature high profile with regard to member action, since personal initiative is called for (investigations do not happen naturally; someone has to spark and carry them), and dramatic exposure tactics that draw attention and shape opinion are often key to the art.

Figure 2 shows the two-century American "investigate" data display. High-publicity investigating has always been an avenue for members' entrepreneurialism, but, perhaps surprisingly, such activity did not fully blossom until the twentieth century. From the vantage point of today, the 1910s through the 1970s looks like a long age of congressional exposure. Entrepreneurs serving on House and Senate committees forged techniques of day-by-day, week-by-week revelation to rivet public attention on various alleged malperformance or misbehavior in the society or the government. The effects were often pronounced. There seem to have been three phases. From roughly 1913 through 1937, the Progressive left on Capitol Hill supplied the energy and inventiveness. Private corporations became a choice target: for example, Senator Thomas Walsh (D-Mont.) pursued (in fact, largely created) the Teapot Dome scandal involving relations between oil companies and the administration of President Warren G. Harding in the mid-1920s, and Senator Robert La Follette Jr. (R-Wis.) hammered various firms for their labor practices in a consequential locale-by-locale exposé that dovetailed with the national organizing drive of the Congress of

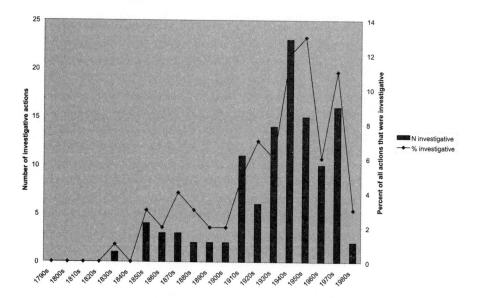

Figure 2   Investigative Actions

Industrial Organizations (CIO) in 1936–1937. Then the conservative side took the lead. Congressman Martin Dies (D-Tex.) pioneered the investigation of un-American activities ("naming names" on the witness stand arose as a technique) starting in 1938, Congressman Howard Smith (D-Va.) harried several New Deal and war agencies around 1940, Senator McCarthy pursued alleged Communists in the State Department and the army in 1953–1954, and Senator John McClellan (D-Ark.) exposed certain culpable practices of labor unions in the late 1950s. Then the initiative went back to the left. The cold war "imperial presidency" came under fire as Senator J. William Fulbright (D-Ark.) staged damaging hearings on the Vietnam War starting in 1966, Senator Sam Ervin (D-N.C.) brought a folksy charm to the televised Watergate probe that crippled the Nixon administration in 1973, and Senator Frank Church (D-Idaho) exposed certain practices of the intelligence agencies in 1975.

That is a formidable record. It exhibits the power and potential of members' investigative action. In Figure 2, the reading for the 1980s is modest by comparison. Is this an indication of slippage in the investigative domain? It would seem so, notwithstanding such eye-catching enterprises of recent times as the probe led by Senator Fred Thompson (R-Tenn.) in 1997 into the Clinton administration's campaign finance practices (the alleged sale of the Lincoln bedroom, the White House coffees, the Buddhist nuns as alleged donors, and the rest), and the House Judiciary Committee hearings chaired by Henry Hyde (R-Ill.) in 1998, ending in Clinton's impeachment.[31] Here is the point. Since the mid-1970s, the process of day-by-day exposure has largely moved elsewhere. Investigative journalism came into its own with Watergate. Special commissions have been set up to study the *Challenger* disaster, the September 11 intelligence failure, and other events of recent decades. Independent counsels entered the scene in the 1970s. Note that by the time the House Judiciary Committee inherited the Clinton imbroglio in mid-1998, there was virtually nothing left to reveal or expose. An independent counsel's office plus the media had already performed the labor. In earlier decades, members of Congress as diverse as Walsh, Dies, McCarthy, Fulbright, and Church might have been taking the lead. It is a difficult question whether today's relative eclipse of member investigative action, if that is what is being witnessed, has left the country better off. To look at it one way, camera-seeking senators versus runaway independent counsels is not an easy choice.

Taking Stands

Taking stands is one of the fundamental activities that members of Congress engage in.[32] Looked at one way, politics is an unending sequence of contributions to a national conversation—an often cranky and contentious one, to be sure. Members of Congress, validated as they are by having won elections and gifted with formal powers that can back up speech, are in a privileged position to make contributions that can swerve or move along that conversation. Many of them perform accordingly, often with consequence.

As a conceptual or coding matter, "taking stands" has blurrier boundaries than, say, legislating or investigating, which are linked reasonably clearly to formal procedures. In principle, taking stands simply means registering a position on some matter before some audience. The reelection drive can animate it, but so can other aims including trying to shape national opinion. For the latter purpose, being a member of Congress supplies an effective platform and some members have famously used it—Congressman James Madison, for example, in propagandizing for a new Jeffersonian Republican party in the 1790s, Senator Charles Sumner (D-Free Soil, then R-Mass.) through his antislavery speeches in the 1850s, and Senator Gerald P. Nye (R-N.D.) in conducting his isolationist crusade in the 1930s.

In the author's study, taking stands could overlap other kinds of member activity, and it often did—notably legislating. An action counted as both "legislating" and "taking a stand" if a member of Congress was documented as making some parliamentary move but also expressing a view—as did Senator Russell, for example, in both formally impeding and rhetorically assailing the civil rights measure in 1964. Altogether, a total of 1,081 of the 2,304 member-action items from 1789 through 1988 qualified as "taking a stand." Of these, 427 or 40 percent were also coded as "legislating." In the residual 60 percent of these items emerges an inventive variety of techniques and venues used by members to get their points across. Table 1 presents a selection of those nonlegislative expressions exhibiting their variety. Much of the prominent public history of the two centuries surfaces in this list.

In recent years, congressional stand taking has continued alive and well. An update of Table 1 might include the following: In 1991, Congresswoman Barbara Boxer (D-Calif.) led a march by women House members to the Senate to protest the way the hearings to confirm Clarence Thomas as a Supreme Court justice were being conducted (controversial testimony by Anita Hill was involved). In 1993 Senator Sam Nunn (D-Ga.) threw cold water on the Clinton administration's gays-in-the-military policy. At a critical moment in 1994, Senator Moynihan called for an independent counsel to investigate the Clintons' Whitewater entanglement. In 1995 came the Contract with America. Two years later, the Republican Revolution having wound down, Congressman Lindsey Graham (R-S.C.) led an abortive coup against Speaker Gingrich. That same year, Congressman Bob Barr (R-Ga.) called for the impeachment of President Clinton, and Senator Jesse Helms (R-N.C.) defiantly blocked the nomination of Governor William F. Weld (R-Mass.) as ambassador to Mexico. Also, Senator Lieberman publicly chastised the president after the Monica Lewinsky revelations broke. In 1999 Senator McCain emerged as the leading proponent of all-out American military intervention

TABLE 1
Selected instances of non-legislative MC stand-taking

1798	Matthew Lyon (DR–VT)	H	spits in the eye of ideological foe Roger Griswold (F–CT)
1801	Theodore Sedgwick (F–MA)	H	boycotts Jefferson's inauguration as Federalist gesture
1814	Timothy Pickering (F–MA)	S	promotes secessionist Northern Confederacy
1825	George Kremer (D–PA)	H	charges (in newspaper) corrupt deal between H. Clay & J.Q. Adams
1831	John Quincy Adams (NR–MA)	H	introduces his first antislavery petition to House
1856	Preston Brooks (D–SC)	H	canes Charles Sumner on the Senate floor after Kansas speech
1858	Stephen A. Douglas (D–IL)	S	takes part in Lincoln–Douglas debates
1858	William Seward (R–NY)	S	delivers his "irrepressible conflict" speech in Rochester, NY
1860	Robert Toombs (D–GA)	S	issues a secession manifesto
1861	Clement Vallandigham (D–OH)	H	as "Copperhead," backs obstruction of northern war effort
1867	William D. Kelley (R–PA)	H	tours South to carry GOP doctrine to freedmen audiences
1868	Benjamin Butler (R–MA)	H	waves a bloody shirt (literally) as Johnson impeachment manager
1872	Charles Sumner (R–MA)	S	backs Democrat Greeley over Republican Grant for president
1874	Lucius Q. C. Lamar (D–MS)	H	eulogizes deceased Sumner in North–South reconciliation speech
1881	Roscoe Conkling (R–NY)	S	resigns Senate seat in a huff over Garfield's patronage turndowns
1889	Henry Cabot Lodge (R–MA)	H	writes *North American Review* piece backing House rules reform
1892	William B. Cockran (D–NY)	H	delivers anti-Cleveland oration at Demo. national convention
1896	David B. Hill (D–NY)	S	boycotts New York City speech of pres. candidate W. J. Bryan
1901	Benjamin Tillman (D–SC)	S	assails Theodore Roosevelt for inviting blacks to the White House
1910	Nelson W. Aldrich (R–RI)	S	moves to fund orthodox GOP congressional candidates

TABLE 1 (continued)

1910	Jonathan Dolliver (R–IA)	S	dares Taft to try to expel Progressives from GOP
1917	Henry Cabot Lodge (R–MA)	S	runs to shake Wilson's hand after presidential speech proposing war
1920	Andrew J. Volstead (R–MN)	H	co-leads a church service to celebrate Prohibition
1922	Robert La Follette, Sr. (R–WI)	S	calls national conference of Progressives
1926	Fiorello La Guardia (R–NY)	H	stages news conference to mix an (anti-Prohibition) illegal drink
1934–35	Huey Long (D–LA)	S	promotes his Share Our Wealth program nationwide
1936	Ellison D. Smith (D–SC)	S	walks out of Democratic convention as black preacher speaks
1937	Josiah W. Bailey (D–NC)	S	co-drafts anti–FDR Conservative Manifesto
1940	Gerald P. Nye (R–ND)	S	helps found America First movement
1944	Alben Barkley (D–KY)	S	resigns Democratic leadership post in tiff with FDR over taxes
1943	Arthur Vandenberg (R–MI)	S	presses anti–isolationist resolution at GOP Mackinac Island meeting
1950	William Jenner (R–IN)	S	denounces General Marshall as a front man for traitors
1951	Joseph Martin (R–MA)	H	assails Truman administration after General MacArthur firing
1952	Henry Cabot Lodge, Jr. (R–MA)	S	promotes pro-Ike "fair play" reso. at GOP national convention
1952	Wayne Morse (R–OR)	S	defects from GOP over McCarthyism
1956	Albert Gore (D–TN)	S	won't sign segregationist Southern Manifesto
1956	Adam Clayton Powell (D–NY)	H	endorses Republican Eisenhower for reelection
1957	Eugene McCarthy (D–MN)	H	takes lead in founding liberal Democratic Study Group
1962	Barry Goldwater (R–AZ)	S	author of foreign policy work *Why Not Victory?*
1962	Kenneth Keating (R–NY	S	charges JFK administration tolerates Soviet missiles in Cuba

TABLE 1   (continued)

1964	Kenneth Keating (R–NY)	S	leads walkout of moderates from GOP national convention
1968	Robert F. Kennedy (D–NY)	S	celebrates Easter mass with labor organizer Cesar Chavez
1968	Eugene McCarthy (D–MN)	S	won't back Humphrey after Democratic convention in Chicago
1970	Gaylord Nelson (D–WI)	S	suggests celebration of Earth Day (and it happens)
1973	Lowell Weicker (R–CT)	S	assails Nixon administration in Watergate hearings
1974	Hugh Scott (R–PA)	S	as leader of Senate GOP, calls Nixon tapes disgusting
1975	Bob Carr (D–MI)	H	puts Vietnam $ cutoff reso. through House Democratic Caucus
1978	Edward Kennedy (D–MA)	S	attacks Carter admin. from the left at midterm Dem. conference
1983	Phil Gramm (D–TX)	H	switches to GOP, resigns House seat, and is reelected
1984	Barry Goldwater (R–AZ)	S	fumes at CIA mining of Nicaragua harbors
1984	Jesse Helms (R–NC)	S	backs right-wing El Salvador leader D'Aubuisson
1987	Edward Kennedy (D–MA)	S	leads fight against Bork nomination to Supreme Court

in Kosovo to ward off Serbian genocide there.[33] Instances of prominent stand taking for the George W. Bush years have already been mentioned, including Senator Kennedy's cry of fraud on the Iraq War. For a good instance of membership in Congress as an avenue to a national audience, consider Congressman Kucinich's propagation of his many views during the Democrats' presidential nominating season of 2003–2004.

Foreign Policy

Congress is ordinarily seen as a domestic institution, yet a healthy share of member action has gone to foreign policy—defined here as all items pertaining in any way to the conduct of U.S. foreign or defense policy. The share is 23 percent, with 539 items from 1789 through 1988. Figure 3 gives the time series. The highlights are the 1790s and 1800s, at least in a relative sense since foreign policy dominated a lean congressional agenda back then, and the two decades of the world wars, yet also the run-up to World War II and the time span of the Vietnam War. Perhaps this foreign policy emphasis is surprising. It stems from not seeing Congress as just a lawmaking body. Some two-fifths of the foreign policy actions also code as "legislate" (as in treaty ratifications), but more than that proportion also code as "take stand" and many also code as "investigate."[34] It is impossible to appreciate the place of members of Congress in foreign policy history without considering these non-lawmaking roles. In the investigative realm, for example, Senator Nye's high-publicity probe of munitions-makers in the mid-1930s probably delayed an acceleration of American involvement in World War II, and Senator Fulbright's televised hearings in the 1960s probably hastened a deceleration of the Vietnam War. Even without chairing committees, aggressive congressional stand takers can help to crystallize opinion constituencies—as in the cases of isolationist senators such as William E. Borah (R-Idaho) and Burton K. Wheeler (D-Mont.) around 1940 and dovish senators such as George McGovern (D-S.D.), Eugene McCarthy (D-Minn.), and Robert F. Kennedy (D-N.Y.) in the late 1960s.

Foreign policy went into eclipse after the close of the cold war, but it has resurged, and stand taking by members of Congress has helped shape the contexts of the recent White House–led wars in Yugoslavia, Afghanistan, and Iraq. On Yugoslavia, Senator McCain pressed the Clinton administration from the hawkish side. On Iraq, Senators Kennedy, Kerry, Edwards, Daschle, and others

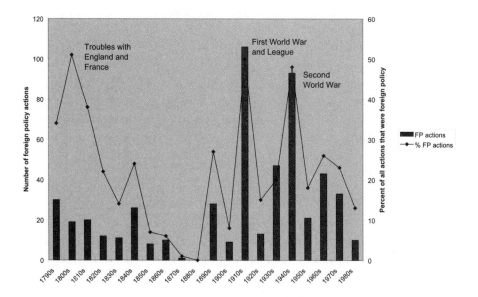

Figure 3   Foreign Policy Actions

pressed the Bush administration from the dovish side in 2002–2003 as Senator Lieberman and Congressman Gephardt assisted from the center. All this is standard congressional action.

Ideological Impulses

Additional kinds of member action have inhered in specific processes or contexts—for example, moves to impeach presidents or to run for the presidency oneself (as with the six Democratic candidates in 2003–2004). Yet two categories of a more omnibus quality may be worth dwelling on. The first is *ideological impulses*. This category covers just the twentieth century, since the overall "action" counts needed to motor it were considerably more numerous than in the nineteenth century. In principle, any kind of standard move by a member of Congress could be coded additionally as "ideological impulse"—legislate, investigate, take stand, and the rest. Isolated in this study were subsets of twenty-five or more temporally clustered member actions in which members pursued the same policy goals or ideological cause.[35] The goal here was to accommodate major political impulses that have surged in importance at particular junctures and that have extended beyond single issues to embody something like passionately expressed belief systems. The Progressivism of the early twentieth century is an example, or New Deal liberalism, or the isolationism of the 1930s (the foreign policy area can generate passionate belief systems, too), or the Great Society liberalism of the 1960s, or the Contract with American conservatism of the mid-1990s.

The fifteen clusters that met the criteria are listed in Table 2. Chronologically, they range from the old guard conservatism promoted by Senator Nelson W. Aldrich (R–R.I.) and Speaker Joseph G. Cannon (R–Ill.) at the beginning of the century through the Democratic liberalism championed by Speaker Thomas P. O'Neill (D–Mass.) and others in the 1980s. In ideological direction, the clusters range from the Aldrich-Cannon conservatism and the "Asia first" anticommunism expressed by Senators Joseph McCarthy, Patrick McCarran (D–Nev.), and others around 1950 through, say, the Progressive insurgency spearheaded by Senator Robert La Follette (R–Wis.) around 1910 and the left-populist challenge to the New Deal staged by Senators Huey Long, Burton K. Wheeler, Elmer Thomas (D–Okla.) and others in the early to mid-1930s. In generational terms, some of the "impulses" centered in high-seniority congressional veterans—the Aldrich-Cannon conservatism, the O'Neill liberalism, the cross-party opposition to the liberal domestic reforms of the 1960s. Some of them centered in feisty newcomers—the Progressive insurgency around 1910, the Asia-first anticommunism around 1950, the opposition to the Vietnam War around 1970. Occasionally, one impulse countered another—as with the Aldrich-Cannon conservatism versus the La Follette Progressivism.

In substantive terms, these impulses could entail either domestic or foreign policy, and they varied accordingly. Five of the fifteen were dominantly

TABLE 2

Major MC ideological impulses in the twentieth century

Years	N	Ideological impulse	Notable participants
1901–10	37	Old Guard domestic conservatism under Theodore Roosevelt and Taft (on currency and tariff legislation, regulation of RRs, etc.)	Nelson W. Aldrich (R–RI), Joseph G. Cannon (R–IL), John C. Spooner (R–WI)
1905–12	34	Progressive insurgency under late TR, Taft (on tariff duties, RR regulation, Cannon's Speakership, etc.)	Albert Beveridge (R–IN), Jonathan Dolliver (R–IA), Robert La Follette (R–WI), George Norris (R–NE)
1912–17	41	New Freedom domestic reform under Wilson (plus warmup for it in 1912–13)	Claude Kitchin (D–NC), Robert La Follette (R–WI), Oscar Underwood (D–AL), many single-shot actors
1917–20	32	Antiwar and anti-League opposition to Wilson's foreign policy	William Borah (R–ID), Robert La Follette (R–WI), Henry Cabot Lodge (R–MA)
1921–31	41	Promotion of Progressive causes under Harding, Coolidge, and early Hoover	Robert La Follette (R–WI), George Norris (R–NE), Thomas J. Walsh (D–MT), Burton Wheeler (D–MT)
1931–37	73	New Deal domestic reform under FDR (and warmup under late Hoover admin.)	Edward Costigan (D–CO), R. La Follette, Jr. (I–WI), David J. Lewis (D–MD), Robert F. Wagner (D–NY)
1933–38	39	Left-populist challenge to New Deal: more inflation, nationalization, relief, wealth-taxes or anti-monopoly than FDR wanted	Hugo Black (D–AL), Huey Long (D–LA), Elmer Thomas (D–OK), Burton K. Wheeler (D–MT), William Lemke (R–ND)
1934–39	36	Right opposition to New Deal (incl. to court-packing & govt. reorganization)	Josiah Bailey (D–NC), John J. O'Connor (D–NY), Burton K. Wheeler (D–MT) after 1936
1933–41	28	Isolationist opposition to U.S. involvement in internat'l. orgzns. and European affairs	William E. Borah (R–ID), Hiram Johnson (R–CA), Gerald P. Nye (R–ND), Burton K. Wheeler (D–MT)
1945–54	30	Foreign-policy internationalism under late FDR, Truman, Eisenhower (pro UN, Marshall Plan, NATO, vs. McCarthyism)	Thomas Connally (D–TX), Arthur Vandenberg (R–MI)

TABLE 2   (continued)

Years	N	Ideological impulse	Notable participants
1947–54	40	Isolationism, Asia-Firstism, and disloyalty hunting under Truman and early Ike admin.	Patrick McCarran (D–NV), Joseph McCarthy (R–WI), Richard E. Nixon (R–CA), Robert A. Taft (R–OH)
1961–68	29	Domestic reform under JFK and LBJ (civil rights, Medicare, etc.)	Hubert Humphrey (D–MN), Mike Mansfield (D–MT), Wilbur Mills (D–AR), Edmund Muskie (D–ME)
1961–68	26	Conservative opposition to domestic reforms of the 1960s	Harry F. Byrd (D–VA), Barry Goldwater (R–AZ), Richard Russell (D–GA), Howard Smith (D–VA)
1964–75	36	Opposition to the Vietnam War and the national security establishment that conducted it	Frank Church (D–ID), J. W. Fulbright (D–AR), Robert F. Kennedy (D–NY), Eugene McCarthy (D–MN), Geo. McGovern (D–SD)
1981–88	34	Pursuit of Democratic foreign and domestic policies under Reagan	Edward Boland (D–MA), Patrick Moynihan (D–NY), Thomas P. O'Neill (D–MA), Claude Pepper (D–FL), Daniel Rostenkowski (D–IL)

the latter. Finally, in process terms the impulses could accommodate lawmaking as their chief content, but they were not limited to that. Ample place is given here to the energetic legislating of the 1910s, 1930s, and 1960s carrying out the Democrats' domestic programs of those times (the congressional side of the New Deal leads the list with seventy-three member actions). But there is room also for impulses tilted toward investigating or taking stands— for example, those embodying the opposition to the Vietnam War or the outburst of Asia-first anticommunism. In a rich and variegated action mix, the former impulse also included antiwar bids for the presidency—by Democratic senators Eugene McCarthy, Robert F. Kennedy, and George McGovern. The America-first anticommunist drive is a choice instance of a dominantly *non*-domestic-policy and *non*-lawmaking ideological impulse. Witness its action ingredients in Table 3.[36]

Much of the cut and thrust of twentieth-century public affairs is incorporated in these fifteen ideological impulses. Where did they come from? To a large degree, to be sure, they have been emanations of public sentiment or accommo-

TABLE 3

The isolationist, Asia–First, anti–disloyalty impulse of 1947-54

Year	Member	Age	Cong. term	H/S	Action
1947	Walter Judd (R–MN)	49	3	H	claims State Department sold out China
1947	John Rankin (D–MS)	65	14	H	role in HUAC investigation of Hollywood
1947	Robert A. Taft (R–OH)	58	5	S	has reservations about Truman Doctrine
1948–49	William Knowland (R–CA)	40	2	S	notable Asia Firster
1948	Karl Mundt (R–SD)	48	5	H	Mundt–Nixon bill re internal security
1948	Richard M. Nixon (R–CA)	35	1	H	Mundt–Nixon bill re internal security
1948	Richard M. Nixon (R–CA)	35	1	H	pursues Alger Hiss in HUAC investigation
1948	J. Parnell Thomas (R–NJ)	53	6	H	chairs HUAC probe of espionage
1948	Robert A. Taft (R–OH)	59	5	S	chief congressional critic of Marshall Plan
1949	Karl Mundt (R–SD)	49	6	S	spokesman for "China lobby"
1949	Robert A. Taft (R–OH)	60	6	S	argues against NATO treaty
1950	Styles Bridges (R–NH)	52	7	S	backs McCarthy's anti-Communist drive
1950	Homer Capehart (R–IN)	53	3	S	makes key speech about internal subversion
1950	William Jenner (R–IN)	42	3	S	an emerging McCarthyite leader
1950	William Jenner (R–IN)	42	3	S	says Gen. Marshall is front man for traitors
1950	Patrick McCarran (D–NV)	74	9	S	McCarran Internal Security Act
1950	Joseph McCarthy (R–WI)	42	2	S	his Wheeling speech launches McCarthyism
1950	Joseph McCarthy (R–WI)	42	2	S	makes accusations before Tydings Committee
1950	Joseph McCarthy (R–WI)	42	2	S	intrudes into CT and MD Senate elections
1950	Richard M. Nixon (R–CA)	37	2	H	runs "pink lady" campaign vs. H.G. Douglas

TABLE 3 (continued)

Year	Member	Age	Cong term	H/S	Action
1950	Robert A. Taft (R–OH)	61	6	S	backs McCarthy's anti-Communist drive
1950	Robert A. Taft (R–OH)	61	6	S	favors lower military spending
1950	Robert A. Taft (R–OH)	61	6	S	demands Cong. role in Korean War policy
1950-51	Robert A. Taft (R–OH)	61	6	S	takes part in major debate re foreign policy
1950	Kenneth Wherry (R–NE)	58	4	S	backs McCarthy's anti-Communist drive
1951	Joseph Martin (R–MA)	67	14	H	leaks MacArthur anti-Truman letter re Korea
1951	Joseph Martin (R–MA)	67	14	H	attacks Truman admin. after MacArthur firing
1951-52	Joseph McCarthy (R–WI)	43	3	S	attacks Marshall, Acheson, others
1951-52	Richard M. Nixon (R–CA)	38	2	S	attacks Acheson, others
1952	Patrick McCarran (D–NV)	76	10	S	McCarran–Walter Immigration Act
1952	Karl Mundt (R–SD)	52	7	S	his "Korea/Communist/corruption" slogan
1952	Francis Walter (D–PA)	58	10	H	McCarran–Walter Immigration Act
1953-54	John Bricker (R–OH)	60	4	S	Bricker Amdt. to restrict pres. treatymaking
1953-54	William Knowland (R–CA)	46	5	S	hardline anti-coexistence foreign policy
1953	Joseph McCarthy (R–WI)	45	4	S	opposes Chas. Bohlen as ambassador to USSR
1953	Joseph McCarthy (R–WI)	45	4	S	gets Greek shipowners to stop China trade
1953	Joseph McCarthy (R–WI)	45	4	S	hunts Communists in State Department
1954	John F. Kennedy (D–MA)	37	4	S	only Demo. senator silent on McCarthy censure
1954	Joseph McCarthy (R–WI)	46	4	S	chairs Army–McCarthy hearings
1954	Joseph McCarthy (R–WI)	46	4	S	is censured by Senate

dations to moves by the White House, yet, in line with the central argument here, they are also partly an accomplishment of congressional entrepreneurialism. The causation needs to be shared. It is a good bet that American opinion has been shaped by these clusters of congressional moves as well as embodied in them. A better advertisement for that idea could scarcely be imagined than the conservative "revolution" led by Newt Gingrich on Capitol Hill in the mid-1990s. Probably this has been the only post-1988 cluster of member actions, given an appropriate search for evidence, that would merit an entry in an updated Table 2. The excitement of Gingrich conservatism radiated out from Washington, D.C. It even seems to have spilled over into the province of Ontario, affecting an election and a government there.[37] It was probably the twentieth century's sixteenth and last "ideological impulse." Its successors of the twenty-first century will no doubt materialize sooner or later.

Oppositions

The second omnibus category is *opposition*. Notwithstanding the importance of Congress, the presidency is ordinarily the center of power, energy, initiative, and attention in the American system. Few would disagree with that reading. Accordingly, the White House draws opposition year in and year out, and Congress has historically been the chief supplier of it. Coded here as "opposition" was "any effort by a member of Congress to thwart the aims or impair the standing of a presidential administration." That came to 511 member actions or 22 percent of the dataset from 1789 through 1988. All these items were also coded more basically as legislate, investigate, take stand, or something else directly behavioral.[38] In a separation-of-powers system like the American one, this definition of opposition is generous yet realistic. It accommodates major legislative disagreements yet also verbal assaults, hostile investigations, and even moves to impeach. It is true that "opposition" as defined here is not quite the same thing as "the loyal opposition" of a kind found in British-style parliamentary regimes—that is, leadership formations of the party out of power that perform in parliament as something like full alternative governments. In contrast, American congressional oppositions can be more fragmentary, inconstant, and reckless—but they can also be more versatile and variegated, and often they can cause a change of policy without a change of government.[39]

To put some familiar meat onto this framework, just over half of the 511 opposition items could be sorted into clusters. The criterion was that the historical works that were consulted treated certain items as ingredients of a single, interrelated, time-specific effort. The resulting eighteen clusters, which can be said to document eighteen distinct congressional "oppositions," to use a plural formulation, are listed in Table 4.[40] They sprawl across the two centuries—from James Madison's pioneering use of the House as an opposition site in the 1790s and Henry Clay's similar use of the Senate in the 1830s through the familiar institutional clashes since World War II. Once again, foreign policy surfaces as a motif. It dominates five clusters and enters into another four—including, during the twentieth century, every entry from the isolationism of the late 1930s through the Watergate crisis of the 1970s. Note that some of these eighteen oppositions mattered a great deal more than others, even if all of them can be said to have met a plausible threshold of prominence. In Table 4, that variation is signaled through a designation of magnitude that resembles a restaurant rating system. Roughly, the number of asterisks accompanying an opposition indexes its volume of member actions. In the four- or five-asterisk range are the Reconstruction opposition to Andrew Johnson in the 1860s, the antiwar and anti–League of Nations opposition to Wilson in the 1910s, the isolationist, Asia-first anticommunist opposition to Truman and Eisenhower around 1950, and the anti–Vietnam War opposition to Lyndon Johnson and Nixon in the 1960s and 1970s.[41] These are the historical high points. Still, it was unpleasant for a president to experience even a one-asterisk member challenge like those of the La Follette Progressives to Taft around 1910 or Huey Long to FDR in the 1930s.

For Congress's place in the American regime, possibly nothing has been more important than these exercises of opposition. Often they have been consequential—consider the policy aggressiveness directed against the White House during the Reconstruction era, the senators' mobilization of public sentiment against FDR's court-packing plan in 1937, and a later generation of senators' mobilization of public sentiment against the Vietnam War. Oppositions like these have offered the regime a kind of flexibility: It has been possible to push presidents to the wall not just during elections, and not just by members of the non–White House party. Voters were assisted to draw the inference that more than normal party-versus-party scrapping was at issue when, for example, Senator Stephen A. Douglas (D-Ill.) broke ranks with President Buchanan, a fellow Democrat, over Kansas statehood with its slavery implications in 1857, Senator Wheeler broke with fellow Democrat FDR over packing the Supreme Court in 1937, Senator Fulbright broke with fellow Democrat LBJ over Vietnam in 1966, and Senator Barry Goldwater (R-Az.) informed the Watergate-beleaguered Nixon that it was time to quit in 1974. All these were devastating moves.

As for recent years, the Republican assault against the Clinton administration during 1994–1998 qualifies as a full-blown opposition cluster. That would be the nineteenth in American history.[42] Uncommon intensity and energy went into opposing the Clinton White House. It was a time of high-publicity moves by members of Congress involving lawmaking, taking of stands, investigations, and finally impeachment. Gingrich, Dole, and other members such as Henry Hyde became household names. Afterward, the early years of the George W. Bush administration brought single-shot opposition moves of significance—as in Kennedy crying fraud on the war—but probably not enough to form a cluster. Even so, like ideological impulses, opposition clusters probably have a future in the twenty-first century.

TABLE 4
Clusters of opposition actions

Years	Leading actors	Cause	Magnitude
1790-93	James Madison (DR-VA)	vs. Hamilton's Treasury program	★★
1793-96	James Madison (DR-VA)	vs. Washington admin.'s pro-England foreign policy	★★
1803-08	John Randolph (DR-VA) Nathaniel Macon (DR-NC)	"Quid" opposition to Jefferson's policies	★
1832-36	Henry Clay (W-KY) Daniel Webster (W-MA) John C. Calhoun (W-SC)	Whig opposition to Jackson administration	★★★
1857-60	Stephen A. Douglas (D-IL)	vs. Buchanan admin.'s pro-South slavery policies	★
1864-68	Thaddeus Stevens (R-PA) Charles Sumner (R-MA) Benjamin F. Wade (R-OH)	congressional vs. presidential Reconstruction policy; impeachment of Andrew Johnson	★★★★★
1869-72	Charles Sumner (R-MA) Carl Schurz (R-MO) Lyman Trumbull (R-IL)	Liberal Republican opposition to Grant administration	★★
1877-81	Roscoe Conkling (R-NY)	patronage showdowns with Hayes & Garfield admins.	★
1906-12	Robert La Follette, Sr. (R-WI) Jonathan Dolliver (R-IA)	Progressive insurgency	★
1917-20	Robert La Follette, Sr. (R-WI) Henry Cabot Lodge (R-MA) William E. Borah (R-ID)	antiwar opposition in 1917 blends into anti-League opposition led by Lodge in 1919	★★★★

TABLE 4 (continued)

Years	Leading actors	Cause	Magnitude
1922-24	Robert La Follette, Sr. (R–WI) George Norris (R–NE) Thomas J. Walsh (D–MT)	Progressive oppo. to Harding and Coolidge admins.; Teapot Dome probe	★★
1934-35	Huey Long (D–LA)	populist "Share Our Wealth" challenge to FDR	★
1937-38	Josiah W. Bailey (D–NC) Burton K. Wheeler (D–MT) John J. O'Connor (D–NY)	break with FDR over court-packing, executive reorganization, unions, minimum wage; the "Conservative Manifesto"	★★★
1939-41	Gerald P. Nye (R–ND) Arthur Vandenberg (R–MI) Burton K. Wheeler (D–MT)	isolationist opposition to involvement in Europe	★★
1938-44	Martin Dies (D–TX) Howard Smith (D–VA) Harry F. Byrd (D–VA) Kenneth McKellar (D–TN)	conservative assault on New Deal and war agencies; many investigations	★★
1947-54	Joseph McCarthy (R–WI) William Knowland (R–CA) William Jenner (R–IN) Patrick McCarran (D–NV)	anti-Communist loyalty probes blended with Asia First policy critique; "Who lost China?" "Who promoted Peress?"	★★★★★
1964-72	J. William Fulbright (D–AR) Eugene McCarthy (D–MN) George McGovern (D–SD)	vs. Vietnam War and national security establishment; the government's "credibility gap"	★★★★
1972-74	Samuel Ervin (D–NC)	Watergate	★★★

High Performers

The continual mention of Senator Edward Kennedy herein signals that some members of Congress have produced more actions than others. That is over-whelmingly true. In the action realm, radical inequality among members has been one of the first facts of congressional life.[43] Consider Table 5, which lists all of the forty-four members of Congress who performed ten or more actions between 1789 and 1988. (An "action career" in the last column supplies the dates of a member's first and last actions on Capitol Hill.) All told, almost a third of the dataset's 2,304 items involved just these forty-four individuals. In order, they range from Henry Clay with forty items down through a handful of chiefly twen-tieth-century members with ten apiece. The thrusts of the various high-perform-ers have varied in kind—some as lawmakers, some as opinion leaders, some as all-around politicians whose careers included White House bids. Notably, as with American presidents, everyone on the list is a white male (more about this in a moment), and virtually all the surnames are northwestern European—Senator Edmund Muskie (D-Maine) seems to be the only exception.

TABLE 5

Members of Congress who performed ten or more "actions"

N actions	Member	Chamber	Action career
40	Henry Clay (DR,W-KY)	H,S	1811–1850
37	Henry Cabot Lodge (R–MA)	H,S	1890–1921
30	Robert A. Taft (R–OH)	S	1939–1953
27	William E. Borah (R–ID)	S	1917–1939
27	Robert La Follette, Sr. (R–WI)	S	1906–1924
27	Charles Sumner (D/FS,R–MA)	S	1851–1872
24	George Norris (R,I–NE)	H,S	1909–1940
23	John Sherman (R–OH)	H,S	1856–1897
22	Stephen A. Douglas (D–IL)	S	1845–1861
21	Nelson W. Aldrich (R–RI)	S	1899–1910
21	Daniel Webster (DR,W–NH,MA)	H,S	1813–1850
20	Robert F. Wagner (D–NY)	S	1927–1949
19	James Madison (DR–VA)	H	1789–1796
17	Samuel Rayburn (D–TX)	H	1914–1961
17	Arthur Vandenberg (R–MI)	S	1933–1948
16	John C. Calhoun (DR,W,D–SC)	H,S	1811–1850
16	Lyndon B. Johnson (D–TX)	S	1953–1960
16	Thomas P. O'Neill (D–MA)	H	1967–1985

TABLE 5   (continued)

N actions	Member	Chamber	Action career
15	William Seward (W,R–NY)	S	1849–1861
15	Thaddeus Stevens (R–PA)	H	1861–1868
14	John Randolph (DR–VA)	H,S	1800–1826
14	Burton K. Wheeler (D–MT)	S	1923–1941
13	James G. Blaine (R–OH)	H,S	1872–1881
13	Barry Goldwater (R–AZ)	S	1960–1984
13	Matthew Quay (R–PA)	S	1887–1902
12	J. William Fulbright (D–AR)	H,S	1943–1968
12	Hiram Johnson (R–CA)	S	1919–1945
12	Lyman Trumbull (R–IL)	S	1861–1872
11	John Quincy Adams (F,DR,NR,W–MA)	H,S	1803–1842
11	Thomas Hart Benton (D–MO)	S	1829–1848
11	Harry F. Byrd (D,I–VA)	S	1937–1964
11	Arthur P. Gorman (D–MD)	S	1881–1904
11	Henry Jackson (D–WA)	S	1957–1976
11	Edward Kennedy (D–MA)	S	1968–1987+
11	Robert La Follette, Jr. (R,I–WI)	S	1928–1939
11	Mike Mansfield (D–MT)	S	1962–1973
11	Edmund Muskie (D–ME)	S	1963–1980
11	Thomas B. Reed (R–ME)	H	1889–1897
11	Benjamin F. Wade (R–OH)	S	1851–1868
10	Hubert H. Humphrey (D–MN)	S	1949–1977
10	Huey Long (D–LA)	S	1932–1935
10	Wilbur Mills (D–AR)	H	1960–1972
10	Richard Russell (D–GA)	S	1948–1970
10	Samuel Smith (DR–MD)	H,S	1800–1827

Since 1988, the best candidates for congressional high performers (all white males still) would seem to be Senator Kennedy, who already appears in Table 5, Speaker Gingrich, and Senator McCain. Kennedy, in the wake of mounting a damaging challenge to President Carter from the left-liberal side of the Democratic Party in the late 1970s, stage-managing the defeat of Robert Bork for a Supreme Court justiceship in 1987, and many other early and midcareer moves, has kept it up. He has effectively maneuvered across party lines to help advance the Americans with Disabilities Act in 1990, the Kassebaum-Kennedy health portability insurance act of 1996, a measure providing health care for children in 1997, the No Child Left Behind Act, and (to his regret) the Medicare prescription drugs measures under George W. Bush, and he has regularly taken prominent positions, as on Iraq.

Gingrich, in a House career spanning a decade and a half, launched the Conservative Opportunity Society (a House Republican activist group of the 1980s), made use of C-SPAN inventively (along with Robert Walker, R-Penn.) to reach out to a small but engaged national audience, stirred up damaging media exposure of Speaker Jim Wright's (D-Tex.) finances in 1989 (Wright reacted by resigning from the House), wrecked a cross-party deal for a George H. W. Bush administration budget in 1990, drummed up candidates and money for the Republican takeover of the House in 1994, coauthored and marketed the Contract with America, presided over House enactment of that program in 1995, shook up the House leadership structure in 1995, confronted Clinton over the budget in the winter of 1995–1996, and championed the president's impeachment in 1998. That is a considerable résumé. Senator McCain has, among other things, pressed the case for war in Yugoslavia, shepherded an ambitious tobacco deal in 1998 (it didn't quite win), bid for the presidency himself in 2000, helped maneuver a patients' bill of rights bill through the Senate in 2001, and guided campaign finance reform to completion.[44]

Member Actions in the Twenty-first Century

Enough of data displays and anecdotes: In the end, why is the realm of member action important? Certainly it is a major aspect of the only political system the United States has had or is ever likely to have. It has helped encase the country's basic separation-of-powers arrangements in a kind of public sphere that has been central to the functioning and stability of those arrangements.[45] The roots of these relationships seem to go back to Stuart and Tudor times: There is the instance of William Pym using his House of Commons office to mobilize the English public against the crown in the 1640s. Granted, it is possible that the U.S. Constitution was a wrong historical turn. Parliamentary government as it evolved in Britain might have been a better option.[46]

As a practical matter, however, that seems to be an irrelevant consideration at this time. American presidents, senators, and House members, legitimized as they are by direct popular choice at all points of nomination and election, are very likely here to stay. Moreover, as indicated in a national survey of public opinion conducted in 2004 by Annenberg's Institutions of American Democracy project, the contemporary American public strongly endorses Congress's place in the system. In answer to the question: "When it comes to making important policy decisions, do you think that decisions should be made by the Congress or by the

93

president?" the response was 59.4 percent by Congress, 20.5 percent by the president, 13.9 percent by both. (An unsurprising partisan tilt emerged in these results, with Republican respondents leaning more toward the president, who was George W. Bush at the time, but pluralities of both Republican and Democratic respondents opted for Congress.) In addition, the public emphatically endorsed the idea of checks and balances—as least as it is indexed in the following survey question: "Which view is closer to yours—legislative checks are good, or legislative checks cause gridlock and inaction?" Favoring "checks are good" were 69.9 percent of the public; favoring "cause gridlock and inaction" only 19.8 percent. Furthermore, there is a healthy, perhaps surprising, appreciation of the non-niceties of the legislative process. In answer to the question: "Which one do you agree with most? A) Conflict is a natural part of the legislative process, or B) Members create conflict where there need not be any," 62.7 percent of respondents chose option A; only 31.5 percent chose option B. These various results speak well for continuing public appreciation of the role of Congress. For all its problems, the American separation-of-powers system is a tough, durable one that anybody living under might as well sign on to and try to make the best of.

Tough as it may be, and improvable though it may be in certain ways, the system also needs to be tended and maintained. Not least, as the twenty-first century gets under way, the realm of legislator action could use some tending and maintaining—or at least some thoughtful examination. Is it in decent enough shape? What are the threats to it? Note that the place of legislative branches in public life is not guaranteed. A theme of twentieth-century scholarship is that they, after all, tend to decline. Legislatures can fail to attract talented members. They can come to be ignored by the media. Regardless of constitutional provisions, they can hemorrhage power to executive branches and as a consequence fall from public attention. All of these things can happen. Consider the apparent trajectory of city councils in America's big cities during the twentieth century. For the twentieth-first century, a good bet for the chief menace to the American institutional mix is the White House's continuing flexing of military muscle in imperial enterprises abroad. On the record, that kind of activity, however well-advised on policy grounds, is not auspicious for a balanced constitution.[47] Congress, the courts, and popular rule all tend to pale before it. A dismal scenario for the year 2100, even lacking any formal constitutional changes, would be a U.S. Congress bereft of member actions as they have been described here—a body diminishing to city-council status, deprived of talent, media coverage, public attention, and real power as the executive branch expands to conduct an imperial role.

With the future trajectory of member action in mind, at least four areas of concern may be worth broaching—media connections, academic culture, congressional membership diversity, and second-order institutions. In the area of *media connections,* a decent supply of information flow from officials to citizens is obviously needed to keep a public sphere going. In particular, media coverage is crucial. Yet in today's environment there are problems. Coverage of Congress seems to have grown scantier in recent times. On network television, at least, there is less of it. Going by testimony supplied by Capitol Hill staff members in a survey conducted by Annenberg's Institutions of American Democracy project in 2004, that falloff in coverage seems to have affected the House of Representatives more than it has the Senate. Asked whether they agreed that "The reduced coverage of public affairs in the news media has made it harder for members of Congress to get media attention for their politically important activities," 63.7 percent of House aides agreed and 34.3 percent disagreed, although Senate aides divided evenly on the question. That is not good news for "the people's body"—the traditional designation of the House given its constitutional design. Beyond questions of volume, media coverage of Congress has also grown more negative. In general, in an environment of channel specialization and proliferation, it is hard for ample, coherent coverage of public affairs to materialize and have reach. For these reasons, and no doubt many others, today's young people, according to survey data, "are more withdrawn from public affairs than earlier birth cohorts were when they were young."[48]

On the brighter side, it is also true that no stable golden age of media connections has ever existed. From 1789 onward, members of Congress have continually needed to invent new ways to get themselves across as media technologies have relentlessly evolved.[49] In recent times, the members' moves have included C-SPAN, talk-show appearances, and the Internet (note Senator Byrd's website). Perhaps such catching up will keep occurring, but this is a front worth constant monitoring.

As for *academic culture,* the chief problem here is that the country's long tradition of writing American public affairs history has fallen on hard times. In general, historians in today's academic departments have shifted their tastes elsewhere. Figures of previous generations such as John Morton Blum and William E. Leuchtenburg are not being replaced. One gets the sense that the history profession has largely given up on the idea of the United States as a self-governing republic whose relations between public and government need to be investigated and recorded. Certainly elected officials as consequential actors, presidents aside, have gone into eclipse. Formal processes are out, protest and other emphases are in.

History texts for elementary and secondary schools have followed the trend. The *National Standards for United States History,* offered in 1994 as a guideline for teaching American history in grades five through twelve, was officially censured in the U.S. Senate by a vote of 99–1 in 1995 (possibly partly as a statement of institutional self-regard). It is a 246-page document awash in the names of historical personages. To be sure, it lacks the detail that the actual history books have. It is suitably workmanlike on major events. But its emphasis, or rather the lack of it, comes through. Huey Long is the only member of Congress mentioned in connection with the New Deal era; there is no sign of Senator Wagner. Senators Blanche Bruce and Hiram Revels, the African American Republicans from Mississippi, are the only members mentioned in connection with Reconstruction; there is no sign of Charles Sumner or Thaddeus Stevens (R-Penn.). Overall for the two centuries, Senator Joseph McCarthy receives by far the most attention of any member of Congress. There is no sign of Daniel Webster (W-Mass.), John Quincy Adams (W-Mass.) in his antislavery phase as a House member, Stephen Douglas, John Sherman (R-Ohio), Robert La Follette, George Norris, Martin Dies, Robert Taft, Arthur Vandenberg (R-Mich.), Sam Rayburn (D-Tex.), Adam Clayton Powell, Jr. (D-N.Y.), J. William Fulbright, Edmund Muskie, Eugene McCarthy, or Edward Kennedy. At issue is the following: How much grasp of public affairs history do American students require in order to become watchful citizens? Fortunately, academic fashions come and go.[50] Perhaps a new generation of historians will compensate.

Still, it is well to appreciate one reason for this laundering of the past. It is dead white males who are being laundered out through, to be sure, a standard exercise of political correctness by academics. But on this topic the academics may be acting as a kind of soured proxy for American society, or at least for substantial parts of it. One threat to the future of congressional member action is Congress's lack of *membership diversity*. American society has changed a great deal in recent times, as has the electorate. In the 1990s, for example, Americans voting in presidential elections hit an all-time peak as a fraction of the resident U.S. population (regardless of age or citizenship), and that participatory achievement probably also indexed a peak in voter diversity, variously considered.[51] But Congress has changed less. Women members of Congress constitute only some 15 percent of the House and Senate. Owing partly to demographics and the accidents of state boundaries, there were no Hispanics or African Americans in the Senate at the beginning of the twenty-first century, although Barack Obama (D-Ill.), Mel Martinez (R-Fla.), and Ken Salazar (D-Colo.) joined the chamber in January 2005. A lag on these fronts is probably diminishing the public sphere. The legitimacy of, regard for, and attention accorded to Congress and its members may be suffering. What can be done? For one thing, a surge in women representatives in the Congress, not to mention women members taking the lead in future "ideological impulses" and "oppositions," might do wonders for the realm of member action. Nancy Pelosi is a start. So would statehood for the District of Columbia, by no doubt fostering the election of two African-Americans to the Senate. Arguably, an important missing voice in that body during the 1980s and 1990s was the Reverend Jesse Jackson.

The last rubric is *second-order institutions*, by which is meant institutions and procedures that are important yet fall short of constitutional standing. This is a tricky subject, but here are two ideas. First, exceptionally strong political parties are probably not good news for the realm of member action. For the American public sphere to function as it has traditionally done, in the context of the nation's complicated presidential system, members of Congress need to be able to perform as individuals, and the public needs to be able to witness them performing as individuals. In recent times, partisanship has reached one of its all-time extremes on Capitol Hill, and that development should give pause. On the House side in particular, staff members of that body reported in the Institutions of American Democracy project survey: "The increased influence of the party leaders has made it harder for other members of Congress to undertake politically important activities." Agreeing with this judgment were 67.2 percent of the aides, disagreeing 32.2 percent.[52] A caution-signal to high-minded advocates of strong parties might be: Beware of getting what you wish for. From the standpoint of a healthy realm of legislator action, an appealing feature of the McCain-Feingold campaign-finance reform, however that measure might be evolving since passage, is that it aimed to weaken the parties. "Soft money" wielded by centralized parties was coming to look like a threat to member individualism. For a century, an underappreciated—and important—feature of campaign-finance regulation in the United States is that it has channeled money to individual candidates, not parties.

Second, getting rid of the Senate filibuster would arguably be bad news for the American public sphere. How can this be? The familiar mathematical case indicts the filibuster, or the stiff cloture requirement underlying it, as an impediment to majoritarian democracy. For better or worse, these practices can *block* public opinion. But this assumes that public opinion is structured in some primordial fashion external to the actions of politicians, which often it is not. In the operation of the U.S. Senate, legislative delays of weeks, months, even years can also assist the *formation* of public opinion as political actors inside and outside Congress make their cases before the public. On this reckoning, the important aspect is the delay, not the roll-call arithmetic. An example is the gradual mobilization of opposition to FDR's court-packing plan in 1937. Actions by individual members of Congress seem to have played a major role.[53] Even in the instances of the great civil rights enactments of the mid-1960s, the lengthy Senate debates probably helped ease the white South's acceptance, more or less, of the results.[54] In the American system, the likeliest beneficiary of strict, quick majority rule in both houses of Congress would be the White House. Presidents would find it easier to plead emergency or mandate and get they want, quickly and without much discussion.

These concerns having been expressed, there is no sign that public awareness of members of Congress has been decreasing during the last half century. In various spot-checks of national public awareness or knowledge of members of Congress (the survey questions vary), representatives registering below 25 percent though well above zero have included Senator Henry Jackson (D-Wash.) in the immediate postwar decades, Congressman Jack Kemp (R-N.Y.) around 1980, and Senator Richard Lugar (R-Ind.) and the unflamboyant Speaker Foley in more recent times. Scorers in the 25 to 50 percent range have included Senator Harry F. Byrd (D-Va.), Senator Fulbright, and Speaker Carl Albert (D-Okla.) before 1980 and Speaker Jim Wright and Senator Jesse Helms since then. Scorers above 50 percent have included Senators Taft and John Bricker (R-Ohio) in the 1940s, Senators Joseph McCarthy and Estes Kefauver (D-Tenn.) in the 1950s, Senator Goldwater in 1963, Speaker O'Neill in the 1980s, Senators Orrin Hatch (R-Utah), Joseph Biden (D-Del.), Arlen Specter (R-Penn.), Alan Simpson (R-Wyo.), and other participants in the Thomas hearings in 1991, as well as Newt Gingrich, Henry Hyde, Bob Dole, and Dick Gephardt later in the 1990s.[55] A range of plausible and reassuring recognition rates emanated from the survey of national opinion conducted by the Institutions of American Democracy project in 2004—Edward Kennedy at 95 percent, John McCain at 84 percent, Orrin Hatch at 56 percent, and Congressman Barney Frank (D-Mass.) at 36 percent. Again, newspaper sources could be used to flesh out information like this, at least by inference, throughout American history.

A final bit of evidence regarding public opinion and legislator action. In a national survey in April 1995, respondents exhibited a deft sense of causation that extended to a counterfactual: "If Newt Gingrich had not been Speaker of the House, do you think the Republicans would have been able to pass as many bills as they did, or don't you think so?" This was just after the Contract with America zoomed through the House. The answers were: Yes, would have, 19 percent. No, would not, 60 percent. No opinion, 11 percent.[56] That judgment seems about right.

Notes

★ The author is indebted to Matthew Glassman, Paul Quirk, and Charles Stewart for their helpful comments on this work.

1. Edward Walsh and Juliet Eilperin, "Gore Presides as Congress Tallies Votes Electing Bush; Black Caucus Members Object as Fla. Numbers Are Accepted," *Washington Post,* January 7, 2001.

2. Kirk Victor, "Lott's Big Gamble," *National Journal* (January 20, 2001), 170–73, quotation at 171.

3. David E. Rosenbaum, "Georgia Democratic Senator Unapologetic in Aiding Bush," *New York Times,* January 23, 2001; David E. Rosenbaum, "Two Leaders of Tax Panel Agree on a Bill," *New York Times,* May 12, 2001; Helen Dewar, "Baucus Deal on Tax Cut Upsets Senate Democrats," *Washington Post,* May 12, 2001; John F. Harris and Dan Balz, "Delicate Moves Led to Tax Cut," *Washington Post,* May 26, 2001.

4. Mike Allen and Ruth Marcus, "GOP Missteps, Jeffords's Feelings about Agenda Led toward Exit," *Washington Post,* May 24, 2001.

5. Lexington, "King of the Hill," *Economist* (January 12, 2002), 33. See also James A. Barnes, "Action versus Inaction," *National Journal* (March 9, 2002), 688–692. The vote was 381–41 in the House and 87–10 in the Senate. On Kennedy's general record: Albert R. Hunt, "The Liberal Lion Roars Louder Than Ever," *Wall Street Journal,* February 19, 1998; "Sen. Kennedy Thrives in Opposition," *New York Times,* January 30, 2001.

6. Richard L. Berke, "A Flurry of Hugs for 'Gang of Five' in Capital," *New York Times,* October 23, 2001.

7. Peter Carlson, "The Solitary Vote of Barbara Lee," *Washington Post,* September 19, 2001; "Congresswoman Lee: Hero of the Left."

8. Paul Alexander, *Man of the People: The Life of John McCain* (Hoboken, N.J.: Wiley, 2003), 182–184, 200–201. On Shays and Meehan: Mary Leonard, "After Months, a Triumph for Meehan," *Boston Globe,* August 4, 1998; Bob Hohler, "Shays Feels GOP Heat over Campaign Bill," *Boston Globe,* July 22, 1998. On McCain and the debate: John Lancaster, "Campaign Bill Unearths a Senate Relic: Debate," *Washington Post,* March 23, 2001. On the town halls: Alexander, *Man of the People,* 340. On McCain's stewardship: John Lancaster and Helen Dewar, "Luck, or Fate, Helped Guide Campaign Bill," *Washington Post,* March 31, 2001. On House passage: Alison Mitchell, "House Backs Broad Change in Financing of Campaigns: Fast Senate Action Sought," *New York Times,* February 15, 2002.

9. Spenser S. Hsu and Kathleen Day, "Senate Vote Spotlights Audit Reform and Sarbanes," *Washington Post,* July 15, 2002. See also David S. Hilzenrath and Jonathan Weisman, "How Congress Rode a 'Storm' to Corporate Reform," *Washington Post,* July 28, 2002.

10. Michael Barone, with Richard E. Cohen and Grant Ujifusa, *The Almanac of American Politics 2004* (Washington, D.C.: National Journal, 2003), 1701.

11. Jim VanderHei and Juliet Eilperin, "GOP Leaders Tighten Hold in the House," *Washington Post,* January 13, 2003; Richard E. Cohen, "Hastert's Hidden Hand," *National Journal* (January 20, 2001), 174–177, quotation at 176.

12. Tom Daschle with Michael D'Orso, *Like No Other Time: The 107th Congress and the Two Years That Changed America Forever* (New York: Crown, 2003), 10.

13. David Firestone, "For Homeland Security Bill, a Brakeman," *New York Times,* July 31, 2002; David Rogers, "Byrd Unleashes Oratorical Fury," *Wall Street Journal,* May 21, 2003.

14. David Rogers, "Medicare Proposal Yields an Odd Couple: Bush and Sen. Kennedy Back the Plan, But with Opposite Views and Expectations," *Wall Street Journal,* June 16, 2003. See also Carl Hulse, "Kennedy's Stance on Medicare Angers Allies," *New York Times,* June 22, 2003. On the Hastert count: David S. Broder, "Time Was GOP's Ally on the Vote," *Washington Post,* November 23, 2003. See also Robert Pear and Robin Toner, "Sharply Split, House Passes Broad Medicare Overhaul," *New York Times,* November 23, 2003; R. Jeffrey Smith, "GOP's Pressing Question on Medicare Vote," *Washington Post,* December 23, 2003.

15. Andrew Miga, "Ted K Rips Bush for 'Selective' Intelligence," *Boston Globe,* November 17, 2003. See also Helen Dewar, "Kennedy Hits Bush on War," *Washington Post,* January 15, 2004.

16. Editorial, "Tom DeLay's Down-Home Muscle," *New York Times*, July 17, 2003. The mid-decade location of this Texas gerrymander was novel, although in ambition, ruthlessness, and possible implications for long-term party control of the House, DeLay's move resembled that of a previous House leader, Philip Burton (D-Calif.), who had brought off an inventive gerrymander of California's congressional map in the early 1970s. On Burton: Michael Barone and Grant Ujifusa, *The Almanac of Politics 1996* (Washington, D.C.: National Journal, 1995).

17. Four years later, in January 2005, during the counting of the electoral votes cast in 2004, Senator Barbara Boxer (D-Calif.) would take the initiative to advance a similar appeal. By this time, the Senate had come to have one African American member—Barack Obama (D-Ill.).

18. In general, the typical, or median in an ideological sense, stances of the congressional parties do not have that kind of influence. A majority party can suffer defections of its centrist members to the opposition side on particular issues. See the argument in Keith Krehbiel, *Pivotal Politics: A Theory of U.S. Lawmaking* (Chicago: University of Chicago Press, 1998).

19. See Matthew Yglesias, "Bad Max: It's a Tempting Story Line That Sen. Max Baucus Has to Cast All Those Pro-Bush Votes because of Pressure Back Home in Montana. It's Just Not True," *American Prospect* (February 2004), 11–13.

20. On this question, see Michael Graetz and Ian Shapiro, *Death by a Thousand Cuts: The Fight over Taxing Inherited Wealth* (Princeton, N.J.: Princeton University Press, 2005).

21. Agenda manipulation is said to make a difference. But in theory, that ordinarily takes place in a context of ready-made, exogenously determined distributions of ideal points.

22. Terry M. Moe and Scott A. Wilson have written, "The transaction costs of moving a bill through the entire legislative process are enormous. . . . The best prediction is that, for most issues most of the time, there will be no affirmative action on the part of Congress at all. The ideal points [of the members of Congress] may logically support a given outcome, but in reality *nothing will happen*." ("Presidents and the Politics of Structure," *Law and Contemporary Problems* 57 [1994], 26–27).

23. On interactive rather than one-way: Fenno, *Home Style*. On not just targets of vectors: In terms offered by Jane Mansbridge, the balance tilts away from "promissory representation" toward "anticipatory" and "gyroscopic" representation. ("Rethinking Representation," *American Political Science Review* 97 [2003], 515–528.) On shaping opinion: Lawrence R. Jacobs, Eric D. Lawrence, Robert Y. Shapiro, and Steven S. Smith, "Congressional Leadership of Public Opinion," *Political Science Quarterly* 113 (1998): 21–41. On policy reputations: Edward G. Carmines and James H. Kuklinski, "Incentives, Opportunities, and the Logic of Public Opinion in American Political Representation," chapter 10 in *Information and Democratic Processes*, edited by John A. Ferejohn and James H. Kuklinski (Urbana: University of Illinois Press, 1990), 252–256. On entrepreneurs: Joseph A. Schumpeter, *Capitalism, Socialism, and Democracy* (New York: Harper and Brothers, 1950), 252–264.

24. Mayhew, *America's Congress*, 5, 6.

25. Ibid., 9.

26. See the discussion of the data source in Mayhew, *America's Congress*, chapter 2. The resulting dataset is available at http://pantheon.yale.edu/~dmayhew/data4.html.

27. Here, for coding purposes, it can also mean becoming memorialized in an eponymous bill title such as the Wilmot Proviso or the Taft-Hartley Act. Such items account for about 10 percent of the "legislate" items in the dataset. See Mayhew, *America's Congress*, 78–81.

28. Each of these twenty decades except the first and last accommodates five Congresses elected in years ending in 0, 2, 4, 6, and 8. That is out of respect for the commonsense meaning of "decade." But an embarrassment consequently arises. The initial decade here actually accommodates the six Congresses meeting from 1789 through 1801, the last decade just the four Congresses meeting from 1981 through 1988.

29. On Clinton's drive for health-care reform, see Johnson and Broder, *The System*. On Senator Gramm's role in banking reform, see Kirk Victor, "Loan Star Phil," *National Journal*, October 30, 1999.

30. See Mayhew, *America's Congress*, 81–90.

31. On Thompson: Francis X. Clines, "Money and Politics: Capitol Sketchbook—The Scene; Partisan Maneuvering for Hearing's Spotlight," *New York Times*, July 9, 1997. On Hyde's role, see Peter Baker et al., "The Train That Wouldn't Stop: Key Players Thwarted Attempts to Derail Process," *Washington Post*, February 14, 1999.

32. See Mayhew, *America's Congress*, 90–102.

33. On Boxer: Maureen Dowd, "7 Congresswomen March to Senate to Demand Delay in Thomas Vote," *New York Times*, October 9, 1991. On Nunn: Michael Wines, "This Time, Nunn Tests a Democrat," *New York Times*, January 30, 1993. On Moynihan: Gwen Ifill, "Moynihan Urges Prosecutor to Study Clinton Land Deal," *New York Times*, January 9, 1994. On Graham: Jim VandeHei and Francesca Contiguglia, "A Year Later, Rebels' Work Isn't Done: On Anniversary of Coup, Conservatives Say They've Matured," *Roll Call* (July 13, 1998), 1, 30. On Barr: "Clinton Critic Requests Inquiry for Impeachment," *Quincy (Mass.) Patriot Ledger*, March 15, 1997. On Helms: Donna Cassatta, "Helms Lashes Back at Critics, Holds Firm in Blocking Weld," *Congressional Quarterly Weekly* (September 17, 1997), 2159–2160. (This was a formal parliamentary move as well as a stand.) On Lieberman: Chris Black, "Lieberman, in Senate, Denounces President," *Boston Globe*, September 4, 1998. On McCain: Alison Mitchell, "McCain Presses His Case for Sending Ground Troops," *New York Times*, April 4, 1999.

34. For the coding of the "foreign policy" category, see Mayhew, *America's Congress*, 103–106. The items thus coded are all parasitic. That is to say, all of them are also coded as something more concretely behavioral—legislate, investigate, take stand, run for president, etc. The 23 percent share figure of the "foreign policy" category rises to 34 percent if items associated with the Civil War and military occupation of the South (6 percent) and those for tariffs and other foreign trade policies (4 percent) are added in. Note that there is possible overlap among the various code categories. For example, an item might code plurally as foreign policy, take stand, and investigate.

35. See Mayhew, *America's Congress*, 197–211. Like "foreign policy," the category of ideological impulse is parasitic. Each of its items had to have a primary anchor in a behavioral category like legislate or investigate. No item could be coded as *only* "ideological impulse." An especially useful guide for much of the century is Horowitz, *Beyond Left and Right*.

36. For each relevant member-of-Congress action, Table 2 supplies the year in which it occurred, the member who performed it, the age of the member at the time, the number of Congresses the member had served in at the time (whether in the House or Senate), whether the individual was a House or Senate member at the time, and the gist of the action.

37. On the Gingrich-led impulse of the mid-1990s, see Dan Balz and Ronald Brownstein, *Storming the Gates: Protest Politics and the Republican Revival* (Boston: Little, Brown, 1996). On the possible Ontario connection, see W. Bilal Syed, "Ontario's Elite Still Can't Smell the Coffee," *Wall Street Journal*, June 16, 1995; Allan Fotheringham, "Score One for the Angry White Guys," *Maclean's* (June 19, 1995), 64.

38. For this category, see Mayhew, *America's Congress*, 106–122. The "opposition" category is parasitic like those for "foreign policy" and "ideological impulse." Quotation on the coding, 107.

39. Still, it is possible for British MPs to oppose their government in a non–"loyal opposition" way. American-style versatility is available in a parliamentary system also. During the twentieth century in Britain, possibly no exercise of parliamentary opposition, by any definition of that term, was more important than back-bencher Winston Churchill's searing criticism of Prime Minister Neville Chamberlain's policy of appeasing Nazi Germany in the late 1930s. Both Chamberlain and Churchill were Tories at the time.

40. There is an overlap in certain particulars between the oppositions presented here and the ideological impulses presented earlier, yet note that the oppositions range over two centuries rather than just one, much of the action content of the ideological impulses would not qualify as oppositional, and in general the standards for selection of items differ. In principle, oppositions had to be indicated reasonably clearly by the relevant historians in order for them to be denominated as an opposition cluster in Mayhew, *American's Congress*, whereas the author used his own judgment in drawing the lines around the ideological clusters.

41. For readers wishing to follow this rating system to ground, here is the procedure. In Table 3.3 on pages 111–112 of *America's Congress*, any A item was counted as 5, any B item as 3, and any C item as 1. This allowed a weighted score for each opposition. Then the eighteen oppositions were ranked according to their scores and divided into categories at plausible junctures. If the two Madison-led oppositions of the 1790s are joined to compose one, which they could be (this is a matter of judgment), there is a respectable case on the evidence for awarding four asterisks to the joint product.

42. It should be noted that the dataset is a bit ragged for the 1980s, as is discussed in *America's Congress*. That owes to the diminishing utility of history books as sources for times after the 1970s.

43. See Mayhew, *America's Congress*, 169–176.

44. On Kennedy and Bork: Linda Greenhouse, "Senators' Remarks Portend a Bitter Debate over Bork," *New York Times*, July 2, 1987. On Kennedy in general: "Sen. Kennedy Thrives in Opposition." On Gingrich through 1995: Balz and Brownstein, *Storming the Gates*, chapters 1, 3. On restructuring the House in 1995: David Rogers,

"GOP's Rare Year Owes Much to How Gingrich Disciplined the House," *Wall Street Journal,* December 18, 1995. On the showdown over the budget: Michael Weisskopf and David Maraniss, "Endgame: The Revolution Stalls," *Washington Post National Weekly Edition,* January 29–February 4, 1996. On McCain and tobacco: Alexander, *Man of the People,* 184–187. On McCain and the patients' rights bill: Helen Dewar and Amy Goldstein, "Senate Passes Patients' Rights Bill," *Washington Post,* June 30, 2001.

45. On the contribution to stability, see Mayhew, *American's Congress,* 216–224.

46. On the Stuart era: Mayhew, *America's Congress,* 123–128. On the Tudor era: Samuel P. Huntington, "Political Modernization: America vs. Europe," *World Politics* 18 (1966): 378–414. For a thoughtful recent critique of certain provisions of the U.S. Constitution, see Robert A. Dahl, *How Democratic Is the American Constitution?* (New Haven, Conn.: Yale University Press, 2003). Notwithstanding the U.S.-U.K. dissimilarities in institutions, it is worth noting that a well-functioning parliamentary system has its own important brand of individual "MP action." In the politics surrounding the Iraq intervention during 2002 and 2003, alert Americans became acquainted with many British MPs: Tony Blair, the prime minister; Jack Straw, the foreign secretary; Geoffrey Hoon, the defense secretary; Gordon Brown, the second-ranking Laborite who occasionally threw his weight around in Blair's interest; Clare Short and Robin Cook, the antiwar defectors from the party cause; George Galloway, the Laborite MP accused of consorting with the Saddam Hussein regime, and others. For a Briton, watching and reacting to what these various people were doing and saying was central to being a citizen during the Iraq affair.

47. On this point, see Hugh Heclo, "What Has Happened to the Separation of Powers?" in *Separation of Powers and Good Government,* edited by Bradford P. Wilson and Peter W. Schramm (Lanham, Md: Rowman & Littlefield, 1994), at 153–164.

48. On the decline of television coverage of Congress: Greg Schneiders, "The 90-Second Handicap: Why TV Coverage of Legislation Falls Short," *Washington Journalism Review* (June 1985): 44–46; S. Robert Lichter and Daniel R. Amundson, "Less News Is Worse News: Television News Coverage of Congress, 1972–1992," in *Congress, the Press, and the Public,* edited by Mann and Ornstein, 133–135; Stephen Hess, "The Decline and Fall of Congressional News," in *Congress, the Press, and the Public,* edited by Mann and Ornstein, chapter 6. On the increasing negativity of coverage: Lichter and Amundson, "Less News Is Worse News," 137–139; Mark J. Rozell, "Press Coverage of Congress, 1946–1992," in *Congress, the Press, and the Public,* edited by Mann and Ornstein, 109–110; John R. Hibbing and Elizabeth Theiss-Morse, "The Media's Role in Public Negativity toward Congress: Distinguishing Emotional Reactions and Cognitive Evaluations," *American Journal of Political Science,* 42 (1998): 481–484. "In this post-Woodward-and-Bernstein era, rewards seem to flow toward reporters or accentuate 'scandal and sloth.'" John R. Hibbing and Elizabeth Theiss-Morse, *Congress as Public Enemy: Public Attitudes toward American Political Institutions* (New York: Cambridge University Press, 1995), 62, and more generally chapters 4, 5. On young people withdrawing: Stephen Earl Bennett, "Young Americans' Indifference to Media Coverage of Public Affairs," *PS: Political Science and Politics* 31 (1998): 535–541, quotation at 535.

49. See the discussion in Mayhew, *America's Congress,* 228–232.

50. The study: *National Standards for United States History: Exploring the American Experience* (Grades 5–12 Expanded Edition) (University of California at Los Angeles: National Center for History in the Schools, 1994). In all, the author counted mentions of thirty-one members of Congress in the *National Standards*. Twelve are eponymous, as in cases of the McCarran-Walter Act 1952 and the Dawes Severalty Act of 1887. Eighteen instances are pre-1900, thirteen post-1900. Only two are post-1960: the Ervin committee in 1973 and Thomas O'Neill's opposition speakership of the early 1980s. On history texts following the trend: Diane Ravitch, *The Language Police* (New York: Knopf, 2003), 135. On the Senate censure: Ravitch, 137. On changing academic fashions: Frances FitzGerald, *America Revised* (New York:Vintage, 1980).

51. The high point was 1992, the year of Clinton's first victory, when 42 percent of the resident population voted. (Possibly the 2004 election has now edged out that of 1992.) Figures for the nineteenth century when white males aged twenty-one largely exhausted the voter rolls are low by comparison—19.5 percent, for example, in 1896. See Charles A. Kromkowski, "Electoral Participation and Democracy in Comparative-Historical and Cross-National Perspective: A New Conceptualization and Evaluation of Voting in Advanced and Developing Democracies, 1776–2002," paper presented at the annual meeting of the American Political Science Association, Philadelphia, August 31, 2003, 28.

52. Here is an interesting historical question: In what era has party discipline peaked on Capitol Hill as an effective override to congressional representatives' personal or constituency preferences? Nobody really knows, but the answer may be the 1850s, when White House patronage maneuvering seems to have had a quite surprising influence over congressional copartisans. It is difficult otherwise to explain the votes of northern Democrats for the inflammatory Kansas-Nebraska Act. Why didn't the northerners block it?

53. See David R. Mayhew, "Supermajority Rule in the Senate," *PS: Political Science and Politics* 39 (2003), 31–36.

54. So far as is known, civil rights enactments were never enforceable in the Deep South at any time before the 1960s absent military occupation. Even in the fringe South, it took federal troops to integrate the Little Rock schools in 1957. Earlier, military occupation had ceased being a live option for northern opinion in the 1870s.

55. The sources are: Michael X. Delli Carpini, *What Americans Know about Politics and Why It Matters* (New Haven, Conn.:Yale University Press, 1996), 73–79, 311–317; *Gallup Poll Monthly*, #313 (October 1991), 27; #352 (January 1995), 24; #353 (February 1995), 25; #397 (October 1998), 34–35.

56. *Gallup Poll Monthly*, #355 (April 1995), 12.

Bibliography

Bauer, Raymond A., Ithiel de Sola Pool, and Lewis Anthony Dexter. *American Business and Public Policy: The Politics of Foreign Trade*. New York: Atherton Press, 1963. A classic treatment of the relations between society and Congress.

Cook, Timothy E. *Making Laws and Making News: Media Strategies in the U.S. House of Representatives.* Washington, D.C.: Brookings Institution Press, 1989. The leading work on this subject.

Fenno, Richard F., Jr. *Home Style: House Members in Their Districts.* New York: Longman. Repr. 2003. The classic work on how members present themselves to their constituencies.

Horowitz, David A. *Beyond Left and Right: Insurgency and the Establishment.* Urbana: University of Illinois Press, 1977. A model treatment of ideological impulses as they invested Congress during the first half of the twentieth century.

Johnson, Haynes, and David S. Broder. *The System: The American Way of Politics at the Breaking Point.* Boston: Little, Brown, 1996. In this subject area, a good case study is essential reading. This is the best one available. It addresses Clinton's abortive drive for health care reform in 1993–1994.

Mann, Thomas E., and Norman J. Ornstein, eds. *Congress, the Press, and the Public.* Washington, D.C.: American Enterprise Institute and Brookings Institution, 1994. The authoritative work on how the media cover Congress.

Mayhew, David R. *America's Congress: Actions in the Public Sphere, James Madison through Newt Gingrich.* New Haven, Conn.: Yale University Press, 2000.

Peters, Ronald M., Jr. *The American Speakership: The Office in Historical Perspective.* Baltimore: Johns Hopkins University Press, 1990. On House Speakers as major political actors from Henry Clay through Tip O'Neill.

Zaller, John R. *The Nature and Origins of Mass Opinion.* New York: Cambridge University Press, 1992. Essential reading on the subject of elite shaping of mass opinion.

Zelizer, Julian E. *Taxing America: Wilbur D. Mills, Congress, and the State, 1945–1975.* New York: Cambridge University Press, 1998. Academic historians seldom write about Congress. This is distinctively a historian's work, and a distinguished one.

ELECTIONS AND REPRESENTATION

4

MODERN CAMPAIGNS AND
REPRESENTATION

Gary C. Jacobson

F ROM THE BEGINNING, AND OF NECESSITY, DEMOCRACY
in the United States has been *representative* democracy. James Madison,
explaining the Constitution in *The Federalist Papers*, adopted the term
republic to emphasize the distinction between democracy as eighteenth-century
Americans understood it and the proposed new system:

> The two great points of difference between a democracy and a republic
> are: first, the delegation of the government, in the latter, to a small num-
> ber of citizens elected by the rest; secondly, the greater number of citi-
> zens, and greater sphere of country, over which the latter may be
> extended.[1]

The sheer size of the new nation meant that if the American people were to
govern themselves at all, they would have to do it indirectly, by delegating
authority to a small number of representatives to act on their behalf. But delegation raised the unavoidable risk, immediately acknowledged by Madison, that
representatives might use their authority to serve themselves rather than the people they were supposed to represent: "Men of fractious tempers, of local preju-
dices, or of sinister designs, may, by intrigue, by corruption, or by other means,
first obtain the suffrages [votes], and then betray the interests of the people."

The Constitution's solution to the delegation problem inherent in representative institutions is regular, free, competitive elections. Elections are meant to
empower ordinary citizens to control their representatives, enabling them to
vote for the candidate they think is best able to serve their values and interests,
with the candidate with the most popular support getting the job. The prospect

of future elections gives officeholders who want to keep (or improve) their jobs a motive to appear as faithful, competent representatives. And elections provide powerful incentives for one set of citizens—those who want to replace the current officeholders—to keep a close eye on representatives and to report any malfeasance they detect. Ideally, elections make representatives accountable to citizens, who exercise control through informed selection and sanctioning; insofar as the process succeeds, self-government is more than a patriotic myth.

Today, many Americans believe that the electoral process falls well short of this ideal. Although public support for the basic institutions of government is broad and deep, polling data reveals widespread discontent about many components of the electoral process: the choice among candidates, the roles of parties, interest groups, money, and the media, and the volume and content of campaign messages.[2] The voters themselves come in for considerable criticism for ignorance and apathy as well. Discontent about the performance of representative institutions is also common, and the electoral process is an obvious target for blame, for the way in which members of Congress win and hold their jobs has a profound effect on their individual and collective activities in Washington. This chapter will examine the processes by which senators and representatives are elected, to provide a fuller understanding of how and why these processes create problems for representative government (real and perceived), and what, if anything, might be done to improve them.

At the center of the analysis are the candidates themselves, for their response to electoral incentives drives both congressional election politics and representational activities in Washington. Winning election or reelection is by no means their only objective, but it is essential to the others (making good public policy, gaining power and respect on Capitol Hill, winning higher office), so electoral considerations permeate congressional politics.[3] The "ambition" that Madison assumed to be inherent in the pursuit of electoral office may be a constant, but the strategic environment in which it is expressed is not. The electoral context presents a complex aggregation of evolving opportunities and constraints. Thus to understand the development of current electoral practices, we have to understand the context to which they are adapted.

The context of congressional elections is a product of institutional features of the electoral system, available communication technology, and local and national public opinion. As this context changes, so do the behavior of members, the internal politics of Congress, and Congress's relations with other political institutions, especially the presidency—and thus the whole structure of representation. Of primary importance is the degree to which the context is conducive to a more candidate-centered or more party-centered electoral process. Collectively, voters in congressional elections decide two things simultaneously: who will represent them in the House or Senate and which party will control each chamber. But they are free to focus their attention more heavily on one decision or the other, and the balance struck between the two has profound consequences for how citizens are represented.

To the extent that elections are candidate centered, the winners have powerful incentives to be individually responsive to the local voters who elected them and to people who finance and otherwise support their campaigns, but much weaker incentives to concern themselves with the collective performance of their party or of Congress as a whole. To the extent that elections are party centered, members of Congress are rewarded or punished at the polls for their collective performance, giving them stronger incentives to contribute to the shared goal of making their party (in Congress and in the White House) look good, but weaker incentives to deliver local services and benefits and to put constituents ahead of party when conflicts arise. Although the balance between these alternatives has varied over time, both candidates and parties continue to matter in congressional elections, creating an inherent tension between individual responsiveness and collective responsibility.

Formal Context of Elections

The formal structure of American electoral politics has always been more open to candidate-centered electoral politics than, for example, systems using proportional representation and party lists. The Constitution's system of representation was designed before parties were invented, and subsequent developments have reinforced its fundamentally territorial character. Although multimember House districts and statewide at-large elections were not uncommon in the early decades of the Republic, they became rarer over time and were finally outlawed by a 1964 Supreme Court decision, *Wesberry v. Sanders,* which required states to draw districts with equal populations. Now all House members are elected from single-member districts by plurality vote.[4] Senators were initially chosen by state legislatures, but since the adoption of the Seventeenth Amendment in 1913 they have been elected by the state's citizens.

Congressional Districts

Each chamber's structure of representation presents its own peculiarities. House districts are now essentially arbitrary constructs subject only to the requirement of equal district populations. District boundaries are not politically neutral and are open to partisan manipulation whenever a single party controls the redistricting process. A partisan gerrymander (the traditional term for the artful drawing of election districts) maximizes the number of seats the controlling party can win, given the number and distribution of its usual voters. The idea is to concentrate the opposing party's voters in a small number of districts that that party can win by large margins, thus "wasting" many of its votes, and to create as many districts as possible in which the controlling party has a secure, though not wastefully large, majority. If neither party has full control of the process, districts are often drawn to favor incumbents of both parties. Gerrymandering has also been used to create districts favoring the election of racial or ethnic minorities, although recent Supreme Court decisions have sharply circumscribed this practice.[5]

The most recent (post–2000 U.S. Census) round of redistricting demonstrated how profoundly the drawing of district lines can affect representation. First, redistricting had a major effect on the party balance. If one makes the reasonable assumption that the 2000 presidential vote accurately measures the basic partisan divide among voters, then it is clear that Republicans used redistricting to increase the structural advantage they already enjoyed from a more efficient distribution of their voters. Although Al Gore outpolled George W. Bush by about 540,000 votes out of the approximately 101,450,000 cast for major-party candidates in 2000, Bush won more votes than Gore in 228 districts, while Gore outpolled Bush in only 207 districts. When the new districts were redrawn after the census, successful Republican gerrymanders in Michigan, Ohio, Pennsylvania, and Texas produced 240 Bush-majority districts, leaving only 195 Gore-majority districts. Democrats mounted a constitutional challenge to the Pennsylvania gerrymander but failed to convince the Supreme Court.[6]

Redistricting for 2002 also gave both parties safer districts. Of the twenty-five districts Republicans had won in 2000 with less than 55 percent of the vote, nineteen were strengthened by increasing the proportion of Bush voters; of the nineteen similarly marginal Democratic districts, sixteen were given a larger share of Gore voters. The net result was a sharp reduction in the number of competitive seats. Estimates of the number of House seats currently winnable by either party vary, but there is no question that the number has fallen sharply since the previous redistricting in 1992. In 2004, *CQ Weekly* identified only 37 of the 435 contests as competitive (either without a clear favorite or leaning slightly to one of the parties), the lowest number in the more than three decades that *Congressional Quarterly* has been handicapping House races.[7]

These two changes left the Republicans with a substantial advantage in the battle to control the House and made the partisan distribution of House seats considerably less sensitive than before to national shifts in voters' sentiments. Insofar as voters treat House elections as a national referendum on the performance of the governing party, the Republican majority installed in 2002 was well insulated against any but strongly contrary national tides. With the electorate evenly split in 2004 between sharply polarized parties, this is no small advantage. And by eliminating the need for moderation on the part of the majority and frustrating the minority's hopes of taking over, these changes are likely to intensify partisan polarization in the House.

A final point on districts: Originally, states were given one House seat for every 30,000 people. With restrictions on suffrage, district electorates numbered from a few hundred to a few thousand. By 2004 the average House district contained more than 670,000 residents, 500,000 or so of voting age, more or less arbitrarily thrown together to meet population and political criteria. Since *Wesberry v. Sanders* mandated equal-population districts, few have encompassed any sort of natural community of interests or coherent political identity. A growing proportion of Americans live in anonymous ring cities and suburbs embedded in large metropolitan media markets where House members are rarely deemed newsworthy. In this context, it is a formidable challenge for representatives to get to know their constituents' diverse needs and values and for constituents to learn much about the person representing them.

States

States are peculiar electoral units for a different reason than are districts: their extraordinary diversity in population and geography. A senator from California represents more than 35 million people, seventy times as many as a senator from Wyoming. New Jersey's population density is one thousand times that of Alaska's. Two hundred and fifty Rhode Islands could fit into Texas. Variations across these dimensions create vastly different electoral contexts—media markets, costs, voter expectations—and representational possibilities. This diversity is a major source of idiosyncrasy among Senate elections and senators themselves. Equal state representation also results in an extravagantly malapportioned upper chamber: the nine largest states are home to 51 percent of the population but elect only eighteen of the one hundred senators; the smallest twenty-six states elect a majority of senators but hold only 18 percent of the population.

In the early years of the twenty-first century the Republicans enjoy a structural advantage in the Senate as well as in the House—Bush, though losing the popular vote nationally in 2000, won more votes than Gore in thirty of the fifty states—but states remain substantially more competitive than House districts. Over the past twenty years, thirty-eight states have chosen senators from both parties, and all of the remaining states have elected governors of the party opposite their senators'. Typically, about half of the contests for the Senate are relatively hard fought, expensive, and close. Because a larger proportion of Senate seats are usually in play, the Senate is potentially more sensitive than the House to national shifts in partisan sentiment, although responsiveness is of course limited by the fact that only one-third of the Senate is at stake in any election year.

Rise of Candidate-Centered Elections

Although the territorial basis of representation in the House and Senate has always been open to candidate-centered electoral politics, not until the post–World War II period was this potential fully realized. Emerging communication technologies and the advent of professional campaign outfits available for hire made traditional party organizations (many already in decline) less essential to campaigns and allowed candidates more direct access to voters. At the same time, the post–New Deal political agenda featured conflicts over such issues as civil rights, the Vietnam War, Great Society programs and their cost, the sexual revolution, and environmental regulation that divided the party coalitions, particularly the Democrats, making the party cue less informative and weakening voters' party loyalties, leaving them more susceptible to candidates' personal appeals. Although party identification remained the single best predictor of an individual's vote in House and Senate elections, party-line voting declined significantly, while the influence on the vote choice of the voter's knowledge and evaluations of the particular congressional candidates grew.[8] National political forces also lost influence relative to state or district factors, leading, among other things, to a near doubling of ticket-splitting—voting for different parties for president and Senate or House—between the 1950s and the 1970s.[9]

Under these conditions, the personal images, political skills, and campaign resources of the individual candidates became more important in determining election results. Because incumbents typically enjoy an advantage in all three, the electoral value of incumbency rose. So did the importance of campaign money; access to the new communication technologies and professional campaign staff did not come cheap, and the economies of scale once provided by joint campaigns for entire party tickets were lost. The content of campaigns became more personal, emphasizing the candidate's local roots, individual character, and personal services to constituents, thereby increasing incentives for negative personal attacks, for an obvious strategy for defeating a candidate whose primary electoral asset is a good personal reputation is to destroy it.

Within Congress, candidate-centered electoral politics encouraged members to focus on activities that enhanced their personal reputations back home. To the ever-popular pursuit of pork barrel projects—the dams, highways, and federal installations whose benefits are enjoyed locally but paid for nationally— was added a relentless search for publicity and legislative credit. Senators and representatives voted themselves sharply increased resources for doing casework, traveling home, and communicating with constituents, and used them assiduously. They also spent an increasing amount of time raising the money to finance their individual reelection campaigns.

The effort seemed to pay off. Members of Congress became increasingly adept at carving out personal political franchises, insulating themselves from national partisan tides. Democrats in particular continued to win districts and states in which Republican presidential candidates routinely outpolled their Democratic opponents. The remarkable success of House Democrats first elected in 1974 in the wake of the Watergate scandal epitomized this pattern; seventy-four of the seventy-six won reelection in 1976, including forty-eight of the forty-nine who had taken seats from Republicans.

The style of representation emerging from these efforts was brilliantly described by Richard F. Fenno Jr. in a classic 1978 study.[10] Fenno traveled extensively with eighteen House members as they made the rounds of their districts, interacting with groups and individuals in a variety of contexts in a ceaseless effort to maintain political support. By different means, all sought the same end: to inspire trust among constituents. In Fenno's words, "The ultimate response House members seek is political support. But the instrumental response they seek is trust." Trust is crucial, because voters know little about what their representatives do or why they do it and are understandably skeptical of what they hear from people soliciting their votes. The members Fenno followed built trust by emphasizing their personal qualifications, including moral character, by identifying with their constituents, and by working to develop bonds of empathy with people and groups they met. They also highlighted their accessibility and willingness to listen. And they spent a lot of time just showing up, being present and visible in the district. For most, issues, policy, and partisanship were not prominent objects of discussion with constituents and were not used to elicit support. Even members who took an issue-oriented approach used issues primarily to cement ties of trust; how they addressed the issues rather than the issues themselves was what mattered. Fenno's conclusion was that these continuing efforts to maintain electoral support were essential to representation. A member of Congress "cannot represent any people unless he knows, or makes an effort to know, who they are, what they think, and what they want; and it is by campaigning for electoral support among them that he finds out such things."

Fenno also traveled with several senators, observing that their typically larger constituencies made it harder for them to cultivate firm ties to constituents. Senators' contacts with voters were more often mediated by television and newspaper reporters; there was less direct interaction. Issues and policy were more prominent in their interchanges, and they did not have as much detailed knowledge of their more heterogeneous constituencies. They were thus less successful than their House counterparts in carving out personal political franchises that could protect them from contrary partisan tides.[11]

Responsiveness versus Responsibility

The drawback to a highly personal approach to winning reelection is that it encourages individual responsiveness at the expense of collective responsibility. For example, members have every reason to promote narrowly targeted programs, projects, or tax breaks for constituents but little incentive to consider the impact of such measures on spending or revenues. Recipients notice and appreciate such specific and identifiable benefits and show their gratitude to the legislator responsible at election time. Because the benefits come at the expense of general revenues (money supplied by the taxes that everyone pays), the cost of the specific project or tax break is borne by the public at large. Thus it makes political sense for members of Congress to pursue local or group benefits that are paid for nationally even if the costs clearly outweigh the benefits. Conversely, no obvious payoff arises from opposing any particular local or group benefit, because the savings are spread so thinly among taxpayers that they go unnoticed. Logrolling (reciprocal support among legislators for pet projects) is the natural outcome. But when members in large numbers follow this individually productive strategy, spending rises, revenues fall, deficits accumulate, and inefficient government programs and projects proliferate. Individual responsiveness leads to collective irresponsibility.

The same logic makes members of Congress hesitate to impose direct costs on identifiable groups in order to produce greater, but more diffuse, benefits for all citizens. For example, laws designed to clean up the environment, a collective good, impose direct costs on industrial firms, such as those incurred in installing antipollution equipment. The cost of compliance is clear to every firm affected, but the benefit of any firm's investment is diffused across so many people that few are likely to appreciate it. Members of Congress, then, fear retaliation from the losers without a compensating increase in support from the winners.

Congressional majorities find ways to get around these problems, but doing so usually requires extraordinary commitment and effort by policy entrepreneurs and party leaders.[12] Even as the electoral process has grown more party-centered in recent decades, and even with the ascension of Republican congressional majorities avowedly hostile to "big government," enthusiasm for pork barrel projects and other particularized benefits—notably tax breaks—has scarcely abated.[13]

Campaign Money and Its Regulation

The rise of candidate-centered elections fueled a sharp increase in campaign spending, which has continued almost uninterrupted to this day, although, as Figures 1 and 2 indicate, the trend has been more erratic in Senate than in House campaigns, and steeper for incumbents and candidates for open seats than for challengers. Preliminary data for 2004 indicates that the average winning House candidate spent more than $1 million, up from an inflation-adjusted $284,000 in 1976; the average Senate winner spent $6.5 million, compared with $2 million in 1976.[14] Although campaign expenses vary greatly by district, it now costs at least $700,000 to run a serious House campaign in most places; every one of the forty-two successful House challengers from 1996 through 2004 spent more than this amount, although only 15 percent of all challengers did so. Full-scale Senate campaigns in any of the larger states can cost more than $20 million. Spending in a few recent Senate races has reached absurd levels; in 2004, for example, Republican John Thune spent $14 million challenging Democratic Senate minority leader Tom Daschle of South Dakota, who spent $19 million in a futile attempt to retain his seat, astonishing sums in a state with only 502,000 registered voters.

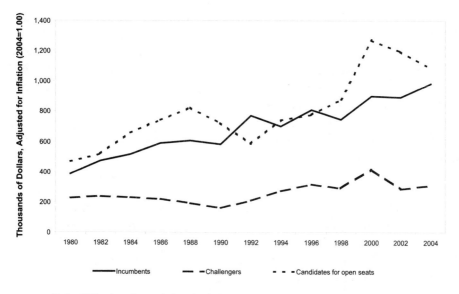

SOURCE: Federal Election Commission data

Figure 1   Campaign Spending in House Campaigns, 1980–2004

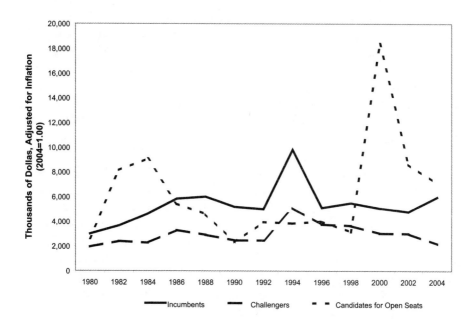

SOURCE: Federal Election Commission data

Figure 2   Campaign Spending in Senate Campaigns, 1980–2004

Responding to the growing importance of money and thus potential for corruption, Congress passed the Federal Election Campaign Act (FECA) in 1971, with major amendments made in 1974. The law required full disclosure of sources of campaign contributions and restricted the size of contributions that individuals, organized groups, and parties could contribute to congressional candidates.[15] FECA was intended to rein in campaign costs and reduce the influence of wealthy interests. The opposite occurred, partly because the Supreme Court, in 1976 in *Buckley v. Valeo,* declared limits on campaign spending to be an unconstitutional violation of the First Amendment,[16] partly because the law itself, by establishing a clear legal framework for campaign finance activities, invited parties and political action committees (PACs) to flourish. As the demand for campaign funds continued to grow, limits on the size of contributions forced candidates to pursue contributions from a larger variety of sources and thus to devote more time to fund-raising. Senators and Senate candidates from large states faced the greatest fund-raising pressure, because contribution limits did not vary by chamber or state population.

FECA's disclosure requirements exposed campaign-contribution strategies that are for the most part pragmatic and thus reinforcing of candidate-centered, incumbent-friendly electoral politics. This is clearest in the pattern of contributions from PACs, the source of about 40 percent of House campaign funds and 20 percent of Senate campaign funds. Many business corporations, labor unions, and trade associations organize PACs mainly to assist traditional lobbying for narrowly focused economic interests. They contribute to candidates not so much to affect the outcome of an election as to gain access and curry favor with the winners. The popularity of this approach explains why PAC contributors as a group have always strongly favored incumbents. In elections since 1978, 75 percent of PAC donations to House candidates went to incumbents, only 12 percent to challengers, and 13 percent to candidates for open seats. PAC contributions to Senate candidates have been less lopsided only by comparison, with 59 percent going to incumbents, 21 percent to challengers, and 20 percent to candidates for open seats.[17]

A few PACs do pursue broad ideological agendas. Like parties, they aim to maximize the number of seats held by members of Congress who support their views, so these PACs support promising nonincumbent candidates and concentrate their resources in close races, where money might make a difference. Conservative PACs are the natural allies of Republicans, and liberal and labor PACs of Democrats, and although ideological zeal occasionally conflicts with the party's exclusive interest in winning seats even if that means backing moderates, their involvement generally reinforces party strategies.

Other PACs pursue both short- and long-term political goals. Many business-oriented PACs, for example, supported incumbent Democrats as long as they were in the majority and likely to remain in power, although they were willing to back promising Republican challengers when the Democratic candidate appeared vulnerable. After the 1994 election, they scrambled to atone for years of supporting Democratic incumbents by helping newly elected Republicans retire their campaign debts and prepare for 1996. Without majority status and committee power to attract contributions from business interests, the balance of PAC campaign resources shifted against the Democrats; in the four elections prior to 1994, Democrats received 66 percent of the PAC money donated to House candidates and 51 percent donated to Senate candidates; since 1994, these figures have fallen to 50 percent and 41 percent, respectively.[18]

Although they attract the most attention, PACs have never been the most important source of campaign funds; private donors have always held that distinction, although they, too, are sometimes identified with specific economic or ideological interests. More important, individual donors also tend to distribute their funds strategically, generally supporting incumbents and ignoring all but the most promising challengers and candidates for open seats.

The only source of campaign money that is not invariably affected by the strategic calculations about the prospects is the candidate's own bank account. The Court's *Buckley* decision voided FECA's limits on candidates' donations to their campaigns (on the ground that the only justification for limiting contributions was "corruption or the appearance of corruption," and candidates cannot corrupt themselves), liberating wealthy candidates to spend all they wanted of their own funds to get elected. This clearly gives multimillionaires a leg up in financing campaigns—the record is held by the investment banker Jon Corzine, who spent $60.2 million winning a New Jersey Senate seat in 2000 (hence the extraordinarily high average for Senate open seats for 2000 in Figure 2)—but wealthy candidates are by no means always successful. One study found that only five each of the top twenty self-financers in both House and Senate contests from 1990 through 1998 won, and two of the Senate winners were incumbents.[19]

The Influence of Money

Multimillionaire candidates like to claim that self-financing frees them from obligations to contributors so that they can more faithfully serve the interests of ordinary people. The implication, widely believed by the public and people in the news media, is that campaign contributions buy favors of one sort or another and thus impair or distort representation. In its strongest form, the argument is that contributions corrupt the entire legislative process, giving citizens "the best Congress money can buy," because members vote with an eye more to the interests of their donors than to those of their constituents or the nation.[20] The evidence usually offered for this charge, however, is largely circumstantial or anecdotal. An investigative reporter or a campaign-reform group reports that members supporting legislation desired by some interest group—milk producers, used-car dealers, physicians, the banking industry, and the National Rifle Association are examples—got more campaign money from PACs representing the group than did members who opposed the legislation, and deduces that money influenced the vote.

Such evidence is inconclusive, however. Contributors say that they are merely helping to elect legislators who share their conception of the public good. And it would be bizarre indeed to find that donors distributed money randomly to friend and foe alike. In fact, no simple matching of contributions to roll call votes or other activities can prove that contributions buy influence. More careful scholarly studies have generally found that PAC and other contributions from identifiable interests exert, at most, only a modest effect on a legislator's decisions, which are largely shaped by party, ideology, and state or district preferences. However, on issues that attract little public attention and do not divide members along party or ideological lines, votes appear to reflect, in a modest way, prior contributions. All things being equal, members of Congress favor interests that help finance their campaigns. But all things are rarely equal. Despite the many tales of members who vote to please financial backers or who demand money from lobbyists in return for help, there is little reliable evidence that policy is being bought wholesale by special interests.[21]

This is not to say, however, that campaign contributions do not have other effects on some members of Congress. Both members and contributors admit that, at minimum, contributions ensure access—a necessary if not sufficient condition for insider influence. Doors are open to lobbyists representing groups that have supported members' campaigns (of course, members are also quick to say that the door is open to any constituent). Furthermore, roll call votes are by no means the only important decisions shaping legislation. Crucial choices are made before bills reach the floor, but little is known about how campaign contributions influence the preliminary stages of the legislative process.[22] It would be strange if interest groups put much time, energy, and money into campaign activities without some perceived legislative payoff.

Still, there are some formidable barriers to using campaign contributions to shape policy. Many important issues generate conflicts among well-organized interests, giving members access to money no matter which side they take and thus freeing them to take whatever side is consistent with their personal or constituency preferences. Given the variety of sources of campaign money available to incumbents—private individuals and parties as well as the thousands of PACs—most have little difficulty financing campaigns without putting their principles on the block. Furthermore, campaign money is a means to an end—winning votes and elections—not the end in itself. For incumbents, the marginal return on campaign spending is small; the prospective value, in votes, of even the maximum PAC contribution ($10,000) is tiny.[23] It makes no sense for a member, to please a PAC or other contributor, to take a stand that produces even a small net loss of voter support. Thus the sentiments of a member's constituents, when they can be estimated, far outweigh campaign contributions in determining roll call votes.

Finally, members of Congress are in a much stronger position to influence contributors than contributors are to influence members of Congress. Like other forms of lobbying, the activities undertaken by PACs are largely defensive. PAC members ignore invitations to fund-raisers at their peril because they risk losing access and putting the interests they represent at a competitive disadvantage. Yet for politicians, granting access is relatively cheap; it does not promise action, merely the opportunity to be heard.

Strategic Politicians

The growing centrality of candidates and importance of campaign money reinforces the crucial importance of strategic behavior in shaping congressional representation. The more voters focus on candidates, the more the quality, skills, and resources of the individual candidates affect election results. The quality of candidates and quantity of campaign resources in turn depend on the prior decisions of potential candidates and contributors, decisions that are strongly influenced by electoral expectations. The high level of success typically enjoyed by officeholders—since 1970, 94 percent of representatives and 81 percent of senators who sought reelection have succeeded—makes incumbency the primary source of electoral expectations. Incumbents who can convince potentially formidable opponents and their potential backers that they are invincible are likely to avoid serious challenges and so will be invincible—as long as the impression holds.

Other things being equal, the strongest congressional candidates are those for whom politics is a career. They are most likely to have experience in raising funds, running campaigns, reaching out to voters, and serving in public office. But their assets—their elective office, reputation as a campaigner—are at risk if an attempt to win higher office fails. Thus the best-qualified congressional aspirants also make the most considered and cautious judgments about when to try for a seat in the House or Senate.

Incumbency is central to their strategic calculations. Politically knowledgeable people are fully aware of the advantages of incumbency and of the long odds normally faced by challengers, and they adjust their behavior accordingly. Hence, for example, typically more than half the candidates for open House seats have previously held an elective office, while such experienced candidates comprise less than a quarter of the candidates challenging incumbents. Within this larger pattern, experienced challengers are more likely to run against incumbents who had closer contests in the last election.[24] Senate contests attract a higher proportion of experienced challengers than House candidates, because a larger proportion of states than House districts have sufficient partisan balance to be competitive, and the track record of Senate challengers is considerably better than that of House challengers.

The career strategies of potential candidates are reinforced by the strategies of individuals and groups who control campaign resources. Resources are limited, and most contributors deploy them where they have the greatest chance of affecting the outcome or currying favor with the winner. No one wants to waste money on hopeless candidacies. Consequently, money is raised most readily by incumbents, candidates for open seats, and challengers facing incumbents who for one reason or another appear vulnerable.[25]

Thus a system of mutually reinforcing decisions and expectations links candidates and contributors with one another and with perceived electoral prospects. The better the electoral odds, the more likely the race is to attract a high-quality nonincumbent candidate, and the more money will be contributed to his or her campaign. Furthermore, high-quality candidates themselves attract campaign money, and the availability of campaign money attracts high-quality candidates. The worse the odds, the more likely a party's nomination will go to a candidate lacking the background or resources to mount a serious campaign, if indeed anyone pursues it at all.

Strategic decisions of potential candidates and contributors thus determine the choices faced by voters on Election Day. As electoral research has become more sophisticated and campaigns more expensive, resources (quality candidates, and money and other forms of assistance) have become increasingly concentrated in the most promising races, where full-scale, often extravagant campaigns on both sides are now the norm. The other contests are effectively conceded to the dominant party. Either one party fields no candidate at all (the number of uncontested House seats is highly variable but has averaged sixty-three since 1980) or the candidate who does run lacks the experience and resources to mount a viable campaign. Primary elections, aside from those for nominations to open seats, are also largely uncontested. In 2004, only about two dozen of the more than 400 House incumbents seeking reelection faced serious challenges.

Representation by Anticipation

The scarcity of viable challengers to incumbents leaves most voters with little effective choice in the voting booth. Does the absence of choice undermine representation? Not necessarily. Seats go uncontested because potential candidates and other activists anticipate, with great if not perfect accuracy, what choice a majority of voters would make if a contest did take place. Incumbents make themselves appear impregnable not simply by holding office, but by taking great care to maintain the support of constituents by delivering desired projects and services, pushing locally popular legislation, and casting votes consistent with constituents' preferences. The surest route to reelection is avoiding a strong challenge; staying in solid with voters is the best way to discourage a strong challenge; and delivering satisfactory representation is the best way to keep voters content. Even if most citizens most of the time pay no attention to what their representatives are doing in Washington, local activists and potential rivals continually keep score, obliging members to anticipate how constituents would view their actions should they learn of them in some future campaign. It is the potential for serious competition, not its ubiquity, that aligns representatives with constituents. After all, Senate contests are far more likely to be competitive than House contests, but there is no evidence that representatives are less responsive than senators to constituents.

Representation by anticipation does not work perfectly, to be sure, and the absence of acceptable alternatives sometimes frustrates voters. In 1990, for example, Congress passed highly unpopular spending cuts and tax increases in late October, long after strategic decisions had determined the competitive situation in each district, leaving most voters without a viable way to vent their anger at the polls.[26] More generally, the lack of a real choice may frustrate citizens even if their preferences are perfectly anticipated, for there is something annoying about having one's decisions presumed in advance even if the presumption is entirely warranted. It is difficult to argue that candidates, activists, and parties should invest scarce resources in hopeless causes just to make voters feel better. But too much aversion to risk sometimes results in missed opportunities for candidates and voters alike, fueling public discontent with the electoral process. More important, if strategic politicians fail to anticipate the effects of national partisan tides, then the translation of shifts in public sentiment into change in Congress is inhibited.[27]

Revival of Partisanship

The trend toward increasingly candidate-centered electoral politics reversed in the 1980s, and the relative importance of partisanship and party campaigning has been growing ever since, although it had not, by 2004, returned to the levels of the 1940s and 1950s. The widely noted increase in unity within the congressional parties, and the ideological polarization between them, both stimulated and reflected important changes in electoral politics. The relationship between voters' party identification and ideology tightened, and the electoral influence of both ideology and party increased. The incidence of ticket-splitting declined, and the proportion of districts and, to a lesser extent, states with majorities that preferred presidential candidates of one party and House or Senate candidates of the other diminished.[28] The impact of national political forces grew, presidential coattails lengthened once again, and it became increasingly difficult for candidates to win states or districts against the partisan grain no matter how hard they worked to differentiate themselves from their national parties.

Some but by no means all of this growth in partisan coherence reflected the gradual realignment of the South, where the civil rights revolution moved conservative whites to abandon their ancestral allegiance to the Democratic Party in favor of the ideologically and racially more compatible Republicans. In-migration also contributed to an increasingly Republican electorate, which gradually replaced conservative Democrats with conservative Republicans in southern House and Senate seats. The constituencies that elected the remaining Democrats became more like Democratic constituencies elsewhere, giving the House and Senate parties more homogeneous (and more liberal) electoral coalitions. In regions outside the South, meanwhile, Democrats gradually supplanted most remaining liberal and moderate Republicans.[29]

The growing partisan divide was driven by a variety of forces in addition to this regional realignment. Among them were bitter conflicts in Washington (contested House election recounts, scandal-mongering aimed at party leaders, battles over Supreme Court appointments, disruptive guerilla tactics of disgruntled minorities, the impeachment of President Bill Clinton) and a contentious national agenda (social issues, particularly abortion and gay rights, and ideological struggles over taxes and deficits). These events and issues sharpened party differences in voter's minds and brought new ideologically driven activists into electoral politics.

As a consequence of these developments, the respective electoral coalitions of the House and Senate parties diverged sharply. Back in 1972, for instance, the vote for Richard Nixon was only 7.6 percentage points higher in districts won by Republicans than in districts won by Democrats. After a steep increase between 1992 and 2004, the difference in presidential vote between Republican and Democratic districts rose to more than 20 percentage points (Figure 3).[30] Similarly measured, the electoral bases of the Senate parties have also become more polarized, although in absolute terms the differences are considerably smaller than in the House (Figure 4).[31] Differences of this sort in the respective congressional parties' electoral bases are strongly related to party differences in roll call ideology and presidential support, so these trends have contributed strongly to partisan polarization in Congress.[32]

Parties and Elections

Intensified party conflict in Washington and competition for control of the House and Senate spurred deeper involvement by national party organizations in electoral politics. Although FECA severely limited direct party contributions to campaigns (in this respect, the law treated a candidate's party as just another PAC), it allowed the parties to spend additional money on behalf of candidates under a ceiling that rose with inflation. The original limit of $10,000 set in 1974 had by 2004 grown to $37,310. The ceiling on coordinated spending by Senate candidates varies with the state's population; in 2004 it ranged from $74,620 in the seven least populous states to $1,944,896 in California. State party committees may spend the same amount as national party committees on coordinated

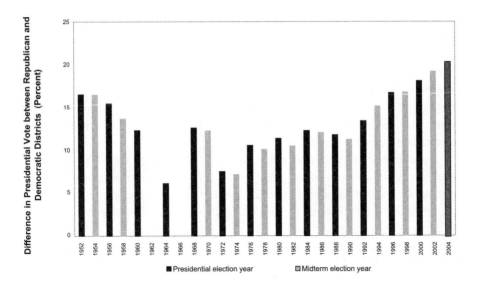

NOTE: Entries for midterms are from the previous presidential elections; 1962 and 1966 are omitted because of missing data. The entry for 2004 is based on the 2000 presidential results pending the release of district-level presidential vote data for 2004.

Figure 3   The Polarization of U.S. House Districts, 1952–2004

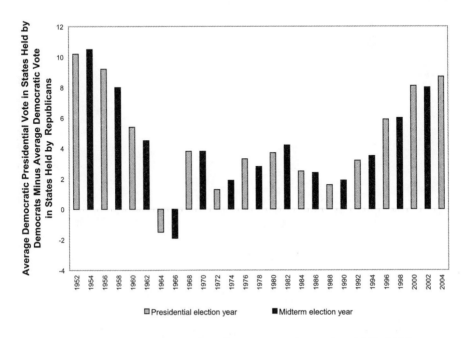

Figure 4   The Polarization of State Constituencies, 1952–2004

spending, and the latter may act as the state party's agent for raising and spending the money, effectively doubling the amount the national parties may spend for candidates. Direct and coordinated party spending reached a peak in the early 1990s, when both parties had enough money to support their most competitive candidates to the legal limit. A 1996 Supreme Court decision allowed parties to spend money for (or against) candidates independently of their campaigns,[33] which they did with abandon in 2004 after campaign finance reform provisions were enacted (see Figures 5 and 6).

Coordinated party expenditures can be made for almost any campaign activity; the only condition is that the party must retain control over how the money is spent. The effort is led by the "Hill" committees—the campaign committees run by both parties in both chambers.[34] Initially, the Hill committees paid for polling, ad production, and media buys; later they added a variety of other services, including programs to train candidates and campaign managers in all aspects of campaigning: fund-raising, personnel management, legal compliance, advertising, press relations, and so on. They also assumed a central role in helping candidates raise money from PACs and other contributors, serving as matchmakers between potential contributors and promising but needy candidates. Hill committee staff also help candidates find suitable managers, consultants, pollsters, media specialists, direct mail outfits, and other campaign professionals.

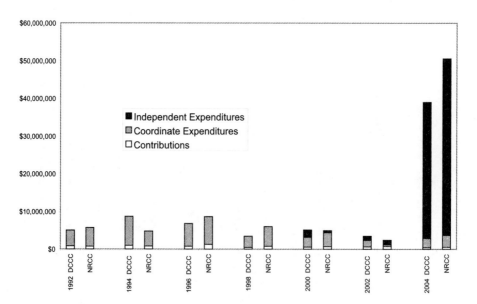

NOTE: DCC = Democratic Congressional Campaign Committee; NRCC = National Republican Congressional Committee

**Figure 5   House Campaign Committee Spending, 1992–2004
(through 20 Days after the Election)**

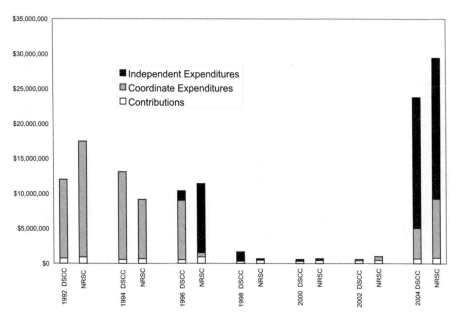

NOTE: DSCC = Democratic Senatorial Campaign Committee; NRSC = National Republican Senatorial Committee

**Figure 6   Senate Campaign Committee Spending 1994–2004
(through 20 Days after the Election)**

Coordinated spending by parties declined after 1994, but only because the parties had developed an even more effective way to get money into congressional campaigns. Congress had liberalized FECA in 1979 to allow unrestricted spending for state and local party building and get-out-the-vote activities. Contributions and expenditures for these activities were not limited by FECA and were dubbed "soft money" to distinguish them from the "hard money" raised and spent under FECA restrictions. Beginning in 1996, the Hill committees began exploiting the soft money option more vigorously, and by 2002 transfers of both soft and hard money to state parties to be used to promote the election of House and Senate candidates had come to dwarf all other party assistance. Figures 7 and 8 display the striking increase in hard and soft money spending by the Hill committees between 1992 and 2002. The ban on soft money imposed by the Bipartisan Campaign Reform Act (BCRA) that took effect for the 2003-2004 election cycle was a response to this explosive growth; by sharply increasing their hard money resources, the parties were able to compensate, although by no means completely, for this new restriction.

Yet another source of party money grew steeply beginning in the 1990s. With control of both the House and Senate up for grabs every two years, members have powerful interest in helping fellow partisans win elections. Not

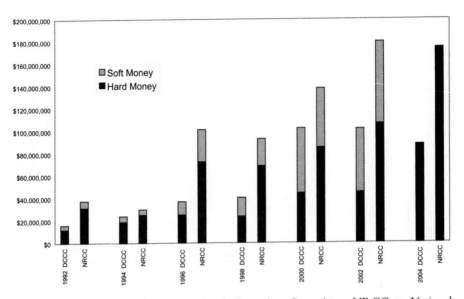

Figure 7 **Hard and Soft Money Spent by House Campaign Committees, 1992–2004 (through 20 Days after the Election)**

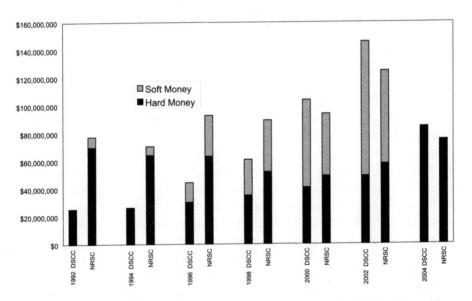

NOTE: DSCC = Democratic Senatorial Campaign Committee; NRSC = National Republican Senatorial Committee

Figure 8 **Hard and Soft Money Spent by the Senate Campaign Committees, 1992–2004 (through 20 Days after the Election)**

a few also aspire to leadership positions in their party. Because in any given election, most face little electoral risk themselves, they use their fund-raising prowess as incumbents to help their party and themselves by funneling money into the campaigns of colleagues in competitive races. Some form their own "leadership" PACs to pass out funds, make contributions directly from their own campaign committees, or help attract contributors to other candidates' fund-raising events. House members' contributions to other candidates grew from $2.7 in 1990 to $23.8 million in 2002. Members' contributions to their party's campaign committee have also grown, from almost nothing in 1990 to $24.5 million in 2002, when such contributions accounted for 12 percent of the National Republican Congressional Committee (NRCC) and 24 percent of the Democratic Congressional Campaign Committee (DCCC) hard money receipts.[35]

The growing awareness of the stakes involved in the party's collective electoral performance has thus led to a remarkable increase in national party involvement in congressional campaigns. This involvement does not by itself necessarily shift the focus of electoral politics away from individual candidates and back to parties, for many of the parties' activities are explicitly designed to produce candidates who are more competitive in a candidate-centered system. But the mere existence of a centralized source of advice on campaign management, strategy, and tactics imposes some uniformity across campaigns. And party contributions often come with strings that severely limit the recipient's autonomy in campaigning. Indeed, the national party has virtually taken over some recent House campaigns. For example, in the extremely tight race for Colorado's Seventh District in 2002, NRCC officials funneled about $2.4 million into the campaign of Republican Bob Beauprez, eventual victor by a bare 121 votes. Along with the money came continuing NRCC oversight of Beauprez's campaign; the state party's executive director reported that the NRCC specified how the money was to be spent "down to the dollar."[36]

On the whole, the explosion of national party activity—financial and otherwise—in congressional election politics has strengthened the hand of party leaders and fostered more unified and polarized parties in both chambers. Successful candidates, especially those in the most competitive races, enter office obligated to party leaders and colleagues for crucial assistance. It is no accident that former Speaker Newt Gingrich's most enthusiastic followers were the Republicans newly elected in 1994 with help from Gingrich's GOPAC. The national party's strategic and tactical guidance encourages candidates to take positions and make promises consistent with the party's core ideology. Heavy party involvement is thus a cause as well as a consequence of sharpened partisan divisions in Congress. As such, it promotes collective responsibility but diminishes members' individual responsiveness to their constituents. The intense and almost totally successful leadership pressure on House Republicans to vote to impeach Bill Clinton in

1998 even when their constituents were overwhelmingly opposed to the move is a striking example.[37]

In the late 1990s, Richard Fenno traveled with the successor to one of his earlier subjects who, in contrast to the representatives Fenno had studied in the early 1970s, "sought political involvement [with constituents] that centered on matters of public policy, especially where he could represent (as he saw it), the strong conservative preferences he shared with a majority of his constituents." This representative presented himself to constituents as the staunchly loyal Republican that, with a 95 percent party unity score, he clearly is.[38] The change noted by Fenno exemplifies the shift to a mode of representation in which party and ideology play much larger roles. Although individual candidates still matter a great deal, the relevant question for voters is now not so much which candidate is the more trustworthy representative or better able to deliver local services and benefits, but which party voters want to control the House and Senate.

Parallel Campaigns

Candidates have never enjoyed exclusive control over congressional campaigns; generic party advertising and independent campaigns conducted by PACs have been part of the process since the adoption of FECA. But their part has been minor. Independent spending has never accounted for more than 3 percent of total campaign spending and in most elections has been closer to 1 percent. Generic party advertising promoting the whole national ticket has waxed and waned in fashion but has usually been quite modest. In the 1990s, however, interest groups and parties developed a new avenue for large-scale involvement in electoral politics beyond the control of the candidates. The Court's *Buckley* decision construed FECA "to apply only to expenditures for communications that in express terms advocate the election or defeat of a clearly identified candidate for federal office." Subsequent decisions confirmed that the First Amendment protected the right to conduct unrestricted so-called "voter education" or "issue advocacy" campaigns, even if clearly intended to influence voters (by, for example, tendentious comparisons of candidates' issue positions), as long as such terms as "vote for," "elect," "vote against," "defeat," or "reject," were not used.

Such prominent organizations as the Christian Coalition, AFL–CIO, Sierra Club, Americans for Limited Terms, as well as more shadowy groups of unknown provenance, such as Americans for Job Security (the First Amendment protects the anonymity of contributors to advocacy campaigns that might not be effective if the biases of their sponsors were known), began investing heavily in "voter education" and "issue advocacy" in recent campaigns. Given a green light by the courts, the parties also jumped in; one memorable effort was the $10 million Republicans spent on television ads during the final weeks of the 1998 campaign, attacking Bill Clinton for his involvement with Monica Lewinsky.

Precise spending figures for these campaigns are often unavailable because they do not come under the Federal Election Commission's jurisdiction, but one research group concluded that interest groups and parties spent $509 million on them during the 1999–2000 election cycle, up from the estimated $260–$330 million spent in 1998 and $135–$150 million spent in 1996.[39] By taking this route, groups were able to spend unlimited and unreported sums on behalf of candidates. They could also conduct stealth campaigns behind innocuous-sounding fronts or without any acknowledgment of responsibility at all; some Democratic House candidates in 2002 were hammered in the last weeks of the campaign by thousands of automated telephone messages (some featuring the voice of Barbara Bush, the president's mother) for which no one has, to this day, taken responsibility.[40] BCRA tightened the rules on independent spending by advocacy groups, but they continued to thrive in a new form as "527 committees" (named for their tax code designation), which collectively spent more than $524 million on federal elections in 2004.[41]

Congressional elections have come to both reflect and reinforce a high level of partisan and ideological conflict in national politics, giving representation a far more partisan and ideological cast in 2004 than it had just a few decades earlier. Although some scholars have argued that polarization is an inside-the-Beltway phenomenon with little popular resonance, the evidence suggests the opposite. Survey data show that the electoral coalitions that members of Congress rely on to keep their jobs have also become more sharply divided by party and ideology. Polarization in Congress has not distanced members from their own supporters, but it has moved them away from the rest of their districts' voters. The voters with reason to be unhappy with the greater party loyalty and ideological extremism displayed by their representatives are those who did not vote for them in the first place.[42] The focus on parties enhances collective responsibility, but it also leaves voters for the losing side more reason to feel unrepresented.

Contemporary Campaigns

Developments since the 1980s have culminated in a bifurcated electoral process. In a large proportion of races there is no real contest. The dominant candidate, most often an incumbent, still conducts a campaign (even unopposed incumbents reported expenditures averaging more than $625,000 in 2004), but the actual vote is a formality. The state or district's representation was decided earlier, when lines were drawn, when voters had rendered judgment in earlier primary or general election contests, when potential candidates and contributors had opted out. Aside from a perfunctory story or two, the news media ignore the races and the candidates.

In those districts and, more frequently, states thought to be in play, however, campaigns can become very intense indeed, with millions of dollars spent on both sides. These are the contests that reveal the essence of modern congressional campaigns. They are fully staffed with campaign professionals of all sorts: campaign managers, accountants, media consultants, pollsters, fund-raisers, researchers, and the like. National party committees are often heavily involved, as are outside groups, so that two or three campaigns for (or against) the same candidate may take place simultaneously.

Voters in the targeted districts and states endure saturation multimedia campaigning. In some highly competitive 2002 races, the competing congressional campaigns bought up virtually all the available TV advertising spots.[43] The Senate campaigns in Minnesota broadcast more than 12,400 ads in the Minneapolis–St. Paul area alone.[44] In one survey, Missouri voters reported seeing twelve to thirteen ads per day during the last week of that state's Senate campaign.[45] In the battle for a South Dakota Senate seat, won by incumbent Democrat Tim Johnson by a margin of only 524 votes, the candidates ran their first spots a year in advance of the election, eventually producing more than one hundred separate spots. For every vote cast for senator, $33 was spent on TV ads.[46] The 2004 race between Daschle and Thune in the same state, resulting in the ouster of former Senate minority leader Daschle, is sure to surpass this total, though the final figures were not available at the time of writing.

Competitive campaigns also made heavy use of direct mail, especially in those House districts where broadcasting is inefficient because the district's voters comprise only a small proportion of the total audience. Direct mail pinpoints the district's voters, and it can be targeted to specific subgroups in the electorate. In a sample of hotly contested House and Senate races in 2002, the candidates and parties combined to send an average of 44 unique mail pieces during the campaign; voters reported receiving 3 or 4 pieces a day during the last week of the campaign. Some campaigns greatly exceeded these averages. In the 2002 contest for South Dakota's Senate seat, some voters reported receiving as many as 10 pieces of mail per day. The 174 unique direct mail pieces distributed during this race were, according to one analysis, "primarily visual, usually filled with distorted images of opponents, babies, or the candidate and his family. The messages lacked substance and most were brief enough to be read on the way to the trash can."[47] Some campaigns also used automated telephone calls as another route to targeted voters. "A telephone call, as unwelcome as it may be, cuts through . . . apathy and cynicism by forcing voters to listen to a political message," or so its practitioners claim.[48] Campaigns that deluge voters with broadcast ads, mailings, and phone calls may just turn many of them off. The political scientists who studied the 2002 South Dakota Senate campaign concluded that "in the end, most voters probably tuned out the commercials, turned off the phone, and placed all the mail in the trash," citing as an example "one woman [who] wrote and explained that she started to watch public television and stopped answering the phone in the evening."[49] Any reasonably sophisticated observer of politics would certainly understand. But of course campaigns are not aimed at sophisticated observers or even regular voters. As one campaign consultant put it, "Most of the people we are trying to reach with our message don't think about [campaigns] at all until late October. They don't read all the news magazines, the *Wall Street Journal,* and two local dailies. They don't watch CNN and C-SPAN. They watch 'Wheel of Fortune' and then think about politics and campaigns less than five minutes a week."[50] Simplicity, repetition, exaggeration, and symbolism (images of home, hearth, neighborhood, and flag) are therefore staples of political advertising. Campaigns targeting the subset of voters who are only marginally interested in politics and therefore open to persuasion by mass advertising are not likely to edify the majority of people who actually participate in elections.

Personal Campaigning

The heavy reliance on the mass media does not mean that candidates have given up trying to make personal contact with potential voters. Most politicians have faith in the personal touch; if they can just talk to people and get them to listen, they can win their support. The difficulty with this approach is that even the average House district now contains more than 660,000 people, and states can be much more populous. It is simply impossible to meet more than a small fraction of the electorate during a single campaign. This approach is often emphasized by poorly funded challengers whose only advantage may be the time they can devote to one-on-one campaigning. But even lavishly funded campaigns use the personal touch when it is feasible, and with adequate research resources, the touch can be personal indeed. According to two political scientists who studied it, Tim Johnson's successful campaign for reelection to the Senate in 2002 "made an effort to personally visit as many households as they could. When either the candidate or campaign worker was going door to door, they carried nine different scripts that contained different issues. Before knocking on the door they already knew something about the occupant and selected the script designed for that demographic."[51]

Many of the candidate's activities are designed to reach voters beyond those in the immediate audience by attracting the attention of the news media. Indeed, campaigns work so hard to get "free" media exposure that campaign professionals refer to it as "earned" media.[52] Campaign events are designed not so much for the immediate audience as for the larger audience watching television or reading the newspaper at home. Not surprisingly, campaign gimmicks designed to attract attention are common.[53] Paid campaign ads may also be used to gain media exposure; one consultant recommends using "shock mailers" to provoke opponents into outraged responses, which then give the charges much wider publicity when the news media report the squabble.[54]

Campaign Messages

Along with letting voters know who the candidate is (voters are notoriously reluctant to support candidates whose names they do not recognize), the campaign is designed to persuade them to vote for him or her. There is no magic formula for appealing to voters; what works in one district or election year may not work in another. Nonetheless, according to campaign professionals, to be effective, every campaign needs to develop and project *some* consistent campaign theme. The theme explains why the candidate should be elected and why the opponent should not. It attempts to frame the choice—to establish what the election is *about*—in a way that underlines the candidate's strengths and plays down the candidate's weaknesses. The goal is not to change people's political attitudes, but rather to define the choice so that a vote for the candidate is consistent with them.[55] The choice of campaign themes is largely an exercise in opportunism: campaigners grab onto whatever issues happen to be available at the time.

Challengers face the special task of getting voters to reject senators and representatives they have supported in the past. They look for vulnerable points to attack: personal scandals, junketing, association with unpopular presidents, unpopular roll-call votes, signs of being out of touch with constituents. Knowing this, incumbents take great pains to make their presence felt back home and to build defensible voting records. They avoid casting other than "explainable" votes;[56] that is, any vote likely to offend important groups in the member's electoral coalition or in the district at large will be cast only if it can be plausibly explained to constituents if it is questioned. Supplying plausible explanations is thus essential to effective coalition-building by party leaders, presidents, and other policy entrepreneurs in Washington. In the same vein, majority-party leaders are expected to protect their people from having to cast unpopular votes by keeping politically difficult issues off the agenda. The minority's strategy is to force votes on issues that will either embarrass majority members back home or force them to vote against their party's position. A great deal of the maneuvering in Congress is aimed at forcing or avoiding such votes, particularly during election years.

General ideological or partisan attacks have been a mainstay of challengers' campaigns for decades. Incumbents are criticized for being too liberal or too conservative for the constituency or for their guilt by association with unpopular parties, causes, or leaders. This approach lost some of its punch in the 1960s and 1970s, as members strove to avoid ideological categorization or personal responsibility for party decisions when it would hurt them politically back home. As electoral politics began to take on a more ideological cast in the 1980s, incumbents—particularly Democrats—found it more difficult to sidestep attacks of this sort, and since then the number of members representing states and districts where a plurality of voters identify with the other party has declined.

Increasingly bitter ideological and partisan conflict has encouraged campaigns to "go negative" at the slightest provocation. Until the 1980s, harsh personal attacks on an opponent were considered a sign of desperation, ineffective and likely to backfire. Challengers on the ropes sometimes resorted to them; their targets ignored the attacks, on the theory that reacting would only bring them unwarranted attention. They were most common in campaigns of "sure losers." No longer. Campaign consultants have become convinced that negative advertising works: "People say they hate negative campaigning. But it works. They hate it and remember it at the same time. The problem with positive is that you have to run it again and again to make it stick. With negative, the poll numbers will move in three or four days."[57]

In close races where party organizations are heavily involved, a division of labor often emerges: the candidate's campaign takes the high road, while the party does the dirty work. Commenting on the 2002 campaign in New Mexico's Second District, the Democrats' political director asserted that "the party's job was to act 'as the bad guy,' so Democratic candidates could focus on a more positive message"; his Republican counterpart agreed: "Negative advertising is the job of the party, leaving candidates to stay above the fray longer."[58] Still, candidates are not above going negative themselves; Saxby Chambliss's successful 2002 Senate challenge of Georgia Democrat Max Cleland, who lost both legs and an arm in Vietnam, featured a television ad that followed footage of Osama bin Laden and Saddam Hussein with an unflattering shot of Cleland and a voiceover claiming that he had "voted against the president's vital homeland security efforts."[59]

The logic, if not the civility, of attacking opponents is compelling in a system of candidate-centered electoral politics. If members of Congress win and hold office by eliciting trust and regard as individuals, then the way to undermine their support is to destroy their constituents' trust and regard. Even national issues unfavorable to the incumbent's party—bad economic news, scandals, failed policies, an unpopular president—need to be personalized to be used effectively to weaken an incumbent. A focus on issues and ideology also inspires negative attacks via distortion of positions or voting records and charges of extremism.

Despite their high rates of success, incumbent members of Congress face an uncertain electoral world. Each election may present a new challenge and a new set of electoral variables. Since incumbents can never be sure which of their actions got them elected previously, they cannot be sure what combination of campaign activities will serve them in altered circumstances. Although in a normal election year most members are reelected easily (at least in the House), most of them have had close calls at one time or another, and all have vivid memories of seemingly entrenched colleagues who suffered sudden massive vote losses and unexpected defeats.

Because of uncertainty, members tend to exaggerate electoral threats and overreact to them. They are inspired by worst-case scenarios—what would they have to do to win if everything went wrong?—rather than objective probabilities. Hence, we find members who conduct full-scale campaigns even though the opposition is nowhere to be seen. The desire to win decisively enough to discourage future opposition also leads many incumbents to campaign a good deal harder than would seem objectively necessary. The specter of fickle electorates, combined with active organizations ready to mobilize extensive campaign resources against them should they show signs of vulnerability, evidently undermine whatever confidence comfortable reelection margins might otherwise inspire. The electoral shakeups of the early 1990s are a reminder that it is wise to take nothing for granted.

Getting Out (or Suppressing) the Vote

Full-scale campaigns invest heavily in getting supporters to the polls. Indeed, a special effort to mobilize voters may be essential to offset any inclination to withdraw in disgust from the mean-spirited campaigns now typical of competitive races. Labor unions lead the effort to get the vote out for Democrats, giving the party its traditional superiority in this area. But Republican officials have recently ratcheted up their turnout efforts. In 2002, the Republican National Committee financed a seventy-two-hour preelection drive to mobilize voters in key contests, using some fifteen thousand volunteers and paid workers in the effort. In Colorado's Seventh District, for example, thirteen hundred Republican volunteers visited the homes of an estimated three hundred thousand Republican-leaning registered voters in the three days before the election.[60] Such campaigns can be effective; an experimental study conducted in 2000 indicated that face-to-face mobilization can raise turnout by as much as 9 percentage points, although telephone and direct mail have little effect.[61]

For purposes of winning an election, reducing the other side's vote by a given number is as valuable as raising one's own by the same number. Because voting, as a duty and a right, is such a potent symbol of democracy, no campaign ever admits openly to trying to keep the other candidate's supporters from the polls. Nonetheless, Republican operatives are regularly suspected of trying to dampen turnout in minority neighborhoods, as they were in 2002, when an unsigned flier appeared in minority neighborhoods in Baltimore reading, "URGENT NOTICE. Come out to vote on November 6th. Before you come to vote make sure you pay your parking tickets, motor vehicle tickets, overdue rent and most important any warrants."[62] The election was actually on November 5.

Senate Campaigns

House and Senate campaigns are similar in goals and strategies, but their contexts are often quite different. As already noted, Senate elections are, on average, considerably more competitive than House elections. Senate incumbents win less consistently and by narrower margins than do House incumbents, and most states are potentially winnable by either party. Closer partisan balance by itself makes Senate elections more competitive, but it also creates a strategic electoral environment that enhances competition in several ways.

First, Senate incumbents are usually faced with more-formidable opponents.[63] About two-thirds of Senate challengers in recent elections had previously held elective office. Among the successful first-time candidates have been two former astronauts (John Glenn and Harrison Schmitt), a former basketball star (Bill Bradley), a lawyer-turned-actor (Fred Thompson), and several prominent millionaire businessmen.

Formidable challengers attract campaign resources. Senate campaigns in general attract proportionately greater contributions because the donations are, in a sense, more cost-effective, especially in smaller states.[64] Senate contests are usually closer, so campaign resources are more likely to affect the outcome. Parties and groups with particular policy agendas are aware that, when it comes to passing legislation, 1 senator is worth 4.35 representatives. A party has to defeat far fewer incumbents to take over the Senate than to take over the House. It makes strategic sense for campaign contributors to focus on the Senate, and that is what they have done.

Senate challengers can also use their campaign resources more effectively. Most Senate constituencies have the size and structure to make television advertising cost-efficient. Resources are usually sufficient to justify using campaign professionals and the technical paraphernalia of modern campaigns: computers, polls, direct mail advertising and solicitation, and so forth. The news media are much more interested in Senate campaigns, so much more free attention and publicity is bestowed on Senate candidates than on their House counterparts.[65] Moreover, Senate incumbents find it much more difficult to develop and maintain the kind of personal relationships with constituents; their activities in Washington are also more conspicuous. Action in the Senate is more visible; the Senate has fewer members, and they are given more attention by the news media.[66] Senators are thus more likely to be associated with controversial and divisive issues.[67]

Given House-Senate differences in electoral competition, it is no accident that from 1980 to 2004, control of the Senate changed hands five times, control of the House, only once. Nor is it surprising that senators show somewhat greater independence and more resistance to party leadership than representatives.

Reforms

Modern campaigns and elections do not lack articulate critics. Reformers currently target the financing, conduct, and content of campaigns; primary election rules; redistricting practices; the incumbency advantage; and district-based House elections and Senate malapportionment. The reform impulse has become institutionalized in a variety of self-appointed public interest organizations, including the Center for Responsive Politics (campaign finance reform), the Alliance for Better Campaigns (candidate accountability for advertising content; greater access to the airwaves for candidates), Citizens for Approval Voting (advocates of an alternative voting system), the Center for Voting and Democracy (proportional representation), and the Reform Institute for Campaign and Election Issues (increasing participation).

Deliberately or not, reform proposals often have implications for the balance between individual responsiveness and collective responsibility on the Hill. A shift to proportional representation, for example, would dramatically increase pressures for collective responsibility because the voters would be choosing among parties rather than candidates. Approval voting, on the other hand, puts a premium on voters' second or third choices and would encourage candidates to solicit support across party lines. The prospect of wholesale constitutional change along either of these lines, while of interest to democratic theorists and students of comparative politics, is remote, if only because any reform would have to win the support of the very people whose power and career paths it would threaten. But as the enactment of the Bipartisan Campaign Reform Act of 2002 (BCRA) has shown, incremental tinkering with the rules of the game is occasionally feasible.

BCRA was a response to the huge expansion of soft party money and various forms of independent spending that had effectively shredded the regulatory system governing congressional campaign finance imposed back in the 1970s by FECA and its amendments. The bill was intended to restore FECA's original regulatory scheme by prohibiting national parties from spending soft money for federal candidates, limiting all contributions to national parties, and restricting contributions to state and local parties for federal election activities.

It also sought to restrict and disclose corporate and union spending on "issue advocacy" or "voter education" used for electioneering (banning such ads during a thirty-day period prior to a primary election and sixty-day period prior to a general election) and to compel disclosure of sources of other independent campaign spending. It raised the limit on individual contributions from $1,000 to $2,000 and indexed it to inflation. And it provided for higher contribution limits for candidates facing self-financed opponents.[68]

BCRA was immediately challenged in court, as Republican leaders sought to overturn soft money restrictions and ideological groups sought to defend their right to unrestricted advocacy on First Amendment grounds. The Supreme Court, however, upheld its major provisions as necessary to prevent "corruption or the appearance of corruption" in federal elections, which the Court defined broadly. The characterization of BCRA as "the most far-reaching and controversial attempt to restructure the national political process in a generation" is accurate only because the legislation has no competitor.[69] In fact, if 2004 is any guide, it is likely to affect the cost, conduct, and content of congressional campaigns only marginally, if at all. Some critics argued that BCRA's ban on soft money would diminish the parties' role in campaigns (thus leaning against "responsibility" in favor of "responsiveness"), but there is no evidence that it did so in 2004. Even before its constitutionality was determined, quasi-party organizations that could finance campaigns with soft money outside the formal party apparatus were already on the drawing boards.[70] The 527 committees mentioned earlier ended up spending more than $500 million during the 2004 election, mostly in the presidential election but with plenty spilling over into House and Senate campaigns. The regular party committees, revving up their hard money fundraising, also spent more than $100 million on independent campaigns for or against candidates in tight races. The sums raised and spent by the candidates continued their upward trajectory as well, with some minor assistance from the higher individual-contribution limits.

At most, BCRA returned campaign finance practices to where they were a decade earlier. Further tinkering is possible, but absent the Court's abandonment of *Buckley* or a constitutional amendment allowing spending limits, fundamental change is unlikely. The realities are that modern campaigns are expensive because communicating with voters is expensive; limits on campaign spending are unconstitutional unless accepted voluntarily in return for public funds; financing congressional campaigns with tax dollars has no effective constituency; and campaigns must therefore depend on private sources of money, which will always be suspect.

Ordinary Americans, bombarded with annoying political ads, believe that too much money is spent on campaigns and support spending as well as contribution limits by wide margins. But the real problem is that in most races one side lacks the wherewithal to get its story out to the voters. In most cases this is of little practical consequence, but there are always at least a few contests where the outcome would be in doubt if both candidates were adequately funded. Because challengers have virtually no chance of winning without having a lot of money to spend, any reform that makes it harder to raise money threatens to reduce competition. BCRA has not, by the evidence of 2004, made it any harder to mobilize campaign resources, so in this regard at least, its designers have obeyed the dictum "First, do no harm."

Stand by Your Ad

One component of BCRA targeted negative campaigning: the provision requiring candidates to be accountable for their advertising content, or to "stand by" their ads. Broadcast ads must include a "clearly identifiable" image of the candidate and statement by the candidate that he or she has approved the communication. The idea is to discourage mudslinging by forcing candidates to take direct personal responsibility for their commentary. Some observers judged that the requirement had reduced negative personal attacks during the 2004 Democratic primaries, although outside groups continued to make them freely, and candidates can still use direct mail and phone banks to flay opponents without taking responsibility. The provision has probably sharpened the division of labor by which candidates take the high road while allied organizations do the dirty work.[71] Whether it will make campaigns less nasty overall is extremely doubtful.

Redistricting Reform

The decline in competitive districts following the post-2000 redistricting has sparked proposals for reform of this process as well. States set their own redistricting procedures, and all but a handful leave it up to the normal legislative process (with courts intervening if for some reason there is an impasse). State legislators are reluctant to put themselves at the mercy of a blindly impartial process, so this is unlikely to change except where ballot initiatives allow voters to bypass the legislature. California may soon provide a test. Its legislature negotiated a bipartisan map for 2002 that carved out nineteen U.S. House districts with less than 46 percent Democratic major-party registration, all won by Republicans, and thirty-four districts with more than 56 percent Democratic registration, all won by Democrats—and not a single district in the competitive 46 to 56 percent range.[72]

A petition was circulating in 2005 for an initiative that would hand California redistricting chores to a panel of retired judges. While success might lead to a few more competitive House districts, the national impact would be modest at best. A deliberate effort to maximize competition everywhere with carefully designed districts could certainly make a difference in the level of competition for House seats, but the political feasibility of such a project is zero; incumbents of both parties would strenuously object to a deliberate increase in their electoral risk, and Republicans are not about to relinquish their current structural advantage. Still, the dearth of competitive seats becomes increasingly problematic as elections become increasingly party-centric. With few seats in play, the electorate's ability to enforce collective responsibility by changing party control in the House diminishes, while the abundance of safe seats encourages party polarization because so few members have to reach out to independents or the other party's supporters to survive.

Open Primaries

Reformers have also sought to reduce partisan polarization in Congress by changing the primary election system to allow any voter to vote in any party's primary or to list all candidates of all parties on a single primary election ballot, with the top two vote-getters competing in the general election regardless of party (Louisiana currently uses a variant of this scheme). Primaries that restrict the choice of primary ballots to a single party, especially those only open to voters who have already registered with a party, are thought to encourage polarization because the nomination is controlled by committed partisans who chose extremists over moderates. Allowing voters of all persuasions to participate in the nomination would produce more moderate representatives. It would also encourage independence, increasing responsiveness while diminishing party loyalty and thus responsibility. The Supreme Court threw out one version of the blanket primary (whereby all voters would receive the same ballot and could vote for different parties' candidates for different offices) adopted by initiative in California,[73] but a version closer to the Louisiana system, already upheld by the Court, was on the November 2004 California ballot. Opposed by virtually all parties, it failed to pass. Although there is some evidence that open primaries produce more moderate representatives, the collateral damage—under the California scheme, for example, third-party candidates would almost never appear on the general election ballot—may be substantial.

Term Limits

Some critics who despair of reducing the structural or financial advantages that make incumbents so difficult to defeat have turned to term limits as a solution. The public strongly backs the idea. Opinion surveys typically find large majorities in favor of limiting legislative terms, and term-limit measures have passed in every state where they have been put to a popular vote. By 1995, when the Supreme Court struck down state-imposed term limits on federal officials as unconstitutional, twenty-two states had adopted them.[74]

The logic behind term limits is dubious at best. Supporters claim that the high success rates of incumbent House candidates has yielded an ossified ruling clique, out of touch with voters and responsive only to the special interests whose money keeps them in office. The only way to ensure change is to limit tenure. But Congress has scarcely been starved for new blood; as recently as the 105th Congress (1997–1998), a majority of House members had been in the House for less than six years, and nearly two-thirds of the senators were in their first or second term. Moreover, in 1992 and 1994, voters demonstrated that they could limit terms the old-fashioned way, by voting out incumbents or compelling them to retire in the face of almost certain defeat.

Beyond that, it seems odd to expect better representation from members who must give up their seats regardless of how well they perform; what quality of work should be expected from an employee who is sure to be fired no matter how well the job is done? Moreover, it is most doubtful that someone soon to be looking for a new job, probably in the private sector, will be less solicitous of "special interests" than someone whose future is controlled by voters. It seems equally doubtful that citizens would receive better representation from elected officials inferior in knowledge and experience to bureaucrats, congressional staff, and lobbyists. Finally, it seems unlikely that representatives would be more responsive to district sentiments when casting votes or taking positions in Washington if the political cost of ignoring constituents were reduced.

Term limits would have their most profound effect on representation, however, by diminishing members' opportunities and incentives for developing strong ties with constituents. As Fenno noted, it takes years of time and effort simply to learn who one's constituents are, what they want, what they need. Even after this has been accomplished, keeping in touch is an endless, labor-intensive chore. Only the prospect of a lengthy series of future elections makes the effort worthwhile. Given the size and diversity of most present-day House districts, not to mention whole states, authentic "citizen legislators" would begin with little knowledge of the opinions, lives, and values of most of their constituents. With a limited electoral future in the district, they would have little reason to invest in learning more. The only "people" they would perhaps be closer to are those in their own limited social or occupational circles. This hardly seems a recipe for better representation for everyone else.

Constituents, from their side, would know even less about their representatives than they do now, in part because the faces would change more often, in part because incumbents would put less effort into making themselves known. With less information, voters would hence be more reliant on party labels to sort out candidates. Term limits would thus make for a much more party-centered process, no small irony considering that the populist advocates of term limits are no fonder of parties than of career politicians.

Conclusion

In upholding the BCRA, the Supreme Court took a surprisingly permissive view of how far Congress could go in regulating campaign money and speech to protect the integrity of the electoral process. Although little more is likely to be done on this front until the BCRA's effects have been fully digested or under a Republican regime that did not want reform in the first place, a future Congress will no doubt find new loopholes to close and new circumventions to thwart. Some state experimentation with the reapportionment system may be at hand as well. Other changes in the electoral process are likely to come, as they have in the past, from technological changes, innovations by losers looking for ways to become winners, and, most importantly, voter response to campaign strategies and tactics. Campaigns are intensely pragmatic affairs, managed by aggressive, ambitious people whose paramount goal is to win. The most important constraint on them is imposed by the voters, whose approval or disapproval guides how the race is run.

Notes

1. Alexander Hamilton, James Madison, and John Jay, *The Federalist Papers* (New York: New American Library, 1961), 82.

2. A sampling of opinion on these matters may be found at http://pollingreport.com /institut.htm and http://pollingreport.com/politics.htm.

3. The classic statement of this argument is David R. Mayhew, *Congress: The Electoral Connection* (New Haven, Conn.: Yale University Press, 1974).

4. The exception is Louisiana, where the top two candidates, regardless of party, compete in a runoff election if none receives an absolute majority in the general election.

5. Gary C. Jacobson, *The Politics of Congressional Elections,* 6th ed. (New York: Longman, 2004), 8–13.

6. *Vieth v. Jubelirer,* 241 F. Supp. 2d 478 (2004).

7. The average number of competitive races from 1982 through 2000 was seventy-two; for the 2004 list, see the *New York Times,* "2004 Election Guide," http://www .nytimes.com/packages/html/politics/2004_ELECTIONGUIDE_GRAPHIC /index_HOUSECQ.html; for earlier years, see the special edition of the *Congressional Quarterly Weekly Report* published in October of the election year.

8. According to National Election Studies data, the proportion of party identifiers voting for their own party's House candidate fell from 88 percent in the 1956/1958/1960 elections to 76 percent in the 1976/1978/1980 elections; on the Senate side, loyalty rates fell from 87 percent to 78 percent over the same period.

9. According to National Election Studies data, the proportion of voters choosing different parties in presidential and House elections rose from 13 percent in the 1950s to 26 percent in the 1970s; for president and senator, the comparable rise was from 14 percent to 25 percent.

10. Richard F. Fenno Jr., *Home Style: House Members in Their Districts* (Boston: Little, Brown, 1978).

11. Richard F. Fenno Jr., *The United States Senate: A Bicameral Perspective* (Washington, D.C.: American Enterprise Institute, 1982).

12. R. Douglas Arnold, *The Logic of Congressional Action* (New Haven, Conn.: Yale University Press, 1990).

13. See, for example, Jill Barshay, "Corporate Tax Bills Stuffed, Scorned—and Supported," *CQ Weekly,* June 26, 2004, 1540–1543.

14. Computed from data in Harold W. Stanley and Richard G. Neimi, *Vital Statistics on American Politics, 2003–2004* (Washington, D.C.: CQ Press, 2003), Table 2-7.

15. The FECA limited contributions from individuals to $1,000, and from PACs to $5,000 per candidate per campaign; the primary and general election campaign count separately, so the effective limits are $2,000 and $10,000 unless there is a runoff primary, which also counts as a separate election. Party limits are discussed below.

16. *Buckley v. Valeo,* 96 S. Ct. 612 (1976).

17. Computed from data in Stanley and Neimi, *Vital Statistics,* Table 2-16.

18. Ibid.

19. Jennifer Steen, "Self Financing Candidates in American Elections," Ph.D. diss., University of California at Berkeley, 1999.

20. See, for example, Philip M. Stern, *The Best Congress Money Can Buy* (New York: Pantheon, 1988); Brooks Jackson, *Honest Graft: Big Money and the American Political Process* (New York: Knopf, 1988); Elizabeth Drew, *Politics and Money: The New Road to Corruption* (New York: Macmillan, 1983).

21. John R. Wright, *Interest Groups and Congress: Lobbying, Contributions, and Influence* (Boston: Allyn and Bacon, 1996), 136–145; Frank J. Sorauf, *Inside Campaign Finance: Myths and Realities* (New Haven: Yale University Press, 1992), 163–74.

22. Richard L. Hall and Frank W. Wayman, "Buying Time: Moneyed Interests and the Mobilization of Bias in Congressional Committees," *American Political Science Review* 84 (September 1990): 797–820.

23. Jacobson, *The Politics of Congressional Elections*, 42–47.

24. Ibid., 39.

25. Ibid., 40.

26. Gary C. Jacobson, "Deficit Cutting Politics and Congressional Elections," *Political Science Quarterly* 108, no. 3 (1993), 375–402.

27. Gary C. Jacobson and Samuel Kernell, *Strategy and Choice in Congressional Elections*, 2nd ed. (New Haven: Yale University Press, 1983), 90–91.

28. Gary C. Jacobson, "The Electoral Basis of Partisan Polarization in Congress," paper presented at the Annual Meeting of the American Political Science Association, Washington, D.C., August 31–September 3, 2000; Gary C. Jacobson, "Terror, Terrain, and Turnout: Explaining the 2002 Midterm Elections," *Political Science Quarterly* 118, no. 1 (2003), 16–18.

29. Jacobson, "The Electoral Basis of Partisan Polarization."

30. Entries for midterm elections are calculated from the presidential vote in the previous election, adjusted for changes in district boundaries, if any; the statistic could not be calculated for 1962 and 1966 because information for reconfigured districts is not available; the entry for 2004 is based on the 2000 presidential vote, as the district-level presidential vote for 2004 was not available at time of writing.

31. The presidential vote gap between the parties' Senate constituencies is smaller than for House districts, in part because, with two senators each, some states have split delegations, netting out to zero. But the growth in electoral consistency has also produced a decrease in the proportion of split Senate delegations; at the high point in the 96th Congress (1979–1980), 54 percent of the states' Senate delegations were split between the parties; by the 108th Congress (2003–2004), only 24 percent remained split, the lowest proportion since the mid-1950s.

32. Gary C. Jacobson, "Partisan Polarization in Presidential Support: The Electoral Connection," *Congress & the Presidency* 30, no. 1 (2003), 19–22.

33. *Colorado Republican Federal Campaign Committee v. Federal Election Commission*, 116 S. Ct. 2309 (1996).

34. The House committees are the Democratic Congressional Campaign Committee (DCCC) and National Republican Congressional Committee (NRCC); the Senate committees are the Democratic Senatorial Campaign Committee (DSCC) and the National Republican Senatorial Committee (NRSC).

35. Jacobson, The *Politics of Congressional Elections*, 78–83; at the time of writing, data for 2004 was not yet available.

36. Daniel A. Smith, "Strings Attached: Outside Money in Colorado's Seventh District," in *The Last Hurrah? Soft Money and Issue Advocacy in the 2002 Congressional Election,* edited by David B. Magleby and J. Quin Monson (Center for the Study of Elections an Democracy, Brigham Young University, 2003).

37. Gary C. Jacobson, "Public Opinion and the Impeachment of Bill Clinton," *British Elections and Parties Review,* vol. 10, edited by Philip Cowley et al. (London and Portland, Ore.: Frank Cass, 2000), 1–31.

38. Richard F. Fenno Jr., *Congress at the Grassroots: Representational Change in the South, 1970–1998* (Chapel Hill: University of North Carolina Press, 2000).

39. Figures for 2002, "Annenberg Public Policy Center Tracks over $509 million in Reported Expenditures on Issue Advocacy," Annenberg Public Policy Center news release, February 1, 2001, at http://www.appcpenn.org/political/issueads /pressrelease020101.pdf, accessed May 16, 2003. By comparison, independent spending by PACs explicitly endorsing or opposing candidates and so reported to the FEC amounted to only about $21 million in 2000, and $14 million in 2002.

40. John Roos and Christopher Roderiguez, "Indiana Second District—Hoosier Values and Outside Money," in *The Last Hurrah?,* edited by Magleby and Monson, 228.

41. Center for Responsive Politics, "527 Committee Activity," http://www.opensecrets .org/527s/527cmtes.asp?level=E&cycle=2004, accessed December 10, 2004.

42. Jacobson, "The Electoral Basis of Partisan Polarization," 7–9.

43. Jay Barth and Janine Parry, "Provincialism, Personalism, and Politics: Campaign Spending and the 2002 U.S. Senate Race in Arkansas," in *The Last Hurrah?,* 61.

44. William H. Flanigan, Joanne M. Miller, and Jennifer L. Williams, "The Minnesota U.S. Senate Race and the Second Congressional District Race," in *The Last Hurrah?,* edited by Magleby and Monson, 102.

45. E. Terrence Jones et al., "The 2002 Missouri Senate Race," in *The Last Hurrah?,* 130.

46. James Meader and John Bart, "South Dakota: At-Large and Senate Race 2002," in *The Last Hurrah?,* 164.

47. Ibid.

48. John Jameson, Chris Glaze, and Gary Teal, "Effective Phone Contact Programs and the Importance of Good Data," *Campaigns & Elections* (July 1999), 64–71.

49. Meader and Bart, "South Dakota," in *The Last Hurrah?,* 170.

50. Joel Bradshaw, "Who Will Vote for You and Why: Designing Campaign Strategy and Theme," paper presented at the Conference on Campaign Management, American University, Washington, D.C., December 10–11, 1992, 114.

51. Meader and Bart, "South Dakota," in *The Last Hurrah?,* 165.

52. Craig Varoga, "Lone Star Upset: Six Strategies behind Democrat Ken Bentsen's Improbable Victory against a Big-Spending Republican in Texas," *Campaigns & Elections* (March 1995), 35.

53. For samples, see Jacobson, *The Politics of Congressional Elections,* 86–91.

54. Eva Pusateri, "Shock Mailers That Jolt Your Audience," *Campaigns & Elections* (May 1995), 41.

55. Bradshaw, "Who Will Vote for You and Why."

56. John W. Kingdon, *Congressmen's Voting Decisions* (New York: Harper and Row, 1973), 46–53.

57. Alan Ehrenhalt, "Technology, Strategy Bring New Campaign Era," *Congressional Quarterly Weekly Report*, December 7, 1985, 2561.

58. Lonna Rae Atkeson, Nancy Carrillo, and Margaret C. Toulouse, "The 2002 New Mexico Federal Races," in *The Last Hurrah?*, 276.

59. CBSNews.com, "Big Brother Lends a Hand," October 17, 2002, http://www.cbsnews.com/stories/2002/10/28/politics/main527101.shtml, accessed May 15, 2003.

60. Associated Press, "GOP Will Continue to Stress Voter Turnout Programs," December 9, 2002.

61. Alan S. Gerber and Donald P. Green, "The Effects of Personal Canvassing, Telephone Calls, and Direct Mail on Voter Turnout: A Field Experiment," *American Political Science Review* 94 (September 2000): 653–663.

62. See Howard Libit and Tim Craig, "Allegations Fly as Election Day Nears," *Baltimore Sun*, November 4, 2002, http://www.baltimoresun.com/news/elections/bal-te.md.turnout04nov04,0,732693.story?coll=bal-election-governor, accessed May 16, 2003.

63. Peverill Squire, "Challenger Quality and Voting Behavior in U.S. Senate Elections," *Legislative Studies Quarterly* 17 (1992), 247–264; David Lublin, "Quality, Not Quantity: Strategic Politicians in U.S. Senate Elections," *Journal of Politics* 56 (1994): 228–241.

64. David Magleby, "More Bang for the Buck: Campaign Spending in Small-State U.S. Senate Elections" (Paper delivered at the Annual Meeting of the Western Political Science Association, Salt Lake City, March 30–April 1, 1989).

65. Kim Fridken Kahn, "Senate Elections and the News: Examining Campaign Coverage," *Legislative Studies Quarterly* 26 (August 1991), 349–374.

66. Timothy Cook, "House Members as Newsmakers: The Effects of Televising Congress," *Legislative Studies Quarterly* 11 (May 1986), 211.

67. Barbara Sinclair, "Washington Behavior and Home-State Reputation: The Impact of National Prominence on Senators' Visibility and Likability," *Legislative Studies Quarterly* 15 (November 1990), 486–490.

68. For detailed analysis of this complicated piece of legislation, see the Campaign Finance Institute, Campaign Finance eGuides, http://www.cfinst.org/eguide/index.html.

69. Daniel R. Ortiz, "The Unbearable Lightness of Being *McConnell*," *Election Law Journal* 3, no. 2 (2004), 299.

70. Derek Willis, "Critics Say Political Groups Formed to Evade New Fundraising Rules," *CQ Weekly*, November 30, 2002, 3112–3113.

71. Brooks Jackson, "Are Candidates Swearing Off 'Attack Ads?' Maybe This Reform Is Working," at http://www.factcheck.org/specialreports137.html, February 4, 2004.

72. Gary C. Jacobson, "All Quiet on the Western Front: Redistricting and Party Competition in California House Elections," in *Redistricting in the New Millennium*, edited by Peter F. Galderisi (Lanham, Md.: Lexington Books, 2005).

73. On the ground that it interfered with the party's freedom of association; see *California Democratic Party v. Jones* (99-401) 530 U.S. 567 (2000).

74. *U.S. Term Limits v. Thornton*, 514 U.S. 779 (1995).

Bibliography

Abramowitz, Alan I., and Segal, Jeffrey A. *Senate Elections*. Ann Arbor: University of Michigan Press, 1992.

Busch, Andrew E. *Horses in Midstream: U.S. Midterm Elections and their Consequences, 1894–1998*. Pittsburgh: University of Pittsburgh Press, 1999.

Campbell, James E. *The Presidential Pulse of Congressional Elections*. Lexington: University of Kentucky Press, 1993.

Canon, David T. *Race, Redistricting, and Representation*. Chicago: University of Chicago Press, 1999.

Cox, Gary W., and Katz, Jonathan. *Elbridge Gerry's Salamander: The Electoral Consequences of the Reapportionment Revolution*. Cambridge: Cambridge University Press, 2002.

Fowler, Linda L., and McClure, Robert D. *Political Ambition: Who Decides to Run for Congress*. New Haven, Conn.: Yale University Press, 1989.

Kahn, Kim Fridkin, and Patrick J. Kenney. *The Spectacle of U.S. Senate Campaigns*. Princeton, N.J.: Princeton University Press, 1999.

Herrnson, Paul S. *Congressional Elections: Campaigning at Home and in Washington,* 3rd ed. Washington, D.C.: Congressional Quarterly Press, 2000.

Jacobson, Gary C. *Money in Congressional Elections*. New Haven, Conn.: Yale University Press, 1980.

Jacobson, Gary C. *The Politics of Congressional Elections*, 6th ed. New York: Pearson, 2004.

Jacobson, Gary C., and Samuel Kernell. *Strategy and Choice in Congressional Elections*, 2nd ed. New Haven, Conn.: Yale University Press, 1983.

Kolodny, Robin. *Pursuing Majorities: Congressional Campaign Committees in American Politics*. Norman: University of Oklahoma Press, 1998.

Krasno, Jonathan S. *Challengers, Competition, and Reelection: Comparing Senate and House Elections*. New Haven, Conn.: Yale University Press, 1994.

Magleby, David B., and J. Quin Monson, eds. *The Last Hurrah? Soft Money and Issue Advocacy in the 2002 Congressional Elections*. Washington, D.C.: The Brookings Institution, 2004.

Westlye, Mark C. *Senate Elections and Campaign Intensity*. Baltimore: Johns Hopkins University Press, 1991.

5

ELECTIONS, PARTIES, AND GOVERNANCE

Sarah A. Binder

WHEN WE CALL CONGRESS AN INSTITUTION OF democracy, we make a critical assumption: elections—free, regular, and competitive—are the lifeblood of the institution. To understand and evaluate Congress's performance as a democratic body, we must perforce explore the impact of elections on Congress. Do elections matter? If so, how, when, why, and in what ways do they matter? To be sure, elections can affect Congress in myriad ways—shaping both institutional performance and individual behavior. Indeed, as Gary Jacobson observes in Chapter 4, the electoral connection infuses the legislative arena—molding legislators who excel at individual responsiveness and strongly shaping the structure of representation.

This chapter focuses on the impact of elections on Congress's performance as a policy maker, exploring the conditions under which electoral change may foster collective responsibility by Congress. Particular attention is paid to the ways in which elections shape partisan fortunes and consequently mold Congress's governing capacity. Although scholars and observers of American politics have historically placed their faith in robust, cohesive political parties, this chapter suggests that polarized parties may in fact diminish Congress's capacity as a lawmaking body. Rather than encouraging compromise, today's competitive balance between the parties often promotes disagreement even when consensus is within reach. Elections certainly matter, but in potentially unexpected ways.

Why Might Elections Matter?

In evaluating the impact of elections on Congress as an institution of democracy, we are assessing how partisan dynamics shape governance. Because the majority party organizes each chamber, retains a disproportionate share of legislative resources, and exerts extensive influence over both chambers' agenda, the impact of elections on democratic governance runs through the conduit of the parties.[1] To be sure, elections over the past half-century have often been more candidate- than party-centered: the importance of traditional party organizations to candidates in elections has waned as incumbency advantage has grown.[2] But even in a world of candidate-centered contests, the impact of elections on Congress will largely be felt through the fortunes of the two political parties. Elections in short are the proving grounds for the two major parties, offering them a recurring chance to make headway in gaining control of the House, Senate, and White House. National tides of sufficient breadth and depth to bring major partisan change may be rare, but elections are nonetheless consequential for the two major parties.

How might elections be pivotal for the parties, and thus potentially for Congress's lawmaking responsibilities? First, the most basic impact of elections is to determine the number of seats held by the two majority parties in the House and Senate, thus shaping the partisan balance until the next election. Second, elections determine whether control of the government will be unified within a single political party or divided between the two major parties. Third, elections shape the distribution of policy views within and across the two political parties—setting the ideological density and spread of both parties. Elections determine whether a moderate center will reign in a given Congress, or whether the parties will occupy polar extremes. Fourth, elections can alter the bicameral character of Congress, as the policy views of the House and one-third of the Senate are up for grabs every two years. Finally, elections can yield mandates, a claim by the winning party that the public overwhelmingly supports the agenda of the newly elected president or congressional majority. These partisan ramifications of elections are explored below, with an eye to understanding how Congress's capacity to govern may be shaped by the collective decisions of the electorate.

United We Govern?

For much of the latter half of the twentieth century, scholars and observers of Congress indicted split party control of Congress and the presidency as the central cause of legislative inaction. In this view, elections mattered because coherent policy making was said to be impossible if the two parties divided up control of the branches of government. That indictment of divided government was rooted in nearly a century-long commitment of political scientists to the strength and vitality of American political parties. That commitment to parties—reaching back to the early twentieth century—grew out of the origins of American political science as a profession. For Woodrow Wilson, Henry James Ford, Frank Goodnow, and others—some of the "founding fathers" of political science as a discipline—political parties were seen as essential for achieving unity of purpose and action in American governance.

Why had these early political scientists been so committed to parties? The argument was put best by Wilson: "The degree of separation now maintained between the executive and legislative branches of our government cannot long be preserved without very serious inconvenience resulting. . . . What we need is harmonious, consistent, responsible party government, instead of a wide dispersion of function and responsibility; and we can get it only by connecting the President as closely as may be with his party in Congress."[3]

This view of parties as governing instruments had been enshrined by the mid-1940s as the *doctrine of responsible parties*. Parties, as articulated by its most forceful and eloquent proponent at the time, were essential to the stability of democratic life. "The political parties created democracy," E. E. Schattschneider observed in his 1942 classic *Party Government*, "and . . . modern democracy is unthinkable save in terms of the parties."[4] Only parties could claim legitimate authority to rule in a democracy, Schattschneider argued, because they were organized to assemble broad majorities to win elections. The necessity of building a majority coalition in a diverse country meant that the parties had to build diverse coalitions with an eye to the interests of both the advantaged and disadvantaged. Pressure groups might have been an alternative to parties, but Schattschneider viewed them as organization with narrow policy aims, little capacity to build electoral majorities, and hence no legitimate claim on the public use of power.

Responsible party government advocates worked in the 1940s in a climate of unified control; divided government occurred only three times between 1900 and 1946. Writing in the aftermath of the World War II—with the devastation of Europe after totalitarian rule—it is not surprising that political scientists under the umbrella of the responsible party government advocates looked first to the political parties as the engine of legislative performance. Accounts of government performance, James Sundquist noted, "identified the political party as the indispensable instrument that brought cohesion and unity, and hence, effectiveness, to the government as a whole by linking the executive and legislative branches in a bond of common interest."[5] Democracy, Schattschneider had argued, was unthinkable except in terms of parties. For responsible party theorists, it was clear that *American* democracy—with its separated institutions sharing constitutional powers—was unthinkable except in terms of unified party government. Although unified control was never considered *sufficient*, it was almost uniformly viewed as *necessary* for ensuring responsive government.[6] V. O. Key, writing in the 1960s, offered the now classic view: "Common partisan control of executive and legislature does not assure energetic government, but division of party control precludes it."[7]

Why is unified party control considered so essential for successful governance? The logic of the argument is pretty simple. Unified party control of government provides an additional bridge between the president and his congressional majority. Operating under a shared electoral interest, unified party control ensures that considerations beyond policy will influence the legislative strategies of legislators and presidents. Presidents have an incentive to work toward the election and re-election of their party's congressional majority, and legislators accrue an incentive to work towards enacting the president's party agenda. Electoral incentives also alter the strategies of legislative leaders. Under unified government, party leaders inside Congress have an incentive to apply their (limited) tools and resources to enact a large share of their party's legislative agenda. Strong policy records create good party reputations, and such reputations purportedly pay off at election time.[8]

In contrast, divided party government reinforces policy disagreements between the branches, and makes it difficult to assemble the policy majorities necessary to forge major legislative change. Under this view, when Congress and the White House are controlled by two different parties, the electoral incentive of both parties is to regain control of government, rather than to work toward enacting major policy change.[9] Building a party reputation based on policy change in theory no longer makes sense for the congressional majority under divided government, as credit for the new initiatives would be shared by both parties. Divided government thus makes policy disagreements between the branches more likely (particularly when differences between the party bring different views about policy), and reinforces those disagreements with an electoral disincentive to cooperate. Thus, according to the conventional wisdom, elections should fundamentally affect legislative performance by determining whether party control will be divided between the two parties or concentrated within a single majority party.

Despite its canonical status among political scientists, no rigorous test of the impact of divided government occurred until David Mayhew's 1991 work, *Divided We Govern*. Mayhew asked a seemingly simple question: Does more get done in Congress during periods of unified or divided control? To answer the question, Mayhew developed a way to identify landmark laws enacted over the second half of the twentieth century, relying on both the contemporary judgments of Washington reporters and the retrospective views of policy specialists.[10] He then tested whether the presence of divided government reduced the number of major laws enacted during each Congress.

Divided We Govern absolved divided government of blame for legislative deadlock. In a striking finding, Mayhew found that unified party control of Congress and the president failed to boost legislative productivity in Washington. According to Mayhew's study, it does not matter whether a single party controls the White House and Congress or not: about the same amount of important business gets done under unified and divided control. Mayhew suggests a number of other forces that may shape Congress's performance, including shifting public moods, presidential cycles, and the rise of issues that cut across the traditional ideological spectrum.

Mayhew concludes that analysts have tended to overestimate the capacity and intentions of American political parties.[11] In other words, elections might indeed matter for shaping Congress's governing performance, but not in the ways that observers typically think. When parties are viewed as "governing instruments," we expect them to yield substantial dividends during unified government, an unrealistic expectation in Mayhew's view. Mayhew instead counsels a less commanding view of parties as "policy factions," coalitions that can muster results regardless of the regime of party control. The American political system is at its heart a pluralist system, and parties adapt in such a system to the multiple cross-cutting currents within the American polity. Political observers and scholars alike, Mayhew suggests, demand more from parties than they can deliver in a system of separated powers.

To understand the impact of elections and parties on Congress's performance, we need to revisit Mayhew's inquiry, method, and conclusions. Has Mayhew asked the right question about the impact of divided government on Congress? In what other ways might elections matter in shaping Congress's capacity? These questions are returned to below as part of a broader exploration of the ways in which elections may affect democratic governance.

The Impact of Pluralist Parties

Mayhew's emphasis on the American political system as a pluralist polity is important. One of the most visible displays of political pluralism appears in the ideological reach of the two major parties. The broad sweep of the two parties quite often leads party scholars to note the parties' "umbrella" character. Given an electoral system that strongly encourages a two-party system, the ideological reach of both parties is necessarily quite wide in a heterogeneous polity.

Congressional elections are important because they determine the distribution of ideological views within each party. Congressional scholars typically distinguish between two stylized arrays of citizens' and legislators' policy views. Sometimes partisans' policy views will be *polarized*, with legislators from each party situated at opposite ends of an underlying left–right ideological spectrum. From the 1980s until the present, Democrats and Republicans in both chambers have been remarkably polarized: Democrats cluster on the far left of the ideological spectrum and Republicans occupy the far right, with just a few legislators filling the ideological center. At other times, partisan *moderation* dominates, with a greater number of legislators standing close to the ideological center between the parties. Although polarized parties may in fact have quite a few centrist legislators, more often the size of the political center runs in tandem with the ideological gulf between the parties.[12] There are typically very few centrist legislators when the parties are polarized.

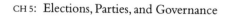

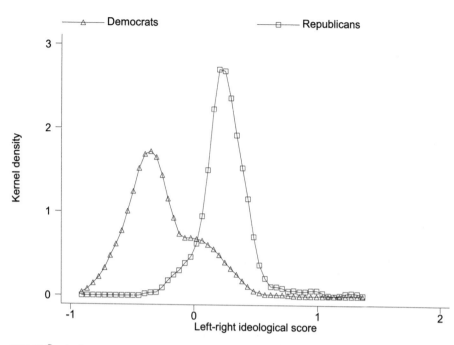

SOURCE: See text.

Figure 1   Ideological Distribution of the Parties in the U.S. House (1969–1970)

Figures 1 and 2 depict these two stylized patterns, using a scoring system based on roll call votes that place legislators along a liberal-conservative spectrum.[13] Figure 1 shows the alignment of House members in the 91st Congress (1969–1970) along the conventional left-right spectrum. In this first term of the Nixon administration, both parties showed moderation, with substantial overlap between Democrats' and Republicans' right- and left-most members respectively. Figure 2 shows the ideological distribution of House members by party during the 106th Congress (1999–2000) in the last two years of the Clinton administration. There is virtually no ideological common ground shared by the two parties in Figure 2, demonstrating polarized parties. Only four Democrats stand to the right of the left-most Republican, Connie Morella, R-Maryland.[14] A large ideological middle dominates the House in the late 1960s; thirty years later, the two parties are strongly polarized.

Why does it matter whether elections produce moderate or polarized parties? There is good reason to suspect that major policy change is hindered when the political center disappears, an apt characterization of today's highly polarized parties. First, and most important, the U.S. political system typically requires broad—and usually bipartisan—coalitions to enact major policy change. Such policy coalitions are more difficult to build when no legislators occupy the polit-

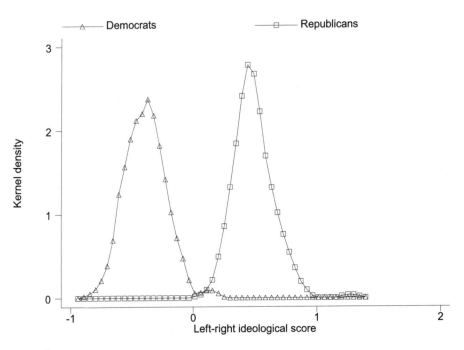

source: See text.

Figure 2   Ideological Distribution of the Parties in the U.S. House (1999–2000)

ical center. Second, when constituencies polarize, parties have an electoral—as well as policy-based—incentive to distinguish their records and positions, and a lesser incentive to bargain and compromise.[15] As Democrat Barney Frank of Massachusetts observed in 1999, "Right now, the differences between the two parties are so great, it doesn't make sense for us to compromise. We'll show where we stand, and let the people decide."[16] This helps to explain why President George W. Bush's push for Social Security reform after the 2004 elections gained little traction among Democrats: With few centrist legislators seeking bipartisan solutions, the parties preferred to stake out different grounds on reforming the program. In short, elections may matter to congressional performance because they determine patterns of party control, as well as the array of policy views between the parties.

The impact of polarization on Congress may seem intuitive to recent observers of congressional politics, who have witnessed the disappearance of the political center and a concomitant decline in the ease of lawmaking.[17] The rise of polarization is seen quite starkly in Figure 3, which shows the percentage of ide-ological moderates in each chamber over the past four decades.[18] As explored in Chapter 4 and elsewhere in this volume, there has been a marked and rapid decline in the size of the political center over the period in both chambers—as a competitive Republican Party took root in the South, the Democratic Party lost its conservative flank.[19] Despite the Senate's staggered elections, polarization has increased in lockstep in both chambers.

The conventional wisdom suggests that today's legislative stalemate is caused in large part by the rise in polarization—a plausible hypothesis, but one that runs counter to a key assumption of the responsible party school. Party government school theorists were attentive, by and large, to the characteristic weaknesses of American political parties.[20] Indeed, these scholars recognized that American political parties were bound to be broadly representative of the public—at least in comparison to interest groups that pursued narrow economic interests. But they held as a matter of faith that reformed parties—unified, disciplined, and coherent—were the key to effective governance. Disciplined parties—organizing around and standing for party positions on major policy matters—were necessary for responsible party government. Only then could collective responsibility by parties replace individual responsibility of legislators. As the parties polarized—and came to stand for different policy agendas—accountability to the electorate would necessarily increase. The parties would stand coherently for different policy prescriptions, voters would choose between stark alternatives, and the winning party would both receive a mandate to carry out that program and take responsibility for the government's action or inaction in the next election.

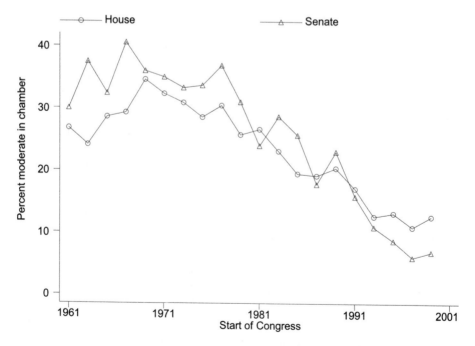

Figure 3 Decline of the Political Center, 1961–2000

If polarization is likely to bring deadlock, rather than action, then the argument of the responsible party school is turned on its head. Given the institutional structure of Congress and the separation of powers that distributes vetoes across the political system, party polarization might ironically make major policy change less, rather than more, likely. Moreover, the emergence of ideologically polarized parties may have the paradoxical effect of *deepening* support for divided government. As Gary Jacobson has argued, "the more divergent the parties' modal ideological positions, the more reason the remaining centrist voters have to welcome the moderating effect of divided government."[21] It remains an open question how elections affect congressional performance: Does electoral moderation improve or harm the prospects for major policy change?

Bicameral Differences

Elections may also affect Congress's performance because of the ways in which they shape the policy views of House and Senate members. Because of the differences in the electoral constituencies of homogeneous districts and heterogeneous states, House and Senate members—even from the same state and party—are unlikely to have entirely overlapping political views. A House Republican from a rural Indiana district represents a constituency that is conservative and homogenous. But a Republican senator from Indiana may face some moderating pressures given the big Democratic cities in northern and central Indiana. The contrast between an intensely conservative Indiana Republican like Dan Burton and a more moderate Republican senator like Richard Lugar illustrates how constituencies may produce legislators with divergent policy views even within the state party. Senators are not always more moderate than House members from their same state and party, but there is a good chance that differences in House and Senate electoral constituencies will lead legislators of the two chambers to stake out different policy agendas and political positions. Such differences become apparent in issues such as immigration policy, on which conservative House Republicans after the 2004 elections preferred an approach that focused on border control to limit illegal immigration while many Senate Republicans preferred an approach that loosened restrictions to meet the demands of employers.

The timetable for House and Senate elections also contributes to bicameral differences. Facing election every two years, House members are more likely to feel compelled to respond to national electoral tides. With staggered elections, the Senate more slowly incorporates and reflects national electoral trends. Not only is just one-third of the Senate up for re-election every two years, but presidential influence over senators is likely to be diluted given their differing electoral times lines. After all, a senator elected for six years on the same ballot as a new president will never appear on the ballot with that president again, as a president can be elected for at best only two four-year terms.

Institutional differences between the House and Senate may exaggerate policy differences between the chambers established by elections. As Steven Smith and Barbara Sinclair show elsewhere in this volume, the influence of the majority party on policy choices in the two chambers differs quite starkly. Majority parties can quite successfully set and secure partisan goals in the House. In the Senate, rules and practices of the institution enhance the power of individual senators and the minority party, and thus typically require bipartisan supermajorities to set the agenda and pass favored legislation. As a result, even if a House majority party can secure support for a legislative priority of the party without support of the minority, the Senate is unlikely to concur. The size of President Bush's tax cut package in 2001, for example, was whittled down significantly after conservative Democrats and moderate Republicans exploited their influence under Senate rules and objected to the price tag of the House-passed tax cut.

For several reasons then, the House and Senate rarely exhibit identical views about public policy. Even though elections have the potential to generate shared ideological views between the two chambers, more often differences between the chambers emerge—regardless of whether a single party controls both chambers. The limited success of House Republicans in enacting most of their Contract with America after the 1994 elections illustrates the bicameral hurdle. Although the House passed nearly 95 percent of its agenda, the Senate balked at many of the House's priorities including a balanced budget amendment, regulatory reform, and other issues.[22]

In thinking about the ways in which elections shape Congress's performance, it is important to assess the impact of bicameral differences on the legislative process. At times, the two chambers will be quite close in their ideological views—a period in which we would expect a quite productive Congress. When the two chambers diverge in their policy views, deadlock should occur more often.

Electoral Mandates

Election outcomes may also shape Congress's legislative capacity by producing so-called electoral mandates. Although there is little agreement on what constitutes mandates, let alone on how or when they might occur, the term *mandate* captures the idea that elections may send a signal about citizens' support for change in public policy.[23] Mandates thus entail elite interpretations of elections: did citizens deliver a policy message in casting their votes? As such, mandates are created both by election results and by elite chatter—in the cloakrooms on Capitol Hill, in the pages and broadcasts of the national press. If elections can generate mandates and if legislators respond to such signals, bursts of electoral change should leave a visible mark on Congress's agenda and its legislative record.

Claims of electoral mandates are most likely when a new congressional majority takes office, particular after a long hiatus in the political wilderness. When a party has been in the minority for a long time, it likely has a greater incentive to legislate efficiently when it regains control of Congress. When a Republican congressional majority took control of Congress in 1948 for the first time since before the New Deal, for example, the *New York Times* suggested that the new majority would likely claim a mandate for change:

> The Republicans took control of Congress on the basis of an obvious popular revulsion against some of the policies of the Roosevelt-Truman administrations. There was no landslide but there was a perceptible movement of the political terrain. The new legislators certainly had a mandate to liquidate some war measures, to loosen some New Deal controls, to check some New Deal projects and to effect practicable economics.[24]

Congressional claims of an electoral mandate also emerged as Republicans interpreted the 1994 election results. That election handed control of Congress to Republicans after forty years as the House minority party and nearly a decade as the Senate minority. House Republicans claimed a mandate to pursue more conservative economic and social policies, arguing that voter disgust with long-term Democratic control of the House would support a sharp reversal in the ideological tenor of policymaking. Even if the influence of a mandate dissipates over time, elections nonetheless create an opportunity for the electorate to shape congressional action.

Although Republicans after the 1994 elections tended to justify their conservative legislative agenda in terms of voter demand, there was also pent-up supply of conservative policy ideas. In fact, the longer a new congressional majority has been out of power, the more dissatisfied it should be with existing policies, and thus the greater its incentive to produce legislative change upon gaining control of both chambers. Long journeys in the minority wilderness also fuel an electoral incentive for the majority to prove it can govern. With the new majority's party reputation hanging in the balance, such electoral incentives further increase the chances for major policy change.[25] If elections can create mandates and influence the course of congressional action, then we should find improvements in congressional performance when new congressional majorities emerge after long periods in the minority wilderness.

Testing for Electoral Effects

To determine the impact of elections for Congress's performance, we need some way of monitoring and measuring congressional action. When new or recurring problems arise on the nation's agenda, is Congress able to muster a timely, responsive, and responsible solution? Granted, reasonable people can disagree about whether a problem truly exists and, if it does, what constitutes an appropriate solution. Moreover, congressional inaction need not be a sign of failure. Views about congressional performance, not surprisingly, tend to vary with one's political circumstance: "If you're against something," former Senate Majority Leader Robert Dole once observed, "you'd better hope there's a little gridlock."[26]

To test for the effects of elections on Congress, a yardstick of congressional performance can be designed. The basic approach is to identify issues that are commonly perceived as significant national problems, and then to assess whether Congress acted to address those problems and whether seasoned observers believed that the solution was well targeted to the problem. When we say that Congress deadlocked on an issue, we mean that legislators and the president were unable to reach a compromise that significantly altered the policy status quo. Successful coordination on a policy solution, in contrast, is deemed evidence of strong congressional capacity. This yardstick of congressional performance thus tallies the share of salient issues on the nation's agenda left in limbo at the close of a Congress.

Constructing a Yardstick

In *Divided We Govern*, David Mayhew defined the challenge for evaluating congressional performance: we are interested in "some actually-did-pass numerator over some all-that-were-possibilities-for-passage denominator."[27] So to evaluate Congress's performance, we need to know what issues are on the nation's policy agenda and we need to know how Congress performed on those issues.

Numerators are easier to build in this context than denominators. Although reconstructing the legislative record over a half-century is no easy task, the raw material (enacted legislation) is tallied in many places. One devises criteria to help select from the hundreds of laws enacted each year, and then applies the criteria in searching the historical record. Mayhew pioneered this method in his analysis of the consequences of divided government, yielding the important finding that not much more gets done under unified than divided control.

Denominators present more of a challenge since we are interested in both what happened and what did *not* happen—bills that failed to become law and issues that failed to attract legislators' attention. To determine the set of issues on the nation's agenda—what Mayhew calls the "all-that-were-possibilities-for-passage denominator"—newspaper editorials written by the *New York Times* between 1947 and 2000 can be used.[28] The editorials capture the broadest range of issues considered pertinent by the nation's elite for Congress to address.

From the editorial pages of the *New York Times*, the issues that plausibly constitute the nation's policy agenda (albeit the agenda of political elites) are extracted by coding the legislative content of each editorial that mentions Congress, the House, or the Senate. The number of editorials written by the *Times* on each issue in each Congress is also tallied. For example, the *Times* editorialized sixty-five times about the successful Civil Rights Act of 1964 (which it favored), forty-eight times about the Tax Reform Act of 1986 (which it also favored), and eight times about the failed constitutional amendment to require a balanced budget (which it opposed) in the 97th Congress (1981–1982). The number of editorials per issue provides a proxy for the public or political salience of the issue, a proxy that can be used to divide the agenda into progressive levels of significance. Most importantly, the *New York Times* takes stands on both legislative proposals they support and those they oppose, meaning that the agendas culled from the editorial page encompass a broad ideologically array of contemporary problems.

Once the agendas are compiled for each Congress, the disposition of each issue is researched to determine if it was eventually incorporated into a bill and enacted into law or whether no definitive action was taken in that Congress. With a record of congressional action on the universe of important issues in each Congress, a gridlock score is calculated for each Congress: the percentage of agenda items that failed to be enacted into law by the end of the Congress. By comparing different Congress's gridlock scores, a yardstick is created to measure and assess Congress's legislative performance over the latter half of the twentieth century.

Patterns of Congressional Performance

Figure 4 shows the landscape of congressional performance between 1947 and 2000, focusing on the most salient legislative issues.[29] The most productive Congresses in this period were the 80th (1947–1948), 88th (1963–1964), and 89th (1965–1966), the last known as the "Great Society" Congress under Lyndon Johnson. Those Congresses stalemated on less than one-third of their agendas.[30] In contrast, the least productive Congress was the 106th (1999–2000), a Republican Congress that faced off against a Democratic Bill Clinton; stalemate occurred on over 70 percent of its agenda. The 105th (1997–1998) and 102nd (1991–1992) were close contenders for the worst performing Congresses. As the *Washington Post* opined after the 105th Congress, "the barrenness of the legislative record is unmatched in recent memory."[31] Conclusions from the yardstick offered here comport nicely with conventional wisdom about congressional capacity across this long period.

Is Congress particularly prone to stalemate today? Critics of Congress who claim so are partially right. Gridlock has trended upward over the period, with the frequency of gridlock on the most salient issues in the 1990s double what it was in the 1940s. Even with the brief appearance of unified government under Bill Clinton and congressional Democrats after the 1992 elections, gridlock remained at a historic high, with over half of its agenda left in limbo when the

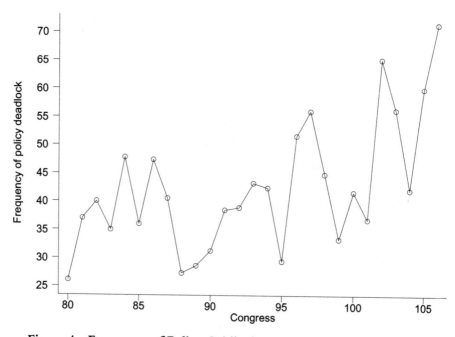

Figure 4   Frequency of Policy Gridlock on Salient Issues, 1947–2000

103rd Congress adjourned. But the level of gridlock does not simply trend upward. After its then unprecedented high in the 103rd Congress, gridlock on the most salient issues dropped fourteen points in the 104th Congress (1995–1996), reflecting election year compromises on reforming welfare, health care, immigration, and telecommunication laws, as well as increasing the minimum wage. Still, no recent Congress has matched the performance of the Great Society, four years of legislative prowess in which Presidents Kennedy and Johnson and their Democratic Congresses stalemated on only fourteen of the fifty most salient issues of those four years.

When Does Congress Govern Well?

What role do elections and party competition play in determining Congress's legislative performance over time? Table 1 shows the results of a statistical model that estimates how electoral and partisan forces jointly shape the frequency of deadlock over the postwar period. The left-most column shows the impact of these forces on all the issues on the agenda of Congress. As one moves from left to right across the table columns, the issues considered in each model increase in salience (and decrease in number). In other words, the right-most column evaluates the impact of elections and parties on Congress's ability to legislate on the most salient issues of the day.

TABLE 1

What Shapes the Frequency of Legislative Gridlock?
(By varying degrees of issue salience, 1953–2000)

		Degree of Gridlock			
Independent variables	All issues	Less salient	Moderately salient	Strongly salient	Most salient
Divided government	.306*	.432***	.418**	.421**	.416*
	(.122)	(.119)	(.151)	(.151)	(.167)
Partisan moderation	-.006	-.012**	-.012*	-.016**	-.014*
	(.004)	(.004)	(.006)	(.006)	(.006)
Bicameral differences	5.867*	7.514**	11.201**	7.502*	8.444*
	(2.739)	(2.739)	(3.570)	(3.626)	(3.954)
Time out of majority	.010	-.009	-.012	-.050ª	-.073*
	(.024)	(.025)	(.034)	(.035)	(.039)
Budgetary situation	.005	.012	.024	.017	.021
	(.007)	(.008)	(.011)	(.011)	(.013)
Public mood (lagged)	-.007	.001	.005	-.004	-.011
	(.012)	(.011)	(.015)	(.015)	(.016)
Constant	.100	-.466	-.973	-.160	.111
	(.790)	(.746)	(.975)	(.985)	(1.052)
N	24	24	24	24	24
F	2.96*	5.81**	3.97**	3.64**	2.99*
Adjusted R-squared	.339	.556	.437	.408	.341

NOTE: Cell entries are weighted least squares logit estimates for grouped data (standard errors in parentheses). * $p < .05$, ** $p < .01$, *** $p < .1$; one-tailed t-tests.

The models suggest that divided government appears to bring on more frequent bouts of stalemate. In each of the models, deadlock is significantly higher in periods of divided party control than in periods of unified control.[32] Although Mayhew convincingly showed that divided and unified governments do not differ in the *quantity* of landmark laws enacted, divided government does appear to affect the broader ability of the political system to address major public problems. Once we incorporate a denominator that captures the national agenda, it appears that split party control increases the likelihood that more issues on the agenda will end in stalemate. We can think of the impact of divided government as a force that erects another barrier in the legislative process: it traps issues that might otherwise have been enacted were control of government unified in a single political party. In this sense, the "party-government school" that advocated "responsible" parties is vindicated. As Woodrow Wilson and many other party scholars argued over the past century, legislative deadlock grows more likely when the two major parties split control of government. Elections thus affect legislative performance when they allocate procedural control of the executive and legislative branches to opposing parties.

Elections also matter by shaping the array of policy views within and between the two parties. Most striking is the impact of polarized parties. In four of the five models, as Congress moderates ideologically, stalemate becomes less likely. Only in the first model, covering all issues on the congressional agenda, does moderation not appear to reduce stalemate. The strong impact of moderation on legislative performance is a striking result because it runs counter to the expectations of the party government school. Despite the faith of responsible party advocates in disciplined and cohesive political parties, the results suggest instead that policy change is *less* likely when the parties stand for different policy agendas. Although single-party control of the branches may help to break deadlock, there are clearly limits to the power of political parties to smooth the way for legislative agreement. Intense polarization seems counterproductive to fostering major policy change.

The models also allow us to estimate how bicameral differences influence congressional capacity.[33] In all five models, increases in the ideological gap between the two chambers lead to more frequent bouts with stalemate. Even after we account for the impact of elections through party control and partisan alignments, policy differences between the House and Senate created by elections still matter. The ability of bicameral differences to bog down the legislative process may help explain why students of Congress may have been "overly optimistic" about the prospects for governance under unified government in the 103rd Congress (1993–1994).[34] Policy disagreement between the two chambers reached 11 percent in that Congress, its highest level since the last period of unified control under the Democrats in the late 1970s. No wonder seasoned observers concluded at the close of the 103rd Congress: "The only good news as this mud fight finally winds down is that it's hard to imagine much worse."[35] The decline in legislative performance associated with bicameral disagreement also helps to explain the several impasses Republicans encountered in the 108th Congress upon gaining control of the White House, Senate, and House. Among other issues, bankruptcy overhaul, corporate tax reform, and the annual budget resolution encountered significantly delays as House and Senate Republicans could not reach common ground on each others' legislative solutions.

Do electoral mandates make a difference? When new congressional majorities take office after a long sojourn in the minority wilderness, stalemate occurs less frequently only on the most salient issues. This might reflect new majorities' efforts to prove their governing capacity on showcase issues high on their agenda.[36] But there is little evidence that the policy environment affects legislative performance. Improved fiscal discipline does not make it easier to reach agreement on policy disputes. Nor does the liberalness of public opinion matter. As the public's preference for activist government increases, congressional performance seems not to change.

In real terms, what impact do changes in the electoral environment have on legislative performance? We can simulate the frequency of gridlock under different electoral scenarios.[37] Using the past half-century as our guide, we can expect divided control of government to increase the frequency of stalemate by roughly 11 percent. Given on average fifty-five issues on the agenda during each Congress, divided government should block resolution of six additional issues. Increases in polarization show similar effects, raising the incidence of deadlock by roughly 9 percent—thus blocking five additional issues. Such results confirm the sentiments of many members and observers of Congress who claim that partisan polarization limits the legislative capacity of Congress.[38] The "incredibly shrinking middle"—as Senator John Breaux (D-Louisiana) called it in 1995—hampers legislators' ability to compromise on major issues. Finally, bicameral differences have the greatest impact on congressional performance: when the frequency of policy disagreement between the chambers doubles, the frequency of stalemate goes up by 12 percent. Although scholars and observers of Congress often blame inter-branch disputes for policy stalemate, intra-branch disagreements also limit Congress's governing performance. When elections yield ideologically distinct chambers—and that ideological gap is exacerbated by the differing rules and practices of the two chambers—bicameral disputes diminish congressional capacity.

Partisanship, Competition, and Republican Government

After the Supreme Court cemented his election in 2000, George W. Bush declared that it was time to "move beyond the bitterness and partisanship of the recent past."[39] By most accounts, however, congressional partisanship continued to rise. Democrats charged that Bush pursued a polarizing agenda of tax cuts and other measures, after his hair-splitting election arguably called for a more conciliatory approach. Republicans countered that a move toward the center would have damaged the Bush presidency, and that there was little Bush could have done given the competitive balance of the two ideologically charged parties.

The terror attacks of 11 September 2001 brought a temporary respite from the intense partisanship of Congress. Swift agreement was reached on several measures directly related to the recovery effort in Washington and New York and legislators from both parties supported the initial foray into Afghanistan to attack the Taliban regime and al Qaeda. But bipartisanship was confined to those issues most closely related to the war on terrorism, and it seemed to dissolve as the war on terror wore on. By the end of 2003, it was hard to imagine worse relations in the House. After Republicans held open the vote on a controversial Medicare reform package for three hours starting at 3 A.M. to squeak out a bare majority, House Minority Leader Nancy Pelosi (D-CA) charged that "this vote was stolen from us by the Republicans."[40] Relations were no better in the Senate. Democrats found themselves excluded from conference committees, and Republicans excoriated Democrats for what they saw as unconstitutional filibusters against the president's judicial nominees and relentless obstruction of Republican priorities. Those and other bitter contests that year led Senate Minority Leader Tom Daschle (D-SD) to declare 2003 the "single most partisan session" of Congress in which he had served.

Why has such tight partisan competition between two polarized parties been so debilitating for Congress and demoralizing for the minority? First, it is extremely difficult to build bipartisan coalitions when the ideological gap between the parties is so large. The narrowness of Republican majorities in both chambers no doubt exacerbated the situation, as there were few votes to spare when Republicans aggressively sought to secure the off-center policies sought by their base. Second, polarization also affects congressional capacity by limiting legislators' incentives to compromise. Especially in today's electoral environment when both parties attempt to solidify their party ranks by gerrymandering congressional districts, incentives to compromise are few—even when acceptable agreements may be in reach.

The electoral logic at work here bears some more attention. When we think about political disagreements, we typically assume that they are caused by genuine disputes about policy ends and means. Political disagreements may also be strategic in nature. Sometimes legislators prefer disagreement over compromise, even when consensus is in sight. As John Gilmour observes, there may be a "disinclination to compromise," when the pursuit of political gain encourages opponents to avoid otherwise reachable agreements.[41] If there is little hope that elections will deliver a new majority party, for example, legislators are unlikely to block policy change in anticipation of regaining control of their chamber. There is little perceived political gain under such conditions for the minority to block otherwise acceptable compromises. In contrast, if the electoral environment is highly competitive, then political parties may prefer disagreement to compromise. Once the political stakes increase, strategic disagreement becomes a more prevalent strategy for ambitious politicians—particularly for those in narrow majorities with a fragile hold on the majority.

The tendency toward strategic disagreement does not bode well for Congress's performance. Because no party holds an unbeatable advantage with the electorate today, both sides believe that the next election could be the one that provides an electoral breakthrough for their party. Driven by intense ideological disagreements, neither side wants to give the other party a break. To be sure, Republican majorities have been able to enact a number of major reforms—including an education package that secured bipartisan support, a raft of tax cuts endorsed by Republicans and many Democrats, and Medicare reform (with predominately Republican votes). At the same time, however, Congress failed several times under Republican majorities to pass a budget blueprint, the federal deficit has soared, and overhaul of the nation's welfare, energy, social and health insurance, and immigration policies remains in limbo. Perhaps most harmful to the institution, legislators on both sides of the Capitol and the partisan aisle bemoan a decline in trust between the parties—a commodity legislators typically deem essential for making a complex legislative process work.

Prospects for Reform

Elections undoubtedly affect congressional performance—determining patterns of party control, creating party mandates, shaping the ideological reach of parties and chambers, and molding the electoral context until the next election. These forces in turn have a heavy hand in shaping what Congress achieves, bringing resolution of some public problems into reach while pushing other solutions aside. Granted, elections alone do not determine whether and when legislators will broker the compromise necessary for major policy change; as many chapters in this volume attest, the rules and practices of the House and Senate matter too. The rules of the game in the House allow slim majorities to successfully pursue stridently partisan agendas, while the Senate's lax limits on debate allow and encourage minorities to rein in majorities and their partisan agenda. So elections—filtered through institutions—influence Congress's capacity to secure major policy change.

Can Congress be made more productive? That is a volatile question, as a reasonable case can be made that congressional inaction is evidence that the framers' system of checks and balances is working just fine. Because constitutional powers are both separated and shared within and across the branches, a slow moving Congress may be precisely what the framers of the Constitution had in mind. Failure to compromise may signal sincere disagreement about the means and ends of public policy. If the electoral context encourages deadlock, so be it: the public interest is well served by stalemate in Washington.

That view makes some strong assumptions. First, it assumes that the framers uniformly sought to limit the new government's capacity to legislate. Although the framers certainly preferred a limited government, they also acted in the shadow of the Confederation Congress—a legislature that more often than not found itself mired in deadlock.[42] Creating a new government freed from the procedural traps prevalent under the Articles of Confederation was a priority for the framers. Second, this view assumes that majorities are able to work their will on Capitol Hill. If a majority prefers a particular course of action, it will succeed. Given the rules of the game in the Senate that require supermajorities to overcome minority obstruction, majority support is often insufficient to secure major policy change.[43] Political will to secure policy change is rarely enough in an institution that widely disperses political power. Third, it assumes that disagreements on Capitol Hill are sincere expressions of disagreement over policy ends and means. But in today's world of near-parity parties, disagreement will often be strategic. Unwillingness to broker compromise may reflect parties' competitive electoral strategies more than their policy differences.

So perhaps improving congressional productivity is a reasonable goal. If so, the challenge remains to devise a pragmatic course of reform. In general, reforms that might encourage the process of compromise would be desirable. In the electoral realm, more competitive elections could make a difference. As Gary Jacobson observes in Chapter 4, only a handful of House races are truly competitive. Because the majority party largely holds safe seats, there is little incentive for the party to reach out to moderate voters or independent voters. Playing to the base and pouring millions of dollars into the remaining competitive races are instead the orders of the day. Redistricting reform—such as the use of bipartisan or nonpartisan redistricting commissions—is one potential approach to boosting competition in House races, although the likelihood of such reform is low.[44]

Inside the institution, change in rules and practices may have some impact on Congress's productivity. Reforms of the Senate debate rules (detailed in Chapter 9), changes in the confirmation process (advocated in Chapter 14), broadening of the minority party's participation in the House (suggested in Chapter 8)—each of these reforms might improve the deliberative process in the two chambers and make policy agreements more reachable and sustainable. Congress might also follow the lead of state and local legislative bodies that have brought outside negotiators into the chambers to facilitate compromise.[45] One could imagine the use of "negotiated consensus" methods at the committee level and again in conference. Although such reforms would be incremental in their effects, they are unlikely to be embraced by members and senators. Delegating influence over the course of negotiations to outside participants is unlikely to be an attractive alternative—given the political and policy consequences of compromise in an intensely partisan and competitive environment. In such times, making compromise more attainable may be a low priority for parties and their leaders in Congress. This is unfortunate—both for the welfare of the American public and for the strength of its most reliably democratic institution.

Notes

1. On House majority parties as instruments of agenda control, see Gary C. Cox and Mathew McCubbins, *Setting the Agenda* (Cambridge, U.K.: Cambridge University Press, forthcoming).

2. See Gary Jacobson, "Modern Campaigns and Representation" in this volume, and Gary C. Jacobson, *The Politics of Congressional Elections*, 6th ed. (New York: Pearson Longman, 2004).

3. "Mr. Cleveland's Cabinet," in *The Public Papers of Woodrow Wilson: College and State*, edited by Ray Stannard Baker and William E. Dodd (New York and London: Harper and Brothers, 1925–1927), vol. 1, 221–222, as cited in Austin Ranney, *The Doctrine of Responsible Party Government: Its Origins and Present State* (Urbana: University of Illinois Press, 1954), 32.

4. E. E. Schattschneider, *Party Government*, 1.

5. James Sundquist, "Needed: A Political Theory for the New Era of Coalition Government in the United States," *Political Science Quarterly* 103 (1988), 613–635, at 614.

6. For a careful delineation of what party theorists meant by responsive government, and thus the relevance of unified party control, see John J. Coleman, "Unified Government, Divided Government, and Party Responsiveness," *American Political Science Review* 93 (Dec. 1999), 821–835.

7. V. O. Key, Jr., *Politics, Parties, and Pressure Groups*, 5th ed. (New York: Crowell, 1964), 688.

8. On the electoral relevance of a policy-based party reputation, see Gary Cox and Mathew McCubbins, *Legislative Leviathan: Party Government in the House* (Berkeley: University of California Press, 1993).

9. The argument is summarized and critiqued in Morris Fiorina, *Divided Government* 2nd ed. (New York: Longman 2003), chap. 6.

10. For details, see Mayhew, *Divided We Govern*, chap. 3.

11. See in particular Mayhew's conclusion in chap. 7.

12. See Sarah A. Binder, *Stalemate*, chap. 4.

13. The scores used here are dubbed DW-NOMINATE, and were developed by Nolan McCarty, Keith Poole, and Howard Rosenthal, *Income Redistribution and the Realignment of American Politics*, AEI Studies on Understanding Economic Inequality (Washington, D.C.: AEI Press, 1997). Figures 1 and 2 are density plots, which are essentially smoothed histograms. They can be read as if they were histograms: the higher the plot, the greater the number of members assigned that ideological score.

14. The four Democrats were Gene Taylor of Mississippi, Jim Traficant of Ohio, Ralph Hall of Texas, and Virgil Goode of Virginia. Goode became a Republican in 2002; Hall, 2004.

15. John Gilmour, *Strategic Disagreement*.

16. Michael Grunwald, "Gephardt's Tireless Quest: Put Democrats atop House," *Washington Post*, July 12, 1999, A1.

17. See Richard E. Cohen, Kirk Victor, and David Baumann, "The State of Congress," *National Journal*, January 10, 2004.

18. Ideological moderates are identified by their roll call behavior, as measured by Poole and Rosenthal's NOMINATE scores. Moderates are those legislators whose voting records place them closer to the midpoint of two parties than to their own party's median. For details on measurement, see Binder, *Stalemate*, chap. 4. NOMINATE scores are introduced in Keith Poole and Howard Rosenthal, *Congress: A Political-Economic History of Roll Call Voting* (New York: Oxford University Press, 1997).

19. Reasons for the polarization are explored in chap. 4 in this volume. On the political transformation of the South, see Nelson W. Polsby, *How Congress Evolves* (New York: Oxford University Press, 2003), David Rohde, *Parties and Leaders in the Postreform House* (Chicago: University of Chicago Press, 1991), David Lublin, *The Republican South: Democratization and Partisan Change* (Princeton, N.J.: Princeton University Press, 2004), and William Lowry and Charles Shipan, "Party Differentiation in Congress," *Legislative Studies Quarterly* 27, no. 1 (2002), 33–60.

20. See Coleman's discussion in "Unified Government, Divided Government, and Party Responsiveness."

21. See Jacobson, "Party Polarization in National Politics: The Electoral Connection," in Bond and Fleisher, *Polarized Politics.*

22. See David Baumann, "Grading the Class of '94," *National Journal* (April 30, 2004).

23. Mandates are explored most recently in Patricia Conley, *Presidential Mandates: How Elections Shape the National Agenda* (Chicago: University of Chicago Press, 2001), and David A. M. Peterson, Lawrence J. Grossback, James A. Stimson, and Amy Gangl, "Congressional Response to Mandate Elections," *American Journal of Political Science* 47 (July 2003), 411–426.

24. "Eightieth Congress: To Date," *New York Times* editorial, June 20, 1948.

25. There is, however, a countervailing force that works against policy success. A new, inexperienced majority may also face the countervailing difficulty of "learning to govern," lacking legislators with the pragmatism and experience necessary to master lawmaking in a complex congressional environment. See Richard F. Fenno, Jr., *Learning to Govern: An Institutional View of the 104th Congress* (Washington, D.C.: Brookings Institution Press, 1997).

26. William Safire, *Safire's New Political Dictionary: The Definitive Guide to the New Language of Politics* (New York: Random House, 1993), 305.

27. David Mayhew, *Divided We Govern*, 34.

28. On the choice of the *New York Times* and details on how the editorials were selected and coded, see Binder, *Stalemate*, chap. 3 and Appendix B.

29. The scores include only those issues on which the *Times* wrote four or more editorials in the Congress.

30. With typical bravado and remarkable foresight (just a mere percentage point off), Johnson predicted in 1964 that "when the record of this [88th] Congress is complete, it will place the 88th Congress in the record books as the most constructive of the twentieth century" ("Salute to Congress," *The New York Times*, August 20, 1964). Although President Harry Truman terms the 80th Congress the "do nothing" Congress, that may have been more strategic than true. As David McCullough in his 1992 biography of Truman suggests, legislation passed included the Marshall Plan, National Security Act, Taft-Hartley Labor Act, Reciprocal Trade Agreements, and Selective Service Reform. See David McCullough, *Truman* (New York: Simon and Shuster, 1992), 696.

31. "A Retrograde Congress," *The Washington Post* [editorial], October 11, 1998, C6.

32. For details on measurement and estimation of the models, see Binder, *Stalemate*, chap. 4.

33. The measurement of bicameral differences in discussed in Binder, *Stalemate*, chap. 4.

34. See James Sundquist, *Back to Gridlock: Governance in the Clinton Years* (Washington, D.C.: Brookings Institution, 1995), 10.
35. "Perhaps the Worst Congress," *The Washington Post*, October 7, 1994, A24.
36. On the challenges faced by new congressional majorities, see Fenno, *Learning to Govern.*
37. The statistical technique used is discussed in detail in Binder, *Stalemate*, chap. 4. Here, the frequency of gridlock is predicted over a broad range of agenda issues (those that were the target of at least two *Times* editorials).
38. See for example William S. Cohen, "Why I am Leaving," *The Washington Post*, January 21, 1996, C7; Lloyd Grove, "The So-Long Senators," *The Washington Post*, January 26, 1996, F1; and Marilyn Serafini "Mr. In-Between," *National Journal*, December 16, 1996, 2080–2084.
39. Dana Milbank and David S. Broder, "Hopes for Civility in Washington Are Dashed," *The Washington Post*, January 18, 2004, A1.
40. See Cohen, Victor, and Baumann, "The State of Congress," 84.
41. See Gilmour, *Strategic Disagreement*, 10.
42. See Calvin Jillson and Rick K. Wilson, *Congressional Dynamics: Structure, Coordination and Choice in the First American Congress, 1774–1789* (Stanford, Calif.: Stanford University Press, 1994).
43. Exploitation of Senate rules to block majority-preferred measures is explored in Sarah A. Binder and Steven S. Smith, *Politics or Principle? Filibustering in the United States Senate* (Washington, D.C.: Brookings Institution, 1997).
44. See Jaime L. Carson and Michael H. Crespin. "The Effect of State Redistricting Methods on Electoral Competition in United States House Races." *State Politics and Policy Quarterly* 4, No. 4 (2004), 455–469.
45. Such negotiation practices are discussed in Binder, *Stalemate*, chap. 6.

Bibliography

Binder, Sarah A. *Stalemate: Causes and Consequences of Legislative Gridlock.* Washington, D.C.: Brookings Institution Press, 2003.

Bond, Jon R., and Richard Fleisher, eds. *Polarized Politics: Congress and the President in a Partisan Era.* Washington, D.C.: CQ Press, 2000.

Gilmour, John B. *Strategic Disagreement: Stalemate in American Politics.* Pittsburgh: University of Pittsburgh Press, 1995.

Krehbiel, Keith. *Pivotal Politics: A Theory of U.S. Lawmaking.* Chicago: University of Chicago Press, 1998.

Mayhew, David R. *Divided We Govern.* New Haven, Conn.: Yale University Press, 1991.

Schattschneider, E. E. *Party Government.* New York: Farrar and Reinhart, 1942.

6

REPRESENTING RACIAL
AND ETHNIC MINORITIES

David T. Canon

SINCE ITS INCEPTION IN 1970, THE CONGRESSIONAL BLACK caucus (CBC) has been known as the "conscience of Congress." In fighting for civil rights, voting rights, and government programs for the poor and unemployed, the CBC's institutional clout has grown over the decades. The number of African American House members has tripled since 1970, and the Hispanic Caucus has emerged as an important ally. However, the question of how to best represent racial and ethnic interests in Congress is far from settled. In 1993, in *Shaw v. Reno,* the Supreme Court challenged the new black-majority and Latino-majority congressional districts that were created in 1992, calling them "political apartheid."[1] The very notion of "minority interests" is rejected by those who call for a "color-blind" approach to politics.

Representing minority interests in a majority-rule institution such as Congress poses problems that touch on all of the themes presented in this volume: constitutional design, democratic values, policy making, and adaptation and reform. The topic of minority representation also provides an excellent example of the interplay of Congress and the courts in shaping institutions. Specific questions addressed in this chapter include: How does the constitutional system of checks and balances and separation of powers, and the competing democratic values of majority rule and minority rights that this system was intended to address, influence the representation of minority and ethnic interests in Congress? What conceptions of racial representation are prevalent in the United States today, and how well are they achieved? How have the electoral reforms of past decades altered the functioning of and prospects for minority representation? How have the courts altered those electoral reforms? What does the future hold for the representation of black and Latino interests in Congress?

Constitutional Design, Democratic Values, and Minority Representation

In *The Federalist Papers,* James Madison described the central problem posed by a political system governed by majority rule as the potential for "majority tyranny"; that is, majority "factions" could impose their selfish interests on the rest of the country in a way that harmed the public good. Minority factions could be controlled by the republican principle (the majority could simply out-vote the minority), but majority factions could not be so easily restrained. The constitutional design of checks and balances and separation of powers, which divided power among the three branches of government and across national, state, and local governments, was the main institutional solution to the problem of majority tyranny.

Hailed by generations of political scientists, the competitive political process of checks and balances was thought to produce reasonably fair and democratic results. Pluralist politics characterized by overlapping memberships, crosscutting cleavages, and responsiveness to intense preferences would create a republic in which "minorities ruled," to use Robert Dahl's famous phrase.[2] However, schol-ars and politicians have concluded since at least the mid-twentieth century that the system did not adequately represent the interests of racial and ethnic minori-ties.[3] The Madisonian system could not, for example, prevent the tyranny of slav-ery and the Jim Crow laws that subjugated African Americans from the beginning of the nation's history until the mid-1960s.

A necessary starting point in a discussion of minority representation is to define the nature of minority interests. If racial minorities and whites shared all the same interests, this volume would not need to address the way in which minorities are represented in Congress. However, voluminous research has demonstrated differences in the objective circumstances of racial minorities and whites (poverty, health care, crime, etc.) and in the subjective interests of blacks and whites.[4] The adequate representation of the substantive interests of racial and ethnic minorities requires that serious attention by legislators be paid to issues in which race plays a role, such as antidiscrimination laws in employment, housing, and the financial sector, affirmative action, social welfare policy, support for the inner cities, especially for urban schools, as well as more general issues that are of interest to all constituents (building highways, providing clean air and water, national defense, quality education, etc.).

The obvious question is how to provide the institutional context within which these distinctive interests can be adequately addressed. Different concep-tions of racial representation provide different answers to that question. These conceptions vary according to the importance they place on descriptive representation and substantive representation and the position they take on the politics of commonality or difference. *Descriptive representation* refers to having representatives who mirror the demographic characteristics of their constituents. Black constituents would be represented by African American representatives, whites by whites, Latinos by Latinos, and so on. At the institutional level, a descriptively representative Congress would "look like" America: that is, it would have about the same demographic profile as the nation.

Based on the 2002 U.S. Census population estimates, that means the House would be comprised of 301 whites, 59 Latinos, 52 African Americans, 17 Asian Americans, 4 Native Americans, and two others (of an undetermined race). The actual numbers in the 109th Congress (2005–2006) fell well short of this descriptive ideal but demonstrated that substantial gains had been made in recent years: there were 23 Latinos (one shy of the record), 40 African Americans (an all-time high), five Asian or Native Hawaiian/other Pacific Islander heritage, one Asian Indian, and one Native American in the House of Representatives. There were two Native Hawaiians, two Latinos, and one African American in the Senate.[5]

Substantive representation refers to a requirement that representatives are responsive to voters' interests across a range of issues. The extent to which representatives are responsive to racial and ethnic interests will be discussed below. The immediate concern is to discuss the varying conceptions of the substantive representation of racial interests: the central divide is between those who view it in terms of the politics of difference and those who see it as the politics of commonality.

Those who view politics through the lens of race and require representation of distinctive black interests by black representatives are practicing the politics of difference. Descriptive representation becomes critical if inherent differences are recognized in terms of identities and shared experiences rather than ideas and opinions.[6] From this perspective, white politicians cannot provide substantive representation for minorities because they cannot understand what it means to be black or Latino, despite their best intentions and efforts. However, descriptive representation does not guarantee substantive representation. Advocates of this view argue that in their legislative roles Republican African American Representatives such as Gary Franks of Connecticut and J. C. Watts Jr. of Oklahoma did not provide substantive representation for African Americans. Thus, the politics-of-difference perspective would see descriptive representation as a necessary but not sufficient condition for substantive representation of racial and ethnic interests.

Shifting to the opposite end of the spectrum, the extreme version of the politics of commonality is the deracialization, or color-blind, perspective. This perspective holds that the race of a member of Congress does not matter because racial issues are no longer central (or at least *should* not be) to American politics.

One variation of this view holds that while there still may be some issues that divide Americans along racial lines, politicians should attempt to find common ground and represent the interests of all their constituents. Furthermore, the race of the member is irrelevant in providing substantive representation because policy positions and ideas matter more than the color of one's skin. That is, descriptive representation is not a necessary condition for substantive representation.

A middle-ground approach is the "balancing perspective" of the politics of commonality.[7] This conception of racial representation holds that there are distinct racial interests and that the optimal style of representation for a member of Congress is one that recognizes those differences and tries to balance the various needs and interests of one's constituency. In contrast, the politics-of-difference approach argues that minority representatives should focus on the needs of their minority constituents because their white constituents are represented by other members of Congress. The color-blind approach to commonality does not recognize the representational issues posed by racially heterogeneous districts because it ignores distinctive racial interests.

The balancing perspective produces a different policy focus and a more pragmatic approach to the legislative process than is true of the confrontational and symbolic approach adopted by some practitioners of a politics of difference, and is more sensitive to racial interests than the color-blind approach. The balancing approach also values biracial coalitions, both in the electoral and institutional context. Descriptive representation is not a necessary condition for substantive representation from this perspective, but rather it is an empirical question whether a representative's race has an impact on how they represent their constituents' racial interests. As the evidence presented below indicates, African American members of the House do a better job than white representatives of balancing the distinctive interests of their black constituents and the more general nonracial interests of their districts.

Eras of Electoral Reform

Changes in the conceptions of racial representation reflect the evolving nature of racial politics in the United States, the shifting balance of partisan power in Congress, and changes in the composition of the Supreme Court since the mid-twentieth century. This evolution is also reflected in electoral reforms related to racial representation and the Court's response to those reforms. There are two periods of electoral reform concerning racial representation and two distinct approaches taken by the Court in response to those reforms, each reflecting different norms and goals. Reforms have sought, respectively, access to the voting booth (from roughly the end of Reconstruction through 1975) and electing "candidates of choice" (from the late 1960s through 1993). The Court's responses may be categorized as the "color-blind" approach (from 1993 until

2001) and the mixed approach, in which race can be a factor in drawing district lines and explicit consideration must be given to how the substantive representation of minority interests can be maximized (from 2001 through today). The central point of contention since 1992 is whether majority-minority districts (congressional districts in which a majority of the voting-age population is a racial minority) can be a tool for enhancing minority representation in Congress. However, competing goals for minority representation have been present since the 1960s. For example, advocates of electing more minorities to office did not give up during the "color-blind" period. The periods are defined by which conception of racial representation and which tool of reform were endorsed by Congress and the Supreme Court.

The goal of reformers during the first period of electoral reforms was to give minorities access to the voting booth. From the end of Reconstruction after the Civil War through the middle of the twentieth century, blacks in the South were almost completely disenfranchised through the imposition of residency requirements, poll taxes, literacy tests, the grandfather clause, physical intimidation, and other forms of disqualification, and later the white primary (in white primaries only whites were allowed to vote in the Democratic primary; given that the Republican party did not exist in most southern states, blacks were effectively disenfranchised by this practice). While these provisions claimed to be race-neutral, their impact fell disproportionately on black voters. The most obvious of these was the grandfather clause, which enabled illiterate whites to get around the literacy test.[8] Many states also had "understanding" or "good character" exceptions to the literacy tests, which gave election officials substantial discretion over who would be allowed to vote. These obstacles virtually eliminated black voting; for example, only 6 percent of blacks were registered to vote in Mississippi in 1890 and only 2 percent were registered in Alabama in 1906. After the last post-Reconstruction black legislator left the House in 1901, it was seventy-two years until another black represented a southern district in Washington, D.C. These practices continued well into the twentieth century. In Mississippi, for example, one county in 1947 had thirteen thousand blacks who were eligible to vote but only six were actually registered. Despite the constitutional guarantees of the Fourteenth and Fifteenth Amendments, blacks had been effectively removed from the political system.

This all changed with the passage of the Voting Rights Act (VRA) in 1965. The VRA suspended literacy tests, provided for federal marshals to oversee the voting process in "covered" states, mandated that voting could not be denied on the basis of race or color, and stated that any changes in electoral practices in covered states had to be "precleared" by the Justice Department or a federal court in Washington. Hailed as one of the most significant pieces of civil rights legislation in American history, the VRA permanently altered the political landscape of southern politics, which in turn had a significant impact on national and congressional politics.

The statistics on the explosion in black participation in the South after the passage of the VRA are impressive. The most dramatic gains came in Mississippi, where black registration increased from 7 percent before the VRA to 60 percent in 1967. As one political scientist noted, "The act simply overwhelmed the major bulwarks of the disenfranchising system. In the seven states originally covered, black registration increased from 29.3% in March, 1965, to 56.6% in 1971–72; the gap between black and white registration rates narrowed from 44.1 percentage points to 11.2."[9]

The last step in the first period of reform was extending the VRA to cover Latinos and other "language minorities" in 1975. Congress found that voting discrimination against language minorities "is pervasive and national in scope." The amendments applied the VRA to parts of the country "with significant numbers of voters with limited or no English proficiency" and required these jurisdictions "to provide voting materials and assistance in relevant languages in addition to English." In a passage that echoed the assessment of African American participation in the electoral process in the South before the VRA, Congress found, "Through the use of various practices and procedures, citizens of language minorities have been effectively excluded from participation in the electoral process. . . . It is necessary to eliminate such discrimination by prohibiting these practices, and by prescribing other remedial

| | March 1965 | | | November 1988 | | |
	Black	White	Gap	Black	White	Gap
Alabama	19.3	69.2	49.9	68.4	75.0	6.6
Georgia	27.4	62.6	35.2	56.8	63.9	7.1
Louisiana	31.6	80.5	48.9	77.1	75.1	–2.0
Mississippi	6.7	69.9	63.2	74.2	80.5	6.3
North Carolina	46.8	96.8	50.0	58.2	65.6	7.4
South Carolina	37.3	75.7	38.4	56.7	61.8	5.1
Virginia	38.3	61.1	22.8	63.8	68.5	4.7

SOURCE: U.S. Department of Justice, adapted from Bernard Grofman, Lisa Handley and Richard G. Niemi. *Minority Representation and the Quest for Voting Equality*. New York: Cambridge Press, 1992, 23–24. Available at: http://www.usdoj.gov/crt/voting/intro/intro_c.htm#note1 #note1.

Figure 1   Voter Registration Rates before and after the Voting Rights Act

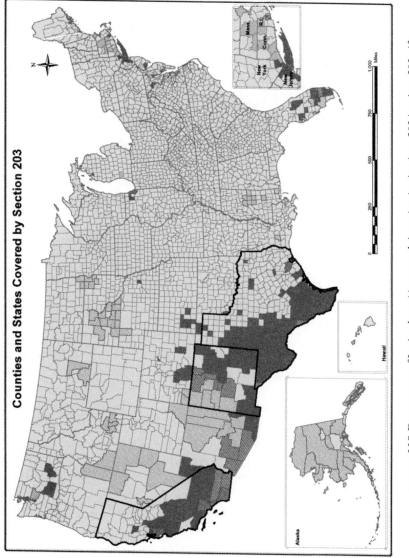
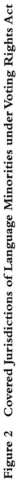

Counties and States Covered by Section 203

SOURCE: U.S. Department of Justice, http://www.usdoj.gov/crt/voting/sec_203/section_203.gif.

Figure 2 Covered Jurisdictions of Language Minorities under Voting Rights Act

devices."[10] These amendments were put into effect for ten years and then extended for ten years in 1982 and for another fifteen years in 1992 to make the extension consistent with the twenty-five-year extension that other central parts of the VRA received in 1982.

This first era of reform reflected increased congressional involvement in the area of civil rights and voting rights. Through the 1950s and early 1960s the Supreme Court was the primary vehicle for advancing civil rights, because southern Democrats, who favored racial segregation, controlled many of the key committees in the House and Senate. Therefore, civil rights advocates often found a more sympathetic hearing from the more liberal Supreme Court, which was led by Chief Justice Earl Warren, a strong supporter of civil rights. In the 1960s and 1970s the power in Congress tipped to more liberal Democrats who supported civil rights policies, as shown by the passage of the 1964 Civil Rights Act, the 1965 VRA, and the VRA amendments of 1975 and 1982.

Despite the stronger role for Congress in civil rights policy, the courts continued to play an important role through the 1970s by interpreting the VRA in a variety of contexts. While minority voters gained more access to the polls, they faced subtle forms of discrimination, including changing electoral practices such as jurisdictions shifting from district to at-large elections (mostly in local elections) or the redrawing of district boundaries to dilute black voting power. An important Supreme Court case, *Allen v. State Board of Elections* (1969), held that "the preclearance provisions were applicable, not only to changes in laws directly affecting registration and voting, but all changes 'which alter the election law of a covered State in even a minor way.'"[11] As *Allen* was applied, covered practices, that is, changes in election procedures that had to be approved or "precleared" by the Justice Department under Section 5 of the VRA, not only included literacy tests and other practices that directly restricted access to voting, but also actions such as switching from single-member to at-large elections, switching from elective to appointive office, qualifications for independent voters and write-in votes, redistricting, and annexation or other voting practices that could *abridge* the right to vote based on race or color.[12] Redistricting cases were primarily of the former type (practices that directly restricted access to voting), while the vote-dilution cases typically involved the types of practices outlined in *Allen*. The *Allen* decision took the first step toward the second period of electoral reform for minority representation by embracing the concept of a "meaningful vote." That is, access to the voting booth was not enough to guarantee that minorities would actually have a say in the political process, if white politicians used a variety of mechanisms to undermine the value of their votes.

The second period of reform was a reaction to a Supreme Court decision interpreting the VRA which challenged the concept of a meaningful vote. In 1980, the Court ruled that someone who challenged an electoral law or practice as being discriminatory would have to prove that its *intent* was to dilute the voting power of minorities rather than to show merely that it had that effect.[13] In the 1982 VRA amendments, Congress strongly disagreed with this interpretation of the VRA and reinstated the "effects" standard for proving vote-dilution claims. The amendments also required that minorities have an equal opportunity to participate in the political process and to "elect representatives of their choice." The Senate committee that crafted this language also included a sentence indicating that nothing in the law established a right to proportional representation for racial and ethnic minorities. This part was necessary to attract the votes of some moderate Republicans who were afraid that the "representatives of choice" clause could lead to an expectation of proportional representation. Critics continued to assert that it was a "quotas bill" and "affirmative action for minority politicians," but the 1982 VRA amendments were passed by the Republican-controlled Senate and Democratic House and signed into law by President Ronald Reagan.[14]

The reformers' central goal during the second era of electoral reform was electing more minority candidates to office. The 1982 amendments went into effect too late to affect the 1980s round of congressional redistricting, but there was one important development in 1986 that shaped the next round of drawing districts: a Court decision, *Thornburg v. Gingles,* that specified the conditions under which minority voters would have to be given an opportunity to elect representatives of their choice. Specifically, if minority voters were sufficiently compact in their geographic distribution, if they voted cohesively for candidates of their choice, and if whites voted as a bloc to deny them an opportunity to elect candidates of their choice, minority voters could claim under Section 2 of the VRA that their votes had been diluted.[15] This court decision, along with its interpretation by the Justice Department, created an expectation for the 1990s round of redistricting that states would create minority-majority districts whenever feasible.

Politics and Policy in Majority-Minority Districts

As expected, in 1992 state legislatures (and in some cases the courts) created fifteen new U.S. House districts that were specifically drawn to help elect African Americans and ten districts that were drawn to provide an opportunity to elect new Latino members. The 1992 elections produced a 51 percent increase in the number of African Americans and Latinos in Congress (from thirty-seven to fifty-six)—the largest infusion of new minority members in the history of Congress. This section will examine how this change in the composition of the House changed the nature of institutional politics and policy outcomes in Congress.

The Peak of Power: The 103rd Congress

The central conclusion of most research on the representation of racial and ethnic interests is that race matters in the House of Representatives, both at the institutional and individual levels, and that the 1982 VRA amendments and the

1992 redistricting has shaped the impact of race in congressional politics. A 1999 study by the author (hereafter referred to as the Canon study), the results of which are summarized below, shows that this was especially true in the 103rd Congress (1993–94).[16]

At the institutional level, the Congressional Black Caucus (CBC) and Congressional Hispanic Caucus (CHC) are highly cohesive but increasingly diverse, largely due to the class of 1992, which included many new members from southern rural districts (as opposed to the traditional northern, urban base for the CBC and CHC). The CBC and CHC are strong supporters of minority interests while also being instrumental in helping mainstream Democratic Party positions succeed. CBC members provided the pivotal votes on crucial legislation in the 103rd Congress, served on a broader array of committees than non-CBC members, and played an increasing role in the leadership.

The common wisdom holds (both among academics and House members) that there is a trade-off between cohesion and dispersion. As a group becomes more diverse and its interests more dispersed, its cohesion and ability to speak with one voice declines. In one sense, this is obviously true. More-diverse groups will not be as cohesive by definition. However, it does not necessarily follow that diversity and cohesion cannot peacefully coexist *across a range of issues.* For many members of the CBC, it makes sense to break with the caucus and work with the Democratic leadership on one piece of legislation, while simultaneously speaking out for minority interests on another. The 1999 Canon study shows that this is exactly what members of the CBC do: they distribute their efforts and time over a broad range of concerns. They attempt to balance their legislative efforts by addressing nonracial issues that appeal to all constituents and racial concerns that are especially important for the African Americans in their districts, consistent with the politics-of-commonality approach. Most importantly for the policy debates surrounding black-majority districts, the CBC *can* have its voice heard in a majority-rule institution (counter to the arguments of Lani Guinier, Bill Clinton's original nominee for Assistant Attorney General of the Civil Rights Division of the Justice Department, and others). The Canon study's analysis of 2,751 bills in the 103rd Congress showed that bills that had a black sponsor had a significantly higher chance of making it through the legislative process than those that did not. Furthermore, legislation that had explicit or implicit racial content (and was typically sponsored by a member of the CBC) received as much support on roll call votes as bills that had no racial content.

Systematic differences can be found among CBC members who practice a politics of difference and those who practice a politics of commonality. These two types of members were identified by the racial composition of the electoral coalition that put the member in office. Commonality members were elected with biracial coalitions, while difference members appealed primarily to African American voters.[17] The electoral coalition had an impact on the members' behavior: "difference" members were somewhat more likely than "commonality" members to spend more time on legislation with racial content, make speeches on the floor that made references to racial politics, and have high levels of support on roll call votes supported by the CBC. However, these relatively small differences among CBC members are dwarfed by the gap between white and black members' focus on racial issues. Blacks were disproportionately represented on committees that addressed black interests, their speeches touched on racial issues more frequently than whites, and a far greater proportion of the bills they sponsored and cosponsored had racial content. For example, 42 percent of the bills sponsored by CBC members had some racial content, compared with only 5 percent of bills sponsored by white members of Congress who represented significant African American populations.

This is strong evidence against the "no racial difference" hypothesis. While white members certainly *can* represent black interests, as Carol Swain, a political scientist at Vanderbilt University, has shown, on average, the white members in the 103rd Congress who represented districts that were at least 25 percent black did not show much interest in racial issues. This evidence supports the argument made by Bernard Grofman, Lisa Handley, and Richard Niemi in their book on minority representation: "Although we recognize that white liberal legislators may vote similarly to their black counterparts on roll call votes, this does not mean that they have the same commitment to a leadership role on civil rights or on economic issues of concern to the black community."[18]

The Collapse of Power: The Court Responds

The peak of power for the CBC and CHC was to be fleeting. The first session of Congress with the new contingent of minority members was barely underway when the rug was pulled out. In a series of decisions starting with the 1993 landmark case *Shaw v. Reno,* the Supreme Court's adherence to a color-blind jurisprudence threw the constitutionality of minority districting into doubt. These court cases were brought by white voters and supported by various conservative interest groups to challenge the majority-minority districts that were created in 1992. In her majority opinion, Justice Sandra Day O'Connor had some strong words for minority districts, comparing them to "political apartheid" and saying that classification based on race had to meet the "strict scrutiny" standard, meaning that it would be allowed only if it served a "compelling state interest." The Court agreed with the white plaintiffs' claim that their Fourteenth Amendment guarantee of equal protection of the laws had been violated by their being placed in a black-majority district. Therefore, unless the state could come up with a "compelling interest" that was served by the minority districts, such districts would be unconstitutional.

Shaw v. Reno created a controversial new version of "standing"—the legal term for the requirements for having the right to sue. The accepted version of standing before *Shaw* required that the plaintiff show some actual harm that he or she suffered because of the object of the lawsuit. But the white plaintiffs in *Shaw* were not required to prove that they were actually harmed by the black-majority districts. Instead the Court accepted their claims of a "generalized stigmatic harm." If the Court had required the white plaintiffs to demonstrate any actual harm, they would have been hard-pressed to come up with the evidence. CBC members elected in the new black-majority districts were more likely to practice a politics of commonality than a politics of difference.[19] Thus Justice O'Connor's assertion, "When a district obviously is created solely to effectuate the perceived common interests of one racial group, elected officials are more likely to believe that their primary obligation is to represent only the members of that group, rather than their constituency as a whole," was simply not supported by the evidence.[20] Commonality members of the CBC clearly do not fit this mold, and even the difference members who may have *campaigned* by appealing to black voters spend a majority of their time in Congress on issues that have nothing to do with race (though, as noted above, they spent more time on racial issues than commonality members and much more than white members).

In general, *Shaw* was a muddled mess that raised important questions but provided no answers. While the case questioned the constitutionality of black-majority districts, it gave no guidance to state legislatures in terms of how race *could* be considered. *Shaw* was also critical of the arbitrary shapes of the gerrymandered districts, saying that "appearance matters," but gave no indication of how it matters. Also, it appeared that four justices wanted to go even further than the majority opinion (written by the swing voter, Sandra Day O'Connor), and challenge key parts of the VRA itself. Subsequent cases clarified some of these issues, holding that race could not be the "predominant factor" in drawing district lines.[21] While the existence of minority districts was threatened at the close of the twentieth century, the VRA itself appeared to be in no danger. In 2000 there were at least five votes on the Court to uphold the VRA, and Sandra Day O'Connor had made it clear in *Bush v. Vera* (1996) that black-majority districts are legal as long as they are "done right."[22] However, through the 1990s, none of the states whose districts were challenged were able to convince the Court that they had done it right: black-majority districts were struck down in North Carolina, Georgia, Louisiana, Virginia, Texas, and Florida.

As the next round of redistricting began, it appeared that states were going to be sued no matter what they did. There were citizens who wanted to sue the state if it considered race *too much* (if race became the "predominant factor"), thus violating the Fourteenth Amendment protections for white voters, and others who would sue if the state did not consider race *enough* (under Section 2 of the VRA, which was still in force).

The last case of the 1990s round of redistricting, *Easley v. Cromartie*, which actually was not heard until the next round of redistricting had almost started, sorted out some of these ambiguities.[23] For the first time in the *Shaw* line of cases, Justice O'Connor voted with the liberals and upheld an African American influence district. At issue was an incarnation of the infamous "I-85 district," (Figure 3) the target of *Shaw v. Reno* (the North Carolina Twelfth). The district got its name because as it wound its way from Durham to Charlotte, at times it was no wider than the width of Interstate 85. This was the fourth time that the district was before the Supreme Court. This version of the district had been pared back to 47 percent black voting-age population, but the federal district court still found that race was the predominant factor in the creation of the district. The Supreme Court disagreed, saying that the lower court decision was "clearly erroneous" because it had not proven that race rather than partisan motivations was dominant. The majority opinion pointed out that "racial identification correlated highly with political affiliation" and that the state legislature was attempting to create districts that protected incumbents and were reliably Democratic.[24] Given that about 95 percent of African Americans in North Carolina register in the Democratic Party and about 97 percent vote Democratic, a district that may *appear* to have been created for racial reasons

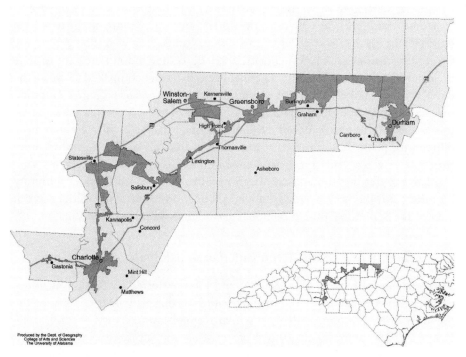

SOURCE: University of Alabama, http://alabamamaps.ua.edu/politics/states/ncdistrict12.jpg.

Figure 3   North Carolina Twelfth U.S. Congressional District, 1992

could have been drawn for partisan reasons. The Court said, "Those attacking the district have the demanding burden of proof to show that a facially neutral law is unexplainable on ground other than race."[25] That burden was not met.

Easley v. Cromartie does not provide definitive guidance on how to balance the Voting Rights Act's requirement to provide minority voters an equal opportunity to elect candidates of their choice and the *Shaw* line of cases' prohibition against race as the predominant factor in creating districts. However, if map drawers respect traditional districting principles and balance partisan and racial motivations so they are clearly complementary or even indistinguishable from one another, African American districts are likely to pass constitutional muster. Given the lack of "bright line" distinctions, congressional and state legislative districts will be decided on a case-by-case basis and litigation in this field is not likely to dissipate any time soon. Indeed, thirty-six states have already had to deal with more than one hundred redistricting cases in state and federal court since 2001 and many of these involved race.

Despite a flurry of litigation following the post–2000 Census round of redistricting, no white plaintiffs have been able to prove that race was the predominant factor in creating a district and few minority voters have been able to prove that their voting rights were violated. Thus, the legal disputes surrounding racial redistricting are starting to reach some type of uneasy equilibrium. Why? One reason is that the state legislators who draw the district lines are adapting to the new legal standards. In the 1990s, state legislators did not think they were doing anything wrong by creating the black-majority districts, so they did not attempt to hide their motivations. Indeed, many states believed they were compelled to create the districts based on the 1982 VRA amendments and *Thornburg v. Gingles.* But then the rules of the game changed with the *Shaw* line of cases. Now that state legislators are aware that race cannot be the predominant factor it will be much more difficult for plaintiffs to prove that a district "is unexplainable on ground other than race." Even a "smoking gun" e-mail in the *Cromartie* case, in which a state legislative staffer mentioned that he "moved the Greensboro Black community into the 12th, and now need[ed] to take about 60,000 out of the 12th" was not seen by the Supreme Court as compelling evidence that race predominated.[26]

Minority and Ethnic Representation in a Republican Congress

The "collapse of power" for the CBC and CHC referred to above was not as much a consequence of the Court's decisions on minority districting as of the Republican Revolution of 1994, in which Republicans regained control of the House and Senate for the first time in forty years, and cut minorities and liberals out of the agenda-setting and decision-making process. Some have argued that minority districting itself may have caused the collapse in power by helping Republicans win seats from white Democrats who had been weakened by losing

African American and Latino voters to the new districts. While the exact number is in dispute, it is clear that the massive defeat of wounded white Democratic incumbents did not materialize in 1992 as only a few were defeated due to racial redistricting.[27] The larger impact of black-majority districts on white Democrats may have been greater in 1994, but it is difficult to separate the effect of having new constituents from the influence of the general Republican landslide.[28] The estimates of Democratic losses caused by racial redistricting in 1994 vary, from the National Association for the Advancement of Colored People's estimate of one seat, to David Lublin's estimate of between seven and eleven seats, to Carol Swain's estimate of twelve seats.[29] In any event, it seems clear that white incumbents have not been as harmed as Democratic partisans feared, nor as much as Republican partisans hoped.

Furthermore, the anticipated Democratic payoff from dismantling some of the black districts did not materialize in 1996. In Georgia, where the shift of black voters to white-majority districts was most dramatic, all Republican incumbents survived. The longer-term impact of dismantling minority-majority districts may be to reduce the number of minorities in the House: when CBC and CHC incumbents in these districts retire and seats become open, minority candidates may not be able to win in districts that are no longer minority-majority.

Whatever the causes of the shift in control of the House to the Republicans, the consequences for minority representation were very clear. One immediate impact of being in the minority party was that CBC members had to relinquish three committee chairs and fifteen subcommittee chairs along with the rest of the Democrats. The Republicans abolished three committees (Post Office and Civil Service Committee, the District of Columbia, and Merchant Marine) as part of the reorganization of the House. The former two were especially important for the CBC: Post Office and Civil Service because it was viewed as an important constituency committee and the D.C. Committee because of the large African American population of the District and continuing issues concerning "home rule" and possible statehood. Missouri Democrat William Clay, a member of the CBC, had been the chair of the Post Office Committee. The other immediate change, which was widely perceived as an attempt by the Republican leadership to remove rival power bases, was the elimination of congressional funding for congressional legislative service organizations such as the CBC and CHC.[30]

The central long-range impact of Republican control of Congress is on the issues that make it onto the political agenda, the modification of bills in committee and on the floor, and the content of the bills that are enacted into law. In each instance, minorities in Congress were better off under Democratic control than under Republican control.

It became even more difficult for the CBC and CHC to have a voice in Congress after George Bush won the presidency in 2000. President Bush's policy agenda was generally not favored by minorities, despite the campaign rhetoric of Bush being a "compassionate conservative." Also, while President Bill Clinton was able to help move legislation in the direction favored by minorities in Congress (as with the welfare reform bill, which Clinton ended up signing only after getting some concessions from Republican leaders), Bush and congressional Republicans showed little inclination to work with Democrats, especially the more liberal wing of the party represented by the CBC and CHC.

Despite this general inclination, there is a range of issues upon which Republicans in Congress and President Bush attempt to appeal to minority voters. Some of these issues have popular support among minorities despite opposition from minority leaders (school vouchers, being "tough on crime," the faith-based initiative); other issues emphasized by Republicans have strong support among the minority mass public and leadership (increasing home ownership among the poor, more foreign aid for Africa, and eliminating racial profiling). However, much of this effort to expand the base of the Republican Party got lost in the focus on the war on terrorism, the war in Iraq, and tax cuts.[31] For example, no direct policy action has been taken to follow up on President Bush's strong stand against racial profiling or in support of more foreign aid for Africa.

One other issue that Republicans in Congress and President Bush pursued to some political advantage among minorities, especially African Americans, is their position against gay marriage. CBC leaders were upset when John Kerry, the 2004 Democratic candidate for president, compared the fight for gay marriage with the civil rights movement of the 1950s and 1960s. In a town hall meeting in Jackson, Mississippi, Kerry was asked if it was appropriate for leaders of the gay-marriage movement to make references to the leaders of the civil rights movement, such as Rosa Parks and Martin Luther King Jr.[32] Kerry, who opposes gay marriage and favors "civil unions" for gay couples, said that he saw similarities between the movements. This did not go over well with some members of the CBC. Arthur Davis, an Alabama Democrat, asserted, "The civil rights movement was more of a movement for the equal rights of all Americans: education, voting rights, jobs. Whereas gay rights in terms of gay marriage is a movement for a special group of Americans. So I would not compare civil rights with gay rights." Representative Albert Wynn, a Maryland Democrat, pointed out that many African Americans are quite conservative on the issue of gay marriage, in fact they are less supportive of the idea than whites. While it is difficult to know how much these issues played in minority voters' decisions in 2004, President Bush did substantially better among Latino voters in 2004 (44 percent) than in 2000 (35 percent); however, Bush made little headway with African American voters, winning only 11 percent of their votes in 2004 compared with 9 percent in 2000.

Future analysis will uncover how patterns of racial voting may have changed in congressional elections in 2004. What is clear is that Bush's success in attracting Latino voters has contributed to a new dynamic in congressional politics on issues that are important to Latinos. In the past, Republicans have supported strong immigration laws and promoted English as the official language of the United States and have not been as supportive of English-as-a-second-language programs as Democrats. However, in an effort to expand the base of the Republican Party, President Bush favors more liberal "guest worker" policies for resident aliens, which has put congressional Republicans in a bind. While some, such as Judiciary Committee chair James Sensenbrenner, Republican from Wisconsin, continue to push for tough immigration laws, other Republicans voice support for the "big tent" strategy.

For the most part, the CBC and CHC will continue to be shut out of the major policy debates as long as they remain the minority party in Congress. Therefore, they will play their role as the "conscience of the House." They have had some success in this regard, for example helping to force the resignation of Senate Majority Leader Trent Lott in December 2002. When Lott made favorable references to Strom Thurmond's 1948 segregationist campaign for president as a "Dixiecrat," CBC leaders kept the heat on until President Bush finally made it clear that he believed that Lott had become a liability to the party. The CBC has continued to speak out on a range of foreign policy issues such as civil wars and instability in Haiti, Liberia, and Sudan and domestic issues such as taxes, health care, and education in addition to the more traditional civil rights issues.

The Future of Racial Redistricting: Assessing Substantive Representation

What does the future hold for racial and ethnic representation in Congress? While an equilibrium has been reached in the racial gerrymandering and voting-rights cases, there is a new area of litigation concerning the effort in several states in the 2002 round of redistricting to eliminate some minority-majority districts and create more minority-influence districts in their place (for example, taking two 60 percent black-voting-age-population districts and turning them into three 40 percent districts).

This approach to redistricting raises an interesting set of questions that reside at the intersection of partisan and racial politics. In an odd reversal of their normal positions, the Republicans have defended the majority-minority districts and portrayed themselves as champions of minority representation while the Democrats have tried to dismantle the districts. The key decision in this emerging area of law is *Georgia v. Ashcroft* (2003).[33] In that case, the state of Georgia was being sued by the Justice Department under Section 5 of the VRA on the grounds that black voters in the state had suffered "retrogression" (that is, the position of black voters was worse off after redistricting than before) when the state's redistricting plan reduced the number of state senate districts with a majority-black voting-age population from eleven to eight, while increasing the number of black-influence districts (those between 30 percent and 50 percent black-voting-age population) by five.[34] The Republican Justice Department wanted to preserve the black-majority districts while the Democrats in Georgia wanted to create more black-influence districts. While motivations are always difficult to determine, it is clear that both parties in the case were influenced, at least in part, by partisan calculations. Republicans figured that they would be better off with the black-majority districts because Democratic voters would be more concentrated and they would have a better chance of winning the surrounding districts. Democrats, conversely, believed that they would be better off with the black-influence districts, in which Democratic voters would be spread more evenly across a larger number of districts.

The Supreme Court's 5–4 decision divided the Court along typical ideological lines, with Chief Justice William Rehnquist joined by the conservative jurists Clarence Thomas, Antonin Scalia, Anthony Kennedy, and O'Connor against their liberal counterparts, Justices David Souter, John Paul Stevens, Ruth Bader Ginsburg, and Stephen Breyer. What was not typical in this case was that the conservative five had voted with the State of Georgia and the Democratic Party's position, and the liberal four had voted with the Justice Department and the Republican Party's position. It was a rare instance in which a highly ideological and partisan court (the Court of *Bush v. Gore*) was not swayed by partisan forces. This reversal of partisan allegiances shows the central place that differing conceptions of racial representation have had on the Court: indeed, on this issue race trumps party.

The evolution of law in this area will have an important impact on racial representation in the U.S. Congress over the next generation. Given the importance of the case, and the explicit trade-off between descriptive and substantive representation that the Court is allowing (and indeed even encouraging), it is essential to examine the case in more detail and explore the tricky issue of how the overall representation of minority interests can be measured.

Unlike *Shaw v. Reno*, the Court in *Ashcroft* explicitly requires a detailed examination of substantive representation of minority interests (recall that in the *Shaw* case the Court did not require white plaintiffs to demonstrate any actual harm and simply accepted their claim that their equal protection rights had been violated by being in a black-majority district). The majority opinion in *Georgia v. Ashcroft* notes, "While we have never determined the meaning of 'effective exercise of the electoral franchise,' this case requires us to do so in some detail."[35] Specifically, to demonstrate that a plan is nonretrogressive, the state must show that any loss of descriptive representation that comes from "unpacking" safe black-majority districts must be offset by gains in substantive representation that come from the creation of a greater number of influence and coalitional districts.[36] ("Safe" districts are those in which the incumbent won with at least 60 percent of the vote in the previous election.)

While the Court did not provide detailed guidance on how to assess the trade-off between descriptive and substantive representation, it asserts that states are permitted a choice in maintaining this balance as long as the "overall level of representation" of black voters was not diminished under the plan in question. According to the majority opinion, "Indeed, the States' choice ultimately may rest on a political choice of whether substantive or descriptive representation is preferable. The State may choose, consistent with §5, that it is better to risk having fewer minority representatives in order to achieve greater overall representation of a minority group by increasing the number of representatives sympathetic to the interests of minority voters."[37] In other words, the Court is saying that a state may decide, for example, that black voters will be better off with four sympathetic white Democrats and one African American representative than with three African American representatives.

Consistent with a pragmatic, balancing approach to representation, Justice O'Connor asserted that the analysis of the overall level of representation of black voters should be supplemented by examining representation that is rooted in legislative leadership. While she does not state it quite in these terms, it seems clear that she wants lower courts to consider a broad range of measures of legislative behavior, rather than relying on the standard roll call analyses of legislative behavior. Perhaps reflecting her own experience as a state legislator, Justice O'Connor's discussion of the importance of leadership positions reads like a textbook passage on the legislative process: "A lawmaker with more legislative influence has more potential to set the agenda, to participate in closed-door meetings, to negotiate from a stronger position, and to shake hands on a deal. Maintaining or increasing legislative positions of power for minority voters' representatives of choice, while not dispositive by itself, can show the lack of retrogressive effect under §5."[38] Of course, it would logically follow that if a plan led to a decrease in legislative positions of power for minority voters' representatives of choice, this would be more evidence of a retrogressive effect.

While the general principles of this new analysis for retrogression are clear, the specific application of the principles remains to be worked out. Justice Souter's dissent in *Georgia v. Ashcroft* lays out the challenges posed by this broadened analysis and is worth quoting at length:

Indeed, to see the trouble ahead, one need only ask how on the Court's new understanding, state legislators or federal preclearance reviewers under §5 are supposed to identify or measure the degree of influence necessary to avoid the retrogression the Court nominally retains as the §5 touchstone. Is the test purely *ad hominem,* looking merely to the apparent sentiments of incumbents who might run in the new districts? Would it be enough for a State to show that an incumbent had previously promised to consider minority interests before voting on legislative measures? Whatever one looks to, however, how does one put a value on influence that falls short of decisive influence through coalition? Nondecisive influence is worth less than majority-minority control, but how much less? Would two [minority] influence districts offset the loss of one majority-minority district? Would it take three? Or four? The Court gives no guidance for measuring influence that falls short of the voting strength of a coalition member, let alone a majority of minority voters. Nor do I see how the Court could possibly give any such guidance. The Court's "influence" is simply not functional in the political and judicial worlds.[39]

Souter raises two central points: (1) It is difficult to measure substantive representation, and (2) even if substantive representation can be measured for a specific member, figuring out the trade-off between influence districts and safe minority-majority districts is virtually impossible. While some of the concerns surrounding the first point have merit, there is a large political science literature on the representation of voters' interests in legislatures that can assist in answering Justice Souter's questions.[40] Substantive representation requires that legislators are aware of the preferences of their constituents and take concrete legislative action to address those concerns. Political scientists have studied a broad range of actions that legislators take on behalf of their constituents. David Mayhew examined the "electoral connection" that drives the behavior of members of Congress. In their effort to stay in office, representatives will appeal to their constituents through "advertising, credit claiming, and position taking."[41] Morris Fiorina pointed to the importance of constituency service, especially dealing with bureaucratic red tape, as another dimension of representation.[42] Richard Fenno discussed the range of "home styles" that legislators will cultivate to represent their constituents in a variety of ways.[43] Richard Hall analyzed participation on committees and on the floor to gauge what members of Congress do to represent their constituents' interests beyond simple roll call voting.[44] The Canon study on race and representation in Congress referred to above examined bill sponsorship and cosponsorship, speeches on the floor, roll call voting, committee assignments, leadership positions, and a range of activities in the district to determine how legislators represent racial interests. Claudine Gay has shown that more African Americans participate in the political process when they are represented by blacks in Congress.[45]

The second point raised in the dissent, concerning the trade-off between more minority influence districts and fewer safe majority-minority districts, is not as easy to address. While the representation literature provides the basis for developing quantifiable estimates of the representation of minority voters' interests in influence districts and majority-minority districts, the federal courts, probably with the assistance of political scientists who are experts on the topic, will have to determine how many influence districts are necessary to balance the loss of a majority–minority district.

The difficulty in this latter task comes from the representational benefits that flow from descriptive representation, which are difficult to measure. These benefits are widely accepted by those who study this topic, but difficult to precisely measure. To apply this problem to the analytical task presented in the new retrogression test, consider the following: If an analysis of the more easily measured aspects of substantive representation (such as supporting minority interests on roll call votes) shows that two white Democrats in influence districts provide the same level of substantive representation as one African American legislator in a safe black-majority district, one could conclude that trading one safe district for two influence districts is nonretrogressive *only if* descriptive representation is seen as having no additional value (either from additional difficult-to-measure aspects of substantive representation or from the intrinsic value of representation itself). But nearly everyone who has examined this issue agrees that descriptive representation has some intrinsic value and some tangible but difficult-to-measure aspects. Even a strong critic of black-majority districts, Abigail Thernstrom, argues,

> Whether on a city council, on a county commission, or in the state legislature, blacks inhibit the expression of prejudice, act as spokesmen for black interests, dispense patronage, and often facilitate the discussion of topics (such as black crime) that whites are reluctant to raise. That is, governing bodies function differently when they are racially mixed, particularly where blacks are new to politics and where racially insensitive language and discrimination in the provision of services are long-established political habits.[46]

The problem is how to define the extent of these additional benefits. The benefits of descriptive representation mentioned here by Thernstrom clearly have substantive impact: changing the terms of debate, bringing up issues that would otherwise not be discussed, forcing others in the room to be more inclusive and tolerant, are real, tangible effects but they are very difficult to assess with the typical measures of legislative behavior. Thus the value of descriptive representation can be broken into three parts: the purely symbolic benefits (having positive role models), substantive benefits that are difficult to measure such as those mentioned above, and substantive benefits that can be readily measured (such as roll call votes, leadership positions, sponsored and cosponsored legislation).

Unfortunately, empirical analysis of benefits that are difficult to measure is obviously problematic, and symbolic value is primarily a normative judgment. However, the new analysis of racial representation required by the courts should ideally include these dimensions of descriptive representation or the courts may too easily conclude that it is acceptable to dismantle black-majority districts.

Instead, the best that can probably be hoped for is analysis that will focus on a broad range of the more easily measured aspects of racial representation. This will allow the courts to establish a minimum number of influence districts required to offset the loss of substantive and descriptive representation in safe districts. If for example, the analysis shows that three influence districts are required to produce the same overall level of substantive representation as one safe district, a plan that did not create at least three new influence districts for each safe district would be retrogressive. However, even if the state produced three influence districts per safe district that was lost, the plan still could be retrogressive given the other aspects of descriptive representation that cannot be measured.

One final consideration in determining whether a given redistricting plan is retrogressive is the views of the African American legislators themselves. The Court pointed out that they should have a good assessment of the costs and benefits of reducing the percentage of black voters in their districts. Indeed, in the *Ashcroft* case, all but one of the African American state legislators favored the creation of influence districts. Given the natural bias toward career preservation, this could be seen as evidence that the overall district plan was not retrogressive. The support of African American legislators for influence districts was a reversal from the general pattern in the 1990s round of redistricting when Republicans and African American legislators worked together to create black-majority districts, often over the objections of white Democrats. In the most recent round of redistricting in 2002, African American legislators were concerned about losing majority control of the legislature and thus were willing to give up some of their loyal supporters to help more vulnerable white Democrats in surrounding districts. The same patterns were evident in the New Jersey state legislature, but not in Wisconsin, where African Americans in the Milwaukee area were concerned about reducing the percentage of black voters in their districts due to the highly polarized nature of racial bloc voting in their city.[47]

Conclusion

Balancing racial and party interests is no simple matter in either the electoral or institutional arenas. On the electoral side, advocates of minority interests would be well served to maximize the number of districts that provide a strong opportunity to elect minorities to Congress, unless party control of the institution hangs in the balance. If partisan control is in question, then minorities would be best served by attempting to maximize the number of Democratic seats, given the additional power that would come to the CBC and CHC with Democratic control of the House. The balance between partisan and racial interests on the institutional side also hinges, in part, on which party controls the majority of seats in the House. If the Democrats control the chamber, the CBC and CHC best serve by employing a politics-of-commonality approach that recognizes the importance of racial interests, but with a pragmatic focus of working within the party. When the Democrats are in the minority, the CBC and CHC are more likely to play a symbolic role of voicing various concerns that would otherwise go unheard. The delicate balance will continue to evolve throughout the first decade of the twenty-first century in electoral and institutional politics.

Another issue that will receive increased attention, in the political world and in academic research, is the nature and impact of multiracial coalitions, both in Congress and in the electorate. The Supreme Court did not address this in the *Ashcroft* case because the districts in question did not have a significant number of minority voters other than African Americans. But it is an open question in terms of how Latino voters should be figured into the new analysis concerning retrogression. In many instances Latino voters support African American candidates, but it is not always the case. Similarly in Congress, the CHC and CBC are very strong allies, but there are some issues upon which there are divisions. As the United States becomes an increasingly multicultural and multiracial society, the issues concerning racial and ethnic representation in Congress take on added complexity and importance.

Notes

1. *Shaw v. Reno,* 509 U.S. 630 (1993).
2. Robert Dahl, *A Preface to Democratic Theory* (Chicago: University of Chicago Press, 1956), 124–151. Pluralism refers to the dominant theory of American politics in the mid-twentieth century. It is rooted in desirability of competition between various interests. Of course, pluralist theorists have been guilty of equating parts of Madisonian theory with their own. Most important is the divergent starting point: Madison was concerned with controlling the effects of evil factions, while pluralists embraced factions as the essential embodiment of political action and expression of political interests.
3. For a review of research on this topic see Paula D. McClain and John A. Garcia, "Expanding Disciplinary Boundaries: Black, Latino, and Racial Minority Group Politics in Political Science," in *Political Science: The State of the Discipline II,* edited by Ada W. Finifter (Washington, D.C.: American Political Science Association, 1993), 247–279.
4. See Chapter 1 of Canon, *Race, Redistricting, and Representation,* for a summary of this literature and a presentation of data from the national level outlining the differences between black and whites on racial issues and issues in which race plays a role, and their similarities on nonracial issues. Latino opinion also differs from white opinion on a broad range of social and economic issues, but it is more diverse than African American public opinion.
5. Data for the 109th Congress compiled from www.house.gov and www.senate.gov. While the representation of women's interests is not discussed in this essay, if the House was descriptively representative in terms of gender there would be 222 women and 213 men in the House of Representatives rather than the actual num-

bers of 65 women and 370 men. However, this is a House record, and the number of women (14) serving in the Senate ties the all-time high. Several of the delegates to the House are also women and minorities: there are three women, one African American, one Latino, and two Pacific Islanders.

6. Anne Phillips, *The Politics of Presence* (New York: Clarendon Press/Oxford University Press, 1995), 6.

7. The author has embraced this balancing perspective in his work on this topic; see Canon, *Race, Redistricting, and Representation*.

8. V. O. Key Jr., *Southern Politics in State and Nation* (New York: Knopf, 1949), 538. For example, the Louisiana grandfather clause read, "No male person who was on January 1, 1867, or at any date prior thereto, entitled to vote under the Constitution of the United States, wherein he then resided, and no son or grandson of any such person not less than twenty-one years of age at the date of the adoption of this Constitution, . . . shall be denied the right to register and vote in this State by reason of his failure to possess the educational or property qualifications." Grandfather clauses, as they applied to voting, were ruled unconstitutional in 1915.

9. Chandler Davidson, "The Voting Rights Act: A Brief History," in *Controversies in Minority Voting: The Voting Rights Act in Perspective,* edited by Bernard Grofman and Chandler Davidson (Washington, D.C.: Brookings Institution, 1992), 21.

10. U.S. Department of Justice, http://www.usdoj.gov/crt/voting/sec_203/activ _203.htm.

11. *Allen v. State Board of Elections,* 393 U.S. 544 (1969). The quote is from *Voting Rights Act, Hearings before the Subcommittee on the Constitution of the Committee on the Judiciary,* No. J-97-92, U.S. Senate, Ninety-seventh Congress, 2nd session (Washington, D.C.: Government Printing Office, 1982), 1073.

12. *Voting Rights Act Extension, Report of the Subcommittee on the Constitution of the Committee on the Judiciary.* U.S. Senate report 97-417, Ninety-seventh Congress, 2nd session (Washington, D.C.: Government Printing Office, 1982), 6–9.

13. *City of Mobile v. Bolden,* 446 U.S. 55 (1980).

14. *Voting Rights Act Extension,* 95–101.

15. *Thornburg v. Gingles,* 478 U.S. 30 (1986).

16. The analysis referred to in this section is drawn from Canon, *Race, Redistricting, and Representation.* In this comprehensive study of racial representation in Congress, the author examined many aspects of behavior in the 103rd and 104th Congresses, including roll call voting and committee and leadership positions for every member of the House. For a subset of members who represented districts that had at least 25 percent African American population (and all members of the CBC), examined were all of the speeches these members made on the floor (3,722 speeches), and all the bills they sponsored (720) and cosponsored (14,560). Also examined were many aspects of the linkages to the constituency from members in districts with 25 percent African American population, including the racial composition of the members' staff, the location of their district offices, the content of their district newsletters, and the newspaper coverage they received in the district from the large-circulation papers and the smaller African American weekly papers.

17. See Chapter 3 of Canon, *Race, Redistricting, and Representation,* for a discussion of the "supply-side" theory of racial representation. This chapter explains in more detail the process for identifying the "commonality" and "difference" members.

18. Bernard Grofman, Lisa Handley, and Richard G. Niemi, *Minority Representation and the Quest for Voting Equality* (Cambridge, U.K., and New York: Cambridge University Press, 1992).

19. See Chapter 4 of Canon, *Race, Redistricting, and Representation.*

20. *Shaw v. Reno,* 2827.

21. *Miller v. Johnson,* 515 U.S. 900 (1995).

22. *Bush v. Vera,* 517 U.S. 952 (1996).

23. *Easley v. Cromartie,* 532 U.S. 234 (2001).

24. Ibid., 1453.

25. Ibid., 1454.

26. Ibid., 1464.

27. Bob Benenson puts the number at three in "GOP's Dreams of a Comeback via the New Map Dissolve," *Congressional Quarterly Weekly Report* 50 (November 7, 1992): 3580–3581; Kevin Hill gives four in "Does the Creation of Majority Black Districts Aid Republicans? An Analysis of the 1992 Congressional Elections in Eight Southern States," *Journal of Politics* 57 (1995): 384–401; Carol M. Swain gives five in "The Future of Black Representation," *American Prospect* (fall 1995): 78–83; and David Lublin argues "five or six" in *The Paradox of Representation,* 112.

28. Richard L. Engstrom makes this point in "Voting Rights Districts: Debunking the Myths," *Campaigns and Elections* (April 1995): 24–46; John R. Petrocik and Scott W. Desposato conclude that national tides had a greater impact on Democratic losses in 1994 than minority districting, in "The Partisan Consequences of Majority-Minority Redistricting in the House, 1992 and 1994," *Journal of Politics* 60 (1998): 613–633.

29. See "Report of the NAACP Legal Defense and Educational Fund: The Effect of Section 2 of the Voting Rights Act on the 1994 Congressional Elections," November 30, 1994, Lublin, *The Paradox of Representation,* 114 (and pp. 111–14 for a summary of this conflicting research), and Swain, "The Future of Black Representation," 78–83.

30. Susan Webb Hammond, *Congressional Caucuses in National Policy Making* (Baltimore: Johns Hopkins University Press, 1998).

31. See David T. Canon and Katherine Cramer Walsh, "George W. Bush and the Politics of Gender and Race," in *The George W. Bush Presidency: Appraisals and Prospects,* edited by Colin Campbell and Bert A. Rockman (Washington, D.C.: CQ Press, 2004), 265–297, for a discussion of how President Bush has tried to use these issues to appeal to minority voters.

32. Brian DeBose, "Black Caucus Resists Comparison of Gay 'Marriage' to Civil Rights," *Washington Times,* March 15, 2004, http://washingtontimes.com /national/200403151225033346r.htm.

33. *Georgia v. Ashcroft,* 539 U.S. ___ (2003). While the context for this discussion of retrogression is state legislatures, these same issues will certainly come up with respect to congressional redistricting, if not in a challenge to some current plan, certainly in the next round of redistricting.

34. Retrogression is a legal standard established by the Supreme Court in its interpretation of Section 5 of the VRA. The Court has held that a "covered jurisdiction has the burden of establishing that a proposed redistricting plan does not have the purpose or effect of worsening the position of minority voters when compared to that jurisdiction's 'benchmark' plan." *Reno v. Bossier Parish School Board,* 120 S. Ct. 866, 871-72 (2000). http://www.usdoj.gov/crt/voting/sec_5/fedregvoting.htm. If the jurisdiction does not meet this burden, then the plan will be seen as retrogressive and will not be approved by the Department of Justice or the D.C. District Court. Also see *Beer v. United States,* 524 U.S. 130, 141 (1976).

35. *Georgia v. Ashcroft,* 15 (page number from the slip opinion).

36. An influence district is one in which a minority candidate is not elected, but the candidate who wins is sympathetic to minority interests. A coalitional district is one in which minority candidates *may* win with a coalition of minority voters and white voters, but sometimes they will lose. One of the challenges of the *Ashcroft* line of cases is to provide concrete, operational definitions of these terms. The majority opinion tends to conflate coalitional and influence districts. While the two are conceptually distinct, the discussion here focuses on influence districts.

37. *Georgia v. Ashcroft,* 19 (page number from the slip opinion).

38. Ibid., 4 (page number from the slip opinion).

39. Ibid., Souter dissent, 5 (page number from the slip opinion).

40. Warren E. Miller and Donald E. Stokes, "Constituency Influence in Congress," *American Political Science Review* 57 (1963): 45–56; Christopher H. Achen, "Measuring Representation," *American Journal of Political Science* 22 (1975): 475–510; a review essay by Donald R. Matthews, "Legislative Recruitment and Legislative Careers," *Legislative Studies Quarterly* 9 (1984): 547–585, on this subject that was written twenty years ago and had twenty pages of references and research on the topic has proliferated since then. Several review essays that focus explicitly on racial representation include hundreds of references on the topic (see McClain and Garcia, "Expanding Disciplinary Boundaries"; David T. Canon, "Electoral Systems and the Representation of Minority Interests in Legislatures," *Legislative Studies Quarterly* 24, no. 3 (1999): 331–385; Seth C. McKee, "The Impact of Congressional Redistricting in the 1990s on Minority Representation, Party Competition, and Legislative Responsiveness," paper presented at the Southern Political Science Association Meeting, New Orleans, January 2004).

41. David R. Mayhew, *Congress: The Electoral Connection* (New Haven, Conn.: Yale University Press, 1974).

42. Morris P. Fiorina, *Congress: Keystone of the Washington Establishment,* 2nd ed. (New Haven, Conn.: Yale University Press, 1989). Fiorina also discusses the negative consequences of this behavior: the desire to provide constituency service (because it is a relatively costless way to win votes) means that legislators will tolerate or even encourage inefficiencies in the bureaucracy to provide more demand for their services.

43. Richard F. Fenno Jr., *Home Style: House Members in Their Districts* (Boston: Little, Brown, 1978), and Fenno, *Going Home.* The latter book, published in 2003, examines how several African American members of Congress represent their constituents in

their districts and in Washington, D.C., both through their "home styles" and a range of legislative activities.

44. Richard L. Hall, *Participation in Congress* (New Haven, Conn.: Yale University Press, 1996).

45. Claudine Gay, "The Effect of Black Congressional Representation on Political Participation," *American Political Science Review* 95 (2001): 589–602.

46. Thernstrom, *Whose Votes Count?*, 239.

47. The New Jersey case was *Page v. Bartels,* 248 F.3d 175, 198 (3d Cir. 2001) and the Wisconsin case was *Baumgart et al. v. Jensen et al.* (ED Wisc. 2002).

Bibliography

Canon, David T. *Race, Redistricting, and Representation: The Unintended Consequences of Black-Majority Districts.* Chicago: University of Chicago Press, 1999.

Clay, William L. *Just Permanent Interests: Black Americans in Congress, 1870–1991.* New York: Amistad Press, 1992.

Fenno, Richard F. *Going Home: Black Representatives and Their Constituents.* Chicago: University of Chicago Press, 2003.

Lublin, David *The Paradox of Representation: Racial Gerrymandering and Minority Interests in Congress.* Princeton, N.J.: Princeton University Press, 1997.

Swain, Carol M. *Black Faces, Black Interests: The Representation of African Americans in Congress.* Cambridge, Mass.: Harvard University Press, 1993.

Tate, Katherine. *Black Faces in the Mirror: African Americans and Their Representatives in the U.S. Congress.* Princeton, N.J.: Princeton University Press, 2003.

Thernstrom, Abigail. *Whose Votes Count?: Affirmative Action and Minority Voting Rights.* Cambridge, Mass.: Harvard University Press, 1987.

Whitby, Kenny J. *The Color of Representation: Congressional Behavior and Black Interests.* Ann Arbor: University of Michigan Press, 1997.

STRUCTURES AND PROCESSES

7

COMMITTEES AND POLICY
FORMULATION

David W. Rohde

FTER THE TERRORIST ATTACKS OF SEPTEMBER 11, 2001, the U.S. Congress was forced to confront the issue of domestic security. Although the House and the Senate addressed the issue differently, the basic approach was the same in both bodies: they utilized their committee systems. Since the adoption of the Constitution in 1787, the Congress has used committees as the basic organizational device for analyzing and articulating policy solutions to national problems. This essay will examine how the committee system developed, how it affects the performance of Congress, and how proposals for changing the committee system might affect Congress's effectiveness.

The most important feature of the committee system is that it is a *designed* institution. That is, the system did not come about by accident, but because of the deliberate decisions of members of Congress. The original committees were created to serve the perceived interests of the members and of the institution as a whole, and when changes occurred in the committee system they happened for similar reasons. This was often because members believed that previously existing arrangements had (perhaps unintended) consequences that frustrated the achievement of their goals within the legislature.

The Committee System: Development and Change since World War II

One of the most important aspects of the development of the committee system has been the ebb and flow of the relationship between the committees and the majority-party leadership. After the committee structure coalesced in the early 1800s,[1] the influence of the majority party over it increased until the revolt against Speaker Joseph G. Cannon in 1910, whereby a coalition of progressive Republicans and minority Democrats was able to change House rules, effectively stripping the Speaker, popularly known as "Czar Cannon," of much of the power he had wielded over the committee system. Thereafter, partly because committee leaders were selected by seniority without regard to party interests, the committees proliferated and became more independent and autonomous.

The time of disproportionate committee power and independence became known as the period of "committee government," and it was in full flower by the late 1940s. Concerns about the efficiency of Congress in the light of an overabundance of committees resulted in the Legislative Reorganization Act of 1946, which reduced committee numbers to fewer than twenty in each chamber and authorized each committee to hire professional and clerical staff, under the control of the committee chairman. This enhanced the capabilities of the committees and the power of the chairs. Committee chairs shaped committee agendas, appointed subcommittees, and decided whether hearings would be held and how bills would be handled. In the Senate, the power of chairmen was reinforced by an "interlocking directorate" of senior members who chaired one committee and served as members of a number of others.

These institutional arrangements were resented by liberal members, mostly Democrats, who believed that the structure was biased against their policy preferences. They thought that committees were dominated by a "conservative coalition" of Republicans and like-minded Democrats (mostly southerners). Because of the lack of two-party electoral competition in the conservative South at the time, southern Democrats were more likely to build up seniority than their northern colleagues, and thus were more likely to become committee and subcommittee chairmen. Then, because of the seniority norm, conservative chairs were free to work with Republicans without fear of losing their positions.

The first break in conservative dominance came in the wake of John F. Kennedy's election as president in 1960. In the House, the Rules Committee had been a roadblock for liberal legislation because of its size and membership. Made up of eight Democrats and four Republicans, two conservative southerners could join with the four GOP members and refuse to report a special rule for floor consideration of any bill that met with their opposition. (Almost all major bills that come to the House floor need a special rule that specifies the length and procedures for floor debate. If no rule is reported by the Rules Committee, the bill cannot be considered.) Fearing that the committee would obstruct the Kennedy administration's legislative program, Speaker Sam Rayburn of Texas led a successful fight (instigated by an organization of House liberals called the Democratic Study Group) to expand the committee by three members. With the addition of two Democrats loyal to the national party program, the ability of Rules to block legislation was reduced, although its independence was preserved.

The power of committees was also affected by provisions of the Legislative Reorganization Act of 1970, which made it possible to obtain roll call votes on amendments and set the stage for the use of electronic voting in the House (cutting the time for votes from about forty minutes to fifteen or fewer). These new procedures led to an explosion of amending activity on the House floor and reduced committee dominance over legislative outcomes.[2]

Despite these gains, the alliance between Republicans and conservative Democrats limited the ability of liberal Democrats to secure procedural reforms if they required a vote of the full House membership. To overcome this strategic disadvantage, in the early 1970s the Democratic Study Group spearheaded the fight for a series of reforms within the Democratic Caucus, where (because only Democrats could vote) liberals had a majority. The reforms relating to committees followed two main tracks.[3] The first sought to neutralize the independence of committee chairs by undermining the automatic nature of the seniority system. The Democratic Caucus adopted proposals that provided for a secret-ballot vote on nominees for chairmanships of standing committees at the beginning of every Congress. Many senior members regarded these new rules as an empty threat until the 1974 elections sent to Congress a large group of new liberal Democrats who supported challenges against a number of southern chairs, three of whom were removed and replaced by members who would be likely to support the policies favored by northern Democrats.

The second reform track struck directly at the power of committee chairs, who (on most committees) dominated the handling of legislation and staff. The main device was a set of procedures called the "Subcommittee Bill of Rights." This reform guaranteed that subcommittees would be allocated jurisdictions, and bills would be referred to the subcommittees under them. Subcommittee chairs were given the right to appoint their own staff, breaking the committee chair's monopoly. More importantly, committee members would bid for subcommittee chairs in order of seniority, ending appointment by full-committee chairs. Thus subcommittees, more likely to be headed by liberals, secured some independent control over legislation.

Finally, reforms strengthened Democratic Party leaders relative to committees. The Speaker was given the power to appoint and remove Democrats on the Rules Committee, including its chair. Also, the assignment of members to other committees was vested in a new Steering and Policy Committee, most of whose members were party leaders or responsible to them.

The Partisan Era and Committee Realignment Efforts, 1974–1994

The cumulative effect of House reforms up to 1974 was to shift the balance of power away from committee chairs to both rank-and-file members and to party leaders. The latter effect came gradually and was hard to discern early in the postreform period because the Democrats' intraparty divisions were still too strong to permit the leadership full advantage of the new balance of power. The balance continued to shift in favor of the leadership, culminating in the election of 1982, which brought a substantial number of new, more liberal Democrats to the House.

From 1982 on, the majority leadership was increasingly aggressive in the use of its new powers, especially employing the Speaker's control over the Rules Committee to structure the floor agenda in ways that fostered Democratic unity and reduced the Republicans' capacity to compete legislatively. These strategies included restricting the minority's ability to offer amendments to bills, and packaging party priorities that might be difficult to pass alone together with proposals that members strongly desired, forcing members to accept or reject the combination. The removal of the three southern conservative committee chairs in 1974, mentioned earlier, gave subsequent chairs strong incentives to be responsive to the collective will of the majority, and party leaders used other powers (such as influence over legislation and committee assignments) to encourage party support among members at large.

The discussion up to this point has focused on the House, because committees have historically been more central to the organization of that chamber as compared with the Senate. There are many reasons for this, but the most important involve sharp differences in the respective institutional environments. The substantial differences in the size of the two chambers forced the House to develop procedural controls on the length of debate and on amending activity to avoid gridlock over legislation, while the smaller Senate was able to take a more relaxed approach. As a result, the Senate developed the tradition of unlimited amending activity and substantial hurdles to shutting off debate. The latter fact created the weapon of the "filibuster," by which a group of members can use continuous debate to delay or completely block a vote on a proposal they oppose. To stop such debate normally takes sixty votes. Thus the House is a majoritarian institution with restricted access to legislating, while the Senate has more unrestricted access and vests blocking power in minorities.

Differences between the chambers will be discussed further below, but this contrast is sufficient to understand the divergent paths the House and Senate took regarding reforms in the 1970s and later. Because of the power that the Senate rules vested in minorities, it was not feasible for the majority leadership to be strengthened the way it was in the House. And because senators were freely able to propose changes to committee proposals on the floor, Senate committees and their chairmen did not have the kind of legislative dominance their House counterparts did, and thus there was no need to seek changes in institutional rules to undermine them. Senate leaders did receive some additional advantages during the reform era, but they were limited and were not mainly designed to deal with committee power.

There was one similarity in the reform paths of the House and the Senate; both tried to deal with restructuring committee organization and jurisdictions. Because the Senate had to handle essentially the same legislative jurisdiction as the House with less than a fourth as many members, senators served on many more committees and subcommittees. They acutely felt, therefore, the burdens of uneven committee workloads and overlapping jurisdictions. In 1977 the Senate passed a significant restructuring of committees by a nearly unanimous vote. Three standing committees and most of the chamber's special and select committees were abolished, and major jurisdictional changes occurred among the surviving committees. Because neither senators' reelection chances nor their ability to influence policy were as closely tied to the status quo of the committee structure, significant changes in that structure were feasible.

The story was quite different for the House. Reformers wanted to restructure the committee system in order to make committee workloads more even and to reduce the degree to which jurisdiction over particular issues was spread across multiple committees. They thought such changes would improve committees' capacity to make policy. Several major efforts were made to deal with the committee system, but the sum of their consequences fell far short of the Senate's revisions in a single effort. In 1974, a major attempt was made to rationalize committee jurisdictions and to equalize workloads, but a divided Democratic Caucus substituted a proposal that resulted in only minor adjustments in the committee system.[4]

The Congress did not return to a serious consideration of committee reform until 1992, when the chambers together created a bipartisan Joint Committee on the Organization of Congress.[5] Some reform-oriented members believed that the overlaps and conflicts in committee jurisdictions required a wholesale realignment such as the 1946 Reorganization Act. However, party leaders had no enthusiasm for the idea, and a coalition of House committee chairmen developed a collective strategy to resist changes that would undermine their committees' influence over policy. The House and Senate members of the joint committee went their separate ways, but in neither chamber did the reform package reach the floor for consideration. Reform would have to await the tidal wave of change in the wake of the 1994 elections.

Reform under Republican Rule

In November of 1994, Republican candidates won majorities in both houses of Congress for the first time in forty-two years. The new majorities of this "Republican Revolution" desired major changes in substantive government policy, and in the House they believed that this end also required major changes in how the chamber operated. The "Contract with America" (the platform on which GOP House candidates ran in 1994) had promised a set of congressional reforms, some of which related to the committee system. These pledges were kept at the opening of the 104th Congress. The House Republicans limited full committee and subcommittee chairs to six-year terms. They abolished three full committees and limited members to two committee and four subcommittee assignments. Full committee chairs were empowered to appoint their subcommittee chairs. Independent subcommittee staffs were abolished, total committee staffs were cut by about one-third, and proxy voting (whereby committee members could delegate their voting rights to committee chairs) was eliminated.

While these changes streamlined the committee system and recentralized some power in committee chairs, it was clear that the House Republicans' intent was not to enhance committee independence. To the contrary, other actions increased the influence of party leaders over committees. Most importantly, the GOP permitted (without any rules change) Speaker-presumptive Newt Gingrich of Georgia to name the chairmen of a number of important committees even though his choices were not the most senior Republicans on the committee. The automatic nature of the seniority norm was terminated, and the newly empowered committee chairs would have strong incentives to be responsive to the party leadership. Gingrich additionally proposed, and the party adopted, a new committee-assignment system that gave the Speaker much more influence over assignments. The Republicans also confirmed the Speaker's right to appoint the party's members of the Rules Committee, maintaining his control of floor procedures and the legislative agenda.

House Republicans were willing to strengthen their party leaders' powers relative to committees in order to enhance the chances of passing their legislative program. Members were not, however, willing to accept large-scale reform of the committee system and its jurisdictions. Representative David Dreier of California, who had been the Republican vice chair of the Joint Committee on the Organization of Congress in 1994, tried to persuade Gingrich to seek major jurisdictional revisions, and he was asked to prepare four progressively more ambitious plans for consideration. The most ambitious proposal, and the one Dreier favored, called for the abolition of five committees and major redistributions of jurisdictions. This plan encountered major resistance, especially from the incoming chairs of the committees that would be most affected and from interest groups. In the end Gingrich and the other leaders decided not to push for major reform, and adopted instead a version of Dreier's least-ambitious plan. This proposal called for the elimination of three committees (mainly those oriented toward Democratic interests), and allocated their responsibilities to other existing committees with relatively few other jurisdictional changes.

The 1994 Republican takeover in the Senate had little organizational impact on committees as compared with the House's efforts. No significant reform occurred at the outset, but a partisan fight in March 1995 over a constitutional amendment to require a balanced budget precipitated some changes. Mark

Hatfield of Oregon, the chairman of the Appropriations Committee, cast the deciding vote against the amendment despite overwhelming support among Republicans. As a consequence, Majority Leader Bob Dole authorized a task force to develop proposals that would make committee chairs more responsive to the GOP leadership. As a result of this effort, in July, Senate Republicans adopted six-year term limits for all committee chairs and agreed that committee members would vote by secret ballot to select committee leaders, followed by a secret vote in the full Senate Republican Conference. In addition, members were limited to one full or subcommittee chairmanship on all but one committee. These changes reduced the independence of committee chairs and, as with reforms undertaken by House Democrats in the 1970s, were accomplished by altering party rules, not the rules of the chamber.

Committees and Congressional Performance

As we have seen, Congress's committee system was established to accomplish certain ends for the membership: to gather information and to shape legislation for the committees' parent chambers. Committees served these interests well because they stretched the capacity of each chamber through division of labor (so only part of the membership had to work on each issue) and fostered the development of expertise (which would happen naturally if members focused disproportionate time and attention on the subjects of their committees' jurisdictions). Over time the members altered the committee structure to better serve that and other interests, including enhancing the members' reelection efforts and their partisan policy goals. These patterns reflect well the analysis of political scientist Richard Fenno, who argued that most members of Congress pursue one or more of three main goals: reelection, power within the institution, and good public policy.[6] Committees are one of the most important institutional structures through which members pursue their goals, a matter that will be returned to shortly.

One might wonder whether having many members with a variety of goals would undermine the capacity of committees to produce legislation that can be enacted into law. Indeed some acute observers of the Congress believe that the committee system faces severe challenges in its ability to perform its jobs. The journalist Richard Cohen, who writes about Congress for the magazine *National Journal,* has characterized the situation as the "Crackup of the Committees."[7] In Cohen's view, committee power has eroded to the point where it has largely collapsed. Among the many problems with committees that Cohen has pointed to are bills that come to the floor without committee consideration, "stage-managed" hearings on bills that members cannot rely on for information, party-driven legislation brought hastily to the floor without any effort at compromise to build support, and a lack of real deliberation in committee or on the floor.

Is the situation as bad as Cohen and other critics have suggested? To be sure, the way committees operate has changed in the wake of the historical changes in structure outlined earlier. However, many of the changes that have occurred are responses to shifts in the makeup of the Congress's membership and in the larger political context. The increase in partisanship in Congress
. since the 1980s has shaped the operations of committees related to many important bills, and has reshaped the relationship between the committees and party leaders. Many of the changes in committees reflect efforts to grapple with the new environment and to solve the problems that stem from it. In addition, some of the difficulties critics observe are the consequence of earlier efforts to remedy other negative aspects of the committee system. Moreover, the perceived problems do not apply universally to all committees or all kinds of legislation.

Committees and Variations in the Legislative Agenda

The following discussion will focus on the consequences of increased partisanship in the legislative process in recent decades and on the increased power of majority-party leadership relative to committees. It is important to recognize at the outset, however, that partisanship is not central to all legislation. Indeed, most bills the Congress considers are neither partisan nor controversial. This point is illustrated by evidence from a study of legislation in the House in three congresses: the 96th (1979–1980, before the reforms had full effect), the 100th (1987–1988, when the Democratic majority leadership was at its strongest), and the 104th (when Newt Gingrich first led the Republican majority). In the 96th Congress, only 31 percent of the bills that reached the House floor exhibited controversy either in committee or on the floor.[8] In the 100th Congress the corresponding percentage was 23 percent, and in the 104th Congress—generally recognized as one of the most partisan Congresses in the last half of the twentieth century—the proportion of controversial bills was only 32 percent.

If the Congress has become increasingly partisan since the 1980s, why does less than one-third of the legislative agenda exhibit even a small amount of controversy? It is because that agenda is diverse and multifaceted, and only a portion of it relates to matters that provoke disagreement between the parties or other groups of members. The parties care intensely about issues that relate to divisions between their respective groups of candidates or party activists. These include matters such as levels of taxation, the scope of federal government power, regulation of business, and social issues such as abortion and gay rights. When these kinds of issues arise, the majority party is likely to try to use its institutional advantages to shape outcomes to its benefit and partisan conflict is likely to erupt. Sometimes controversy will arise from sources other than party, such as regional or urban–rural conflicts.

Most legislation, however, does not relate to these sources of divergent preferences. Many bills involve the renewal and revision of existing programs with wide support in the country and the Congress, or the proposal of new policies with many perceived benefits. This type of bill offers members the opportunity to enhance the welfare of their constituents and, as the congressional scholar David Mayhew has suggested, to claim credit for that enhancement and thus improve their chances for reelection.[9] Since members do not run directly against one another, one member's ability to gain favor with his or her constituents does not prevent another from doing so as well, and thus all members can potentially benefit from the adoption of a piece of legislation. As a consequence, in the weeks leading up to the hard-fought congressional elections of 2002, with party control of both houses very much in doubt, the House overwhelmingly supported passage of bills dealing with overhaul of the nation's election procedures (357–48), Defense Department appropriations, including $71.5 billion for procurement (409–14), and programs dealing with rural and community health care (392–5). Meanwhile the Senate passed the election-overhaul bill (92–2), and the Defense appropriations bill (93–1). So not all legislation engenders controversy, and partisan conflict does not always permeate the working of the legislative process and impede the passage of important legislation.

Committees, Jurisdictions, and Members' Goals

It is clear that committees have important implications for members trying to achieve various ends through the legislative process. For members focusing on reelection, their committees offer a locus where they have the chance to pursue all three of the major activities that David Mayhew has argued are beneficial to their electoral fortunes: advertising, credit claiming, and position taking. Indeed, Mayhew contended that the desire of members to enhance their reelection chances is the principal reason the Congress is structured as it is.

First, committees offer the opportunity for members to advertise themselves (that is, to have themselves perceived in a positive light unrelated to issue positions). Committee activity such as hearings and bill drafting attracts attention when it relates to issues that interest the media. Committee members have the opportunity to demonstrate that they are involved with, and working hard on, matters that are important to their constituents and the country. Committee activity also gives members occasions to self-advertise by issuing press releases related to their work.

Second, members can use committee work for credit claiming, whereby they assert to constituents that they are responsible for producing some desired benefit for the constituency. Examples include government programs that closely relate to district interests (such as agriculture policy in a farm district) or new projects that will be constructed in a specific district (such as roads or federal buildings). Because it is substantially easier to include such provisions in a bill when it is being structured initially than to try to add them via amendments when the bill is on the floor, committee members have a distinct comparative advantage.

Finally, committee work offers the opportunity for position taking—members identifying with a particular side on an issue. Committees consider issues and make decisions, and those serving on the committees make strategic choices about when to take a visible position and when to remain in the background.

Committees are also important structures to those members who are interested in achieving policy goals, whether for their own sake or to satisfy electoral constituencies. Some members seek assignment to a committee because its jurisdiction relates to issues about which he or she has experience or expertise. For example, in the 1980s a Democrat who had taught and written about African politics became the chairman of the House Foreign Affairs Committee's subcommittee on Africa. In other instances members acquire expertise on a subject via long service on a committee. It is in the interests of the congressional membership collectively to foster the development of expertise among members, and to encourage committees to share that expertise with the parent chamber through its evaluations of and judgments on prospective pieces of legislation.[10]

In addition to this general interest in enhancing expertise, committees are important vehicles for members who want to enact specific policies. For example, when the Republicans won control of the House in 1994 for the first time in forty years, many GOP representatives strongly desired to reverse Democratic programs enacted in previous decades. It was important to party members and their leaders that committees with jurisdiction over these salient matters would be responsive to what the party wanted.

Finally, committees are important to those members who seek to exercise power within the institution. Committees have a substantial impact on legislative outcomes, and influence over those outcomes within committees is not evenly distributed. It is not the case that committee and subcommittee leaders can simply dictate what their panels will do, but it is true that even after the reforms of the 1970s committee leaders had many assets that gave them disproportionate influence. These included control over staff resources and significant influence over the panels' agendas. Thus power-oriented members would have a substantial interest in achieving—and protecting—leadership positions on committees.

From this analysis it is clear why committee jurisdictions should be so important to members, and why efforts to alter those jurisdictions should be so sensitive. Jurisdictions determine which committees can act on an issue and to which committee a particular bill will be referred.[11] Multiple committees have a potential interest in a single topic. For example, tobacco is a cash crop of interest to Agriculture Committee members, and the source of health problems on which other committees focus. As a consequence, some overlapping of jurisdictions is unavoidable. This is particularly true because the Congress separates the act of authorizing (declaring what government programs will exist) and appropriating (determining how much will be spent on each program). The latter task is centralized in the Appropriations Committees, while the former is divided among the rest. However, the degree of overlapping jurisdictions is a function of how the committee system evolves.

The political scientist David King has argued that one should think in terms of "statutory" jurisdictions (which are specified in the rules of the chamber) and "common law" jurisdictions (which reflect the actual practices of bill referrals). As new issues arise, the parliamentarians of the House and Senate make decisions about where bills relating to them should be referred, and those initial referrals tend to govern future ones. Then eventually these practices are codified in the formal statutory jurisdictions. In this context, committees compete with one another to assert primacy over (or at least a share of) new issues. With the rise of new issues, the system of jurisdictions gradually has become clearly delineated. King contends that formal jurisdictions are almost always mere codifications of this type of evolution.

Yet if the current state of committee jurisdictions and their evolution tend to serve the interests of individual members, there is no reason to believe that they will automatically serve the collective interests of Congress for policy making and oversight. Fragmentation of jurisdiction over an issue among many committees can make it difficult to address the issue comprehensively and coherently. Furthermore, fragmentation multiplies the number of points in the legislative process where proposals to change policy can be slowed or blocked. In addition, some analysts believe that the current arrangements undermine Congress's ability to conduct effective oversight. Regardless of these potential problems, however, members' interests make it difficult to alter existing arrangements to foster the institution's collective goals.

Homeland Security and Committee Jurisdictions

The interplay of members' interests related to committee jurisdictions is illustrated well by the Congress's organizational actions on homeland security after 9/11. To respond to the security concerns about protecting the country from further terrorist attacks, the Bush administration, somewhat reluctantly following congressional urging, proposed consolidating relevant programs in a single cabinet-level Department of Homeland Security (DHS). In the "lame duck" session after the 2002 elections, the president prevailed, the DHS was authorized, and the House and Senate had to decide how to alter the committee system to deal with the event.

The House had been dealing with the issue of homeland security via a temporary select committee established in 2002. It had been chaired by Majority

Leader Dick Armey and had only nine members, drawn mostly from the party leaderships. With the new department, the view was generally shared that this arrangement would no longer be adequate, but there was not agreement on the alternative. Before the new arrangement the White House had estimated that eighty-eight committees and subcommittees (comprising almost all the members of both chambers) had jurisdiction over some aspect of homeland security, and most of these programs had been consolidated in the department. Thus the interests of almost all the congressional membership would be potentially affected by any proposal. This was especially true of the leaders of the committees and subcommittees involved, who were consequently reluctant to support significant changes. Losing part of their jurisdictions to a new committee would reduce their influence and interfere with the ability of their committees' members to achieve any of the three goals of reelection, institutional power, and good public policy.

Speaker Dennis Hastert decided on a compromise arrangement by creating another temporary select committee that had oversight responsibility over the DHS (permitting it to call in department officials and inquire into how they were carrying out their responsibilities), but only shared authorization jurisdiction with other committees. The Republican side of the committee (all appointed by the Speaker) included eight chairs of other committees and other senior members who could continue to look out for their committees' interests. In the spring of 2004, the House began to address the future of the select committee. Many outside the chamber, including the 9/11 Commission (an independent, bipartisan body established by presidential directive to advise the Congress on circumstances surrounding 9/11) and former Speakers Newt Gingrich and Thomas Foley, argued for a permanent standing committee with legislative jurisdiction over the department. In particular, observers argued that the select committee had conducted only about one-third of the House's oversight hearings on homeland security, and that the difficulty of responding to so many entities with jurisdiction over it was impeding the performance of the department.

Not surprisingly, the leaders of other interested committees did not agree. In hearings before the Rules Committee on the fate of the select committee, virtually all the committee chairs who testified opposed the continuation of the committee, and they were even more adamant in opposing its being made a permanent standing committee. Nor was this a partisan matter, because most of the chairs were supported by their committees' ranking Democrats. They argued that the original committees had years of experience and expertise with the programs. For example, Don Young, chairman of Transportation and Infrastructure, contended that only his panel was qualified to oversee the U.S. Coast Guard and the Transportation Security Administration, both of which had been transferred to the new department. Energy and Commerce chair Joe Barton commented that "the select committee's work here is done," and that it "has become an impediment to further progress."[12] The final judgment on this conflict rested with Speaker Hastert (who supported a separate committee) and the Republican Conference at the beginning of the 109th Congress in 2005. The decision was to create a permanent committee, but to leave some of the relevant jurisdiction with the committees that had held it previously.

The response of the House Appropriations Committee to the creation of DHS was less contentious. For many decades the committee had been organized into thirteen subcommittees, with the government's spending divided among them. The committee's chair announced January 29, 2003, that the relevant parts of the jurisdictions of eight subcommittees would be transferred to a new Homeland Security Subcommittee, and that the two smallest remaining subcommittees would be merged, thus maintaining the committee's basic structure. This reorganization was less controversial because it did not interfere significantly with the interests of the members.

Initially in the Senate, there was almost no controversy about what to do, because committee structure has less effect on members' interests. Jurisdiction over homeland security legislation was simply given to one of the existing committees, Governmental Affairs. At the end of 2004, however, when proposals for transferring intelligence oversight from other committees to Governmental Affairs were considered, members' interests were strongly affected. Senior members from other committees largely dismembered the transfer plan, and the committee even ended up losing some authority over security-related budgets. With regard to Senate Appropriations, the committee simply followed the lead of the House committee on restructuring.

Committees in the Partisan Era

During the era of committee government, independent committees and the political priorities of their leaders dominated the legislative process. The institutional structure was intended to foster the reelection interests of individual members. The central features of this arrangement were the protection of the seniority system and of powerful committee chairs. However, because reelection was not the sole interest members had, the institutional structure was changed. This was partly due to an increasing proportion of the membership caring intensely about enacting particular policy preferences. As the policy views of members of each party became more homogeneous, those members increasingly saw their parties as appropriate and useful vehicles for advancing their policy goals. A sufficient number of members were willing to trade the protections of an inviolable seniority system in exchange for greater influence by the majority party over committees and their legislative products.

Another reason for members' willingness to strengthen their party's influence over committees was to enhance its ability to compete effectively in the struggle for majority control of the House and Senate. This has been particularly true since the Republicans' takeover of Congress in the 1990s. Ever since the election of 1994, control of both houses of Congress has been in doubt, and this matter has enormous potential impact on members' goals. Members of the majority have better opportunities than the minority to obtain media visibility and to bring home government projects and contracts—all things that foster a member's chances of reelection. In addition, members of the majority are more likely to see their policy views written into law. Finally, party and committee leaders in the majority have more personal power than their minority counterparts. Thus members have great incentive to strengthen their party's efforts to retain (or to achieve) majority status, and enabling the party to influence committees' activities when necessary is one way to do this.

As this discussion indicates, party influence has been enhanced in various ways over the years. The Democrats in the 1970s removed the absolute nature of the seniority norm and reduced the powers of committee chairs, while strengthening the influence of party leaders. Then the Republicans permitted Speaker Gingrich to assert the right to name some chairs, and they centralized staff resources under chairmen who could be controlled by the leadership. These shifts in the balance of power have continued in subsequent Congresses.

In 1995 the House GOP imposed six-year term limits on committee and subcommittee chairs, and these limits had their impact after the 2000 election. Many chairs sought to evade or abolish these limits, but the leadership pushed ahead and adopted a system under which the Republican Steering Committee (which was itself strongly influenced by party leaders) would interview members who wanted to be candidates for a chairmanship. After the interviews the committee would select a nominee for chair and submit the name to the full caucus of House Republicans for final approval. At the beginning of the Congresses in both 2001 and 2003 the Steering Committee bypassed a number of more-senior moderates in order to choose more-conservative, but more-junior, members for chairmanships. For example, Chris Shays of Connecticut (who had allied with the Democrats to pass campaign finance reform) was skipped over for the leadership of the Government Reform Committee in favor of Thomas Davis of Virginia, even though the latter had served on the committee only half as long. Thus, potential committee leaders were put on notice that their ambitions would depend in part on how supportive they were of party programs, which increased leadership influence.

The substantive effects of term limits on committee performance and legislative output (as opposed to the political interests of individual chairmen) are unclear. Policy expertise is not really lost to the committee (since the former chair remains on the panel), but the political experience regarding procedures and deal making are not transferred automatically to the new chairs.

In addition to altering selection processes for chairs, the majority-party leaders have used their enhanced powers to directly influence committee actions. During the years of Republican control (especially in the Congress after 1994), the leadership pressured the House Appropriations Committee to include important legislative changes desired by Republicans in appropriations bills because they thought the proposals would be easier to pass this way than standing on their own. Normally such efforts would violate House rules, but the Speaker was able to use his control of the Rules Committee to grant exceptions for these party priorities. This strategy was the main thing that led to the confrontations with the Clinton administration that resulted in the government shutdowns in 1995–1996. The House Republican leadership put a number of major policy changes in appropriations bills. When Clinton refused to go along with these changes and vetoed the bills, the government was left without authority to continue spending money for some programs. Eventually the Republicans gave up on many of their proposals, and government offices reopened.

Republican Party leaders also pressured chairs of legislative committees to resolve conflicts on particular bills in ways that benefited the party. In November of 2003, Speaker Hastert and Senate majority leader Bill Frist intervened in the conference committee negotiations on the Medicare reform bill with their own proposal for revisions to break the deadlock. (Conference committees are temporary panels made up of both representatives and senators selected to work out differences on a particular bill passed by both chambers.) Republican representative Bill Thomas, chairman of the Ways and Means Committee and of the conference committee, was angered by the interference with his independence and cancelled further negotiations, but by the next day—after pressure was exerted— he was back at it and eventually accepted terms very close to those proposed by the leaders. In another instance that same month, House leaders successfully pressured the chairman of the Armed Services Committee to compromise with the Senate on the Defense authorization bill by threatening to remove provisions he desired from the version under negotiations.

Another method for party leaders to influence the final content of legislation is through the conference committees. The majority party in each chamber gets a majority of members on the committee. These members are selected by the party leaders, and they can personally influence panels they deem important. For example, Senator Frist selected himself to serve on the Medicare conference, and Speaker Hastert chose then majority whip Tom DeLay to be a conferee in 2002 on a high-priority energy bill. Parties are also increasingly trying to manipulate conference committee participation to their advantage. For example, on the 2003 Medicare bill, Chairman Thomas refused to let any of the House Democrats who were appointed to the conference committee participate in its deliberations, and only two of the most conservative Democratic senators who were appointed were allowed in the room. On the energy bill the same year, no Democrats at all were permitted to participate. The congressional analyst Barbara Sinclair has aptly described these historically unusual strategies as "unorthodox lawmaking," and not surprisingly, they have provoked strong Democratic objections and exacerbated interparty tensions.[13]

Partisanship and Other Member Interests

The preceding discussion has indicated that members have significant incentives to strengthen party influence over committees, but one should not conclude that partisan interests always dominate. Members have other interests that are important to them that are served by committees. When partisan incentives conflict with members' reelection, policy, or power goals, sometimes the partisan aspect will take a backseat. For example, the House Republicans after the 1994 elections sought to downsize committees, partly to persuade the public of their intent to operate a "leaner" government than the Democrats and partly to exert more centralized control of committees. However, committees offer their members opportunities to secure projects and benefits for their constituencies, and one of the best for this is the Transportation and Infrastructure Committee, which, among other duties, authorizes federal highway projects. The opportunities for credit claiming offered by the committee led to great demand for membership among Republicans wanting to enhance their chances for reelection. Thus, even though the GOP leadership tried to hold the line generally on committee expansion, the Transportation Committee grew from sixty-one members in 1995 to seventy-three in 1997, and then to seventy-five in 1999. Reelection incentives trumped the ideological goals of the Republican Revolution.

Similarly, after 1994 the Republicans carried out the promise in the Contract with America to cut committee staff by one-third. This effort was also intended to demonstrate the GOP's intent to be frugal with public money. In addition it restricted committees' ability to be independent and entrepreneurial in policy making. Over the next few years GOP committee leaders found that the cuts had left them short of the resources they needed to process legislation and to conduct oversight of the executive branch. Therefore in 2001 the Republican leadership proposed an 11 percent increase in committee funding, nearly restoring support to the levels before the 1995 cuts. Here policy and power interests outweighed former ideological responses.

It is worth noting here that there has been some disagreement among congressional analysts about the impact of partisan control on the incidence of congressional oversight of the executive. David Mayhew has argued that from 1946 to 1990, there was no relationship between the occurrence of "high-publicity" investigations and whether Congress was controlled by the same party as the president.[14] Mayhew's evidence on unified party government, however, came largely from the period when the Democrats controlled Congress and were ideologically divided. Many observers and participants believe that since the GOP gained congressional majorities in 1994, and particularly under unified Republican control, oversight has become more lax. The 9/11 Commission, for example, contended that "congressional oversight for intelligence—and counterterrorism—is now dysfunctional."[15] Even the Republican chairman of the Finance Committee, Senator Charles Grassley of Iowa, has argued that the minority-party Democrats were better fulfilling their oversight obligations. And Republican Representative Davis of Virginia, chair of the House Government Reform Committee, said that the party that controls Congress and the White House "get[s] less oversight. . . . That's the way it goes."[16] There are, moreover, indications that even in some instances when GOP committee leaders were inclined to conduct investigations of the Bush administration, there was partisan resistance. For example, Senator John Warner of Virginia, chair of the Senate Armed Services Committee, was pressured by Republican colleagues to "tone down" his investigation of the abuse of Iraqi prisoners at Abu Ghraib, and Representative James Greenwood of Pennsylvania, chair of an Energy subcommittee, said that some members of the Republican leadership resisted his planned investigation of the collapse of the energy company Enron.[17] Thus intensified partisan divisions may have reduced the ability and inclination of committees to perform effective executive oversight.

Another example of competition between partisan and other interests was the resistance to major jurisdictional realignment for committees among Republicans after 1994, discussed earlier. David Dreier and other reformers wanted major changes, but the senior members who would be the new committee leaders didn't want their power bases disrupted. For example, the Dreier plan would have significantly reduced the scope of the jurisdiction of the powerful Energy and Commerce Committee. A staff aide to Thomas Bliley of Virginia, the incoming chair of the committee, commented: "Mr. Bliley has not spent 14 years toiling in the vineyards trying to uphold the Republican principle against the best the Democrats had to offer so that we could be robbed of the opportunity of enacting the Republican agenda."[18]

Representativeness of Committees

Given that committees are so important to the legislative process, and that they retain significant (albeit restricted) independence of action in their spheres, some observers have raised the question of whether they are representative of the memberships from which they are drawn. This is a complex matter about which analysts disagree, but the ultimate answer seems to be: sometimes yes and sometimes no. Because members use committees to achieve multiple (and sometimes competing) goals, and because the legislative arena includes many policy dimensions on which members can take positions, it is not probable for committee memberships to be representative of the chamber in all of these different aspects simultaneously.

To take one example, during 1995–1996 the House Republican leadership spearheaded an effort to significantly transform the nature of federal agriculture policy by reducing farmers' dependence on government subsidies. This matter included partisan and ideological interests as well as the narrow economic interests of particular congressional districts (and, by extension, the political interests of their representatives). When the bill (termed the "Freedom to Farm Act") came to the House floor, votes on setting basic government policy produced sharp partisan splits both among committee members and those not on the committee. Thus on the partisan dimension the committee was very representative of the chamber. Other votes, however, dealt with the amount of support for particular agricultural products, and generally involved efforts to cut back those programs. On those votes most committee members of both parties lined up overwhelmingly in opposition, while non–committee members supported many of the changes. So on parochial distributive matters the committee was unrepresentative of the chamber. Thus we can expect committees to be representative or unrepresentative depending on the issue they are considering.

There is another, and perhaps even more fundamental, aspect to the question of committee representativeness. Members of the House and Senate have many responsibilities and demands on their time, and these often compete with one another. Members must continually decide what activities to participate in and what issues to be active on.[19] Thus on a given committee, one member may choose to be very active in connection with Bill A but not on Bill B, while another committee member will make the reverse decision. Evidence indicates that the influence of members on policy outcomes is directly proportional to how much time and effort they devote to a bill. As a consequence, different subsets of a committee's membership will be influential on different bills, and it is extraordinarily unlikely that these various subsets would be equally representative of the committee much less the larger chamber membership. Therefore, unequal participation will lead to variations in a committee's representativeness in its legislative activities even if the makeup of the committee's membership did not. This is one of the many reasons why the matter of committee independence is so consequential with respect to the nature of policy outcomes in legislation.

Senate Distinctions

As noted above, because committees have been more central to the legislative process in the House than in the Senate, this discussion has been disproportionately centered on the House. Before concluding, however, it will be useful to focus briefly on the Senate and its differences. First, Senate committees must cover essentially the same legislative jurisdiction as the House with less than one-fourth as many members, so individual senators must carry a heavier committee load. In 2001, for example, each senator held an average of 3.3 standing committee and 8.9 subcommittee assignments, while the corresponding figures for representatives were 1.9 and 3.6 respectively.[20] On the other hand, almost every senator is the chair or ranking minority member of a committee or subcommittee while the same is true for only about half the House. Thus senators are spread more thinly (and are likely therefore to be less specialized and have less specific expertise), but they are more likely to have an institutional power base on which they can focus.

Another important difference is that Senate rules and traditions vest more power in individual and small groups of members than does the House. The most widely recognized manifestation of this is the ability of a minority to block legislation through a filibuster, but many other tools permit even a single senator to impede and delay the body. As a consequence, while in the House even a narrow partisan majority can ride roughshod over the minority if they stick together, in the Senate the majority must take at least some minority views into account if they want to accomplish things.

Finally, the House majority is able to use its Rules Committee to restrict what amendments can be considered, and regular House rules require that only amendments that deal with the same subject as the bill (termed "germane" amendments) may usually be introduced. In the Senate, on the other hand, amendments can only usually be restricted by unanimous consent of the members, and nongermane amendments are permitted on the floor. Thus it is far easier for senators who do not serve on a committee to influence the content of legislation within its jurisdiction, and it is much more difficult in the Senate to prevent an issue from being taken up and debated.

The consequence of these differences has been that in the Senate *both* parties and committees have been institutionally weaker than in the House, and individual members have been more consequential. Moreover, because the majority party usually had to negotiate with members of the minority, partisan conflict in the Senate tended to be less frequent and less intense. Relative to the past, however, party conflict has heightened in the Senate as well. Like the House, the Senate is closely divided and the parties are competing for majority control. That exacerbates partisan tension and conflict. Also, many senators serving at the turn of the twenty-first century had formerly been members of the House during and after the Gingrich speakership, and many observers think they have carried with them attitudes that reflect the bitterness of the partisan struggles of the larger chamber. As Republican Conference chairman Rick Santorum of Pennsylvania (himself a former representative) said in 2003: "The idea that somehow or other, irrespective of who's in the majority, that this is an egalitarian place

... it's just not the way this place operates. ... The majority means that you win."[21]

Another House-Senate contrast involves the different bases of representation, and this leads to differences in the policies that emerge from their committees. Since House seats are based on population and the Senate's on equal representation, the chambers tend to try to have the distribution of federal benefits depend on the same considerations. Because neither chamber can override the other, policies tend to involve a compromise between the two contrasting impulses. Again, homeland security issues provide a good illustration. The biggest grant in this area (about $2 billion per year) involves funds to equip and train "first responders." Part of the formula for allocating the money uses state equality and part uses population. Thus on a per capita basis the largest allotment is to Wyoming ($35.31 per person) and the smallest is to California ($4.68).[22]

Prospects for Reform

In light of the preceding discussion, we can now return to the concerns of critics such as Richard Cohen and try to assess the likelihood that the Congress will change its practices in ways that would be seen as an improvement. Certainly the prospect of large-scale jurisdictional reform in the House is virtually nil, because, as we have seen, it would disrupt too many members' reelection and power interests. Regardless of the benefits to policy making from achieving coherent jurisdictions, major reform of this type will occur only when (as in 1946) many representatives perceive that current arrangements are undermining the achievement of their goals. Since members' goals are generally well-served by the current committee structure, change is likely to be piecemeal at most.

Other frequently voiced concerns—such as lack of committee consideration of bills, party-driven legislation, and the bypassing of committees entirely—stem largely from the Congress's highly partisan environment and intense interparty competition. The constituency bases of the two parties are increasingly different, partly from realignment of voter sentiments and partly from deliberate partisan design of House districts. Members of each party's congressional delegation hold much more similar policy views than used to be the case, and interparty differences have sharply increased. Those members with the most intense policy commitments believe that their constituents sent them to Congress to enact their party's legislative program, and to prevent the other party from achieving theirs.

Moreover, as has been emphasized here, both parties see majority control of the chambers as constantly at stake. Each congressional party delegation has good reason to believe that, if they choose the right strategies to convince swing voters that the party's policies are the best and that the opposition's are undesirable, the "holy grail" of majority status can be won. Thus, more than used to be the case, every legislative choice by each party is viewed not only in the light of what is substantively desirable, but also with regard to how it may affect electoral fortunes.

Almost all of the concerns about the committee system are the consequence of this situation. When the majority party has a high legislative priority they believe would be beneficial to the country, and they think its potential success will be undermined by committee consideration, they will try to restrict committee action or bypass it. If the minority party believes that a piece of legislation would be damaging to the people it represents, it will try to impede or block the majority's actions. Pursuit of each party's strategy will often make the members of the other party angry if their goals are being frustrated. These are the circumstances that foster partisan conflict and the related personal animosities that observers see as so regrettable. And as long as the parties' constituencies remain so different, and as long as the congressional parties' policy views remain so internally homogeneous and so divergent between them, these circumstances will almost certainly continue to govern congressional activity. The problems with congressional committees perceived by Richard Cohen and others do not stem principally from the nature of the committee system, but from the dynamics of American electoral politics and the parties that structure them.

Regardless, however, of the reasons for which the problems with the committee system occur, the effects persist. Legislative issues that currently divide the parties are even more likely to cause problems for committees than when Cohen wrote in 1999. Committees may find it difficult to take up such controversial bills in the first place, and they are unlikely to be able to draw on the participation and expertise of members from the minority party because the majority will usually not be willing to share policymaking authority or credit. Moreover, it was more probable in 2005 than it was in 2000 that majority-party leaders would alter the decisions of committees after the fact, or to bypass them completely if this was deemed necessary to accomplish party goals. Furthermore, as discussed earlier, executive oversight has continued to atrophy. Thus the historical benefits of specialization and bipartisan expertise that flowed from the committee system are less likely to be found in the processing of high-saliency legislation than had been true before the partisan era.

This should not, however, be taken as a complete counsel of despair. It should be remembered that most of the legislation the committees deal with does not significantly involve party conflicts, and conference committees deal with that more routine part of the agenda quite capably. Moreover, there are benefits as well as problems that stem from the current partisan environment. The electorate is likely to be presented with contrasting ideas for governance by candidates of the two parties, giving voters a clearer choice on the issues. And since the majority party in each chamber has greater influence over committees than in the past, those committees are more likely to produce legislation that reflects the views of the majority party the voters selected. In any event, with its pros and cons, the committee system of the Congress will continue to have a substantial impact on the laws that govern the nation.

Notes

1. For a discussion of the early history of the committee system, see chapter 2 of this volume, "Institutional Development of Congress," by Eric Schickler.
2. A detailed analysis of the growth of amending activity on the floors of both chambers may be found in Steven S. Smith, *Call to Order: Floor Politics in the House and Senate* (Washington D.C.: Brookings Institution, 1989).
3. For details on the adoption and impact of the Democratic House reforms, see David W. Rohde, *Parties and Leaders in the Postreform House* (Chicago: University of Chicago Press, 1991).
4. One significant feature of the proposal was a provision authorizing the Speaker to refer bills to more than one committee (called "multiple referral").
5. An account of the activities of the joint committee, as well as of actions taken in the wake of the subsequent Republican takeover of control of Congress, can be found in C. Lawrence Evans and Walter J. Oleszek, *Congress under Fire: Reform Politics and the Republican Majority* (Boston: Houghton Mifflin, 1997).
6. Fenno, *Congressmen in Committees*, chapter 1.
7. *National Journal*, July 31, 1999, 2210–2217.
8. The data discussed here was taken from Jamie L. Carson, Charles J. Finocchiaro, and David W. Rohde, "Consensus and Conflict in House Decision Making: A Bill-Level Examination of Committee and Floor Behavior," paper presented at the 2001 Annual Meeting of the Midwest Political Science Association, Chicago, Illinois. A bill was classified as controversial if on even one roll call in committee or on the floor there was a minority vote of more than 10 percent.
9. David R. Mayhew, *Congress: The Electoral Connection* (New Haven, Conn.: Yale University Press, 1974).
10. This interest in developing and sharing expertise is the central focus in the "informational" theory of legislative organization presented by Krehbiel in *Information and Legislative Organization*.
11. This discussion of jurisdictions draws on King, *Turf Wars*; Adler, *Why Congressional Reforms Fail*; and Frank R. Baumgartner, Bryan D. Jones, and Michael C. MacLeod, "The Evolution of Legislative Jurisdictions," *Journal of Politics* 62 (May 2000): 321–349.
12. Quoted in *CQ Weekly*, March 27, 2004, 752.
13. Sinclair, *Unorthodox Lawmaking*.
14. David R. Mayhew, *Divided We Govern: Party Control, Lawmaking, and Investigations, 1946–1990* (New Haven, Conn.: Yale University Press, 1991), chapter 2.
15. *CQ Weekly*, August 7, 2004, 1008.
16. Geoff Earle, "Dems Did Oversight Better Says Grassley," *Hill*, May 13, 2004, 1, 6.
17. See David Nather, "Congress as Watchdog: Asleep on the Job?" *CQ Weekly*, May 22, 2004, 1190.

18. Quoted in Evans and Oleszek, *Congress under Fire*, 97.
19. This discussion of participation and representativeness of committees is drawn from Hall, *Participation in Congress*.
20. Norman J. Ornstein, Thomas E. Mann, and Michael J. Malbin, eds., *Vital Statistics on Congress, 2001–2002* (Washington, D.C.: American Enterprise Institute, 2002), 121.
21. Quoted in *CQ Weekly*, November 8, 2003, 2762.
22. *USA Today*, October 30, 2003, 2A.

Bibliography

Adler, E. Scott. *Why Congressional Reforms Fail: Reelection and the House Committee System.* Chicago: University of Chicago Press, 2002.

Deering, Christopher J., and Steven S. Smith, *Committees in Congress.* 3rd ed. Washington, D.C.: CQ Press, 1997.

Evans, C. Lawrence. *Leadership in Committee: A Comparative Analysis of Leadership Behavior in the U.S. Senate.* Ann Arbor: University of Michigan Press, 2001.

Fenno, Richard F., Jr. *Congressmen in Committees.* Boston: Little Brown, 1973.

Krehbiel, Keith. *Information and Legislative Organization.* Chicago: University of Chicago Press, 1991.

Hall, Richard L. *Participation in Congress.* New Haven, Conn.: Yale University Press, 1996.

King, David C. *Turf Wars: How Congressional Committees Claim Jurisdiction.* Chicago: University of Chicago Press: 1997.

Longley, Lawrence D. *Bicameral Politics: Conference Committees in Congress.* New Haven, Conn.: Yale University Press, 1989.

Maltzman, Forrest. *Competing Principals: Committees, Parties, and the Organization of Congress.* Ann Arbor: University of Michigan Press, 1997.

Sinclair, Barbara. *Unorthodox Lawmaking: New Legislative Processes in the U.S. Congress.* 2nd ed. Washington, D.C.: CQ Press, 2000.

8

PARTIES AND LEADERSHIP
IN THE HOUSE

Barbara Sinclair

SINCE EARLY IN ITS HISTORY, THE HOUSE OF REPRESENTA-
tives has relied on parties and committees to provide the structure that
enables it to do its job. Parties organize the chamber and provide coordination; committees do most of the substantive work on legislation. The strength of
the congressional parties and the extent to which they play a significant policy
role have, however, varied widely over time. Since the mid-1980s majority-party
members in the House have worked and voted together at high rates, with the
result that the party position seldom lost in the chamber. In the 1960s and 1970s,
in contrast, the House parties displayed much less internal unity; the majority
Democrats frequently split and consequently often failed to pass legislation that
a majority of the party's members strongly favored. As Figure 1 illustrates, House
political parties that were not all that distinctive in the 1950s and 1960s had
become sharply polarized by the turn of the twenty-first century.

Most scholars believe that the strength of the congressional party is, at least
in part, a function of the homogeneity of the party members' electoral constituencies. Similar constituencies, it is argued, translate into similar legislative
preferences on the part of members. And when members hold similar legislative
preferences, they benefit from their party leaders acting aggressively to facilitate
the enacting of those legislative preferences into law. When, however, members'
legislative preferences are diverse, members are less willing to allow their leaders
to act forcefully, preferring to pursue their policy and electoral goals independently of the party.[1]

This essay will trace the development of parties and party leadership in the
House from the 1950s to the present and then examine how the parties and their

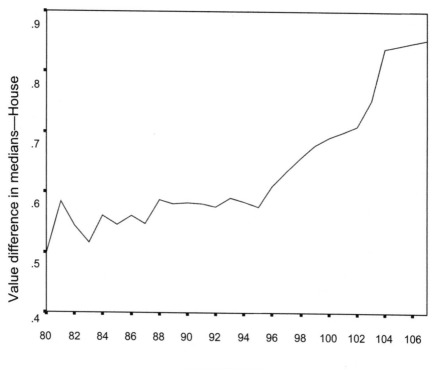

CONGRESS

NOTE: The Poole and Rosenthal DW-nominate scores can be interpreted as locating members of Congress on a left-right dimension. See Keith T. Poole and Howard Rosenthal, *Congress: A Political-Economic History of Roll Call Voting* (New York: Oxford University Press, 1997).

Figure 1

leaderships function in the contemporary House. It attempts to show how changes in the external political context altered members' needs and expectations and how members changed the way the House functions in response. It argues that a substantial increase in constituency-based preference homogeneity was a necessary condition for the development of the highly partisan contemporary House. Problems members encountered in meeting their legislative goals accelerated the development of and then reinforced the need for aggressive party leadership. Thus, Democrats found they could not respond effectively as individuals to the electoral and policy threat posed by the presidency of Ronald Reagan; they realized that collective action was necessary and that that required stronger leadership. For Republicans as the majority party after 1995, extremely narrow margins of control made strong leadership a prerequisite to legislative success. In addition, forces internal to the House amplified the effects of these external forces. The essay closes with a consideration of the consequences of high partisan polarization in the House for how Congress performs as a democratic institution.

Development of the Partisan House

To enable the House to legislate, tasks, powers, and resources are delegated to various subsets of members—committees, committee leaders, party entities, and party leaders—through rules and informal understandings. Members can change these rules and customs. They do so, it can be argued, when an existing set of arrangements no longer serves to advance their goals of policy and reelection.

Party leaders are best seen as agents of the members who chose them. The tasks, powers, and resources that members delegate to their party and its leadership, and members' expectations as to how aggressively those powers should be exercised, depends on members' perceptions of the costs and benefits of a strong congressional party and leadership. An increase in party members' ideological coherence decreases the costs and increases the benefits of a strong party leadership. Strong leaders can pressure committees to report legislation quickly and in a specific form; they can use procedural powers to advantage the party position on the floor; they can employ rewards and punishments to induce members to support the party position. When members' legislative preferences are similar, such assertive leadership action to pass legislation is likely to benefit most members and harm few. The level of ideological coherence is not, however, the only factor determining the costs and benefits of a strong party leadership. In addition, changes in the political environment that alter members' ability to enact the legislation they need to advance their goals may thereby also alter the perceived costs and benefits to members of an assertive or restrained leadership. This may lead members to expand or diminish the powers and resources they delegate to their party leadership and their expectations about the use of leadership powers.

Committee Government and Liberal Discontent

During the period of "committee government" that prevailed from roughly 1920 through the early 1970s, the role of the House majority party and its leadership was restricted. The revolt against Speaker Joseph Cannon in 1910, the result of an ideological split in the then-dominant Republican Party, had stripped the speakership of major institutional resources. By the late 1930s, the Democrats, who were in the majority for most of the period after 1930, were split along largely coinciding regional and ideological lines and this factionalism, pitting conservative southern Democrats against more-liberal northern Democrats, further limited the party and its leadership.

Legislation was the product of a number of autonomous committees headed by powerful chairmen, who derived their positions from their seniority on the committee. The chairmen commanded great organizational and procedural powers; they dictated the subcommittee structure of the committee, assigned members to subcommittees, hired the staff, and determined the agenda. Thus they were able to shape decision making in their committees. For example, Graham Barden, a very conservative North Carolinian who chaired the Education and Labor Committee during the 1950s, kept the committee staff small and, reportedly, incompetent; refused to call committee meetings; and, when committee members attempted to do so, used the chairman's procedural powers to prevent the committee from making decisions—all to prevent the committee from reporting out progressive legislation. The seniority rule for choosing committee chairmen and the norm guaranteeing members the right to stay on a committee once assigned to it meant that party leaders and the party membership as a whole lacked any practical mechanism for holding committees or their chairs accountable. Party leaders seldom if ever interceded in committee to shape legislation; the chairmen's power and norms of deference to committee worked against such involvement.

The Rules Committee, too, was independent during this period, and that limited the party leadership's control over the scheduling of legislation for floor consideration. The committee reports out special rules that allow legislation to be brought to the floor and govern the consideration of each bill on the floor. In the late 1930s, the Rules Committee had come under the control of a bipartisan conservative coalition and thereafter Democratic Speakers often had to bargain with the committee in order to get to the floor legislation supported by a majority of the majority party.

Intercommittee reciprocity, the norm of committees deferring to one another, meant that most committees could expect to pass most of their legislation on the floor without great difficulty; consequently, committees and their chairs did not often require help from the leadership. On the other hand, on those highly controversial issues that were fought out on the floor, the leadership often confronted a deep North-South split and had great difficulty in successfully building winning coalitions.

The committee government system, by allocating key positions on the basis of seniority, produced an ideologically biased distribution of influence that benefited conservative southern Democrats, whose "safe" seats assured them long careers, and disadvantaged liberal northern Democrats, who tended to be from more-competitive districts. The system worked well for southerners, who could afford to bide their time, but much less well for northerners, whose policy and participation objectives were being thwarted. The conservative chairs were often autocratic in how they ran their committees; thus, as Tom Foley, later Speaker of the House, recounts, at Foley's first meeting of the Agriculture Committee in 1965, Chair Harold Cooley told the freshmen that the senior members would ask all the important questions; the new members were expected to keep their mouths shut.

A change in the composition of the House Democratic Party eventually undermined the committee government system. Beginning with the 1958 elections and continuing through the 1960s, the House Democratic membership underwent a transformation; many more Democrats were elected from the North and most of them were liberals; then, as Republicans began to make electoral inroads in the South, the number of southern Democrats shrank.

Reforming the House

The effort to change the House was a long and arduous one, beginning in earnest in the immediate aftermath of the 1958 elections. But it was not until the period between 1969 and 1975 that the reform forces succeeded in making a series of changes in House and party rules that altered how the House functioned.[2] Both policy and participation motives drove the liberal Democrats who spearheaded the reforms. They wanted to make legislative decision makers, especially the committee chairs, responsive to the majority party, which was now clearly, though not homogeneously, liberal. They also wanted to increase the opportunities for rank-and-file members to participate meaningfully in the legislative process.

These dual objectives account for the seemingly contradictory thrusts of the reforms—both centralizing and decentralizing. Committee chairmen and the chairmen of Appropriations subcommittees no longer got their positions purely on the basis of seniority; they had to win majority approval in the Democratic Caucus, a requirement intended to make them responsive to the party majority. When, in 1975, three senior southern chairmen were deposed, all chairs realized that they could no longer ignore the party majority. The provision for regular meetings of the Democratic Caucus provided a forum in which rank-and-file members could inform Democratic committee contingents of their views, and a few instances of the caucus instructing committees put committees on notice that they had better listen to strongly held caucus sentiments. The task of assigning members to committees was shifted from the Ways and Means Democrats to the new Steering and Policy Committee chaired by the Speaker. The Steering and Policy Committee was designed to be both representative and responsive, its membership a combination of members elected from regional groups, elected party leaders, and leadership appointees.

To give the leadership true control over the scheduling of legislation for the floor, Democrats granted the Speaker the right to nominate all Democratic members and the chairman of the Rules Committee, subject only to ratification by the caucus. By making Rules Democrats dependent upon the Speaker for their position on the committee, reformers made the committee an arm of the leadership.

Yet another set of reforms that were implemented at the same time aimed at "spreading the action" and, as such, had decentralizing implications. In 1971 members were limited to chairing only one subcommittee. The 1973 "Subcommittee Bill of Rights" took the power to select subcommittee chairs from committee chairs and gave it to the Democratic caucus of the committee and guaranteed subcommittees automatic referral of legislation and adequate budget and staff. These changes reduced the control of the full committee chair and of other senior committee leaders over the committee's legislative activities.

During this period, in addition, both committee and personal staffs were expanded and distributed much more broadly among members. Even junior members thus gained the resources to exploit their new opportunities for participation. Sunshine reforms allowed for recorded votes in the Committee of the Whole, the proceedings on the House floor during which bills are amended, and opened up most committee markups and conference committee meetings to the media and the public, encouraging members to use these forums for grandstanding as well as for policy entrepreneurship.

By the mid-1970s, the committee-government system was dead and a very different House was emerging. Committee chairmen's powers had been severely curtailed and the bases of committee autonomy undermined. The reforms significantly enhanced the powers and resources available to the party leadership for facilitating the passage of legislation, most notably by giving the Speaker control of the Rules Committee. At the same time, however, rank-and-file members' incentives and capacity for participating in the legislative process had also expanded.

In the immediate aftermath of the 1970s congressional reforms, the decentralizing thrust predominated in the House. The liberal reformers had expected the reforms to both facilitate the making of good—read liberal—pubic policy and increase opportunities for rank-and-file participation in the legislative process. By the mid-1970s, participation by the rank and file at the committee and the floor stage had indeed increased enormously and, combined with the large numbers of inexperienced subcommittee chairmen, had multiplied the number of significant actors and radically increased uncertainty. For example, in 1977 an amendment passed that on the surface appeared innocuous but in actuality would have placed severe restrictions on the political activities of labor unions. The floor manager—the subcommittee chair—was new and no member with the necessary expertise was on the floor to quickly figure out the amendment's real effect and inform Democrats. That vote was reversed, but the example signified a larger problem. Legislation had become increasingly vulnerable to attack on the chamber floor, and Congresses with large Democratic majorities produced disappointing legislative results from the party's standpoint. The Democratic leaders of the mid-1970s believed that their members were unwilling to accept significant constraints on their newly acquired opportunities to participate broadly in the legislative process. Furthermore, the Democratic membership was still quite ideologically diverse. Thus, although the reforms had bestowed new powers on the party leaders, leaders did not perceive a willingness on the part of their members to sanction aggressive use.

By the end of the 1970s, however, many Democrats had become concerned about unexpected consequences of the reforms. Floor sessions stretched late into the night, legislation crafted by now more representative committees was picked apart on the floor, and Democrats were forced to go on the record on politically risky amendments over and over again. In the 1980s, the open, participatory process that the reforms established became even more legislatively problematical. With the 1980 election of Ronald Reagan, House Democrats faced a conservative, confrontational president who threatened both their policy and their electoral goals, a significantly reduced majority, and a Senate controlled by the opposition party.

By the mid-1980s, the legislative difficulties that the reforms and then Reagan created combined with increases in the membership's ideological coherence had altered Democratic members' expectations of their party and their leadership. The change in southern politics that the civil rights movement and the Voting Rights Act set off had, by the early 1980s, resulted in a less-conservative southern Democratic House contingent and, by the mid-1980s, House Democrats were, according to the usual voting measures, more homogeneous than they had been at any time since the New Deal era.

Toward Party Government

Democratic Party leaders responded to their members' changed expectations by becoming more actively involved in the legislative process so as to facilitate the passage of legislation their members wanted and also by taking on agenda setting and public promotion functions new to congressional leaders.[3] To make this enhanced role possible, the leadership and party elaborated party organization and developed new strategies.

The leaders had in the 1970s begun elaborating the party organization that, during the committee government era, had been skeletal and seldom used. The whip system, which was responsible for ascertaining members' voting intentions on key votes, not only became more active but expanded enormously, with most of the growth occurring in leadership-appointed whips. The party leaders also began using leadership-appointed special task forces to mobilize majorities. The uncertainty the reforms created meant the party leadership needed help in gathering the necessary information on member voting intentions and in putting together majorities, and that need stimulated organizational expansion. Additionally, the leaders quickly learned that, by putting members to work in the whip system and on task forces, they provided them with valued opportunities to participate meaningfully in the legislative process—and in ways that helped rather than hurt the party effort. Especially after the 1980 elections, with the loss of the White House and the consequent blow to Democratic morale, caucus meetings became much more frequent and the caucus spawned a variety of committees and task forces, providing still more opportunities for members to participate in the ongoing discussion of how the party should respond to its changed circumstances.

In the late 1970s, in response to member complaints, the Democratic leadership began to use special rules to gain more control over the legislative process at the floor stage. In the difficult political climate of the 1980s, leaders increasingly employed rules that restricted amendments to protect party-supported legislation from being unraveled on the floor and, when possible, to shield their members from politically perilous votes. Over the course of the 1980s, Democratic leaders developed restrictive rules into powerful tools for advancing their members' legislative preferences.

To help Democratic committee contingents and Democratic members pass satisfactory legislation in difficult times, party leaders became more active in the prefloor legislative process as well. When committees were unwilling or unable to put together bills that were satisfactory to most majority-party members and that could pass the House, the majority-party leadership took on the task of superintending the negotiations and sometimes of actually working out the language. With committee chairs now dependent on the party caucus for their positions, leaders could and were expected to pressure committees and their chairs to be responsive to the party membership. Party leaders represented the House in negotiations with the administration and the Senate on the omnibus bills through which Congress increasingly legislated; only they had the legitimacy to speak for their membership.

Members also increasingly expected their leaders to participate in national political discourse and in the setting of the congressional agenda. When the opposition party controls the White House, the congressional majority will usually be dissatisfied with the president's agenda, and Democrats found themselves in that position from 1981 through 1992. Furthermore, given the political climate during this period, House Democrats needed their leadership's aid to get their issues on the agenda; the leaders had some chance of commanding the necessary media attention—individuals had little chance. Speaker Jim Wright in 1987, at the beginning of the 100th Congress, proposed an agenda consisting of issues such as clean-water legislation, a highway bill, and aid to the homeless, which were broadly supported within the Democratic Party. He relentlessly kept the spotlight on those items and used leadership resources aggressively to facilitate their passage. By the end of the Congress, all the items had become law and the Democratic Congress had gained considerable favorable publicity. Thereafter Democrats expected their leaders to engaged in agenda setting activities. When Wright's successor, Tom Foley, was less vigorous about doing so, members criticized him sharply.

President Reagan's success at painting the Democratic Party as "tax and spend" and "soft on defense" taught Democrats the importance of defining issues and party images to the party's benefit. In response, House Democrats came to expect their leadership to participate effectively in national political discourse, influencing the terms of the debate so as to further Democrats' immediate legislative goals and to protect and enhance the party's image.

By the late 1980s, then, the House majority-party leadership was highly active, routinely involved in all stages of the legislative process and much more engaged than its committee government–era predecessors in political discourse on the national stage. Unlike its predecessors of the strong speakership period of 1890–1910, however, this party leadership was neither strongly hierarchical nor highly directive. In response to its members' expectations, it led through a strategy of inclusion: communication between leaders and members was continuous and very much two-way, and those members who so desired were afforded myriad opportunities to participate in the legislative process as part of the party team.

With an activist majority-party leadership leading a relatively ideologically coherent membership, the action on high-profile issues increasingly took place within the majority party, and the minority party was more and more relegated to the sidelines. Changes in the character of the Republican House membership contributed to this trend as well. The Republican Party became more aggressively conservative in the 1980s; not only were fewer moderates being elected, more hard-edged, ideological conservatives were entering the chamber—from the South but from other regions as well. Thus the Republican Party also became more ideologically homogeneous and, as it did so, it too became more amenable to strong leadership, even imitating the majority party in giving its leaders powers and resources such as the power to choose Republican members of Rules. Their irrelevance rankled Republicans and a bitter partisanship became the norm on the House floor.[4]

Ideologically coherent, aggressively led congressional parties, thus, predated the Republican takeover of House control in the 1994 elections. Nevertheless, a new majority of strongly ideological conservatives that believed itself mandated to make fundamental policy change allowed Newt Gingrich as Speaker to exploit leadership tools more aggressively than any of his postreform predecessors. Exercising power well beyond that specified in Republican Conference rules, Gingrich short-circuited the normal process and himself designated committee chairs, bypassing seniority in several instances. Gingrich set the agenda—first through the "Contract with America," the party platform, and then by insisting on balancing the budget; party leaders held the committees to tight schedules and exerted a strong influence on the substance of legislation. Gingrich vigorously performed the role of party spokesman and, during much of 1995, loomed larger in national discourse than the president. Throughout, the leaders acted as agents of an intense and determined membership ideologically committed to passing the legislation at issue and convinced that the party's electoral fate depended on delivering on its promises.

Once the extraordinary sense of mandate dissipated, so did the leadership's complete dominance of the legislative process. Yet though Gingrich left the speakership in 1999 and was replaced with a less-visible and lower-octane leader, Dennis Hastert, the House majority party and its leadership remained central to the legislative process; the leadership continued to be highly active and involved in all stages of the process and the process continued to be highly partisan. Given the Republican Party's narrow margins of control, an active party and strong leadership continued to be prerequisites to legislative success.

Parties and Party Leadership in the Contemporary House

Contemporary members of the House expect their party to take a prominent part in setting the congressional agenda, to engineer the passage of major legislation, and to promote the party's image beyond the chamber. Members believe such collective party action will further their own policy and electoral goals and they expect their party leaders to ensure that these functions are performed in a way that does, in fact, advance those goals. "All of us want a strong leadership because we want to get things done," summed up moderate Republican Chris Shays in 2003.[5]

Members of both parties would like their leaders to advance their policy and electoral goals through agenda setting, constructing legislative majorities, and promoting the party image. Minority-party leaders are, however, severely handicapped by House rules, which empower a reasonably cohesive majority to control the legislative process and prevail without consulting the minority. Minority-party members, of course, know that their leaders are highly constrained, yet dissatisfaction is endemic in the minority party. In the current highly partisan era, minority leaders perforce tend to focus their efforts less on winning legislative battles in the House and more on promoting the party beyond the chamber.

Party Organization

The contemporary House parties are elaborately organized for joint action and for member participation. To carry out the expanded functions expected of it, the party leadership needs the assistance that the various organizational entities can provide. In addition, many of the party organs offer members much-prized opportunities to participate in the legislative process.

The Republican Conference and the Democratic Caucus, the organizations of all party members in the chamber, elect leaders and determine party rules. They also serve as forums for the exchange of information between leaders and members. Each meets at least weekly. Party and committee leaders report on the status of major legislation; they explain strategy; and they exhort and sometimes pressure their members to support the party position. Members express their views and, not infrequently, their complaints to the leadership.

The leaders of the conference and caucus are elected by the party membership and are a part of the extended leadership circle. Beyond holding meetings of the full membership, these leaders are charged with other functions as well and are provided with considerable staff for carrying them out. House Republicans entrust the primary responsibility for communicating the party message to the conference. Staff prepare a blizzard of paperwork—press releases, issue reports, and talking points. Some of these materials are distributed directly to the press, but much is intended as a resource for members to help them effectively communicate the party message in their districts. Thus, "recess packs" with pithy summaries of Republican accomplishments and talking points on the issues leaders want to highlight are prepared before each recess. All recent conference chairs have relied on subsets of members to assist in conveying the message. The "Theme Team," a group of about fifty members, takes responsibility for articulating the message in the one-minute speeches that start the legislative day.

The Democratic Caucus also has message responsibilities, though currently the top leaders play a more visible role on the minority side. Like their Republican counterparts, staff prepare and disseminate information aimed at the media but especially at Democratic members. Eighteen issue task forces are charged with "developing and communicating legislative priorities and party policy for House Democrats."[6] For minority-party members, having an opportunity to develop policy and participate on issues of special interest to the district or to them personally is especially important, and large numbers—over half the Democratic membership—sign up for one or more task forces.

The parties' whip systems are charged with collecting information on members' voting intentions and persuading members to vote the party position. The Republican whip system, which is headed by an elected whip, consists of sixty to seventy members, including an appointed chief deputy whip, approximately twenty regional assistant whips, and a number of appointed deputy whips. The regional whips do the first count of Republicans' voting intentions by polling the members in their state or region; refining the count and the first efforts at persuasion are tasks entrusted to the deputy whips.

The Democratic whip system is even bigger than the Republican one, generally numbering about one hundred members. Regionally elected zone whips do the initial count; appointed whips then refine the count and attempt to persuade the wayward. As a minority in a highly partisan House, the Democratic Party can seldom expect to win floor votes, and party leaders have fewer inducements than their majority counterparts to encourage party voting. Yet the leaders strongly believe that a unified Democratic position on the most salient issues is essential to conveying to the public that the party is presenting a clear alternative to the Republican Party. So even more than on the Republican side, the leadership must rely on persuasion. The senior whips now meet with small groups of members early in the legislative process attempting to build consensus against the Republican position and for a Democratic alternative.

Policy committees, committees on committees, and congressional campaign committees exist and are active and significant in both parties. The Republican Policy Committee, with a diverse and representative membership of forty-eight, is charged with the "enunciation of official Republican policies."[7] In 2001–2002, for example, the committee issued fourteen policy statements on issues ranging from tax policy to the exclusion of Taiwan from the World Health Organization. Subcommittees of the Policy Committee perform much the same function that the Democratic Caucus task forces do; as the committee's website states, they offer "a unique opportunity for participation by members whose legislative ideas do not in every case coincide with their committee assignments."

House Republicans entrust the assignment of members to committees and the nomination of committee chairs to a twenty-six-member Steering Committee made up of the elected leadership, the chairs of the top committees, and representatives chosen by regional and class groups. The Speaker has five votes, the majority leader has two, and seven other party leaders serve on the committee, so the leadership, if it is united, can dominate the process. Yet members do have a say through their elected representatives, and Steering Committee decisions require conference ratification.

House Democrats combine the Committee on Committees function with some of the Policy Committee functions in a Steering and Policy Committee. Its makeup is similar to that of both the Policy and the Steering Committees on the Republican side, consisting of the extended leadership, regionally elected members, and leaders' appointees. So, as on the Republican side, rank-and-file members have input but the leadership can largely control outcomes. The committee seldom promulgates official party positions but does serve as a sounding board for the leader.

The Campaign Committees raise money and provide campaign services to members and nonincumbent party nominees. Services such as opposition research, help with campaign commercials, and field campaign advice are provided by large, expert staffs. Drawing as many members as possible into the effort to raise money for reelecting current members and increasing the membership is a party priority in an era of narrow margins, so both parties' Campaign Committees are large and have a diverse membership. Both parties also put considerable effort into getting members with big campaign treasuries and fairly safe seats to contribute directly to party coffers, and the amounts contributed have become substantial—over $25 million in 1999–2000.[8]

These various party organs, and more informal ones as well, perform specific tasks that aid the party effort; they also provide rank-and-file members with prized opportunities to participate. Leaders learned long ago, in the wake of the reforms, that drawing members into participation on party efforts pays off not just on the immediate endeavor but also in the longer term; members become stakeholders in leadership success and buy into party policy proposals.

Setting the Congressional Agenda and Constructing Majorities

Throughout most of American history, the political party has been the single most common foundation of legislative majorities in the House, and majority-party leaders have had some responsibility for constructing those majorities. In the contemporary House, members expect their party leaders to play a role in setting the congressional agenda and to be highly active in putting together majorities to pass legislation. In both endeavors, members expect their leaders to act as their agents.

Agenda Setting

The House parties construct agendas to guide legislative action and to promote the party image with the public. Rank-and-file members participate in the process of formulating the agenda through the Policy Committee and its subcommittees on the Republican side, the caucus task forces on the Democratic side, and a variety of less formal working groups and arenas. The party retreats held early each year, usually in a resort setting, contribute to the process; members discuss issues, provide feedback, and refine proposals. The party leaders coordinate the process and influence it greatly, through their appointment powers but even more through their informal authority.

The Contract with America is probably the best-known congressional party agenda. Put together in 1994 by Republican whip Newt Gingrich, conference chairman Dick Armey, and a considerable proportion of the Republican minority, it consisted of a list of specific legislative proposals and was intended to serve as a campaign platform for the 1994 elections. The Republican Party even paid to have it printed in *TV Guide*. When Republicans won control of the House, the Contract served as a guide to legislative action. In the 106th Congress, Speaker Hastert reserved the first ten House bill numbers for the top Republican legislative priorities, which were labeled "The Republican Common Sense Agenda." Since the mid-1990s, minority Democrats have presented their agenda under the rubric "Families First."

A cohesive House majority party with a clear agenda of its own can compel a president of the other party to deal with its issues; sometimes, when the public strongly supports its proposals, the party can even coerce the president into accepting legislation he dislikes. Thus majority Democrats forced onto the agenda in the late 1980s and early 1990s plant-closing notification, a minimum-wage increase, and a reversal of the Supreme Court decision in *Grove City College v. Bell*, which limited civil rights law in education. Reagan reluctantly allowed plant-closing-notification legislation to become law without his signature; he vetoed the Grove City bill but was overridden. George H. W. Bush forced a scaling back of the Democrats' minimum-wage increase but, even there, Democrats believed they had won a public relations victory. Majority Republicans repeatedly put tax-cut legislation and bills outlawing "partial birth" abortion on President Bill Clinton's desk, forcing him into vetoes. On their third try, they got Clinton to accept a welfare-reform bill that many of Clinton's core supporters strongly opposed.

When the House majority and the president are of the same party, the president's agenda tends to dominate. Because the political parties are now quite ideologically coherent, the president and the members of his party in the House are likely to have similar legislative preferences. In fact, the president is likely to have adopted some of his agenda from that of his congressional party, as George W. Bush clearly did with tax cuts.

During the Bush presidency, House Republicans continued to develop agendas but ones that were somewhat more general, specifying aims rather than specific bills, and tracked the president's program closely. The low-numbered bills were reserved for major presidential initiatives; in the 108th Congress, HR1 and S1 were the Medicare/prescription drugs bills and HR2 and S2, the Bush tax cut.

Congressional party leaders of the president's party believe that the congressional party's electoral success depends heavily on the president's policy success; "Members desert their president at their peril," a high-ranking leadership aide argued. Consequently, leaders will put presidential proposals on the congressional agenda even if some of their members are opposed and, having done so, will work hard to pass them. A significant faction of the Republican House membership opposed adding a prescription drugs benefit to Medicare, but the party leadership pulled out all the stops to pass Bush's proposal in 2003. Nevertheless, congressional leaders are agents of their members and there are limits to how far they can deviate from member preferences, even to support their president. A politically adept president understands that, even though in a period of high partisan polarization he has great influence with his fellow partisans in Congress, there are limits to that influence. He can help them by being perceived as a successful president and by bestowing a variety of favors ranging from fund-raising help to district projects; yet he cannot guarantee them reelection. To ensure reelection, members need to satisfy their constituents by promoting their interests and reflecting their views. Thus a president will take advice about the agenda from the congressional party leadership.

Prefloor Legislative Process

On major legislation of importance to the party, the House majority-party leadership oversees the legislative process from the beginning. The Speaker often sets rough timetables for when legislation should be reported out of committee.

Through staff, the leaders monitor committee proceedings; they periodically discuss progress with the chair. By and large, the majority-party members of most committees—and especially of the most important committees—hold legislative preferences that are similar to those of the leadership and the conference. Most committee chairs are responsive to their party leaders' advice and counsel.

When problems arise that threaten the passage of legislation important to members individually or the party collectively, and committees are either unwilling or unable to handle them on their own, more overt leadership involvement in the prefloor legislative process becomes necessary. Sometimes because of internal conflicts, internal leadership problems, or an unrepresentative membership, a committee produces legislation the leadership considers problematical or fails to produce a bill at all. In 1991, Speaker Foley prevailed upon a reluctant Ways and Means Committee chairman to move legislation extending unemployment benefits, "must" legislation for Democrats from high-unemployment areas. Required by the budget agreement to pay for an extension with new taxes, the chairman had been loath to take on that fight. In 1995 the constitutional amendment imposing term limits on members of Congress, a major plank of the Contract with America, emerged from the Judiciary Committee in a form that the majority of the Republican Party found unacceptable. The Rules Committee, at the direction of the leadership, dropped the committee draft and substituted another version. In 2001 the House Judiciary Committee unanimously reported a consensus antiterrorism bill that the Bush administration believed was too weak. Speaker Hastert substituted a bill closer to the Senate legislation that the White House supported and brought that to the floor.

Salient legislation needs to be substantively acceptable to the bulk of the party membership and also defensible in the public arena. The civil rights bill that the liberal Judiciary and Education and Labor Committees reported in March 1991 was too easy a target for President George H. W. Bush, who had vocally and repeatedly labeled similar legislation a "quota bill," thus putting Democrats on the defensive. Working with committee Democrats and with other members, especially southerners, concerned about supporting legislation that could be labeled a quota bill, the leadership worked out a compromise that included an explicit ban on quotas. The resulting legislation satisfied at least minimally both the strongest civil rights supporters and the Democratic membership as a whole and it passed easily.

When several committees have jurisdiction over legislation, leadership coordination and often mediation efforts may be necessary to get one bill to take to the floor. During the 101st Congress, the Ways and Means Committee and the Education and Labor Committee were at loggerheads over childcare legislation; each came up with a distinct approach and refused to budge. The Speaker intervened to break the stalemate, and that intervention involved making substantive adjustments to the legislation. In 1995 the House Republican leadership produced the party's welfare reform bill by combining bills passed by three committees and, in the process, altered some controversial provisions.

Omnibus bills, that is, bills that address numerous and not necessarily directly related subjects, issues, and programs and thus are long and highly complex, usually demand leadership involvement. Whether or not they are formally multiply-referred, their complexity often means that success depends on a coordinator from outside the committees. Even more important in dictating leadership involvement is the status of many such bills as party-agenda legislation. Budget resolutions, which set out a blueprint for overall spending and taxing and priorities for spending in twenty or so broad areas, and reconciliation bills, which make the changes in law required by the budget resolution, are a de facto statement of the majority party's priorities and are often the vehicle for making non-incremental policy change. The 1990 budget deal between President George H. W. Bush and the congressional Democratic majority, Clinton's economic program in 1993, the Gingrich balanced budget plan in 1995, the balanced budget compromise between congressional Republicans and Clinton in 1997, and George W. Bush's tax cuts in 2001 and 2003 were enacted (or, in the 1995 case, passed Congress) through reconciliation bills. Majority-party members of the House are unwilling to entrust to committees and their chairs full responsibility for drafting measures such as these with their far-reaching substantive effects and enormous electoral implications; they expect their elected party leaders to ensure that such legislation satisfies their individual policy and electoral needs and enhances their party's reputation.

The Medicare/prescription drugs bill passed in 2003 illustrates the varieties of leadership involvement in the prefloor process on controversial legislation crucial to the party's reputation. The bill was a top presidential priority; were it to fail the president and the Republican Party would look ineffective, incapable of delivering on their promises. So instead of a bill being introduced and then referred to committee, the party leadership and the top Republican leaders on Ways and Means and Energy and Commerce, the two committees with major jurisdiction over health care, met and reached an "agreement in principle" on a proposal before any committee action took place. After the committees reported legislation, the committee chairmen got together with Speaker Hastert and other Republican Party leaders to work out a final bill to take to the floor. Their aim was not only to meld the two committee's bills into one but also to make changes that would pick up the support of various groups of disgruntled Republicans. Over the course of several days, the party leaders met with small groups of members, attempting to persuade them to vote for the bill and, when necessary, negotiating changes to get their vote.

Contemporary party leaders can exercise so much influence in the legislative process at the prefloor stage because they are fulfilling the expectations of their members in a period of high intraparty ideological homogeneity; their clout with committee members and chairs ultimately depends on their acting as effective and faithful agents of their members. Gingrich's extraordinary sway over committee decision-making in 1995 was quite clearly a result of his enormous prestige as the "majority maker" and of the sense of mandate that animated the Republican membership. In addition, however, leaders possess more immediate bases for persuading and pressuring committees and their chairs. Party leaders have much greater influence over committee assignments than they used to and they are willing to use that influence to reward the loyal and disadvantage—if not punish—the disloyal. Members know that their chances of gaining assignment to the most coveted committees depend on their party loyalty. Once Democratic committee chairs had to win caucus confirmation by a majority secret-ballot vote at the beginning of each Congress, caucus disapproval of an unresponsive chair became a real possibility and leaders could intimate that a recalcitrant chair risked such action, as Speakers Tip O'Neill and Wright each did on occasion. In recent years, Republican Speakers gained direct influence over the choice of chairs. When the six-year term limit on committee chairs, which the Republicans wrote into House rules after their 1994 electoral victory, claimed its first victims in 2000, Speaker Hastert instituted a new procedure for choosing chairs, one that reinforced members' incentives to be responsive to the party and the leadership. Chair aspirants were required to appear before the Steering Committee, which nominates chairs to the conference. There they were put through a rigorous interview about their legislative and communication strategies and their proposed agendas. Twenty-nine members interviewed for the thirteen vacant chairmanships; and the Steering Committee did not follow seniority in choosing the new chair for six of the thirteen vacant positions. On two important committees, a fairly moderate member was passed over for a less-senior conservative. However, the best predictor of who got chairmanships was how much money they had raised for fellow House Republican candidates.[9] In filling four vacant chairmanships at the beginning of the 108th Congress, Republicans again passed over two moderates and installed less-senior but more-conservative members.

Interviews for sitting chairs are usually a formality, but Chris Smith, who had first been chosen to head the Veterans Affairs Committee in 2000, was warned during his 2002 interview that he needed to be more of a team player. In late 2004, evidently not having heeded the warning sufficiently, he was stripped of his chairmanship. Republican Conference rules were altered in late 2002 to give the Steering Committee the right to pick the "Cardinals," the chairs of the Appropriations subcommittees. Previously, party rules allowed the full committee chair to pick the subcommittee chairs. "The goal," said a GOP aide, "is to make these folks accountable."[10] Clearly, party rules and procedures for selecting committee leaders provide those who hold or aspire to committee leadership positions with strong incentives toward responsiveness and thereby amplify the effects of intraparty ideological homogeneity.

Strategy and Persuasion at the Floor Stage

The majority-party leadership's goal is to assure that, before it takes major legislation to the floor, the legislation is in a form that is acceptable to most of the party membership, that it will pass the House, and that preferably it will benefit and certainly not damage the party's reputation. Although its ideological coherence lets the Republican majority in 2005 aspire to passing legislation that meets these criteria, narrow margins in the House mean that doing so is seldom easy. Certainly in the American context, ideological homogeneity never means identical legislative preferences; even members who agree on most issues may find that constituency interests or personal policy preferences split them occasionally. Consequently, party leaders often need to employ both procedural strategies and persuasion to pass major legislation in an acceptable form.

CRAFTING THE RULE. Control over the special rules that are used to bring most major legislation to the floor provides the party leadership with its single most potent strategic tool; through carefully constructed rules, the leaders can structure choices on the floor so as to advantage the majority party.

Since the later 1970s, majority-party leaders have increasingly restricted the amendments that may be offered on the floor; in 1977–1978, only 14 percent of rules substantially restricted amendments; by the 1990s and 2000s, over half did. On major legislation the use of substantially restrictive rules has gone up even more over this period, from 21 percent to, on average, 67 percent.[11] Restricting amendments through a rule reduces uncertainty on the floor; the minority is prevented from offering a stream of amendments, hoping to find one that will split the majority. Large, complex bills such as budget resolutions are now always considered under highly restrictive rules, often allowing the minority only one amendment—a comprehensive substitute, that is, an alternative version of the entire bill. Increasingly, other legislation that is a part of the party agenda is also considered under such rules. Allowing the minority to offer only a comprehensive substitute forces them to also confront the tough tradeoffs that the majority faced in putting together its bill. Furthermore, because it is a comprehensive minority-party proposal rather than a more limited amendment, majority members are less likely to defect and vote for it.

Special rules, as they have evolved since the 1980s, are useful strategic tools because they can be tailored to the particular problem a specific bill faces.[12] Thus, restrictive rules can sometimes be used to prevent a vote on an amendment the party leadership opposes but fears would pass or to make a vote on such an amendment obscure and thus difficult to use in an election campaign against its members. The Republican tax bill in the 104th Congress placed a $200,000 cap on the income of families eligible for a $500-per-child tax credit. Democrats and many Republicans were on the record as supporting a reduction in the cap to

$95,000, so if an amendment reducing the cap had been offered on the floor, it would have passed. The rule did not allow that amendment, and the bill passed with the higher cap. Speaker Gingrich correctly assumed that those of his members who supported the lower figure would not be willing to defect from the party position and hand the party a highly visible defeat on a bill central to the party agenda. When House Republicans brought their prescription drugs bill to the floor in the summer of 2002, they forced the Democrats to offer their alternative, which provided more generous drug benefits, not as an amendment but through a motion to "recommit with instructions." The difficulty of explaining that arcane procedural motion to voters would protect their members who voted against the higher benefits, the Republican leadership figured. The leadership can also make a specific amendment in order to provide "cover" for its members; when the Democratic leaders made an order to the 1991 civil rights bill an amendment specifically prohibiting the use of racial or gender quotas the purpose was to give their members a counter when opponents accuse them of voting for a "quota" bill.

By using a restrictive rule to allow only an up-or-down vote on a bill, leaders can engineer passage of measures that have to pass but that members dislike voting for, such as increases in the debt ceiling, by packaging them with ones the members very much want. (If the debt ceiling is not raised when it is reached, the United States would default on its debt.) In 1996, for example, the Republican leadership added the line-item veto as a sweetener to the debt-limit-increase bill, giving members only a vote on the package.

A majority of the full House membership must approve each rule, so the leadership cannot impose restrictive rules on an antipathetic membership. In crafting rules, the leadership must be sensitive to its members' needs and wants. To be sure, as the parties have become more coherent, the expectation that members will support the party position on procedural votes such as rule votes has become increasingly strong. Republican Party leaders impress this expectation on their freshmen members during orientation sessions and make it a requirement for service in the whip system. Nevertheless, if members believe a rule coerces them in a manner they find unacceptable, they can and do vote against it. For example, in late 2002, a group of vehemently antiabortion Republicans voted against the rule for the bankruptcy reform bill conference report and thus killed the bill. The conference report included a Senate provision preventing antiabortion groups from using bankruptcy to get out of paying court-awarded damages to abortion clinics.

Rules seldom fail. In crafting rules, what the leadership is trying to do is make it easy for their members to vote in such a way that the party-preferred policy is the outcome and, given homogeneity, that is what most of their members want—even if sometimes, without a cleverly crafted rule, it would be hard for them to vote that way.

WHIPPING AND PERSUADING. The whip system is central to the effort to assure a floor majority and one that includes most majority-party members. How long before planned floor consideration the effort starts depends on how difficult the task is expected to be and how important to the party the bill is. After the regional whips conduct the initial count of how party members intend to vote, appointed whips refine the count, contacting members who were missed or undecided on the first go-around, checking any reports that seem suspect, and then attempt to persuade members to vote the party position. Because the whip systems are so large, an effective effort can be mounted without every whip participating in every case, and so multiple efforts can be waged without exhausting the whips.

If the need for an all-out campaign can be anticipated, the leadership and the whip system will work with allied interest groups from early in the process. Groups that have ties to members because they represent an important constituency interest, because they are major financial donors, or because they share intensely held policy preferences can be highly effective advocates for the party position. Such groups have probably always been involved in majority-building campaigns, but the effort to enlist them has become increasingly routinized and sophisticated. Leaders meet with closely allied interest groups on a regular basis and expect those groups to help in persuasion. Republican whip Roy Blunt and his "deputy whip in charge of coalitions" form coalitions of interest groups to work with the whip system on specific major Republican initiatives. For example, in 2003, such groups were set up to work the energy bill, the medical liability bill, the bankruptcy bill, and the tax package.

If the outcome still appears too close for comfort, the top party leaders become directly engaged in persuasion and, if the president is of the same party and the bill at issue is of high priority, he may as well. Of course, the top leaders have been planning strategy and overseeing the majority-building effort from early in the process; administration officials have also usually been involved in strategy and in some persuasion. Cabinet secretaries and other high-ranking officials may well have argued the administration's case before the Policy Committee and sometimes to a meeting of the full conference.

Shortly before a showdown vote on major legislation, the party leaders often call a special meeting of the conference to lay out their case. The leaders present their best arguments, both substantive and political, and make sure that members understand the costs of losing the vote. Such conferences often take on the character of a pep rally and exert considerable peer pressure on the holdouts.

On the toughest votes, the Speaker and the majority leader engage in one-on-one persuasion as well. They are the big guns and are saved for the hardest cases so that their persuasion efforts are not expended frivolously. The leaders' first arguments are usually party-loyalty based; but if appeals to not letting your colleagues, your president, and the party down are unavailing, the leaders will bargain. The bargains necessary to get significant groups of members on board will usually have been made before legislation gets to the floor, in committee or in the postcommittee adjustments leaders often engineer. But, to get the last few votes, the leaders may have to make deals right on the floor. For example, when the Republican House leaders brought up trade-promotion-authority legislation (also known as fast track) in December 2001, they lacked the votes to pass the bill. Party leaders eked out a 215 to 214 victory by making deals with textile-state Republicans reluctant for constituency reasons to vote for the legislation, overriding the committee chairman in at least one case. Similarly, to pass the Medicare/prescription drugs bill in June 2003, a very reluctant Jo Ann Emerson (R.-Mo.) was induced to change her vote in return for a leadership promise to bring to the floor a bill allowing the importation of cheaper drugs from Canada.

When the bill at issue is central to the president's agenda and victory is in doubt, he too becomes directly engaged in the persuasion effort. To pass his economic program in 1993, President Bill Clinton invited House Democrats to the White House in small groups, appeared before the Democratic Caucus to appeal for support, and called sixty members, some repeatedly, for one-on-one persuasion. President George W. Bush used rides on Air Force One and promises of projects to persuade members on the fast-track- authority bill in 2001; to pass the conference report on the Medicare/prescription drugs bill in 2003, he deployed his Health and Human Services secretary, Tommy Thompson, to assist the Republican leadership in last-minute persuasion efforts and backed them up by calling members on their cell phones right on the floor.

The majority's control over procedure confers advantages at every stage of the process. For example, when the fifteen minutes that is allotted for a recorded vote ran out on passage of the Medicare/prescription drugs bill conference report, the Republican position was losing. The leadership held the vote open for almost three hours until enough members could be persuaded to change their vote to reverse the outcome.

Insider Perspectives on the House Legislative Process

A 2004 survey[13] of congressional staff aides provides a perspective on how participants see the contemporary legislative process. A sample of House and Senate staffers were asked:"How often do Republicans and Democrats, in general, agree on important matters [in the issue area you work on]—often, occasionally or rarely?" Staffers reported very considerable though not completely pervasive partisanship, with about half answering that agreement across party occurred "occasionally" and about a quarter each answering "often" and "rarely." House staffers reported considerably more partisanship than comparable Senate staffers. In both chambers, minority Democrats perceived a higher level of partisanship than majority Republicans. Thus, a third (34%) of House Republicans but less than one in five Democrats (17%) said that, in their area, Republicans and

Democrats agreed often. Interviews with House members also indicate that majority and minority party members' notions of what constitutes bipartisanship differ considerably. Bipartisanship is most frequent in the House on the distributive issues of agricultural policy and transportation, according to aides who work on those issues. A majority of House Republican staffers contend that bipartisan agreement occurs often on foreign and defense policy but Democrats disagree, though most agree that agreement does occur occasionally. On social welfare issues, energy and environmental issues and economic policy, partisanship is the norm, staffers of both parties report.

The aides were also asked to assess how much influence various congressional actors had on policy decisions in their area. Almost two-thirds (62%) of Republican and three-quarter (75%) of Democratic staffers attributed "a great deal" of influence to the Republican House leadership; and both saw the leadership as more influential than the committees on balance; 55 percent of Republican staffers and 42 percent of Democratic staffers characterized the committees as having a great deal of influence. Perceptions of leadership influence varied across issues, being seen as highest on economic policy, which includes taxes, and lowest on distributive issues and, by Republicans, on foreign and defense policy issues. Overall, the Republican leadership was rated highly influential on most issues and in comparison to other key congressional actors. Sixty percent or more of House Democrats saw the Republican leaders as having a great deal of influence in each of the issue areas and, in every area, saw the leadership as more influential than the committees. House Republicans judged their leaders to be more influential than the committees in each of the issue areas except distributive policy and energy and environmental policy and well over half said their leaders had a great deal of influence on every issue except foreign and defense policy (where 47% responded "a great deal" and 47%, "a fair amount").

Members of the House largely concur with the staffers surveyed, interview evidence and public statements indicate. The House legislative process is partisan and majority party leaders wield a great deal of influence over policy. Democrats perceive somewhat more partisanship than Republicans, but what really distinguishes members of the two parties is how they evaluate the situation. Republicans believe they are running the House efficiently and as fairly as possible given their narrow margins. Democrats believe Republicans are displaying a greater arrogance of power after ten years in the majority than Democrats did after forty. They argue that inordinate party leadership power erodes the committees' legislative capacity and that the leadership's heavy handed way of controlling the floor is fundamentally undemocratic.

Relations with the Senate and Post-Passage Politics

To become law, legislation has to pass both chambers in identical form. This constitutional requirement provides an incentive for cooperation between the chambers, especially when both are controlled by the same party. However, the two chambers' very different rules create continuous tension between them and make sustained cooperation difficult. House rules empower a reasonably cohesive majority to work its will expeditiously; Senate rules allow an individual or small group to delay action and a large minority to block it altogether. The Speaker can make commitments about when and in what form the House will pass a bill that the Senate majority leader cannot. Majority-party members of the House feel that they are required to "do the heavy lifting" and "take the tough votes" while their Senate colleagues "hog the spotlight" and yet are often unable to deliver on legislation.

An unusually public venting of House-Senate tensions occurred in spring of 2003. Senate majority leader Bill Frist, new to the position and inexperienced in leadership, promised the House Republican leadership that the Senate would approve $550 billion (of the $726 billion Bush initially proposed) for tax cuts, but when it became clear the bill would not pass with that figure, he gave Finance Committee chairman Charles Grassley the go-ahead to agree to a $350 billion cap. Republican House leaders were very publicly furious; to get the votes of some of their most conservative members, they had assured them of a $550 billion figure.

House members often feel put-upon and sometimes betrayed by the Senate. During the first Congress of the Clinton presidency, House Democrats passed the president's stimulus plan intact and his economic plan with an unpopular BTU tax; the Senate killed the stimulus plan and, to get the vote of a recalcitrant Democratic senator, Clinton agreed to scuttle the BTU tax. House Republicans passed all but one of the party's Contract with America items in the first one hundred days as they had promised, only to see many of them die in the Senate. During the George W. Bush presidency, House Republicans were repeatedly called upon to pass extremely conservative bills so as to provide the administration with the strongest possible bargaining position vis-à-vis the Senate. A small but important group of moderate House Republicans were forced to vote for legislation considerably to the right of their average constituent, while conservatives were later disappointed with the watering down of the legislation necessary for Senate passage.

House majority-party leaders nevertheless need to work with their Senate counterparts. Since the 1980s or before, meetings between House and Senate party leaders have occurred on at least a semiregular basis. High-ranking leadership staffers are in touch, most often by phone, routinely. Toward the end of a congressional session or whenever major bills important to the party reach the interchamber reconciliation stage, the leaders will be in almost constant contact with one another.

The same factors—high partisan polarization, weaker committees, multiple referral—that drew the party leadership into the prefloor legislative process also necessitated the leaders taking a more central role in the post-passage process. The Speaker now regularly appoints the majority leader or whip to conference committees on legislation of major significance to the party. Thus, in 2002, Tom DeLay, then majority whip, served on the energy bill conference; the next year, DeLay, now majority leader, served on the Medicare/prescription drugs bill conference. Informal involvement by the leadership is even more frequent and is not a recent innovation. In 1987 Speaker Wright not only appointed Majority Leader Foley as a conferee but, before officially designating them conferees, he extracted certain promises from the other Democrats who would serve on a conference to revise the Gramm-Rudman deficit-reduction act.

The heightened partisan polarization in the 1990s and beyond has made reaching conference agreements that can then pass both chambers more difficult. During the period of split partisan control of the House and Senate from June of 2001 through the end of 2002, major legislation such as the patients' bill of rights and an energy bill died at the conference stage because the differences between the Democratic Senate bill and the Republican House bill were irreconcilable. But even when the two chambers are controlled by the same party, the Senate's supermajority requirement can complicate the process. To get an agreement that assures passage in the Senate requires that House Republicans not only satisfy the Republican majority in the Senate but some Democrats as well.

Yet Republicans are increasingly responding to the problems that the Senate's supermajority requirement creates for them by using conferences to recoup losses they suffered in the Senate. During the latter years of Democratic control of Congress, when the party had become more ideologically coherent, the actual compromises between House and Senate, just as those within the chambers, were most often made within the Democratic Party. Recently, Republicans with much narrower margins of control have taken to excluding most Democrats from conference negotiations altogether. In 2003, no Democrats were allowed to participate in the energy bill conference and only two who were considered accommodating were admitted to the negotiations on the Medicare/prescription drugs bill. Republican leaders took a highly active role in working out a final deal on the Medicare/prescription drugs bill, with Speaker Hastert and Majority Leader Frist conducting the final negotiations personally; and the conference reports on both the energy bill and the Medicare/prescription drugs bill tilted strongly toward the more-conservative House versions. Republicans gambled that Senate moderates of both parties would be loath to vote against bills on such important issues even if those bills were considerably further to the right than they preferred. On the Medicare/prescription drugs legislation, the wager paid off, at least in the short run, and the bill passed the Senate easily. The energy bill, in contrast, was blocked by a filibuster.

PR Politics

House members expect their party to develop an appealing message and their party leaders to orchestrate the dissemination of the message beyond the chamber. The parties engage in "public relations politics" with both electoral and policy goals in mind and with the hope of affecting public opinion in both the short run and the longer run. If public debate on a salient issue can be framed so as to favor a party's position, that party is greatly advantaged in the immediate legislative battle and gains near-term electoral benefits from promoting the issue. By taking part in national political discourse in a way that enhances the party's image in the public's mind—by associating the party with popular positions, by portraying it as responsible and competent, and by painting its opposition in negative terms—the congressional party can gain policy and electoral benefits over the longer term as well. Intraparty ideological homogeneity has made agreeing on a message easier; partisan polarization has made disseminating a party-enhancing message more vital, especially to the party that does not hold the presidency. Even a majority party with a same-party president now engages in PR politics.

The top party leaders on both sides of the aisle perceive media relations as a key part of their job and equip themselves with extensive media operations, including multiple press aides. Thus, when Nancy Pelosi was elected Democratic leader in late 2002, she made the hiring of an experienced, savvy communications strategist a top priority, and she regularly speaks out on the issues before Congress. However, neither leaders nor members believe the top leadership can or should carry the PR burden alone, and members are urged and given multiple opportunities to participate. The parties regularly organize subsets of their members to deliver the one-minute speeches that begin the legislative day, with the result that they sometimes take on the character of set-piece battles with waves of well-trained troops from the two parties waging intense rhetorical combat. Democratic Caucus task forces play an important role in publicly promoting the policy proposals they have developed. In 2003, new House Republican Conference chair Deborah Pryce created a "Message Action Team" of thirty members of varying seniority and expertise. "It's sort of an inner circle of people that are willing to meet and talk about the message and help develop it and deliver it," Pryce explained. "These are people who are good on camera and good on their feet."[14]

The congressional parties have become adept at orchestrating events to garner press coverage. To attract media attention to their effort to increase aid for the homeless in the winter of 1987, House Democrats organized "the Grate American Sleep Out" in which a number of members of Congress—including whip Tony Coelho—joined the homeless to sleep outside—on a grate. In an attempt to shore up the GOP's image on education, House Republican leaders in 2002 instructed committee and subcommittee chairmen to hold hearings dedicated to publicizing education initiatives and accomplishments.

The parties also make frequent and often concerted efforts to get their members to promote the party message in their districts. The mass of information that various party entities—especially the caucus/conference—produce for dissemination to the membership is intended to provide members with talking points and arguments most favorable to the party's position and thereby make it as easy as possible for members to convey the party message to their constituents and their local media. As part of the 2002 effort to enhance the Republican Party's image on education, for example, the Republican leadership put out a memo titled "Weekly Education District Action Items," providing their members with a variety of suggested activities: visit a classroom once a week; read a story to elementary school students; give a civic lecture to older students; hold a meeting for parents and teachers, preferably in the school gym, to discuss education; present flags flown over the Capitol to schools for special events. In mid-July 2003, when the battle over the Medicare/prescription drugs bill raged in Congress, at least seventy-five House Democrats held district town hall meetings criticizing the House Republicans' bill. "Democratic members are taking the prescription drug issue straight to seniors to explain what Democrats are fighting for, and the irresponsible plan that Republicans are trying to push through Congress," explained a spokeswoman for House minority whip Steny Hoyer (D-Md.)[15] Nor did this PR battle end when the bill became law. Democratic leaders continued to encourage their members to hammer on the issue during their trips home; Republican leaders urged their members to hold district workshops and tape public-service announcements extolling the law.

PR strategies are especially important to the minority party, since the minority's influence within a highly polarized House is so limited. Because, on so much major legislation, decision making in committee, on the floor, and in conferences is highly partisan, the minority-party position almost never prevails. Minority members believe their views are not seriously considered and that consequently the interests of their constituents and allies are given short shrift. Painting a positive picture of their own party and its issue stances and a negative portrait of the opposition and its record is, of course, a component of the minority party's electoral strategy. In addition, however, the minority's only real shot at affecting the legislative agenda and outcomes is by bringing public pressure to bear on the majority. Thus, Democrats believe that their successful PR efforts induced reluctant House Republicans to bring up an extension of unemployment insurance and the extension of the child tax credit to the poor in 2003.

Party Influence and Its Limits

Extreme partisan polarization characterizes the legislative process and outcomes in the contemporary House of Representatives. The result is that the majority party seldom loses and the minority seldom wins. But is this simply a reflection of electorally induced member preferences or do internal arrangements contribute to partisan polarization? The answer to this question should be of interest beyond academics, because it affects whether proposed reforms might have the impact intended.

Constituency-based ideological homogeneity that is high by American standards is a necessary condition for the sort of polarization seen today. The national parties aid their members' election efforts more now than they ever have, but they do not control the party nomination nor can they assure a member of reelection; that still depends on a member's relationship with his or her constituency. Only when the legislative preferences that stem from electoral needs and policy goals are quite homogeneous within the party do members gain from a strong party and a strong party leadership in the chamber.

High constituency-based ideological coherence provides the basis for the development of internal arrangements that amplify its effects and so translate into more extreme partisan polarization than one might expect from homogeneity alone. As this discussion has shown, party leaders now possess control over resources that they can and do use to induce party-preferred behavior—by committee leaders as well as by rank-and-file members—and to structure decisions so as to advantage the party position. In addition, members now spend most of their Washington time with their party colleagues, not with members of both parties, and advancement in the House, whether in the committee or party hierarchy, is dependent on a member's reputation with his or her party colleagues. The incentives for being a member in good standing of the party team are strong.

Ideological coherence as well as the internal incentives to party regularity work to the advantage of a president of the same party as the House majority and to the detriment of a president of the opposition party. Members are likely to share policy goals with a president of their party; they are likely to see his policy success as affecting, if not their own electoral fate, at least that of some of their party colleagues and possibly determining House control. Members asked to save their president from an ignominious defeat must weigh not only their own policy views and electoral advantage but also their reputations within their House party. So, when her vote proved to be decisive, Marjorie Margolies-Mezvinsky (D-Penn.) voted for Clinton's economic program, even though she had promised her constituents she would not vote to raise taxes. Many conservative Republicans opposed to any expansion of entitlement programs voted for the Medicare/prescription drugs bill, which did exactly that, because the alternative was handing Bush and their leadership a devastating defeat.

Members' willingness to support their leaders or their president is not without limits, however. Few will gravely endanger their own reelection and most will swallow strong policy reservations only so often. When their constituents became seriously concerned about Clinton's major health reform proposal in

1994, House Democrats were unwilling to go along with their own party leaders or with the president and a plan was never even brought to the House floor. In 1996, nervous House Republicans capitulated to Clinton and congressional Democrats who had waged an effective PR battle on the issue and raised the minimum wage. Speaker Hastert failed to keep off the floor and prevent passage of a campaign finance reform bill, even though the Republican leadership, most of the membership, and President Bush opposed it. In the end, party and party leadership power depends on member acquiescence.

Consequences and Possible Reforms

What are the consequences of the institutional arrangements and the policy process in the contemporary House for how Congress performs as a democratic institution? We value a legislative process that fosters deliberation, that is open to public scrutiny, and that takes into account the interests and demands of all segments of society; but we also want a process that has the capacity to make decisions relatively expeditiously. Current arrangements promote the latter value more than the former. Ideologically coherent parties and stronger, more centralized leadership in the House facilitate timely and definitive decision making; gridlock is seldom a problem *within* the House. Furthermore, the current process is relatively inclusive within the majority party; decision making is not highly hierarchical.

The current process, however, tends to exclude the minority party and the interests and segments of society it represents. The result is severe disaffection among minority-party members. Deliberation is, at best, truncated; and, at times, it is sacrificed for speed, even within the majority party. Highly partisan decision-making can lead to extreme policy incapable of surviving the legislative process, especially the Senate, where a bare majority is seldom enough.

Partisan polarization may have its most deleterious process effects on congressional oversight of the executive. Once Bush became president, congressional Republicans largely abdicated their oversight responsibilities. When members of the congressional majority party and the president strongly perceive themselves as members of the same "team" in a high-stakes battle against an opposition team, the lack of serious oversight should come as no surprise. Ferreting out corruption or incompetence in the administration of their team's leader is unlikely to strike majority-party members as a winning strategy.

Are these negative consequences something about which we should be concerned? One might argue that since the Senate grants minorities considerable power, there is little cause for worry. Certainly "reforms" instituting significant supermajority requirements in the House would produce much greater problems than they would solve. So are there changes in rules and procedures that could promote more deliberation and greater participation by the minority without a major impact on the chamber's decision-making capacity? If the argument that contemporary internal arrangements amplify the effects of constituency-based ideological coherence is correct, then the answer is yes; however, if the argument that internal arrangements reflect the preferences of majority party members is correct, the likelihood of such changes actually being made is low.

What sort of changes would foster deliberation and give minority-party members a greater role in the process? Minority members could be guaranteed adequate time to study draft legislation and to propose and debate amendments in committee; floor consideration of legislation not first considered in committee and of bills changed in a major way after committee consideration could be disallowed; special rules that severely restrict amendments could be limited. But why should one expect the majority party to institute such rules, to abide by them if instituted, and to treat them as other than an annoying formality if abided by? To be sure, the fear of negative publicity restrains the majority to some extent and the threat of greater media scrutiny might well act as an incentive to greater minority inclusion. Furthermore, current rules and customs do provide some important protections for the minority. Thus the minority is allotted one-third of committee staff budgets and the minority leadership is quite generously funded; the minority is guaranteed the right to call its own witnesses at committee hearings and can ask the Government Accountability Office to conduct investigations of the executive branch. Yet, in a period of high partisan polarization, expecting consensualist democracy in the House is probably unrealistic.

Notes

1. There is some controversy over whether parties and leaders have an impact on how members behave and on what the House decides, beyond passively channeling homogeneous preferences. Keith Krehbiel argues that members' preferences—not party—drive the vote and that what appears to be partisanship is actually "preferenceship." See Krehbiel's *Information and Legislative Organization* (Ann Arbor: University of Michigan Press, 1991) and "Where's the Party?" *British Journal of Political Science* 23 (1993): 235–266. Proponents of the partisan model argue that the majority party and its leadership influence outcomes through structuring the legislative process and through directly influencing members' legislatively relevant behavior, especially when legislative preferences within each party are homogeneous and differences between the parties substantial. See Joseph Cooper and David W. Brady, "Institutional Context and Leadership Style: The House from Cannon to Rayburn," *American Political Science Review* 75 (1981): 411–25, Gary W. Cox and Mathew D. McCubbins, *Legislative Leviathan: Party Government in the House* (Berkeley: University of California Press, 1993, and David

W. Rohde, *Parties and Leaders in the Postreform House* (Chicago: University of Chicago Press, 1991).

2. Burton D. Sheppard, *Rethinking Congressional Reform: The Reform Roots of the Special Interest Congress* (Cambridge, Mass.: Schenkman, 1985).

3. Barbara Sinclair, *Legislators, Leaders and Lawmaking: The U.S. House of Representatives in the Postreform Era* (Baltimore: Johns Hopkins University Press, 1995).

4. Richard B. Cheney, "An Unruly House," *Public Opinion* 11 (1989), 41–44, and William F. Connelly, Jr., and John J. Pitney, Jr., *Congress' Permanent Minority?: Republicans in the U.S. House* (Lanham, Md.: Rowman & Littlefield, 1994).

5. *Congressional Quarterly Weekly* (March 29, 2003), 748.

6. Democratic Caucus website.

7. 108th House Republican Conference rules.

8. Bruce Larson, "Incumbent Contributions to the Congressional Campaign Committees," *Political Research Quarterly* 57 (March 2004), 156.

9. Paul R. Brewer and Christopher J. Deering, "Musical Chairs: Interest Groups, Campaign Fundraising, and Selection of House Committee Chairs," in *The Interest Group Connection: Electioneering, Lobbying, and Policymaking in Washington,* edited by Paul S. Herrnson, Ronald G. Shaiko, and Clyde Wilcox (Washington, D.C.: CQ Press, 2005), 141–63.

10. *Roll Call,* January 6, 2003.

11. Data are for the 103rd–105th and 107th Congresses; substantially restrictive means closed, modified closed, and what Republicans called "structured."

12. See Barbara Sinclair, *Unorthodox Lawmaking: New Legislative Processes in the U.S. Congress.* 2nd ed. (Washington, D.C.: CQ Press, 2000).

13. Survey conducted by the Annenberg Public Policy Center.

14. *Roll Call,* April 21, 2003.

15. *Roll Call,* July 21, 2003.

Bibliography

Aldrich, John, and David Rohde, "The Consequences of Party Organization in the House: Theory and Evidence on Conditional Party Government." in Jon Bond and Richard Fleisher, eds. *Polarized Politics: Congress and the President in a Partisan Era.* Washington, DC: CQ Press, 2000. A concise statement of the conditional party government variant of partisan theory by its two of its major proponents.

Bolling, Richard, *House Out of Order.* New York: Dutton, 1965. A description and critique of the House in the 1950s by a member who played an important role in the reform movement.

Cooper, Joseph, and David W. Brady, "Institutional Context and Leadership Style: The House from Cannon to Rayburn." *American Political Science Review* 75 (June 1981). An early statement of the conditional party government thesis and an excellent analysis of the changing distribution of influence in the House from the late 19th century through the 1970s.

Cox, Gary, and Mathew McCubbins. 1993. *Legislative Leviathan: Party Government in the House.* Berkeley: University of California Press, 1993. The originators' statement of the cartel variant of partisan theory.

Sinclair, Barbara, *Legislators, Leaders and Lawmaking.* Baltimore: Johns Hopkins University Press, 1995. A description and analysis of how the House and the Democratic party leadership changed over the course of the 1970s, 1980s and early 1990s.

Sinclair, Barbara, "Transformational Leader or Faithful Agent? Principal Agent Theory and House Majority Party Leadership in the 104th and 105th Congresses," *Legislative Studies Quarterly* 24 (August 1999). Description and analysis of the Gingrich speakership with an emphasis on its similarity and differences from its predecessors.

9

PARTIES AND LEADERSHIP IN THE SENATE

Steven S. Smith

NEARLY UNIQUE AMONG THE WORLD'S NATIONAL LEG-
islative bodies, the United States Senate allows a minority of its members to prevent a vote on regular legislative business. The Constitution
implies that a majority of senators present and voting can pass legislation, but the
Senate has adopted rules that require, under most circumstances, its presiding
officer to recognize a senator who seeks to speak and to allow that individual to
continue speaking for as long as he or she desires. Because a senator can entertain
questions from colleagues and eventually yield the floor to a colleague, the
debate can continue indefinitely—a filibuster. The filibuster, or threatened filibuster, is what provides the ultimate protection for extended debate and the
preservation of individual and minority rights. It is what gives the Senate its
unique character, one that many praise and undoubtedly more despise.

Nearly all senators—Democratic and Republican, majority party and
minority party—bemoan obstructionism in the chamber. In recent decades,
each new Senate majority-party eventually has deplored the blockage of legislative business by the minority. In late 2003 Senator Evan Bayh (D-Ind.), a minority Democrat complaining about Republican charges of minority obstruction,
pleaded:

> We must stop this cycle of constant recrimination, a process in which the
> minority obstructs to gain power and then turns around and complains
> about obstruction once power has been obtained. It makes us all look
> bad. If hypocrisy had a monetary value, we could easily erase the Federal
> deficit because of debates such as the one we are engaged in tonight.[1]

Bayh's critique is no doubt valid, but he fails to note that from time to time even majority party leaders have blocked votes on minority party proposals in fear that the proposals might win a majority, which in turn produces a stalemate over action. Proposals to break the cycle of obstructionism and recrimination are filibustered. The Senate is caught in a procedural vise created by its own history.

This essay outlines the strengths and weaknesses of Senate policy making. It examines why the Senate has not accomplished significant reform of its decision-making processes in the face of widespread criticism of its rules by senators, presidents, and many others. A brief review of the development of Senate decision-making processes reveals that obstructionism and weak leadership are endemic to the institution. Several fundamental conditions have shaped the modern Senate process: the gradual elaboration of leadership positions and party organization, changes in the rule (Rule 22) governing the breaking of filibusters, new scheduling practices, and evolving leadership tactics, including new provisions in unanimous-consent agreements and holds. The essay concludes with an analysis of the Senate's ability to improve its decision-making processes.

Development of Senate Decision-Making Processes

The Senate's rules were different from those of the House of Representatives from a very early point. In 1806, with no debate and no apparent awareness of the long-term implications, the Senate eliminated its rule on the previous question. The House, just a few years later, strengthened its previous question rule, which provided that a majority of legislators could close debate and move to a vote on the bill, amendment, or other motion at before the chamber. This rule proved critical to the adoption of measures to overcome obstructionism in the late nineteenth century. In the Senate, the absence of a previous question motion proved critical to minorities seeking to obstruct majorities on both substantive and procedural matters. Not until 1917, under quite unusual circumstances, did the Senate adopt Rule 22, which provided a means for a two-thirds majority of senators present and voting to end debate. Senate minorities have successfully blocked efforts to impose general limits on debate or amendments. In 1975, the Senate reduced the threshold for cloture to three-fifths of all senators (except for matters changing the Senate's rules, for which the threshold of two-thirds of senators present and voting was retained).

The absence of general limits on debate and amendments limits the value of majority status and having a strong majority leader. Under precedent established in the 1930s, the majority leader is recognized to speak or make a motion before other senators seeking recognition. This privilege gives the majority leader the opportunity to move that the Senate take up certain legislation, offer an amendment, propose a unanimous-consent agreement, or address a subject of the leader's choice. The right of first recognition does not guarantee that the Senate will vote on the majority leader's proposals. The minority party, if cohesive, may block legislation by filibuster, even by refusing to allow a vote on the motion to proceed to the consideration of a measure.

Preventing Senate consideration of a policy proposal, even if opposed by a majority, is generally not possible. Any senator may offer an amendment on any subject to most legislation. That is, nongermane amendments are allowed on most measures. As a general rule, therefore, the majority leader is unable to prevent certain subjects from receiving floor consideration. The leader can filibuster an amendment or take the underlying bill off the floor (by unanimous consent), which produces a stalemate.

The Senate lacks a powerful leader comparable to the House of Representatives' Speaker, who is both the presiding officer and leader of the majority party. The vice president, who is president of the Senate, is not a member of the Senate, may be of a party different from the Senate majority, and cannot be disciplined or removed by the Senate. The president pro tempore ("pro tem" in everyday Senate usage) is the most senior member of the majority party and presides in the absence of the vice president. In practice, junior majority party senators take turns presiding because the president pro tempore, who typically is a committee chair and has other responsibilities, cannot be present at all times. Consequently, the Senate has not granted much authority to its presiding officer and Senate parties have not made the presiding officer the top party leader with responsibility for setting party strategy as has the House majority party.[2]

While Rule 22 is often cited as the Senate rule that most defines the character of the Senate, the importance of Rule 12, governing voting procedure and unanimous consent agreements, must not be overlooked. Many observers of the modern Senate make the mistake of assuming that the Senate's practice of organizing floor activity under unanimous-consent agreements (UCAs), which set the terms for the consideration of bills or other measures, dates to its early days. In fact, UCAs, proposed by the majority leader or bill manager to limit debate or amendments, became common only in the late nineteenth century. By the start of the twentieth century, UCAs limiting debate and amendments had developed a standard form. Agreements that provided for a vote on a bill and pending amendments at a specific time were a regular part of floor-management practice at the turn of the century. However, until 1914, UCAs were not enforced by the Senate's presiding officer and, oddly, could not be modified, even by unanimous consent. In the late nineteenth century, senators considered UCAs to be informal "gentleman's agreements"—agreements among senators on the floor at a particular moment—that could not be enforced by the presiding officer and could not be modified by senators who happened to be on the floor at a later time. These circumstances limited the use of UCAs as devices for expediting the business of the chamber. The functionality of UCAs improved greatly with the adoption of new provisions to Rule 12 in 1914. The new rule made UCAs orders of the Senate, which meant that they were enforceable by the presiding officer, and stipulated that they could be modified by unanimous consent.[3]

Senate policy-making processes emerged in an institutional context in which the majority party's leaders had limited ability to control the policy agenda and influence outcomes. It is reasonable to assume that the institutional context limited the incentives to create powerful leadership posts. Authority granted to a central leader by the party would not translate into significant influence over the Senate, because of the minority's ability to offer amendments and conduct extended debate. Any move by the majority party to create a rule that would enhance the power of the majority leader would be filibustered by the minority. In fact, formal floor leadership posts were not developed until the twentieth century, long after such positions were adopted by House parties. Senate party caucus chairs were mere presiding officers and real political leadership arose only informally. "Floor leaders" were informally recognized, at least among Democrats, in the last few years of the nineteenth century; only gradually between 1900 and the 1930s did most of the duties of the modern floor leader emerge. And even then, scheduling was a matter of gaining unanimous consent to bring up legislation and give some order to its consideration, at least in the absence of invoking cloture, which limits debate and requires amendments to be germane.

Senator Joe Robinson (D-Ark.) is recognized as the first modern Senate leader. Robinson assumed personal responsibility for chairing his party conference, managing the floor and negotiating UCAs, and representing his party colleagues before reporters and at the White House. He was the first floor leader granted the right of first recognition and he proved to be ever-present on the floor. Since Robinson's time, the burden of managing the Senate in the face of potential obstructionism, with weak parliamentary tools for scheduling Senate action, has fallen on the shoulders of the majority leader.

Throughout the Senate's history, many observers have argued that the Senate is what senators want it to be. A "deliberative body" that "protects the rights of minorities," serves as the "brakes on the runaway train of government," and "allows issues and opinion to mature" before action are the acquired rationalizations for the Senate's procedures, its tolerance of obstructionism, and its weak leadership. In fact, from time to time Senate majorities have attempted to modify the chamber's rules to allow for a vote on legislation or executive business only to find that minority obstructionism prevented action on their proposals. Most recently, Senate Majority Leader Bill Frist sought a rule that would allow the Senate to eventually vote on presidential nominations, only to find minority objection to the consideration of the resolution approved by a majority of the Committee on Rules and Administration. As Senator Bayh implies, politics, not procedural principle, has dictated the path of development in the Senate's policy-making process.

Key Features of Contemporary Senate Politics

Scholars frequently characterize the decision-making processes of the House of Representatives as varying along a historical continuum from decentralized to centralized policy making. At the decentralized end, House decision making is centered in standing committees, as it was during the mid-twentieth century. At the centralized end, the leadership of the majority party directs the legislative process, as it did during the speakership of Newt Gingrich (R-Ga.).

The Senate, however, has not seen such swings between decentralization and centralization. Rather, the absence of rules limiting floor debate and amendments has constrained just how committee-oriented or leader-dominated Senate legislating can be. Senate floor leaders and bill managers are more likely than their House counterparts to face uncertainty about what will transpire on the floor. Individual legislators, factions, and the minority party carry greater weight on the Senate floor than on the House floor. Consequently, the Senate process might be characterized as generally more floor-oriented or collegial than the House process, where legislating is more strongly directed by committee or party leaders.

At the same time, both houses have been forced to adapt to a number of key features of modern congressional politics. The most important features are individualism, the preeminence of budget measures, frequent divided-party control of the House, Senate, and presidency, and an intense partisanship that has worked to transform governing into campaigning.[4]

Individualism has long been a distinctive characteristic of the Senate. The chamber has long been known for its oversized personalities and its iconoclasts. For many generations, the Senate floor, in the absence of germaneness and general time limitations on debate, has provided a platform for senators to promote themselves and reach a national audience.

Individualism in both houses of Congress has ratcheted up a few notches since the 1960s due to developments in and out of Washington, D.C. Congressional candidates create their own campaign organizations, raise their own money, and set their own campaign strategies. This independence from the national political parties tends to carry over when the winners take office. Once in office, legislators use official resources and exploit their relationships with interest groups and political action committees for political advantage. They hire professional campaign managers, consultants, and pollsters. And they absorb public opinion polls, utilize the latest communications technologies, travel to their home states most weekends, and spend a great deal of time raising money. Senators now raise about twenty thousand dollars for each week of their six-year terms on average, with only minuscule contributions to party organizations. These developments draw legislators' attention away from the halls of Congress, from their committee work, and from the leaders. They breed hypersensitivity to public opinion, grandstanding, rigidity, and paralysis.

The large federal budget deficit was a dominant force in legislative politics during the period from 1980 to 1995. The respite from deficits in the late 1990s ended early in the administration of President George W. Bush in the aftermath of deep tax cuts and sharply increased spending on national security and defense following the 9/11 attacks. Government spending and tax policy are central to the differences between the two parties and so contributed to heightened partisanship in Washington. The budget process pushed key policy decisions into the hands of central budget and party leaders, who often consulted with one another and with administration officials behind closed doors. The parties' casting of and avoiding blame for the deficits, and disagreements over the required legislative response, sharpened partisanship.

The domination of budget deficits on the congressional agenda further restricted the discretion to Senate (and House) committees. Spending caps limited the number and size of new policy initiatives. Reconciliation instructions, put in place almost every year through budget resolutions designed by budget committee and party leaders, frequently required committees to report legislation that cut spending on programs in ways that the committees would not have supported otherwise. Only bills of the appropriations committees, which had to juggle spending priorities under spending caps, were generally protected from major challenges on the floor. In the Senate, the caps were backed by budget enforcement rules that provided points of order against amendments violating the caps; a sixty-vote majority was required to overrule the presiding officer on such points of order.

Perhaps the most conspicuous feature of Senate politics in recent decades has been the close division between the two parties. After twenty-six years of Democratic control, the Republicans won a Senate majority in the 1980 elections, only to lose their majority in the 1986 elections. The Republicans regained a majority in the 1994 elections, but majority status switched back to the Democrats in 2001 after Senator James Jeffords of Vermont gave up his Republican affiliation, declared independence, and caucused with the Democrats. Republicans regained a bare majority after the 2002 elections.

Political scientist Richard F. Fenno Jr. has argued that frequent changes in party control is a check on the majority party.[5] Such changes reduce the temptation for a new majority to overreach itself once in office. For the minority, the likelihood of a return to majority status in the foreseeable future encourages responsible behavior. If Fenno is right, then alternating control of Congress produces greater flexibility in party policy positions, more pragmatic party strategies, greater civility in political discourse, and perhaps greater public support for the institution. A political "uncertainty principle"—that an uncertain electoral future breeds political moderation—may operate in Congress.

However, while there have been signs that minority-party leaders want to appear responsible and deserving of majority-party status, the general pattern appears to be one of mutual recrimination as the parties seek to gain or maintain majorities. The oppose-at-every-turn tactics advocated by Newt Gingrich to promote the Republicans' interest in gaining a House majority in the 1980s and early 1990s were employed by Democrats in both houses a few years later. While senators sometimes insisted that the Senate should not become a "partisan cesspool" like the House, many complained that it became one and sometimes blamed this on the number of senators who had served in the House during the Gingrich era. The volume of partisan rhetoric in both houses was as high at the turn of the twenty-first century as any sitting member could remember.

Underlying the rhetoric appears to be a real polarization in the policy preferences of the two senatorial parties. Figure 1 shows the pattern of Senate voting behavior measured on a liberal-conservative continuum in the period after World War II. Beginning in the late 1980s, the central tendencies of the Senate parties began to diverge and the intraparty cohesiveness of both parties increased. The pattern in the House (not shown) is similar, which suggests that both houses have experienced intensified party polarization for similar reasons, whatever they may be. The consequence is that party leaders were pushed harder and harder by party colleagues to avoid compromise with the opposition, to

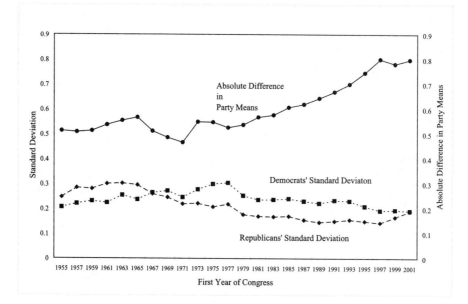

NOTE: Scores based on DW-NOMINATE scores.

SOURCE: http://voteview.uh.edu/dwnomin.htm.

Figure 1   Inter-Party Differences and Intra-Party Standard Deviations in Liberalism Scores, 1955–2002

brand the opposition as the enemy of the public good, and to score political points against the opposition whenever possible. Both professional and personal relations across party lines reached a very low point.

The causes of congressional partisanship take us beyond the scope of this essay, but a little speculation is in order. It appears that public opinion may have polarized in the early 1990s—after congressional parties began polarizing in the 1980s.[6] A reasonable speculation is that the groups important to nomination politics within each party—for example, the Christian right, gun owners, and anti-abortion groups for Republicans, reproductive-rights activists, environmentalists, and labor groups for Democrats—played a pivotal role in pushing less-moderate candidates in each party. And congressional activists, such as Newt Gingrich on the right, actively recruited like-minded candidates in the two parties. The result was more-polarized pairs of candidates in congressional election contests. In this way, most winners, especially new legislators, contributed to the partisan polarization that emerged in the halls of Congress. But there appears to be more to it than the electoral coalitions of the parties. The competitive balance of the two parties nationally, producing narrow majorities in Congress and extremely tight presidential contests, appears to produce an emphasis on exaggerating differences between the parties, giving up on compromise, and scoring political points against the opposition at every opportunity.

Obstructionism on presidential nominations and other matters has further intensified partisanship in the Senate. While partisanship is visible across a wide range of issues, it has been most frequently noted on judicial nominations. Senators of both parties have obstructed floor action on large numbers of the judicial nominees of opposition presidents. The contending forces in the battle over judicial nominations are typically backed by well-financed outside groups on both the left and the right, which see the appointment of certain federal judges, who hold their posts for life, as a threat to the groups' respective social and political agendas.

In the face of Democratic obstructionism on judicial nominations during the presidency of George W. Bush, Senate Republicans threatened the "nuclear option." The strategy proposed a ruling by Vice President Richard Cheney, in his capacity as presiding officer, that cloture could be invoked on judicial nominations by a simple majority, which could be backed by a majority to table an appeal of the ruling. In the view of Democrats, this would be a gross violation of the precedents of the Senate and might encourage the Democrats to obstruct action on all other legislation—that is, to "go nuclear." The Republicans resisted the temptation to use that option, but threat of its use hardened partisan feelings. A crisis over the nuclear option was averted in 2005 when a group of Democrats and Republicans promised to allow some nominations to come to a vote and to oppose a ruling by the vice president to allow a simple majority to invoke cloture.

In 2003, the Senate's majority-party Republicans took the unusual step of excluding Democrats from conference-committee discussions on key bills. Democratic leader Tom Daschle (D-S.D.) was among the banned conferees. Democrats responded by filibustering motions to appoint conferees on other bills. In 2004 Senate Republican leader Bill Frist (R-Tenn.) took the unusual step of appearing at a rally and fund-raiser for Daschle's opponent in the South Dakota senatorial race, hardly consistent with the traditional practice of not campaigning in person against a fellow leader with whom good working relations are necessary. With a fifty-one-seat majority, Frist apparently decided that promoting Daschle's opponent and retaining control of the Senate warranted this breach of tradition. Senators continue to report that personal relations across party lines are poor. Both parties have been creating precedents they hardly want the other side to follow when majority control is reversed.

How does partisan polarization, high since the 1980s, mix with the individualism that emerged in the 1960s and 1970s? On the face of it, partisanship seems to imply disciplined party action, which is seemingly contrary to the exercise of individualism (see Jacobson in this volume). There really is no incompatibility, however. In recent Congresses, the vast majority of senators both voluntarily supported the party line on substantive issues and continued to build their own campaign organizations, raise record campaign contributions, and cater to the swarm of organized interests that hover over the Senate. Party-line votes and aggressive individualists are the everyday features of the contemporary chamber.

Leadership in the Contemporary Senate

Senate parties and leaders adapted to the conditions shaping modern Senate decision-making processes in many ways, including an elaboration of leadership positions and party organization, the evolution of unanimous-consent agreements and holds, and the centralization of some of the most legislatively important functions in the position of floor leader. These developments represent reasonable adaptations by senators and their parties to evolving circumstances, but they have often intensified the effects of individualism, obstructionism, and partisanship that have marked the Senate in recent decades.

Floor Leaders

In the contemporary Senate, the floor leader assumes personal responsibility for party strategy. The floor leader is expected to direct all major activities of party leadership—managing the floor, serving as party spokesman, working with the president, building winning coalitions, and electioneering. Responsibilities that were once the province of a steering or policy committee now rest squarely with the floor leader. To be sure, party committees and task forces have some significance in collective party efforts, but their job has been to assist the leader rather than to replace him or her.

Scheduling floor activity is the central function of the modern leader. The fact that the majority and minority leaders often are called the "floor leaders" reflects the traditional importance of this task.[7] Since the days of Joe Robinson (D-Ark.) in the 1930s, floor leaders have been the most visible senators on the floor. In the modern era, floor leaders have averaged more than four times as many entries for floor remarks in the index of the *Congressional Record* as the average senator. Senator Robert Byrd (D-W.V.) relished his floor duties; more recent leaders have turned over to assistant leaders responsibility for being on the floor during routine debate.

Serving as party spokesman emerged as a vital role in parallel to floor duties for the majority and minority leaders. The number of mentions of floor leaders' comments in the major newspapers and electronic media routinely exceed those for other senators in recent decades.[8] Since the 1970s, leaders have been expected to be effective on television. Being likeable and articulate and "looking good in a blue suit" are a central theme of discussions of leaders' qualities. Senator Byrd, an incumbent leader, was not particularly telegenic and was even challenged for reelection to his leadership post on the grounds that his party needed a more effective spokesman Byrd survived the challenge but retired from the position to make way for a new leader two years later. As the most visible partisans in a partisan era, leaders also have become high-priority targets for opposition leaders and radio talk show hosts.

All recent floor leaders of the president's party have been the primary conduit for communication between the White House and their Senate party colleagues. While all leaders say their loyalty belongs to their party colleagues and their institution, most leaders of the president's party assume that helping the president succeed is in the interest of their colleagues and give this operational function high priority. The reason is plain to all senators—the president's popularity influences senatorial electoral prospects. Championing the president's legislative program, promoting the president's interests by holding press conferences and addressing the public through floor speeches, and making television appearances to argue for the president's policies are regular fare for recent leaders.

During most of the Senate's history, responsibility for building legislative coalitions was assumed by bill managers, typically chairs of the committees originating legislation. Even under Democratic leaders Mike Mansfield (D-Mont.) and Byrd in the 1960s and 1970s, bill managers usually took the lead in rounding up votes. But since that time the burden has shifted to floor leaders for the most important legislation. The concentration of the legislative agenda in a few budget and tax measures of overriding importance to the president and fellow partisans, the difficulty of overcoming obstructionism on many measures, and the polarization of the parties have contributed substantially to the importance of building coalitions for or against legislation. This duty is integrated with the floor leader's responsibilities for scheduling, public relations, and coordinating with the White House.

Majority and minority leaders are intimately involved in fund-raising efforts and, because of their visibility in the media, are popular speakers at the fund-raising events of their colleagues. Leaders have been particularly important in persuading their partisans to contribute from their personal campaign bank accounts to the campaigns of colleagues up for reelection. "Leadership PACs"— political action committees created by legislators—have facilitated fund-raising for party colleagues while promoting the senators' own efforts to run for leadership posts or the presidency. Such PACs have been created by a large number of senators, extending far beyond the top leaders, but the leaders' ability to draw an audience and raise money keeps them central to party fund-raising efforts. Both Senate campaign committees target their money to close contests, with incumbents given some priority over challengers and open-seat candidates.[9]

Challenges of Managing the Floor

Rule 22 has not changed since 1975, when the Senate reduced the threshold for cloture to a three-fifths constitutional majority (sixty votes if all seats are filled). Nevertheless, starting with the Reorganization Act of 1939 and expanding into many policy areas since the 1970s, the Senate has supported limits on debate and amendments for specific types of legislation. The most conspicuous special process applies to budget measures, but the Senate has accepted debate limits in many other policy areas—many involving the delegation of authority to the executive branch, in which the Senate seeks to guarantee that it makes an affirmative decision to stop or allow a planned executive action. No overriding commitment to unlimited debate was apparent in Senate action on these procedural constraints. No concern about the preservation of the deliberative character of the Senate—or even to the interests of the minority, geographical areas of the country, or small states—seemed to exist among a majority of senators when these provisions were enacted.[10]

Even so, party leaders have confronted more widespread obstructionism since the early 1970s than at any time in the Senate's history. Measuring the number of filibusters is a tricky business. Obstructionism may come in the form of threatened filibusters. Cloture motions, which can be counted, may be used more than once for the same bill, and they may be used to prevent nongermane amendments rather than to limit debate. And cloture petitions may not be filed in the face of a filibuster when the proponents of a measure know that they do not have votes to adopt the cloture motion. Nevertheless, the number of cloture motions (see Figure 2) is a crude indicator of trends in the majority leader's efforts to overcome obstructionism, which typically is a product of minority-party objections to unanimous-consent requests to consider or to provide for a final vote on measures.

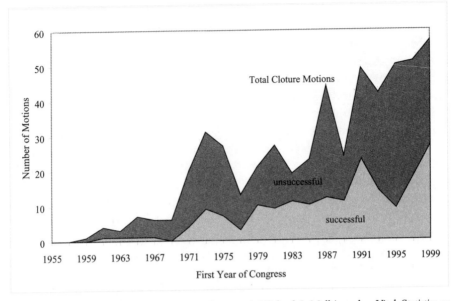

SOURCE: Norman J. Ornstein, Thomas E. Mann, and Michael J. Malbin, eds., *Vital Statistics on Congress, 2001–2002* (Washington, D.C.: AEI Press, 2002).

Figure 2 Number of Successful and Unsuccessful Cloture Motions, 1955–2000

In addition to obstructionism, demands of other kinds have increased the burdens of floor leaders. Senators have placed more demands on floor leaders to schedule floor action to their convenience. Advances in transportation technology allow most senators to return to their home states on weekends, which has encouraged them to accept speaking invitations and attend other events and, in turn, made it important to seek an abbreviated workweek in Washington and insist that floor action be more concentrated in midweek. At the same time, floor leaders must accommodate Senate action on more legislation and provide time for more amendments and speeches. Senate leaders must work around obstructionist colleagues whose leverage is increased by the scarcity of time for floor sessions.

Since the adoption of the modern rule on unanimous consent agreements in 1914 and the emergence of the modern floor leader in the early decades of the twentieth century, the complex unanimous-consent agreement—those limiting debate or amendments in some way—has become the most important scheduling tool of the majority-party leader. Lyndon Johnson (D–Tex.) has been given credit for great innovation in Senate leadership, including his use of UCAs. Congressional observers have noted Johnson's aggressiveness in seeking unanimous consent, showing that when he overcame objections he immediately went

266

to the floor, gained consent for a time limitation, bullied colleagues into with-holding amendments, and rammed the bill through the Senate.[11] Evidence of Johnson's distinctiveness as a floor leader is evident in Table 1. More frequently than his predecessors, Johnson successfully propounded time-limitation agreements before the motion to proceed on a measure was offered, divided control of time for general debate on a bill between the floor leaders, and barred nongermane amendments.[12]

Johnson was the exception to the rule that leaders have had to accommodate the demands of their colleagues, but his successors have made the negotiation of debate and amendment limits the central part of their scheduling activity. Faced with senators who aggressively sought to protect their parliamentary options, majority leaders devised more and more complicated UCAs to limit debate and amendments to push legislation forward as quickly as possible. Standardized provisions were replaced with provisions tailored to the demands of senators on the bill at hand (see Table 1). Beginning in the mid-1980s, UCAs providing for the consideration of a single amendment were more common. The greater frequency of provisions barring second-degree amendments reflected the leaders' efforts to more fully structure the floor agenda whenever possible. Such provisions were almost always accompanied by provisions barring other motions, appeals, and points of order. At times, although for only a small fraction of bills, amendments to certain sections of bills were barred by UCAs.

Modern Senate UCAs come in all shapes and sizes, but the complex UCAs that are most important limit debate and amendments in some way, as is shown in this 2003 excerpt from the *Congressional Record*:

> Mr. McConnell: Madam President, I ask unanimous consent the Senate now proceed to the consideration of S. 1215, the Burma sanctions bill; that there then be 60 minutes of debate equally divided under the control of myself and the Democratic leader or his designee; further, that no amendments be in order other than a substitute amendment and a technical amendment to that substitute. I ask unanimous consent that following the debate time and the disposition of the above amendments, the bill be read a third time and the Senate proceed to a vote on the passage of the bill, with no intervening action or debate.[13]

Typical of many modern UCAs, this UCA closed possible loopholes for delay with the last provision that the Senate move to a vote "with no intervening action or debate."

While UCAs are often tailored to individual measures or amendments, they also have been used to establish a comprehensive floor agenda for a measure, or even a set of measures, in delicate legislative situations. UCAs have the virtue of being difficult to modify (only by unanimous consent, of course), so they provide a particularly useful means for cementing arrangements intended to guar-

TABLE 1

Selected Provisions of Senate Unanimous Consent Agreements (UCAs), 1935–2000.

Congress	Majority leader	Number of complex UCAs	Set one standard limit for debate on all amdmts.	Set a specific limit for debate on one or more amdmts.	Allow only specified amdmts. to be offered	Bar second degree amdmts.
74th (1935-1936)	Robinson (D-Ark.)	20	55.0	0.0	0.0	0.0
77th (1941-1942)	Barkley (D-Ky.)	12	50.0	0.0	0.0	0.0
82nd (1951-1952)	McFarland (D-Ariz.)	45	68.9	11.1	2.2	0.0
83rd (1953-1954)	Taft (R-Ohio)/ Knowland (R-Calif.)	30	73.3	0.0	0.0	0.0
84th (1955-1956)	Johnson (D-Tex.)	92	78.3	4.4	6.5	0.0
85th (1957-1958)	Johnson (D-Tex.)	36	69.4	5.6	8.3	0.0
88th (1963-1964)	Mansfield (D-Mont.)	96	38.5	35.4	2.1	0.0
92d (1971-1972)	Mansfield (D-Mont.)	378	32.8	47.9	0.3	1.3
96th (1979-1980)	Byrd (D-W.Va.)	407	10.8	46.9	7.1	5.9
98th (1983-1984)	Baker (R-Tenn.)	148	3.4	26.4	29.7	16.2
100th (1987-1988)	Byrd (D-W.Va.)	86	2.3	34.9	14.0	30.2
102d (1991-1992)	Mitchell (D-Maine)	103	2.9	20.4	16.5	49.5
104th (1995-1996)	Dole (R-Kans.)	98	4.1	10.2	18.4	27.6
106th (1999-2000)	Lott (R-Miss.)	105	11.4	33.7	11.4	30.5

antee votes on certain measures or amendments or preclude votes on others. But the need to acquire unanimous consent places a burden on the Senate's floor leaders and gives senators a source of leverage over each other.

Emerging with more creative uses of UCAs in the 1960s and 1970s was the practice of holds. A hold is a threat to block a motion to proceed to the consideration of a bill or resolution. It is communicated, usually in writing, to a floor leader, and recorded on the daily calendar of legislation that is ready for floor action. Generally, the identity of the senator placing the hold is kept confidential. On the majority side, the majority leader takes holds into account when scheduling floor action. On the minority side, the minority leader must object to acting on a measure if a hold has been forwarded to him. Holds have no status in Senate rules or precedent. Rather, they are an informal practice within each of the Senate parties.

Increasingly restrictive UCAs have encouraged senators to request that their floor leaders protect their opportunities to debate, offer amendments, or exploit other parliamentary privileges. The desire to expedite floor activity led floor leaders to seek clearance from their party colleagues and the leader of the minority party for legislation they intended to bring to the floor soon. This process became regularized under the guidance of Byrd when he served as assistant to Mike Mansfield.

Since the 1970s, holds have become more common. Quite frequently, holds are used for purposes unrelated to the measures on which the holds are placed, such as to gain a committee hearing on an unrelated matter, secure the nomination of an individual for an executive position, or simply to register an objection to the behavior of a committee leader or executive official. Holds had become so numerous and troublesome by the 1980s that every majority leader since Howard Baker (R-Tenn.), who served as the Republican majority leader for the 1981–1984 period, has attempted to persuade his colleagues to exercise greater restraint in using them. Leaders also have reiterated their intention to ignore holds at their own convenience and to disclose the identity of senators placing holds, but without exception they have found it difficult to ignore the demands of their party colleagues for observance of their requests and confidentiality.

Elaboration of Party Organization

Individualism, by its nature, intensifies the problem of coordination. Senators are more demanding but more distracted. Moreover, individualism raises the cost of solutions to collective-action problems. Sacrifice for the common good, whether it is a policy position or a commitment of time and effort to party activities, is more difficult to motivate as the opportunity costs increase. As a party seeks to address the competitive challenges as it pursues its collective policy and electoral goals, it must do so by developing more elaborate coordination mechanisms (committees, task forces, leadership positions) and by offering stronger incentives for a few members to devote their energies to the party's welfare. In addition, in an individualistic Senate, entrepreneurial senators, either in the interest of a party faction or in their personal interest, can promote the creation of new party units, positions, and services designed to address these concerns. Indeed, self-driven senators may actually have greater needs for certain kinds of services—public relations, electronic technology, policy research—that party leaders and staffs can be motivated to provide.

Public funding for party organs reflects the expanded activity of the parties. Party spending on staff and services increased slowly through the 1970s, showing little more than inflationary increases. In the 1980s, when Republicans became the majority, party spending began to escalate rapidly. The Republican majority made cuts in party spending in 1995, as part of their effort to meet their promise to reduce Congress's spending on itself, but they quickly returned to the established pattern of expanding party spending. Spending on Senate parties has increased by several orders of magnitude since the early 1980s, reaching about $1.2 billion by 2000.

Senate party organs now provide a wide range of services for senators and their leaders. The Republicans took the lead. Republicans separated their conference and Policy Committee (RPC) staffs in 1979 under conference chair Robert Packwood (R-Ore.), and then proceeded to expand the functions of both staffs. The RPC initiated RPC-TV in 1987 to provide information about floor activity and party functions to offices through the Capitol cable television system. RPC's publication program expanded to many more policy reports and advisories and a new telephone system was created to provide information on floor activity. More election-oriented services were added—media consultation, graphics design, and electronic facilities. An RPC task force on economic policy helped committee leaders on the relevant committees coordinate party activity. And a weekly program, coproduced with the conference, was created and aired on the Senate's cable system. After the Republicans regained a majority in the 1994 elections, RPC staff supported the task forces appointed by floor leader Robert Dole (R-Kans.) and worked more closely with the House Republican Policy Committee on joint hearings, publications, and talking points for senators in an effort to produce a coherent Republican message.[14] At the same time, conference chairs turned the conference office into a large communications center for the party and senators. Under floor leader Trent Lott (R-Miss.) and conference chair Connie Mack (R-Fla.), conference and RPC responsibilities were redistributed so that most media and electronic services were consolidated in the conference staff. The RPC staff then was more focused on research and position papers, developing Web-based resources for Republican offices, and supporting the leadership's policy task forces. This arrangement was retained when Bill Frist replaced Lott as majority leader.

Democrats were slower to develop the range of services for senators and organized collective efforts than the Republicans, primarily because of leader Robert Byrd's lack of interest in doing so in the late 1970s and 1980s. In the late 1970s, Byrd started weekly luncheons for the party under the auspices of the party's Policy Committee (DPC), which he chaired (the Republican

Conference had been meeting weekly since the mid-1950s). But, after making few other changes as majority leader in 1977–1980, Byrd moved after the elections of 1980 not only to vitalize the DPC but to involve more Democrats through task forces and a Democratic Leadership Council. He also hired a politically experienced staff director. But, while the DPC staff began to publish a few more reports, the range of services was limited in comparison with the hundreds of publications and communications services that the Republican party organization offered. The election of George Mitchell (D-Maine) in late 1988 as Democratic leader led to a sharp break with past practices of the DPC. The party had lost another presidential election and was eager to redefine its public image. Mitchell rewarded Tom Daschle (D-S.D.), seen as a moderate, as DPC cochair, the first co- or vice-chair ever appointed for the DPC. Mitchell retained control of the floor staff and foreign policy staff that operated under the auspices of the DPC under Byrd, while Daschle took responsibility for the domestic policy staff and communications staff. The staff supported the many task forces that Mitchell had established. At the same time, an annual issues conference was initiated by Daschle and his staff, and the publication, public relations, and office services program was expanded to match the scope of the Republicans' operations. The DPC-TV operation was expanded in 1989. Daschle soon encouraged the development of "message boards," ad hoc, self-appointed discussion groups of senators with interests in major issues.[15]

Daschle was elected Democratic leader in late 1994 upon Mitchell's retirement and following the loss of Democratic majorities in the House and Senate. The effectiveness of the House Republicans' "Contract with America" platform and weakness of the Clinton administration led Senate Democrats to seek to improve their own public relations efforts. Daschle created a new Committee on Technology and Communications and appointed Jay Rockefeller (D-W.V.), a supporter of his leadership bid, to be its chair. The committee was charged with improving the party's electronic technology, expanding radio and television services for senators, and developing a more expansive public relations effort.[16] Daschle continued the cochairmanship arrangement (with Nevada's Harry Reid, a Daschle supporter), but in 1999 gave up the cochairmanship of the DPC and left Byron Dorgan (D-N.Dak.) to chair the committee by himself. By the late 1990s, Senate Democrats had matched Republicans in the range of publications, public relations support, and electronic media services provided by party committees.

In addition to expanding services with enlarged party staffs, the Senate parties added leadership positions and broadened participation within party councils. Task forces on public relations and key policy initiatives are now common. Democratic leader Mike Mansfield (D-Mont.) and his successors expanded their party's Steering Committee, to accommodate a wider range of partisans in the committee assignment process. Democratic leader Mitchell appointment the first assistant floor leader who, in addition to the elected whip, helps the floor leader cover floor activity. Daschle continued the practice. Under Daschle, the leader gave up the chairmanship of the Steering Committee and broadened its jurisdiction, renaming it the Steering and Coordination Committee. Hillary Clinton (D-N.Y.) was named to head the committee, and a new post, chief deputy for strategic outreach, was created for Barbara Boxer (D-Calif.).

On the Republican side, leadership positions had long been shared more widely, but the party conference moved to limit the independence of the chairs of standing committees. In response to frustration with the voting behavior of a committee chair, the Republican Conference required that secret ballots be cast in committee contingents and then in conference on committee chairmanships and set a six-year term limit on committee chairs and party leaders other than the floor leader. The move created more opportunities for participation while establishing higher expectations for adherence to party positions.[17]

Finally, the senatorial campaign committees have greatly expanded their operations. As for the House parties' campaign committees, Senate campaign committees nearly tripled their receipts between the late 1980s and the 2003–2004 election cycle. The staff for the campaign committees now numbers in the dozens. The leaders and staff continue to focus on reelecting incumbent partisans, but they now play a much larger role in recruiting candidates to challenge opposition-party incumbents and to run in open seats. They provide a full array of campaign services, although the direct campaign contributions are more important as start-up money and add up to only a small fraction of what candidates raise on their own.

Efforts toward Reform

A sensible hypothesis about the condition of the modern Senate is that it is tolerated by senators because, at least on balance, it serves their interests reasonably well. Intraparty reforms to improve the accountability of committee leaders to the parent parties and the expansion of party services have been accepted without much fanfare. Reform of the Senate's rules is another matter. The record shows that even when a majority of the Senate appears eager to relieve its frustration with obstruction, it is unable to get even the most modest changes adopted.

Senators periodically call for reform and reform efforts have been undertaken. Proposals to create new means for limiting debate have been offered by senators and others. Some efforts to limit debate for specified purposes, such as budget measures, have been adopted and have proven important. In recent years, reform of the practice of holds has been demanded, but efforts at reform have failed. The root cause is Rule 22. Two recent proposals for reform that went nowhere illustrate the problem.

In 2003 Senators Chuck Grassley (R-Iowa) and Ron Wyden (D-Ore.) proposed a new rule that they hoped would limit the harm done by the practice of holds. Under the proposed rule, senators would be required to disclose holds in the *Congressional Record* no later than two session days after providing notice to the party leadership. The proposal promised to enhance the accountability of senators placing holds to Senate colleagues and to the American people. In the view of the sponsors, disclosure would speed negotiations to remove obstacles to floor action and may reduce the incentives to place holds in the first place. These are laudable goals, but the proposal had serious flaws: No effective means of enforcement was proposed, holds would be given official status in the Senate's rules for the first time, the new rule would encourage senators to wait until the last moment to place holds in order to avoid premature disclosure of their identity, and the proposal did not guarantee disclosure for senators placing holds through intermediaries other than party leaders, such as through faction leaders.

Ultimately, the Senate Committee on Rules and Administration took no action on the proposal. While many senators seemed to favor limiting the use of holds, the proposed rule was likely to be ineffective. The procedural foundations of holds are (a) the possibility of obstruction by filibuster, (b) the necessary reliance of floor leaders on obtaining unanimous consent to consider most measures and to expedite debate and amending activity, and (c) the desirability of anticipating objections to unanimous-consent requests. The effectiveness of holds is enhanced by the coordinating role of floor leaders and by secrecy. The willingness of floor leaders to observe holds is understandable but greatly reduces the costs to senators who seek to block floor action. Secrecy increases the effectiveness of holds by reducing accountability and slowing the process of removing obstacles to floor consideration of legislation or nominations. The Grassley-Wyden proposal addressed secrecy but not the facilitating role of floor leaders. It is likely that secrecy remains because it is convenient for both leaders and their party colleagues. Senators sometimes conjecture that leaders appreciate the secrecy of some holds. Minority leaders, in particular, find it convenient to attribute to an anonymous colleague an objection to action on a measure or nomination. This helps them deflect a charge of partisan obstructionism. If, under a regime structured by obstructionism and unanimous-consent agreements, secrecy suits the needs of both a party leader and his party colleagues, there is reason to be skeptical about the ability of the Senate to successfully demand disclosure or reduce the use of holds.

Another reform proposal, this one authored by Majority Leader Frist in 2003, was aimed at eliminating obstructionism on presidential nominations, one of two classes of executive business under Senate rules (the other being treaties). Specifically modeled after a proposal authored by Senators Tom Harkin (D-Iowa) and Joseph Lieberman (D-Conn.) years earlier that applied to all motions, the Frist proposal would allow a cloture petition to be filed after twelve hours of debate on a presidential nomination and, starting with the standard three-fifths (sixty) constitutional majority requirement for cloture, reduce to fifty-seven, fifty-four, and fifty-one votes as the number required to close debate over successive two-day periods and to a simple majority of senators present and voting thereafter.

Frist's proposal, under Rule 22, would have been filibustered and killed had the majority leader demanded Senate action on it. The Republican leader hoped that by limiting the possibility of simple majority cloture to nominations that he could attract votes to have the new rule adopted. But, surely as he expected, Frist never scheduled the resolution for floor consideration because it would have been filibustered by the Democrats. Democrats Harkin and Lieberman, by then in the minority party, did not testify at the committee hearing on the Frist proposal or address the issue on the Senate floor. Instead, Harkin railed against the hypocrisy of the Republicans for condemning the Democrats for blocking judicial nominations by filibuster.

Why doesn't the Senate majority simply force extended debates that either wear down the opposition or make the minority pay a bigger political price for obstructionism? This "tough guy" solution is the advice that every majority leader gets from frustrated party colleagues who believe that the minority can be forced to back down one way or another. Majority leaders very seldom take the advice, for two reasons. First, in the individualistic Senate, leaders are under considerable pressure to make the Senate's schedule "family friendly"—that is, to keep a civil schedule that allows senators time to spend at home (or, as the cynics say, campaigning). Second, however long the majority leader keeps the Senate in session, he or she is unlikely to overcome the obstacles to the measures at issue, is likely to delay consideration of other legislation and further complicate scheduling problems, and the leader and the leader's party may be blamed for their inability to govern effectively, whoever is actually at fault in the matter at hand.

Rule 22 has its proponents. The argument is that the rule preserves the deliberative character of the Senate by allowing senators to speak at length without interruption. In this way, Senate debate serves to slow decision making and allow the public to be educated on the great issues. Furthermore, it is said that Rule 22 protects sizable minorities from legislative measures that mean-spirited or vindictive majorities might pass. The House of Representatives, under the influence of the large states, must be balanced with the supermajoritarian Senate in order to protect the interests of small states and minority groups. Moreover, it is often argued, the framers of the Constitution intended for the Senate to be different and their scheme should not be tampered with except under the most exceptional of circumstances.

However, many of the standard arguments against reform of Rule 22 are not viable.[18] In practice, little meaningful deliberation occurs on the Senate floor. On only the rarest of occasions, such as the debate over the 1991 resolution on the

Persian Gulf War, do senators engage in extended, thoughtful exchanges before a full chamber. Instead, under pressure to attend committee meetings, raise campaign funds, meet with lobbyists and constituents, and travel home, senators deliberately minimize the time they spend on the floor. To be sure, obstructionism can extend debate and draw attention to the Senate, but seldom is a filibuster or threatened filibuster used for that purpose. Indeed, even with limits on debate, the Senate can arrange for a lengthy debate at any time by unanimous consent or suspension of the rules. As for small-state senators, they have never banded together to protect Rule 22; rather, their separate partisan interests generally have dictated their positions on reform. Historically, minority interests—slaveholding states, anti–civil rights forces, and many others—have been protected with some frequency. And there is no evidence that the framers of the Constitution intended that measures could be prevented from coming to a vote in the Senate. Instead, the framers sought protection against unwise majorities by building a separation-of-powers, bicameral system. Other than providing for supermajorities on constitutional amendments and the approval of treaties, the framers did not address extended debate and put in place one rule allowing both houses of Congress to choose their own rules. Brass-knuckle politics, not high procedural principle, has kept the filibuster in place.

Senators have an obligation to continue to explore proposals for limiting the harm of Senate obstructionism and in encouraging quality public deliberation in the one national institution in which it is feasible. This goal is hardly original; Henry Clay and Daniel Webster sought the same thing. While there is no reason to be optimistic that they will be adopted, reasonable proposals that achieve a new balance between preserving deliberation and minority rights, on the one hand, and improving legislative efficiency on the other, are available and deserve support. As long as lengthy, exhaustive debate is preserved, there is little reason to prevent the majority from eventually casting a vote on an amendment, bill, nomination, or treaty.

The plan proposed by Senators Harkin and Lieberman remains a viable scheme for balancing the competing values underlying majority rule and extended debate. By ratcheting down the number of votes required for cloture over a determined period of time, the Senate would preserve the right to lengthy and exhaustive debate while allowing the majority to eventually pass a motion. A second consideration is the advance notice required before a vote occurs on a cloture petition. To lengthen the period for a cloture petition to ripen as the threshold for cloture is reduced makes sense. The minority gains additional time to persuade the public and perhaps Senate colleagues of the virtues of their position as the Senate moves closer to simple majority action on a measure. Another reasonable step is to allow simple majorities to limit debate for limited purposes, such as consideration of a specified set of amendments, in order to expedite Senate action without eliminating the possibility of a filibuster of the underlying bill.

Conclusion

The job of leading the Senate has been likened to the herding of cats. If only it were so easy. Leaders struggle with far more than the stubbornness and idiosyncrasies of members. They must operate in an institution constrained by the supermajority requirement of Rule 22 and, whenever they can, by the necessity of gaining unanimous consent. But, remarkably perhaps, the Senate is not entirely ungovernable. Most senators do not fully exploit their parliamentary prerogatives; they do not have the time to do so. But more senators have exploited those prerogatives more frequently in recent decades, creating a body that has often been nearly dysfunctional.

The contrast between the modern Senate and the modern House of Representatives is stark, even considering that both houses are deeply affected by new-styled election campaigns, polarized parties, and intense partisanship. The House has seen an ebb and flow in the degree of centralization and decentralization in its policy-making processes but seldom obstructionism. Polarized parties tend to empower their leaders and the majority party manages to get most of its program passed. If House rules allow minority obstructionism, the rules get changed. The ability of the majority to impose rules and gain votes allows it to run roughshod over minority rights.

For the Senate, partisanship and obstruction breed stalemate. It is not an institution that comes close to meeting its oft-claimed special purpose of preserving deliberation in the policy-making process. Instead, the institution is frequently hijacked by senators eager to pursue their individual policy and electoral goals and by concerted party action to score points against the opposition. The Senate's inherited rules limit the degree to which policy making can be pushed off the floor to committees or to central leaders. The possibility of a filibuster and the offering of nongermane amendments keeps senators focused on the floor as a location where they can modify the details of legislation. Thus the Senate, in contrast to the majoritarian House, remains a more floor-oriented, collegial institution.

Notes

1. *Congressional Record* 164 (November 12, 2003), S 14543.
2. Still, senators often sought solutions to institutional problems by experimenting with enhanced authority for their presiding officer during the nineteenth century. Maintaining order on the floor and assigning senators to committees proved difficult at times before the Civil War, while managing the floor agenda and implementing unanimous-consent agreements were vexing problems in the last decades of the century. On matters concerning basic features of Senate floor procedure, such as maintaining order and enforcing unanimous-consent agreements, the presiding offi-

cer was eventually granted clear authority. But the authority was nondiscretionary. And, on other matters, such as setting the agenda and making committee assignments, senators and their parties eventually invented other means for solving these problems. See Gerald Gamm and Steven S. Smith, "The Emergence of Senate Party Leadership."

3. Gamm and Smith, "The Emergence of Senate Party Leadership."

4. For an extensive treatment of changes in the Senate's political environment, see Barbara Sinclair, *The Transformation of the U.S. Senate.*

5. Richard F. Fenno Jr., *Learning to Govern: An Institutional View of the 104th Congress* (Washington, D.C.: Brookings Institution, 1997).

6. Gary C. Jacobson, "Party Polarization in National Politics," 1–30.

7. Gamm and Smith, "The Emergence of Senate Party Leadership."

8. Stephen Hess, *The Ultimate Insiders*; Steven S. Smith, "Congressional Leaders and Foreign Policy," in *Congress and the Making of Foreign Policy*, edited by Paul E. Peterson (Norman: University of Oklahoma Press, 1984).

9. Paul Herrnson, *Congressional Elections*, 2nd ed. (Washington, D.C.: CQ Press, 2000), 84–119.

10. Sarah Binder and Steven S. Smith, *Politics or Principle: Filibustering in the United States Senate* (Washington, D.C.: Brookings Institution, 1997).

11. Robert A. Caro, *The Years of Lyndon Johnson*; Rowland Evans and Robert Novak, *Lyndon B. Johnson: The Exercise of Power* (New York: New American Library, 1966).

12. Steven S. Smith and Marcus Flathman, "Managing the Senate Floor: Complex Unanimous Consent Agreements since the 1950s," *Legislative Studies Quarterly* 14, no. 3 (August 1989): 349–374.

13. *Congressional Record* (June 11, 2003), S7690.

14. William P. Connelly, "Party Policy Committees in Congress," paper presented at the annual meeting of the Western Political Science Association, Seattle, Washington, March 21–23, 1991; Samuel C. Patterson and Thomas H. Little, "The Organizational Life of the Congressional Parties," paper presented at the annual meeting of the Midwest Political Science Association, Chicago, Illinois, April 9–11, 1992; and Donald A. Ritchie, *A History of the United States Senate Republican Policy Committee, 1947–1997* (Washington, D.C.: Government Printing Office, 1997).

15. Personal interview, George Mitchell, March 28, 1992; Connelly, "Party Policy Committees in Congress"; Patterson and Little, "The Organizational Life of the Congressional Parties"; Sean Q. Kelly, "Democratic Leadership in the Modern Senate: The Emerging Roles of the Democratic Policy Committee," paper presented at the annual meeting of the American Political Science Association, New York City, September 1–4, 1994.

16. Sean Kelly, "Passing the Torch: Generational Change and the Selection of the Senate Democratic Leader in the 104th Congress," paper presented at the annual meeting of the Midwest Political Science Association, Chicago, April 6–8, 1995.

17. Helen Dewar, "Senate Republicans Put a Lid on Seniority by Limiting Terms of Chairman," *Washington Post*, July 20, 1995, A25.

18. Binder and Smith, *Politics or Principle.*

Bibliography

Aldrich, John H. *Why Parties? The Origin and Transformation of Political Parties in America.* Chicago: University of Chicago Press, 1995.

Ansolabehere, Stephen, James Snyder Jr., and Charles Stewart III. "The Effects of Party and Preferences on Congressional Roll Call Voting." *Legislative Studies Quarterly* 26, no. 4 (2001): 533–572.

Bawn, Kathleen. "Congressional Party Leadership: Utilitarian versus Majoritarian Incentives." *Legislative Studies Quarterly* 23, no. 2 (1998), 219–243.

Brady, David, David Epstein, and Mathew McCubbins, eds. *Party, Process, and Political Change in Congress.* Stanford, Calif.: Stanford University Press, 2002.

Caro, Robert A. *The Years of Lyndon Johnson: Master of the Senate.* New York: Alfred A. Knopf, 2002.

Cox, Gary, and Mathew McCubbins. *Legislative Leviathan: Party Government in the House.* Berkeley: University of California Press, 1993.

Cox, Gary, and Mathew McCubbins. *Legislative Leviathan Revisited.* Cambridge, U.K.: Cambridge University Press, forthcoming.

Froman, Lewis, Jr., and Randall Ripley. "Conditions for Party Leadership: The Case of the House Democrats." *American Political Science Review* 59, no. 1 (1965), 52–63.

Gamm, Gerald, and Steven S. Smith. "The Dynamics of Party Government in Congress." In *Congress Reconsidered*, 7th ed., edited by Lawrence C. Dodd and Bruce I. Oppenheimer. Washington, D.C.: Congressional Quarterly Press, 2001.

Gamm, Gerald, and Steven S. Smith, "The Emergence of Senate Party Leadership," in *Senate Exceptionalism*, edited by Bruce I. Oppenheimer. Columbus: Ohio State University Press, 2002.

Hess, Stephen. *The Ultimate Insiders: U.S. Senators in the National Media.* Washington, D.C.: Brookings Institution Press, 1986.

Jacobson, Gary C. "Party Polarization in National Politics: The Electoral Connection," in *Polarized Politics: Congress and the President in a Partisan Era*, edited by J. Bond and R. Fleischer. Washington, D.C.: Congressional Quarterly Press, 2000.

Maltzman, Forrest. *Competing Principals: Committees, Parties, and the Organization of Congress.* Ann Arbor: University of Michigan Press, 1997.

Ripley, Randall B. *Majority Party Leadership in Congress.* Boston: Little, Brown, 1969.

Sinclair, Barbara. *Transformation of the U.S. Senate.* Baltimore: Johns Hopkins University Press, 1989.

POLICY AND PERFORMANCE

10

INTERESTS, CONSTITUENCIES, AND POLICY MAKING

Frances E. Lee

If we can not at once . . . make our government what it ought to be, we can at least take a stand against . . . any prostitution of our Government to the advancement of the few at the expense of the many.
—President Andrew Jackson, veto of the Bank Renewal Bill, 1832

I F THE VOLUME OF POLITICAL RHETORIC ON A TOPIC indicates its importance, then the undue influence of "the few" is one of the most serious and long-standing problems facing American government. Since the time of Andrew Jackson and before, politicians have been promising to take the government back from narrow interests and return it to its rightful owners, the American people. Politicians perennially make these promises because they recognize that a substantial portion of the voting public believes that American governing institutions too frequently sacrifice or neglect the interests of "the many" in order to serve the interests of "the few." Of all the institutions of American government, the U. S. Congress is typically perceived by the public as most ensnared and corrupted by the influence of narrow interests.[1]

The U.S. Constitution charges the Congress with providing for the "general welfare," with legislating in the interest of the whole. As a democratic institution, however, Congress faces enormous and continuous pressure to respond to narrow interests. One can distinguish between two types of inducements to put narrow interests ahead of the general. First, all members of Congress are lobbied by the representatives of organized interests. Organization obviously has its advantages. By organizing, individuals or businesses with a common interest are able to ensure that their concerns are heard and that policy makers take them into account. Members of the broad, unorganized public naturally fear the consequences of those advantages and suspect that policy makers will ignore their interests in favor of the louder, more insistent voices of the organized.

A second type of inducement for Congress to prefer the narrow to the general interest—parochialism—is built into the system of representation itself. Each member of Congress is individually elected by a geographically defined constituency. As such, each member represents only a part of the national whole. The pressures created by geographic representation do not draw the ire of the public the way that organized interests do, but they have broad-ranging effects on congressional politics and policy making. Under this electoral system, "the typical Congressman is primarily a Washington representative for his district, not a national legislator."[2] Individual members can neglect the national interest with impunity as long as they can win a voting plurality of their local constituents. Not surprisingly, studies of legislative decision-making have shown that members of Congress "consider the constituency interest first."[3]

This essay assesses parochial and interest-group pressures on Congress in light of members' electoral and career interests—identifying the sources of these pressures, the factors that strengthen or weaken their influence, and the effects each is likely to have on congressional policy-making. The overall picture that emerges suggests that members of Congress have much greater incentive to attend to geographic interests than to organized interests generally. Also examined are the incentives of members of Congress to take a wider view of national policy and the likelihood that these will counterbalance pressures from narrow interests. The essay closes with an examination of the effects of parochialism on congressional policy-making. Although these effects are often misrepresented in popular media treatments of Congress, they are pervasive and important. In broad terms, the conclusion is that congressional policy-making is not hostage to narrow interests. The influence of narrow interests—especially those of the parochial variety—does impair Congress's capacities as a national policy-making institution. However, members have both motive and means to take action in pursuit of their view of the national interest, particularly on issues that clearly implicate their own ideological or partisan commitments.

Geographic Politics

Every senator here is judging the legislation and the amendments thereto on the basis of how his state is going to fare. . . . That is what senators are paid $100,000 a year to do, to look out after their people.

—Senator Dale Bumpers (D–Ark.)

All members of Congress jealously guard their local constituencies' interests. They do so not only because of their electoral self-interest but also because the structure of representation makes parochialism normative. Members are always recognized as the senator or representative from a particular place, and they understand their jobs in these terms. The salaries of members of Congress may be paid out of the federal treasury, but—as with respect to Senator Bumpers above—the system of geographic representation ensures that they view themselves, at least in part, as attorneys for their constituencies. Legislators representing geographic constituencies around the world feel obligated to protect local constituent interests. During Prime Minister's Questions, British members of Parliament demand explanations for government cutbacks in their local constituencies. Canadian members of Parliament rank protecting the interests of their ridings as one of their most important legislative duties. Parceling out representation to geographic constituencies creates legislators who see serving the particular interests of their narrow constituencies as an appropriate and fundamentally important part of their role in the political system.

Parochialism in Comparative Perspective

Compared with other democracies, the U.S. system seems designed to maximize attention to local interests at the expense of national concerns. Most democratic systems today do not elect legislators from single-member districts. Most democracies that still use single-member districts also select national representatives by other means, usually by proportional representation from party lists in large multimember districts. In such "mixed-member" electoral systems, legislators elected from single-member districts have incentives to focus on local constituency service, but they are counterbalanced by legislators whose electoral fortunes are more closely tied to the voters' views of the parties.

In the only two other advanced democracies that still elect all their national representatives from single-member districts, Canada and the United Kingdom, important features of the governmental system sharply curb legislators' parochialism. In these parliamentary systems, policy making is highly centralized in the executive. The executive is able to pass its program with little input from rank-and-file legislators, provided the government can maintain the confidence of its majority in the parliament. Given the hierarchical nature of the process, individual legislators have little leverage to obtain parochial concessions for their constituencies. Moreover, voters in these systems recognize the centralized character of the policy process and see a close link between their local representative's party affiliation and the outcomes of national policy. As a result, they choose candidates overwhelmingly on the basis of their partisan preferences. A legislative candidate's reputation for service to the district, incumbency status, and presentation of self are rarely consequential for winning office. From the viewpoint of individual members, loyalty to party over constituency is encouraged because their path to power is controlled by the party, from their initial election to positions in the cabinet. While rank-and-file members of Parliament have little legislative influence, appointment to a cabinet position means, as Canadian prime minister Pierre Trudeau observed, going "from being a 'nobody' to being a somebody." Ambitious politicians are keenly aware of these facts, and, given these electoral and career incentives, it is hardly surprising that "many Canadians [perceive] that members place constituency views second to party loyalty and do not fully represent local interests when they are forced to choose between the two."[4]

By comparison, legislators seeking a long and successful career in the U.S. Congress have virtually no electoral incentive and little career incentive to put either partisan or national interests ahead of local concerns when the two come into conflict. In electoral terms, it is difficult to imagine a political system that better rewards legislators for focusing on constituency matters. Indeed, one study rank-ordered electoral systems worldwide on the basis of legislators' incentives to cultivate a personal reputation distinct from party and concluded that only one existing type of electoral system (used in the Philippines) clearly places a greater premium on this behavior than the U.S. Congress.[5] Candidates for Congress organize and fund their campaigns largely on the basis of their own efforts as individuals. Once elected, they have many avenues to policy influence. Given the dispersion of power in the Congress, individual members can wield meaningful influence even without obtaining a committee chairmanship or party leadership position. Just winning reelection repeatedly enables a member to build seniority, which remains a path to power even in the more partisan contemporary Congress. Although party loyalty does help members obtain desirable committee positions and other promotions, party leaders in the United States tolerate far more intraparty dissent than is permitted in parliamentary systems, and they generally allow even their most disloyal members to retain their committee assignments.

Differences across Members

Although all members of Congress have strong incentive to attend to constituency concerns, a focus on local matters is especially useful for members serving constituencies that are difficult to represent in other ways. In constituencies that are ideologically heterogeneous or closely divided in party affiliation, virtually any position on national policy that a member takes has the potential to exacerbate divisions in the constituency. Constituency service, by contrast, has the virtue of making friends without simultaneously making enemies. It has a "lowest common denominator" appeal to diverse constituents. A number of studies have shown that electorally vulnerable members obtain more parochial projects for their constituencies.[6] The electoral value of attending to narrow, parochial interests was in evidence during the difficult reelection campaign of Senator Mary Landrieu (D-La.) in 2002. In a state that only two years previously had voted for President Bush by a nine-percentage-point margin, Landrieu was faltering until, just days before the election, she seized upon a "secret deal" purportedly arranged by Bush to increase Mexico's sugar export quota to the United States, a decision that would cut into the profits of Louisiana's $1.7 billion sugar industry. Her new campaign slogan, widely credited with helping her to a narrow victory: "We need a senator who will put Louisiana *first.*"

Salience of Geographic Issues

Many policy issues do not have obvious consequences for geographic constituencies. For parochial pressures to come into play, the policy must involve concentrated benefits or costs that affect groups unified by their geographic location.[7] Policies of this type arise under two conditions: when Congress makes explicit choices about how to distribute federal benefits in geographic terms, and when general provisions of public policy will have markedly different effects in different regions or states.

The system of representation in Congress ensures that members of Congress will be exquisitely sensitive to the geographic effects of federal policies. Members take a strong interest in policy outcomes whenever Congress considers legislation involving the geographic distribution of benefits, even when there is little or no conflict about that distribution. Conflict is often muted in this area because deciding how to distribute federal dollars does not necessarily mean facing tradeoffs. Members of Congress will see one constituency's gain as another's loss only when the structure of the program requires them to do so. Congress has two ways of allocating federal projects and grants (when it does not delegate the task to executive agencies): on an individual basis, as earmarked projects for specific entities or locations within congressional districts, or on the basis of formula. Members of Congress find formula distributions, which are used to allocate most intergovernmental grant money, attractive because they appear to treat all areas fairly: every constituency receives its amount on the basis of objective, quantitative measures of need. However, tradeoffs become apparent when a formula is used because the choice of formula directly affects the amount constituencies receive, with one's gain necessarily another's loss. Disputes over formulas can be difficult to resolve and may degenerate into what Senator John Warner (R-Va.) has dubbed the "battle of the charts," in which senators "put up a matrix which benefits their state a little bit more . . . at the detriment of someone else." Unlike in most policies, such conflicts do not break along partisan lines. "There are no Republicans and no Democrats in this debate," Senate minority leader Bob Dole quipped during consideration of a formula. "If I get $100 more under this formula, I am for it."

When Congress allocates projects as individual earmarks, members do not confront tradeoffs. This is the common pattern in water resource, public lands, and military construction authorizations. Thousands of earmarks are also included in the regular appropriations bills Congress passes annually. A cursory glance at such legislation reveals that there is no apparent limit to the number of projects that can be included. Such bills are often referred to as "Christmas trees" because they bestow gifts on everyone, and no member has a reason to regard another's project as a threat to his or her own. When allocations will be made in this manner, members submit their project proposals to the committees of jurisdiction and expect that, within reason, their requests will be accommodated.

Geographic issues also become salient to members of Congress when public policies will have markedly different effects in different regions or states. Unlike decisions about the allocation of federal benefits, these issues arise as side effects, often accidental, of proposed national policies. For example, Federal Energy Regulatory Commission (FERC) chairman Pat Wood in 2003 sparked a regional dispute in Congress by proposing a new regulatory regime for high-power transmission lines. The new regulations were developed to implement a policy of energy competition, and, according to Chairman Wood, were designed to benefit consumers nationwide: "Fair and fully competitive markets work in the best interests of retail consumers no matter what part of the country they live in." Although a nationalized market in electricity interested states with higher-than-average energy costs, it did not appeal to states, especially in the Southeast, that have long enjoyed lower energy costs. Members of Congress from these states opposed the FERC's new regime because it would have reduced the competitive advantage that low energy prices provide in recruiting manufacturers to their states, no matter what benefits the policy might have produced nationally. Similar difficulties arise in many policy areas, including agricultural and mass-transit subsidies, tobacco regulation, labor laws, and environmental protection. Regardless of the proposal's merits from a national perspective, members of Congress in such cases have every incentive to step out of their role as national policy-makers and step into the debate as local advocates.

It is important to note that the type of policy is not entirely fixed from the outset of its consideration. Under the U.S. system of representation, organized interests exploit the privileged place of geographic interests by highlighting any differences across states and regions as members of Congress consider national policies. As a result, issues that might not be seen in geographic terms under a different system of representation become framed as constituency matters in the United States. For example, a major bone of contention in Medicare policy is how to calculate payments to teaching hospitals. The underlying question is the degree to which the Medicare program should subsidize the high costs of medical education. But the debate plays out in Congress in a regional manner, with hospital associations in areas of the country with large numbers of teaching hospitals balking at the pain that cutbacks would cause for their regions. From a national perspective, the real policy issue is how the United States should pay for medical education, but the representational system encourages organized interests to dodge the national policy question and seek out ways to emphasize regional differences so as to enlist advocates in Congress.

House versus Senate

Although House members and senators are both concerned with how public policies will affect their constituencies, the different bases of representation in the House and Senate mean that parochialism will have different effects in the two chambers. Senators represent states, the fundamental building blocks of the federal system. Most federal domestic-assistance funds go to state governments, which often possess wide discretion over their expenditure. With the exception of the seven single-district states, however, House districts are nothing more than electoral entities. They are not administrative units and—in most cases—are not even coterminous with local government entities. As such, Senate constituencies are often the direct recipients of federal funds but House constituencies are not.

This difference in the two chambers' bases of representation has important consequences for congressional parochialism. Because of this difference, House members and senators need to use different policy tools in order to provide benefits to constituents and claim credit for doing so. House members must either earmark funds directly to particular organizations or locations in their constituencies or construct narrow grant programs administered by federal bureaucrats whom they can influence. Senators, by contrast, are able to claim credit for the large grants to states that account for most domestic-assistance money. Whenever Congress considers the many important federal programs that distribute funds to states—including Medicaid, welfare, foster care, rehabilitation services, social services, and highway programs—senators take a strong interest in the distribution of funds and typically vote for whatever proposed alternative provides their state with the most money. Accordingly, conflict over geographic distribution in these programs occurs far more frequently in the Senate than in the House.

House members, however, find that money granted to state governments often does not trickle down to their districts, and even when it does they are not in a good position to take credit for it. A great enthusiast of the pork barrel, Representative James A. Traficant Jr. (D-Ohio) explained this difficulty: "We would fight to get the money for the states. The local politicians would have press conferences and announce the projects. Then they would brag about how they got the money. . . . And then they will run against us." House members' electoral interests are more closely tied to the narrow programs for which they can claim credit, even though such programs account for a much smaller proportion of federal grant dollars. When the Congress reauthorized surface transportation programs in 1998, for example, individual House members' support for the legislation was strongly associated with their receipt of earmarked projects for their districts but not with the level of funding for their states as a whole, even though only 5 percent of transportation funds were distributed by earmark and 88 percent went to state departments of transportation.

The Senate's greater interest in the allocation of federal funds to states takes on additional importance because of that chamber's remarkable apportionment scheme. Each state is represented by two senators, regardless of population—granting equal weight to Wyoming's half million residents and California's 33.8 million. States with small populations thus have much greater power in the Senate than in the House. This affects Senate decisions about geographic allocation in two ways. First, it shapes the politics of building winning coalitions in the Senate. When legislators divide a fixed sum of federal dollars (as in conflict over formulas), coalition builders seek support from small-state senators because their funding demands can be accommodated at much lower cost than those of senators representing large-population states. Second, the Senate as a body prefers to distribute funds in ways that disproportionately benefit small-population states. Combined with the Senate's greater interest in state-level funding, Senate preferences for distribution in such programs are more likely to prevail in conference committee negotiations.[8]

Interest-Group Politics

There are few subjects on which the perceptions of political scientists and the American public diverge more than on the influence of organized interests over the shape of public policy. Overwhelming majorities of the public agree with the statement that "Congress is too heavily influenced by interest groups."[9] Political rhetoric often turns on the distinction between "the public interest" and the "special interests," or, in Andrew Jackson's terminology (quoted at the start of the chapter), the "few" versus the "many." It portrays the two types of interests as unalterably at odds with one another, with organized groups rent-seeking at the expense of the broader public.

Among political scientists, there is little consensus on the precise extent of interest-group influence in Congress. The question has, according to a comprehensive review of the literature, yielded "more debate than progress, more confusion than advance."[10] Regardless of their disputes, however, political scientists reject as crude and exaggerated the popular view of overwhelming interest-group influence. The strongest theoretical argument for excessive interest-group influence, examined below, does not offer a complete account of the role of organized groups in congressional policy-making. Interest-group influence is likely to be less problematic than the worst-case scenario because interest groups do more than rent-seek; most public policy issues do not generate systematic advantages for narrow interests; and interest group influence over members of Congress is limited and counterbalanced by other considerations, including public opinion and members' own policy beliefs and partisan goals.

The Case for Excessive Influence of Narrow Interests

Interest-group influence has great potential to create problems for congressional policy-making because not all societal interests are represented by organized groups. Therefore, if interest groups wield influence over the congressional agenda or policy decisions, public policy outcomes will be biased in favor of organized groups and against interests that fail to organize effectively. Mancur Olson's seminal 1965 analysis systematically expounds the problem. Organizations do not necessarily develop just because people share a common goal or interest. Organizing requires sacrifices of time and money, and individuals understand that their contribution will rarely be decisive or even significant in producing the good. They also have great incentive to free ride on the work of others. If an organization comes into existence to advance a particular goal, the benefits cannot be confined to the group's members alone. If, for example, a Sierra Club campaign successfully preserves a wilderness area, anyone can enjoy it, regardless of whether they made any contribution to the effort. The organizational hurdles are higher for large groups than for small groups and are at their highest in the case of nonexcludable public goods such as environmental protection and consumer safety. Organizing is easier for small groups with a strong material stake in policy outcomes, especially if the cost of organizing is small enough and the potential gains large enough that one individual would benefit even by bearing the costs of spearheading the organizational efforts alone. If this logic holds, then, "there is a systematic tendency for 'exploitation' of the great by the small."[11]

From this perspective, Congress sits at the center of a biased interest-group universe in which members receive too much input from myriad narrow groups and not enough input from groups representing broad, diffuse societal interests. Consistent with this view, there do appear to be systematic biases in the composition of the interest-group world. One comprehensive survey found that business interests comprise 72 percent of all interests having Washington representation.[12]

An imbalance of organizational strength will be more likely to affect policy outcomes in certain types of public policy disputes. James Q. Wilson distinguishes policy proposals on the basis of whether their effects fall on the few or the many.[13] When the benefits or costs of a policy are concentrated on a small group of individuals or organizations, the affected group is likely to have strong preferences on the issue and to find it relatively easy to organize to articulate those preferences. By contrast, policies that involve general benefits or costs affect much larger groups and create lower stakes for each individual affected. As a consequence, these larger groups are less likely to organize and therefore less likely to be represented among the interests before Congress.

This imbalance can have serious consequences for public policy. Policy proposals that involve either concentrated benefits paid for by costs diffused over the general public or diffuse benefits paid for by costs concentrated on a narrow group are likely to create unequal contests in organizational terms. Narrow groups expecting to receive concentrated benefits or pay concentrated costs have strong incentive to organize on behalf of their interests, while the broad groups that would receive the diffuse benefits or bear the diffuse burdens are less likely to organize and act effectively on their own behalf. This pattern is certainly in evidence when Congress considers narrowly framed tax loopholes or subsidies benefiting small, identifiable groups. Sugar and milk subsidies, for example, significantly inflate the costs of these staple products for the American consumer. That Congress retains these subsidies year after year probably results from both the intense pressure that the affected producer groups are able to exert on their own behalf and the anemic opposition to policies that impose such diffused costs. Based on this reasoning, one might expect to see similar asymmetries in organizational strength when Congress considers new health, antidiscrimination, environmental, or safety regulations that would impose costs on specific industries or economic interests in order to provide diffuse benefits for consumers, the disabled, women and minorities, national park users, or endangered species.

In sum, this theory provides a convincing account of some congressional policy-making, most notably the multitudes of tax loopholes and small grants targeted at narrow groups. But it also overlooks some important countervailing considerations. First, interest groups do not merely organize for material goals, and their aims may or may not involve rent-seeking. Second, relatively few public policies can be classified as disputes in which only narrow interests stand to gain (or lose) on one side, and only broad publics stand to lose (or gain) on the other side. Third, whatever biases exist in the interest-group world, there are important limitations on the ability of organized interests to influence members of Congress. Each of these issues is examined below.

Interest Groups and Representation

Organized interests play an important representational role in American politics. The interests of the organized few are not always adverse to the disorganized many. The theory of collective action raises great concerns about interest-group exploitation because it emphasizes collective goals, especially material gain, as the motive for political organization, and because narrow groups are easier to organize on this basis. However, individuals often join groups even if they do not believe that their contribution will have a significant impact on the achievement of collective goals. They will join for purely other-directed or altruistic motives, simply because they believe in the cause.[14] People also join political organizations to enjoy the satisfactions obtained from participating itself, a motive that Wilson in 1974 identified as the "solidary" pleasures of working with like-minded people. Political entrepreneurs who take the lead in organizing induce support by appealing to people's ideological, policy, and solidary motives, in addition to their use of selective, material incentives to group membership.

Because of the multiple motives for organizing, interest-group influence on Congress will not necessarily bias public policy toward narrow interests and away from the diffuse interests of the broader public. Rent-seeking does not occur every time a group influences policy-making. Even when groups get what they ask for in policy terms, careful empirical analysis is necessary before concluding that the policy benefited a narrow group at the public's expense.

With respect to the representative role of interest groups, it is useful to distinguish between interest groups whose members have a direct economic stake in government policy, and public interest groups that pursue goals that "will not benefit selectively either the membership or the activists of the organization."[15] These two groups can be identified by their membership structure. A group that confines its membership to businesses or individuals engaged in particular trades or economic enterprises, such as the American Financial Services Association or the National Beef Cattlemen's Association, presumably has as its foremost goal promoting the interests of that narrow interest. On the other hand, public interest groups, whose membership is open to anyone willing and able to make a contribution (usually financial) to the cause, seek policy goals that will appeal to a large base of potential members. In that sense, public interest groups represent more diffuse or general interests in society, while narrow producer or trade groups represent more narrowly defined interests.

Membership structure provides important evidence about a group's goals, but it does not dispose of the question of who will benefit from the policies the group pursues. Interest groups play a representative role that cannot be explained solely by reference to their organizational structure. Public interest groups do not exclusively represent broad, diffuse interests. Public interest groups can and do push for policies that provide direct and immediate benefits to narrow groups. For example, during the 2002 debate on national tax policy, many conservative public interest groups pressed for tax cuts heavily tilted toward the richest households in the United States, including the complete elimination of the estate tax, a levy that affected only the wealthiest 1.9 percent of all estates. Many public interest groups, in turn, rely on corporations and associations for financial support, and fund-raising from these sources undoubtedly shapes their policy agendas in ways that diminish their distinctiveness from producer groups or trade associations. Some ostensible public interest groups are entirely bankrolled by a handful of moneyed interests seeking to mask their influence.

Meanwhile, narrow economic interests and trade associations, like public interest groups, can play a useful representative role in policy making. They possess important information about the likely effects of government policy in their areas of concern, information that often cannot be obtained from any other source. Public policy can often be better designed as a result of their input.

Federal rulemaking processes require public comment periods to allow interested parties an opportunity to voice concerns before new regulations go into effect, and hearing from them often results in better regulatory policy. Similarly, Congress calls on organized groups for information and testimony, not merely as quid pro quo for gaining political support, but often because they can make a valuable contribution to effective policy design and implementation.

Furthermore, even the narrowest organized groups active in politics claim a broader representative role that cannot be dismissed out of hand. All groups press their case by depicting "win-win" scenarios under which policy makers can advance the group's particular goals and help the broader public simultaneously. Such claims may often be self-serving, but sometimes the policy arguments they make are empirically valid. Scientists ask for increased funding for medical research, arguing that it will lead to life-saving breakthroughs. Small businesses seeking accelerated depreciation for new investments contend that the tax incentive will promote job growth. Oncologists protesting a reduction in Medicare reimbursement rates maintain that it will limit their patients' access to the newest, most effective medications. The advocacy of narrow groups demanding attention and funding for specific needs and causes may very well result in policy that is better both for the group and for the diffuse interests of the broader public.

The only way to determine whether organized interests seek policies that benefit society generally or only the narrow interests of group members is to analyze the costs and benefits involved. One cannot conclude that rent-seeking has occurred merely by showing that narrow groups have been able to get what they want from government; one must go on to show that those group demands would have been rejected by the broader public had it been fully informed and adequately organized. For example, farm groups may get the subsidies they seek from government, but in order to demonstrate that they have "captured" public policy, agricultural economists and other policy analysts must show that the inefficiencies and excess costs to the public outweighed the benefits from those subsidies associated with price and production stability. Without this kind of empirical analysis, it is not possible to conclude that interest-group influence was detrimental to the diffuse interests of the general public.

Organizational Incentives in Policy Making

Relatively few public policies give rise to clearly biased organizational incentives. The mohair subsidy, the contemporary rural electrification program, and the oil depletion allowance are not emblematic of public policy generally. As Arnold observes, "most policies embrace all . . . types of costs and benefits"—costs and benefits for the general public and for identifiable groups.[16] Government programs usually involve a variety of benefits and costs for both the general public and particular groups, not merely benefits for narrow interests, paid for at broad public expense. They are thus not likely to give rise to unequal fights with well-organized representation on only one side, allowing interest groups to capture public policy-making without effective challenge. Highway spending provides narrow benefits to highway contractors, but broad benefits for economic development. It also comes at a cost to general revenue, as well as to interest groups advocating higher expenditures on mass transit or containment of urban sprawl. Food stamps and other low-income nutrition programs provide concentrated benefits for commodity producers, but diffuse benefits for the large number of adults and children eligible for assistance. Food stamps come at taxpayer cost, as well as that of state governments, which must administer the program. Government spending on the Strategic Defense Initiative provides concentrated benefits for defense contractors, but (if the technology can be made to work) broad benefits in increased security against ballistic missile attack. At the same time, it is a very costly program in overall budgetary terms, and undoubtedly starves funding for weapons programs that other defense contractors would like to develop or sell.

Public policies usually involve a complex mixture of costs and benefits that result in politics with no predetermined set of outcomes. Even in policies where the mix of costs and benefits confers organizational advantages on one side of an issue, outcomes will not necessarily be stable over time. Programs with narrow benefits can and do become the target of opposing interests, good-government reformers, and groups acting on behalf of taxpayers or broad social interests.[17]

Sources of Interest-Group Leverage

Regardless of the composition or competitiveness of the interest-group universe surrounding Congress, what can members of Congress gain from acceding to interest-group demands? The reason members of Congress respond to parochial pressures is obvious. Protecting constituency interests is both an electoral imperative and a normative ideal. The relationship between members' goals and the pressures of interest groups is not so clear. Indeed, if members' own statements are any guide, their understandings of their job description cut against interest-group influence. After all, no one runs for office arguing that she will be especially accessible to lobbyists. Promises to "stand up to the special interests" are hackneyed in political advertising.

Interest groups, however, have resources that make it worthwhile for members to pay attention to them. With respect to the public's most prominent concern, money, organized interests are indeed a valuable source of campaign funds. Political action committees (PACs), the electioneering arm of interest groups, provide on average 40 percent of the campaign funds for incumbent House members and 25 percent for incumbent senators.[18] Many of these interest groups have a stake in issues before Congress and contribute to campaigns to enhance their access to members to lobby them about these issues.

In addition, lobbyists and interest-group representatives provide members with information on public policy issues, information that is crucial for members to achieve their policy goals. A member of Congress cannot become an influential player on a particular set of policy issues until he is both knowledgeable about them and perceived by other members as such. Group representatives stand ready to offer expert information about issues, the policy alternatives being considered, the arguments that the opposition will advance, and judgments about the political stakes involved. In short, they present members with "actionable intelligence" on public policy. The best-funded groups maintain a constant presence on Capitol Hill, monitoring congressional activity and expressing their preferences on every issue that affects their group's goals.

Although interest-group resources are valuable, they have only limited leverage over individual members of Congress. After all, the number and diversity of such groups has exploded since the 1960s. In this "hyperpluralist" environment,[19] there is no shortage of organized interests to whom members of Congress can turn for information and campaign funds. As Gary Jacobson observes, "Incumbents can raise whatever [amount] they think they need."[20] Because there are so many groups making demands on Congress, members enjoy wide freedom in choosing among them. The proliferation of groups dilutes their influence individually.[21]

In many cases, interest groups are less of a pressure on members of Congress than a resource to be exploited. Members of Congress turn to lobbyists and groups with whom they are sympathetic and use them as a "service bureau" to supplement their own staffs. In such circumstances, a lobbyist's success does not come from pressure, but simply from being able to identify and work with members who are already predisposed toward the group's goals. A great deal of empirical research going back to the 1960s suggests that this pattern accounts for much of the perceived influence of interest groups.[22] Contemporary research on the effect of PAC contributions on roll call votes has yielded contradictory findings but, at minimum, should put to rest the simplistic relationship between money and votes that too many journalists and citizens assume. A number of major studies, in fact, have found no causal connections whatsoever between PAC contributions and individual members' votes.[23]

When thinking about interest-group influence on Congress, it is important to note that the pressure runs in both directions. Interest groups usually have more to gain (or lose) from legislative action than legislators have to gain (or lose) from interest-group action. "In dealings between legislators and lobbyists, the legislator is almost always the dominant party," writes Alan Rosenthal. "Each needs the other, but lobbyists are far needier than legislators."[24] The public perceives members of Congress as at the mercy of interest groups, when the reverse is more often the reality.

It would be impossible to explain the amount of money and resources that interests devote to lobbying if it had no impact on congressional behavior. Under the right conditions, groups may sway undecided members, reframe issues to enlist new support, mobilize supporters, or demobilize opposition.[25] But interest groups can hardly ever credibly threaten members of Congress with loss of an election, and empirical studies yield virtually no evidence of lobbyists converting outright opponents. Interest groups have no choice but to deal with members of Congress, especially those in key positions of influence affecting their interests, but members are free to pick and choose whom to support.

Public Opinion and Issue Salience

When members of Congress perceive that a policy issue is or may become publicly salient, the influence of organized interests generally wanes. In such cases, members of Congress cannot afford to confine their attention to organized interests—because of their interest in reelection, if for no other reason. Interest groups with the capacity to mold public opinion, however, are able to benefit from heightened salience. Public interest groups probably enjoy an advantage over other types of interest groups in this regard. Many public interest groups enjoy considerable credibility on their issues, and some of these possess the financial resources and access to news media to effectively disseminate their views. Such groups' ability to shape public opinion and discourse on their issues affords them a source of power over members of Congress. Members of Congress hesitate to run afoul of Common Cause on lobbying and ethics issues, and actively seek support from the American Association of Retired Persons (AARP) on proposals affecting Medicare and Social Security for precisely this reason.

Economic interest groups can also exploit public salience if they can frame issues effectively and overcome natural skepticism about their motives. A coalition of automobile, boat, aircraft, jewelry, and fur interests, for example, waged a successful public campaign to repeal the luxury excise tax that Congress imposed on those products in its 1990 budget agreement. By drawing attention to subsequent job losses in those sectors, the affected interests managed to build opposition to a tax that members of Congress had initially expected to be either uncontroversial or perhaps even popular, one that was narrowly targeted on items associated with the excesses of wealth. Congress repealed every one of the luxury tax increases over the course of the 1990s. Most interest groups, however, do not possess the public credibility or financial resources necessary to wage successful campaigns to shape public opinion.

Public opinion creates a firm limit to interest-group usefulness to members of Congress: no member ever wants to be perceived as putting narrow interests ahead of the public good. If an interest group is unable to frame its position in a way that the public could conceivably accept, it should expect members of Congress to withhold their support should the issue ever become or threaten to become publicly salient. Interest groups have little to offer that could compensate members for any loss in reputation or public support. Indeed, members of Congress—often envisioning worst-case electoral scenarios—prefer to avoid the risk. As one lobbyist put it, "A legislator is going to listen to his own constituents any day over me."[26] Whenever issues appear to have even the potential to engage broader public attention, members will want to act in ways that will be "explainable" to constituents.

Once again, the contrast with parochialism is instructive. When members of Congress perceive that a policy issue under debate directly implicates parochial interests in their state or district, they must act on behalf of these narrow interests. As Barbara Sinclair observes, "When an issue seriously affecting a key state interest arises . . . senators cannot stay on the sidelines; they have no choice but to become involved."[27] For the same reason that an issue's salience increases members' incentive to act on behalf of parochial interests, it decreases their incentive to respond to most other narrow interests. Members' safest course of action is to attend to constituency interests: it never hurts and always has the capacity to help. Depending on the circumstances, association with particular interest groups can be either helpful or harmful. Members must handle organized interests with care.

Constituency Connections and Iron Triangles

Lobbyists understand that the system of representation in the United States creates a unique access point for them in Congress: their ability to frame issues as constituency matters. Members of Congress do not owe them loyalty or attention as representatives of organized interests, per se. But, across the board, members feel a special obligation to attend to constituency interests. Textbooks therefore advise the would-be lobbyist to find a local angle. Focus on members whose constituencies are clearly affected: "If a member represents a district or state that harbors your client . . . he or she is a primary target."[28] Prepare materials documenting how issues affect local constituencies: "Know a member's district like he knows it himself. . . . Nothing, nothing is more effective."[29] Bring a constituent along to meetings with members as "the best way to guarantee that the point of view will be heard."[30] Not all issues can be framed as local matters, but the system rewards creativity.

On some issues, organized interests bend public policy so much toward their interests that they appear to monopolize policy making in those areas. Interest groups seem to dictate policy in areas where their interests happen to coincide with those of influential congressional and agency policy-makers. In such policies, self-serving networks comprised of organized interests, members of relevant congressional committees, and agency bureaucrats—often termed "iron triangles"—capture public policy. The classic example is national water development policy.

The key interest groups involved—farmers, developers, and barge shipping—all share a common economic interest in constructing large-scale water projects. Meanwhile, members of Congress use these projects to forge ties with prominent constituents and claim credit for "bringing home the bacon." Finally, the Army Corps of Engineers—the administrative agency in charge of building and maintaining these projects—expands its budgets by, as one internal Corps memo put it, "form[ing] a stronger partnership with Congressmen and their staffs so that we become their agency of choice."

Iron triangles do not characterize most policy making, but they account for some patterns quite well. To varying degrees, the concept successfully describes policy making with respect to agriculture, water development, Native American affairs, defense procurement and military bases, public lands, and transportation.[31] The common element across these policies is their strong geographic content. Each is, in some sense, tied to the land. Making policy in these areas is foremost about distributing goods to geographic constituencies. As such, each of these policies affords organized interests easy opportunity to capitalize on the favored place of geography in the U.S. system of representation. Each generates strong incentive for members of Congress to focus on providing local benefits. At the intersection of private interests and local constituencies, these policies maximize both interest-group and parochial pressures on Congress, leading to predictable and biased policies that shortchange national interests.

Members' Wider Views

Despite the constant lobbying by narrow interests, members of Congress have important incentives to take a wider view of policy. Members of Congress are hardly so passive that they do nothing other than respond to organized interests and parochial demands. They are also legislative entrepreneurs with their own ideas of the public interest—creative, ambitious individuals who "persuade, connive, hatch ideas, propagandize . . . and in general cut a figure in public affairs."[32] Congress is not merely a black box processing demands from outside itself. Members of Congress have policy and partisan goals of their own. They have ideas about good national policy, ideas that perhaps prompted them to get involved in politics in the first place. And members also want to work with their fellow partisans to produce a legislative record that will either improve their party's collective image or damage the other party's image. These motives lead them to take a more comprehensive view of policy making than if they devoted all their attention to demands from narrow group and constituency interests.

Policy Goals

For a significant number of members of Congress, winning office is a means to an end. Members of Congress seek office, often forgoing wealth or other career opportunities, because they have beliefs about what government should do and how it should do it. Political scientists usually understand such beliefs in terms of political ideology, defined as abstract beliefs about the proper role of government, typically conceptualized on a political spectrum ranging from left to right. This is a useful, but often overly deterministic, view. Many policy issues do not involve a high level of ideological content. Members of Congress attend, endure, and participate in hearings on such unglamorous topics as financial management at the Department of Defense, assessment in early-childhood education, and telecommunication law and economics. Members actively seek committee positions in which they will work on similarly low-profile, technically complex issues. And, in many of these cases, members make policy determinations neither on the basis of external constituency demands nor abstract ideologies, but "on the merits."[33]

Ideology may have become a more important consideration for members of Congress in recent years. With few exceptions, members of Congress are drawn from the ranks of the politically active. Since the decline of patronage and other material incentives for political participation the reasons for getting involved in American politics may have shifted more toward the expressive and the ideological.[34] Furthermore, the proliferation of explicitly ideological think tanks, foundations, and media outlets has heightened the ideological content of the political agenda generally. Members of Congress who first became involved in politics for ideological reasons and invested the time and energy required to win office will not be inclined to devote all their time to constituency service. Such members will want to engage in legislative combat to write those ideological visions into law. Whenever Congress considers issues related to fiscal policy (especially budgets), redistribution across classes (especially income taxes and entitlement programs), and the social and cultural issues closely associated with liberalism or conservatism (e.g., gay rights, abortion, gun control), the ideological motivations that individual members bring with them to Congress are very important for understanding policy outcomes.

Partisan Motives

In addition to members' ideological beliefs, congressional policy choices are also shaped by members' investment in their own political parties. Given party leaders' very limited arsenal of sanctions and their reluctance to use them against disloyal members, party influence does not derive from "the whip," the punishments that legislative leaders can impose on members. Nevertheless, members of Congress recognize that a great part of their political support derives from their association with one of the national parties. Indeed, recent evidence suggests that voters' views of parties are becoming a better predictor of their assessments of particular congressional candidates,[35] and that, as a result, individual members are likely to see their own personal fortunes as tied to the success of their parties. Individual members of Congress thus have a stake in cooperating with fellow partisans to improve their party's image and public record.[36] Despite the lack of collective responsibility in Congress compared with other legislatures around the world, members do have incentives to link their party in the public mind with effective government and desirable policy outcomes and, if possible, to associate the opposing party with opposite characteristics.

Members' partisan goals are likely to predominate on the relatively small number of agenda items that members perceive as defining their party's record. The nature of these issues depends on a variety of factors, including the president's use of the bully pulpit in setting the agenda. Legislative issues central to the parties' agenda are often signaled by early introduction in the Congress and identified with low bill numbers (e.g., HR1, S2, etc.).

Distinctly partisan motivations in policy-making are most visible on the rare occasions when party leaders push their members to support legislation at odds with the party membership's ideological beliefs. For example, President George W. Bush and Republican congressional leaders made the passage of a prescription drug benefit for Medicare recipients a top priority in 2003. A central part of the Republican strategy to improve the party's collective reputation on health care policy, enacting such legislation under unified Republican government would, as President Bush explained, "enable [Republicans] to say to seniors we kept our promise." Republican Party leaders had to apply tremendous pressure to the party's conservative wing to induce support for a policy that, whatever else it included, was indisputably a major expansion of an entitlement program. As freshman representative Tom Feeney (R-Fla.) said, "I came to Washington to reform Great Society programs, not to ratify and enlarge them." House leaders were able to pass the bill only after holding the vote open for almost three hours and persuading a handful of members to change their votes. In this case, leaders asked their fellow partisans to put aside their personal ideological preferences in favor of the party's collective image, and, with some difficulty, persuaded enough of them to do so.

It is not easy, particularly in the contemporary Congress, to distinguish between members' partisan and ideological motivations in policy making. Party leaders and members usually seek to enhance their parties' public reputations on policies that are consistent with shared ideological goals. Leaders need not apply pressure to gain party members' support in such cases, but this does not render partisan motives unimportant. Republicans do not merely prefer "smaller government" as individual legislators, they also want to take credit as a party for the passage of specific tax cuts. Democrats not only believe in helping "working families," but also want to take credit as a party for the passage of minimum-wage increases or the provision of health insurance for all children. Belonging to a party and having a common stake in collective action facilitates the coordination among members necessary to deliver on specific policies, even where there is substantial agreement on abstract ideological principles.

Conflict between Narrow Interests and National Policy

Members of the contemporary Congress have stronger reasons than in the past to view policy from a national perspective. Both the high level of ideological polarization and the majority's narrow margin of control have raised the policy and partisan stakes. In the current environment, a shift of a few seats would yield outcomes dramatically more favorable or unfavorable to most members' policy preferences or party image. At the same time, members are subjected to more demands from narrow interests than ever before. How do members react when their national policy or partisan goals come into conflict with the interests of constituents or particular interest groups?

It is better for everyone involved to damp down these kinds of conflicts whenever possible. For their part, interest groups typically work through the political party that is friendlier to their goals. Organized interests cannot expect members of Congress to back them if they are at odds with members' partisan or national policy goals. They have limited leverage over members of Congress in any case, but especially in high-profile matters involving political ideologies, party leaders, and presidential politics. Many interest groups, a sizable proportion of the public interest groups, become so closely allied with one of the parties that one could almost say that the group belongs to the party. Activist Grover Norquist's Wednesday Group—a weekly gathering of business lobbyists, conservative public-interest-group representatives, and Republican officeholders—merely exemplifies this pattern. Members of Congress respond in kind by accommodating demands from their interest-group allies in ways that are also broadly consistent with their ideological inclinations. Republicans rarely see a tax loophole entirely without policy merit; Democrats draw few distinctions between the national interest and the interests of labor unions. This is not to deny that conflicts arise between the political demands of interest groups and the ideological and partisan commitments of members, but everyone involved—interest groups and officeholders alike—benefits from keeping these conflicts to a minimum.

Parochial interests present members of Congress with more difficult dilemmas than interest groups do. As with favored interest groups, members usually manage to minimize conflict between their constituents' interests and "good public policy." Members who think that the North American Free Trade Agreement is bad for their constituents typically maintain that free trade is bad national policy, too. But if the conflict is salient or undeniable, members have strong electoral incentives to bow to parochial interests. Parties do not reelect members; constituents do. Members with a reputation as party mavericks tend to perform better electorally than loyal partisans.[37] Senator Mark Pryor (D-Ark.)

was not taking a courageous stand when he declared in a 2002 campaign commercial, "People matter more to me than a political party. And like this sign that is on my father's [a former senator from Arkansas] desk says, 'I will always put Arkansas first.'"

The fate of energy legislation between 2001 and 2004 illustrates the difficulties parochial interests create for a party's collective goals. Shortly after taking office, President George W. Bush unveiled a national energy policy with an emphasis on boosting domestic production. Three years later the massive conference report was still bogged down over a parochial matter as minor as a liability waiver for the producers of MTBE, a fuel additive produced in Gulf Coast states that is also a groundwater contaminant in the Northeast. Despite a remarkable record of Republican unity throughout the 108th Congress, direct intervention by Vice President Dick Cheney, Speaker Dennis Hastert, and Majority Leader Bill Frist could neither induce six northeastern Republican senators to support the bill containing the MTBE liability waiver nor persuade key southern House power brokers Tom DeLay (R-Tex.) and Billy Tauzin (R-La.) to drop it. Because of its close connection to congressional parochial interests, energy policy has long been a graveyard for ambitious initiatives.

Curbing Narrow Interests

Members of Congress seeking to deliver on national policy goals despite contrary pressure from narrow interests have two courses of action available to minimize political liability for themselves: they can either diminish congressional authority over the policy or obscure their responsibility for it. To diminish authority, Congress can delegate policy decisions to the executive branch or a special commission. After members of Congress realized that it was so politically damaging to close military bases in their constituencies that—left to their own devices—no obsolete or unnecessary base would ever be closed, they adopted a procedure by which a commission recommends a slate of base closures that go into effect unless Congress passes legislation rejecting it in total. Fast-track authority for presidents to negotiate trade agreements similarly provides members of Congress "plausible deniability" for adverse local consequences of trade policy. But members of Congress are naturally reluctant to relinquish authority to outsiders on any matter of importance to them. Alternatively, Congress can adopt procedures equivalent to chaining the refrigerator door—such as adopting points of order against earmarked projects in legislation or bringing tax bills up for House floor consideration under closed rules. As with dieters' refrigerators, Congress can unlock these restraints with decisions reached by a majority vote.

Obscuring congressional responsibility means adopting procedural or policy mechanisms that make it difficult to hold individual members accountable for policies. Congress can choose from a wide variety of techniques, including slow phase-ins, "hold harmless" provisions, triggers, and sunset provisions. In 1983, for example, Congress sought to improve the financial solvency of the Social Security program by increasing the retirement age for benefit eligibility from sixty-five to sixty-seven. To limit the electoral ramifications of imposing benefit cuts on a visible group, Congress legislated a gradual phase-in of the change over a twenty-two-year period ending in 2022. Most of those who voted for the change were no longer even serving in Congress when the first retirement age increases began to kick in.

Legislative procedures can also be used to similar obfuscatory effect. One common tactic is to package otherwise controversial items in omnibus legislation that commands wide support. During the 2003 consideration of an $87 billion emergency supplemental appropriation for military action and reconstruction in Iraq, Republican leaders wanted to deliver the entire amount requested by the Bush administration, even though the $20 billion for reconstruction projects in Iraq was decidedly less popular in Congress and with constituents than the money for the U.S. military. House leaders packaged the Iraq reconstruction money with the military funds and brought the bill up under a closed rule, allowing supporters to claim that their vote was merely to provide "support for the troops." After fending off an amendment to split the two parts into separate bills, Senate leaders obtained unanimous consent to pass the whole package with an unrecorded voice vote, leaving the matter of who supported it ambiguous.

Creative legislators can thus devise strategies to mitigate the negative political fallout from congressional actions. The question is whether Congress uses them primarily to restrain narrow interests, or whether they are more often employed to avoid accountability with constituents generally. Such strategies are useful whenever congressional actions might be unpopular, either with broad publics or particular groups. In the Iraq supplemental case, for example, they were used to approve spending that was unpopular with a majority of many members' constituents. Indeed, one might argue that obfuscatory tactics would be most useful when members of Congress take actions that are broadly unpopular. It is not possible to give a definitive accounting. It is clear, however, that special rules limiting amendments in the House—which are often (but not always) designed to protect majority-party members from explicit votes on unpopular parts of their proposals—have become important tools enabling the majority party to prosecute its agenda. They facilitate members' ability to make national policy; to the extent that this conflicts with narrow interests, they help members of Congress curb their influence. The larger point is that members have policy goals of their own and access to mechanisms that give them political leeway to pursue them.

Assessing Congressional Parochialism

Given members' incentives under the U. S. system of representation, the kind of narrowness of vision more likely to afflict congressional policy-making is parochialism, not interest-group particularism generally. Interest groups unquestionably have an impact on congressional policy-making, although the scope of that influence has proven difficult to document and contentious among scholars. But parochialism is the "failing" built into the structure of Congress itself. Because of the multiplicity of competing organized interests, members of Congress stand apart from them and make choices about which ones to support. These choices are guided and constrained by members' ideological and partisan commitments, as well as their understanding of the public interest. By contrast, members do not stand apart from parochial demands to any substantial degree. They are elected by and advocates for one particular constituency, and it always makes political sense for members to prioritize their constituents' interests. As such, geographic representation raises unique questions about Congress's ability to legislate in the general interest. It is impossible to measure precisely how detrimental parochialism is to congressional policy-making, but it creates important institutional biases, though not—as shown below—the bias most commonly associated with it, fiscal profligacy.

The Myth of an "Out Of Control" Congress

I will continue to fight vigorously both against too much government spending and for the largest slice of the pie possible for Maryland's Sixth District.
—Representative Roscoe Bartlett (R-Md.)[38]

A conventional criticism of Congress is that every member seeks benefits for his own constituency but no one pays attention to the aggregate cost of these benefits, thus leading to excessive expenditures. As far back as 1937, a reporter could casually refer to a "pork barrel demonstration in the ancient manner of Congress" and blame congressional pork barreling for "a number of very bad chapters in our nation's fiscal history."[39] Journalists decrying the latest example of pork barrel spending today regularly connect Congress's interest in parochial benefits with the federal government's overall budgetary health. Political scientists have formalized this logic, developing models that show why distributive logrolling in Congress "makes it so difficult to balance the federal budget."[40]

Despite the intuitive logic, parochialism in Congress has never been the cause of large national budget deficits. Overall fiscal policy simply does not bubble up from the uncoordinated behavior of individual members of Congress. Congress observes budget procedures by which overall spending levels are set; these are not always followed, but they produce significant constraint in any case. Congress determines bottom-line expenditures on discretionary programs with one eye toward the president's budget and the other toward last year's outlays. Furthermore, there is simply too little money at stake in all the projects and programs for which members can individually claim credit for these programs to drive federal budgets. Two-thirds of federal spending does not even fall within

Congress's annual discretionary review. These automatic expenditures, including entitlement programs, government pensions, and interest on the national debt are, along with the state of the economy and the level of tax revenues collected, the most important determinants of the nation's fiscal well-being. Even if Congress had not funded a single nondefense discretionary program in fiscal year 2003, there would still have been a national budget deficit.

The data in Figure 1 shows that one cannot understand congressional policy-making by reducing it to the logic of individual actors seeking constituency benefits. Figure 1 tracks congressional earmarking in appropriations legislation and overall government outlays from 1992 to 2003. Earmarks designate funds to institutions and projects in particular locations; these are the type of expenditures for which individual members can most easily claim credit. Media coverage of Congress typically presents earmarks as exemplary of a much larger problem with pork barrel spending. As this figure reveals, earmarking has exploded since the early 1990s. The number of individual earmarks and their

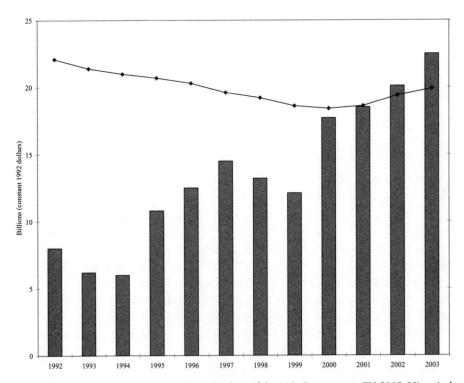

SOURCE: Citizens against Government Waste; Budget of the U.S. Government FY 2005, Historical Tables.

Figure 1   Earmarking in Appropriations Legislation and Federal Outlays, 1992–2003

total cost in constant dollars have gone up more than 180 percent over the period. However, government spending as a whole has not grown during this time frame; overall outlays actually declined as a proportion of GDP every year between 1992 and 2000 and, despite a rebound, were still lower in 2003 than in 1992. The data in Figure 2 reinforces the pattern. Figure 2 displays trends in expenditures for the types of program thought to be most vulnerable to parochial pressure: transportation, community development, water projects, and military construction. In every case other than community development, spending in 2003 was lower as a proportion of GDP than it was in 1962. Community development spending has also seen dramatic cuts from its highs during the late 1970s and early 1980s. Note further that the declines in spending on programs distributing geographic benefits are greater than the decline in overall outlays, meaning that such programs constitute a smaller proportion of federal spending today than in earlier periods.

It is easy to scoff at Representative Bartlett's promise to fight "against too much federal spending" and for the "largest share of the pie possible" for his constituents. But, in all fairness, he is right: members of Congress can do both these things simultaneously with a minimum of hypocrisy, because policy mak-

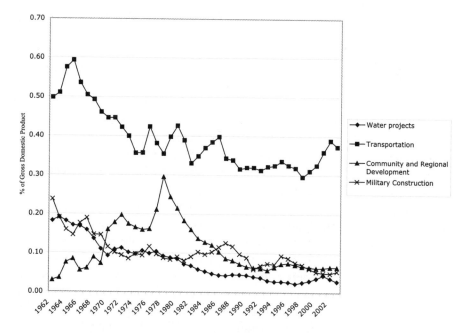

source: Budget of the U.S. Government FY 2005, Historical Tables.

**Figure 2   The Shrinking Pork Barrel, Outlays for Geographic Benefits,
1962–2002**

ing operates on multiple levels. Members make decisions about overall expenditures based on ideological preferences, calculations of partisan advantage, and other national policy considerations. Within that larger pie, members then set aside spending to claim credit for providing local benefits. Trends in earmarking mean that a greater proportion of discretionary spending is allocated on the basis of earmarks today, but parochial pressures do not drive budgetary policy.

Inequitable and Inefficient Distribution

Every square inch of Wyoming is as vulnerable as every inch of New York. If you say there are not terrorists in Wyoming, that's just where they'll strike.
—Joe Moore, Wyoming's director of homeland security[41]

Although parochialism cannot explain overall levels of spending, it does cause inequitable patterns in federal expenditures and poor program design. Congress has repeatedly shown itself unable to target funding in a particular program to areas in greatest need, with the politics of coalition building in Congress expanding the number of program beneficiaries and diluting the program's effectiveness. This pattern is notable in policies designed to promote regional economic development (e.g., enterprise zones, model cities) and to provide for public infrastructure and services (water and sewer grants, transit subsidies).[42]

In addition, inequities in funding result when members advantaged by seniority, committee membership, or majority-party status secure disproportionate amounts for their constituents. A vast literature on this subject reveals that these kinds of representational advantages create biases in some programs, but the extent of this problem is easily exaggerated. Representational power in Congress has its greatest effect on the relatively small amount of funds distributed on the basis of congressional earmark. In such cases, advantaged members—particularly those in the majority party and on the committee of jurisdiction—reserve a disproportionate share for themselves.[43]

The small-state advantage in Senate representation creates funding inequities that are greater and more widespread than those associated with party, seniority, and committee membership. Small-population states enjoy measurable advantages over large-population states in the distribution of federal dollars across most categories of distributive policy, with the small-state advantage most pronounced in the programs over which Congress retains tightest control.[44] In some cases, the inequities are surprisingly large. Under the formula grants to states for homeland security, for example, high-terror-risk states such as New York and California receive less than $5.50 per capita from the federal government to prevent and respond to terrorists attacks, while a low-risk state such as Wyoming receives $38.31 per capita.

Recent trends in grants-in-aid spending are likely to exacerbate the effects of congressional parochialism. Congress has converted a number of categorical grants and individual entitlements into block grants, and many members have been pushing for the creation of additional block grants, including for Medicaid, foster care, and Head Start. As it does so, the policy choices before the Congress will deal less with program design and administration—those issues are devolved to the states—and more explicitly and exclusively with allocating lump sums to states. Although legislators' preferences for devolution and block grants often stem from their views of the proper role of the federal government, a side effect of any such reforms is that the federal programs in these areas are likely to take on a deeper imprint of congressional parochialism.

Parochial Dimension to Decision Making

More difficult to measure—but potentially most important—is the effect of parochialism on how members of Congress make decisions on policies that do not have a geographic dimension. Geographic representation creates a second decisional criterion for members of Congress in addition to their policy preferences: What is in it for my constituency? In this sense, parochialism is problematic not only because it affects congressional decision making on policies that distribute federal benefits or affect different regions of the country differently, but also because it affects policies that have no inherent connection to geographic politics whatsoever.

When Congress decides on national policy, it ideally should do so on the basis of what at least a majority of members believe is in the national interest. Although no consensus definition of "the national interest" exists—it is a classic example of an "essentially contested concept"[45]—it is certainly not equivalent to the sum of all local constituency interests. It is neither possible nor desirable to eliminate all potential sources of compromise that enable Congress to negotiate agreements, but geographic representation creates a systematic reason for lawmakers to make decisions on national policy for reasons that are irrelevant to national interests.

Coalition leaders frequently exploit this extra dimension of congressional decision making to build legislative majorities. By targeting benefits to particular members' constituencies, leaders can induce them to support a policy that, for whatever reason, they are reluctant to support on its merits.[46] For example, even though Senator Norm Coleman (R-Minn.) told voters during his 2002 campaign of his opposition to oil drilling in the Alaskan National Wildlife Reserve (ANWR), he was led to reverse his position when Senator Pete Domenici (R-N.M.) inserted a provision for $800 million in loan guarantees for the construction of a power plant in an economically depressed area of Minnesota. The outcomes of national policy can be determined by parochial bargains like this if a decisive number of members accept side payments for their constituencies.

Whenever high-profile legislation is closely fought, media reports of such deals surface. "The end of a session often takes on the mood of a festive bazaar," begins a typical article. "Lawmakers are courted with promises of special projects . . . in exchange for their votes."[47] Even when such deals are struck, however, it is not possible to know how often members merely withhold support from measures they actually favor in order to extract concessions from leaders.

One indirect indicator of the importance of this kind of deal making is the incidence of close votes potentially decided by side payments. Transaction costs are high enough that it would be extremely difficult for leaders to use side payments to assemble large coalitions. Table 1 displays the size of the winning margin on key congressional votes in the 103rd–107th Congresses. These data reveal that on most important, controversial policy matters, it is unlikely that side payments had a decisive impact. Outcomes in most of these votes were decided by lopsided majorities: the median margin of victory in the House over the period was sixty-seven votes, and in the Senate it was seventeen. However, using as an indictor the number of votes decided by margins of ten or less in the House and five or less in the Senate, side payments could have played a role in as many as 10 to 25 percent of key votes; included among these are some highly consequential matters of fiscal and budgetary policy.

TABLE 1
Size of Winning Margin on Key Congressional Votes★

Margin (Number of Votes on Winning Side)					
House			Senate		
Congress (# key votes)	% marginal votes (decided by < 11 votes)	Median House margin	Congress (# of key votes)	% marginal votes (decided by < 6 votes)	Median Senate margin
103rd (31)	13	55	103rd (31)	25	18
104th (33)	6	94	104th (33)	29	13
105th (27)	18	52	105th (27)	17	18
106th (25)	16	111	106th (25)	28	14
107th (24)	20	30	107th (24)	17	20
Total	13%	67		22%	17

SOURCE: The *Congressional Quarterly Almanac* is used to identify key votes and vote tallies.
★The data takes into account the number of votes needed to win. For example, in the Senate, 51 votes is counted as a one-vote margin when a simple majority is required; 60 votes is counted as a one-vote margin when a three-fifths majority is required.

Conclusion

The House will always be made up of 435 members who'll be ever-hesitant to resist a parochial interest.

—Rep. Les AuCoin (D-Ore.)[48]

Congressional policy-making cannot be understood without taking into account both the structural incentives in the institution and external influences upon it. Geographic representation, single-member districts, and the decentralized character of electoral politics combine to put enormous pressure on Congress to respond to local interests. Members of Congress also cope with a wide and growing array of organized interests making demands. The American public tends to reserve special indignation for organized interests, and there is a long-standing tradition of populist rhetoric in American politics that stokes this indignation. The analysis provided in this essay suggests that this anger is misdirected. Parochial and interest-group pressures do not exert equal influence on members. Members' loyalty to narrow constituent interests is built into the representational system, whereas organized interests usually need to find some special "hook"—a local angle, a partisan or ideological tie—to warrant any loyalty at all.

No systematic empirical analysis suggests that organized interests always or even usually seek policies that confer narrow benefits at the expense of broad publics. Public interest groups, in particular, play a vital role in developing and building support for policies that have broad public constituencies. Even narrowly constituted organized interests seek policies that they can justify in public policy terms. Organized interests check and balance one another, and the proliferation of organized interests in recent years has diluted their individual influence. Setting aside their goals, organized interests have limited leverage over members of Congress. Members rarely need support from any particular organized interest for reelection purposes; they are able to raise the campaign funds they need elsewhere, and thus they pick and choose among groups, working most closely with those interests with which they are personally comfortable. One cannot deny that organization confers significant advantages to groups, but the public's fear and loathing of organized interests is out of proportion to all of the empirical evidence regarding their goals and influence.

Meanwhile, congressional parochialism demonstrably undermines Congress's capacity to legislate in some matters, creating especially serious difficulties for policies that distribute governmental benefits geographically. In a world that becomes smaller and more interconnected all the time, the United States' exclusive use of geographic representation seems increasingly anachronistic. Selecting representatives from geographic constituencies has some virtues: it works to make legislators more accessible to citizens, and it ensures that national policies that have any differential effects across different geographic areas will be carefully considered. But it comes with a serious cost. It creates a system of divided loyalty for all members of Congress, who are asked to serve simultaneously as national lawmakers and as advocates for local interests. Local interests should undoubtedly be weighed in the balance—along with other narrow or minority interests—as members make national policy, but the U.S. system seems engineered to put supreme emphasis on them.

Reform of congressional representation is almost certainly outside the realm of political possibility. Although it would not require a constitutional amendment for states to select some or all of their House representatives on the basis of proportional representation, the basis of Senate representation is one aspect of U.S. government that probably cannot be changed even with a constitutional amendment. Regardless of the legal niceties involved, Americans show no inclination to get behind any movement for representational reform in any case. At all governmental levels, they tend to think of representation in geographic terms. Moreover, Americans are notoriously conservative with respect to their political institutions, and overwhelming majorities believe that the U.S. constitutional system is already the best in the world.

In the end, congressional policy-making is *influenced* but not *determined* by structural incentives and external pressures. Members of Congress themselves cannot be left out of the picture. Most members of Congress have preferences about national policy, shaped by their ideological beliefs and partisan commitments. In addition, Congress at all times contains some highly ambitious, entrepreneurial, and talented politicians whose ideas about public policy have independent effect. Finally, Congress has at its disposal the policy and procedural tools that grant members electoral leeway to pursue their vision of public policy in the national interest.

Notes

1. John R. Hibbing and Elizabeth Theiss-Morse, *Congress as Public Enemy: Public Attitudes toward American Political Institutions* (Cambridge, U.K., and New York: Cambridge University Press, 1995.)
2. George B. Galloway, *The Legislative Process in Congress* (New York: Crowell, 1953), 375.
3. John W. Kingdon, *Congressmen's Voting Decisions* (New York: Harper and Row, 1981), 248.
4. F. Leslie Seidle and David C. Docherty, eds., *Reforming Parliamentary Democracy* (Montreal and Ithaca, N.Y.: McGill-Queen's University Press, 2003), 9–10.
5. John M. Carey and Michael Soberg Shugart, "Incentives to Cultivate a Personal Vote: A Rank Ordering of Electoral Formulas," *Electoral Studies* 14, no. 4 (1995), 417–439.

6. See Stein and Bickers, *Perpetuating the Pork Barrel*, 118–131, and Frances E. Lee, "Geographic Politics in the U.S. House of Representatives: Coalition Building and Distribution of Benefits," *American Journal of Political Science* 47, no. 4 (2003), 713–727.

7. See Arnold, *The Logic of Congressional Action*, 25–28.

8. A study of interchamber conflict in forty-two state-based federal grant programs reveals that the Senate's preferences prevail more than twice as often as those of the House. See Frances E. Lee and Bruce I. Oppenheimer, *Sizing Up the Senate: The Unequal Consequences of Equal Representation* (Chicago: University of Chicago Press, 1999), 216.

9. Hibbing and Theiss-Morse, *Congress as Public Enemy*, 63–65.

10. Baumgartner and Leech, *Basic Interests*, 13.

11. Mancur Olson Jr., *The Logic of Collective Action: Public Goods and the Theory of Groups* (Cambridge, Mass.: Harvard University Press, 1965), 29.

12. Schlozman and Tierney, *Organized Interests and American Democracy*, 77.

13. See Arnold, *Logic*, and James Q. Wilson, *Political Organizations* (New York: Basic Books, 1974), 330–337.

14. See Terry M. Moe, "Toward a Broader View of Interest Groups," *Journal of Politics* 43, no. 2 (1981): 531–543, and Terry M. Moe, *The Organization of Interests: Incentives and the Internal Dynamics of Political Interest Groups* (Chicago: University of Chicago Press, 1980).

15. Schlozman and Tierney, *Organized Interests and American Democracy*, 29.

16. See Arnold, *Logic*, 26–27.

17. See Gary Mucciaroni, *Reversals of Fortune: Public Policy and Private Interests* (Washington, D.C.: Brookings Institution Press, 1995).

18. Paul S. Herrnson, *Congressional Elections: Campaigning at Home and in Washington.* 2nd ed. (Washington, D.C.: CQ Press, 1998).

19. Allan J. Cigler and Burdett A. Loomis, "Always Involved, Rarely Central: Organized Interests in American Politics," in *Interest Group Politics*, edited by Cigler and Loomis, 6th ed. (Washington, D.C.: CQ Press, 2002), 381.

20. Gary Jacobson, "Money in the 1980 and 1982 Congressional Elections," in *Money and Politics in the United States: Financing Elections in the 1980s*, ed. Michael J. Malbin. (Washington, D.C.: American Enterprise Institute for Public Policy Research, and Chatham, N.J.: Chatham House, 1984), 57.

21. Robert H. Salisbury, "The Paradox of Interest Groups in Washington—More Groups, Less Clout," in *The New American Political System*, edited by Anthony King, rev. ed. (Washington, D.C.: AEI Press, 1990).

22. See Raymond A. Bauer, Ithiel de Sola Pool, and Lewis Anthony Dexter, *American Business and Public Policy: The Politics of Foreign Trade* (New York: Atherton Press, 1963), Charles L. Clapp, *The Congressman: His Work as He Sees It* (Washington, D.C.: Brookings Institution, 1963), Lester W. Milbrath, *The Washington Lobbyists* (Chicago: Rand McNally, 1963), and Harmon Zeigler, *Interest Groups in American Society* (Englewood Cliffs, N.J.: Prentice-Hall, 1964).

23. Janet M. Grenzke, "PACs and the Congressional Supermarket: The Currency is Complex," *American Journal of Political Science* 33 (1989), 1–24, Lawrence S.

Rothenberg, *Linking Citizens to Government: Interest Group Politics at Common Cause* (Cambridge, U.K., and New York: Cambridge University Press, 1992), and John R. Wright, "Contributions, Lobbying, and Committee Voting in the U.S. House of Representatives," *American Political Science Review* 84 (1990), 417–438

24. Alan Rosenthal, *The Third House: Lobbyists and Lobbying in the States,* 2nd ed. (Washington, D.C.: CQ Press, 2001), 215.

25. Richard A. Smith, "Advocacy, Interpretation, and Influence in the U.S. Congress," *American Political Science Review* 78, no. 1 (1984): 44–63, and Richard L. Hall and Frank W. Wayman, "Buying Time: Moneyed Interests and the Mobilization of Bias in Congressional Committees," *American Political Science Review* 84, no. 3 (1990), 797–820.

26. Rosenthal, *The Third House*, 215.

27. Barbara Sinclair, *The Transformation of the U.S. Senate* (Baltimore: Johns Hopkins University Press, 1989), 144.

28. Bruce C. Wolpe and Bertram J. Levine, *Lobbying Congress: How the System Works.* 2nd ed. (Washington, D.C.: CQ Press, 1996), 61.

29. Schneier and Gross, *Legislative Strategy*, 142.

30. Jeffrey H. Birnbaum, *The Lobbyists: How Influence Peddlers Get Their Way in Washington* (New York: Times Books, 1992), 6.

31. For each policy area, see, respectively: William P. Browne, *Private Interests, Public Policy, and American Agriculture* (Lawrence: University Press of Kansas, 1988), Arthur Maass, *Muddy Waters: The Army Engineers and the Nation's Rivers* (Cambridge, Mass.: Harvard University Press, 1951), J. Leiper Freeman, *The Political Process* (Garden City, N.J.: Doubleday, 1955), Barry S. Rundquist and Thomas M. Carsey, *Congress and Defense Spending: The Distributive Politics of Military Procurement* (Norman: University of Oklahoma Press, 2002), Grant McConnell, *Private Power and American Democracy* (New York: Knopf, 1966), and Robert J. Dilger, *American Transportation Policy* (Westport, Conn.: Praeger, 2003).

32. David R. Mayhew, *America's Congress: Actions in the Public Sphere, James Madison through Newt Gingrich* (New Haven, Conn.: Yale University Press, 2000), 9.

33. See Martha Derthick and Paul J. Quirk, *The Politics of Deregulation* (Washington, D.C.: Brookings Institution, 1985), 140–146.

34. See Morris P. Fiorina, "Parties, Participation, and Representation in America: Old Theories Face New Realities," in *Political Science: The State of the Discipline*, edited by Ira Katznelson and Helen V. Milner (New York: Norton, 2002), 511–541.

35. Gary C. Jacobson, *The Politics of Congressional Elections.* 6th ed. (New York: Pearson Longman, 2004), 136–43.

36. Gary W. Cox and Mathew D. McCubbins, *Legislative Leviathan: Party Government in the House* (Berkeley: University of California Press, 1993), 109–135.

37. Robert S. Erikson and Gerald C. Wright, "Voters, Candidates, and Issues in Congressional Elections," in *Congress Reconsidered*, edited by Lawrence C. Dodd and Bruce I. Oppenheimer, 5th ed. (Washington, D.C.: CQ Press, 1993), 103–108.

38. Roscoe Bartlett, in David Baumann's article "Take your Omnibus and Shove . . . Some Cash into It for Me," *National Journal* (December 18, 2003).

39. See, respectively, Arthur Krock, "In Washington," *New York Times* (June 2, 1937) and "In Washington," *New York Times* (May 28, 1937).

40. Charles Stewart III, *Analyzing Congress* (New York: Norton, 2001), 36–40.
41. Joe Moore, in Brian Kates, "We get $5-a-head for Security," *New York Daily News,* (November 24, 2003), 8.
42. See Arnold, *Congress and the Bureaucracy: A Theory of Influence,* especially chapters 7 and 8.
43. For majority-party benefits, see Steven J. Balla et al., "Partisanship, Blame Avoidance, and the Distribution of Legislative Pork," *American Journal of Political Science* 46, no. 3 (2002), 515–525. For committee benefits, see Rundquist and Carsey, *Congress and Defense Spending,* John A. Ferejohn, *Pork Barrel Politics: Rivers and Harbors Legislation, 1947–1968* (Stanford, Calif.: Stanford University Press, 1974), and Richard F. Fenno Jr. *The Power of the Purse: Appropriations Politics in Congress* (Boston: Little, Brown, 1966).
44. See Cary M. Atlas et al., "Slicing the Federal Government Net Spending Pie: Who Wins, Who Loses and Why," *American Economic Review* 85, no. 2 (1995), 624–629, and Frances E. Lee, "Representation and Public Policy: The Consequences of Senate Apportionment for the Geographic Distribution of Federal Funds," *Journal of Politics* 60 (1998), 34–62.
45. W. B. Gallie, "Essentially Contested Concepts," *Proceedings of the Aristotelian Society* 56 (1955/1956), 167–198.
46. Diana Evans, *Greasing the Wheels: Using Pork Barrel Projects to Build Majority Coalitions in Congress* (Cambridge, U.K., and New York: Cambridge University Press, 2004).
47. Deborah McGregor, "Thanksgiving Brings Feeding Frenzy Round the Pork Barrel," *Financial Times* (November 26, 2003), 2.
48. Les AuCoin, in James M. Naughton, "The Lost Innocence of Congressman AuCoin," *New York Times Magazine* (August 31, 1975), 171.

Bibliography

Arnold, R. Douglas. *Congress and the Bureaucracy: A Theory of Influence.* New Haven, Conn.: Yale University Press, 1979.

Arnold, R. Douglas. *The Logic of Congressional Action.* New Haven, Conn.: Yale University Press, 1990. A broad ranging analysis of the factors that enable Congress to make policy in the service of general, rather than narrow, interests.

Baumgartner, Frank R., and Beth L. Leech. *Basic Interests: The Importance of Groups in Politics and in Political Science.* Princeton, N.J.: Princeton University Press, 1998. A comprehensive review of empirical research on interest groups.

Cain, Bruce, John Ferejohn, and Morris Fiorina. *The Personal Vote: Constituency Service and Electoral Independence.* Cambridge, Mass.: Harvard University Press, 1987. A comparison and contrast of the constituency-orientation of legislators in the United States and Great Britain.

Mayhew, David R. *Congress: The Electoral Connection.* New Haven, Conn.: Yale University Press, 1974. A classic treatment of how congressional institutions and policy-making are shaped by member's pursuit of reelection.

Schlozman, Kay L., and John T. Tierney. *Organized Interests and American Democracy.* New York, Harper and Row, 1986.

Stein, Robert M., and Kenneth. N. Bickers. *Perpetuating the Pork Barrel: Policy Subsystems and American Democracy.* Cambridge, U.K., and New York: Cambridge University Press, 1995. A comprehensive examination of the connection between congressional interests and the geographic distribution of federal funds.

11

DELIBERATION AND
DECISION MAKING

Paul J. Quirk

I F YOU TUNE IN TO C-SPAN'S TELEVISION COVERAGE OF CON-
gress, you are likely to find someone talking about public policy. It may be
a member explaining an amendment on the House or Senate floor; an
executive-branch official answering questions at a committee hearing; or a
party leader making a statement to reporters, among other possibilities. If you
visit the Capitol and wander into the working area of a Congress member's
office, you encounter mountains of paper, much of it about public policy:
committee reports, transcripts of committee hearings, studies by consultants or academics, memos, letters, and email print-outs. You may find the
member receiving a briefing from a staff aide, listening to a lobbyist, glancing
at the previous day's *Congressional Record*, or reviewing a memo prepared by
staff.

All these activities—the speaking and listening, reading and writing, and the
thinking that goes with them—perform a central function of Congress. To perform effectively as a policymaking institution, Congress cannot simply identify
the policy preferences of various constituencies, form coalitions among their
supporters, and count up the votes. Rather, a key part of Congress's task is
develop alternatives, collect and evaluate information, and weigh consequences—in short to deliberate about public policy.[1]

Such deliberation is important in at least three ways. First, thorough discussion in Congress makes policies more legitimate. Opponents of a policy will
accept the fact of its adoption more readily if they have had a reasonable chance
to change people's minds about it. Second, congressional debate about a legislative issue will, to some degree, educate the public about it. The news media

report highlights of a legislative debate, and attentive citizens learn something about the issue. Finally, well informed, thorough deliberation will help Congress reach intelligent decisions. It can prevent mistakes—unaffordable tax cuts, useless expenditures, unworkable programs, and unnecessary wars. It can also expose an unsatisfactory status quo. In the 1960s, congressional debate focused the nation's attention on the discrepancy between the nation's fundamental values and widespread, legally sanctioned racial segregation—facilitating the adoption of major civil rights laws.

The constitutional structure of Congress promotes deliberation in several respects.[2] To enact a law both chambers and the president must concur (unless Congress overrides a presidential veto). The members of the Senate and House are elected separately from each other, and from the president—with each office having terms of different length, and different geographic constituencies. As a result of these structures, Congress has been prone to work slowly; to delay responding to changing public sentiment; to take into account a wide range of interests and perspectives; and to debate issues thoroughly, or at least at length.

Nevertheless, Congress's performance as a deliberative body often leaves much to be desired. The discussion of issues may be dominated by uninformative, emotional rhetoric, and misleading or tendentious claims. It may overlook important aspects of decisions. As the framers feared, Congress may defer to an overexcited, uninformed public opinion or to pressure from organized groups.

This chapter examines how the institutions of Congress—the rules, procedures, and organizational structures through which decisions are made—affect its performance in legislative deliberation. Beyond that, it also examines how these arrangements develop and change. What forces and interests drive the development of congressional institutions for deliberation? Finally, it asks a practical question: Can Congress adopt institutions that will enhance its deliberative capability and reduce the threat of deliberative failures?

The chapter (an extension of my work with Gary Mucciaroni)[3] argues that several features of congressional institutions affect its capability for deliberation. But in making decisions about those institutions, members usually do not seek to enhance that capability. Instead, they design and struggle over institutional arrangements with a view toward achieving other goals. For the past two decades, party regulars—liberal Democrats and conservative Republicans—have effected changes designed to concentrate influence in the party organizations and party leadership. The trends toward dominant parties and severe party conflict have had significant costs for deliberation. In the concluding section, we corroborate these conclusions with some findings from the 2004–2005 Annenberg Survey of Congressional Staff. The survey shows that most Democrats and even many Republicans take a dim view of the contemporary Congress's methods and performance in deliberation.

How Congress Deliberates

The concept of deliberation is rarely the central focus of scholarly or journalistic discussion of the institution. Nevertheless, the function of deliberation is crucial to legislative performance. And Congress uses a variety of processes to accomplish it.

The predominant images of Congress, in both academic and popular accounts, focus not on deliberation but rather on lobbying, coalition building, and political power.[4] On this view, members pursue policies that are demanded by powerful groups or their constituencies. In debating bills, they seek only to justify and advertise their positions, not to learn or to reconsider the merits of issues.

This conception fits a good deal of what goes on in Congress. But it over-looks the important role of deliberation. Members often make their own judgments about legislation. Those motivated by a desire to adopt good policy will do so simply to figure out their own policy preferences. But even those mainly concerned about reelection need to judge which policies will actually benefit their constituencies or affected interest groups. If a member votes for a measure that turns out badly, an election challenger is very likely to point it out. Whatever the member's motivation, therefore, making a decision on legislation requires a judgment on the merits.

In this chapter, the term *deliberation* refers to the intellectual process of identify-ing alternatives, gathering and evaluating information, weighing considerations, and making judgments about the merits of public policies. This usage follows the dic-tionary definition of the verb, *to deliberate*, that is, "to think carefully and often slowly, as about a choice to be made."[5] In deliberating about public policy, legislators deal with both *substantive* considerations (such as social or economic consequences) and *political* ones (such as feasibility and electoral effects). They may seek to strike a bal-ance between substantive and political goals. In this chapter, however, we set aside political deliberation and focus entirely on substantive deliberation.

Importantly, the term *deliberation* does not refer to any particular social or institutional process, such as formal debate or group discussion.[6] Indeed, Congress can use a variety of organizational processes to perform the necessary intellectual tasks. It can arrange for collective discussion and exchange of infor-mation among members. It can delegate the task of deliberating to smaller groups of members, such as committees. It can rely on each member to gather information and deliberate separately. In truth, Congress usually employs a com-bination of all of these processes.

In the context of policy decisions, then, deliberation includes several ele-ments, each of which may be performed well or poorly.

1. *Identifying and developing alternative policies.* A satisfactory or effective deliberation requires that legislators consider a sufficient range of alternatives to avoid getting locked in on an inferior option.

316

2. *Estimating the consequences of those policies.* Legislators need to identify and compare the important substantive consequences of alternative policies, including the existing policy.
3. *Assessing the ethical or emotional significance of policies and consequences.* Legislators should weigh moral issues sufficiently to arrive at judgments that will stand up to their own or their constituents' further reflection.
4. *Refining provisions.* Whether policies succeed or fail will sometimes depend on specific provisions of the legislation. High-quality deliberation includes careful craftsmanship in bill drafting.

Each of these tasks involves obtaining facts, arguments, and other information; assessing the value of that information; and using it to make the respective judgments. Congress deliberates competently or effectively, then, when a decisive group of members performs these tasks well—obtaining the best available information and interpreting it reasonably. Effective deliberation will promote intelligent decisions on legislation.[7]

The primary vehicle for congressional deliberation is legislative debate, broadly defined. Members listen, and may contribute, to a stream of discourse about policy choices. Other actors—such as the president, other executive branch officials, interest group representatives, and various experts—also contribute. The content of this discourse ranges from casual speculation, to practitioners' expertise, to results of systematic research. Some of the contributors, such as nonpartisan congressional staff agencies, seek to provide objective, politically neutral advice. But most of the discourse consists of persuasive argument: Sponsors of bills advocate them. Opponents criticize them. Affected groups defend their interests. Undecided members try to sort out the conflicting claims.

Legislative debate takes place in various settings, both formal and informal. Although House and Senate practices differ in important respects, there are three major formal settings in each chamber: committee hearings, committee markups (or bill drafting sessions), and floor debate. All three occasions produce written information for the benefit of other members and the public. Hearings immediately yield prepared statements by most witnesses, and complete transcripts are published eventually. When a bill drafting session ends in approval of a bill, the committee prepares a report of its recommendations, often including dissenting views. Floor debate is recorded and published in the *Congressional Record*, available to members the next day.

A great deal of communication and deliberation, however, occurs outside formal settings. Lobbyists for interest groups, White House staff, and other executive branch officials visit members to explain their positions and urge support. They also present supporting documents. Bill sponsors and leading opponents send "Dear Colleague letters" to the entire membership. In recent years, party caucuses and committees have provided increasingly important additional venues. A multitude of interest- or ideology-based caucuses also discuss legislation—among them, the Congressional Black Caucus, the Congressional Steel Caucus, and the Congressional Sex and Violence in the Media Caucus (whose members *oppose* the sex and violence).[8] Of course members receive all the media that ordinary citizens do—from editorials in the *New York Times* to Rush Limbaugh's radio talk show.

The different settings for debate are largely interchangeable, providing roughly similar content. Sponsors of a tax cut, for example, will not predict a 5-percent increase in economic growth in a letter to all members and then tout a 10-percent increase in a floor speech. Opponents would seize on the discrepancy to discredit the speaker. A member will learn much the same thing, therefore, by reading the letter or listening to the speech.

Congressional debate also affects the broader deliberative process among the public. Hearings and floor debate receive media coverage and stimulate additional coverage of the policy issue. Bill sponsors and opponents appear as "talking heads" on television news and public affairs programs. Indeed, as research has shown, the news media often use congressional debate to define the range of relevant positions about a major national issue.[9] In the period leading up to the war in Iraq, for example, Congress accepted the Bush administration's unsupported claims about Iraq's possessing weapons of mass destruction. Leading news organizations, including the *New York Times* and the *Washington Post*, followed the example. They highlighted the administration's claims and relegated even serious challenges by reputable observers to the back pages.

How Deliberation Fails

If Congress has so many sources of information and occasions for debate, it might seem certain to make reasonably well informed, intelligent decisions. How does it sometimes fail to deliberate adequately? That is, in what sense does it fail, and what accounts for the failure?[10]

Defining Failure

A failure of deliberation has not occurred, of course, merely because a decision turns out badly. Policies, like best-laid plans, often go awry unforeseeably. When Congress allowed the Medicaid program to cover long-term care, it set guidelines to ensure that people would first use their own assets to buy care. It did not foresee that clever lawyers would find ways for well-off elderly to transfer assets and qualify for coverage, vastly increasing the program's cost.

Rather, a failure of deliberation occurs when Congress, or a decisive group of members, ignore relevant considerations; overlook pertinent information; or distort the significance of such information—and thus make substantially inaccurate judgments concerning a policy choice. In 1981 Congress acted on promises by President Ronald Reagan, inspired by a fringe group of economists, that a 25-percent tax cut would increase revenues. The tax cut produced a budget deficit that policymakers struggled to overcome for twenty-five years. In 1992 Congress overlooked the lack of competition in cable television markets when it deregulated cable television rates. The result was a dramatic rise in rates and a rapid repeal of the measure. In debating repeal of the inheritance tax in 2001, for example, advocates of repeal drastically overstated the adverse impact of the tax on the ability to inherit family farms and businesses. The distortion probably affected Congress's decision to repeal the tax.[11]

Congress may also fail to deliberate effectively in a different way. Even if members are well informed and have realistic judgments about the merits of a policy, they may distort the reality in their public statements. For example, they may justify a costly subsidy for a narrow group by claiming, without credible grounds, that it will produce large benefits for the economy. As a result, Congress may adopt a policy that it would clearly reject if the members were forced to portray it candidly.

Identifying failed deliberation in particular cases of policymaking is often controversial.[12] For one thing, staunch partisans almost always defend the policies that their side was responsible for—almost regardless of the results. Fortunately, this chapter refers to cases of apparent deliberative failure only for illustration. The argument does not depend on assessments of deliberation in specific cases.

Barriers to Deliberation

Fundamentally, deliberative failure results from three kinds of barriers to deliberation.

SUBSTANTIVE DIFFICULTY. First, and easy to overlook, attempting to sort out the merits of a policy decision may encounter a great deal of sheer substantive difficulty. It may require considerable effort and intelligence. The issue may be complex or technical. It may require difficult comparisons between competing values, or different types of risk. There may be numerous scenarios to consider or outcomes to weigh. When Congress passed the Occupational Safety and Health Act in 1970, for example, it faced the massive task of defining appropriate safety standards for a multitude of affected industries. To speed up the work, it authorized the Occupational Safety and Health Administration (OSHA) to adopt existing industry standards as mandatory federal standards through a radically simplified process. Unfortunately, many of these standards were outdated or downright silly and had been long ignored by the industries. OSHA's efforts to enforce them virtually destroyed its credibility.

The difficulty of deliberation is increased if there are severe time constraints or if other circumstances cause exceptional stress. It may be extreme, therefore, in a perceived crisis—as in the congressional vote to authorize military action in Vietnam in 1964, or in the development of the USA Patriot Act in the aftermath of the 9/11 terrorist attacks. Time constraints also arise from political considerations and the legislative process. Presidents want Congress to pass their programs during their first months in office. Sponsors of bills adopt major amendments, not previously discussed, at late stages of the legislative process. Congress legislates in enormous detail, and it folds vast amounts of policy into omnibus bills. In all these circumstances, deliberation is rushed.

Another kind of difficulty exists when an issue is prone to elicit psychological bias. There are well documented, systematic, and often powerful tendencies toward bias and error in human judgment.[13] Some biases reflect the mental strategies that people use unconsciously for simplifying judgments and decisions. For example, experimental research demonstrates that people estimate the frequency of an event largely by noticing how easily they can remember instances of it. Because crashes of commercial airliners are heavily covered in the media—even though very rare—people vastly overestimate the risk of such accidents, and regulatory policies have required disproportionate investments in airline safety. Other types of psychological biases that affect policy judgment include stereotyping, wishful thinking, and avoidance of cognitive dissonance.

CONFLICT. Second, deliberation may be hindered by severe conflict between individuals or groups.[14] Participants in deliberation will exchange information, keep their minds open, and focus on problem solving if they believe they have important interests in common. If they believe their interests are mostly in conflict, they will make exaggerated and misleading claims, focus their attention on relative outcomes, and neglect whatever interests they do have in common. As conflict-laden debate proceeds, it generates anger and rigid commitment that exacerbate these tendencies.

Although conflict is endemic to political decision making, the level of conflict varies. Policy issues that pit labor unions against management—chronic opponents in the political arena—generate posturing and mutual accusations, without much deliberation. More generally, policy issues that divide Democrats and Republicans very sharply will inhibit deliberation. Instead of trying to understand problems and find workable solutions, each party focuses on pressing its demands and scoring points. As we have noted, partisan conflict has been exceptionally intense in the late 1990s and early 2000s.[15]

PRESSURE. Third, and most obvious, legislative deliberation may be distorted by political pressure to adopt certain policies, and thus to endorse claims and arguments that support them.[16] The main pressures come from powerful constituencies—interest groups, the general public, and increasingly the core groups and activists of each party. They can induce legislators to endorse dubious claims, avoid inconvenient questions, or simply cut short deliberations. In the mid-1990s, for example, a wave of drug-related street violence left the public gripped by fear of crime. Congressional advocates of tough crime bills, pandering to the fears, pushed for lengthy mandatory sentences for broad categories of drug offenses. Few members had the temerity to resist. The measures produced an unprecedented increase in the prison population—much of it representing mere addicts locked up for decades on conviction of minor drug offenses.

On some types of legislation, members' responses to narrow constituency interests overwhelm all pretense of deliberation. In an essentially obligatory political role, members seek federal funds and projects targeted upon their states or districts.[17] Coalitions form to enact pork barrel spending on highways, sewers, post offices, and water resource projects, and sometimes to block base closings planned by the Defense Department. Discussion of these measures is dominated by the arithmetic of state and district benefits, with scant attention to the national interests they affect.

Members also face pressures to support the agendas of their party leadership and especially, for members of his party, the president's program. After President Lyndon Johnson proclaimed a "War on Poverty" in his 1964 State of the Union Address, the Democratic Congress hastily enacted a broad array of complex programs within two years. Many elements of the program were widely criticized and later abandoned.[18]

The Changing Political Environment

The capability for deliberation is not a fixed feature of Congress, hard-wired into the fundamental constitutional provisions. For one thing, as Gary Mucciaroni and I show in a forthcoming study of congressional floor debate on three major bills, congressional advocates argue far more responsibly and accurately on some issues than others.[19] They make a trade-off between maintaining credibility and producing compelling rhetoric. And their choices depend, for example, on which audiences are most crucial for the given issue and the likelihood of dubious claims being refuted effectively. More important for this chapter, however, Congress's capability for deliberation also will vary over time. Several developments in American politics over the past four decades have affected it.

One development is certainly beneficial: there has been an explosion of empirical research on public policy.[20] Centered in think tanks, schools of public policy, and university-based public affairs institutes, this research sometimes answers questions that policymakers of the past could only speculate about. In the early 1960s, advocates of the Head Start program could make bold claims that it would dramatically improve academic performance for low-income children. By the 1990s, well-designed studies of actual results documented definite, though somewhat modest, benefits.[21] Of course the findings of policy research are often controversial. They may reflect the political views of the researcher. But some policy research produces results of undeniable importance for intelligent policymaking.[22]

There has also been an explosion of interest-group lobbying, with mixed implications for the pressures on members.[23] Both producer groups, such as business and professional associations, and ideological and public-interest groups have proliferated. Whereas in the 1950s or 1960s a few business groups dominated lobbying on transportation, banking, or nuclear energy, for example, in the 2000s literally dozens of groups lobby Congress in any significant policy area. The groups' proliferation does not imply that they dominate the legislative process. Paradoxically, it should help members resist pressure from any one or few groups. It may increase pressure, however, on issues where a multitude of groups stand together—for example, on tax breaks that benefit a wide range of businesses.

Interest groups' methods of exerting influence have also changed. Interest-group contributions to political campaigns have grown dramatically since enactment of the first major federal campaign finance law in 1974, and the growth has not subsided after the Bipartisan Campaign Reform Act (BCRA) of 2002. Judging from the empirical evidence, however, campaign contributions have only modest effects on members' legislative decisions.[24] More important, interest groups that have potentially effective public appeals have increasingly emphasized "outside lobbying."[25] Instead of working the halls of Congress—the inside approach—they sponsor issue advertising to go over the heads of Congress members and win support from the mass public. In 1998 the tobacco industry defeated a major increase in federal cigarette taxes by running advertisements that solicited sympathy for low-income smokers. The combination of a well-financed lobby group and an effective media campaign can generate a great deal of pressure.

The mass media and the general public have also changed. Some of these changes are likely to create additional obstacles to deliberative policymaking. Despite a dramatic increase in levels of formal education, citizens score no higher than they did sixty years ago on tests of political and policy information.[26] Fewer people get the news from high-quality media, such as newspapers. More people use entertainment-oriented, so-called "soft media," from *The Daily Show* to Oprah Winfrey or *People Magazine*, as their main source of information, and the television network news broadcasts have moved toward a larger proportion of soft news. The more informed citizens often get news from highly ideological or polarized programs, like Rush Limbaugh or *Crossfire*, which treat every issue as a matter of partisan warfare.

At the same time, new communications technology has made it easier for ordinary citizens to express political opinions and lobby Congress. Advocates for causes implore people to email their Congress members, providing easy links to the members' addresses. The effects of these changes are hard to measure. But Congress probably encounters more frequent and intense pressure from poorly informed citizens than it did a few decades ago.[27]

Finally, trends in electoral politics from the 1980s to the present have posed additional challenges for deliberation. A gradual realignment of party geography has sharpened the ideological differences between the Democratic and Republican parties in Congress.[28] In 2004 congressional Democrats and Republicans had wider ideological differences than they had had in almost one hundred years. Both congressional parties have given their respective leaders greater power to determine and enforce party positions.[29] And during the George W. Bush administration, congressional Republicans have given extraordinary deference to the president.

These changes in the media, interest-group strategies, public opinion, and party politics, taken together, have given rise to a new style of policymaking in Washington. In what observers have called the "permanent campaign," the policy debate on major issues increasingly consists of presentations for the media by the president and the leadership of the congressional parties.[30] The president makes trips to give speeches and appear at staged media events. After President George W. Bush announced a measure to reform Social Security in early 2005, he spent much of the next three months on tour to promote the plan. The party leaders in each chamber provide a stream of statements and appearances, hoping for a snippet of national news coverage of their message-of-the day. Meanwhile, interest groups run television advertisements, coordinated with the party messages, in the states and districts of undecided Congress members.

This media-oriented debate creates difficult conditions for deliberation. The participants, divided largely into two party coalitions, compete to find messages that push the right buttons with core constituencies and the mass public. They rely heavily on tendentious symbolism and misleading claims. "The Bush benefit cut would be the largest in history for middle-class seniors," said Senate Minority Leader Harry Reid of Bush's 2005 Social Security Plan, even though the benefits were to continue rising faster than prices. With party leaders in charge of strategy, committees and the full chambers lose control of policy. The requirements for effective media appeals drive out sober analysis.

Congressional Institutions and Deliberation

Some policy issues challenge Congress's capability for deliberation, pushing it to act hastily or on dubious grounds. How do Congress's rules, structures, and procedures affect its ability to deal responsibly and intelligently with those issues? To the extent that institutions matter, does Congress adopt those that enhance deliberation?

Institutional Effects

Any legislature whose members have significant independence will deliberate about policy choices. Some will favor a policy change. Others will oppose it. And both sides will seek to persuade the undecided. But institutional arrangements will also shape Congress's capability for deliberation and determine how thoroughly it deliberates, especially when a majority is eager to act.

More specifically, the rules, structures, and procedures of Congress can influence the quality of deliberation in a variety of ways. Among the most important:

1. They affect the amount of *time and attention* that Congress gives to a decision. In the House, the Rules Committee recommends and the whole chamber adopts special "rules" allocating floor time for the consideration of bills. Senate rules allow any forty-one of the one hundred senators to prolong debate indefinitely. The duration of committee deliberations is generally at the discretion of committee leaders. Giving an issue more time and attention will usually improve the quality of the deliberation.

2. They determine the available *resources and expertise* for deliberation. A strong system of standing committees ensures that some members have expertise in each area of legislation. A sizable staff gives members the ability to deal competently with more subjects. Such resources and expertise can help Congress master difficult issues, and make it easier to avoid erroneous judgments.

3. They may shape the *information* available for decision. House and Senate rules require that budget documents project revenues, expenditures, and deficits for a ten-year period. Many statutes require the executive branch to collect data and report to Congress. The Congressional Budget Office (CBO) provides budget estimates—including long-term revenue and expenditure projections—from an official, nonpartisan source. Forcing or facilitating awareness of good information helps prevent reliance on bad information.

4. They create *opportunities for communication, criticism and rebuttal*. In the House, for example, most debate consists of five-minute speeches, resulting in a series of brief, repetitive, statements. In the Senate, speeches are often much longer, providing opportunity to discuss an issue in depth. The annual adoption of a concurrent budget resolution ensures that Congress will debate and decide overall fiscal policy before it takes up particular programs and tax provisions. Both

chambers have norms of formality and politeness that help to avoid personal attacks and emotionally charged conflict.

5. They regulate *constituency access and members' autonomy*. For example, regulations on lobbying practices and campaign contributions attempt to limit the power of interest groups. Prior to the 1970s, rules that permitted closed meetings and unrecorded floor votes insulated members from both interest group and mass-public constituencies. Regulating constituency access may enhance deliberation. Unfortunately, it also may diminish accountability and interfere with constructive forms of constituency influence.

6. Finally, congressional institutions affect members' *incentives for deliberative effort*. The seniority rule for selecting committee chairs, observed without exception in the mid-twentieth century, made it worthwhile for senior committee members to invest effort in developing substantive expertise and skills in committee leadership. Term limits on committee chairmanships, imposed by the Republicans in the mid-1990s, reduce the payoffs for such investments. The contemporary Senate's frequent adoption of major floor amendments reduces the committees' incentives to deliberate carefully.

Deliberation and Institutional Choice

In all, then, Congress has a wide range of institutional levers for enhancing the quality of deliberation. Unfortunately from this standpoint, however, it does not organize itself with the primary objective of enhancing legislative performance. As Eric Schickler has shown, congressional institutions develop in response to demands made by changing coalitions of members in pursuit of several distinct goals—a complex pattern of action that he calls "disjointed pluralism."[31] The same account applies to institutions that affect deliberative capability.

To be sure, Congress members have reasons to prefer better deliberation, rather than worse. They want policies to succeed and to benefit their constituencies and the country. They also want Congress to work well, to be respected, and to have a major role in policymaking. Most members, however, are even more strongly committed to certain specific interests and types of policies. Members of a conservative Republican majority, for example, want Congress to enact its policies. Members with farm constituencies want it to pass bills reported by the agriculture committees. Junior members want a chance to influence legislation. Nearly all members want to get home for long weekends. In general, members will give higher priority to their distinct partisan, ideological, and constituency interests and to various personal interests, and lower priority to the diffuse interest of all members in improved deliberation.

Congress will adopt rules or structures for the specific purpose of improving deliberation, therefore, only in special circumstances. First, it will do so when the deliberation-enhancing rule or structure has minimal cost for competing objectives. For example, Congress readily provides members with staff, computers, and research services. It frequently adopts provisions requiring the executive branch to collect and report information. Second, Congress will adopt deliberation-enhancing measures that are needed to avoid gross deficiencies in performance. For example, it requires sponsors of taxing and spending proposals to use economic projections by the CBO, rather than whatever projections they find convenient. In particular, Congress will act to avoid deficiencies that threaten its role in policymaking—as when the president might point to congressional incompetence to justify taking unilateral action.

Third, Congress will adopt deliberation-enhancing measures that impose essentially equal burdens on both parties or on both liberal and conservative interests. In 1990, Congress established a *pay-as-you-go* rule requiring that proposals for tax cuts or spending increases incorporate offsetting tax increases or spending cuts.[32] The rule forced Congress to face the consequences of its actions. It constrained budget strategies. Yet it was acceptable to both Democrats and Republicans because it inhibited tax cuts and spending increases in exactly the same way.

For the most part, however, institutional decisions that affect deliberative capability—to its benefit or detriment—are intended for other purposes altogether. Congress responds to constituency demands about rules and structures—such as public-interest group pressure for open proceedings. It abandons legislative proceedings on Mondays and Fridays for the sake of members' personal convenience. Each party pushes for campaign finance policies that strengthen its electoral prospects.

Most important, Congress designs institutions that reflect and shape a changing internal distribution of influence.[33] Junior liberal Democrats wrested power from conservative committee chairs in the 1970s. Both parties gave more leverage to party leaders in the 1980s and 1990s. The Republican majority in the House used special rules to roll over the Democratic minority in the late 1990s and 2000s; Senate Democrats expanded the filibuster to avoid the same fate.

The institutions of deliberation in Congress are, therefore, largely by-products of other goals and demands. The demands that strengthen deliberative capability are generally those of the minority party, which seeks to slow action and disperse power. The majority party tries to simplify procedures and concentrate power, with the frequent result of short-circuiting the consideration of issues. In recent years, the Democrats and Republicans in Congress have fought intense battles over these issues.

Institutional Developments

The period from the late 1960s to the early 2000s has brought notable change in congressional institutions. The changes have concerned all of the general features of institutions listed above as likely to affect deliberation. However, as we would expect, they have not been designed to promote deliberative performance.

Managing Resources and Workload

Effective deliberation requires, perhaps more than anything else, time to think and discuss legislation. To deliberate effectively, Congress must balance the time that members have available for policy decisions with the number and complexity of those decisions. Unfortunately, for the quality of deliberation, Congress puts too much legislative business on its plate for the commitment of time that members make.

Early in the twentieth century, Congress was able to debate issues at length, handle all of the year's legislative business, and yet allow members several months off between sessions. As the volume of legislative business increased with the growth of government, however, dealing with all of it grew steadily harder. As Connor and Oppenheimer's data on the House of Representatives in the 68th Congress (1923–1924), the 84th Congress (1955–1956), and the 96th Congress (1979–1980) indicate, the number of public bills considered annually increased substantially over this period.[34] The House adjusted to the rising volume of bills by staying in session for longer periods and putting in more workdays. Until the last two decades of the twentieth century, the demands of fund-raising and campaigning for office were sufficiently modest, and the congressional work year sufficiently short, that the House could lay on more days and weeks of work without encountering much resistance. By the 1990s, limits were reached: The annual session essentially lasted all year, and the numbers of workdays days leveled off at about 130–140 per year—three days per week, with a few weeks off—the apparent limit of members' willingness to show up.[35]

Although the number of bills also leveled off in the 1990s, the volume of legislating continued to increase. Up to 1984, the maximum number of pages of legislation enacted in one Congress was 5400; in the 1990s it twice exceeded 7500. The 105th Congress (1997–1998) enacted twenty-five pages of legislation for every day it was in session.

With workdays at a limit, further adjustment to the increased workload has taken other routes. For one thing, the House has dramatically increased the length of the formal daily session—from about four hours in 1981 to about eight hours in 2000.[36] Added to the hours of meetings and other activities that take place after the daily adjournment, the result has been an inordinately long unofficial workday. Some members have abandoned congressional careers, complaining about the working conditions and quality of life.

In addition, the House has cut corners in the work of deliberation. It has developed the habit of doing business on the floor with few members in attendance.[37] And it deals with a great deal of legislation very quickly—often under special procedures, such as *suspension of the rules*, that provide for only an abbreviated debate. It evidently has not neglected major bills. Judging from the debates on three key bills in each of five years from 1983 to 1999, the House has not cut the time for debate on such bills.[38] But Congress has packed more legislating into one bill. Some bills have reached well over one thousand pages in length. Omnibus appropriation bills, in particular, are huge measures that incorporate appropriations and often significant policy changes spanning a vast range of government programs.[39] Decisions on these bills are orchestrated by the party leaders. Few other members even know their important provisions, much less consider them seriously.

In principle, Congress has two alternatives to the current regime of long daily sessions, poorly attended debates, and massive bills—but neither is likely to gain support. It could resume increasing the number of days in the annual session, which, at this point, would require attendance on Mondays or Fridays. Under the pressures of the constant campaigning of recent years, members would dismiss that idea out-of-hand. Alternatively, Congress could reduce its volume of legislative business—considering fewer bills or making those bills shorter, and in a word, making less policy. To do so, it would have to delegate more decisions to the executive branch, and members would have to forgo opportunities for claiming credit. Members will not make these sacrifices of political power. Rather, they will continue passing a massive amount of legislation, without taking more time to do it, and hope for the best.

The trends in Congress's legislative workload and work schedule are not likely to produce careless decisions on the major issues of the day. Congress reserves time for those issues. Rather, high-volume legislating makes Congress vulnerable to haphazard or ill-considered decisions on lesser, even though important, matters, which necessarily receive less attention. In one common scenario, an influential legislator slips a special-interest provision into an omnibus bill, and Congress enacts it without noticing it.

Regulating Constituency Pressure

The most important threat to effective deliberation in Congress in general is probably pressure from powerful constituencies. On issues that are sufficiently salient, the pressure comes primarily from the mass public. On other issues, it comes mainly from interest groups. Congress has limited means to regulate those pressures, which are essential features of a democratic political system. In any case constituency demands and partisan electoral goals have also constrained efforts to do so.

THE MASS PUBLIC. Prior to 1970, much congressional activity was not readily observed by ordinary citizens. Many committee meetings, including most bill-drafting or "markup" sessions, were closed to the public. Floor debate was not televised. Many important floor votes were conducted as unrecorded voice votes, with the presiding officer simply calling for the *yeas* and *nays* and judging which were louder. The public learned only which side had won, not how their representatives had voted. As Bessette points out, the closed arrangements had the advantage of permitting members to deliberate with some autonomy.[40] But they were effectively attacked as protecting cozy relationships with special interests. They probably had both effects in different circumstances.

A movement for "government-in-the-sunshine" in the late 1960s and early 1970s, promoted by public-interest groups such as Common Cause and Ralph Nader's Public Citizen and supported mainly by liberal Democrats, swept away most of the barriers to observation.[41] Reform measures opened most committee meetings to the public and reporters, provided for C-SPAN's television coverage of floor debate, and mandated that nearly all floor votes be recorded and published. The reforms catered to an expectation that greater openness would benefit consumer, environmental, and other liberal causes. They were controversial in Congress, with even some liberals objecting to the loss of institutional autonomy. A liberal Democratic House committee chair criticized television coverage of floor debate as putting members "in a goldfish bowl." But with Democratic majorities in both chambers, and favorable coverage of the reforms in the media, Congress sided with the reformers. Since the 1990s, the Republicans—advocating tax cuts and conservative positions on hot-button social issues—have probably gained more than the Democrats from Congress's direct exposure to the mass public. In any case, the public has become accustomed to the openness. For better or worse, going back to a more closed and insulated Congress is not on anyone's agenda in Washington.

INTEREST GROUPS. Organized interest groups have two means of imposing pressure on legislative deliberations that are potentially subject to congressionally devised constraints: contributing to election campaigns and lobbying the members. Congress has passed statutes designed to regulate both; but neither effort has been effective. Interest groups' third means of imposing pressure discussed above—issue advertising—is constitutionally beyond the reach of legislative constraints.

The history of congressional efforts to regulate campaign contributions has been a tale of frustration.[42] Congress enacted the first major limitations on campaign contributions in the Federal Election Campaign Act Amendments of 1976. But interest-group contributions to congressional candidates, instead of shrinking, grew dramatically. In the Bipartisan Campaign Finance Reform Act of 2002, Congress closed some of the loopholes in the 1976 Act. But the main result has been the channeling of private money into independent advertising, compromising candidates' responsibility for appeals made on their behalf.[43]

In the end, the limitations of campaign-finance reform reflect the centrality of partisan interests in institutional decisions that affect those interests. Several states have passed measures that limit the role of private money by providing public financing tied to voluntary spending limits. But in addition to facing a lack of public support at the national level, almost any public-financing measure will give an electoral advantage to one of the parties, most likely the Democrats. Republicans have vigorously opposed public financing, and it was never on the table in the discussions leading to the 2002 act.

Judging by how interest groups allocate their resources, their most effective tool of influence is not contributions but rather lobbying: They spend more on lobbying by a ratio of about 10:1.[44] Popular suspicion of lobbyists has made it easy to adopt restrictions on certain aspects of lobbying. Congress has passed laws strictly limiting lobbyists' ability to provide members with gifts—with a limit of $50 per gift (the price of a moderately good restaurant meal in Washington), and an aggregate limit of $99 per year.

But these laws have not touched—and constitutionally cannot touch—the main source of lobbying pressure: that a well-heeled industry can send dozens and, for a key vote, hundreds of representatives to meet with Congress members and staff, make the case for the group's policies, and ask for support. Interest-group lobbying is protected by the constitutional right of citizens to "petition the government." Up to a point, it is a useful source of information for members.[45] Unfortunately, there is no apparent way to bar lobbying that goes beyond that point.

Policy Development: Committees and Parties

The deliberative heavy lifting in Congress, and especially the House of Representatives, has traditionally been performed in committee. Both chambers have maintained systems of standing committees—almost essential for effective deliberation in a large assembly—since the early nineteenth century.[46] Because other goals largely drive institutional change, however, Congress has often failed to manage or use the committees in ways that serve their deliberative function.

COMMITTEE APPOINTMENTS AND CHAIR SELECTION. For a committee to deliberate competently, its members should be sufficiently concerned about the policies in its jurisdiction to invest effort in learning about them and yet reasonably representative of the entire chamber. Committee leaders, especially the chair, should have expertise in the policy area and skill in running committee processes. Lengthy committee experience is generally helpful.

The so-called textbook or pre-reform Congress of the mid-twentieth century had important weaknesses in committee recruitment practices.[47] Many committees were dominated by members whose states or districts were especially affected by committee bills—the agriculture committees by members with farming constituencies, Housing and Urban Affairs by members from urban states or districts, and so on. Because these members were highly engaged with their committee work, such committees had the advantage of deliberating carefully. But they did so from an unrepresentative point of view. The House and Senate often faced choices whether to pass bills severely biased toward committee constituencies or rather to rewrite them, without benefit of committee deliberations, through floor amendments.

Committee chairs were selected on the basis of committee seniority. The seniority system avoided divisive fights over chairmanships. It ensured that chairs had long experience and the relative autonomy associated with winning reelection several times. And it made chairs independent, both of party leaders and of other committee members. But it did not ensure that chairs would have outstanding or, necessarily, even average skills. When the famously effective Ways and Means Committee chair, Wilbur Mills, left the House in 1975, he was succeeded by a series of less capable chairs, and the committee's work deteriorated.[48]

In the reform and post-reform periods, the congressional parties have made important changes in committee appointments and especially the selection of chairs.[49] These changes reflected the greater ideological uniformity within each party and the parties' enlarged roles in policy making. Prompted by demands from junior liberal Democrats, the House Democratic Caucus in 1975 voted out three notoriously conservative and authoritarian Southern Democratic committee chairs. After the Republican takeover of Congress in 1995, the Republican leadership in both chambers asserted increasing control over committee appointments. More important, they established election of chairs by the party conferences as standard procedure. Although they have followed seniority in most cases, they have used the leverage of election to ensure that committee chairs faithfully pursue the party's agenda.

The election of committee chairs should have mixed effects on the committees' deliberative functions. On the positive side, it will help ensure the chairs' competence. By making the committees responsive to the majority party, it should also reduce the need to rewrite bills on the chamber floor. On the negative side, the committee chairs will have less taste for conducting independent deliberation on bills that are high on the party agenda.

The House Republicans also adopted rules limiting committee chairs to a single six-year term. The term limitation serves the attractive goal of distributing power more widely among members. Unfortunately, it also reduces the incentives of a committee chair to develop expertise and to maintain the committee's reputation for competence.

COMMITTEE ORGANIZATION AND JURISDICTION. An effective committee system has to divide all of government's subject matter into coherent, independent chunks—committee jurisdictions—and then adjust the divisions occasionally as various linkages among policies and programs rise and decline in importance. Congress members, however, fiercely resist changes in committee jurisdiction.[50]

Jurisdictional changes disrupt their relationships with constituencies, waste their subject-matter expertise, and dissipate their influence. Almost invariably, the chambers defer to the members' resistance and refuse to realign committee portfolios. With some exceptions, committee jurisdictions still follow the scheme established by the Legislative Reorganization Act of 1946.

The lack of occasional realignment affects deliberation adversely. For one thing, it creates imbalances in committee workloads. The House Ways and Means Committee, for example, has jurisdiction over taxation, the Social Security system, Medicare, Medicaid, and the welfare system—a large fraction of the most complex and important domestic policies. For another, it increases the likelihood that a single bill or program will affect the jurisdictions of two or more committees in each chamber. The House deals with such conflicts, moderately effectively, through a rule that permits referral of a bill to multiple committees. But from the standpoint of orderly, coherent deliberation, there is no substitute for committee jurisdictions that line up with the major activities of the government.

Despite the normal resistance, Congress has sometimes been strongly motivated to reorganize committees in particular areas. Until the 1974 Budget Reform, each of thirteen appropriations bills and usually one or more tax bills came to the chamber floors separately—with no prior plans on the allocation of resources among broad areas or on the overall balance of revenues, expenditures, and budget deficits. These broad allocations and fiscal balances were not even decided directly, much less carefully deliberated. Congressional support for reform was not motivated by these deliberative deficiencies, but rather by their effect on the institutional rivalry with the president. Republican President Richard Nixon cited the Democratic Congress's failures of fiscal control as justification for impounding funds that it had appropriated. To defend its authority, Congress reformed the budget process. It created the Budget Committees and gave them jurisdiction over an annual concurrent budget resolution to set guidelines for taxing and spending bills. Since then, Congress has first decided the general framework of the budget—ensuring that the broadest issues receive direct consideration—and only then has made specific decisions on taxing and spending.[51]

Thirty years later, Congress swallowed some of its objections to jurisdictional realignment in creating the Department of Homeland Security and establishing new committees to deal with the department. In this case, Congress was motivated by the obvious urgency of dealing coherently with terrorism. Even so, it left many responsibilities for the new department scattered across the committee system.[52]

In short, then, Congress has accepted substantial realignment of committee jurisdiction only in response to extraordinary circumstances. In normal times, the members' stake in maintaining their turf trumps efforts to overcome confusion and duplication in jurisdictions.

IMPLEMENTING COMMITTEE PROCESSES. For committees to provide the benefit of careful and competent deliberation, they must have considerable independence in their legislative actions, and the chambers must normally rely on their recommendations. On the other hand, however, if party leaders or caucuses take over the function of policy development, then the quality of deliberation depends on the capabilities and efforts of those entities.

In the pre-reform period, Congress consistently protected the committees' policy development role. The members' motivation for defending it, however, was mainly to protect their turf. Non-committee members sometimes attempted to invoke procedures, such as the discharge petition, that would bring bills to the floor without committee approval. But the chambers rarely went along with rolling the committee.[53] Congress usually has preferred to let committees block widely supported legislation rather than compromise their prerogative not to act. In votes on these petitions, members look out primarily for their interests as committee members.

Since the 1995 Republican takeover, however, committee turf has given way to the movement toward stronger parties. Especially in the House, Republican leaders have often given legislative committees specific instructions on a bill. In this approach, the leadership makes the main policy decisions; the committee works out the details; and the committee minority is reduced to the role of critic. In some episodes of what Barbara Sinclair calls "unorthodox legislation," party leaders have drafted bills and taken them to the floor without even bringing them to the committee.[54] The broadest incursion into legislative committee responsibility has been the practice of putting substantive legislation into appropriations bills—including omnibus bills that accomplish much of a session's significant legislating in a single stroke. Omnibus bills serve the leadership's convenience by bringing a massive amount of legislating onto a single track, which leaders can easily direct.

On its face, the takeover of the committees' role in policy development by party leadership represents a degradation of the deliberative function. As discussed below, how far the apparent degradation is real depends on what kind of deliberation the parties undertake behind the scenes.

Providing Information

Congressional institutions can also affect legislative deliberation by specifying particular information, or information from a particular source, to be made available for consideration. Congress has created specialized staff agencies whose findings and reports have special authority, owing to the agencies' nonpartisan structures and accountability to Congress: the Congressional Budget Office (CBO), the Congressional Research Service (CRS), the Government Accountability Office (formerly General Accounting Office, GAO), and the short-lived Office of Technology Assessment (OTA), created in 1972 and abolished in 1995. Congress can choose to give prominence to the high-quality, non-partisan information that these agencies produce. For example, it has given the CBO a mandate to prepare cost estimates for pending legislation; and it debates budget policies on the basis of ten-year projections provided by the CBO and the administration. Such requirements ensure that certain considerations are raised; make high-quality information prominent; and give it a presumption of validity in relation to any conflicting claims.

The potential benefits of these information-providing measures are limited, however, for two reasons. First, general rules cannot specify the essential information for a wide range of issues. They can specify some crucial information for budgeting: ten-year revenue and expenditure projections; current-services budgets; assumptions about economic growth, inflation, employment; and so on. But even in that highly repetitive context, the effort to specify information is only moderately successful. Budgets hold deficits to acceptable levels, according to the standard wisecrack, "by smoke and mirrors." Put differently, the numbers often do not really represent what the rules intend. In other policy contexts—say, in education, or criminal justice, or foreign aid—rules that specify mandatory information have little or no relevance. Every bill poses different issues.

Second, Congress is not inclined to elevate the role of nonpartisan policy analysis to an extent that would generally constrain legislative debate. Policy debates often turn, in large part, on factual or analytic issues: Does capital punishment deter crime? Does the minimum wage cause unemployment? If it wished to do so, Congress could assign a staff agency to provide expert nonpartisan assessments of the best available evidence on the main analytic issues for every major policy decision. Congress has not chosen to generalize the role of staff agencies in this way, however. But those assessments would often fail to resolve important questions—just as forecasts by the CBO often fail to predict the economy accurately. In addition, they would create a burden for legislators who chose to argue outside their range. It is likely that members value the opportunity to make claims more freely without bearing that burden. If nothing else, it facilitates effective posturing with constituencies.

Thus Congress has established the staff agencies for narrower purposes and kept them on a shorter leash. The CBO was established as part of the 1974 budget reform to help Congress compete with the president in shaping the budget. The CRS performs studies by request for particular congressional clients (who may choose not to release them), and the GAO reviews executive agencies' administrative performance.

The OTA's abbreviated existence illustrates the limits of Congress's desire for nonpartisan analysis.[55] OTA performed studies, at Congress's request, to assess scientific and technological issues relevant to congressional decisions. It adopted an explicit strategy of avoiding controversial findings whenever possible. Nevertheless, even though OTA's analyses were highly regarded, it was unable to avoid partisan recriminations, and disaffected Republicans eventually killed it.

Debating Bills on the Floor

Although the deliberative heavy lifting is done in committee, the final stage of deliberation occurs in debate on the House and Senate floor. That is also the stage that captures most of the attention of the media and ordinary citizens.

Floor debates vary considerably, however, in their value for deliberation. To maximize that value, the floor should consider a modest number of significantly different alternatives—for example, a committee bill, a few major amendments, and the status quo. It will not attempt to deal with a wide range of fundamental alternatives, or to decide numerous details. A useful debate will feature direct confrontation between opposing claims, with substantial presentation of reasoning, evidence, criticism, and rebuttal. Finally, it will go on for a reasonable period and then end with a decision. An inability to reach a decision is a defect of the arrangements for deliberation.

In managing floor debate, however, congressional leaders do not worry a great deal about the quality of deliberation. Rather, they use procedures primarily to shape legislative outcomes. Their strategies for doing so and the resulting character of debate differ considerably between the House and Senate.

AMENDMENTS AND CLOSURE: THE HOUSE. Floor debate in the House is regulated mainly by special "rules" that the Rules Committee recommends, and the floor approves by majority vote, for each bill. In addition to allocating the time for debate, a rule may limit the amendments that can be proposed on the floor, or even permit none at all. The nature of floor deliberation in the House depends, therefore, largely on the Rules Committee's practices in designing these rules.

In much of the textbook-Congress era, the Rules Committee, despite having nominal Democratic majorities, was controlled by a pivotal group of conservative Southern Democrats, who often formed coalitions with the Republicans. The committee sometimes constrained the House agenda, especially on civil rights, by blocking liberal measures that the full chamber might have passed. But it usually devised rules that permitted the whole House to deliberate coherently and work its will, rather than merely favoring a particular result. It prohibited amendments on certain subjects, especially taxes, where it judged that floor amendments could lead to chaos. Barring amendments on tax bills kept the floor from giving away the store. The Rules Committee sometimes identified a handful of permissible amendments, presenting the main outstanding controversies for resolution on the floor. It often imposed no restrictions on amendments—a workable practice in a period in which the whole House generally deferred to the legislative committees.

In the reform era, the Rules Committee responded to the demands of junior rank-and-file members, mostly liberal Democrats, for more opportunities for participation and influence by accommodating a dramatic increase in the number of floor amendments. The House took the attitude, Steven Smith remarked, "Why don't we do it on the floor?" The result was a swashbuckling amending process that often threw overboard the advantages of committee expertise.[56] In the post-reform and party era, especially after 2000, the Rules Committee has become a tool of the majority party leadership. It designs special rules primarily to protect the Republican majority's bills from destructive floor amendments. It often limits the Democratic minority to offering a single amendment, usually a substitute for the entire bill.[57] The minority gets a chance to display its alternative and debate its merits. But the majority leadership has little difficulty keeping its members in line on an amendment to substitute an entire bill.

This partisan use of special rules serves deliberation in one sense: It results in debate that puts the fundamental issues dividing the parties on public display. But it precludes separate consideration of any additional specific issues addressed in a bill. And it does not enable a floor majority (regardless of party) to determine its preferences. The House will decide, for example, between a Republican and a Democratic plan for Social Security Reform. Republicans who oppose creating private investment accounts will not have a chance to express their view.

Whether considering few or many amendments, the House conducts legislative business on a firm schedule. When the majority leadership is ready to act—usually because it expects to win—there are few obstacles to reaching a decision.

AMENDMENTS AND CLOSURE: THE SENATE. In most cases, floor action on a bill in the Senate is regulated by a *unanimous consent agreement*. Such agreements are negotiated by party and committee leaders and adopted, as the name indicates, by unanimous consent of the full Senate. Much like a House special rule, a unanimous consent agreement controls the consideration of floor amendments and the time allowed for debate. In the absence of such an agreement, senators retain the right to unlimited debate. And the minority party or any sizable group of senators may use that right, if they so choose, to block or substantially delay action by means of a filibuster or the threat of a filibuster.

Under favorable circumstances, these methods of regulating floor debate promote thorough and informed deliberation. In negotiating a unanimous consent agreement, each party seeks to maximize its influence on the bill at hand, without worrying about deliberation. But the minority party, and often other senators with special concerns, have incentives to insist on adequate opportunity for amendment and time for debate. The requirements of effective deliberation are well served. The difficulty with these arrangements, however, is that they depend on moderation and self-restraint on all sides.

Through most of U.S. history, the Senate's consensual methods of regulating floor debate worked reasonably well. Senate debates had the reputation of being thorough; yet filibusters were generally infrequent. Senators generally observed a norm of resorting to filibuster only on very serious matters. Southern senators, for example, filibustered Civil Rights measures that they felt would undermine the fabric of Southern society. Majorities usually trimmed their ambitions to avoid provoking that response. In these circumstances, the institution of the filibuster served useful deliberative purposes. It helped a legislative minority draw attention to the weaknesses of a bill otherwise headed toward rapid enactment. If the pressures to adopt such a bill come from narrow groups, it helped expand the scope of conflict—the scenario portrayed in the classic film *Mr. Smith Goes to Washington*. Above all, delay by filibuster or by the threat of filibuster sometimes countered the impulse to act in a politically inspired rush.

In the past decade, however, these institutions have broken down. With increasingly severe differences over policy, and stronger constituency pressures to press those differences, the parties have more often failed to achieve a mutual accommodation. And the minority party—whether Republican or Democratic—has asserted its procedural rights increasingly aggressively. Resort to the filibuster has become fairly routine.[58] Indeed, commentators have simply assumed that enacting a bill requires the support of sixty senators—the number of votes currently required to invoke *cloture* and thus end debate. They take for granted that senators will support a filibuster to block any bill that they prefer not pass.

Apart from filibustering, the minority party and other senators have insisted on so much amending opportunity, and adopted floor amendments so readily, that bills essentially have been rewritten on the Senate floor—rendering the committees' work largely irrelevant. In some cases, committees that expected such treatment have not bothered to draft fully developed proposals.[59]

The Senate floor in the early 2000s has become a problematic, often unworkable, institution. On the one hand, with a disaffected Democratic minority increasingly seeking merely to obstruct, it is often incapable of acting at all. The impasse that resulted with respect to confirmation of judicial nominations during the second Bush administration led to a crisis that threatened the foundations of the Senate as an institution.[60] On the other hand, when it does act, the floor sometimes takes on most of the responsibility of drafting bills. Unfortunately, floor debate on a raft of amendments is no substitute for the deliberative function of the committees.

Consequences and Prospects

Even though the basic constitutional design of Congress ensures a good deal of deliberation, some policy issues present serious barriers to deliberating intelligently. Various rules, structures, and practices of Congress also affect its capability for deliberation. But the development of those institutions is driven mainly by other concerns—with deliberative capability largely a by-product of those other concerns.

Several trends of the past two decades have tended to weaken Congress's deliberative capability. In the House, the majority party has wrested much of the responsibility for policy development from the standing committees. It also has severely restricted the opportunity of the full chamber to consider amendments. The majority party, especially its leadership, calls the shots on legislation. In the Senate, with rules that prevent majority-party domination, the greatest difficulties arise from exploitation of those rules, mainly by the minority party. The Democratic minority has forced consideration of dozens of amendments in floor debate on a controversial bill—the opposite extreme from the restricted amendments in the House. In effect, the Senate writes some bills on the floor, without benefit of committee deliberation. In other cases, the minority blocks action altogether. In both chambers, the polarization of party conflict along with the increasing pressures of public opinion, media politics, and the permanent campaign have made constructive discussion more difficult. On the face of it, Congress has become less capable of deliberation.

The difficulties with deliberation in the contemporary Congress emerge clearly in the findings of the 2004–2005 Annenberg Survey of Congressional Staff.[61] As one would expect, Republican and Democratic staff differ sharply in their views of congressional decision making, with the Democratic minority far more critical. House and Senate staff also differ, reflecting the greater accommodation of the minority in the Senate. Nevertheless, large proportions of the respondents—often including overwhelming majorities of the Democrats—endorse statements suggesting important deficiencies in deliberative performance. Substantial majorities of each party in each chamber say that the majority party leadership makes most of the important decisions (see Table 1). Most Democrats say in addition that "the majority party makes policy decisions regardless of the minority's views." In the House, almost half the Republicans agree. And majorities of Democrats and some Republicans deny that "the decision making process faithfully follows established rules and procedures." Despite the differences in perceptions between the parties, these findings point to Republican majorities pushing bills through Congress without accommodating Democratic views or providing for full and orderly consideration.

Many respondents report corresponding deficiencies in the substantive content of deliberations. The problem is not with the availability of information. Majorities in all groups say that the House or Senate often or almost always has the information it should have about the consequences of policies. Rather, as one would expect, the difficulties arise in how Congress uses that information. Almost two-thirds of House Democrats and half of Senate Democrats deny that

TABLE 1

Staff Perceptions of Decision Making Deliberation

Thinking about policymaking by the House/Senate in the area mentioned by respondent:

The majority party leadership makes most of the important policy decisions.

	agree	disagree	DK/other
House Republicans	77%	19%	4%
Senate Republicans	66	29	6
House Democrats	92	8	0
Senate Democrats	83	17	0
All	83	15	2

The majority party makes policy decisions regardless of the minority's views.

	agree	disagree	DK/other
House Republicans	43%	47%	10%
Senate Republicans	14	86	0
House Democrats	90	7	3
Senate Democrats	90	10	0
All	65	31	4

The decision making process faithfully follows established rules and procedures.

	agree	disagree	DK/other
House Republicans	81%	12%	7%
Senate Republicans	71	23	6
House Democrats	29	67	4
Senate Democrats	47	50	3
All	53	42	5

Policy decisions are the result of careful analysis, discussion, and deliberation.

	agree	disagree	DK/other
House Republicans	91%	8%	1%
Senate Republicans	74	17	9
House Democrats	33	62	4

TABLE 1 (continued)

Senate Democrats	50	47	3
All	59	37	4

Policies are based on ideological beliefs rather than evidence.

	agree	disagree	DK/other
House Republicans	38%	61%	1%
Senate Republicans	49	49	3
House Democrats	89	9	2
Senate Democrats	83	13	3
All	67	31	2

In making policy decisions in the respondent's area, the House/Senate a) looks at the relevant information quite objectively OR b) often overlooks or distorts relevant information.

	quite objective	overlooks or distorts	DK/other
House Republicans	82%	11%	7%
Senate Republicans	60	34	6
House Democrats	14	79	8
Senate Democrats	43	43	13
All	45	47	8

The [House/Senate] has the information it should have about the likely consequences of different policy options.

	often/ almost always	sometimes not too often/ never	DK/other
House Republicans	80%	17%	3%
Senate Republicans	89	12	0
House Democrats	58	41	1
Senate Democrats	67	30	3
All	70	28	2

SOURCE: The Annenberg 2004–2005 Survey of Congressional Staff. N=242. Group Ns: House Republicans, 74; Senate Republicans, 35; House Democrats, 103; Senate Democrats, 30.

"policy decisions are the result of careful analysis, discussion, and deliberation." Indeed, about one-quarter of Senate Republicans also deny it or withhold judgment. About two-thirds of all respondents, including sizable proportions of every group, say that "policies are based on ideological beliefs rather than evidence." And substantial proportions—including 78 percent of House Democrats—say that their chamber "often overlooks or distorts relevant information." Although we do not have comparable data from earlier periods, the survey findings corroborate the indications of significant deficiencies of deliberation in the contemporary Congress.

It is hazardous to attribute specific policy decisions of recent years to Congress's methods or capabilities for deliberation. For one thing, the George W. Bush administration even more than Congress was severely criticized as having defective deliberative processes; acting on uninformed, ideological views of the world; and relying on wishful thinking. And it pressured Congress to go along with its decisions. Whatever the effect of presidential pressure, Congress approved the war in Iraq without undertaking a serious examination of evidence that Iraq had weapons of mass destruction. It also approved a series of tax cuts, spending bills, and budgets that produced unprecedented long-term deficits. It funded the war in Iraq and expanded the Medicare program to provide coverage of prescription drugs without making plans to pay for them. The fiscal results alarmed informed commentators across the political spectrum. The nonpartisan controller general of the United States and head of the Government Accountability Office, David Walker, observed that 2004 may have been the most fiscally reckless year in the nation's history. To some degree, these policy decisions probably reflect recent deterioration in Congress's capability for deliberation.

The practical question is whether Congress can adopt institutional changes that will improve that capability. As the chapter has shown, many institutional features affect it. The Republicans, for example, could eliminate or modify the term limitations for committee chairs. The House and Senate could experiment with debate formats that encouraged more direct and immediate confrontation over competing claims. The main problem, as we have seen, is that Congress rarely makes important institutional changes mostly to improve deliberation. It makes them mainly to achieve other, seemingly more pressing, objectives.

Taking this constraint into account, there are three main approaches worth considering. First, the two parties could negotiate agreements in each chamber that defined moderate, workable participation rights for the minority party— that is, guaranteeing the minority greater participation in the House, and limiting minority obstructionism in the Senate. On the face of it, however, there is virtually no rationale for the House majority or for the Senate minority to surrender power for these purposes. The public is not demanding either change.

An interesting logical possibility is that the two parties could strike a bargain that covered both chambers—with the majority party giving up some control of the House in exchange for the minority party giving up some power to obstruct action in the Senate. But there is no tradition of such cross-institution bargaining on rules or structures. In managing the House, for example, House Republicans look after their own interests, not those of Senate Republicans. If the political parties continue to become stronger and more centralized, however, a grand House-Senate compromise on minority participation could become conceivable in the future.

If Congress wanted to reduce the intensity of party ideological conflict, it would have at least one means to do so. It could set federal requirements for the decennial processes of redrawing House district lines in each state to prevent the political parties from dominating the redistricting. Nonpartisan redistricting commissions, for example, would probably create a larger number of competitive districts than have existed in recent House elections. (They could hardly create fewer.) And these competitive districts would often elect moderate members of either party. If the House had a healthy contingent of moderates, bill sponsors and advocates would have to appeal to these moderates. Their doing so would change the tone of debate. The House, at least, would spend more time deliberating about common interests, and less time using divisive appeals to rally opposing constituencies.

Neither party in Congress has shown any interest in changing a redistricting process that has produced safe districts for all but a handful of House members. Redistricting reform might become politically feasible, nevertheless, if reformers somehow got citizens exercised about the virtual disappearance of competitive House elections.[62]

Finally, Congress should and will adjust to the presence of polarized parties, prone to dominate policy making, by building up the deliberative capability of party organs. In due course, the parties will develop stronger advisory and decision processes, with larger, more specialized staff, and more formal procedures. If parties take over the deliberative tasks of committees, in other words, they eventually will have to gear up for committee work. Even with improved staff and procedures, however, party organs are unlikely to incorporate ideas and information from the full range of perspectives that the committees and the respective chamber floors dealt with in less partisan times.

Notes

* Joseph Cooper provided exceptionally detailed and constructive criticism of an earlier draft of this chapter, leading to many important improvements. George Connor provided data and advice that helped a then-undergraduate student, Nicholas Caccamo, update a 1993 study by Connor and Bruce Oppenheimer; I have benefited from Caccamo's work. Above all, my thinking about many important issues in this chapter was developed in collaboration with Gary Mucciaroni, with whom I am coauthor of *Deliberative Choices:*

Debating Public Policy in Congress. The present chapter would have been better if other commitments had not precluded his working on it as coauthor.

1. The pioneering studies of Congress as a deliberative institution are Arthur Maass, *Congress and the Common Good*; Joseph Bessette, *The Mild Voice of Reason*; and Keith Krehbiel, *Information and Legislative Organization*.

2. Bessette, *The Mild Voice of Reason*.

3. Gary Mucciaroni and Paul J. Quirk, *Deliberative Choices* (forthcoming). The main concepts and definitions used in the present chapter follow those developed in the book. The book, however, takes on tasks that are mostly distinct from those of the chapter. In particular, the book develops an empirically grounded approach to evaluating the intelligence of congressional debate, employs that approach in case studies of three major policy decisions, and develops a theoretical analysis for explaining differences in the quality of debate from one issue to another. It also addresses effects of institutional structures and possibilities for institutional reform, although considerably more briefly than the present chapter. For alternative approaches to measuring or assessing deliberation in Congress, see Edward L. Lascher, Jr., "Assessing Legislative Deliberation: A Preface to Empirical Analysis," *Legislative Studies Quarterly* (1995): 501–519; and Marco R. Steenbergen et al., "Measuring Political Deliberation: A Discourse Quality Index," *Comparative European Politics* 1, no. 1 (2003): 21–48.

4. David J. Vogler, *The Politics of Congress*; Gary W. Cox and Mathew D. McCubbins, *Legislative Leviathan*; Philip M. Stern, *Still the Best Congress Money Can Buy*.

5. *The American Heritage Dictionary of the English Language*, 4th ed. Available at http://www.dictionary.com, c. February 2005). Our usage is consistent with the use of the term in research on cognitive psychology. See Ziva Kunda, *Social Cognition: Making Sense of People*.

6. For a variety of perspectives on deliberation, see Jon Elster, ed., *Deliberative Democracy*. Some scholars use the concept of deliberation in a far more restrictive sense—to refer only to group discussion or to certain well regulated forms of such discussion. But the broader, dictionary definition enables us to consider the complex and variable processes by which Congress actually performs this function.

7. Competent deliberation does not guarantee correct judgments, of course. It does not abolish uncertainty. Indeed one mark of competent deliberation is that it recognizes uncertainty where it exists, rather than drawing firm conclusions that are unwarranted. We also distinguish deliberation from decision. This permits us to recognize, for example, that incompetent deliberation may produce a good decision. For example, Congress may wildly overestimate the long-term financial problems of the Social Security program and yet make desirable adjustments of benefit schedules as a result.

8. Susan Webb Hammond, *Congressional Caucuses in National Policymaking*.

9. Lance Bennett, "Toward a Theory of Press-State Relations," *Journal of Communication* 40, no. 2 (1990): 103–125.

10. For a generally similar approach to deliberative failure, see Marc K. Landy, Marc J. Roberts, and Stephen R. Thomas, *The Environmental Protection Agency*.

11. See Mucciaroni and Quirk, chaps. 5 and 6.

12. Identifying cases of deliberative failure requires the analyst to make judgments both about the significance of available information (for example, what consequences members should have foreseen) and about members' goals (what consequences they would have chosen). We cannot know these things with precision or certainty. As a result, we can ascribe deliberative failure persuasively only in relatively extreme cases—when legislators overlook obviously important information, with obviously unsatisfactory results.

13. Daniel Kahneman, Paul Slovic, and Amos Tversky, eds., *Judgment under Uncertainty*; Massimo Piatelli-Palmarini, *Inevitable Illusions*.

14. This effect has been studied extensively in the literature on the social psychology of negotiation and bargaining. See, for example, Dean G. Pruitt and Peter J. Carnavale, *Negotiation in Social Conflict*.

15. See Binder, Chapter 5 of this volume.

16. Anthony King, *Running Scared*; Martha Derthick and Paul J. Quirk, *The Politics of Deregulation*; Paul J. Quirk and Joseph Hinchliffe, "The Rising Hegemony of Mass Opinion," *The Journal of Policy History* 10, no. 1 (1998), 19–50; John Mark Hansen, *Gaining Access: Congress and the Farm Lobby, 1919–1981* (Chicago: University of Chicago Press, 1991). An important question, not yet addressed in the literature, is to what extent constituency pressure affects outcomes by distorting deliberation and judgment, or only acts directly on legislators' incentives and decisions. Does a major lobbying campaign by powerful groups change legislators' beliefs? To the extent that constituency pressure works by distorting deliberative processes, measures that somehow protected those processes would also affect outcomes, without requiring broader changes in the distribution of political power.

17. See Lee, Chapter 10 of this volume.

18. Gareth Davies, *From Opportunity to Entitlement*.

19. Mucciaroni and Quirk, *Deliberative Choices*.

20. Andrew Rich, *Think Tanks, Public Policy, and the Politics of Expertise*.

21. Sherri Oden, Lawrence Schweinhart, and David Weikart, *Into Adulthood*.

22. A case in point was the role of economic analysis in the reform of anticompetitive regulatory regimes in the 1970s and early 1980s. For an account, see Derthick and Quirk, *The Politics of Deregulation*.

23. Allan J. Cigler and Burdett A. Loomis, eds. *Interest Group Politics*; Paul Herrnson, Ronald Shaiko, and Clyde Wilcox, eds. *The Interest Group Connection*.

24. See Jacobson, Chapter 4 of this volume.

25. Ken Kollman, *Outside Lobbying*.

26. Michael X. Delli Carpini and Scott Keeter, *What Americans Know about Politics and Why It Matters*.

27. There is no consensus on the overall influence of public opinion. As their title suggests, Lawrence Jacobs and Robert Y. Shapiro, *Politicians Don't Pander* (Chicago: University of Chicago Press, 2000) argue that policymakers generally are not influenced by public opinion. For an opposing view, see Quirk and Hinchliffe, "The Rising Hegemony of Mass Opinion." For a review of the relevant literature, see Jeff Manza and Fay Lomax Cook. "A Democratic Polity? Three Views of Policy

Responsiveness to Public Opinion in the United States," *American Political Research* 30 (2002), 630–667.

28. See Binder, Chapter 5 of this volume.

29. See Sinclair and Smith, Chapters 8 and 9 of this volume.

30. Norman J. Ornstein and Thomas E. Mann, eds., *The Permanent Campaign and Its Future.*

31. See Schickler, Chapter 2 of this volume. See also, Eric Schickler, *Disjointed Pluralism.*

32. See Patashnik, Chapter 13 of this volume.

33. Ibid.

34. George E. Connor and Bruce I. Oppenheimer "Deliberation: An Untimed Value in a Timed Game," *Congress Reconsidered*, 5th ed., edited by Lawrence C. Dodd and Bruce I. Oppenheimer (Washington, D.C.: CQ Press, 1993). This section also draws on an unpublished undergraduate paper, Nicholas Caccamo, "Measuring Deliberation in the House of Representatives," University of Illinois at Urbana-Champaign, May 2004.

35. Norman J. Ornstein, Thomas E. Mann, and Michael J. Malbin, *Vital Statistics on Congress, 2001–2002* (Washington, D.C.: American Enterprise Institute, 2002).

36. Ornstein et al., *Vital Statistics.*

37. Connor and Oppenheimer, "Deliberation: An Untimed Value in a Timed Game."

38. Caccamo, "Measuring Deliberation in the House of Representatives."

39. Glen S. Krutz, *Hitching a Ride.*

40. Bessette, *The Mild Voice of Reason.*

41. Roger H. Davidson and Walter J. Oleszek, *Congress against Itself*; Quirk and Hinchliffe, "The Rising Hegemony of Mass Opinion."

42. See Jacobson, Chapter 4 of this volume.

43. Glen Justice and Jim Rutenberg, "Senators Say Political Groups Are Circumventing Finance Law," *New York Times*, March 10, 2004, A26.

44. Steven Ansolabehere, James M. Snyder, and Micky Tripathi, "Are PAC Contributions and Lobbying Linked? New Evidence from the 1995 Lobby Disclosure Act," *Business and Politics* 4, no. 2 (2002), 135–155.

45. Jane Mansbridge, "A Deliberative Theory of Interest Representation," in *The Politics of Interests: Interest Groups Transformed*, edited by Mark P. Petracca (Boulder, Colo.: Westview Press, 1992).

46. Joseph Cooper, *The Origins of the Standing Committees and the Rise of the Modern House* (Houston: Rice University Studies, 1970); see also Schickler, Chapter 2 of this volume.

47. Christopher J. Deering and Steven S. Smith, *Committees in Congress*, 3rd ed.; Kenneth A. Shepsle, *The Giant Jigsaw Puzzle.*

48. Randall Strahan, *New Ways and Means.*

49. See Rohde, Chapter 7 of this volume.

50. E. Scott Adler, *Why Congressional Reforms Fail*, chap. 16.

51. Chap. 13; James L. Sundquist, *The Decline and Resurgence of Congress.*

52. See Rohde, Chapter 7 of this volume.

53. Walter Oleszek, *Congressional Procedures and the Policy Process.*

54. Barbara Sinclair, *Unorthodox Lawmaking.*
55. Bruce A. Bimber, *The Politics of Expertise in Congress.*
56. Stanley Bach and Steven S. Smith, *Managing Uncertainty in the House of Representatives* (Washington, D.C.: Brookings Institution, 1988); Oleszek, *Congressional Procedures and the Policy Process.*
57. Richard E. Cohen, Kirk Victor, and David Baumann, "The State of Congress," *National Journal* (10 January 2004).
58. Sarah Binder and Steven S. Smith, *Politics or Principle?.*
59. Cohen, Victor, and Baumann, "The State of Congress."
60. See Maltzman, Chapter 14 of this volume. This crisis can best be understood as the effect of a vicious cycle of partisan conflict. President George W. Bush selected a number of exceptionally conservative judicial nominees, and the increasingly disciplined and conservative Senate Republicans prepared to confirm them. Faced with potentially drastic effects on the judiciary, the Senate Democrats resorted to an unprecedented, repeated use of the filibuster to block the confirmation of several of these nominees. The Republicans, in turn, threatened to use an unprecedented, dubiously legitimate procedure to abolish the filibuster on judicial nominations. This procedure would have relied on a mere majority vote to impose a limitation on senators' right of debate. If the procedure were defined as legitimate, it could be used to impose broader limitations on the right of debate, and ultimately to abolish the distinctive character of the Senate.
61. Telephone interviews were completed with 204 staff from members' offices, including 65 in the Senate (35 Republicans and 30 Democrats), and 177 in the House (74 Republicans and 103 Democrats). Respondents were employed as Administrative Assistants (the top staff position in a congressional office), Legislative Directors, Legislative Assistants, or in equivalent positions—usually with no more one staffer per member's office. Each respondent was asked several questions about decision making in their own chamber and in the policy area of his or her own responsibility. The findings thus reflect staffers' observation of congressional decision making in all areas of legislative activity.
62. Patrick Basham and Dennis Polhill, *Uncompetitive Elections and the American Political System.*

Bibliography

Adler, E. Scott. *Why Congressional Reforms Fail: Reelection and the House Committee System.* Chicago: University of Chicago Press, 2002.

Basham, Patrick, and Dennis Polhill. *Uncompetitive Elections and the American Political System.* Policy Analysis No. 547. Washington, D.C.: Cato Institute, 2005.

Bessette, Joseph. *The Mild Voice of Reason: Deliberative Democracy and American National Government.* Chicago: University of Chicago Press, 1994.

Bimber, Bruce A. *The Politics of Expertise in Congress: The Rise and Fall of the Office of Technology Assessment.* Albany: The State University of New York Press, 1996.

Binder, Sarah, and Steven S. Smith. *Politics or Principle? Filibustering in the United States Senate.* Washington, D.C.: Brookings Institution, 1995.

Cigler, Allan J., and Burdett A. Loomis, eds. *Interest Group Politics*, 6th ed. Washington, D.C.: CQ Press, 2002.

Cox, Gary W., and Mathew D. McCubbins. *Legislative Leviathan: Party Government in the House.* Berkeley: University of California Press, 1993.

Davidson, Roger H., and Walter J. Oleszek. *Congress against Itself.* Bloomington: Indiana University Press, 1977.

Davies, Gareth. *From Opportunity to Entitlement: The Transformation and Decline of Great Society Liberalism.* Lawrence: University Press of Kansas, 1996.

Deering, Christopher J., and Steven S. Smith, *Committees in Congress.* 3rd ed. Washington, D.C.: CQ Press, 1997.

Delli Carpini, Michael X., and Scott Keeter. *What Americans Know about Politics and Why It Matters.* New Haven, Conn.: Yale University Press, 1996.

Derthick, Martha, and Paul J. Quirk. *The Politics of Deregulation.* Washington, D.C.: Brookings Institution, 1985.

Elster, Jon, ed. *Deliberative Democracy.* Cambridge, U.K., and New York: Cambridge University Press, 1998.

Hammond, Susan Webb. *Congressional Caucuses in National Policy Making.* Baltimore: Johns Hopkins University Press, 1997.

Herrnson, Paul, Ronald Shaiko, and Clyde Wilcox, eds. *The Interest Group Connection: Electioneering, Lobbying, and Policymaking in Washington.* 2nd ed. Washington, D.C.: CQ Press, 2005.

Kahneman, Daniel, Paul Slovic, and Amos Tversky, eds. *Judgment under Uncertainty: Heuristics and Biases.* Cambridge, U.K., and New York: Cambridge University Press, 1982.

King, Anthony. *Running Scared: Why America's Politicians Campaign Too Much and Govern Too Little.* New York: Free Press, 1997.

Kollman, Ken. *Outside Lobbying: Public Opinion and Interest Group Strategies.* Princeton, N.J.: Princeton University Press, 1998.

Krehbiel, Keith. *Information and Legislative Organization.* Ann Arbor: University of Michigan Press, 1992.

Krutz, Glen S. *Hitching a Ride: Omnibus Legislating in the U.S. Congress.* Columbus: Ohio State University Press, 2001.

Kunda, Ziva. *Social Cognition: Making Sense of People.* Cambridge, Mass.: MIT Press, 1999.

Landy, Marc K., Marc J. Roberts, and Stephen R. Thomas. *The Environmental Protection Agency: Asking the Wrong Questions.* New York: Oxford University Press, 1990.

Maass, Arthur. *Congress and the Common Good.* New York: Basic Books, 1983.

Mucciaroni, Gary, and Paul J. Quirk. *Deliberative Choices: Debating Public Policy in Congress.* Chicago: University of Chicago Press, forthcoming.

Oden, Sherri, Lawrence Schweinhart, and David Weikart. *Into Adulthood: A Study of the Effects of Head Start.* Ypsilanti, Mich.: High/Scope Press, 2005.

Oleszek, Walter. *Congressional Procedures and the Policy Process.* 6th ed. Washington, D.C.: CQ Press, 2004.

Ornstein, Norman J., and Thomas E. Mann, eds. *The Permanent Campaign and Its Future.* Washington, D.C.: American Enterprise Institute, 2000.

Petracca, Mark P., ed. *The Politics of Interests: Interest Groups Transformed.* Boulder, Colo.: Westview Press, 1992.

Piatelli-Palmarini, Massimo. *Inevitable Illusions: How Mistakes of Reason Rule Our Minds.* New York: Wiley, 1996.

Pruitt, Dean G., and Peter J. Carnavale. *Negotiation in Social Conflict.* Pacific Grove, Calif.: Brooks/Cole, 1993.

Rich, Andrew. *Think Tanks, Public Policy, and the Politics of Expertise.* New York: Cambridge University Press, 2004.

Schickler, Eric. *Disjointed Pluralism: Institutional Innovation and the Development of the U.S. Congress.* Princeton, N.J.: Princeton University Press, 2001.

Shepsle, Kenneth A. *The Giant Jigsaw Puzzle: Democratic Committee Assignments in the Modern House.* Chicago: University of Chicago Press, 1978.

Sinclair, Barbara. *Unorthodox Lawmaking: New Legislative Processes in the U.S. Congress.* 2nd ed. Washington, D.C.: CQ Press, 2000.

Stern, Philip M. *Still the Best Congress Money Can Buy.* Washington, D.C.: Regnery Gateway, 1992.

Strahan, Randall. *New Ways and Means: Reform and Change in a Congressional Committee.* Chapel Hill: University of North Carolina Press, 1990.

Sundquist, James L. *The Decline and Resurgence of Congress.* Washington, D.C.: Brookings Institution, 1982.

Vogler, David J. *The Politics of Congress.* Boston: Allyn and Bacon, 1974.

12

FOREIGN AFFAIRS AND WAR

Christopher J. Deering

DEBATE REGARDING THE RELATIVE BALANCE OF POWER among and rightful authority of the three branches of government is endemic to the Constitution. But in the modern era it has been particularly persistent and vigorous in the realm of foreign affairs and war. Likewise, and despite episodic shifts in institutional dominance, the reshaping of power in foreign affairs and war has been more dramatic and more fundamental than in any other area of constitutional authority.

This shift in power, which distinctly advantages the executive, can be attributed to no single cause and no single source. Each of the three branches has made important, indeed historic, contributions. Congress's contribution to this state of affairs centers on the establishment of the contemporary national security state—a congeries of institutions that includes the National Security Council, the Departments of State and Defense, a large standing army, nearly a dozen intelligence organizations, and, with its establishment in 2002, the Department of Homeland Security.[1] Although some view the shift as alien to the intent of the framers and to an "original" interpretation of the Constitution, the Supreme Court also has made an important contribution by shifting from a traditional interpretation of foreign policy power in the Constitution, one that views the executive as constrained to a prerogative interpretation, which permits substantially more leeway to the executive.[2] And, almost needless to say, modern presidents have aggressively expanded and utilized the resources of the office to articulate a powerful, even "imperial," presidency.[3]

This essay focuses upon the character and consequences of this shift in power and assesses its implications for democratic governance and the vitality of Congress as a representative institution. What was the original distribution of powers where foreign affairs and war are concerned? How has that distribution been altered during more than two centuries of American history? Does the contemporary Congress possess the institutional and political capacity to exercise properly its constitutional powers? And what reforms might be desirable or possible to improve Congress's ability to discharge its duties?

In brief, this essay advances the following argument. First, the constitutional arrangements adopted by the founders gave more power to the executive where issues of diplomacy were concerned—those being naturally the province of executives—and, correspondingly, more power to the legislature where defense and commerce were concerned—those being naturally dangerous to trust solely to the executive. Second, with some ebb and flow, this balance of authority remained intact into the twentieth century. At that point, however, the establishment of a large standing army and the various elements of the national security presidency provided the foundation for a much more powerful executive in both foreign affairs and war. Third, although Congress attempted to reassert its authority during the post-Vietnam era by bolstering its legislative tools, those attempts generally fell short of restoring the status quo ante. This shortfall results from Congress's inability to marshal either the institutional or political will necessary to redress the balance of power. Thus, the essay concludes by laying out a case for why reform efforts are unlikely to change these circumstances in the near future.

War and Foreign Affairs in the Constitution

Although foreign relations occupied the Constitutional Convention remarkably little, the founders did face one very basic question: In a world largely populated by undemocratic states, how could popular principles be embraced in the making of U.S. policy with respect to war and foreign affairs? The answer to that question follows, in two parts. First, the founders adopted an approach to policy that might be called consolidated deterrence. This approach combined fiscal and commercial prudence with modest military capacity to discourage interference by the United States's principal rivals. In addition, it was based upon an adherence to a protectionist or mercantilist trade policy popularly called the American system. Second, the founders adopted a constitutional division of labor regarding "security against foreign danger" and "intercourse with foreign nations," by which the former would be dominated by the legislative branch and the latter would be dominated by the executive.[4] These two matters are treated in turn below.

Consolidated Deterrence in a Mercantilist Age

The founders' overall approach to external affairs had two components: consolidated deterrence and the American system.[5] As stated by John Jay (*Federalist* No. 4), consolidated deterrence combined "trade prudently regulated," a "militia properly organized," and "finances discreetly managed."

If [foreign powers] see that our national Government is efficient and well administered—our trade prudently regulated—our militia properly organized and disciplined—our resources and finances discreetly managed—our credit re-established—our people free, contented, and united, they will be much more disposed to cultivate our friendship, than provoke our resentment.[6]

Consolidated deterrence was a means of combining national strengths in order to deter foreign aggression, diminish national weaknesses, and induce cooperation and trade. Nascent, provincial, and indebted, the new republic had neither the capacity nor the inclination for empire building. Insulated by a spacious western frontier and a wide ocean to the east, the founders hoped that the United States could mature in relative isolation from the rest of the world. A strong, unified national government and an attendant strength in commerce, largely through self-sufficiency, were the two most important requirements for safety from America's British, French, and Spanish rivals. For the ardent nationalist Alexander Hamilton, a well-organized professional army and a competent navy would provide additional security if they were authorized.[7]

As Hamilton saw it, a principal virtue of the new union was the strength to be drawn from free and unfettered trade within and among the component states. Indeed, Hamilton sounds very much the free trader in describing the salutary features of a "common market": "An unrestrained intercourse between the States themselves will advance the trade of each by an interchange of their respective productions, not only for the supply of reciprocal wants at home, but for exportation to foreign markets."[8] Although a free trader at home, Hamilton, who became the first secretary of the treasury, was a mercantilist when it came to foreign commerce.[9] Mercantilism sought to harness "economic life in the interests of political and national strength and independence," including military strength.[10] It envisioned a central role for the national government in shaping commercial policy vis-à-vis other nations. The maintenance of a positive balance of trade was of particular importance, along with self-sufficiency in those items essential to national defense. Alexander Hamilton is regarded as the "pioneer advocate" of protectionism, particularly for infant industries, and Congress would become the principal architect of a policy that the economist Friedrich List would call the American system.[11]

External Power and the Constitution

Congress's powers with respect to foreign affairs and war are contained in Article I, Section 8 of the Constitution. Congress's authority to declare war, establish an army and a navy, control immigration, regulate foreign commerce, and even such relative obscurities as granting letters of marque and reprisal appear in clauses 1–17. Section 8 then concludes, of course, with the sweeping "necessary and proper" clause (clause 18). By contrast, the president's authority over foreign and national security policy appears as a brief grant in Article II, Section 2. The president's duties and responsibilities appear in Section 3. The chief executive is granted two consequential diplomatic powers that signal the unique position of that office: to make treaties and to appoint ambassadors (each with the advice and consent of the Senate). The president also is vested generally with the "executive power." Section 3 adds the diplomatic responsibility of "receiving ambassadors and other public ministers" and the admonition to "take care that the laws be faithfully executed."[12] The president's only explicit national security authority consists of the following: "The President shall be Commander and Chief of the Army and Navy of the United States, and of the Militia of the several States, when called into the actual Service of the United States." (Art. II, Sec. 2, clause 1).

Contemporary proponents of an energetic and independent executive role in war and foreign affairs rarely make a sharp distinction between foreign policy and military policy—between diplomacy and defense, that is. But the founders did make such a distinction. Although it is sometimes suggested that the founders faced a simpler world and therefore saw no point in making such distinctions, a fair reading of their thoughts on the matter suggests otherwise. Diplomacy and defense are both addressed, and addressed quite distinctly, in the Constitution and in *The Federalist Papers*. The founders' familiarity with the character of diplomacy and war as practiced under eighteenth-century international law is evidenced by numerous references to a variety of technical matters regarding the "intercourse among nations." Moreover, the fact that these discussions appeared in *The Federalist Papers* further suggests that they had every expectation their audience would have little trouble following along.

In *Federalist* No. 23, Alexander Hamilton asserts that the new union would provide for four essential functions: (1) the common defense; (2) preservation of the public peace from internal or external attacks; (3) the regulation of commerce both internal and external; and (4) the superintendence of political and commercial intercourse.[13] Simplifying a bit, Hamilton later tells us (in No. 41) that the powers regarding external matters conferred upon the government by the new Constitution can be divided into two classes—security, on the one hand, and foreign political and commercial intercourse, on the other hand.[14]

Thus, with Hamilton leading the way, the founders instituted different foundations for the practice of foreign policy and for making defense and commercial policy. In foreign policy, which involved treaty making and diplomacy generally, executive authority and capacity would predominate. In defense and commercial policy, which necessarily involved taxation and legislation, Congress would predominate. In the former case Congress, and primarily the Senate, would function as adviser and critic. In the latter case, the president would perform the executive function, taking care that the laws be faithfully executed. This division of labor was based upon a fairly straightforward rationale. First, a strong aversion to executive (i.e., monarchical) control of the military meant that Congress should predominate on questions of security. To the extent that policy regarding foreign commerce rested upon the power of taxation, a similar rationale obtained there. And, second, direct dealings with other nations, particularly the negotiation of treaties, required the "perfect secrecy and immediate dispatch" that only a seasoned diplomatic corps and a unified executive could supply. To be sure, negotiations regarding affairs of trade and navigation were to be "cautiously formed and steadily pursued"—executive attributes. But the concurrence of the Senate in these affairs would provide an essential protection.[15] And in any case, the House would dominate actual policy making by taking the lead with respect to any implementing legislation.

To emphasize, Congress's foreign and national security powers are granted explicitly. The Constitution also grants Congress broad authority to make all laws necessary and proper to carry out these functions. In contrast, the president's constitutional authority is restricted to a few specific diplomatic functions and the broad responsibility of commander in chief during times of war. But even that power was no different from what was invested in most of the states' governors. And there is no evidence that they were expected to go marching off to war. Thus, the commander in chief's role, as it was well understood at the time, was that of the chief political authority.

As noted above, the distinction between diplomacy and defense is not often emphasized. And yet Hamilton and Jay both discuss the president's peculiar diplomatic advantages in some detail while writing little about the military power. *The Federalist Papers* scarcely mention the president's role as commander in chief.[16] To be sure, Hamilton dearly hoped for the establishment of a professional military along the Prussian model. But that had nothing to do with presidential authority. So while modern commentators are fond of quoting Jay's call for "secrecy and dispatch" as signal advantages in chief executives and defects in legislatures, they fail to note that Jay's reference is to treaty making and not at all to war making (No. 64). If we take this distinction, or division, between diplomacy and defense seriously, therefore, a strong case can be made for Congress as the primary locus for the war power and the presidency as the primary locus for intercourse with foreign countries.

Although the founders' intent in this seems clear enough, there has been substantial evolution in military policy and the institutional apparatus supporting it since the adoption of the Constitution. This change has proceeded with Congress establishing the national security state and the courts carving out a wide ambit of authority for the chief executive.

Emergence of the National Security State

As noted at the outset, this essay argues that the balance of constitutional power in foreign affairs and war has been substantially altered over the course of the nation's history. That alteration is not a result of constitutional amendment. Rather, it is the result of accumulated legislative change, executive activity, and, to a lesser extent, Court decisions. This section outlines these changes and examines their consequences.

From the adoption of the Constitution until the middle of the nineteenth century, Congress, the Court, and most presidents adhered to a Madisonian, that is to say, limited, view of constitutional authority in foreign and military affairs. In brief, Congress legislated in a generally clear fashion, executives rarely stretched their authority in an aggressive fashion, and, when they did, the Court held that legislative authority was preeminent. From the Civil War until after World War II, legal and political doubts about the president's freedom to use American troops declined steadily as the traditional view was replaced by what political scientist Gordon Silverstein calls the "prerogative view" of foreign policy.[17] After the Civil War, the courts adopted an increasingly Hamiltonian, or executive-centered, point of view. This trend culminated in Justice George Sutherland's 1936 opinion in *United States v. Curtiss-Wright Export*. Sutherland's opinion for the Court is infamous and expansive in articulating a plenary and exclusive power for presidents in international relations—one that Sutherland located in the very sovereignty of the nation and not in the Constitution itself.[18]

In order to engage troops abroad, before World War II at least, presidents required some means of raising the requisite number and then providing their equipment and transportation. Put simply, presidents needed Congress's approval. If not legally, therefore, presidential prerogative was at least practically constrained by the lack of a large standing army and the absence of substantial numbers of U.S. troops stationed abroad.[19] Thus, when President Theodore Roosevelt sent the Great White Fleet (a fleet of battleships assembled to display American naval power) around the world in 1907 his authority to do so was still something of an open question. But when Congress balked at the expense, Roosevelt simply asserted that he had enough money to get the fleet to the Pacific Ocean. Congress could pay for its return or it would stay in the Philippines. Roosevelt's move was something of a stunt, and public opinion was very much on his side, but it was a precursor to the sort of independence that would soon be common for chief executives.

Circumstances in the post-World War II era were quite considerably different. Having already supplied the troops, agreed to the bases, produced the equipment, and consented to the alliance structures necessary to pursue military policies abroad, Congress had put itself into a reactive role. That is to say, a strong presumption came to exist that presidents might employ U.S. military forces as they saw fit. Meanwhile, Congress now carried the burden of proof to demonstrate why executives should not be engaged in foreign military activities. Historically speaking, this reversed the roles of these two institutions. Two twentieth-century developments define this state of affairs: the post-World War II standing army and the establishment of an institutionalized national security presidency. The statutory basis for each is a product of congressional deliberation—a fairly reasoned response to circumstances emanating from the cold war. In combination, however, they had the unintended consequence of a substantial shift in authority for foreign affairs and war from Congress to the president.

The Standing Army

For more than 150 years the practice of maintaining a small- to moderate-sized standing army, adhering to a policy of neutrality, and creating only modest-sized civilian institutions for the military's support was common except during times of war. The peacetime establishment of a substantial standing army with institutional and intelligence support in the context of multilateral treaty commitments after World War II therefore marked a significant shift in U.S. posture and policy. In the decade prior to the war, active-duty military forces of the United States averaged about 275,000 personnel per year.[20] From 1946 to 1950 the average was 1.8 million personnel, an increase of 6.6 times the prewar level. Prior to World War II, the largest previous increase in the standing military from a prewar to a postwar period had occurred after the Spanish American War, from about 43,000 personnel to about 132,000 personnel, or 3 times the prewar size. By any reckoning, therefore, this was an unprecedented complement of land, air, and naval forces for the United States. And it was fully and enthusiastically authorized by Congress.

Why maintain a large standing army? The onset of the cold war gives a shorthand answer. Not only did the United States need troops in Germany and Japan for some period after the war's end, but new alliance structures, the inability of allies to provide for their own defense, and a series of brushfire conflicts linked to decolonization necessitated a U.S. military structure capable of being used in a variety of ways, part of a policy known as "flexible response." U.S. hegemony simply meant that if there was a problem, America likely would be viewed as part of the solution. But the presence of this same standing army, a large portion of which was forward deployed near potential flashpoints, also had the practical effect of greatly reducing Congress's influence in decisions about how and when to commit U.S. troops abroad. Combat operations in both Korea and Vietnam proceeded without a formal declaration of war and, initially in both cases, without congressional consultation or authorization. True to the founders' expectations, Congress has virtually never led America into war. But it played a positive role by providing presidents with the resources necessary to fight wars. Since World War II, however, congressional participation in military policy is no longer primarily *ex ante*. Rather it tends to be *ex post,* as Congress ratifies executive decisions or stands silent in acquiescence. Short of an all-out conventional war requiring more resources than exist in the standing army or a conflict known to be likely well in advance, the 2003 invasion of Iraq for example, Congress is now severely constrained when it comes to war-powers decisions.

Even the earliest presidents, John Adams and Thomas Jefferson for example, proved that military action without consultation or authorization was possible. But modern communications and transportation permit the movement and insertion of military force in ways that could not have been dreamed of in an earlier age. So in addition to the sheer size of the military, which has actually declined since the mid-1990s, mobility adds a new dimension. None of these would be of consequence, however, if the expansionist orientation of modern chief executives had not combined with the political reticence of legislators to intervene when troop commitments are imminent or when Congress is faced with a fait accompli.

The Institutionalized National Security Presidency

By itself, the large peacetime standing army likely was insufficient to establish the national security presidency. But to it Congress also added a bureaucratic apparatus of enormous consequence. This apparatus ultimately included a group of (frequently competing) intelligence operations—the Central Intelligence Agency (CIA), the Defense Intelligence Agency (DIA), the National Security Agency (NSA), and the Federal Bureau of Investigation (FBI), among others— along with the Department of Defense (DoD), the Joint Chiefs of Staff (JCS), the National Security Council (NSC), and, since 2002, the Department of Homeland Security. Thus the post-World War II period also witnessed the establishment of a complex, well-staffed, and entrenched policy planning and intelligence bureaucracy. While this process of institutionalization is certainly not confined to national security, it is perhaps most obvious in that realm. And while the National Security Act of 1947—which, by itself, provided the DoD, NSC, JCS, and CIA—is the cornerstone event in this process, it was preceded and followed by additional legislative action, which also redounded to the executive's advantage.[21] Layered onto this were U.S. agreements to the North Atlantic, Southeast Asian, and Central Treaty Organizations that committed America to a series of multilateral military alliances for the first time in the nation's history.

As with many legislative acts of the twentieth century, the creation of a large standing army and its accompanying civilian establishment worked to the disadvantage of Congress by delegating statutory authority to the executive branch. The Budget and Accounting Act of 1921, the Executive Reorganization Act of 1939, and the Employment Act of 1946 are the other prominent examples of this trend. The shift took place over at least a half century; it was not a consequence of constitutional amendment, let alone some bloodless coup d'état. Rather, as the political historian James Sundquist has argued cogently, it was assembled gradually from statutes, executive orders, and written and unwritten understandings between the branches.[22]

Modern publics have come to expect presidents to act decisively on virtually all policy matters, but the demands are even more apparent during crises. The commander in chief must protect American interests, property, and citizens wherever they might be. Contemporary polling data exhibit broad support for President George W. Bush's aggressive and determined posture regarding the war on terrorism and the conflict in Iraq. Meanwhile the bureaucratic apparatus provided him with the tools to act in a fairly unilateral fashion—a move that the administration implied it would make with or without congressional support. The result is an institutionalized national-security presidency.

Tools of the Trade in Foreign Affairs and War

By the close of the 1960s Congress had established, and the executive had readily embraced, the national security state. This shift in power and influence, described in the foregoing sections, was highly consequential and it was in no way ephemeral. But it did not leave Congress wholly without influence in matters of war and foreign affairs. By the early 1970s a majority of legislators concluded that the delegation of power to the executive had gone too far. As a consequence, the House and Senate set about reclaiming congressional authority from the president. In this section, Congress's attempt to restore a balance of power is examined. Discussed are the various legislative tools that Congress has to make or to influence foreign affairs and war. The argument is that Congress's attempt to reclaim power fell far short of its goals because it lacked sufficient political will, or bipartisan will, to do so.

The most direct route for Congress to reassert influence over decisions on war and foreign affairs was simply to legislate—with or without the president's consent. And up to a point, that's precisely what the Democratic Congress did in the waning years of the presidential administration of Richard Nixon and into that of Gerald Ford. To do so, however, Congress needed to marshal veto-proof majorities, a circumstance requiring the cooperation of the minority Republicans. On many matters, Republicans were remarkably willing to oblige. But the differences between the two parties were sufficiently great that legislative bargains had to be struck. And the resulting bills were never quite so strong or quite as coherent as the statutes that had delegated power to the executive in the first place. Thus, Congress also attempted to exploit its authority over trade and tariff authority, on treaties and nominations, and through investigations as added means for reining in the executive branch. For a variety of reasons these too met with limited success. Each is treated in turn below, with a concluding section on the special case of war powers.

Authorizations and Appropriations

Congress's authority to "make all laws that are necessary and proper" and its companion authority to draw funds from the Treasury pursuant to "appropriations made by law" are the bulwarks of its national authority. Put simply, absent statutory authority and the funds to execute that authority nothing should happen. In addition, Article I, Section 8 carries the special restriction that "no appropriation of money to [the Army] shall be for a longer term than two years" (clause 12). But Congress has long since taken that basic safeguard a step further by appropriating virtually all government monies annually. Thus, the legislature's powers to authorize programs and to appropriate funding are absolute—so long as Congress and its component committees choose to use those powers.

From the early nineteenth century until nearly the end of the Vietnam War, Congress and its committees did not always exploit these powers. Rather, the legislature tended to give open-ended authorizations to the military departments—authorizations that sketched out general missions and persisted from year to year. Moreover, for most of this period, those same military departments were run on the so-called bureau system, which bestowed substantial authority on bureau chiefs answerable neither to the military's chain of command nor to Congress as a whole—though they were frequently cozy with the relevant committee chairs. During wartime an expanded defense establishment operated with enhanced authority. But after each conflict, demobilization returned the military to its previously diminished state. In the immediate post-World War II era, little had changed with respect to open-ended grants.[23] But these grants of authority and the presence of a large standing army greatly reduced the role of the House and Senate Armed Services Committees in national security policy making.

By the early 1960s, therefore, the committees faced a dual threat to their power. The Pentagon was authorized to operate with very permissive programmatic authority, a circumstance that reduced the Armed Services Committees to the status of defense cheerleaders. Meanwhile the three defense-oriented Appropriations subcommittees—Procurement, Personnel, and Military Construction—continued the practice of annual appropriations, a process that frequently also included programmatic guidance. This practice further reduced the influence of the authorizing committees. In response, the Armed Services Committees seized upon a similar procedural device by annually reauthorizing various military programs, this to enhance the committees' capacity to participate in defense policy making. The trend toward annual reauthorization began in 1959 with the so-called Russell Amendment, which was named after the venerable chair of the Senate Armed Services Committee, Democrat Richard Russell of Georgia. The Russell Amendment required annual statutory authorization for the procurement of aircraft, missiles, and naval vessels. Those authorizations also set limits on how much could be spent to do so. From 1962 through 1982 the annual authorization requirement was expanded eleven more times. By one estimate, only 2 percent of defense appropriations required annual authorization in 1961, virtually all accounted for by military construction. By 1982 the figure stood, effectively, at 100 percent. Each year, therefore, the Armed Services

Committees produce a "must pass" piece of legislation, the annual defense authorization bill.

By contrast, during the immediate post-World War II period the annual foreign aid authorization bill produced by the House Foreign Affairs and Senate Foreign Relations Committees provided these two panels with a consistent opportunity to influence policy. But as Armed Services' role expanded through the late 1960s and into the 1970s the two foreign policy committees suffered a comparable decline. Ideological and partisan differences regarding foreign aid ultimately ended in stalemate as the committees were unable to report a foreign aid bill that could garner majority support in the chamber. Foreign aid programs did not disappear, but the committees' influence was ceded to the Foreign Operations subcommittees of the Appropriations Committees. Weakly led and without an annual authorization bill, Foreign Relations and Foreign Affairs became a shadow of their former selves. As Senator Christopher J. Dodd (D-Conn.) put it in 1985: "By frittering away its authorizing function, the Foreign Relations Committee became a largely irrelevant debating society."[24]

In an attempt to arrest this decline the foreign policy committees simply emulated the Armed Services Committees by expanding their use of the State Department authorization bill.[25] Starting in 1972, the two committees required periodic reauthorization of, among other things, the State Department, the United States Information Agency, and the Arms Control and Disarmament Agency. Previously, State and its constituent foreign policy components operated under open-ended authorizations of the traditional sort. Pursuant to the new requirement, Congress then passed the necessary reauthorizing legislation for the various foreign relations activities. Two years later, Congress extended the requirement by instructing the president to submit three major pieces of legislation each year—a foreign aid proposal, a military aid proposal, and a foreign relations proposal.

Although a State Department authorization has passed nearly every year since then, the bill's impact has been limited. More importantly, Congress has failed to pass a foreign aid bill in almost every year during the same period. That bill, of course, would authorize most of the spending controlled by the foreign policy committees. And this potential but unrealized influence means that the authorizing committees have ceded their leverage, and a perfect opportunity to perform oversight. The vacuum is filled, if it is filled at all, only by the Appropriations subcommittees.[26] On balance, therefore, attempts by the (now renamed) International Relations and Foreign Relations Committees to assert their authority have fallen far short of what some activist members had hoped for. Partly this is due to the long-recognized fact that the foreign policy committees simply do not have any pork to distribute—no juicy procurement contracts, no large construction programs. Absent that, the panels are good platforms for position taking by policy mavens or members attempting to burnish their foreign policy credentials but otherwise unattractive to a broad cross section of the membership. But it also is the case that both committees have suffered from a lack of strong leadership or an engaged membership more generally.

During the immediate postwar period Foreign Relations Committee chair and ranking minority member Senator Arthur G. Vandenberg (R–Mich.) was an invigorating force for bipartisanship and interbranch cooperation. For their part the Democrats provided at best a checkered group of leaders until Senator J. William Fulbright (D–Ark.) similarly marshaled the committee to play an important role in debates about U.S. policy in Southeast Asia. But the decades since the 1970s are more like the norm as Foreign Relations' effectiveness has been limited under leaders such as Senators Jesse A. Helms (R–N.C.) and Claiborne D. Pell (D–R.I.)[27] Helms, it is said, viewed Foreign Relations as a brake on policy change, more likely to utilize its negative power—blocking nominations or funding for various activities—than its positive power.

Meanwhile, leadership of the House committee was lackluster for most of the postwar years. Neither Thomas E. Morgan (D–Penn.) nor Clement J. Zablocki (D–Wis.), two long-serving chairs, provided particularly aggressive guidance during the long period of Democratic control. During the post-Vietnam era, to be sure, both Dante Fascell (D–Fla.) and Lee Hamilton (D–Ind.) may be regarded as exceptions to that pattern but exceptions nonetheless. On the minority side, committee Republicans were either quietly cooperative with the committee majority or simply ciphers for various Republican administrations.

By contrast, the House and Senate Armed Services Committees have been led by an all-star cast of strong, indeed famously strong, chairs who fashioned reputations for influence, expertise, bipartisanship, and pork barreling. The Senate committee was led by a string of luminaries: Senators Richard B. Russell (D–Ga.), Leverett Saltonstall (R–Mass.), John C. Stennis (D–Miss.), John G. Tower (R–Tex.), Barry G. Goldwater (R–Ariz.), and Sam A. Nunn (D–Ga.). Though perhaps not comparably blessed, House Armed Services also was led by a fair number of energetic, astute, and policy-oriented leaders—Carl Vinson (D–Ga.), L. Mendel Rivers (D–S.C.), F. Edward Hebert (D–La.), and Les Aspin (D–Wis.). Again, the Armed Services panels' role in annual authorizations helped to carve out a more stable and influential institutional role, one less dependent on personality, aided by a cold war consensus on defense issues, and buttressed by a uniformly conservative membership. As a result, even the least distinguished of its chairs maintained an air of authority within the chamber.

In sum, attempts by Congress, and its authorizing committees, to regain power in the last three decades of the twentieth century were at best only marginally successful. Leadership capacity enhanced the role of the military committees, but those leaders were mostly inclined to leave power with the Pentagon. In contrast, leadership incapacity was, for the most part, an outright barrier to influence for the foreign policy panels. But both chambers found it difficult to write into law changes in foreign and military policy, a far more difficult task than delegating power. As important, both chambers found it increasingly difficult to bridge an ever-widening partisan gap—narrowest in the 1970s and widening thereafter. For a brief period, elements of both parties found a common foe in President Nixon. But with Nixon's departure that window of opportunity closed rather quickly.

Tariff and Trade Authority

Authority and initiative for tariff and trade policy belong unambiguously to Congress. Article I, Section 8, clause 3 gives Congress the power "to regulate Commerce with foreign Nations, and among the several States." Inasmuch as tariff legislation is tax legislation, it could hardly be otherwise. For most of American history, therefore, trade legislation has been initiated and dominated by Congress—from the Tariff of 1816 and the 1828 Tariff of Abominations right on through Fordney-McCumber in 1922.[28]

This trend culminated in 1930, when the Republican-controlled Seventy-first Congress passed and President Hoover signed the Smoot-Hawley Tariff Act, widely regarded as one of the most protectionist tariff structures in American history.[29] Just four years later, however, in 1934, the Democratic-controlled Seventy-third Congress passed and President Roosevelt signed the Reciprocal Trade Agreements Act, which gave the president broad authority to negotiate trade agreements and then implement them via executive order. This sea change, which lasted until 1974, marked a long period of legislative delegation to executive agents insofar as trade policy was concerned. For a large portion of this period, however, Congress and the presidency were controlled by the same party.

By 1974 an era of divided government had commenced, legislative distrust of the president was at its apex due to the Watergate scandal, and trade negotiations had shifted from tariffs to nontariff barriers. Congress had rethought its position. It did not, however, revert to its parochial and protectionist ways. Rather, through the Trade Act of 1974, it delegated negotiating authority to the executive branch, but retained its own veto option through a mechanism commonly called fast-track authority.

Under fast track, the president was permitted to negotiate trade agreements but required to submit those same agreements to Congress for review and approval by an up-or-down vote. Absent the prospect of amendment, it was assumed, negotiated agreements would not fall victim to Congress's parochial tendencies. But in a time of divided government neither would an administration be able to ignore blithely the views of legislators. Moreover, the negotiation process would include a congressionally created agent, the U.S. trade representative, and it further provided for hearings, reporting requirements, and participatory conduits for stakeholders in the process. Fast track was subsequently renewed, though in somewhat altered form, by the Trade Agreements Act of

1979 and the Omnibus Trade and Competitiveness Act of 1988. Thus, by various means it remained in place through April 1994, at which point ideological and partisan disagreements produced a stalemate. It would be another eight years, August 2002, before the various factions could agree upon legislation reinstating fast-track authority.[30]

Congress's solution to trade legislation is emblematic of recent trends. It may be called byzantine. Mindful that its own parochial tendencies can be damaging, it delegates trade authority. Distrustful of the chief executive as its agent, it institutes *ex ante* controls by instructing negotiators to include particular provisions in agreements while at the same time establishing complex mechanisms to assure timely decisions via expedited procedures.[31] Trade legislation is hardly unique in this respect. The budget process, arms exports, war powers, covert actions, and base closures all include similar mechanisms. Attendant legislation becomes more complex. Trade bills themselves are more complex (and longer). And the compromises enshrined within them make for less coherent policy.[32]

These procedures empower the executive to do its work and subsequent approvals permit at least halting policy progress. The imbalance of influence and initiative is not redressed. But Congress keeps its hand in the game, at least at the margins, by ensuring review and approval mechanisms. Delegation with constraints is the norm. Congress becomes the brake but not often the accelerator in this version of the policy process.

Advice and Consent: Appointments and Treaties

If the positive power associated with legislating proves difficult, perhaps the Senate's negative power through advice-and-consent proceedings might be an effective tool for influencing foreign affairs. And, because a minority of senators can have disproportionate influence via the filibuster, this might prove especially useful to the minority party. Indeed, the Senate has attempted to exploit this procedure since at least the early twentieth century when it refused to ratify President Woodrow Wilson's much-wanted Versailles Treaty. Unfortunately, at least from Congress's perspective, presidents have circumvented this constitutional requirement by employing greater numbers of executive agreements and by empowering their national security advisers—neither requiring advice-and-consent approval from the Senate.

The Senate's advice-and-consent authority reflects a political compromise, as do many aspects of the Constitution. Formally, the Constitution provides for the nomination by the president and confirmation by the Senate of ambassadors, public ministers and consuls, justices of the Supreme Court, and all other officers of the United States as established by law. Likewise, it provides that the president may make treaties "by and with the advice and consent of the Senate." These executive powers, conditioned as they are by Senate approval, evidence the caution with which authority was invested in the chief executive under the

Constitution. In general, and in subsequent practice, presidential freedom was preferred while the Senate's advice and consent would merely deter the chief executive from offering up "unfit characters" or, in the case of treaties, assure products that are "cautiously formed and steadily pursued."[33] And so it has been, as the Senate has given its prompt and overwhelming consent to the vast majority of appointments and treaties submitted by the president.

Although the Senate has somewhat rarely utilized its advice-and-consent authority to influence foreign and defense policy, the politics of the appointment process has received much more attention by pundits and scholars since the 1970s. The withdrawal of Earnest W. Lefever (assistant secretary of state for human rights) during the Reagan administration, the rejection of John Tower (nominated as secretary of defense) during President George H. W. Bush's administration, and the withdrawal of both Bobby Ray Inman (secretary of defense) and Anthony Lake (director of Central Intelligence) during President Bill Clinton's administration provide prominent recent examples. Survivors of the process, such as Paul Warnke, who became President Jimmy Carter's arms control negotiator despite forty nay votes in the Senate, can enter a president's administration severely weakened. Meanwhile all nominations, even if overwhelmingly successful, can become a referendum on an administration's foreign and defense policy, particularly for members of the president's so-called inner cabinet—State, Defense, Treasury, and Justice.

From the end of World War I onward, major treaty ratifications have been highly politicized events. And although few treaties are rejected, Senate influence through amendments, reservations, limitations, and understandings is far from trivial. Moreover, since many treaties require implementation measures passed by Congress (the Panama Canal Treaty, for example), even the House has occasion to become an important player in this postratification process.

Like nominations, treaties are communicated to the Senate by the White House, whereupon they are numbered, placed on the executive calendar, and referred to the appropriate committee—in this case Foreign Relations. Also like nominations, the committee may simply ignore the submission—in which case it is likely dead—or hold hearings, of greater or lesser duration, prior to returning it to the floor with a positive or negative recommendation. Unlike nominations, however, a resolution of consent may contain the aforementioned additional provisions. The most severe of these, amendments, require renegotiation of the treaty. But any of them can be politically consequential for the incumbent administration. In anticipation of additional provisions, modern presidents and their advisers have been far more solicitous of the Senate's advice during the negotiating phase of contemporary treaties.

A systematic study of treaties from 1947 to 2000 found that treaties addressing "high politics" (security and sovereignty) were much more likely to be the subject of Senate reservations than those that focused upon economics or international norms. Also, treaties during the cold war were less likely to be targeted in this way. By itself, divided government had no significant impact on the likelihood of treaty reservations, but as the ideological distance of the president and the pivotal senator diverged, the likelihood of reservations increased.[34]

It cannot be said that Congress has suddenly seized the upper hand where advice and consent is concerned. And as previously noted, presidents have found ways to circumvent the power that does exist. But legislators, particularly individual members, have seized upon the opportunities presented to pressure the executive branch generally and the president in particular on policies that resonate with their constituencies. With most appointments foreordained to succeed and few highly consequential treaties even presented, the opportunities are far from frequent. And, as with oversight, which is treated next, the best that Congress can sometimes hope for is the spotlight of media coverage for a short period of time.

Legislative Oversight

If Congress's function as architect and financier of government activity is well founded, then so too is the legislature's responsibility to oversee, control, and correct executive implementation.[35] And by wide agreement, the precedent for the legislature's role in this activity was established in 1792 when Congress undertook an investigation into the disastrous military campaign of General Arthur St. Clair against Native Americans in the Northwest Territory (near present-day Fort Wayne, Indiana). During the course of its investigation St. Clair was largely exonerated for any culpability in the loss of more than half of his troops while very serious shortcomings in the military's supply and ordnance capacity were uncovered. In the actual event, newspaper reports of the military defeat spread faster than official reports through government channels and were, therefore, partly responsible for Congress's investigation. More than two centuries later, Congress continues to respond in similar ways whenever foreign or military crises hit the headlines—the Iran-contra affair and the Abu Ghraib prisoner-abuse scandal being prominent recent examples. Indeed, some would argue that most oversight is of that nature.

What, then, is the best approach to this oversight responsibility? Should it be done retrospectively by investigating administrative malfeasance and shirking? Or should it be done prospectively through legislative design and statutory guidance? In 1984 Mathew McCubbins and Thomas Schwartz introduced a now widely used metaphor to capture Congress's alternatives. Legislators might engage in "police patrols," by the routine review of programs, or they might simply investigate whenever things go awry, by responding to "fire alarms."[36] McCubbins and Schwartz argue that Congress prefers the efficiency of alarms to the drudgery of patrols. As a result, they assert, patrols are likely to be outnumbered by responses to alarms. (See Shipan in this volume.)

Perhaps recognizing this tendency, Congress adopted a statutory requirement for oversight in the Legislative Reorganization Act of 1946. That act required Congress's standing committees to engage in "continuous watchfulness" over the execution of laws by departments and agencies within their jurisdictions.[37] It was not to be strictly reactive or fire alarm in orientation. In addition, Section 190(d) of the law required each committee to provide a report of its oversight activity for each Congress. In practice, most oversight—comprised of hearings, reports, and draft legislation—is performed by the legislative staffs of the various committees. Committee staffs are frequently experienced, well connected, and substantively knowledgeable. And, because they are well connected, departments and agencies generally are reluctant to try and put anything over on the committees, which, after all, provide them with the legal authority and the funding to carry out their programs.

The available evidence indicates that despite the dictates of the 1946 act Congress performed its oversight role only indifferently through the 1950s and 1960s. As with its legislative role, therefore, Congress sought new ways to enhance its oversight capacity as the Vietnam War and other elements of U.S. foreign policy became more controversial. Thus, during the 1970s, Congress fashioned a more active rather than passive form of oversight. This oversight not only featured third-party informants, to pull fire alarms, but also a form of self-incrimination through executive branch reporting requirements. These reporting requirements, in turn, allowed for actual legislative participation in policy making. This "new oversight" includes annual authorizations along with reporting requirements, notifications, and other anticipatory techniques.[38] The technique was not entirely new, of course; as early as 1951 Congress included language in the Military Construction Act that required military departments to "come into agreement" with the Armed Services Committees prior to completing any real estate transaction in excess of $25,000.[39]

By the 1970s Congress was fully motivated to enhance its consultation and participation through the use of a variety of reporting requirements. Not a few of these, in turn, carried legislative veto provisions. For example, the Case-Zablocki Act of 1972 required that all executive agreements be reported to Congress; the Nelson–Bingham Amendment of 1974 required that all major arms sales be reported to Congress; and the Hughes-Ryan Amendment of 1974 required the president and the CIA to report any covert activity to Congress in a "timely manner." Each of these provisions, and there were more, gave to Congress a formal opportunity to reject, alter, or terminate the activity. And although the Supreme Court invalidated most such vetoes in *Immigration and Naturalization Service v. Chadha* (1983) Congress continues to utilize artfully worded legislative vetoes to force executive agents to report to Congress prior to taking particular actions defined in statutes.[40]

Like the "old" oversight, new oversight techniques require energy, motivation, and staff resources to be successful. But changes in the last decade of the twentieth century militated against such success. First, upon gaining control of the House, Republican leaders redeemed a promise to reduce the size of legislative staffs much as their Senate colleagues had done in the 1980s. As a consequence, the level of oversight necessarily declined without the human resources required to arrange and hold hearings. Second, the distractions of fund-raising, which by all accounts take an ever larger portion of legislators' time, reduced the amount of attention that members could devote to oversight activity. And third, unified (Republican) government eliminated a primary political motivation for investing time and resources in investigatory efforts. Thus, the available data suggests that a long-term increase in oversight efforts—from the 87th to the 100th Congress—was replaced by a slow decline and then a sharp drop in that same effort.[41]

Given these deterrents, an increased emphasis on fire-alarm oversight is hardly surprising. But how does one know it when one sees it? Consider, as an example, the House Armed Services Committee's 1997 oversight plan, which states: "While most of the committee's oversight agenda was designed to serve primarily in support of the annual authorization bill, much of the committee's most demanding oversight activity was *event-driven* and not subject to prior planning."[42] A subsequent section of the same report illustrates what "event driven" means by way of the introductory phrases used for each of a series of hearings:

"In the wake of the devastating bombing of the Khobar Towers complex in Dhahran, Saudi Arabia . . ."

". . . the circumstances surrounding the shootdown of an American F-16 fighter over Bosnia."

"In the wake of the tragic killings of a black civilian couple by three white soldiers from the Army's 82nd Airborne Division . . ."

". . . an in depth review of the April 14, 1994, downing of two Army UH-60 Black Hawk helicopters by Air Force F-15 fighters over Northern Iraq."[43]

Clearly, even though they might not use the police patrol/fire alarm terminology, the Armed Services staff make a distinction between the routine work put into the authorization bill and the work needed to investigate a tragic accident involving sophisticated aircraft of various kinds.

In sum, despite efforts to improve its oversight capacity, Congress continues to be responsive rather than proactive when it comes to the review of policy implementation. To be sure, a cautious executive will behave strategically in such an environment, lest it be called to the Hill to explain itself. But the initiative remains with the executive when it comes to policy implementation. And, given the size and reach of federal programs—both defense and nondefense—the legislature's capacity to overlook exceeds its ability to oversee.

The War Powers Resolution of 1973

The War Powers Resolution of 1973, passed over President Nixon's veto, is the most widely known and widely cited example of the new oversight. In essence, the resolution asserts Congress's Article I authority over United States armed forces and requires that presidents seek prior approval whenever possible before utilizing those forces in combat, in circumstances where combat is imminent, or in circumstances where the introduction of troops would substantially alter the balance of U.S. forces in a particular area. Most importantly, the provisions of the resolution require the president to notify and consult with Congress *prior* to engaging in the foregoing uses of the military.

It is widely known that this resolution was a reaction to the often-secretive usage of U.S. armed forces in Southeast Asia and to a turn in public opinion against U.S. military activities in that region. In addition, of course, the presidency of Richard Nixon had been severely wounded by the events surrounding the Watergate break-in and hostile interbranch relations more generally. So for some members of Congress, at least, the resolution was one more way to embarrass the Nixon administration.

In the message to Congress that accompanied his veto of the War Powers Resolution, President Nixon argued that the act was an unconstitutional infringement on the president's Article II authority as commander in chief. Every president since Nixon, regardless of party affiliation, essentially has agreed. And yet, during that period (November 1973 through March 2004) those same presidents have made 111 reports to Congress "consistent with" the procedures set down in the resolution.[44] These reports covered a wide variety of events that ranged, chronologically, from the removal of refugees from Da Nang, Vietnam (reported by President Gerald R. Ford on April 4, 1975), to the deployment of additional troops and equipment to Kosovo, Yugoslavia (reported by President George W. Bush on November 14, 2003). In virtually every one of these instances the president reported to Congress *after* troops and equipment had been deployed. Thus, the War Powers Resolution clearly did not stop the president from utilizing the military independent of congressional authorization.[45]

During the summer and early fall of 2002, President Bush made clear to Congress and the American people that his administration viewed Iraq's acquisition of weapons of mass destruction as a clear threat to U.S. security. After addressing the United Nations and meeting with congressional leaders, Bush sent to Congress a draft resolution authorizing him to use force in Iraq specifically and in the region generally. Although Bush's resolution was never itself introduced, similar resolutions authorizing the use of force made their way through both the House and the Senate. The House version of this authorization (H.J. Res. 144) ultimately was adopted by both chambers and signed by Bush on October 16, 2002. Under the resolution, Bush was authorized to deploy and utilize U.S. forces not only in Iraq but otherwise without serious limitations in scope or timing. Bush's request was a tacit acknowledgment of the political circumstances and the potential force of the War Powers Resolution. But Congress's preemptive granting of military authority was, equally, tacit acknowledgment of the president's central role in the use of military force.

Were Congress's attempts to regain influence successful? Only at the margin, it appears. Annual authorizations have proven the most effective, but their implementation requires the investment of substantial time, energy, and resources—elements that are not always in abundant supply. Internal partisan divisions also eliminate the institutional will frequently necessary to combat the modern chief executive. The reporting requirements and approval mechanisms attendant to the new oversight also check executive authority by way of at least forcing the president's agents to consider how their initiatives will play on Capitol Hill. That is, an anticipated response mechanism may not provide the Hill with positive influence but it may moderate the executive in some circumstances. Senate hearings and debate on treaties and appointments represent a similarly oblique policy instrument. Presidents may stop to think about how their choices will play on Capitol Hill, but they still get most of what they want. For the most part, initiative remains with the executive despite legislative attempts to regain power.

Institutional Reform

The argument of the preceding sections has been that Congress's role in foreign affairs and war has become increasingly marginalized and, moreover, that it is largely Congress's own fault. Through legislation and precedent Congress simply ceded authority to the executive branch. The executive, for its part, willingly accepted and exploited these delegations and the central position in war and foreign affairs that came with them. And even when moved to respond, Congress has lacked the capacity, that is to say the political will, to redress the balance of power.

Can Congress recover? Can Congress build upon the War Powers Act, the trade act, and other devices designed to recoup lost ground? A fair response to that question is likely to be No. The current war on terrorism is most likely to reinforce Congress's deference to the executive. And the executive's case for "secrecy and dispatch" will resonate with a substantial portion of representatives and senators. But even if that were not the case, Congress faces a series of substantial hurdles that reduce the likelihood of meaningful reform. This, concluding, section first outlines the most important barriers to reform and then lays out three scenarios for a legislative response to the current balance of power in war and foreign affairs.

Reform's Hurdles

Why are reforms unlikely? In a 2002 work, E. Scott Adler argues that congressional reforms are somewhat rare and that those that occur generally fail because they cannot overcome entrenched interests.[46] That is, legislators with a stake in the existing balance of power and the benefits it bestows undermine or simply block the efforts of reformers. Put slightly differently, Adler's argument is that the coalitions required to mount reform movements are very difficult to come by. It is no surprise, therefore, that serious reform movements occur somewhat rarely in an institution's history. And when they do, they are the result of unusual combinations of forces that are difficult to predict. At present, five imposing hurdles to reform stand out—institutional stickiness, turf consciousness, *stare decisis*, legacy programs, and party polarization. These are treated briefly in turn.

INSTITUTIONAL STICKINESS. Institutions are notoriously sticky. That is, once adopted, they persist with a good deal of stubbornness. The Senate will not soon abandon the filibuster or institute a germaneness rule. House Republicans are not going to repeal terms limits for committee chairs anytime soon. None of these, by itself, is responsible either for the current state of affairs or for preventing Congress from playing a more democratic and responsible role in foreign and defense policy. In concert, however, they are part of what makes up the contemporary Congress and its modes of doing business. Institutions are the product of collective decisions that assemble numerous individual interests at particular points in time. The circumstances that permit institutional change are frequently unusual; they are not repeated often. The result here is that institutions such as the filibuster, and institutions generally, tend to provide greater negative power than positive power. And yet the reassertion of legislative influence requires the latter more than the former.

TURF CONSCIOUSNESS. Turf consciousness is a special case of institutional stickiness. Committee turf, the formal legislative jurisdiction controlled by each panel, not only hampers what Congress can accomplish, it also affects and limits what the executive can accomplish—and the likelihood of stepping on a Capitol Hill landmine. In some instances, control over military procurement, for example, legislative turf is well established. In other cases, however, homeland security being the most obvious example, property rights are not yet clearly established or, in the case of the House Select Committee, those rights are undermined by a balkanized membership from other standing committees. Kansas Republican Pat Roberts, chairman of the Senate Intelligence Committee, put it succinctly shortly after the 9/11 Commission report was released in 2004: "The No. 1 issue for any chairman of any committee is that you don't give up your turf under any circumstances—not a spadeful." Turf consciousness has a conservative effect.

Policy making is fragmented, shared across committees, and therefore subject to compromise. Compromise tends to reduce coherence. And reduced coherence limits institutional influence—especially in the eyes of the Court, as is shown next.

STARE DECISIS. To the extent that the current regime has a basis in judicial precedent, there is no reason to think that foundation will change dramatically or change soon. The contemporary state of judicial opinion, as Gordon Silverstein has pointed out, has two components. First, it favors Congress when Congress can act clearly and positively through legislation. Second, in the absence of such legislation, it favors executive prerogative in foreign and defense policy.[47] If Congress delegates broadly or vaguely, the Court has not intervened to rein in executive prerogative. And, with the exception of individual rights and liberties, neither will the Court intervene in the absence of legislative acts. Since at present positive acts by Congress are less likely to emerge, that balance of judicial opinion favors executive predominance. And to the extent that judicial policy changes slowly, an obeisance to stare decisis (abiding by legal precedent), there is no reasonable prospect that that opinion will be supplanted or dislodged anytime soon. This circumstance is further reinforced, in 2005, by the conservative-leaning Supreme Court, the likelihood of openings on the Court in the near term, and Republican control of both the presidency and Congress.

LEGACY PROGRAMS. Bureaucratic pressure, constituent pressure, and interest-group pressure all ensure that Congress will privilege existing programs over new programs if it must choose between the two—no matter how rational or compelling a new program might be. This is the inveterate "iron triangle" of relations among authorizers, providers, and beneficiaries. Thus, programs such as the F-22 advanced tactical fighter and V-22 tiltrotor aircraft are perpetuated while newer programs face fierce budget scrutiny. These "legacy" programs have strong backing from institutionalized backers, turf-conscious bureaucrats, and reelection-oriented legislators. Why are legacy programs problematic? Two reasons stand out. First, in periods of budget constraint, new programs can only be considered if older programs or failed programs are phased out. But if old programs (almost) never die, the budget pressures militate against new endeavors. Second, once political coalitions have been formed, status quo policies tend to stick. These, in turn, constrain Congress's ability to respond rationally to new policy-making environments. The result, according to policy critics of all persuasions, is that contemporary battles are typically hampered by attempts to fight them with dated strategies.

POLARIZED POLITICS. As noted just above, recent Congresses have lacked the political will to recoup power from the executive. That is to say, there is simply no sufficiently large majority of a similar mind to make policy or to unambiguously alter institutional arrangements. The root cause for this lack of collective will lies in the increased conflict between Republicans and Democrats—that is to say, in polarized politics. Polarized politics features narrow majorities with high levels of intraparty cohesion. And so long as party cohesion, and discipline, remain strong, the prospects of a splinter group—moderate Republicans or conservative Democrats, for example—crossing the partisan aisle are diminished substantially. Polarization also fosters a certain level of political hostility, making broad-based coalitions that much harder to form.

The interparty conflict and lack of comity often commented upon as features of contemporary politics did not appear overnight. And they are not likely to disappear overnight. To go from the nadir of modern partisanship in the 1970s—featuring historically low levels of party voting and high levels of cross-chamber cooperation—to the identifiable reemergence of cohesive party politics on Capitol Hill took ten years. Commentary on that emergence and its crystallization into "polarized politics" took nearly another ten years. Current electoral institutions reward incumbents and punish challengers. Thus, there are few incentives for legislators to alter or to moderate their behavior. By one popular measure, the last couple of Congresses featured nearly wholly distinct partisan groupings, with no more than a bare handful of Democrats featuring voting records more conservative than a single Republican. There is no reason to expect that the 109th or the 110th Congresses will be any different. (For ideological trends among the two parties see Figures 1 and 2.)

In sum, institutional imperatives *will* dominate during the coming administration and into the twenty-first century. And yet this is not to say that partisan control does not matter. Conservative Congresses *will* produce markedly different policies than liberal Congresses. They *will* be more supportive of the military, more supportive of a unilateralist approach to security and diplomacy, more trusting of executive prerogatives, and more tolerant of intrusions upon civil liberties in the pursuit of national security. And divided government *will* feature stalemate, or gridlock, on numerous policy fronts—animated by the aforementioned polarized politics.

In the end, there is little reason to predict that the national security state will disappear anytime soon. As noted earlier, international security circumstances and divided public opinion over the United States' role in policing world affairs certainly militate against that. But so too does entrenched congressional and bureaucratic support for existing institutions. And although the policy status quo is more mutable than the institutional status quo, policies also tend to become entrenched. So despite the intentions of the founders, the politics of war and foreign affairs are very much transformed relative to the century following the adoption of the Constitution. The traditional view, dominant during that period, has been muscled aside. And in its place, a prerogative view has gained predominance, the product of practice, precedent, and presidential will.

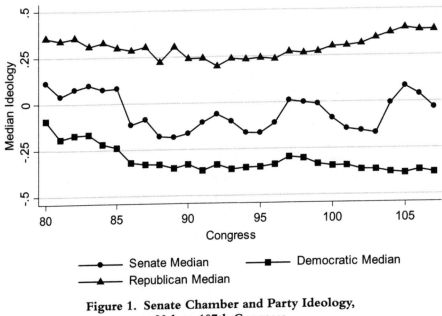

Figure 1. **Senate Chamber and Party Ideology, 80th to 107th Congress**

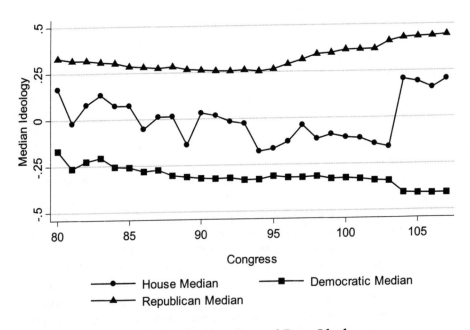

Figure 2. **House Chamber and Party Ideology, 80th to 107th Congress**

Congress and America's Future

What, then, will Congress do during the early part of the twenty-first century? The argument of the previous section suggests that a dramatic resurgence of congressional influence in war and foreign affairs is highly unlikely. But that still leaves substantial leeway for the legislative branch to play a greater or lesser role, and a more or less responsible role, in that same realm. The purpose of this final section is to sketch out three scenarios for the coming decades—an abdicating scenario, a legislating scenario, and a tinkering scenario.

Abdication

In 1965 Samuel P. Huntington wrote a provocative essay, "Congressional Responses to the Twentieth Century," in which he argued that Congress should reshape its role within American constitutional government in a quite fundamental fashion.[48] Huntington's essay was one of eight chapters designed to consider the "vitality and effectiveness" of Congress more than halfway through the twentieth century. It was, in that respect, very much like the present volume. Huntington's contribution to that volume was novel, however, because it was the only chapter written by someone who would not, even then, have been pigeonholed as a congressional or presidential scholar. Perhaps it is not surprising, then, that Huntington advanced the least conventional of all the arguments contained within that volume. In brief, he asserted that Congress should simply abdicate its position as principal policy maker:

> If Congress can generate the leadership and the will to make the drastic reforms required to reverse the trends toward insulation, dispersion, and overseeing, it could still resume a positive role in the legislative process. If this is impossible, an alternative path is to eschew the legislative and to adapt itself to discharge effectively those functions of constituent service and bureaucratic control which insulation and dispersion do enable it to play in the national government.[49]

Huntington's argument was premised on the assumption that Congress had been insulated from the otherwise nationalizing tendencies of national politics, that is, that Congress remained locally oriented, atomized, and decentralized. Needless to say, a change of the sort that Huntington advocated in the mid-1960s would be extraordinarily fundamental. And formal changes of such a magnitude are nearly impossible to contemplate. That said, passive abdication is neither farfetched nor unprecedented.[50]

Abdication today might be either formal or informal. Some critics of the contemporary Congress argue that by doing nothing the institution has run away from its constitutional authority. This would be an informal variant of abdication—the president proposes and the Congress disposes. But there also is a more formal variant wherein Congress delegates power to the executive branch but then fails to oversee the bureaucracy's activities. Congressional critics would view the War Powers Act as a formal abdication of authority inasmuch as it recognizes the president's authority to use U.S. military forces under a wide variety of circumstances.

Legislative Reassertion

In 1969 Theodore J. Lowi argued, in *The End of Liberalism,* that Congress had ceased to legislate in an authoritative fashion.[51] Instead, Congress had come to focus on establishing procedures aimed at delegating authority and ensuring interest-group participation in policy decisions. If Lowi was correct, then the most obvious way for Congress to regain or enhance its influence over foreign affairs is to reassert its lawmaking authority. That is to say, Congress is most powerful and influential when it legislates in a clear and convincing fashion. After a number of abortive tries, it did cut off funding for military activity in Cambodia, Laos, and Thailand in 1970. Despite the president's opposition it did establish a nuclear nonproliferation policy for the United States in 1978. In 1986, again over executive opposition, it passed tough trade restriction against South Africa in support of the antiapartheid movement. And it passed fairly sweeping reorganization plans affecting the Pentagon—the so-called Goldwater-Nichols Act of 1986. These examples demonstrate that Congress can act when properly motivated and that it can do so even in the face of presidential opposition.

Will Congress legislate? For the reasons stated above, that seems unlikely. So long as Republicans hold the White House and control Congress, the likelihood of interbranch disagreement is much diminished—as it should be. Moreover, most Republicans and not a few Democrats are simply content with the current balance of power where foreign affairs are concerned. What would a legislative reassertion of power look like if were to occur? One frequently discussed option would have Congress repeal or rewrite the War Powers Resolution. But several attempts on that front have failed. Alternatively, it could substantially reduce or nearly eliminate the standing army or proscribe its being based overseas. That, admittedly, is an extreme example, and it is extremely unlikely. But for the better part of one and a half centuries it is precisely what Congress did do. Short of such extreme, and likely unwise, measures Congress might still find a way to utilize the annual defense authorization bill, the State Department authorization bill, and even the long-dormant foreign aid bill to influence U.S. policy in war and foreign affairs. Those are proximate, feasible, vehicles for the reassertion of influence. But there is no reason to expect that outcome anytime soon.

Tinkering

The third scenario, a tinkering strategy, is the one most likely to be adopted by Congress. Or, to put it more accurately, it is likely to be the default strategy.

Changes emanating from a tinkering strategy will be incremental because none will constitute a major break with the status quo. Like abdication, legislative tinkering can take two forms. One form involves the alteration of institutional features—rules, structures, procedures, and so forth. The other form involves relatively isolated changes in policy via legislation or other informal mechanisms.

The alteration in small ways of various chamber rules and the statutes-at-large occurs all the time. Not infrequently, today's changes simply undo yesterday's seemingly good ideas. For example, it made good sense for tenure on the intelligence oversight committees to be limited—ultimately to eight-year stints. But the constant shuffling of members and the lack of prestige that attends a limited-tenure committee no longer looks like such a hot idea.[52] Likewise, when the Intelligence Committees were originally created they had oversight responsibility but no legislative responsibility. Not surprisingly, the committees were well informed but only occasionally influential. But in 1992 the addition of authorizing powers over intelligence agencies such as the CIA, DIA, FBI, and NSA bolstered their status substantially.

A somewhat comparable change, also involving the Senate, would be to alter the Foreign Relations Committee's "Super-A" status. Under current Republican rules, members of the Republican Caucus may have only one assignment from among Appropriations, Armed Services, Finance, and Foreign Relations. As a result, Foreign Relations' Republican contingent includes the very senior chair, Richard Lugar (R-Ind.) and a group of members who average only about six or seven years in the chamber. Thus, there is little weight of reputation or institutional memory among the majority group. Demoting Foreign Relations might actually elevate its status.

Legislative tinkering regarding narrow issues also occurs all the time. The intelligence bill passed at the end of the 108th Congress in 2004 included foreign policy provisions on Pakistan, Afghanistan, and Saudi Arabia and it also established the International Youth Opportunity Fund to support American-sponsored schools in Muslim countries. Also in 2004, Congress passed and the president signed the North Korean Human Rights Act. This act featured bipartisan support and was designed to increase pressure on the repressive North Korean regime to improve its human rights policies. The act authorized the appropriation of $24 million over a four-year period. This sort of tinkering is resisted by the executive branch but, ultimately, it is tolerated because it beats the alternative—full-scale legislating by Congress. But, at best, it is an atomized, piecemeal approach to policy making and not one that enhances institutional influence.

In sum, current circumstances suggest that Congress will eschew abdication but find itself without the political will to legislate. The roadblocks to reform, to legislating, are simply too formidable at this point in time. Party polarization means that supermajority coalitions of the sort that briefly emerged in Congress during the 1970s are unlikely. Decades of Court decisions tilt toward the executive in the absence of clear legislation. Institutional features reinforce the parochial electoral motives of individual members in even more pronounced fashion than Huntington observed in the 1960s. And presidents of both parties are fully prepared to press the limits of executive power. Unable to legislate, unwilling to abdicate, Congress likely will tinker, leaving the conduct of foreign affairs and war largely to the discretion of the president.

Notes

1. See Christopher J. Deering, "Congress, the President, and Military Policy," *Annals of the American Academy of Political and Social Science* 499 (September 1988): 136–147, and Deering, "Congress, the President, and War Powers."

2. See Silverstein, *Imbalance of Powers*, 101ff. To be precise, Silverstein argues that the Court continues to back Congress when it clearly opposes the executive; but it has permitted far more discretion to presidents in the absence of clear legislative signals.

3. The notion of the "imperial presidency" is from Arthur M. Schlesinger Jr., *The Imperial Presidency* (Boston: Houghton Mifflin, 1973). For a more recent argument along the same lines see Stephen Graubard, *Command of Office: How War, Secrecy, and Deception Transformed the Presidency from Theodore Roosevelt to George W. Bush* (New York: Basic Books, 2005).

4. These are Hamilton's words from *Federalist* No. 41 and represent the two classes of power conferred upon the government with respect to external affairs. These are discussed further immediately below. Alexander Hamilton, James Madison, and John Jay, *The Federalist Papers* (1788; repr. New York: Bantam Classic, 1982), 244. Subsequent page citations are to this edition.

5. So far as can be determined, this characterization of an early American approach to external affairs is the author's. It is consolidated inasmuch as it combines a series of features—political, military, and economic—rather than simply a strong military to achieve desired goals. It is deterrence because the goal itself is to discourage foreign interference and avert armed conflict. It might be observed that the underlying logic here anticipates what today would be called the democratic peace literature. The Achilles' heel, however, was that U.S. economic policy had a strong mercantilist element—a feature frequently associated with interstate conflict. See Christopher J. Deering, "Principle or Party? Foreign and National Security Policymaking in the Senate," in *The Contentious Senate: Partisanship, Ideology, and the Myth of Cool Judgment*, edited by Colton C. Campbell and Nicol C. Rae (Lanham, Md.: Rowman & Littlefield, 2001), 43–61.

6. *The Federalist Papers*, 20–21.

7. No navy existed at the point that the Constitution was being written, its components having been sold off after the Revolutionary War. So it is no surprise that Hamilton would be an advocate of its early return: "A further resource for influencing the conduct of European nations toward us, in this respect, would arise from the establishment of a federal navy. There can be no doubt that the continuance of the

Union under an efficient government would put it in our power, at a period not very distant, to create a navy which, if it could not vie with those of the great maritime powers, would at least be of respectable weight if thrown into the scale of either of two contending parties." *The Federalist Papers,* No. 11, 60–61.

8. *The Federalist Papers,* No. 11, 63.

9. The case, in this regard, is made by Edward Mead Earle, "Adam Smith, Alexander Hamilton, Friedrich List: The Economic Foundations of Military Power," in *Makers of Modern Strategy: From Machiavelli to the Nuclear Age,* edited by Peter Paret, repr. (Princeton, N.J.: Princeton University Press, 1986), 217–261.

10. J. W. Horrocks, *A Short History of Mercantilism* (London: Methuen, 1925), 1.

11. Hamilton's *Report on Manufactures,* submitted to Congress in 1791 while he was secretary, is regarded as a classic statement on political economy generally and of the American system in particular. That said, Hamilton's advice on this and upon military policy fell largely upon deaf, or antagonistic, ears. Not until 1816 did Congress enact a pronouncedly protectionist tariff scheme, to be followed in 1828 by the Tariff of Abominations. Friedrich List was the primary intellectual proponent of the American system after Hamilton's death in 1804.

12. Hamilton describes this duty as "more a matter of dignity than of authority. It is a circumstance which will be without consequence in the administration of the government; and it is far more convenient that it should be arranged in this manner." *The Federalist Papers,* No. 69, 423.

13. *The Federalist Papers,* No. 23, 133.

14. *The Federalist Papers,* No. 41, 244.

15. The two phrases are from Jay, *The Federalist Papers,* No. 64, 392–393 (emphasis in the original). Jay likens the negotiation of treaties and diplomatic affairs generally to tides of irregular duration, strength, and direction: "To discern and to profit by these tides in national affairs, is the business of those who preside over them; and they who have had much experience on this head inform us, that there frequently are occasions when days, nay even when hours are precious" (393).

16. Hamilton does touch on the president's role in *Federalist* No. 69, in which he characterizes the role as a limited one and compares it at once to the governor of New York and the king of England. He also may have remained silent on the issue for fear of raising a red herring. Either that or he experienced a sudden shift of opinion in his editorializing as "Pacificus" during the debate on neutrality only a few years later.

17. Silverstein, *Imbalance of Powers.*

18. 299 U.S. 304 (1936). For more on Sutherland's point of view see his *Constitutional Power and World Affairs* (1919; repr., New York: Columbia University Press, 1970). For a list of additional cases offering broad delegation arguments see Louis Fisher, "The Legitimacy of the Congressional National Security Role," paper delivered at the National Defense University Symposium, "Congress, the Presidency, the Judiciary, and National Security," Washington, D.C., November 19–20, 1987, 18, note 15.

19. "Army" is used broadly here, to refer to air, ground, and naval forces. The founders feared a large standing ground army and limited appropriations for it to two years. No such restriction exists for a navy (or air force).

20. The figures here and following are from Deering, "Congress, the President, and Military Policy."

21. Although not a component per se of the national security state, the Reciprocal Trade Act of 1934 is an early legislative delegation consistent with this overall trend. The act gave the president nearly complete authority to negotiate bilateral trade agreements. The 1962 Trade Expansion Act altered and extended that authority.

22. James L. Sundquist, *The Decline and Resurgence of Congress* (Washington, D.C.: Brookings Institution, 1981).

23. For example, before 1962 the committees authorized the military services an aggregate active-duty personnel ceiling of 5 million even though actual peacetime active-duty personnel levels rarely reached half these authorized levels. Likewise, the secretary of the air force was authorized to "procure 24,000 serviceable aircraft or 225,000 airframe tons . . . as he may determine."

24. Quoted in John M. Goshko, "Virtuoso Performance Surprises Hill," *Washington Post,* November 3, 1985, A12.

25. The current requirement proscribing the use of any funds appropriated to the Department of State without specific authorization is at 22 U.S.C. §2680.

26. On postwar developments in the foreign policy committees see James M. McCormick, "Decision Making in the Foreign Affairs and Foreign Relations Committees," in *Congress Resurgent: Foreign and Defense Policy on Capitol Hill,* edited by Randall B. Ripley and James M. Lindsay (Ann Arbor: University of Michigan Press, 1993), 118–121.

27. On the impact of Pell's stewardship see Helen Dewar, "Senate Foreign Relations Panel Founders," *Washington Post,* 10 October 1989, A1. On Helms and the brief tenure of Senator Richard G. Lugar as chair see Pamela Fessler "Helms Sweeps through Panel, Fires Nine GOP Staff Aides," *Congressional Quarterly Weekly Report,* 11 January 1992, and John M. Goshko, "Virtuoso Performance Surprises Hill," *Washington Post,* November 3, 1985, A12.

28. A standard on the history of U.S. tariff policy: F. W. Taussig, *The Tariff History of the United States,* 7th ed. (London and New York: Putnam's Sons, 1923).

29. On Smoot-Hawley, see E. E. Schattschneider's classic, *Politics, Pressures, and the Tariff: A Study of Free Private Enterprise in Pressure Politics* (New York: Prentice-Hall, 1935). Schattschneider's work is generally viewed as a case for the triumph of special interests over the national interest and, thus, an indictment of the centripetal nature of Congress.

30. The Trade Act of 2002 (Public Law 107-210). Fast track had received a new moniker, Trade Promotion Authority, and Democrats won some concessions. President Bush received negotiating authority through June 2005, and the likelihood of a two-year extension. Background on fast track and events leading up to passage of the Trade Act can be found in Lenore Sek, *Trade Promotion Authority (Fast-Track Authority for Trade Agreements): Background and Developments in the 107th Congress,* CRS Issue Brief IB10084 (Washington, D.C.: Congressional Research Service, January 14, 2003).

31. On delegation in trade policy, utilizing principal-agent theory, see Sharyn O'Halloran, "Congress and Trade Policy," in Ripley and Lindsay, *Congress Resurgent,* 283–303.

32. These and other conclusions may be found in Destler's review of trade policy during the thirty-year period 1961–1990. I. M. Destler, "Delegating Trade Policy," in *The President, The Congress, and the Making of Foreign Policy*, edited by Paul E. Peterson (Norman: University of Oklahoma Press, 1994), 228–245.

33. Hamilton writes in No. 76 (*The Federalist Papers*, 463) that Senate consent will prevent the president from appointing "unfit characters from State prejudice, from family connection, from personal attachment, or from a view to popularity." Jay's words on treaties are from No. 64 (*The Federalist Papers*, 392–393).

34. David Auerswald and Forrest Maltzman, "Policymaking through Advice and Consent: Treaty Consideration by the United States Senate," *Journal of Politics* 65 (November 2003): 1097–1110. The pivotal senator is the person or persons near the two-thirds point necessary for consent.

35. For a more complete treatment of these developments see Christopher J. Deering, "Alarms and Patrols: Legislative Oversight in Foreign and Defense Policy," in *Congress and the Politics of Foreign Policy*, edited by Colton C. Campbell, Nicol C. Rae, and John F. Stack Jr. (Upper Saddle River, N.J.: Prentice Hall, 2003): 112–138.

36. Mathew D. McCubbins and Thomas Schwartz, "Congressional Oversight Overlooked: Police Patrols versus Fire Alarms," *American Journal of Political Science* 28 (February 1984): 165–179.

37. Today, that language (now reading "shall review and study, on a continuing basis") is at 2 U.S.C. §190d. It was originally contained in Section 136 of the Legislative Reorganization Act of 1946.

38. For further discussion of the "new oversight" see Thomas M. Franck and Edward Weisband, *Foreign Policy by Congress* (New York: Oxford University Press, 1979), 84.

39. Reported by Raymond H. Dawson, "Congressional Innovation and Intervention in Defense Policy: Legislative Authorization of Weapons Systems," *American Political Science Review* 61 (March 1962): 47.

40. On the Court's reasoning in *Chahda* and its aftermath see Louis Fisher, "The Legislative Veto: Invalidated, It Survives," *Law and Contemporary Problems* 56 (autumn 1993): 273–292. Fisher reports, as early as 1993, that Congress had passed into law at least two hundred additional veto provisions. Although presumably unconstitutional, they continued to thrive as a practical accommodation between the branches, unchallenged in court.

41. On this general point see Richard F. Fenno Jr., *Learning to Govern: An Institutional View of the 104th Congress* (Washington, D.C.: Brookings Institution, 1997). For some evidence on the balance of alarms and patrol oversight in a sample of committees see Steven J. Balla and Christopher J. Deering, "Oversight over Time and across Committees: An Operational Measure of Police Patrols and Fire Alarms," paper presented at the annual meeting of the Midwest Political Science Association, Chicago, Illinois, April 19–22, 2001.

42. House Committee on National Security, *Report of the Activities of the Committee on National Security for the One Hundred Fourth Congress*, 104th Cong., 2d sess., 1997, H. Rept. 104-884, 35, emphasis added.

43. Committee on National Security, *Report*, 39–44.

44. It should be emphasized that presidents virtually always report "consistent with" rather than "pursuant to" the act to (*a*) emphasize their position that the statute is unconstitutional, and (*b*) avoid the legal entanglements that would ensue from a report pursuant to its provisions. That same report, Richard F. Grimmett, *The War Powers Resolution after Thirty Years*, CRS Report RL32267 (Washington, D.C., Congressional Research Service, March 14, 2004), identified eighteen additional cases where presidents did not file reports but which, arguably, constituted troop usage as defined in the resolution.

45. But at least one study, by Auerswald and Cowey, makes a strong case that the executive use of force was curtailed by the implicit threat represented by the act and its provisions. Their evidence is developed from thirteen major pre-War Powers conflicts during the twentieth century and fourteen post-War Powers conflicts—where they find conflicts tended to be of more limited duration and featured some congressional opposition. David P. Auerswald and Peter F. Cowhey, "Ballotbox Diplomacy: The War Powers Resolution and the Use of Force," *International Studies Quarterly* 41 (September 1997): 505–528.

46. E. Scott Adler, *Why Congressional Reforms Fail: Reelection and the House Committee System* (Chicago: University of Chicago, 2002).

47. In addition to Silverstein, *Imbalance of Powers*, see Craig R. Ducat and Robert L. Dudley's argument that the judiciary generally and the federal district judges in particular have been deferential to the executive branch throughout the post-World War II era. Ducat and Dudley, "Federal District Judges and Presidential Power during the Postwar Era," *Journal of Politics* 51 (February 1989): 98–118.

48. See Samuel P. Huntington, "Congressional Responses to the Twentieth Century," in *The Congress and America's Future*, edited by David B. Truman, 2nd ed. (Englewood Cliffs, N.J.: Prentice-Hall, 1973).

49. Huntington, "Congressional Responses," 38.

50. See, for example, Louis Fisher's arguments in *Presidential War Power*, 2nd ed. (Lawrence: University Press of Kansas, 2004.

51. Theodore J. Lowi, *The End of Liberalism: Ideology, Policy, and the Crisis of Public Authority* (New York: Norton, 1969).

52. Just such a move was included in the fiscal year 2005 intelligence authorization bill reported by the Senate Intelligence Committee. Helen Fessenden, "Senate Intelligence Committee Advances Authorization Bill, Removes Its Own Term Limits," *CQ Weekly*, May 8, 2004, 1088.

Bibliography

Deering, Christopher J. "Congress, the President, and War Powers: The Perennial Debate." In *Divided Democracy: Cooperation and Conflict between the President and Congress,* edited by James A. Thurber, 171–197. Washington, D.C.: CQ Press, 1991.

Koh, Harold Hongju. *The National Security Constitution: Sharing Power after the Iran-Contra Affair.* New Haven: Yale University Press, 1990.

Lindsay, James M. *Congress and the Politics of U.S. Foreign Policy.* Baltimore: Johns Hopkins University Press, 1994.

Ripley, Randall B., and James M. Lindsay. *Congress Resurgent: Foreign and Defense Policy on Capitol Hill.* Ann Arbor: University of Michigan Press, 1993.

Silverstein, Gordon. *Imbalance of Powers: Constitutional Interpretation and the Making of American Foreign Policy.* New York: Oxford University Press, 1997.

13

BUDGETS AND FISCAL POLICY

Eric Patashnik

C ONGRESS IS AT THE HEART OF THE BUDGET PROCESS. This is not a trivial observation. In most democratic nations, executive actors dominate tax and spending decisions. Legislative bodies typically possess narrow authority over fiscal policy-making. American national government is the exception to this rule. While the executive branch plays an important, often leading, role in the budget process, the Constitution gives Congress the authority to levy taxes and provides that funds cannot be withdrawn from the United States Treasury except pursuant to its appropriations acts. The constitutional framers recognized that the separation of powers would have little meaning unless Congress and the executive shared control over the nation's purse strings.

But formal constitutional authority is one thing. Autonomous budget power and the political capacity to promote fiscal responsibility are quite another. Autonomous budget power exists when Congress can write its fiscal policy preferences into law (whether or not those preferences are fiscally sound).[1] The political capacity to promote fiscal responsibility exists when Congress can balance claims on the federal budget against revenues in order to produce fiscal policy that is sustainable over the long run. While Congress does not have to pass a balanced budget every year, it must avoid creating structural budget deficits, meaning deficits that persist even when the economy is not in a recession. While congressional budget power and responsible fiscal policy-making are distinct concepts, the budget process works best when they are mutually enforcing.

Because it is a highly permeable institution, Congress's budget power and its ability to promote responsible fiscal outcomes are significantly influenced by external factors such as presidential leadership, constituency pressures, elite opinion, and economic performance. Yet Congress's budget power and its contribution to sound fiscal policy-making are also shaped by the workings of the budget process within the institution. The budget process structures the flow of budget information, frames policy debates, and influences Congress's internal distribution of power. Budget rules and procedures can make it easer for lawmakers to close an unwanted gap between revenues and spending—or they can make it harder. The budget process can highlight the fiscal trade-offs across a range of policy options—or they can obscure them. And the budget process can erect or remove parliamentary barriers to the adoption of budget measures supported by narrow legislative factions. In sum, the internal workings of the congressional budget process can promote or inhibit the exercise of collective responsibility and fiscal responsibility in a political body in which lawmakers have powerful incentives to satisfy the demands of constituents and clientele groups.

This essay reviews the development of congressional budgeting and in particular Congress's efforts beginning in the 1970s to strengthen its budget power and promote responsible national fiscal policy. Three major budget reform thrusts—the Congressional Budget and Impoundment Control Act of 1974, the Balanced Budget and Emergency Deficit Control Act of 1995 (known as the Gramm-Rudman-Hollings Act), and the Budget Enforcement Act of 1990—have shaped legislative dynamics and congressional performance since that time. These reforms have had an overall mixed impact. On the positive side of the ledger, the reforms have helped Congress to coordinate its fiscal decisions and made it easier for legislative majorities—when they coalesce—to write their taxing and spending preferences into law. They have also strengthened Congress's analytic capacity by giving it independent sources of budget information. On the negative side, the same centralizing budget reforms that have made it easier for Congress to control itself have also rendered it more susceptible to executive influence, encouraging presidents to use the congressional budget process as a vehicle to advance their own projects, which may or may not be fiscally prudent. The most important limitation of previous budget reforms is that they have arguably left Congress without adequate tools to address the emerging fiscal challenges of the twenty-first century. These challenges include preparing major entitlement programs for the impending retirement of the baby boomers. If Congress decides to confront these fiscal policy tasks in the years ahead, further changes to the budget process may be warranted.

Congressional Budgeting before Reform

Any discussion of Congress's capacity to budget must be placed in historical context.[2] In 1964 the political scientist Aaron Wildavsky published a seminal book, *The Politics of the Budgetary Process,* which provides a convenient baseline for evaluating changes in budgeting dynamics since the 1950s.[3] Wildavsky characterized national budgeting during that era as an "incremental" process of pluralistic bargaining. While the budget process described by Wildavsky was competitive, it was orderly. Because the U.S. economy grew rapidly during the 1950s and early 1960s, and because government expansion was mostly welcomed, budget actors both in the White House and on the Hill were generally content to allow existing programs and expenditures to escape close scrutiny. Their attention—and political conflict—were largely confined to proposed changes at the margin. While federal spending increased steadily over this period, policy makers maintained their capacity to adjust fiscal claims and rations. Congress generally managed to pass budget measures on time and to avoid large peacetime deficits. In sum, collectively responsible fiscal results were produced even though individual members were motivated to spend money on popular programs and deliver benefits to their districts.

For several reasons, this relatively harmonious fiscal world began to crumble in the late 1960s. First, changes in the composition of the federal budget itself reduced Congress's political ability to balance claims and rations. Traditionally, most of the federal budget supported items like national defense and highway building. These annually appropriated programs required budget claimants to petition for "fair share" increases at the margin; claimants had no prior right to more spending. In the 1960s and 1970s, however, the federal government began spending more and more on social welfare transfer programs such as Social Security, Medicare, Medicaid, and food stamps. Many of these programs were established as *entitlements* by which eligible recipients have a legal right to stipulated payments. As long as the underlying authorizations remained law, Congress was obliged to provide sufficient funds to cover benefit promises. The autonomy from normal appropriations review and control afforded by entitlement status reduced political uncertainty for beneficiary groups, but it also impaired the ability of budget actors to decide how incremental resources would be allocated across competing claims. Changes in the level of entitlement spending are largely driven by demographic and technical factors, such as the rate of medical inflation. By 1974, "mandatory" spending for entitlements had climbed to 49 percent of federal spending, up from 32 percent in 1962. In short, almost half the U.S. national budget was beyond Congress's short-term control.

The second key development that eroded Congress's budget power and its ability to pass responsible budgets was the breakdown of elite consensus on what constitutes sound fiscal policy. Beginning in the late 1940s, most economic policy elites were applied Keynesians who believed that recessions were not automatically self-correcting, and that it was appropriate for the government to run deficits during periods of economic contraction. With the enactment of the Employment Act of 1946, the federal government assumed responsibility for keeping the economy near the "full employment" level of production, which Keynesian economists believed they could identify. In 1964 Congress enacted a major tax cut that leading Keynesians promised would give the economy a badly needed jolt. When economic growth accelerated rapidly after the tax cut's implementation, the Keynesian prescription became the new fiscal policy orthodoxy. Over the next decade, however, the Keynesian economic consensus began to decay. In the early to mid-1970s, the U.S. economy simultaneously experienced a deep recession and high inflation—a miserable combination that Keynesian economic models could not easily explain. Members of Congress began receiving a cacophony of economic policy advice. Neoliberal Keynesians argued that fiscal policy remained critical, but that Congress needed to become more nimble and strengthen its ability to adjust to changing economic conditions. "Monetarist" economists such as Milton Friedman, in contrast, argued that countercyclical fiscal policy was bound to be ineffective if not counterproductive, and that responsibility for maintaining economic growth was better left to the Federal Reserve's management of interest rates and the supply of money. By the mid- to late 1970s, supply-side economists were also elbowing their way into this conversation. They argued that the federal government's main fiscal task was to lower marginal tax rates in order to encourage savings and investment. Each group of economists had followers among important policy makers. The political effects of this breakdown of elite consensus on fiscal policy would be intensified and hardened over time by growing ideological polarization and partisan conflict within Congress, as elaborated in more detail below.

The most important reason for the collapse of the budgetary world described by Wildavsky was an institutional struggle between Congress and the president over government spending. This struggle was fundamentally rooted in the incentives for conflict and cooperation embedded in the Constitution. Historically, legislative-executive cooperation prevailed on budget matters. During the late nineteenth century, neither Congress nor the executive even maintained a formal budget system for coordinating taxing and spending decisions. Although the federal government was growing, most policy makers did not yet see the need for formal mechanisms of fiscal integration, meaning each spending bill was considered in isolation. World War I altered those perceptions. Federal spending increased massively to finance the military effort, and the federal government was forced to borrow heavily. After the war, budget reformers convincingly argued that the government lacked the political capacity to manage its huge national debt. To strengthen the president's ability to control spending, Congress passed the Budget and Accounting Act of 1921. The 1921 act required the president to submit an annual, comprehensive budget to Congress, and established the Bureau of the Budget (later renamed the Office of Management and Budget) to help the president decide how much to request for each agency. In sum, Congress viewed a stronger executive as a way to strengthen the government's—and by extension its own—capacity to adopt fiscally responsible budgets.

While executive budgeting was becoming more centralized, legislative budgeting remained fragmented and decentralized. Between the late 1860s and

1974, Congress maintained one legislative process for mobilizing revenues (managed by the House Ways and Means and Senate Finance Committees) and a second for expending money (directed by the House and Senate Appropriations Committees). Without a single legislative panel responsible for taking a top-down look at the total budget picture, Congress was forced to respond to the president's annual budget recommendations in piecemeal fashion. Congress generally deferred heavily to presidential guidance. Indeed, based on a careful empirical comparison between presidential budget requests and subsequent congressional appropriations decisions during the period between 1947 and 1984, Paul E. Peterson found that executive-legislative differences were marginal. While Congress rejected some presidential initiatives and increased spending on some legislative favorites (such as infrastructure projects), Congress generally stuck close to the aggregate level of spending recommended by the president. Peterson found that Congress also mainly followed the presidential lead on tax matters.[4] This informal system of legislative deference to executive leadership worked remarkably well over the postwar era. Between 1947 and 1957, the federal government ran annual budget surpluses five times. During the next decade, the federal government managed to balance its budget only once, but the deficits it produced were almost always quite small (less than one and a half percent of gross domestic product). By deferring to the president, and taking advantage of postwar economic growth, Congress was able to manage the nation's fiscal affairs without creating obvious economic problems or stimulating excessive political conflict.

But legislative-executive cooperation on the budget broke down in the late 1960s and early 1970s. The major culprit was President Richard Nixon's exceptionally aggressive use of the executive's impoundment power. After his election landslide in 1972, Nixon began impounding—simply refusing to spend—billions in congressional appropriations for programs he disfavored. Nixon certainly did not invent executive impoundment power. Congress had traditionally accepted that if an appropriation item was no longer warranted because administrative needs had changed since the budget obligation had been made, the president could usually obtain its permission to withhold the money for the item. Rather than canceling a modest amount of appropriations to promote administrative efficiency, however, Nixon used the impoundment tool as a political weapon, canceling funding for programs he considered unnecessary. Nixon rationalized his attempt to seize control of federal spending by pointing out that Congress was disorganized and lacked an institutionalized process for making responsible budget decisions. Lawmakers viewed Nixon's actions as nothing less than an attack on Congress's standing in the constitutional system. "Once it is widely recognized that a project may be entombed by the executive branch—even when a convincing case has been made before the Congress and after due deliberation monies have been appropriated—the American people will sense the futility of appealing to their elected representatives. They will conclude, if they haven't already done so, that the Executive Branch is the only significant arena for policy making," commented Senator Frank Church (D-Idaho) in 1973.[5]

A consensus emerged that Congress needed to terminate presidential impoundment abuses and strengthen its autonomous budget power. Lawmakers recognized that if Congress was to challenge the president for leadership on fiscal matters, it needed the institutional capacity to articulate a majority position on the budget. In 1972 Congress established a Joint Study Committee on Budget Control, composed of members from the House and Senate appropriations and tax committees as well as two at-large members from each chamber. The committee in 1973 issued a report that emphasized the need to establish a new framework that would allow Congress to coordinate its taxing and spending decisions and bargain on equal footing with the president.

The Congressional Budget and Impoundment Control Act of 1974

The result was the Congressional Budget and Impoundment Control Act of 1974. Signed by President Nixon less than a month before he resigned the presidency, the landmark act gave Congress important new tools for policy coordination. While some members hoped the measure would promote balanced budgets, the act was less a substantive reform than a procedural one. The new framework was extremely flexible—it permitted Congress to adopt any budget position for which a majority coalition could be assembled. If a majority could agree on a set of fiscal policies, the new budget framework would prevent minority factions from defeating it on the chamber floors. But if no majority consensus could be reached, the act could not magically establish one.

The 1974 Budget Act had three key features. First, it created a system of impoundment control to stop presidents from overriding congressional spending wishes. Rather than banning impoundments entirely (which would have eliminated the executive's flexibility to withhold budget resources for legitimate administrative reasons), the Budget Act set forth tight rules governing the conditions under which impoundments could occur.[6] Second, a major new congressional staff organization, the Congressional Budget Office (CBO), was established to give Congress nonpartisan budget advice and technical support. No longer would Congress have to rely on the budget estimates and economic forecasts of the Office of Management and Budget (OMB), whose long-standing reputation for "neutral competence" had been seriously tarnished by the efforts of both the Johnson and Nixon administrations to employ the elite agency as a political arm of the White House.

Third, budget committees were created in each chamber to manage Congress's new budget process. Significantly, the new budget procedures did not eliminate the preexisting tax-writing and appropriations processes. Rather, the new budget process was layered *atop* them in order to maintain opportunities for broad participation by members in a crucial legislative function. In sum, the new congressional budgetary process would feature an important element of centralization, but Congress's traditional institutional character as a collegial body would be preserved. The two budget committees were charged with articulating Congress's overall fiscal policy. After reviewing the president's budget proposals, the House and Senate Budget Committees would draw up a concurrent resolution outlining a tentative congressional budget. The initial resolution (to be passed by May 15) would set target totals for spending, taxes, and the size of the budget surplus or deficit.[7] Within these overall targets, the resolution would break down spending among the functional categories (e.g., defense, health, income security) used in the president's budget. To reflect the congressional committee structure, the budget resolutions (which did not require a presidential signature) would also provide a specific allocation to each committee that considered budget legislation. The budget resolution's aggregate levels of spending and revenues and spending allocations made to congressional committees would be enforced by points of order that could be raised when individual bills were considered on the floor.

After enactment of the initial budget resolution, Congress would start processing the thirteen regular appropriations bills for the upcoming fiscal year through its normal appropriations process. The tax-writing committees would also conduct their business. In September, after Congress had finished action on appropriations, the Budget Committees would take another overall look at the status of the budget. By September 15, Congress was to have adopted a second budget resolution that could either affirm or revise the budget targets set by the initial resolution. Unlike the first resolution, the second resolution was supposed to be binding. If the Budget Committees determined that actions taken by Congress during the year did not fit the final budget resolution totals, they could direct the committees with jurisdiction over appropriations, entitlements, and revenues to submit recommendations for meeting the final targets in a process known as "reconciliation." The Budget Committees would then combine the committee recommendations it received into a single package and report them to the floor as a "reconciliation" bill by September 25, in time for the start of the new fiscal year on October 1.

Congressional Budgeting after 1974

The rules and procedures established in the 1974 Budget Act have endured, but their operation has varied with changes in economic and political conditions. Since 1974, Congress has crafted budgets both with significant input from the president and without it, and in the context of both deficits and surpluses. As lawmakers gained more experience with the new budget framework, they adapted certain of its provisions to new uses. Post-1974 Congresses have also made some significant additions to the original framework. Some—not all—of these modifications have enhanced Congress's autonomous budget power. A congressional budget process less open to revision and experimentation would surely have reduced it.

The first significant revision of the 1974 Budget Act involved the timing of the reconciliation process. Originally, reconciliation occurred late in the year. Its purpose was to enforce the policy changes adopted in the first budget resolution. By the time reconciliation bills were considered on the chamber floors, however, decisions in the appropriations process had already been made. Once constituencies had been promised benefits, it was politically awkward for lawmakers to suddenly change their minds. Because reconciliation came so late, it had no bite. But in 1980 a procedural revolution took place. The Senate Budget Committee decided to move the reconciliation process from the second budget resolution in September to the first budget resolution in May. This meant the Budget Committees could give their recommendations for budget savings to the affected committees *before* the year's funding decisions had been approved.

While budget reconciliation in 1980 constituted a major procedural innovation, its policy impact (about $4 billion in budget savings) was quite modest. The 1981 reconciliation measure—the first adopted during the Reagan administration—was another story entirely. Ronald Reagan entered the White House in January 1981 with three ambitious budget priorities: to dramatically reduce taxes, to increase defense spending, and to curb domestic programs. The budget reconciliation process was an ideal vehicle for advancing this agenda. Reconciliation bills are considered under special rules that limit the scope of floor amendments in the House and under expedited procedures that prevent filibusters in the Senate. In the Omnibus Reconciliation Act of 1981 (OBRA81), a coalition of Republicans and southern Democrats known as "boll weevils" enacted significant reductions in both domestic discretionary items and entitlement programs such as welfare and food stamps. (These southern conservative members defected from the Democratic party to vote with congressional Republicans on budgetary and tax bills in the 1980s. They took their name from the insect that destroys cotton crops in the South.) These budget cuts would almost certainly not have been adopted under the old, piecemeal congressional budget framework. The passage of OBRA81 was a huge victory for the Reagan administration. Its fiscal strategy was to keep the legislative focus on the net budget savings of the reconciliation measure while minimizing the ability of affected groups to protest. "My aim in this tactic was to take the Hill by storm before the interest group opposition to spending cuts congealed," acknowledged David Stockman, OMB director under Reagan. As presidential scholar Stephen Skowronek argues, "Reagan took over the reconciliation procedure in the congressional budget process and turned it into a vehicle for the imposition of his will."[8] Yet, as Joseph White and Aaron Wildavsky argue in their authoritative account of the budget battles of the 1980s, OBRA81 was still Congress's bill. Its contents "defined the boundaries of what Congress was willing to cut from domestic government."[9]

Congress continued to use the reconciliation process during the remainder of the 1980s, but the policy changes it enacted were insufficient to balance the budget. Not only were lawmakers generally unwilling to impose large cuts in entitlement programs, but Congress acceded to Reagan's demand for major tax cuts in 1981. The revenue losses of the Economic Recovery Act of 1981 (about $750 billion over five years) were three or four times larger than the budget savings achieved in OBRA81. In the 1970s, the federal government ran a budget deficit above 3 percent of GDP only twice, even though U.S. economic performance was less than stellar. In the six years between fiscal years 1982 and 1986—a period of economic recovery—the federal deficit *never* fell below 4 percent, and in three of those years exceeded 5 percent of GDP (see Figure 1).

Attempts to make deep reductions in the deficit were stymied by conflict both between Reagan and Congress and within Congress. There is no hard evidence to support claims that Reagan deliberately engineered large deficits to starve the federal government, but when large deficits emerged he refused to sacrifice his defense buildup. Reagan repeatedly called for additional reductions in

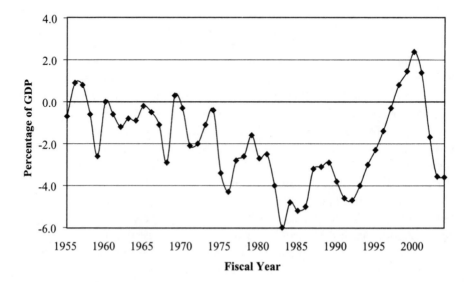

SOURCE: Congressional Budget Office.

Figure 1. Federal Deficits and Surpluses as a Percentage of GDP, 1955–2004

domestic discretionary spending, but Congress refused to approve them. He reluctantly signed several tax increases passed by Congress during the remainder of the 1980s, but the total revenue mobilized through these tax hikes offset only about two-thirds of the money lost to the Treasury in 1981. While both Reagan and key members of Congress decried the deficit, there was no consensus on what to do about it. Despite the frequent resort to bipartisan deficit-reduction summits, conflict, stalemate, and delay were the rule.

By the mid-1980s, many lawmakers believed that additional procedural changes were needed to force themselves (and the executive) into taking the painful steps that would be required to liquidate the deficit. In 1985 Senate freshmen Phil Gramm (R–Tex.) and Warren B. Rudman (R–N.H.) joined with former Budget Committee chairman Ernest F. Hollings (D–S.C.) to introduce what came to be known as the Gramm-Rudman-Hollings (GRH) Act. The measure required the federal deficit to be eliminated gradually over six years, with maximum allowable deficits along the way. If the deficit projected for a given year exceeded that year's deficit target, GRH provided for automatic cuts (through a process known as "sequestration") in various federal programs.[10] The logic of the reform seemed compelling. Either the deficit would be eliminated automatically through across-the-board cuts, or else lawmakers would be motivated into making tough, but more discriminating, cutbacks of their own.

Although GRH may have helped prevent the deficit from exploding during the late 1980s, it failed to achieve its stated goals. One problem was that GRH completely exempted from sequestration many expensive items (such as Social Security, food stamps, and veterans' pensions), thus requiring disproportionate cuts in the rest of the budget. In addition, the measure's focus on projected future deficits invited lawmakers to employ bookkeeping tricks in order to make budget forecasts look more rosy. When Congress found itself unable to meet its deficit target for fiscal 1987, for example, it moved a $680-million installment of the federal revenue-sharing program by five days so that it would fall at the end of fiscal 1986 instead of the following year. The use of countless other gimmicks undermined the integrity of the process and made Congress look feckless. Finally, the deficit targets did not take into account unexpected changes in economic conditions.

After years of evading the GRH framework, Congress finally scrapped it in 1990, but not before President George H. W. Bush and the Democratic-controlled Congress negotiated the Budget Reconciliation Act of 1990 (OBRA90), a huge multiyear package of spending cuts and tax increases that promised to cut $496 billion from deficits over the following five years. To prevent these policy achievements from being chipped away by subsequent legislative actions, Congress passed the Budget Enforcement Act (BEA). The BEA did not call for a balanced budget in any year. Instead, it imposed caps on discretionary spending and created a "pay-as-you-go" (paygo) rule that required tax cuts or entitlement increases to be paid for with other tax increases or entitlement cuts. Sixty votes were required in the Senate to bypass the rule.

An interesting debate has developed on whether the shift to the BEA reflected lessons that members of Congress self-consciously took away from their unsatisfactory GRH experience. Former CBO director Robert Reischauer is skeptical of claims that the progression to the BEA represented "policy learning." He insists that BEA's passage was largely an exercise in political blame-avoidance:

> By 1990, lawmakers had backed themselves into a corner. If they implemented Gramm-Rudman, the across-the-board cuts, the sequester would have been over 30 percent of discretionary spending, excluding defense pay. That was irrational, it would have decimated Head Start and other popular programs. . . . The limits, avoided by Congress in one year, only got harder to adhere to in the next year. So lawmakers would redefine the limits. They were up against the wall in 1990. They would have been hooted out of court if they had said they wanted to revise the limits again. . . .
>
> They got themselves into a situation that was difficult to back out of. They said, "I am going to walk on water," and gathered a crowd to watch them. They had no way to avoid stepping into the lake. It was not necessarily learning, it was painting themselves into a corner. They concluded that for political survival, it was better to bite the bullet than snub their nose yet again at a promise they had made.[11]

Reischauer is certainly correct that lawmakers had gotten themselves into a jam, and that the BEA was more an act of political desperation than the product of formal study. Yet the decision to stop doing something that is not working in order to avoid a negative political reaction may be exactly the way a political institution like Congress discovers how to improve its policy performance. As budget scholar Irene S. Rubin argues, "Embarrassment may have been the reason for the display of political backbone, but, even so, there had to be learning."[12]

An argument can be made that the BEA's pay-as-you-go framework was in fact carefully designed to correct major defects in the GRH structure. The BEA eliminated fixed deficit-reduction targets that prior experience had demonstrated could easily be rendered impracticable by unforeseen changes in economic conditions. Instead of holding Congress hostage to external factors it could not control, the BEA made Congress more accountable for the budget effects of its own decisions. To reduce the incentive for budget gimmickry, the BEA extended the scope of the budget resolution from one to five years and provided for the discretionary-spending caps to be adjusted automatically for changes from the anticipated rate of inflation. Finally, the BEA sought to promote equity in the budget process. Under the GRH rules, discretionary programs could be sequestered even if it entitlement spending was driving the increase in the deficit. In contrast, discretionary spending under the BEA would be sequestered only if the appropriations had not lived within the appropriations caps.

Effects of Congressional Budget Reform

Budget reform had far-reaching effects on Congress's internal dynamics, transforming how lawmakers understood, debated, and voted on budget issues. Since nearly everything Congress does costs money, the political impact of budget reform was profound. First, congressional budget reform altered the distribution of power and roles within Congress. Under the 1974 act, the budget panels became the leading rationers of funds in Congress, upsetting traditional patterns of resource allocation. The appropriations panels were often characterized as being "guardians of the Treasury" in the 1950s and 1960s. Even when they supported program expansions, they sought to root out administrative waste and prevent unnecessary spending. In their postreform role as supplicant to the budget committees, however, appropriators often began acting as claimants or advocates lobbying for maximum funding of the programs under their jurisdiction.[13]

Second, the 1974 Budget Act and its progeny centralized taxing and spending decisions in Congress. The House Speaker and other top party leaders shaped the membership of the budget committees, monitored their activities, and mobilized the winning coalitions needed to pass budget resolutions and reconciliation bills. Because they enjoyed key procedural protections during floor debate, budget resolutions and omnibus reconciliation bills became increasingly important vehicles for moving parties' major agenda items. Both parties have looked to the congressional budget process as a legislative fast-track at a time when the regular committee process in Congress seemed to be disintegrating due to the declining ability of committee chairs to compel compromise solutions as a result of their loss of power following committee reforms of the 1970s. The death knell for the old committee system came in 1995, when the Republicans took over Congress. House Speaker Newt Gingrich of Georgia circumvented the committees by creating Republican task forces and demanding that they produce bills to his liking, which would then be packaged together as omnibus budget measures. Under Gingrich, the new Republican majority tried to use the budget process to cut taxes, terminate programs, reform welfare, restructure Medicare and Medicaid, and send power back to the states.[14] While President Clinton largely succeeded in blocking this ambitious effort, the Republicans' maneuver reinforced the perception that the budget process is the only legislative game in town.

A third effect of congressional budget reform is that it led to the "fiscalization of the policy debate."[15] In the prereform era, lawmakers never voted on budget totals, only on the parts. Votes on budget resolutions and reconciliation bills forced members to go on record on the appropriate size of total spending, total revenues, and the budget deficit. Sharper and more explicit budget trade-offs were required just as the deficit was exploding. Conflicts over the size of funding increments can be resolved by splitting the difference. But when the conflict is framed in terms of a contest between competing visions of the appropriate role of government, the political debate becomes more abstract and acceptable accommodations become far harder to reach. Inevitably, conflict over budget matters intensified.[16]

Fourth, the new budget process forced partisan and ideological conflicts within Congress out into the open. As the new budget process was taking effect, the two parties were drifting apart and becoming more internally homogenous. While liberal and conservative members certainly had their budget fights in the 1950s and 1960s, ideological and partisan conflict over the budget was muted during the postwar era by the distributive nature of most federal spending and the consensus on the priority of defense (then the largest budget item). When political scientist Steven E. Schier conducted extensive interviews with lawmakers in the mid-1980s, however, he found a profound fiscal dissensus. Schier concluded that virtually all members of the House and Senate approached budget issues from ideology-encompassing deep-seated concepts about the appropriate size and role of government. Conservatives believed that defense was a high spending priority and worried about the effect of redistribution on economic incentives. Liberals viewed social spending as more important than defense and were concerned about the achievement of a fair distribution of income. In sum, the two political camps disagreed about the most fundamental budget issues—how large government should be and how taxpayer money should be spent. Some 40 percent of congressional roll call votes on budget resolutions between 1976 and 1990 found 75 percent or more of Republicans opposing 75 percent or more of Democrats. On 10 percent of the roll calls, 90 percent or more of one party opposed 90 percent or more of the other.[17] The budget became the key arena for partisan struggles over the future of activist government. The high political stakes attracted intense media attention. During the 1970s, less than 10 percent of the New York Times's articles on Congress also dealt with the budget. During the 1980s, typically 20–30 percent of stories on Congress were budget-related.[18]

Finally, budget reform elevated the importance of budget forecasts in the CBO and the OMB. Because these budget projections were so critical, politicians have sometimes fought over them—as in the skirmishing over the scoring (estimating the budgetary impacts of pending and enacted legislation as compared to the limits set in the budget resolution) of President Clinton's health reform proposal in 1993–1994. As Theda Skocpol has argued, back in the Progressive Era and the New Deal, lawmakers used to spend a lot of time trying to guess what the Supreme Court would accept as constitutional. In the 1980s and 1990s, lawmakers lived in fear that the CBO would reject their proposals as not "costed out."[19]

From Deficits to Surpluses and Back Again

Since 1974, Congress's capacity to exercise fiscal responsibility by matching spending and revenues has been tested by both deficits and budget surpluses. Perhaps surprisingly, the latter have in some ways proved the tougher political challenge.

Appearances to the contrary notwithstanding, the liquidation of the deficit in 1998 did not happen overnight. A balanced budget would not have been achieved in 1998 without the enactment of OBRA90 and the BEA eight years earlier. The contribution of these measures to deficit reduction was initially obscured, however, by rising health care spending and the impact of the 1990–1991 economic recession. Over the next eight years, congressional Republicans and Democratic president Bill Clinton fought a series of historic budget showdowns.

With the deficit approaching $300 billion in fiscal 1992, the Clinton administration made deficit reduction an early priority. Like Ronald Reagan before him, Clinton viewed the centralized congressional budget process as a valuable tool for penetrating legislative routines and circumventing normal turf battles among congressional committees. While Clinton accepted the need for spending cuts, he proposed attacking the deficit mainly by raising taxes. This was anathema for Republican lawmakers, who were still fuming at President George H. W. Bush's decision to break his "no new taxes" pledge in 1990. Without a single Republican vote, the Democrats in 1993 managed to pass a major deficit-reduction bill that relied heavily on an increase in the top income tax rate. While congressional Democrats celebrated their narrow victory, support for the package proved electorally damaging for a number of the party's incumbents, and in the 1994 midterm elections the Republicans seized control of both chambers. Republicans quickly took up the mantle of deficit reduction for themselves. Their first strategy was to push for a balanced-budget amendment to the Constitution. After the Senate failed by one vote to send the amendment to the states for ratification, Republicans turned their attention to cutting spending on social programs. Under the leadership of House Speaker Newt Gingrich (R-Ga.) and Senate majority leader Robert Dole (R-Kans.), Congress passed a major deficit-reduction bill in 1995, but President Clinton refused to sign it, arguing that the measure cut too much from Medicare, Medicaid, and other domestic programs. When neither side blinked, the fiscal year came to an end without a new budget in place, causing the government to temporarily shut down for an extended period before congressional Republicans abandoned their efforts for the year. Ultimately, Clinton emerged as the political victor in the budget battle, and was easily reelected to a second term in 1996. Yet the deficit remained a salient political issue.

In 1997 Clinton and the Republican Congress finally agreed to a deficit-reduction package. Like the Republican proposals of 1995–1996, the Balanced Budget Act of 1997 featured significant cutbacks in Medicare spending. Unlike the 1990 and 1993 deficit-reduction packages, the measure also contained some tax reductions. The measure was not expected to produce a balanced budget until 2002. Yet the federal government ran a budget surplus in 1998 and again in each of the next three years. Several fortuitous political and economic developments contributed to this stunning budget turnaround. The most important was the extraordinary performance of the U.S. economy. With unemployment low, productivity soaring, and the equity markets reaching historic peaks, the government's tax collections surged. Expenditures for safety-net programs such as food stamps and unemployment insurance declined. Meanwhile, the end of the cold war enabled the federal government to significantly scale back its military spending commitments. Finally, a slowdown in private sector health care cost growth caused the Medicare changes of the 1997 Balanced Budget Agreement to produce even larger budget savings than had been anticipated.

But the deficit was not eliminated through luck alone. Budget reforms also contributed to the fiscal turnaround. The paygo rules of the BEA were remarkably successful in restraining Congress and the president from increasing the deficit through explicit tax cuts or entitlement increases. When Congress did adopt deficit-increasing actions, it found offsets to pay for them. For example, the 1997 tax cut bill was paid for by cuts in entitlement programs, mainly Medicare. In addition, the discretionary spending caps disciplined the annual appropriations process. Between 1990 and 1998, real (inflation-adjusted) discretionary outlays were reduced by 11 percent. While the BEA rules contained potentially exploitable loopholes, legislators declined to take advantage of them. For example, while Congress was free to exempt any spending or tax measure from the BEA's strictures by classifying it as an "emergency item," it invoked this power only for genuine disasters such as the humanitarian crises in Bosnia and Kosovo.[20]

But when a budget surplus unexpectedly emerged in 1998, with projections of ever larger surpluses over the coming decade, Congress and the president found it politically impossible to keep the lid on federal spending. The BEA rules were initially evaded through accounting gimmicks and then allowed to expire in 2003. In 1999 and 2000 Congress enacted "emergency" appropriations totaling $34 billion and $44 billion, respectively, far above the annual average of the previous seven years. A large share of this money went for *predictable* items, including completing the 2000 decennial Census. After the September 11, 2001, terrorist attacks, Congress quickly approved billions in additional spending for homeland security, assistance to the airlines, and military actions in Afghanistan and Iraq. All told, nonentitlement spending rose an average of 12.8 percent a year in 2002 and 2003.

Federal government spending would have risen after 9/11 even if Al Gore had been elected president. By contrast, the two major rounds of tax cuts that Congress passed in 2001 and 2003—along with a smaller tax cut in 2002—would almost certainly *not* have occurred. Largely as a result of legislative changes, federal taxes fell to 15.8 percent of GDP in 2004, the lowest level since 1950 and well below the average level of 18.5 percent of GDP during the period between 1980 and 2003. Bush's stated rationale for tax reduction evolved over time. During the early days of his presidency, Bush stressed that the emergence of a massive budget surplus—estimated at $5.6 trillion over the 2002–2012 period—was proof that Washington was "overcharging" taxpayers. "The surplus is not the government's money. The surplus is the people's money," the president said. After budget deficits returned in 2002, Bush emphasized that tax cuts were needed to jump-start an economy damaged by recession and the 9/11 attacks. Bush's impressive legislative victories demonstrate that when a president asks Congress to cut taxes, lawmakers usually say yes. Unlike the more politically conflicted legislative majorities that Reagan had to bargain with in 1981, however, the Republican majorities in the House and Senate during the Bush years were far less torn about the need for tax reductions. Just as the number of political moderates in Congress has declined, so legislative support for norms of fiscal restraint has evidently waned. What remains uncertain is whether future Congresses and administrations will be able to reduce the long-term claims on the federal budget to match the shrinking of the government's revenue base.

Consequences for Congressional Budget Capacity

This review of the origin and evolution of congressional budgeting since the 1970s suggests several conclusions about the effects of budget reform on congressional budget capacity and fiscal responsibility.

First, budget reform has strengthened Congress's ability to coordinate its fiscal policies. While congressional budget reform has not guaranteed that a majority position on the budget would coalesce on the House and Senate floors, it *has* made it far easier for lawmakers to coordinate their fiscal actions. Budget resolutions, allocations to committees and appropriations subcommittees, reconciliation instructions—each of these devices has helped Congress establish budget goals for the year. Before 1974, members of Congress never had to vote on the budget as a whole. Spending and revenue aggregates were simply the sum of the individual parts. After 1974, they couldn't escape responsibility for these votes. Even when Congress fails to work out interchamber differences on a budget resolution, as happened in 2004, each chamber has the opportunity to deliberate on the appropriate level of revenues and spending. As former CBO director June

O'Neill has argued, "Although the current system is well short of perfect, the Congress now possesses the tools to achieve budget outcomes that are closer to its objectives than has been the case in the past."[21] The fact that Congress has passed budgets with a range of policy objectives demonstrates that fiscal decisions are not immune to legislative control. Yet Congress's ability to alter the size and content of the budget is far from perfect. Increasingly, it is constrained by the composition of the budget itself. The more spending for mandatory entitlement programs grows, the less able are lawmakers—even conservatives who favor smaller government—to determine spending priorities. In short, Congress has much better tools of fiscal management, but its budget work is getting harder.

Second, budget reform has strengthened Congress vis-à-vis the executive by regulating impoundments and giving lawmakers independent sources of budget information. The tough impoundment-control rules that Congress established in 1974 must be counted as a major reform success, even though the shift to a more formal, less flexible impoundment regime entailed significant political and administrative costs. Reining in presidential power was more important to Congress in 1974 than enhancing the executive's ability to manage federal spending, and it has remained so.

Institutional reform has also strengthened congressional budget autonomy by giving lawmakers independent, credible sources of budget information. The lion's share of the credit must go to the Congressional Budget Office. Since the appointment of Alice Rivlin as its first director, the CBO has maintained a strong reputation for neutrality and competence under periods of both Democratic and Republican legislative control. The CBO's macroeconomic projections and policy analyses are similar if not superior in quality to those produced by the OMB. Like the OMB (and private sector economic forecasters), the CBO makes its share of mistakes. But the CBO is more honest and up-front than most forecasters about the sensitivity of its models to changes in the underlying assumptions. This is the hallmark of high-quality analytic work.

From time to time, various legislative factions have complained about the CBO's actions, especially "scorekeeping" decisions, which determine how the economic flows from a proposed policy measure will be counted against the government's official balance sheet. For example, liberal Democrats in 1994 were distressed when CBO director Reischauer announced that he would score key regulatory provisions of President Clinton's health care reform bill as tax increases, and conservative Republicans have frequently complained that the CBO fails to properly count the positive revenue feedbacks from the economic growth produced by tax cuts. The CBO has largely been able to resist such political threats to its professional integrity, maintaining its ability to promote Congress's long-term institutional interest in having access to credible, independent sources of information with which to challenge the executive and inform its own budget decisions.

Third, while congressional budget reform has made it harder for presidents to override the fiscal preferences of legislative majorities, it has also made it easier for skillful presidents to shape those priorities. It goes too far to argue, as some have, that the Congress abdicated its spending authority to the executive when it centralized its budget procedures in 1974.[22] Nonetheless, the centralized budget process can promote executive power both by effectively reducing the number of legislative veto points and by making it easier for presidents to "frame" the fiscal policy debate in broad terms that serve their larger policy agendas. Some presidents have used the congressional budget process to promote budget-balancing. Others have used it to push for costly tax or spending initiatives that contribute to long-term deficits. To the extent that the congressional budget process works, however, *all* presidents have an incentive to make it work for *them*.

Finally, congressional budget reform has permitted Congress to exercise fiscal responsibility—but it has not required it. Since the adoption of the 1974 Budget Act, federal budget deficits have been the rule. The budget surpluses at the end of the Clinton years were the exception. While the superb performance of the U.S. economy was the main reason for the liquidation of the deficit in 1998, congressional budget reform played a contributing role. The BEA's pay-as-you-go requirement framework prevented Congress and the president from using the proceeds from unexpected economic growth to create expensive new budget obligations. When the economy grew faster than the budget baseline, deficits fell.

While budget rules can shape the context in which fiscal decisions are made, they cannot create a legislative will to promote fiscal responsibility where it is lacking. Budget rules are like the serving restrictions of a weight-control diet: empowering for those with the genuine desire to shed pounds, but not particularly effective for dieters who are just going through the motions. After the budget surplus appeared in 1998, and even more so after the terrorist attacks of September 11, 2001, legislative commitment to fiscal responsibility collapsed. Tax reduction and homeland security spending became more important priorities than budget balancing. With no consensus on the appropriate fiscal goals for the new era between Democrats and Republicans or even within the Republican Party, the discretionary spending caps and paygo rules were allowed to expire. In 2004 Congress failed to pass a budget resolution, because Senate and House Republicans could not agree on whether tax cuts needed to be paid for. "The process is broken," lamented former CBO director Alice Rivlin. "The disciplinary mechanisms have disappeared."[23]

The New Fiscal Predicament

At the start of President George W. Bush's second term, the United States found itself at a fiscal crossroads. The federal budget deficit stood at $477 billion. Relative to the size of the American economy, the deficit (4.2 percent of GDP) was not massive. Yet many seasoned budget analysts feared that the nation faced grave fiscal dangers ahead. Projections showed that deficits would not disappear over the next decade even if the economy avoided falling into a recession. Based on reasonable assumptions, budget deficits were projected to climb to an estimated $687 billion in 2014 and accelerating thereafter, just as the baby boom generation began to retire.[24] After that, the fiscal situation was expected to deteriorate rapidly. The costs of Social Security, Medicare, and Medicaid were conservatively projected to rise from 7.0 percent of GDP in 2003 to 17.7 percent in 2050, leaving no room for other spending unless taxes were increased dramatically.[25]

Some analysts argued that fears about the nation's fiscal future were overblown. They claimed that the budget process possesses self-correcting properties. If deficits get too large, these analysts claimed, the government will take the necessary actions to bring revenues and spending into line. The strongest version of this argument is the so-called "starve the beast" theory, which holds that structural budget deficits will not persist, because the level of spending is constrained over time by the level of available tax revenues. According to this model, aggressive tax cuts actually promote long-run fiscal responsibility by reducing the ability of the government to create ballooning spending commitments, which are the main cause of deficits.[26] With the exception of a few true believers such as Milton Friedman, however, few experts at the start of the second Bush administration were so sanguine about the nation's fiscal prospects. In 2004 the libertarian Cato Institute (which would be expected to be sympathetic to the starve-the-beast theory) published a study discrediting its causal assumptions. The study found no significant positive relation between the level of federal spending and the level of federal revenues over the 1949–1980 period, and that there was actually a *negative* relation over the 1981–2000 period, meaning that spending actually rose as taxes were reduced. The study attributed this finding to the growing influence of supply-side economics and the resulting weakening of the traditional norm of budget balancing.[27]

As President George W. Bush was preparing to give his second inaugural address, there were thus good reasons for supporters of bigger and smaller government alike to be worried about the ability of Congress and the president to extricate the nation from its fiscal predicament. To curb structural budget deficits and prepare for the costs of the baby boomers' retirement, responsible policy makers would have to do it the old-fashioned way, through some combination of tax increases and benefit reductions.

Enhancing Congressional Budget Capacity: Possible Reforms

If Congress reaches a political consensus on the need to confront the nation's fiscal challenges, well-crafted budget reforms can help lawmakers establish and enforce needed changes in budget policies. Yet budget reforms can also have unintended consequences, such as shifting power to the executive or (as the Gramm-Rudman-Hollings experience demonstrates) undermining institutional credibility. When Congress examines its menu of reform options, it must choose carefully. Two prominent reform ideas look promising, but four others should be avoided.

Reinstating the Budget Enforcement Act

The single most important step Congress could take to restore fiscal responsibility would be to reinstate the pay-as-you-go requirements of the BEA.[28] While pay-as-you-go rules are not a panacea, they contributed to the fiscal turnaround of the late 1990s. They can do so again. Some House Republicans argue that any new pay-as-you-go rule should exempt all or most tax legislation. The offset requirement would only apply to new entitlement spending. This modification would not only gut the rule's ability to promote fiscal restraint, it would privilege one legislative faction's policy goals over others. In the long run, the most important fiscal challenge the nation faces is unaffordable entitlement spending. But in the short to medium run, the most important challenge is unaffordable tax cuts. To be politically effective and sustainable, budget reforms must be seen as balanced and equitable.[29] This requires that tax cuts and entitlements face the same procedural restraints.

Using Alternative Frameworks to Analyze Budget Prospects

A second sound reform idea is to change the informational context of fiscal policy debates. Congress's budget decisions are largely the product of the information contained in official budget baselines. While the baseline concept ensures that lawmakers work off the same page when making budget decisions, there is more than one way to measure resource flows over time. In recent years, policy analysts have emphasized two alternative frameworks for measuring the government's financial position. The first is accrual accounting. Under the government's regular cash-based accounting system, the costs of long-term policy commitments such as pensions or environmental cleanup programs are recognized when bills actually come due. Under accrual accounting, by contrast, these costs are recognized in the years when the liabilities are incurred (e.g., during the years when a worker's retirement benefits are being earned), rather than when the benefits are actually paid. Accrual accounting can provide decision makers with better information about the future costs of long-term policy commitments.

The second alternative framework is generational accounting. One of the problems with focusing on the government's cash flow is that the deficit does not reveal what implications fiscal policy has for any generation. Not only do tax and spending programs affect people of different ages differently, but the current deficit does not record implicit obligations, such as the unfunded (which is not to say unaffordable) liabilities of the Social Security system. Generational accounting offers insight into these matters by measuring how the burden of taxes and transfer payments are distributed across birth cohorts. If long-term fiscal gaps are identified, it reveals how particular generations will be affected by the required policy changes. In sum, generational accounting can be a tool for increasing the responsiveness of Congress and the executive to an underrepresented political interest, namely, the well-being of future generations.[30] Both accrual and generational accounting rely on controversial empirical and theoretical assumptions that limit their ability to serve as the basis for official actions. If used as conceptual tools for analyzing policy, however, these alternative frameworks can enrich Congress's and the public's understanding of long-term budget prospects.

Capping Entitlements

If Congress decides to curb spending for programs like Social Security and Medicare, it may be tempted to impose a rigid cap on entitlement outlays that would trigger automatic cutbacks if a designated entitlement program's level of spending exceeded a predetermined threshold. While this reform idea is more carefully tailored than was sequestration under Gramm-Rudman-Hollings, it would be hard to implement given the sensitivity of entitlement spending to hard-to-predict factors like the rate of health care inflation. A study of the limited experience with expenditure caps in the food stamp program concluded that while the caps force greater attention to issues of budget cost, they have dubious enforceability. Moreover, their implementation encourages members of Congress and the executive to engage in political brinkmanship. There is an underlying tension between welfare and budgeting, and entitlement caps do not dissolve it.[31] A better approach would be to adopt changes in the structure of the programs themselves, such as increasing the retirement age or increasing beneficiary cost-sharing.

Converting to a Biennial Budget Cycle

Another superficially appealing reform idea is to convert to a biennial budget cycle. Many critics argue that the requirements of the annual budget process are overwhelming. They claim that the need to meet the tight deadlines of the yearly budget cycle crowd out other important legislative activities. If the budget process were converted to a two-year cycle in which substantive legislation were considered the first year and spending bills the second, supporters argue, it would allow Congress to spend more time on long-term planning. While it might be worth experimenting with a two-year budget schedule for some programs with multiyear time horizons—such as military procurement accounts—Congress should not abandon the traditional annual budget cycle lightly. While Congress would still hold the purse strings, biennial budgeting could weaken its ability to control agencies through the appropriations process.

It might also make it harder for Congress to adjust to changing budgetary and economic conditions. By the second year of the biennium, the economic and technical assumptions underlying a two-year budget resolution would likely require extensive changes. If Congress takes the time to make the necessary revisions, much of the efficiency gains from the shift to a biennial budget cycle would be lost. If it fails to do so, however, the information and estimates that policy makers use would become unreliable.

Requiring the President to Sign Budget Resolutions

Congress should not transform the budget resolution from a concurrent resolution (on which the president's signature is not required) into a statute. To be sure, there are reasonable arguments for this proposed change. Because the president has no say over the content of budget resolutions, some experts argue, the two branches follow separate fiscal tracks and often fail to take into account each other's priorities, leading to intense political conflicts over the budget at the end of the year. They contend that subjecting budget resolutions to presidential approval would encourage the two branches to resolve budget conflicts early and reduce uncertainties for agencies. Yet making the president a signatory to a joint budget resolution might not make it any easier for Congress and the executive to resolve conflicts. If disagreements delayed the resolution, legislative action on regular appropriations bills and other matters could stall as well. As Robert J. Greenstein of the Center for Budget and Policy Priorities notes, "Even under current procedures, concurrent budget resolutions that do not require Presidential approval often are not passed by May 15. Requiring the President to sign the resolution would lengthen this process, especially when Congress and the President start from widely diverging positions."[32] In addition, arming the president with veto power over the budget resolution would likely weaken congressional power. The point of congressional budget reform is to *strengthen* legislative budget capacity, not to render the Congress less potent.

Giving Presidents Expedited Rescission Authority

Another reform approach that could lead to an undesirable shift in power to the president would be to create a new executive spending control device to replace the line-item veto (which the Supreme Court invalidated in 1998). One variant would be to give the president "expedited rescission" authority, which would require Congress to vote on the president's proposed cancellations of spending items and targeted tax breaks. Supporters argue that this procedure would serve as a way to root out waste and abuse in the budget. Yet presidents may end up using this expedited rescission authority to strengthen their bargaining position in budget negotiations. The budgets produced under such a regime would not necessarily be any smaller, they would simply be more closely tailored to presidential priorities than legislative ones.

Conclusion

Even if Congress adopts well-designed reforms of the budget process, procedural improvements will not solve the nation's fiscal challenges. Only sound policy decisions can accomplish that. For those who value responsible budgeting, the issue is not whether the United States will be a high tax-and-spend or a low tax-and-spend nation in the twenty-first century. That is a question that is best decided through electoral contestation, partisan competition, and political deliberation. The crucial issue is whether the United States will become a nation simultaneously committed to high federal spending (because of the rising costs of entitlement programs) and low taxation (because of a political unwillingness to make the necessary sacrifices in current consumption to avoid imposing a huge debt on future generations). Avoiding this politically seductive yet economically dangerous path will not only test the technical skill of budget analysts, it will also test the quality of the nation's political leadership and the capacity of Congress and the executive to work together to ensure a fiscally sustainable future.

Notes

1. Allen Schick, *The Capacity to Budget* (Washington, D.C.: Urban Institute, 1990), 12.
2. For a full statement, see Eric M. Patashnik, "Ideas, Inheritances, and the Dynamics of Budgetary Change," *Governance* (April 1999): 147–174.
3. Aaron Wildavsky, *The Politics of the Budgetary Process* (Boston: Little Brown, 1964).
4. Paul E. Peterson, "The New Politics of Deficits," in *The New Direction in American Politics,* edited by John E. Chubb and Paul E. Peterson (Washington, D.C.: The Brookings Institution, 1985), 365–398.
5. *Congressional Quarterly Almanac—1973* (Washington, D.C.: CQ Press, 1974), 255.
6. Under the 1974 Budget Act, the president may delay temporarily the release of appropriated funds—an action known as a "deferral." Deferrals take effect automatically unless either chamber passes a disapproval resolution. If a president wishes to eliminate spending authority permanently (an action known as a "rescission"), he must receive Congress's permission. If Congress does not grant such permission within forty-five days, the president is obligated to release the funds.
7. The budget resolution specifies aggregate levels of both new budget authority (the amount of future spending that may be committed) and outlays (the amount actually spent this year).
8. Stephen Skowronek, *The Politics Presidents Make: Leadership from John Adams to George Bush* (Cambridge, Mass.: Harvard University Press, 1993), 423.
9. Joseph White and Aaron Wildavsky, *The Deficit and the Public Interest: The Search for Responsible Budgeting in the 1980s* (Berkeley: University of California Press, 1989), 155.
10. Initially, sequestration orders were to be carried out by the comptroller general, an official accountable to Congress. In 1986 the Supreme Court held in *Bowsher v.*

Synar that this arrangement unconstitutionally violated the separation of powers. In 1987 the act was modified to give the OMB director sole authority to carry out sequestration orders.

11. Quoted in Irene S. Rubin, *Balancing the Federal Budget: Eating the Seed Corn or Trimming the Herds?* (New York: Chatham House, 2003), 7–8.

12. Ibid., 12.

13. Alan Jay Abramson, "Responsive Budgeting: The Accommodation of Federal Budgeting to Different Programs and Spending Regimes" (Ph.D. diss., Yale University, December 1990), 71.

14. Allen Schick, "The Majority Rules," *Brookings Review* (winter 1996): 42.

15. See Paul Pierson, "The Deficit and the Politics of Domestic Reform," in *The Social Divide: Political Parties and the Future of Activist Government,* edited by Margaret Weir (Washington, D.C.: The Brookings Institution Press, 1998), 126–180.

16. John W. Ellwood, "Budget Control in a Redistributive Environment," in *Making Economic Policy in Congress,* edited by Allen Schick (Washington, D.C.: American Enterprise Institute, 1983), 88.

17. The data is taken from John J. Coleman, *Party Decline in America: Policy, Politics, and the Fiscal State* (Princeton, N.J.: Princeton University Press, 1996), Table 3.1, 75.

18. David W. Brady and Craig Volden, *Revolving Gridlock: Politics and Policy from Carter to Clinton* (Boulder, Colo.: Westview Press, 1998), 56.

19. Theda Skocpol, *Boomerang: Clinton's Health Security Effort and the Turn against Government in U.S. Politics* (New York: Norton, 1996), 67.

20. Robert D. Reischauer, "The Dawning of a New Era," in *Setting National Priorities: The 2000 Election and Beyond,* edited by Henry J. Aaron and Robert D. Reischauer (Washington, D.C., 1999), 5.

21. Statement of June E. O'Neill, director, Congressional Budget Office, before the Subcommittee on Legislative and Budget Process and the Subcommittee on Rules and Organization of the House Committee on Rules, U.S. House of Representatives, July 13, 1995, at http://www.cbo.gov/showdoc.cfm?index = 5500&sequence=0.

22. See for example Louis Fisher, *Congressional Abdication on War and Spending* (College Station, Tex.: Texas A&M University Press, 2000).

23. Richard E. Cohen, Kirk Victor, and David Baumann, "The State of Congress," *National Journal,* January 9, 2004.

24. Alice Rivlin and Isabel Sawhill, eds., *Restoring Fiscal Sanity: How to Balance the Budget* (Washington, D.C.: The Brookings Institution Press, 2004), 3.

25. Ibid., 4.

26. Milton Friedman, "What Every American Wants," *Wall Street Journal,* January 20, 2003.

27. William A. Niskanen and Peter Van Doren, "Some Intriguing Findings about Federal Spending," paper presented at the annual meeting of the Public Choice Society, Baltimore, Maryland, March 11–14, 2004.

28. This discussion of reform options leans heavily on the following sources. "Reforming the Federal Budget Process," statement of Douglas Holtz-Eakin, director of the Congressional Budget Office, before the Subcommittee on Legislative

and Budget Process, Committee on Rules, U.S. House of Representatives, March 23, 2004; Rudolph G. Penner, *Repairing the Congressional Budget Process* (Washington, D.C.: Urban Institute, 2002); Allen Schick, *The Federal Budget,* rev. ed. (Washington, D.C. The Brookings Institution), 2000; and Alan J. Auerbach et al., "Budget Blues: The Fiscal Outlook and Options for Reform," in *Agenda for the Nation,* edited by Henry J. Aaron, James M. Lindsay, and Pietro S. Nivola (Washington, D.C.: The Brookings Institution Press, 2003).

29. One smaller issue that requires attention in any revision of the BEA is an exemption for any spending or revenue legislation declared to be an emergency requirement by the president and Congress. Such an exemption is required to give policy makers the flexibility to adjust to unforeseen events, but if there are no limits on permissible exemptions it creates incentives to game the system. One way to strike a balance would be to set a limit on the amount of funding that could be designated as an emergency requirement, based on annual average levels of emergency spending in previous years. Alternatively, policy makers could agree upon a strict statutory definition of emergencies to guide policy actions.

30. Generational accounting methods have not yet penetrated legislative debates, but have recently begun to appear in the communications of the Social Security Board of Trustees. See, for example, the statement of Thomas R. Saving, public trustee of the Social Security Board of Trustees before the Senate Special Committee on Aging, July 23, 2003. On the politics of Social Security financing more generally, see Eric M. Patashnik, *Putting Trust in the U.S. Budget: Federal Trust Funds and the Politics of Commitment* (Cambridge, U.K.: Cambridge University Press, 2000), chapter 4.

31. Ronald F. King, *Budgeting Entitlements: The Politics of Food Stamps* (Washington, D.C.: Georgetown University Press, 2000).

32. Robert J. Greenstein, "Changing the Budget Resolution to a Joint Resolution That Is Signed into Law," Report of the Center for Budget and Policy Priorities, Washington, D.C., May 7, 2000.

Bibliography

Patashnik, Eric. *Putting Trust in the US Budget: Federal Trust Funds and the Politics of Commitment.* New York: Cambridge University Press, 2000. Explains the budget rules governing long-term programs such as Social Security and Medicare.

Rivlin, Alice M., and Isabel Sawhill, *Restoring Fiscal Sanity 2005.* Washington, D.C.: The Brookings Institution Press, 2005. A sober analysis of the nation's current fiscal challenges.

Schick, Allen. *The Federal Budget: Politics, Policy, Process.* Washington, D.C.: The Brookings Institution Press, 1995. A definitive primer on congressional budget rules and procedures.

Wildavsky, Aaron. *The Politics of the Budgetary Process.* Boston: Little, Brown, 1964. A modern classic that describes legislative-executive bargaining over fiscal matters as an incremental process in which last year's budget is the most important determinant of current decisions.

14

ADVICE AND CONSENT: COOPERATION AND CONFLICT IN THE APPOINTMENT OF FEDERAL JUDGES

Forrest Maltzman

O N SEPTEMBER 4, 2003, MIGUEL ESTRADA, NOMINATED BY President George W. Bush for a lifetime seat on the U.S. Court of Appeals for the District of Columbia, gave up his quest for confirmation. In a letter to the president, Estrada asked that his nomination be withdrawn: "I believe that the time has come to return my full attention to the practice of law and to regain the ability to make long-term plans for my family."[1] The letter came after a two-year struggle for confirmation, a period during which Democrats had exploited Senate rules seven times to block consideration of Estrada's appointment. Noting that a majority of the Senate wanted to see Estrada confirmed, President Bush laid the blame squarely on the shoulders of the Democratic representatives, who had filibustered the appointment. "Mr. Estrada," the president charged, "received disgraceful treatment at the hands of forty-five United States senators."

Within months after Estrada's withdrawal, President Bush used his power to make temporary recess appointments and placed two nominees on the federal appellate bench whose confirmation votes had been blocked by Senate Democrats.[2] Bush justified such rare use of the recess-appointment power by charging that "a minority of Democratic senators has been using unprecedented obstructionist tactics to prevent him and other qualified individuals from receiving up-or-down votes. . . . Their tactics are inconsistent with the Senate's constitutional responsibility and are hurting our judicial system." Such actions, Minority Leader Tom Daschle (D-S.Dak.) shot back on the Senate floor, "not only poison the nomination process, but they strike at the heart of the principle of checks and balances that is one of the pillars of the American democracy."[3] Daschle, with the support of the Senate Democratic Caucus, threatened to block all future judicial nominations unless the White House guaranteed that it would make no more recess appointments.[4]

Although Estrada may have felt that he was being singled out for mistreatment by the U.S. Senate, he was just one of many casualties in the battles waged in recent years over the process of advice and consent. This chapter explores the politics of judicial selection, focusing on partisan and institutional forces that have shaped the fate of presidential appointments to the lower federal courts over the past half-century. Both cooperation and conflict have been the norm in selecting new judges for the federal bench. To the extent that institutional forces have been a perennial source of stalemate in the confirmation process, institutional innovation may be a cure. The chapter concludes with a consideration of potential reforms.

Role of the Senate in Judicial Selection

The Virginia Plan introduced by Governor Edmund Randolph in 1787 at the Constitutional Convention called for judges to be selected by Congress. In reaction, Pennsylvania delegate (and future Supreme Court justice) James Wilson argued that the executive should be responsible for judicial appointments.[5] As Alexander Hamilton explained in *Federalist* No. 76, delegates at the convention recognized that "one man of discernment is better fitted to analyze and estimate the peculiar qualities adapted to particular offices, than a body of men of equal or perhaps even of superior discernment."[6] Subsequently, a compromise was reached in Article II, Section 2 of the Constitution: Presidents would hold the power of appointment, but such appointments would be made "by and with the Advice and Consent of the Senate." Regardless of the motives and intentions of the framers of the Constitution, the compromise embedded in Article II requires that the president and the Senate share the power to appoint federal judges.[7]

The Senate's involvement in the process of advice and consent is shaped in large part by the structure of the federal court system. The organization of the federal bench has evolved episodically over the course of American history, but its basic configuration was set by the Judiciary Act of 1789. In establishing the U.S. District Courts and the Circuit Courts, the act divided the nation into thirteen judicial districts that essentially followed state lines.[8] Because judicial districts were defined territorially, each federal judgeship came to be associated with a home state, and new judges were typically drawn from that state. Because presidents typically did not know potential candidates from those states, political and legal elite from the state—including U.S. senators—came to take the lead in generating candidates for judicial appointments. The geographic character of judicial selection became firmly rooted over time, and was even extended to the Circuit Courts of Appeals that were created by the Judiciary Act of 1891, known as the Evarts Act. Although the new appellate courts covered several states, each appellate judgeship was tied to a particular state, so that states—and their senators—would lay claim to influence over both district and appellate judgeships.

Today, no uniform process for identifying potential judges prevails across the states. In some states, the most senior senator has an informal right to recommend candidates for White House consideration; in most states, only senators or other elected officials from the president's party are allowed to participate— reflecting the nineteenth-century idea that judgeships would be distributed like party patronage.[9] Despite the historically partisan cast of judicial selection, in a few states today—including California and Wisconsin—bipartisan selection commissions generate judicial candidates for the White House to consider. No matter the formal or informal arrangements governing judicial selection in each state, the involvement of senators affords home-state senators influence over the selection of judges in their states.

Presidents, however, are not required to heed senators' preferences in naming appointees. True, the Constitution prescribes both "advice" and "consent" of the Senate. But there are no constitutional requirements that force the president to respect the views of interested senators. Still, presidents typically want to see their nominees confirmed and they know that the full Senate must act to confirm their appointees. This means that presidents theoretically have an incentive to take into account the views of home-state and other senators in selecting nominees. Until recently, senators typically deferred to the views of the home-state senator from the president's party, as captured in the norm of senatorial courtesy. In addition, the Senate Judiciary Committee in the early twentieth century established the "blue slip" to solicit the views of home-state senators—regardless of whether they hailed from the president's party—after nominees had been referred to the committee.[10] The blue-slip procedure has traditionally enabled home-state senators to express their approval or disapproval of judicial nominees. Not only did the blue slip enhance the influence of home-state senators during the confirmation stage, the practice also enhanced the senators' influence during the nomination stage. The threat of the blue slip could be used to encourage the president to consult with the home-state senator before naming an appointee.

The basic outlines of today's judicial selection process took root in the early 1900s. The conventional wisdom suggests that cooperation pervades the advice-and-consent process, since judicial selection has historically rarely attracted national attention and since Senate confirmation has only occasionally triggered open conflict. It is said that the president simply defers to the views of the home-state senator(s) from his party when selecting judges for the federal trial courts, the U.S. District Courts.[11] Former senator Phil Gramm (R-Tex.) even once boasted, "I'm given the power to make the appointment. . . . The people elected me to do that."[12] Presidential deference to the Senate over appellate court judges is said to be less common, but the process has still typically been considered free of conflict.

In contrast to the conventional wisdom, patterns in the Senate's treatment of presidential appointments to the federal bench suggest a severe deterioration in the process of advice and consent. Figure 1 shows the proportion of judicial nominees confirmed in each Congress between 1947 and 2002. There has clearly been a sharp decline in confirmation rates for both district and appellate court appointees, with appellate court nominees harder hit. Whereas the vast majority of circuit court nominees were confirmed in the 1950s, less than 40 percent were confirmed in the 107th Congress (2001–2002). For district court nominees, 94 percent were confirmed between 1947 and 1980, but only 76 percent were confirmed between 1990 and 2002.[13] This data suggests that recent conflict in the Senate over judges comes on the heels of nearly two decades of disputes over judicial nominees. But neither is the process newly politicized, as partisan and ideological disagreements between President Richard Nixon and a Democratic Senate in the early 1970s produced standoffs over some nominees.

It also now takes longer than ever for the Senate to confirm judicial nominees. Figure 2 shows the remarkable increase in the duration of the confirmation process over the latter half of the twentieth century, a measure that

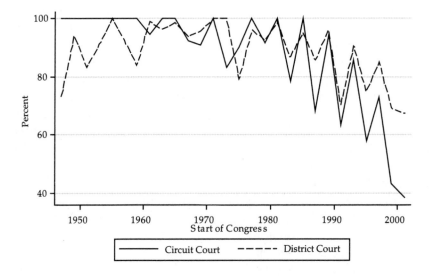

SOURCE: Data compiled from *Final Legislative and Executive Calendars*, Senate Judiciary Committee, 80th–107th Congresses.

Figure 1. Confirmation Rate for Judicial Nominees, 1947–2002

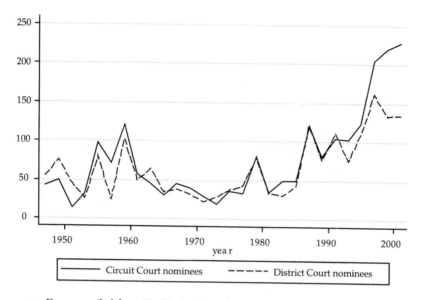

SOURCE: Data compiled from *Final Legislative and Executive Calendars*, Senate Judiciary Committee, 80th–107th Congresses.

Figure 2. Average Confirmation Delay, 1947–2002

likely reflects the degree of conflict in each Congress over the selection of judges.[14] When Ronald Reagan was president, the Senate took on average roughly one month to confirm the typical (district and appellate) judicial nominee during his first term (when the Senate was controlled by Republicans). By the end of President Bill Clinton's second term, the wait for a confirmation decision had increased on average fivefold for district court nominees and sevenfold for appellate court nominees. At least a quarter of Clinton's judicial nominees in the 106th Congress (1999–2000) waited more than six months to be confirmed. Delays in the amount of time it took to get confirmed continued to increase under President George W. Bush, reaching a record in the 107th Congress (2001–2002), when appellate court nominees had to wait on average nearly eight months to be confirmed.

Still, recent delays in the confirmation process are not without precedent. During President Dwight D. Eisenhower's last term, for example, the Democratic Senate took on average four months to confirm the president's judicial nominees. Sometimes it took the Democratic Senate led by Lyndon Johnson longer than seven months to conclude action on nominees slated by Eisenhower for vacancies on the federal bench. Disagreement between the president and Senate over federal judges has historical precedent—even if today's conflicts are more salient than those of years past.

Accounting for the Conflict over Federal Judges

Speculating about the causes of the breakdown of the confirmation process has become sport for political pundits. Many commentators assessing the Senate's treatment of Clinton's nominees typically pointed to poisoned relations between conservative Republicans and Clinton. Personal and political antagonisms between Clinton and hard-right conservatives are said to have led Republicans when they controlled the Senate to derail large numbers of highly qualified nominees. Democratic obstruction of Bush's nominees is thus often viewed as payback for Republicans' ill treatment of Clinton nominees. Although such forces may account for some of the delay, it can hardly account for it all, since the trend toward lengthy confirmation periods was well under way before Clinton took office in 1993 and before Republicans gained control of the Senate after the 1994 elections.

Others suggest that conflict over judges in recent years is a natural consequence of approaching presidential elections. For example, with control of both the Senate and the White House up for grabs in November 2000, it was natural for Republican senators to approach their duties of advice and consent with extreme caution. Rather than confirming an outgoing Democratic president's last judicial nominees, pragmatic politics would dictate that Republicans should save these lifetime appointments for a possible successor of their own party. Not surprisingly, forty judicial nominees remained in limbo until the November election in 2000, and were never confirmed.

The historical record lends support to these hunches. Since the mid-twentieth century, the Senate has treated judicial nominations submitted or pending during a presidential election year differently than it has treated other judicial nominations. First, the Senate does take longer to confirm nominees submitted or pending during a presidential election year than in all other years. Second, presidential-election-year appointees are less likely to be confirmed. For all judicial nominations submitted between 1947 and 2002, appointees pending in the Senate in a presidential election year were 25 percent less likely to be confirmed than nominees submitted earlier in a president's term.

Divided party control of the White House and Senate also strongly affects the fate of judicial nominees. Because presidents overwhelmingly seek to appoint judges who hail from their own party, Senate scrutiny of judicial nominees is particularly tough when different parties control the White House and the Senate. Judicial nominees are less likely to be confirmed during a period of divided government: Over the 1947–2002 period, the Senate confirmed 94 percent of appellate court nominees in periods of unified control, but roughly 80 percent of nominees during episodes of divided rule. Nominees must also wait longer for Senate confirmation in periods of divided control.

When presidents seek to fill vacancies on appellate circuits whose judges are evenly balanced between the two parties, confirmation battles are particularly pitched. Senate majorities are especially reluctant to confirm nominees to such courts when the appointment would tip the court balance in the favor of a president from the opposing party. One of the hardest-hit courts during the Clinton and George W. Bush presidencies was the Sixth Circuit Court of Appeals, spanning midwestern states such as Michigan and Ohio. During much of this period, a quarter of the bench was vacant, including one seat that set empty for over five years. Moreover, the Sixth Circuit was precariously balanced between the parties, with the bench roughly half-filled by judges appointed by Democrats. As a result, nominations to this circuit were seen by many as critical to shaping the bench. Rather than squander an opportunity for a Republican president to move a balanced court into the conservative camp, Republicans derailed nominations to the circuit. Once Bush took office in 2001, the two Michigan senators (both Democrats after the defeat of Republican senator Spencer Abraham in the 2000 elections) went to great lengths to prevent the Senate from taking action on Bush's conservative nominees for that court. In short, both electoral and partisan dynamics shape the fate of judicial nominees before the Senate, raising the bar for presidents seeking to engineer the courts as they see fit.

Delays in the confirmation process should not be solely attributed to electoral forces. The process of advice and consent is also affected by an array of Senate rules and practices, each of which distributes power across the institution. The first hurdle for nominees is securing approval from the Senate Judiciary Committee. This entails both overcoming potential objections from home-state senators via the committee's blue slip and securing support of the Judiciary Committee chair. These are treated in turn below.

Once a nomination is referred to the panel, both of the home-state senators for the judgeship are asked their views about the nominee. Senators can return a committee blue slip, demarking their support of or objection to the nominee, or they can refuse to return the blue slip altogether—an action signaling the senator's opposition to the nominee. A negative blue slip from one home-state senator traditionally was sufficient to block further action on a nominee. Frustration with blue slips from Democratic senators, however, led Judiciary Committee chairman Orrin Hatch (R-Utah) to significantly revise the committee's treatment of home-state senators' objections registered via blue slips. Today, two negative blue slips are required in order for there to be any hope of derailing committee action on a nominee; single objections are insufficient at this writing to defer Senate action on a nominee. Of course, even when blue slips were afforded more deference in the judiciary panel, home-state senators' objections were simply advisory; the committee chair was not required to heed such concerns.

Despite recent changes, ideological differences between the president and the home-state senator for appellate nominees have led to longer confirmation proceedings than normal, suggesting the power of home-state senators to affect panel proceedings. Conversely, the support of one's home-state senator is essential in navigating the committee successfully. Given the often fractured attention of the Senate and the willingness of senators to heed the preferences of the home-state senator, having an advocate in the Senate with an interest in seeing the nomination proceed is helpful in smoothing the way for nominees.

Senate rules are also important because they grant considerable powers to committee chairs. On those occasions when federal judgeships do not attract much attention outside the home state, the Senate largely defers to the Judiciary Committee's judgment on whether or when to proceed with a nomination. Considerable discretion over the fate of each nominee is held by the committee chair, who holds the power to convene hearings and to schedule a vote to report a nomination to the chamber. As a result, policy and ideological disputes between the panel chair and the president show a discernible effect on the course of judicial nominations. When policy differences between the president and the chair of the panel emerge, the committee typically takes longer to act.

Nominations must also make their way onto the Senate's crowded agenda. Both majority- and minority-party coalitions can delay nominations after they clear committee, exploiting both the formal and informal rules of the Senate chamber. The majority leader has the upper hand in setting the chamber's agenda, because he or she enjoys the right of first recognition under Senate precedent. Most importantly, the majority leader controls the executive session agenda, the arena in which nominations are called up for confirmation. When the president's party controls the Senate, nominations are usually confirmed more quickly; under divided control, nominations can be kept off the floor by the majority leader. Such procedural advantages clearly enhance the importance of support from the majority leader in shaping the fate of presidential appointees.

Still, nominations can be filibustered once they reach the floor. Most such disputes are headed off because the majority leader typically seeks unanimous consent of the full chamber before calling up a nomination in executive session. Such consultation between the two parties means that nominations are unlikely to clear the Senate without the endorsement of the minority party. The few exceptions to this usually require a great deal of the majority party's political capital and the chamber's time—as the spring 2005 battles over changing the rules to ban judicial filibusters attest.

So long as the opposing party retains some power over the fate of nominees—even when the opposing party does not control the Senate—the opposing party retains significantly the ability to affect the course of the nomination and confirmation stages. As policy differences increase between the president and the opposing party, that party is more likely to exercise its power to delay nominees. Given the high degree of polarization between the two parties today, it is not surprising that judicial nominations have become such a flash point for the parties.

As discussed below, when Democrats lost control of the Senate after the 2002 elections, the Republican majority attempted to win confirmation by forcing votes on controversial nominees who lacked the support of the minority and occasionally the home-state delegation. This forced the Democrats to turn to new tactics to block confirmation of those nominees they deemed most objectionable, by way of the filibuster. Although Senate majorities have in the past periodically had to fight to close debate via cloture on judicial nominees, successful filibusters are without modern precedent for lower-court nominees. Such extreme tactics clearly result from the increased polarization between the two parties and the rising salience of the federal courts across the interest-group community. Much of the variation in the fate of judicial nominees before the Senate is thus driven by differences in ideological outlook across the branches and political parties.

Presidents can sometimes shape the outcome of advice and consent. Although the president lacks a formal means of pushing nominations through to confirmation, presidents have a few tools for affecting the fate of their appointees. First, better-qualified nominees move more quickly through the Senate, meaning that a higher rating from the American Bar Association (which offers an evaluation of nominees' qualifications for the federal bench) may shorten the time it takes to get confirmed and may increase the probability of confirmation.[15] The type of nominee appointed by the president, in other words, may smooth the way to confirmation. There is little evidence that more popular presidents are able to get their nominees approved more quickly than can less popular ones, perhaps a reason why presidents only rarely use their bully pulpit to draw attention to the plight of their nominees.[16]

Still, as suggested earlier, presidents can have tremendous impact on the fate of a nominee by strategically timing referral of a nomination to the Senate. Nominations made earlier in a president's term tend to move more swiftly, as the duration of the confirmation process tends to drag out when nominations are made or still pending in a presidential election year. Nominations also take longer as the Senate gets mired in considering scores of appointees. The fewer nominees pending, the quicker a nominee will sail to confirmation. All told, presidents likely have some influence over the speed of advice and consent, but their influence seems to be exercised only at the margins of the legislative arena.[17]

Explaining Trends in Judicial Selection

Partisan, ideological, and institutional forces are clearly at play in judicial selection, as political posturing can only explain so much of the Senate's treatment of presidential appointees to the federal bench. To bring greater clarity to the dynamics of the selection process, one can assess how variation in the electoral and institutional context affects the timing and probability of confirmation.

Table 1 focuses on the fate of presidential appointees to the Circuit Courts of Appeals between 1947 and 1998. This data shows the probability that a nominee has not yet been confirmed over the course of the first year following his or her nomination. Thus, the data takes account of the two patterns observed in Figures 1 and 2: how long it takes for the Senate to act on a nomination and whether or not the Senate eventually confirms a nominee. Comparing the probabilities for nominees under different conditions provides a better idea of the degree to which various forces affect the Senate's treatment of presidential appointments to the federal bench.[18]

The data make it clear that electoral and institutional forces strongly affect the fate of judicial nominees before the Senate. In periods of divided government, there is a 54 percent chance that a nominee will still be waiting to be confirmed after 90 days. In contrast, in periods of unified party control, there is only an 18.1 percent chance that a nominee is still awaiting Senate action after 90 days. As the first year after nomination wears on, the difference in the Senate's treatment of nominees grows even wider. After 360 days, nearly every nominee has been confirmed if the same party controls the Senate and the White House; when divided party control prevails, there is a 22.1 percent chance that nominees will still remain in limbo nearly a year after referral to the Senate.

Why might nominees have to wait longer for confirmation in a period of divided government? If the president's opponents control the Senate and they disagree fundamentally with the president over basic public policy issues, the Senate majority party is also likely to be suspicious of the policy views of the president's judicial nominees. The majority party thus may take advantage of its scheduling power to delay confirmation of the president's judicial nominees. Such delays were commonplace when President Clinton needed a Republican Senate to confirm his judicial nominees. Starting in 1995, after Democrats lost control of the Senate, Republicans used their control of the chamber to slow down consideration of Clinton's nominees, particularly once the nominees had been referred to the Senate Judiciary Committee. As Democrats later charged, scores of Clinton nominees were defeated in the late 1990s not because the Senate voted them down, but because the Judiciary Committee dragged its feet so effectively that time ran out in each Congress, with many of Clinton's nominees never making it to the floor for a vote.

The Senate's treatment of nominees also varies quite strongly with the ideological proximity of the president and the opposing party in the Senate. When the parties are quite close in policy outlook, there is only an 18.2 percent chance of a nominee's not being confirmed after 90 days. Compare that to a period of intensely polarized parties: After 90 days, there is an 80.8 percent chance that a nominee will still be waiting for Senate action. After a year with no Senate action, nominees are four times more likely to be awaiting confirmation when the parties are noticeably polarized. Significant delays in confirmation can thus

TABLE 1

Forces Affecting Probability of Senate Action on Appointments to U.S. Circuit Courts of Appeal, 1947–1998*

Variable	90 Days	180 Days	270 Days	360 Days
Party control of White House and Senate				
Divided	.542	.355	.253	.221
Unified	.181	.041	.018	.006
Proportional Difference	2.99	8.66	14.06	36.83
Ideological proximity of president and opposing party				
Distant	.808	.652	.367	.367
Close	.182	.182	.182	.091
Proportional Difference	4.44	3.58	2.02	4.03
Partisan balance of circuit court in period of divided government				
Critical Circuit (closely balanced)	.613	.413	.290	.246
Non-Critical Circuit (lopsided)	.265	.111	.062	.049
Proportional Difference	2.31	3.72	4.68	5.02
Ideological distance between president and home-state senator				
Ideologically distant home-state senator	.80	.80	.80	.80
Ideologically proximate home-state senator	.313	.152	.091	.075
Proportional Difference	2.56	5.26	8.79	10.67
Presidential electoral calendar				
Nomination pending during presidential election year	.630	.513	.430	.363
Nomination pending earlier in president's term	.275	.095	.041	.034
Proportional Difference	2.29	5.40	10.49	10.68
Time trend				
Nominations made after 1980	.551	.343	.240	.220
Nominations made before 1981	.176	.062	.038	.019
Proportional Difference	3.13	5.53	6.32	11.58

*Table shows conditional probability that a nomination has not yet been confirmed at different time intervals, under the specified conditions.

be achieved when the parties are polarized, even in periods of unified government when the presidential opposition fills the Senate minority party. In the 108th Congress (2003–2004), the Senate Democratic minority was able to derail ten nominees by filibusters on the Senate floor and to delay action on several more. Given the rules of the Senate that encourage obstruction by large minorities when the parties are polarized, it is no wonder that judicial nominees are often caught in the middle of partisan wars in the Senate.

Divided government also shapes judicial selection politics in more specific ways. If during a period of unified government the president tries to fill a vacancy on an appellate court that sports roughly the same number of Democratic and Republican judges (a so-called critical circuit), no special attention is typically paid by senators to that nominee. But if the president tries to fill a vacancy on such a critically balanced circuit during a period of divided control, confirmation moves more slowly, since that new judge would tilt the circuit bench against the Senate majority's views. Ninety days after a nomination is made in a period of divided government to a closely divided circuit, there is a 61.3 percent chance that the nominee will still be waiting for the Senate to act. In contrast, nominations to circuits that already favor one party or the other face only a 26.5 percent chance of remaining in limbo after 90 days during a period of divided control. By the end of the first year after nomination, candidates for judgeships on balanced courts are over five times more likely to still be awaiting Senate confirmation.

Ideological objections from home-state senators also can derail confirmation, since ideological foes of the president have historically used the Judiciary Committee blue slip to slow down confirmation for nominees they oppose. As shown in Table 1, when at least one home-state senator is ideologically opposed to the president, there is an 80 percent chance that the nominee will still be waiting for the Senate to act over the course of the first year. In contrast, when the home-state senator is in step ideologically with the president, nominees face only a 31.3 percent chance of waiting for confirmation after 90 days and a less than 10 percent chance of still awaiting Senate action after a year.

The importance of partisanship, critical circuits, and the Judiciary Committee's use of the blue-slip procedure puts into perspective debates in the late 1990s over the makeup of the Sixth Circuit. In 1997 and 1998 the circuit was nearly evenly balanced between Democrats and Republicans, as Democrats made up roughly 45 percent of the bench.[19] The tight ideological balance led the parties to stalemate over additional appointments to that bench, even though nearly a quarter of the bench was vacant. Michigan's lone Republican senator blocked Clinton's nominees by exploiting the blue slip in the late 1990s, and the Republican chair of the Judiciary panel recognized his objections. Michigan's two Democratic senators after the 2000 elections then objected to Bush's appointments to the circuit. General disagreement over the potential judges' policy views fueled the standoff, and the conflict was particularly intense owing to the impact of filling those judgeships on the ideological makeup of that regional bench. Indeed, the National Association for the Advancement of Colored People's legal defense fund quietly encouraged Democratic senators on the Judiciary panel to delay consideration of the Sixth Circuit appointments until after the court had reached a decision on a highly salient case involving the use of affirmative action in admission decisions by the University of Michigan.[20] When appointments will have a visible consequence on the shape of public law, senators are particularly likely to exploit the rules of the game to delay confirmation.

Table 1 also demonstrates that the confirmation process moves more slowly during a presidential election year. The Senate is much more hesitant to act on nominees late as opposed to earlier in a president's term, as opposition-party senators seek to "save" empty judgeships for appointments by a new president of their own party. Finally, the evidence in Table 1 also shows temporal changes in the confirmation process since the 1980s. Before 1981, less than 18 percent of nominees had not been confirmed after 90 days; since 1981, over 55 percent have still been waiting for the Senate to act at the 90-day mark. In other words, in addition to the partisan, ideological, and institutional forces at play, there has also been a secular trend that has lengthened the confirmation process since the mid-twentieth century.

Explaining District and Appellate Court Differences

Although confirmation rates at the district court level are quite variable, the fates of trial court nominees roughly parallel the experience of appellate court nominees before the Senate until the early 1990s. Over time, the confirmation process has become more protracted and less certain for both levels of federal judges. Nevertheless, as the evidence in Table 2 suggests, in recent years district court nominees have been confirmed more expeditiously than have appellate court nominees. What accounts for the difference?

Procedurally, there is no difference in how the Senate treats nominations to the two different levels of the federal bench. Institutionally, the rules and practices that govern Senate consideration of appellate court nominees also apply to the treatment of district court nominees. Judiciary Committee consideration, the blue-slip process, Senate floor practices, and the potential for a filibuster are equally relevant for nominees under consideration for both levels of the federal bench. Likewise, the institutional, partisan, and ideological forces elaborated above that shape the Senate's treatment of appellate court nominees should also likely influence the fate of district court nominees.[21]

But the two types of appointments differ quite radically in the perceived importance of their judgeships. Federal trial-court judges do not have the pol-

TABLE 2

Rate and Duration of Senate Confirmation Process, by Federal Court Level, 1947–2002

Years	Percent nominees confirmed		Time from nomination to confirmation*	
	Circuit Courts	District Courts	Circuit Courts	District Courts
1947–1956	100%	91%	55 days	58 days
1957–1966	99%	96%	60 days	52 days
1967–1976	92%	95%	35 days	31 days
1977–1986	94%	94%	57 days	53 days
1987–1996	73%	81%	105 days	99 days
1997–2002	50%	74%	215 days	145 days

*Average time (in days) from nomination to confirmation for nominees eventually confirmed in the Congress in which they were nominated.

icy-making reach of their appellate court brethren. For one, the rulings made by district court judges are subject to review by the appellate court. The result is that the impact of federal district court decisions is essentially limited.[22] So even though district court decisions affect the enforcement of environmental regulations, treatment of prisoners, desegregation of schools, and many other areas of substantial impact, their impact is felt only within a limited jurisdiction. Finally, district court judges have almost no discretion over their docket. Even judges with an activist orientation are regularly required to hear routine cases the outcomes of which are likely to turn on the facts of the case rather than on issues of law or policy.

The limited policy-making role and impact of federal trial-court judges means that presidents, senators, and organized interests who care about the makeup of the federal bench typically take little interest in nominations to the federal district courts. Nominees to the trial courts thus frequently escape the level of scrutiny felt by nominees to the appellate bench. Recognizing this, senators and presidents have historically given more discretion to home-state (and even hometown) senators when occasions to select trial-court judges arise. Whether the intense polarization of the process for selecting appellate court judges will eventually spill over to the consideration of district court nominees remains to be seen.

Contentiousness of the Debate

Observers of the Senate should not be surprised that the confirmation process is more contentious today than previously, given increased media attention to the wars of advice and consent and the rising salience of confirmation politics in recent years. The increased salience of judicial selection since the 1980s has been pronounced both within and outside the Senate. Within the Senate, both party caucuses have taken an intense interest in the fate of nominees, especially those slated for seats on the appellate bench. Outside the Senate, dueling interest groups now do battle over increasing numbers of judicial nominees. Many point to the 1987 battle over the nomination of Robert Bork to the Supreme Court as a turning point in the involvement of organized interests in judicial selection. But interest groups have kept a close eye on judicial selection for quite some time.[23] Both liberal and conservative groups were involved periodically from the late 1960s into the 1980s. And in 1984, liberal groups under the umbrella of the Alliance for Justice commenced systematic monitoring of judicial appointments, as did conservative groups led by the Judicial Reform Group. Although interest-group tactics may have fanned the fires over judicial selection in recent years, the introduction of new blocking tactics in the Senate developed long after groups had become active in the process of judicial selection.[24] Outside groups may encourage senators to take more aggressive stands against judicial nominees, but by and large, Senate opposition reflects senators' concerns about the policy impact of judges on the federal bench.

Instead of attributing the politicization of the advice-and-consent process to the lobbying tactics of outside groups, the focus should be on three trends that have become particularly pronounced since the 1980s. First, the two political parties are more ideologically opposed today than they have been for the past few decades. From the empirical analysis above, it appears plain that ideological differences between the parties encourage senators to exploit the rules of the game to their party's advantage in filling vacant judgeships or blocking new nominees. Second, the partisan balance on the courts has been nearly even in recent years. As a result, the probability that any appointment will have a substantive impact is enhanced. When Democrats lost control of the Senate after the 2002 elections, the federal courts were nearly evenly balanced between Democratic and Republican appointees: the active judiciary was composed of 398 judges appointed by Republican presidents and 400 judges appointed by Democratic presidents.[25] Having lost control of the Senate, distrusting the ideological bent of Bush appointees, and finding the courts on the cusp of partisan balance, the Senate Democratic Caucus in 2003 made scrutiny of judicial nominees a priority, and it achieved remarkable unity in blocking nominees deemed particularly egregious. Likewise, Republicans have been extremely reluctant to grant Democrats input when candidates are generated for vacancies on the federal bench.

Third, and perhaps most critical, since the 1960s the federal courts have become an increasingly important venue for policy making in the American political system.[26] Groups with an interest in the policy process now routinely seek to use the federal courts to shape policy outcomes. Likewise, Congress has routinely given the courts authority to resolve important policy disputes. Finally, the Supreme Court has opted to reduce the size of its own docket by almost a third since the 1980s. The Supreme Court decided 152 cases during the 1980 term, while during the 2000 term it decided only 87 cases; this increases the importance of circuit courts.[27] The change is particularly dramatic when one considers that over 4,000 cases were appealed to the Supreme Court during the 1980 term and nearly 9,000 cases were appealed to the Court during the 2000 term. As a result, the federal courts of appeals are now more often the final arbiter on consequential issues of public law.

The deterioration of the judicial-selection process is best illustrated by developments in the 108th Congress (2003–2004). Minority-party Democrats calculated that the costs incurred by filibustering a few judicial nominees would be worth the negative publicity associated with such stalling techniques. Starting in 2003, six nominees for judgeships on the Circuit Courts of Appeals were successfully filibustered by Senate Democrats, as a nearly united Democratic Party prevented the Republican majority from invoking cloture. Democrats had so frustrated the majority party after launching four filibusters that Republicans themselves staged a forty-hour talkathon to highlight the Democrats' intransigence. But rather than convincing Democrats to give up their fight, the talkathon ended with Democrats blocking cloture on two more appellate court nominees. Citing the nominees' controversial views on issues such as civil rights, environmental policy, and abortion rights, Democrats maintained that the Bush nominees held views too far from the mainstream to support confirmation. By the end of 2004, ten appellate court nominees had been filibustered by the Democrats, with several others waiting in the wings for action by the full Senate.

Critics of the Democratic-led filibusters charged that the filibusters were both unprecedented and unconstitutional: "The Constitution, fairly read, clearly calls for a majority vote on judicial nominees," argued Senator Jeff Sessions (R-Ala.).[28] If the Constitution is interpreted to require a simple majority vote for confirmation, then any rule or procedure that allows a minority of the body to block a majority from casting a vote on confirmation conflicts with the Constitution. This position led critics of the Democratic filibusters to charge that requiring sixty votes to cut off debate on judicial nominations (under the Senate's Rule 22, the chamber's cloture rule) was plainly unconstitutional.

Whether the Constitution has any bearing on the Senate's rules of debate is a contentious question. The Constitution, in Article I, Section 5, allows each chamber to select its own rules. In that case, the Senate is free to select rules of debate that require supermajority votes to limit consideration of items on the Senate's agenda, just as the House requires supermajority votes for certain motions. Rule 22 in fact states that a cloture petition can be filed "to bring to a close the debate upon any measure, motion, [or] other matter pending before the Senate." Certainly nominations fall within the broad sweep of Rule 22.

Nor is there much basis for the claim that obstruction of presidential appointees was unprecedented before 2004. Before the 108th Congress, numerous judicial nominations had been subject to cloture votes. Granted, motions to invoke cloture may be filed even when no filibuster is under way. But given that cloture is the Senate's only motion in attempting to overcome a filibuster and that most judicial nominees are confirmed by unanimous consent, it is reasonable to suspect that efforts to invoke cloture on judicial nominees were precipitated by threatened or actual filibusters on the Senate floor. Certainly the filibuster against the elevation of Abe Fortas to chief justice of the Supreme Court in 1968 falls in this category, as President Lyndon Johnson withdrew the nomination after the Senate rejected cloture, 45–43. Between the Fortas vote and the 108th Congress, cloture was attempted fourteen times on district and circuit court nominations—including the appointments of Stephen Breyer to the First Circuit Court of Appeals and Richard Paez to the Ninth Circuit (after a four-year wait for confirmation).[29] What is so distinctive about the 108th Congress filibusters is that all of the filibusters were successful. Apart from the Fortas filibuster, no other filibusters of judicial nominations have been successful in the twentieth century.

Moreover, successful obstruction of judicial nominees is not without precedent—even if outright filibusters of judicial nominees was extremely rare before 2003. After all, Republicans successfully blocked scores of Clinton nominees when their party controlled the Senate in the late 1990s: controlling the agenda of the Judiciary panel, Republicans could successfully block nominees simply by refusing to hold hearings or by failing to call nominees up for a confirmation vote after being reported from committee. Successful opposition to confirming new judges is not new, but the tactics of opposition—and their visibility to the public—certainly are. And the result of such obstruction has been to further polarize the process and politics of advice and consent.

Reforming the Process of Advice and Consent

Vexed by successful Democratic filibusters of several appellate court nominees, Republican leaders in the 108th Congress advocated reform of the confirmation process. One reform would implement a sliding scale for cloture on nominations, successively reducing the number of votes needed to invoke cloture as debate goes on. Senate majority leader Bill Frist (R-Tenn.) introduced a resolution in May 2003 that would change the Senate's Rule 22 to create such a sliding scale. Frist's plan closely resembled a reform advocated by Senators Tom Harkin (D-Iowa) and Joseph Lieberman (D-Conn.) in 1995. Under Frist's proposal, the first attempt to invoke cloture would require sixty votes, or three-fifths of the Senate. If the majority failed to muster sixty votes, the number of senators required to invoke cloture would be reduced by three for each subsequent cloture motion. By ratcheting down the number of votes required to limit debate, a majority vote would be sufficient to invoke cloture on nominations on the fourth cloture motion—thus eliminating the filibuster of judicial nominations. Supporters of the sliding scale provision argued that it reconciled the Senate's tradition of extensive deliberation with the constitutional requirement of majority rule.[30]

Adoption of the Frist proposal was highly unlikely. Although the Constitution permits a majority of the Senate to establish its own rules, Senate rules and precedents make procedural changes themselves subject to a filibuster. If the rule change were to be filibustered—which it surely would—then under Senate rules a two-thirds majority would be needed to break the filibuster.[31] Considering that neither party is likely to secure two-thirds of the Senate seats in the near future, reform of Senate rules along the lines of the Frist proposal remains severely unlikely.

A close cousin of the Frist proposal would be creation of a Senate "fast-track" for judicial nominations, akin to the expedited procedures that have become common for consideration of trade pacts and defense base-closing recommendations.[32] Fast-track authority for these and other policy areas have been set statutorily by the Senate, limiting overall debate time on measures and guaranteeing an up or down vote. By creating a fast track for judicial nominations, filibusters would no longer be possible. But the creation of a fast track for nominations would itself be subject to a filibuster, meaning that the Senate is unlikely to adopt this proposal in the current polarized environment. With the perceived stakes of judicial appointments so high, the minority party is unlikely to agree to any procedural reform that extinguishes its right to block confirmation.

Majority Leader Frist in 2003 also proposed eliminating filibusters of judicial nominees through a more radical approach dubbed "the nuclear option." Under this approach, a simple majority of the Senate would seek a ruling from the presiding officer to establish the precedent that filibusters against nominations are unconstitutional. Unlike either the fast-track or decreasing cloture threshold proposals, this procedural approach would circumvent the need for minority concurrence, since a simple majority could table an appeal of the presiding officer's ruling. But the approach was dubbed the nuclear option because of the anticipated consequences if the attempt were to succeed: Democrats vowed to exploit their remaining procedural advantages and shut down most Senate business.[33] As Senator Chuck Schumer (D-N.Y.) remarked, the nuclear option would "vaporize every bridge in sight—bipartisan or otherwise."[34]

When debate over the nuclear option came to a head in May 2005, it was unclear whether Majority Leader Frist would be able to secure the necessary fifty-one votes to change Senate precedents to ban filibusters of judicial nominees. As the controversy steamrolled toward a vote to invoke cloture on the nominations of Priscilla Owens to the Fifth Circuit Court of Appeals, a group of fourteen senators—seven Democrats and seven Republicans—reached a deal that at least temporarily averted the nuclear option.[35] Democrats who signed the compromise agreed not to filibuster three of the contested nominations. In return, the seven Republicans promised not to vote to invoke the nuclear option for the rest of the Congress. The agreement contained an escape hatch for the Democrats, allowing Democrats to filibuster in "extraordinary circumstances." Republicans claimed an escape hatch of their own, retaining the right to vote for the nuclear option should Republicans judge individually that Democrats had failed to uphold their end of the deal. Given the ambiguity of the agreement, the short-term character of the deal, and the deep-seated conflict over the selection of federal judges, the agreement most likely provided only temporary relief in the ongoing wars over advice and consent.

Some senators did advocate longer-term solutions to the confirmation malaise. Most notably, Senator Patrick Leahy (D-Vt.) advocated a solution that he believed would enhance the Senate's provision of "advice" to the president. Under his proposal, senators would designate bipartisan commissions to identify qualified candidates for the federal bench. Presidents would then select their appointees from the pool of candidates endorsed by the bipartisan group. Such a selection process would encourage presidents to select more moderate nominees. Leahy was confident that the Senate would treat such nominees more expeditiously. In reaction, the Bush administration asserted that such a mechanism would usurp presidents' constitutional authority to choose judges.

A potential solution to the partisan wars that have been waged over judicial selection would be to try on a pilot basis a hybrid solution that combines elements of the Leahy and fast-track proposals. The process would start by the Senate detailing procedures for states to establish acceptable bipartisan judicial-selection commissions. The Senate would then treat nominees selected from lists generated by selection commissions more expeditiously than other nominations. If the president selected a judicial candidate from a list of candidates recommended by a bipartisan commission, then the nominee would be afforded fast-track protection throughout the confirmation process. As such, the commission proposal would overcome problems inherent in experiments with selection commissions in the late 1970s. If the president chose instead to nominate someone not recommended by a bipartisan commission, the nominee would not be protected from a potential filibuster.

Presumably, presidents would make a strategic choice of which route to follow for each nomination. If a court was balanced between the parties and if home-state senators for the judgeship were unlikely to support the president, a strategic president would probably opt to rely on the recommendations of a bipartisan commission in order to secure swift confirmation. In other cases, when the stakes of the appointment were not so high, the president might reasonably try his luck without seeking fast-track protection. By providing both parties with an incentive to participate, the hybrid proposal might be attractive enough to secure supermajority support for adoption.

Shy of meaningful procedural innovations, the only other vehicle for overcoming nomination gridlock would be for the Senate to agree on a case-by-case basis to consider packaging nominations. If senators were to put together packages of nominees that included both liberal and conservative nominees, Democratic senators would be likely to tolerate conservative nominees recently favored by Republican presidents. Of course, conservative presidents are unlikely to appoint liberal judges, so the prospects for this type of reform are fairly remote.

More troubling about this proposal is the chance that it would increase the probability of selecting judges ill-suited for lifetime appointments on the federal bench. In *Federalist* No. 76, Alexander Hamilton supported the notion of having nominees selected by one person rather than a collegial body. He argued that the choice made by one was likely to be better than the choices made by "a body of men who may each be supposed to have an equal number; and will be so much the less liable to be misled by the sentiments of friendship and of affection." Hamilton felt that if a group of politicians made the nominations, they would inevitably distribute the positions equally among them. Hamilton did not want judicial nominees filled on the basis of a logroll among politicians who each held a "diversity of views, feelings, and interests, which frequently distract and warp the resolutions of a collective body." When it comes to the federal bench, concerns about logrolls are particularly relevant, since the vast majority of cases are decided by judges on their own.[36] Clearly, if judicial nominees were routinely considered as part of a package, the result might be a judiciary stacked with extremists who individually make decisions that do not take into consideration a diversity of views about the law and its application.

Conclusion

The public nature of the problems associated with the nomination process suggests that the politics of judicial selection have changed markedly over the past half-century. Although enduring political and institutional forces help account for the patterns of advice and consent over that long period, the character of the process seems qualitatively different today than in the past. To be sure, not every nominee experiences intense opposition, as Democrats acquiesced to over two hundred of George W. Bush's judicial appointees over the president's first four years in office. But the degree of conflict seems to have increased sharply over the course of the Clinton and Bush presidencies.

Does it matter that the process of judicial selection has become so polarized in recent years? There are at least four ways in which the battles over advice and consent might have enduring consequences for American political institutions. First, the performance of the federal courts might suffer. There is at least some suggestive evidence that because of vacancies on the federal bench, cases are taking longer to be processed by the appellate court. The Sixth Circuit—handling appeals from the trial courts of Kentucky, Michigan, Ohio, and Tennessee—illustrates the problem starkly. With 25 percent of its bench vacant in 2002, the court was the slowest of all the circuit courts—even though its docket was the fourth smallest. As Michigan's attorney general remarked that year, "None of us is at our best when 25 percent of our colleagues are missing."[37]

Second, the legitimacy of the courts as a democratic institution might be harmed. Although establishing this link is difficult, public opinion polls suggest that the public believes both that politics should not shape the federal bench and that it does shape the bench. When asked in 2002 about Senate consideration of Supreme Court nominees, over half of a Gallup Poll's respondents agreed that senators should consider a nominee's policy views—even if the nominee was qualified legally and ethically for the bench.[38] Nearly 50 percent agreed that senators should vote to reject nominees if they have doubts about the president's choices.[39] Still, when queried about the Senate filibuster over Judge Charles Pickering's nomination to the Fifth Circuit Court of Appeals in 2002, nearly half of respondents believed that the debate was more based on "politics" than on "principle."[40]

Such results suggest that despite the public's view that ideology is relevant in dispensing advice and consent, there is a considerable cost to such debates. Although it is difficult to establish that the public's broader view of the courts is shaped by the media's treatment of the confirmation process, the public's confidence in federal judges is likely shaped by the politics of their selection. The fact that approximately half of the general public views judicial selection as driven by ideological disagreement and that such conflict was appropriate threatens the legitimacy of the judiciary.

Third, recurring battles over advice and consent will be harmful for the Senate as an institution of democracy and for its members. The breakdown in the confirmation process in 2004 sheared what had already been a tenuous relationship between the two Senate parties. Even before the nuclear option wracked the Senate, relations within the Senate Judiciary Committee had deteriorated significantly. In 2004 several Republican committee staff found themselves in criminal jeopardy after hacking into Democrats' computers and helping themselves to staff strategy memos on the president's judicial nominations.[41] In response, one of the Republican staffers under investigation unapologetically asserted that the real crime is the "corruption" associated with Democratic tactics for blocking conservative judicial nominees.[42] The breakdown in party relations might seem old hat for veteran observers of the House. But in the Senate—where unanimous consent across the parties is essential to make the body function—partisan disagreements have the potential to make the Senate unmanageable. That at least was the judgment of the seven Republican senators who bucked their party's leadership in forswearing support for the nuclear option in the spring of 2005.

Fourth, and finally, the cumbersome and uncertain nomination and confirmation process might impose too high a cost on potential nominees, leading them to avoid public service. That is certainly how Miguel Estrada felt, as reflected in his statement asking the president to withdraw his nomination. His future caught up in a gridlocked confirmation process, the lure of a lifetime appointment on the federal bench no longer seemed worth the cost. To what extent such sentiment is felt is difficult to determine, but the potential for discouraging promising federal judges from public service is real.

The confirmation process for federal judicial nominees is today, and has always been, uncertain. But the process has deteriorated significantly since the 1980s. The stakes riding on who sits on the federal bench are simply too high for combatants in the battles of advice and consent. Policy motivations, political incentives, and institutional opportunity will continue to shape the practice of advice and consent. Fortunately, the breakdown in the system has become so apparent that the need for reform is well understood. Unfortunately, there is no agreement over the appropriate reform. Nevertheless, failure to act threatens to harm the United States' democratic institutions.

Notes

1. As cited in Carl Hulse and David Stout, "Embattled Estrada Withdraws as Nominee for Federal Bench," *New York Times,* September 4, 2003.
2. See John King, "Pickering Appointment Angers Democrats," *CNN.com,* January 17, 2004, and Mike Allen, "Bush Again Bypasses Senate to Seat Judge," *Washington Post,* February 21, 2004.
3. Senator Tom Daschle, "Politicization of the Nomination Process," 108th Congress, 2d Sess., *Congressional Record* 150, March 26, 2004, S3200.
4. Sheryl Stolberg, "Senate Democrats Threaten to Block More Bush Nominees," *New York Times,* March 26, 2004.
5. See John Anthony Maltese, "The Presidency and the Judiciary," in *The Presidency and the Political System,* edited by Michael Nelson, 6th ed. (Washington D.C.: CQ Press, 2000).
6. See *Federalist* No. 76, in *The Federalist Papers,* edited by Garry Wills (New York: Bantam, 1981).
7. On disputes among the framers about the wording of the advice-and-consent clause, see John Ferling, "The Senate and Federal Judges: The Intent of the Founding Fathers," *Capitol Studies* 2 (winter 1974): 57–70.
8. Each of the eleven states that had already ratified the Constitution was incorporated into a separate judicial district. The remaining two districts covered Maine and

Kentucky, which were then still part of Massachusetts and Virginia, respectively. District courts for Rhode Island and North Carolina were created in 1790 after both states had ratified the Constitution. See Federal Judicial Center, *History of the Federal Judiciary*, www.fjc.gov/history/home.nsf.

9. On the emergence of federal judgeships as patronage, see Kermit Hall, *The Politics of Justice: Lower Federal Judicial Selection and the Second Party System, 1829–61* (Lincoln: University of Nebraska Press, 1979).

10. See Sarah A. Binder, "Origins of the Senate Blue Slip," paper presented at the annual meeting of the Midwest Political Science Association, Chicago, April 15–18, 2004.

11. See Goldman, *Picking Federal Judges.*

12. As cited in Robert A. Carp and Ronald Stidham, *Judicial Process in America*, 2d ed. (Washington, D.C.: CQ Press, 1993), 232.

13. For a breakdown of confirmation rates by decade, see Table 2.

14. The data includes all nominees for the Federal District and Circuit Courts of Appeals eventually confirmed by the Senate. Nominations to federal district courts in Puerto Rico and the U.S. territories are excluded, as are nominations to the specialized Federal Circuit and other specialized trial courts.

15. See Joel B. Grossman, *Lawyers and Judges: The ABA and the Politics of Judicial Selection* (New York: Wiley, 1965), and Garland W. Allison, "Delay in Senate Confirmation of Federal Judicial Nominees," *Judicature* 80 (1996): 8–15.

16. Presidential reluctance to utilize the bully pulpit in favor of particular nominees inevitably stems in part from the fact that presidents make a large number of nominations and prefer to go public on higher-priority items. For this reason, presidents tend to be much more aggressive in the promotion of Supreme Court nominees than nominees at either the circuit or district levels.

17. For a similar argument regarding a president's ability to promote a policy agenda, see George C. Edwards III, *At the Margins: Presidential Leadership of Congress* (New Haven, Conn.: Yale University Press, 1989), and Mark A. Peterson, *Legislating Together: The White House and Capitol Hill from Eisenhower to Reagan* (Cambridge, Mass.: Harvard University Press, 1990).

18. Probabilities in Table 1 are calculated using the *sts list* command in Stata 8.0. These rates are technically known as "survival probabilities." One could also use multivariate statistical models to predict the conditional probability of a nominee's not being confirmed at certain points in time. Such an analysis appears in Sarah A. Binder and Forrest Maltzman, "Senatorial Delay in Confirming Federal Judges, 1947–1998," *American Journal of Political Science* 46 (January 2002): 190–199. The first five variables in Table 1 were statistically significant at the $p < .05$ level in Binder and Maltzman's analysis. In this analysis, an added variable taps changes over time in the Senate's treatment of judicial nominees. Measurement of variables in Table 1 is discussed in detail in Binder and Maltzman, "Senatorial Delay."

19. The partisan balance of the bench is determined from Gary Zuk, Deborah J. Barrow, and Gerald S. Gryski, *A Multi-User Database on the Attributes of U.S. Appeals Court Judges, 1801–1994*, computer file (Ann Arbor, Mich.: Inter-University Consortium for Political and Social Research, 1997).

20. Charles Hurt, "The Case Was Fixed," *Washington Times*, November 18, 2003.

21. The one exception pertains to the impact of closely divided courts on the Senate's treatment of the nominee. Because district courts do not use a panel when deciding cases, nominations to evenly divided district courts should not be treated any differently than nominations to district courts lopsided clearly in a partisan direction.

22. See Lawrence Baum, "Responses of Federal District Judges to Court of Appeals Policies," *Western Politics Quarterly* 33 (June 1980): 217–224, and Charles A. Johnson and Bradley C. Canon, *Judicial Policies: Implementation and Impact* (Washington, D.C.: CQ Press, 1984).

23. See Gregory A. Caldeira and John R. Wright, "Lobbying for Justice: The Rise of Organized Conflict in the Politics of Federal Judgeships," in *Contemplating Courts*, edited by Lee Epstein (Washington, D.C.: CQ Press, 1995), and Roy B. Flemming, Michael B. MacLeod, and Jeffery Talbert, "Witnesses at the Confirmations?: The Appearances of Organized Interests at Senate Hearings of Federal Judicial Appointments, 1945–1992," *Political Research Quarterly* 51, no. 3 (September 1998): 617–631. See also Lauren Cohen Bell, *Warring Factions: Interest Groups, Money, and the New Politics of Senate Confirmation* (Columbus: Ohio State University Press, 2002).

24. Recent tactics of two leading interest groups are detailed in Bob Davis and Robert S. Greenberger, "Two Old Foes Plot Tactics in Battle over Judgeships," *Wall Street Journal*, March 2, 2004.

25. See Alliance for Justice Judicial Selection Project, *2001–02 Biennial Report* (Washington, D.C.: Alliance for Justice, 2003), Appendix 3.

26. See Kagan, *Adversarial Legalism*, and Thomas F. Burke, *Lawyers, Lawsuits, and Legal Rights: The Battle over Litigation in American Society* (Berkeley: University of California Press, 2002).

27. Data is from the Administrative Office of the United States Courts, Supreme Court Public Information Office.

28. As cited in Jeffrey Toobin, "Advice and Dissent: The Fight over the President's Judicial Nominations," *New Yorker*, May 26, 2003, 47.

29. See Richard S. Beth, "Cloture Attempts on Nominations," CRS Report for Congress, RS20801 (Washington, D.C.: Congressional Research Service, updated December 11, 2002).

30. See John C. Eastman, "Filibuster Preservation: Does the Senate Filibuster Need Reform?," *National Review Online*, May 15, 2003, www.nationalreview.com /comment/comment-eastman051503.asp; Sarah A. Binder and Steven S. Smith, "Filibusters: A Great American Tradition," *Atlanta-Journal Constitution*, May 25, 2003.

31. Although three-fifths is sufficient to invoke cloture on a nomination, the cloture threshold for measures that would change Senate rules is a two-thirds vote of duly elected senators.

32. See Sarah A. Binder and Forrest Maltzman, "A Nomination for Change in the Senate: Process for Confirming Judicial Appointees in Desperate Need of Reform," *Roll Call*, June 19, 2000.

33. Although there are a number of ways to accomplish this, it does not necessarily require more than the support of a few members. For example, one or more members of the minority party might simply refuse all requests for unanimous consent.

Routine requests such as the waiving of the requirement that introduced bills be read on the floor would be rejected.

34. As cited in Helen Dewar, "GOP Votes to Break Nominee Filibusters: Democrats Appear Able to Block Plan," *Washington Post,* June 25, 2003, A21. Although Democrats threatened massive retaliation, they would not need to block literally all Senate business in order to retaliate against the Republican majority. Inevitably, bills with broad popular appeal would be permitted to go forward while Republican policy priorities and routine, low-salience bills (such as funding for Congress and the White House) would be blocked.

35. See Charles Babington and Shailagh Murray, "A Last-Minute Deal on Judicial Nominees," *Washington Post,* May 24, 2005, A1.

36. At the appellate level, cases are normally decided by a three-judge panel.

37. As cited in Terry Kinney, "Sixth Circuit Slowest of Appeals Courts," *Louisville Courier-Journal,* January 10, 2004.

38. See Gallup, CNN, *USA Today* Poll, June 12–23, 2002. Public Opinion Online, Roper Center at University of Connecticut, www.ropercenter.uconn.edu, accession number 0408132.

39. Hickman-Brown Research, July 10–16, 2001. As reported in Poll Track, July 30, 2001, www.nationaljournal.com.

40. Opinion Dynamics Poll, March 12, 2002, Public Opinion Online, Roper Center at University of Connecticut, www.ropercenter.uconn.edu, accession number 0399912.

41. Charlie Savage, "US to Probe Taking of Computer Files: GOP Staff Leaked Democrats' Memos," *Boston Globe,* April 27, 2004.

42. Manuel Miranda, "What Wrongdoing?: Hate to Say It, But: There Is No There There," *National Review Online,* March 11, 2004, www.nationalreview.com /comment/miranda200403111041.asp.

Bibliography

Chase, Harold W. *Federal Judges: The Appointing Process.* Minneapolis: University of Minnesota Press, 1972.

Goldman, Sheldon. *Picking Federal Judges: Lower Court Selection from Roosevelt through Reagan.* New Haven, Conn.: Yale University Press, 1997.

Harris, Joseph P. *The Advice and Consent of the Senate.* Berkeley: University of California Press, 1953.

Kagan, Robert A. *Adversarial Legalism: The American Way of Law.* Cambridge, Mass.: Harvard University Press, 2001.

15

CONGRESS AND THE BUREAUCRACY

Charles R. Shipan

O NE OF THE MOST SIGNIFICANT CONGRESSIONAL LAWS of the 1990s was the 1996 Telecommunications Act, in which Congress set out a fundamental revision of the law that had governed telecommunications policy since the passage of the Communications Act of 1934. To update the regulatory framework for telecommunications policy— a policy area that includes telephone services, radio, television, the Internet, and satellite technology—Congress delegated authority to the Federal Communications Commission (FCC), instructing it to make decisions about a number of policy issues that had arisen in the six decades since the commission was first created.

Some of the provisions in the new law were fairly straightforward. Others, such as how to allocate new portions of the spectrum and how to regulate decency on the Internet, were far more controversial. One issue that seemed relatively clear-cut revolved around media ownership rules, such as the number of television stations that one company could own. In the 1996 act, Congress said that no company could own local stations that reached more than 35 percent of the nation's population. At the same time, Congress also instructed the FCC to revisit and potentially revise this standard every two years.

In 2003, under the authority granted to it by Congress, the FCC issued a new set of ownership rules. By a vote of 3 to 2, with its three Republican commissioners voting against its two Democratic commissioners, the FCC increased the national cap on station ownership from 35 percent to 45 percent. Given that the Republican Party controlled the White House and both chambers of Congress at the time, and that party leaders generally supported the loosening of regulatory restrictions, Michael Powell, the FCC chairman, might have expected little serious resistance to his agency's rule. If that was indeed Powell's expectation, he was in for a surprise. Spurred by an unlikely coalition of liberals and conservatives, pressure began to mount, both outside and inside Congress, to prevent this rule from going into effect.

Within Congress, members who opposed the FCC's action took several approaches to try to overturn it. In both chambers, members introduced bills and committees held hearings. In the House, and eventually in the Senate, members turned their focus toward the budgetary process in an attempt to influence the agency. Other members in the Senate sponsored a "resolution of disapproval," a little-used tactic that allows Congress to strike down agency actions. Still others gave speeches, wrote opinion pieces for newspapers, appeared on television, and sent out press releases decrying the agency's action. Eventually, both chambers agreed, in an appropriations bill, to revise the standard back to 35 percent, but then were forced to increase the cap to 39 percent in order to avoid a presidential veto. Thus, in early 2004, Congress passed, and the president signed into law, a revision of the ownership rule, one that both overturned the FCC's action and revised the 1996 act.

This episode demonstrates how Congress can become involved in agency decision-making. Congress delegated authority to the FCC, but then, unhappy with the commission's action, it pressured the agency to retract its decision. When that failed, Congress passed a new law that simply overturned the agency's decision. While interesting for the substantive aspects of communications policy, this episode is also noteworthy for the questions it raises about the relationship between Congress and the bureaucracy.[1] Do agencies often get to make such important decisions? If they do, then do members of Congress have an incentive to try to influence these actions? What institutional means of influence do members use? How are these strategies affected by institutional and historical changes within Congress? What are the normative implications of these strategies?

The answers to these questions reveal important insights about bureaucracy. But they also extend well beyond bureaucracy. To begin with, they shed light on the roles that parties, committees, and individuals within Congress play in the separation-of-powers relationship between the legislative branch and agencies in the executive branch and elsewhere. Perhaps most importantly, an analysis of these questions brings up issues at the heart of democracy, including expertise, responsiveness, and accountability. Because members of Congress have limited amounts of time, energy, and knowledge, they need to delegate a significant amount of policy-making authority to bureaucracies. The potential benefit of this delegation is that it allows specialists in these bureaucracies to draw on their expertise and respond to changing circumstances when making policy decisions. The downside, from the perspective of members of Congress, is that they may lose control over policy making. Thus, there is a fundamental trade-off that members of Congress face when they choose to delegate. At one extreme, if knowledgeable experts are not given discretion to set policy, then policy making might be uninformed. At the other extreme, if experts are allowed to make policy without being subject to political controls, then policy making might be unaccountable. A focus on congressional influence on the bureaucracy will enable us to better understand how bureaucracy fits within our separation-of-powers system and how this system balances the imperatives of expertise, responsiveness, and accountability.

Scope of Bureaucratic Decision-Making

The FCC's decision regarding ownership rules was unusual for the controversy it generated, but the fact that it made such a decision was *not* unusual. After all, political bureaucracies make the overwhelming majority of public policy decisions in the United States. This is not to deny the importance of policy making by other political actors. The president, for example, has the ability to set policy by issuing executive orders, to deny policy change through the use of the veto, and to place items on the agenda. And throughout the 1990s Congress passed several hundred new laws each year while the Supreme Court issued signed opinions in roughly one hundred cases per session. Yet the sheer amount of policy making done by the bureaucracy dwarfs the output of these other institutions. To cite just one measure, the Federal Register, which lists all proposed and approved regulations issued by the bureaucracy, routinely covers more than sixty thousand pages per year and has grown steadily since the 1980s.

What sorts of policy areas are these bureaucracies involved in? The short answer is: nearly everything. We can see this, first, by looking across agencies, at the breadth of their reach. The tens of thousands of pages in the Federal Register each year contain approximately four thousand new rules (i.e., policies promoted by agencies).[2] Within the executive branch, bureaucracies have responsibility over major policy areas ranging from social security, Medicare, transportation, the environment, and agriculture, to defense, energy, education, and most recently homeland security. Similarly, independent agencies—those that exist outside of the executive branch of government—cover significant policy areas such as consumer products, employee-labor relations, communications, trade, and nuclear power.

For a second, and complementary, view of the extent of agency actions, we can consider the policies covered within specific agencies. Such a focus reveals the depth of an agency's jurisdiction. Consider, for example, the Food and Drug Administration (FDA). We know from the name of the agency that it has jurisdiction over food. But what exactly does this mean? To begin with, in the area of food, the agency regulates the safety of various foods, including canned goods, plant and dairy food, beverages, and seafood. Its food responsibilities extend beyond these safety issues, however, reaching into the areas of nutritional labeling and nutritional products. As seen with its decision in February 2004 to ban products containing ephedra, it also has some authority over dietary supplements, although the extent of this authority remains controversial.

While this seems like an extensive list of policy responsibilities, it represents only a portion of the agency's activities. As its name also suggests, the FDA has jurisdiction over drugs, so companies must obtain the agency's approval in order to sell prescription and over-the-counter drugs. The agency also regulates medical devices, such as contact lenses and pacemakers; biologics, including vaccines; cosmetics; animal feed; and products that emit radiation, such as cell phones and microwave ovens. Finally, the agency has garnered some new responsibilities with the emphasis in the United States post-9/11 on preventing and combating bioterrorism. All told, the agency, according to its own estimates, regulates about twenty-five cents of every consumer dollar.

Congress and the Incentives to Influence

Whether one considers the jurisdiction of a single agency or the range of areas covered by a range of agencies, it is clear that the policy-making reach of bureaucracies is immense. Given that Congress delegates broad responsibility over policy making to agencies, it is natural to question whether Congress influences the actions that these bureaucracies take. To answer this, it is necessary to explore the tools that members can use to influence agency actions. But before the issue of influence is addressed, a precursor question should be considered: Does Congress *want* to influence agencies? That is, given that Congress has delegated policy-making authority to agencies, do members of Congress have an incentive to affect agency actions? Why wouldn't they simply view the policy as being out of their hands?

For starters, bureaucracies are powerful political institutions. They possess independent sources of knowledge, deep reservoirs of expertise, and great familiarity with the policy areas within their jurisdiction. They receive support—and pressure—from interest groups. And the people who work in these bureaucracies bring their own views and policy biases with them when they come to work at an agency. All of these things provide bureaucracies with some power to resist influence from other political institutions. More importantly, they can cause bureaucracies to implement laws in ways that differ from what Congress intended. If bureaucracies were "faithful implementers" of the laws that Congress passes, then Congress would have little need to try to influence agencies; but there is always the possibility that agencies will, if left to their own devices, enact policies that differ from those that Congress prefers.

In general, members of Congress have two sorts of incentives to maintain influence over agencies.[3] One is a purely electoral motive: doing so allows them to claim credit with their constituents and with important interest groups. To begin with, members have an incentive to intervene on behalf of groups or con-

435

stituents in order to correct agency-induced wrongs. In addition to this sort of particularized influence, members have an electoral incentive to engage in influence in a broader sense. Members can take credit for playing a role in adjusting agency actions, broadly construed, that concern their constituents. Granted, the electoral payoffs here are less direct and immediate than those from other sorts of constituency service actions members can take. But still, members do claim credit for influencing agency actions, especially when they are well positioned to do so, as certain committee or majority-party members are. In the case of the media ownership rules, for example, members who opposed the FCC's rule did not hesitate to advertise their opposition to their constituents, either by posting information about their actions on their Web sites, or in mailings to their constituents, or through their other actions.

This first type of incentive is intensified due to the attention that interest groups pay to interactions between Congress and agencies. Members of Congress may hope that by delegating responsibility to agencies they will be able to shift responsibility, deflecting the blame when groups or constituents are dissatisfied with agency actions, and perhaps taking credit for having assigned responsibility to the agency when groups or constituents are pleased with its action.[4] Groups, however, would notice these attempts to shift blame. Thus, once they have delegated to agencies, members of Congress cannot simply wash their hands of the policy area and reap the rewards of having delegated. Instead, they need to make sure that the agency continues to produce the sorts of policies that they intended when they delegated in the first place.

There is a second reason why members of Congress have an incentive to influence bureaucratic actions, a more policy-oriented reason that returns to the trade-off mentioned earlier. Because members of Congress do not have the time or expertise to deal with even the limited set of policy issues that interest them, they need to delegate. Once they have delegated, if they do not put in place mechanisms that will allow them to influence bureaucratic actions, then they run the risk that bureaucracies will make policy decisions that run counter to what members want. To the extent that members are motivated by policy concerns, in addition to re-election—and they clearly are—they need to keep tabs on agency actions.

The discussion so far has referred to members of Congress as a collective, but individual members have differential incentives to engage in activities that will influence agency actions. More specifically, two factors, or institutional positions, influence whether a member is likely to spend time and effort attempting to influence agency actions. First, and most important, is whether a member is on a committee with jurisdiction over the agency. Committees have greater influence, relative to the rest of the chamber, over policies within their jurisdictions.

Consider, for example, policies produced by the U.S. Department of Agriculture (USDA). This agency has a variety of policy responsibilities, including rural development, school lunch and breakfast programs, resource conservation, food safety, and other agricultural services. While many members of Congress will have an interest in the actions of this agency, there is little doubt that the members of the House and Senate Agriculture Committees have a heightened interest, relative to the rest of their colleagues. They have chosen to specialize in this area, after all, by serving on this committee, for either (or both) of the incentives pointed out above—they might have an intrinsic interest in this policy area, perhaps because they have lived on or near farms, or they might have electoral reasons, such as wanting to please their agricultural constituents. In either case, they stand to benefit from making sure that the USDA is taking what they view as appropriate and beneficial actions. Furthermore, they sit on the committee that has primary jurisdiction over this agency, the committee to which most agriculture bills are referred, and as such they are in a better position than noncommittee members to influence the bills that affect the agency, to conduct hearings, and to engage in other types of oversight actions.

A second factor that influences whether a member will have an incentive to attempt to influence an agency is membership in the majority party. Party members have a vested interest in ensuring that their party has a positive image overall, since their electoral fortunes are linked. That is, broad tides tend to favor either Democrats or Republicans, with all members of a party benefiting during years in which their party is perceived positively, and all suffering during years in which their party is perceived negatively.[5] Because the majority party wants to retain its status, it wants to make sure that it passes laws that will be perceived as beneficial, especially to its core constituencies. Often these laws will delegate responsibility to an agency; but in delegating, members will not want to give up control entirely, since the worst case, from the perspective of the party, would be one in which they delegate and the agency takes actions that are viewed as unfavorable by voters. Thus, members of the majority party will take steps to make sure that the agency to which authority is delegated will act as they would, if they were making decisions instead of the agency. These steps can take different forms, which will be discussed in the next section.

The majority party in Congress will have an added incentive to attempt to influence agencies, and more broadly to oversee the actions and activities of these agencies, when the president is of the opposite party. In part this is for policy reasons; policy divergence is most likely to occur under divided government, so the majority party in Congress will want to constrain the agencies under the president's control.[6] In addition, members of the majority party may believe that they can benefit from using active oversight to emphasize policy differences between their party and the president's party, and if in the course of such hearings and investigations they embarrass a president and his agency, this is a not insignificant side benefit.[7]

Means of Influence

Given that members of Congress have the incentive to influence agency actions, and that some have more of an incentive than others, what means do they have at their disposal? The focus in addressing this question is on five mechanisms of control. In the sections below, the consequences of these mechanisms are also assessed, through a consideration of how effective they are as well as which sorts of control they facilitate.

Budgetary Controls

First, members of Congress can rely on budgets to influence the actions of agencies. Consider first the idea of the budget as a resource constraint. Suppose that an agency—say, the Consumer Product Safety Commission (CPSC)—is regulating more aggressively than Congress would like. It might, for example, be pursuing recalls, or even lawsuits, with unusual vigor, at a rate beyond what members of Congress find acceptable. To pursue these recalls and lawsuits, however, requires manpower and resources. That is, the CPSC needs to be able to have enough lawyers on staff to file lawsuits, and it needs to have enough inspectors to determine which products need to be recalled. Furthermore, it needs to have the money available not only to pay these lawyers and inspectors, but also to fund the staff who will work with these other professionals, the costs associated with their tasks, and so on. Thus, Congress can force the agency to reduce the number of recalls, lawsuits, and other enforcement activities by limiting the amount of money it can spend on these activities.

Budgets also can be used to send signals to the agency about the intent and preferences of Congress. An agency might, for example, respond immediately to a decrease or an increase in the amount of money it receives from Congress by either decreasing or increasing the level of its activities. On the other hand, an agency may be attentive not only to the signals contained in the current budget but also to overall trends in the amount of money Congress appropriates (i.e., whether this amount has consistently been increasing or decreasing over time). The agency then can interpret this information over time and adapt its responses in accordance with its interpretation of the overall signal. Recent statistical evidence demonstrates that several actions of the FCC and the FDA—the number of broadcast license denials, ship notices, and broadcast inspections for the former, the number of samples taken and inspections performed for the latter—are consistent with such expectations.[8]

A related, but often overlooked, tool that members of Congress can use is a limitation rider. These are statements inserted into appropriations bills, or amendments to those bills, that restrict the ways in which appropriated funds can be spent and place other constraints on agencies. Although scholars have paid little attention to this form of influence, it has been used widely, and increasingly, by members of Congress. By one count, in 1999 alone there were 611 limitation riders in the eleven bills that appropriated money to federal agencies.[9]

A prominent example of Congress using an appropriations rider to affect an agency's policy action took place in the debate over media ownership rules. When other approaches to overturn the agency's action failed—most notably, when party leaders in the House refused to act on a resolution of disapproval that the Senate had passed, effectively killing it—opponents of the FCC's 45 percent cap turned their attention to the appropriations process. Recognizing that the appropriations bill had to pass in order to keep the government running, in November 2003 Senator Ted Stevens (R-Alaska) attached a rider with a 35 percent cap to the bill that funded the FCC along with the departments of Commerce, Justice, State, Education, Labor, Health and Human Services, Agriculture, and Veterans Affairs. Since the House already had passed essentially the same bill, the 35 percent cap would have become law if the president had been willing to sign it. After he threatened a veto, House and Senate party leaders negotiated the 39 percent compromise with the White House.[10] Still, the measure passed, even in a watered-down form, only because it was included in an appropriations bill that absolutely had to pass in order for the government to keep running.

Congress has created one other institutional change, related to the budget, in order to facilitate its oversight of bureaucratic activities. This change, put into effect by the Government Performance and Result Act (GPRA) of 1993, was stimulated by the goal of creating a link between an agency's performance and the amount of money it receives in appropriations.[11] Agencies, in conjunction with the General Accounting Office, a congressional organization, now develops a set of indicators designed to measure their performance. The FDA, for example, would spell out a plan to evaluate the safety of new food and color additives, set targets for these evaluations (e.g., evaluate 50 percent of these petitions for these additives within 360 days in fiscal year 2001), and then, in its next budget request, notify Congress whether it has met these targets. When funding an agency, Congress thus can tie funding levels to the agency's success in meeting targets that the agency and Congress have agreed on, rewarding agencies whose actions it likes and punishing those it does not.

Using the budget to influence agencies offers Congress two primary benefits. First, budgets can be used to send signals to agencies, which can then take time to adapt to these signals. Thus, the regular pattern of a yearly budget allows for Congress to use the budget not just as a onetime constraint, although it is undoubtedly effective at that. It also allows Congress to present a longer-term approach, such as regularly increasing (or decreasing) appropriations, to which the agency will eventually adapt.[12] Second, as the case of media ownership caps reveals, appropriations bills can provide an excellent vehicle for passing bureaucratic controls that might not be passed otherwise. The budget needs to be passed, agencies need to be funded, and the government cannot be shut down, so if a member of Congress can succeed in attaching a rider to an appropriations bill, he or she might be able to enact a provision that would not have passed on its own.

Of course, the budget has limitations as a mechanism for influence. Although a cut in the amount of money appropriated to an agency can force even an aggressive agency to cut back on its activities, an increase in funding is not as effective at pushing a reluctant agency to do more. This point, while legitimate, is often overstated; the budget is not purely a single-edged sword. It is true that Congress cannot force an agency to do more simply by increasing its funding, but it can appropriate more money in conjunction with other legislative directions that specifically instruct the agency how to be more active, thereby using increased funds to facilitate, rather than constrain, actions. For example, in the next section we will see that Congress was attempting in the early 2000s to force the FDA to allow prescription drugs to be imported from Canada. At the same time, Congress was providing additional money for the agency to hire inspectors, thus demonstrating that different tools, such as the budget and statutory instructions, can complement each other.

Statutory Instructions

A second tool that Congress can use to influence bureaucratic actions is legislation. More specifically, members of Congress can write laws that spell out, in more or less detail, precisely what sorts of actions an agency should take. These "statutory controls" act as constraints on what the agency can and cannot do, sometimes with respect to the agency's actions, other times with respect to the agency's policy decisions.[13]

One useful example of congressional attempts in this direction concerns the purchase of prescription drugs from other countries, especially Canada. As a result of soaring drug prices, many consumer advocates in the United States have pushed the FDA to approve the sale of imported drugs into the United States. Prior to 2000, importation of drugs from other countries had been illegal. A 2000 law, the Medicine Equity and Drug Safety Act (MEDS), then created the potential for U.S. citizens to legally obtain lower-cost prescription drugs from other advanced industrialized countries. Yet this bill also contained a provision that allowed the secretary of the Department of Health and Human Services (HHS) to determine whether or not drugs imported from these other countries were indeed safe, and the secretaries of HHS under both Presidents Bill Clinton and George W. Bush opposed loosening the restrictions on the importation of drugs from other countries on the grounds that the FDA could not ensure that these drugs will be as safe as those produced and sold in the United States.

In response to this situation, in 2003 and early 2004 members of Congress introduced several bills designed to allow consumers to purchase their prescriptions from Canada (and eventually other countries), provided the FDA had approved the drug in the United States and inspected the plant at which the drug is produced. If such a law were to be passed, it would effectively replace the current FDA policy of prohibiting such purchases with a policy that explicitly allows for such purchases under specific conditions. In other words, it would represent a classic example of Congress telling an agency exactly what it should do. The MEDS act had given HHS, and the FDA within HHS, the option to create a system that allowed for legal importation of drugs. When the FDA and HHS failed to move in this direction, Congress began to take steps to require the agency to allow importation. In effect, then, if Congress passes such laws, it will be substituting its own judgment for the agency's.

The downside of this sort of action, of course, is that it can lead to the sort of "micromanagement" that threatens to undercut a primary reason for delegating policy-making authority to agencies in the first place—namely, that these agencies have the time, resources, and expertise needed to address policy. The FDA, for example, which is staffed with experts who devote all of their professional efforts to determining whether pharmaceuticals (among other things) are safe and effective, determined that it cannot ensure the safety of drugs imported from Canada. Yet if Congress passes such a law, the FDA would effectively be required to allow such sales, despite its objections.

Directly telling an agency what to do is the surest way to make sure the agency does what Congress wants it to do. But often Congress is not concerned as much with spelling out a particular policy outcome as it is in providing more general directions about the nature of policy actions. A specific example of this sort of behavior occurred when Congress held a series of hearings on the Occupational Safety and Health Administration (OSHA) in the 1970s. In response to what it learned from these hearings, it proceeded to issue specific guidelines instructing OSHA how to go about its business. OSHA could not, for example, investigate farms or place penalties on employers with fewer than ten employees. Furthermore, Congress instructed the agency to pay for advisory services for employers.[14] With these and other similar actions, Congress acted to constrain—or in some cases, to motivate—bureaucratic actions.

These examples demonstrate how Congress can write specific laws to influence bureaucratic actions. The effect of these sorts of laws is to limit the agency's discretion, and they accomplish this by specifying the minimum or maximum amount of actions, thereby preventing the agency from taking actions beyond those bonds. Other statutes, such as the Kefauver-Harris Amendments in 1962, which prompted the FDA to take a more aggressive and protective view toward the approval of new drugs, and the Magnuson-Moss Act of 1974, which increased the powers of the Federal Trade Commission, are geared to prod the agency into action, rather than to restrict it. In these and many cases, Congress is relying primarily on its power to write laws that influence the general approach that agencies take.

Somewhat surprisingly, little is known about the effectiveness of such statutes, outside of some specific successes and failures.[15] A 2002 study of legislatures other than the U.S. Congress, including both U.S. state legislatures and cross-national parliaments, found that legislatures are more likely to write detailed statutes under certain conditions (e.g., when there is policy disagreement between the legislature and the agency), but this study did not look at the effects of these laws.[16] Detailed statutes are certainly likely to influence agency actions more than vague statutes, but to date no evidence has been brought to bear on this idea.

Agency Procedures and Structures

As the previous section shows, Congress can fill legislation with policy-specific details that tell agencies exactly what sorts of policies they should implement. Writing detailed laws, however, is time-consuming, and members of Congress are often short on time. In addition, writing these sorts of laws subverts one of the main reasons for delegating to agencies in the first place, the idea that agencies possess the necessary expertise, and Congress does not. Furthermore, even if Congress has enough time and expertise to write a law today, conditions might—and probably will—change in ways that it cannot possibly foresee today, in which case any law that it passes may soon be outdated. An agency that possesses policy-making responsibility can quickly adapt to new circumstances; Congress cannot. Indeed, for these reasons and others, some scholars conclude that Congress is unlikely to write detailed laws that will control agency actions.[17]

The conclusion that Congress is unlikely to write detailed statutes seems unwarranted, since many laws are filled with policy details. But at the same time, it is clear that Congress sometimes prefers to write statutes that are general, even vague. In these cases, does that mean that Congress is effectively relinquishing control over the agency? Does delegation under broadly worded statutes imply abdication? A number of studies have answered no. Congress has another option: it can design agency procedures, and create structures, that increase the probability of certain policy actions and outcomes and decrease the odds of others.[18]

What sorts of procedural and structural provisions might Congress put in place? First, Congress can choose the structural location of an agency. It can locate the agency within the executive branch, as it did when placing the Occupational Safety and Health Administration within the Department of Labor. Alternatively, it can create an independent agency, as it did with the Consumer Product Safety Commission. Other options include placing agencies within the Executive Office of the President, or creating government corporations. Not surprisingly, evidence indicates that Congress is more likely to place agencies within the sphere of the executive branch—that is, under the president's direct control—when the same party controls the presidency and Congress.[19] Even though the agency might be under the control of the president, unified control provides for less policy disagreement between the Congress and president than divided control.

Structural controls are fairly obvious. But procedural controls can be equally important, if more hidden from public view. The goal of these procedural provisions (as well as structural provisions) is to increase the likelihood that the agency will faithfully implement that law that Congress has written—that is, that it will make the same decision that Congress would if it were making the decision. Thus, a law might require agencies to issue specific reports that will keep Congress abreast of the agency's actions. It might explicitly require the agency to conduct public hearings. And it might require the agency to consult with specific organizations or groups before reaching a decision. One canvassing of laws and the literature on oversight identified fourteen separate types of provisions that Congress can—and does—place on agencies.[20]

Congress can also enlist the courts in its effort to influence the bureaucracy. For example, Congress can design provisions for judicial review of agency decisions, provisions that will benefit some groups rather than others or that will make an agency's decisions more open or less open to review by the courts.[21] An investigation of the review provisions in amendments to the Clean Air Act demonstrated, for example, that when Democrats control Congress, they are more likely to include provisions that increase the odds of citizen suits and thus push the EPA in a more activist direction.[22]

The goal of these sorts of structural and procedural provisions is to help increase the likelihood of certain outcomes. They are far from deterministic, of course.[23] But they increase the probability of certain types of outcomes, and decrease the probability of others. One way they do so is by favoring the same sorts of groups and constituents that the current Congress favors.[24] They also can put the agency on "autopilot," so that as conditions change, the agency also changes, in the direction that the enacting Congress would prefer—for example, by making sure that the agency always consults with interest groups that Congress favors. And while there is inevitably some trade-off involved, they allow Congress to draw on an agency's expertise, while still maintaining control.[25]

It should be noted that some scholars argue that these procedures do not lead to enhanced congressional control, but rather, because of the multiplicity of actors involved and the differing incentives of these actors, they often lead to agencies that are insulated from political influence.[26] Empirical evidence regarding the strategic use and effects of such provisions has been mixed, with some studies finding little support.[27] Still, others have found grounds for these arguments, including statistical studies and case studies that have demonstrated the ways in which Congress has used such provisions.[28] Furthermore, Congress regularly includes such provisions in law. Along with the appropriations rider that changed the ownership cap to 39 percent, for example, Congress also inserted some other procedural provisions, such as requiring the FCC to review its rules every four years, rather than every two, thereby reducing the likelihood that the agency would be able to increase the cap any time soon.

Congressional Reaction to Agency Actions

Congress sometimes reserves the right to review agency actions before those actions can go into effect. Although these sorts of reviews could conceivably be considered under the previous section, since they are a form of procedure that agency actions must go through in order to become law, they are important enough to discuss on their own. One of these is the legislative veto; the other is congressional review.

The legislative veto, which dates back to 1932, was developed in part to help Congress keep an eye on agencies, but also in part to allow Congress to delegate more freely to the executive branch.[29] Over time, Congress increasingly began to use this tool to influence agency actions. Although there are different versions of legislative vetoes, the basic approach is to allow one or two houses of Congress to reject an agency action, and to have this rejection take legal effect without requiring the president's signature. Thus, the veto provided the House and Senate, either separately or in tandem, with the ability to either approve or disapprove an agency's action, thereby allowing or preventing that action from becoming law. In 1983, however, the Supreme Court ruled in *INS v. Chadha* that legislative vetoes violated the "presentment" clause of the Constitution because they could be passed without the president's agreement, and that they violated the Constitution's "bicameralism" clause because some vetoes were unicameral in nature.[30]

Congress has continued to include variants of legislative vetoes in laws since this decision, and has sought other, similar means by which to control agencies.[31] Still, because of the Court's decision, the constitutional status of many of these veto provisions was in doubt, leading Congress to create a new method to avoid the pitfalls of the legislative veto. In the Congressional Review Act (CRA) of 1996, Congress created an institutional tactic that was intended by Republicans as a way to curb what they viewed as the excesses of agencies in the Clinton administration. Under congressional review, once an agency enacted a rule, Congress could pass a joint resolution—thereby adhering to the Constitution's bicameralism requirement—that would prohibit that rule and any substantially similar one. For example, an early (and unsuccessful) attempt to use the CRA took place in 1997, when Representative Don Young (R-Alaska) introduced a resolution to overturn what he saw as the overly stringent Fish and Wildlife Service rules regulating the importation of sport-hunted polar bear trophies.[32]

444

Overall, tools such as the legislative veto and congressional review provide Congress with another arrow in its quiver that it can use against agencies. Because they are harder to use, these tools are less useful than the budget, or detailed statutes, or structures and procedures, in setting out broad policy controls. But that is not their purpose. What they provide instead is a way for Congress to move quickly in order to prevent specific agency decisions, much as it did when it used the CRA to overturn the Clinton administration's ergonomic standards.[33] More importantly, Congress can include these sorts of provisions, knowing that it will not necessarily need to use them but knowing also that their presence may be enough to ensure agency compliance. In effect, the threat of a legislative veto or resolution of disapproval indicates to an agency that Congress can overturn the agency; and such a threat sets bounds for agency actions, bounds that agencies do not want to overstep.

Oversight

A final category of mechanisms that Congress can use to influence agencies falls under the rather broad umbrella of "oversight." In part, this category includes what is conventionally thought of as active oversight. In part, it also includes more passive forms of oversight. And finally, it includes threats of sanctions if any kind of oversight turns up agency actions that are inconsistent with congressional desires.

Congress has many traditional, active-oversight tools that it can use to attempt to influence agencies. It can conduct hearings in order to learn what agencies have done and what they are planning to do, such as when it held hearings to urge the FCC to delay the imposition of access charges for phone customers.[34] It can conduct investigations into agency actions. It can issue reports on agency actions, or request reports from the agency. It can audit bureaucratic programs. Or it can pass sunset provisions, under which delegation to an agency expires after a certain time period and needs to be revisited and repassed by Congress in order to go into effect again.

When Congress engages in these sorts of actions, it is engaging in what some scholars call "police patrol" oversight.[35] That is, it is searching for evidence of bureaucratic misdoings or, more innocuously, bureaucratic actions that are inconsistent with congressional desires. With this type of oversight, Congress is acting, in effect, like police officers who drive around city streets, making their presence known and searching for problems. When members of Congress engaged in police patrol activity find problems, they can act to correct these problems, often using some of the mechanisms discussed earlier, such as passing new laws or implementing budgetary controls. But they can also utilize informal means, such as verbally telling the agency head (e.g., during a hearing) what needs to be changed.

Although members of Congress clearly do conduct police patrols, scholars have found little evidence that members systematically and rigorously engage in such activity.[36] Police patrols are costly, in terms of both time and effort. Members often want to know what agencies are doing, but they face competing demands on their time and may not be able to spare the staff members needed to prepare for hearings or conduct investigations. This approach to oversight also is inefficient. Much as criminals might avoid police patrols by avoiding streets where patrols are taking place, or by altering behavior when the police do come around, agencies may be able to keep activities that Congress might not like out of view.

Police patrols are only one approach to oversight. Another draws upon a separate metaphor, that of "fire alarms."[37] Rather than cruising around town in their fire engines, looking for fires they might need to put out, fire departments install fire alarms around town that can be pulled when necessary. When the alarm goes off in the station house, the fire department springs into action. In much the same way, Congress can install fire alarms in legislation—that is, they can install the functional equivalent of alarms, which their constituents and favored groups can pull in order to alert them to potential problems. These alarms can take many forms, such as rules and procedures that allow citizens and groups to examine agency decisions, or granting them standing to appeal these decisions, or facilitating actions that allows them to contact Congress or go to court.[38] In the Nuclear Waste Policy Act of 1982, for example, Congress required the Department of Energy to consult with states and Indian tribes that might be affected by the location of waste disposal sites.[39] From the perspective of members of Congress, this more decentralized approach to oversight is far more efficient than police patrol oversight, and just as likely, or perhaps even more likely, to root out problems.

Furthermore, it may not even be necessary for members of Congress to use the tools of active oversight. The existence of these oversight tools, backed up by the threat of *ex post* sanctions (e.g., the passage of new laws, budget cuts, etc.), can impel agencies to pay attention to congressional preferences. In this view, agencies will automatically adapt their actions to make sure that Congress has no need to invoke sanctions, and as a result, evidence of active oversight may not be seen because Congress does not need to engage in such activity. They engage in "contemporaneous" control by relying on the threat of sanctions, which causes agencies to respond to their preferences.[40] Hence, studies have demonstrated that a wide range of agencies, including the Federal Trade Commission, the Environmental Protection Agency, the Equal Employment Opportunity Commission, the Federal Communications Commission, and the Food and Drug Administration, have conditioned their actions on their perceptions of congressional preferences.[41]

Advantages, Disadvantages, and Trade-offs for Members of Congress

Taken together, these various tools and approaches—the budget, legislation, structures and procedures, congressional review, and traditional oversight—

provide Congress with a wide range of opportunities and capabilities for influencing the bureaucracy. From the broader perspective of public policy, these tools advantage some members more than others. To the extent, for example, that tools benefit individual members, they may open up the policymaking process to a broader range of influences, while to the extent that they favor committees, they may reinforce a tendency toward iron triangles or other closed systems. From the perspective of members of Congress, each comes with certain advantages, and each comes with costs. How do members view these mechanisms?

Committees

Within Congress, specific committees have jurisdiction over specific issues and specific agencies. The Judiciary Committees, for example, have primary jurisdiction over many of the policies covered by the Justice Department; the Agriculture Committees oversee the Department of Agriculture; the Energy and Commerce Committee has primary jurisdiction over the EPA's air pollution policies; and so on. Given that specific committees are more likely to pay attention to an agency's action, which control mechanisms benefit committee members the most, and which benefit them the least?

To begin with, committee members clearly are the primary beneficiaries of using detailed statutory instructions to influence agencies. The vast majority of substantive bills come through committees; consequently, committee members are able to play the lead role in designing statutes that spell out specifically what sorts of policies agencies should implement. Especially in eras when committees play a dominant role in the legislative process, then, members of committees will assert control over agencies by writing detailed statutes. And to the extent that Congress as a whole enacts institutional reforms that strengthen committees, it increases the likelihood that such statutes will be used to influence agencies.

Committees also benefit from the use of traditional oversight tools, such as hearings, investigations, and powers to appoint political actors to agency positions. This clearly puts them in a position to play the most central role in using police patrol oversight to influence agencies. Typically, many types of fire alarms, such as those that require agencies to report to or consult with committee members, push the agencies to take committee preferences into account. Furthermore, since these fire alarms are inserted into laws that were created in the first place by the committee, they tend to reflect the goals of committee members and their favored groups and constituents. Finally, many of the threats that cause agencies to be sensitive to changes in committee preferences, threats such as the passage of new laws, or the possibility of embarrassing hearings and investigations, also center around committees. Thus, agencies are likely to be more responsive to the preferences of these committee members than to the preferences of other members of the chamber, particularly when there is at least some shared ideological perspective between a committee and an agency.[42]

Committees do not always benefit from all mechanisms of influence. They could benefit, for example, from a resolution of disapproval, if the resolution comes through the committee. Under the Congressional Review Act, a resolution of disapproval is immediately referred to a committee. If the committee fails to act, however, thirty senators can force the resolution on to the Senate calendar by signing a petition. Thus, a committee has no recourse to block a resolution of disapproval with which it disagrees.

The use of structures and procedures also presents a mixed bag for committee members. They can benefit, of course, by constructing structures and procedures that are likely to benefit them into the future. At the same time, there is an inherent tension between the *ex ante* approach of structural and procedural controls and the contemporaneous nature of oversight controls. Suppose, for example, that the structural and procedural controls work perfectly and the agency does exactly what the committee and Congress that passed the original legislation want it to do. Suppose further that committee membership changes over time, and that this changed committee now wants to influence the agency. It may be unable to do so, at least without great difficulty, given that structures and procedures are pushing the agency toward some outcomes and decisions rather than others. To the extent, then, that structures and procedures are successful at locking in certain sorts of behavior, they also may limit the ability of committees (and others in Congress) to exert power later. Thus, members of committees might prefer to have the option of contemporaneous, or *ex post,* control, while members not serving on those committees might prefer the use of structures and procedures, which is exactly what one perceptive study found when examining delegation to the EPA.[43]

Even worse, from the committee's perspective, is the use of the budget process to influence agencies. Traditionally, committees with oversight over an agency occupy a privileged position in Congress, with the ability to initiate or block bills that change agency policy. To the extent that parties can shape agency actions through the budget, or more importantly, to the extent that individual members can avoid the committees of jurisdiction by attaching riders to appropriations bills, committees can be excluded from the process. Senator John McCain (R-Ariz.), for example, opposed the 39 percent media ownership compromise. This certainly may have represented a sincere preference on his part, as many of his public statements indicated; but it also probably reflected his displeasure that the Senate Commerce Committee, which he chaired and which holds jurisdiction over the FCC, had lost control over this issue.[44] In fact, the use of the appropriations process, and the use of riders within this process, represent the most significant way in which committees can lose the power to influence agencies.

Parties

Parties, and their leaders, similarly benefit more from some mechanisms of influence than others. First, to the extent that majority-party leaders play a primary role in shaping the overall budget and retaining control over the Appropriations Committee, these leaders, along with the rest of their party, can benefit tremendously. Since the budget that emerges from each chamber tends to reflect the priorities and goals of the majority party within that chamber, the budget is a useful tool for the majority party.

Second, although committees can attempt to operate autonomously from parties and leaders, scholars increasingly have provided arguments and evidence indicating that committees often serve as agents of the party.[45] To the extent that committees are doing the bidding of the majority party, then parties benefit from the same approaches as the committees (although parties still exert more influence over the appropriations process than over authorization committees). For example, when parties are dominant, they will tend to rely on detailed statutes and traditional forms of oversight.

As with committees, some of the mechanisms for influence create problems for the majority-party leaders. First, congressional review can advantage individual members, relative to committees and parties, by providing these members with a way to introduce resolutions that can influence, or even overturn, agency actions. Second, while parties may be able to control the overall contours of the budget and the appropriations process, they cannot control all of the details such as riders within those bills. The next section describes how each of these tools can advantage individual members of Congress at the expense of committee members and party leaders.

Individual Members

Individual members, or the floor, stand to benefit most from two mechanisms of influence. First, as discussed earlier, there can be a trade-off between *ex ante* control and contemporaneous control. To the extent that *ex ante* controls, such as structures and procedures, lock in specific behaviors and actions, they limit the ability of future committee members and party leaders to exert influence. At the same time, they provide the floor, which passes the bills that can lock agency behavior into place, with a measure of influence, albeit not as much influence as the committee that first shaped the bill.

Second, the Congressional Review Act also allocates certain limited powers to individuals, or at least groups, who want to buck the majority party. After the Senate passed the resolution of disapproval regarding the FCC's ownership rules in September 2003, Republican leaders in the House, led by Tom DeLay, a supporter of the FCC's new rule, described the resolution as dead on arrival in the House.[46] Still, if the majority leaders in the Senate had been opposed to this resolution, individual members would have had additional options. They could have forced a resolution out of the committee and automatically onto the Senate calendar, without the consent or support of either the committee or the party leaders. And even if the Senate leaders had refused to call the resolution up for consideration or a vote, members could have brought it up through a motion to proceed.

Finally, the use of riders offers individual members the chance to influence agencies. As with pork barrel projects, members often put riders that are geared toward influencing government agencies into appropriations bills, and they do so precisely when they think that the provisions in these riders might not succeed on their own, either because of lack of support from the floor or because powerful committee chairmen or party leaders oppose the provisions. The media ownership rules offer an excellent example of the ability of individual members to use the appropriations process to pass something that party leaders opposed. Had these individual members not been able to include a rider about the media ownership rules in the appropriations bill, the cap almost certainly would have remained at the FCC-imposed level of 45 percent, given the support of party leaders for the FCC's action. They knew, however, that congressional leaders needed to pass the larger appropriations bill and that these leaders would not oppose an appropriations bill that contained a level lower than the FCC's standard, even if they preferred 45 percent.

Institutional Changes

All of the mechanisms for influence discussed above hold appeal for members of Congress. But clearly, some hold more appeal for some members than for others. Just as importantly, institutional changes, both internal to Congress and external, influence their attractiveness. That is, as Congress itself changes, undergoing the sorts of institutional changes documented throughout this volume, and as it reacts to external changes, the relative attractiveness of these various strategies also changes. Congress will, of course, continue to use all of these forms, since they offer different sorts of benefits; but in response to internal and external changes, some will be favored over others. This section briefly traces through these changes and their potential effects on mechanisms of influence.

Internal Changes

In the decades following World War II, and particularly during the 1960s and 1970s, committees dominated the legislative process. Of course, committees had played a major role in the policy-making process for well over one hundred years at this point. And parties, although weaker, did not disappear during the postwar era. But the sense of an institution in which most of the work was done in committees reached a peak in these postwar decades. Not surprisingly, many of the regulatory statutes passed during this time were extremely detailed, an approach favored by the committees that marked up the laws and aided by the increasing prevalence of divided government, which is associated with more detailed statutes.[47]

The reforms of the 1970s, which empowered individuals and subcommittees, led to more decentralization within Congress, at least prior to the mid-1990s. As a result, individual members of Congress became policy entrepreneurs, and could use their powers as subcommittee chairs, especially following the post-Watergate reforms, to advance their favorite causes. In addition, this decentralized entrepreneurship occurred just as activity by government bureaucracies began to expand dramatically. In an attempt to maintain influence, committees more frequently began to develop committee or subcommittee reports as "guidance" for bureaucracy. Congress continued to engage in micromanagement; but instead of writing laws that spelled out policy details, it began to write laws that instead relied even more heavily on rules and procedures to constrain agencies, using what James Q. Wilson calls "rule-oriented micromanagement."[48]

Beginning in the 1980s, and especially during the 1990s, with the Republican takeover of Congress, parties began to ascend once more. As a result, the use of the appropriations process to influence agencies became more common and attractive to Congress. Committees were still important, of course, but especially after the 1994 election, Republican Party leaders attempted to assert their dominance over committees. Thus, the strategies that committees rely on to influence agencies, such as standard oversight, also remained attractive.

The shifts within Congress, from committee dominance to a greater role for the individual to more powerful parties, marked a series of institutional changes that had implications for the relationship between Congress and the bureaucracy. When committees are powerful, they use strategies, such as writing detailed statutes, that benefit committees. When individuals gain more power, a turn can be observed toward Wilson's rule-oriented micromanagement. And when parties ascend, Congress begins to rely more on budgetary tools and appropriations bills to control agencies.[49]

External Institutional Events

Changes outside of Congress also can lead to changes in how Congress has attempted to exert influence over agencies. First, perhaps the most obvious example of such a change was the passage of the Congressional Review Act, which was a response to the Supreme Court's *Chadha* decision. Thus, Congress responded to the invalidation of the legislative veto by implementing an institutional change of its own.

Second, beginning during the administration of President Dwight D. Eisenhower and continuing through the end of the twentieth century, divided government became the norm, with Congress generally in Democratic hands and control over the presidency often residing with Republicans. This created several incentives for members of Congress. It meant that there were battles over the structural location of agencies, with Democrats preferring the creation of independent agencies, in order to avoid putting an agency under the direct control of a Republican president, or placing a new agency in a favorable executive agency (e.g., locating OSHA in the Department of Labor rather than in the less sympathetic Department of Commerce). Also, because Democrats worried about agencies that were in Republican hands, they often wrote extremely detailed statutes, filled with specific policy instructions and guidelines, and also put many rules and procedures in place to benefit Democratic constituencies, such as making it easier for citizens to challenge EPA decisions. Furthermore, to the extent that at least some Republican presidents, such as Ronald Reagan, wanted agencies to do less, rather than more, it increased the impact of the budget as a tool for influencing agencies. More recently, of course, the reappearance of unified government during President George W. Bush's first term and into his second, combined with the resurgence of party control within Congress to make active congressional oversight less common.

Third, the large deficits of the 1980s changed the incentives for members of Congress to engage in oversight. When new programs can be created, members of Congress garner benefits from creating these new programs and have little incentive to engage in active oversight. Yet when deficits began to increase, less money was available for new programs, and members of Congress (and their staffs) were freed up to spend more time overseeing the programs already in existence. Thus, as an accomplished study of congressional oversight activities demonstrates, active oversight increased markedly during the 1980s, as police patrols became more attractive relative to other options.[50]

Transparency and the Mechanisms for Control

Regardless of the internal institutional changes, such as reforms in the committee system or changes in the power of political parties, or of external changes, such as increasing deficits, the rise of divided government, or the actions of the Supreme Court, members of Congress continued to use all of the various strategies discussed in this essay to influence the bureaucracy. What changed, however, were the relative payoffs of each of these strategies. In effect, institutional changes that, except for the *Chadha* decision, were not directly about the relationship between Congress and the bureaucracy ended up affecting the attractiveness of various forms of influence, sometimes for all members, but always for at least some members. As with internal changes, external changes affected the attractiveness of the various options. And since these options vary in their efficacy, as discussed throughout this essay, both internal and external changes affected congressional influence over bureaucracy. Increased party control within Congress, for example, led to increased scrutiny of executive actions by the Republican-controlled Congress during the last six years of the Clinton administration.

Members of Congress delegate responsibility to government bureaucracies in nearly every area of policy making. Once they have delegated, however, they face a dilemma: delegation is necessary, but it threatens to create a situation in which the agencies make policy that Congress disapproves of. This essay describes several general institutional mechanisms that Congress can use in an attempt to influence agency actions, including the budget, detailed statutes, structural and procedural provisions, congressional review, and traditional oversight. The discussion has focused on how different control mechanisms increase Congress's ability to influence agencies, how different members of Congress might benefit from different types of control, and how institutional changes both internal and external to Congress affect the relative attractiveness of the various types of control. All of these represent important ways to evaluate the mechanisms, with a special emphasis on the efficacy of these mechanisms from the point of view of members of Congress. But another highly valued aspect of the policy-making process is transparency, which means that citizens can actually see how policy is being made (and then can respond, if need be). Having more transparency in actions also increases accountability, since citizens who can see how policy is being made are more likely to be able to hold their representatives accountable for these policies.

Transparency is more likely to occur when policy making takes place in the relatively more open process of the legislature than behind the closed doors of a government bureaucracy.[51] To the extent that this is a desirable normative property of policy making, then, the question is which of these mechanisms is most likely to lead to transparency in policy making. More concretely, in which of these areas does Congress play the most prominent and visible role?

To begin with, policy making is most transparent when Congress writes detailed statutes that tell agencies exactly what to do. Committees issue reports, floor speeches are given and then published, debates are held in the open chamber, and votes are public and recorded. Similarly, when Congress relies on the budget process, and on riders, the public can see ahead of time what sorts of constraints are placed on agencies. In each case, the entire process is open to public scrutiny. Of course, in reality it is more complicated than this, with certain aspects of congressional action (e.g., negotiations within committee chambers) taking place behind closed doors, or with items buried deep within bills, but there is little question that this is the most open and transparent way for Congress to influence agencies.

The use of structures and procedures, congressional review or legislative vetoes, and oversight offers less transparency. In the case of structures and procedures, for example, Congress sets broad parameters, and then the agency makes decisions within those parameters. These parameters can lead to policy biases, but these biases tend not to be very visible to constituents (although interest groups are certainly aware of them), nor are the policies themselves debated in, or passed by Congress. Congressional review is different in that it highlights a specific decision that an agency has made, but this review occurs after the fact. That is, Congress first delegates to an agency, then the agency issues a rule. If that rule attracts congressional attention, as the media ownership rule did, then we get a great deal of transparency as the legislature attempts to disapprove of the rule. But otherwise, most bureaucratic decisions are made in the agency, out of the public's view. The use of oversight is similar, in that agencies first make decisions and then Congress responds. With police patrols, at least congressional action is active, and draws attention to bureaucratic actions. But to the extent that fire alarms are used, long periods of time, and large numbers of decisions go by without Congress taking any action, especially if the agency is acting in accord with congressional desires.

Transparency, then, is an attainable goal. Yet to the extent that it is a desirable goal, it conflicts with another valuable normative goal, which is to draw on bureaucratic expertise in order to make "good" policy. Congress delegates to agencies in part to draw on the expertise of these agencies, so when Congress instead gives agencies precise instructions about what to do and how to spend funds, it is not allowing agencies to draw on this valuable resource of expertise. Alternatively, when Congress permits agencies broad discretion to set policy, it reduces the amount of transparency in the policy making process, and potentially also the accountability for policy outcomes and decisions. The ongoing goal for Congress, then, is to find a way to balance these competing needs for transparency, accountability, and expertise.

Notes

*I would like to thank Sarah Binder, Paul Quirk, Forrest Maltzman, and especially Eric Patashnik for helpful comments and advice.

1. *Bureaucracy* is used here to denote both executive branch agencies (e.g., the Department of Energy) and independent regulatory agencies (e.g., the Federal Communications Commission). The terms "bureaucracy" and "agency" will be used interchangeably throughout this chapter in reference to those bureaucratic institutions involved in politics.
2. Clyde Wayne Crews Jr., *Ten Thousand Commandments: An Annual Snapshot of the Federal Regulatory State* (Washington, D.C.: Cato Institute, 2004).
3. For arguments that members do not have the incentive to control bureaucratic policy-making, see Fiorina, "Congressional Control of the Bureaucracy," and Moe, "The Politics of Bureaucratic Structure."
4. Morris P. Fiorina, "The Case of the Vanishing Marginals: The Bureaucracy Did It," *American Political Science Review* 71 (1977): 177–181.

5. Gary Cox and Mathew D. McCubbins, *Legislative Leviathan: Party Government in the House* (Berkeley: University of California Press, 1993).

6. Epstein and O'Halloran, *Delegating Powers*.

7. Seymour Scher, "Conditions for Legislative Control," *Journal of Politics* 25 (August 1963): 526–51.

8. Daniel P. Carpenter, "Adaptive Signal Processing, Hierarchy, and Budgetary Control in Federal Regulation," *American Political Science Review* 90, no. 2 (1996): 283–303.

9. These riders can be broad (e.g., telling multiple agencies that they cannot use any funds to prepare for implementation of the Kyoto Protocol) or exceedingly narrow and specific (e.g., telling the Fish and Wildlife Service that it cannot use funds to block a permit from the U.S. Army Corps of Engineers to the City of Lake Jackson, Texas, for the purpose of building a public golf course between the Brazos River and Highway 322). See Jason MacDonald, "Congressional Oversight Still Overlooked?: Limitations Riders in Appropriations Legislation," unpublished manuscript, Kent State University, Kent, Ohio, 2004.

10. The 35 percent standard would have forced Viacom, which owns CBS and UPN, and News Corp., which owns Fox and other local stations, to sell some of their stations. Viacom and News Corp. each reached just under 39 percent of the national audience. General Electric, which owns NBC, reaches approximately 35 percent, and Walt Disney, which owns ABC, reaches around 25 percent.

11. B. Guy Peters, "Federal Bureaucracy and Public Management," in *Developments in American Politics 4*, edited by Gillian Peele et al. (New York: Palgrave, 2002).

12. Carpenter, "Adaptive Signal Processing."

13. John D. Huber, Charles R. Shipan, and Madelaine Pfahler, "Legislatures and Statutory Control of Bureaucracy," *American Journal of Political Science* 45, no. 2 (2001): 330–345.

14. Graham K. Wilson, *The Politics of Safety and Health*: Occupational Safety and Health in the United States and Britain (Oxford, U.K., and New York: Oxford University Press, 1985); Wilson, *Bureaucracy*.

15. Kenneth J. Meier, *Politics and the Bureaucracy: Policymaking in the Fourth Branch of Government*, 3rd ed. (Pacific Grove, Calif.: Brooks/Cole, 1993).

16. Huber and Shipan, *Deliberate Discretion?*

17. Moe, "The Politics of Bureaucratic Structure"; Terry M. Moe and Michael Caldwell, "The Institutional Foundations of Democratic Government: A Comparison of Presidential and Parliamentary Systems," *Journal of Institutional and Theoretical Economics* 150 (1994): 171–195.

18. Mathew D. McCubbins, Roger G. Noll, and Barry R. Weingast, "Structure and Process, Politics and Policy: Administrative Arrangements and the Political Control of Agencies," *Virginia Law Review* 75 (1989): 431–482.

19. Epstein and O'Halloran, *Delegating Powers*.

20. Ibid.

21. Shipan, *Designing Judicial Review*; Charles R. Shipan, "Interest Groups, Judicial Review, and the Origins of Broadcast Regulation," *Administrative Law Review* 49, no. 3 (1997): 549–584; Charles R. Shipan, "The Legislative Design of Judicial Review: A Formal Analysis," *Journal of Theoretical Politics* 12, no. 3 (2000): 269–304.

22. Joseph P. Smith, "Congressional Manipulation of Judicial Policymaking: Judicial Review under the Clean Air Act," *Legislative Studies Quarterly,* forthcoming.

23. For example, agencies are required to invite and pay attention to comments on proposed rules. Yet in the case of media ownership rules, one study found that 97 percent of the eighteen thousand statements filed electronically with the FCC opposed raising the ownership cap. Clearly, the agency was not bound by these opinions; but they certainly facilitated, and fed, the opposition that arose after the agency voted. John Nichols and Robert W. McChesney, "FCC: Public Be Damned," *The Nation,* June 2, 2003. Available at: http://www.thenation.com/doc.mhtml?i 20030602&s =nichols.

24. McCubbins, Noll, and Weingast, "Structure and Process, Politics and Policy."

25. Kathleen M. Bawn, "Political Control versus Expertise: Congressional Choices about Administrative Procedures," *American Political Science Review* 89 (1995): 62–73.

26. Moe, "The Politics of Bureaucratic Structure."

27. Steven J. Balla, "Legislative Organization and Congressional Review of Agency Regulations," *Journal of Law, Economics, and Organization* 16, no. 2 (2000): 424–48; David C. Nixon, Robert M. Howard, and Jeff R. DeWitt, "With Friends Like These: Rule-Making Comment Submissions to the Securities and Exchange Commission," *Journal of Public Administration Research and Theory* 12, no. 1 (2002): 59–76.

28. Epstein and O'Halloran, *Delegating Powers;* Matthew Potoski, "Designing Bureaucratic Performance: Administrative Procedures and Agency Policy Choice," *State Politics and Policy Quarterly* 2 (2002): 1–23; Bawn, "Political Control versus Expertise"; Charles R. Shipan, "Keeping Competitors Out: Broadcast Regulation from the Federal Radio Act of 1927 to the Telecommunications Act of 1996," in *A Communications Cornucopia: Markle Foundation Essays on Information Policy,* edited by Monroe Price and Roger Noll (Washington, D.C.: Brookings Institution Press, 1998).

29. Jessica Korn, *The Power of Separation: American Constitutionalism and the Myth of the Legislative Veto* (Princeton, N.J.: Princeton University Press, 1996).

30. Joseph Cooper, "The Legislative Veto in the 1980s," in *Congress Reconsidered,* edited by Lawrence C. Dodd and Bruce I. Oppenheimer, 3rd ed. (Washington, D.C.: CQ Press, 1985).

31. James W. Fesler and Donald F. Kettl, *The Politics of the Administrative Process,* 2d ed. (Chatham, N.J.: Chatham House, 1996).

32. Balla, "Legislative Organization and Congressional Review."

33. Cindy Skrzycki, *The Regulators: Anonymous Power Brokers in American Politics* (Lanham, Md.: Rowman and Littlefield, 2003).

34. John Ferejohn and Charles R. Shipan, "Congressional Influence on Administrative Agencies: A Case Study of Telecommunications Policy," in *Congress Reconsidered,* edited by Lawrence C. Dodd and Bruce I. Oppenheimer, 4th ed. (Washington, D.C.: CQ Press, 1989).

35. Mathew D. McCubbins and Thomas Schwartz, "Congressional Oversight Overlooked: Police Patrols versus Fire Alarms," *American Journal of Political Science* 28 (1984): 165–179.

36. Scher, "Conditions for Legislative Control"; Morris S. Ogul, *Congress Oversees the Bureaucracy: Studies in Legislative Supervision* (Pittsburgh: University of Pittsburgh Press, 1976).

37. McCubbins and Schwartz, "Congressional Oversight Overlooked."

38. The fire alarm point of view is related to the arguments about structures and procedures. One difference is that the fire alarm perspective is mostly concerned with addressing agency problems *after* they have occurred—as McCubbins and Schwartz write, it represents how "Congress attempts to detect and remedy executive-branch violations of legislative goals" ("Congressional Oversight Overlooked," 165)— while the structures-and-procedures argument is concerned with exerting influence *before* the agency acts. The former are thus sometimes described as *ex post* controls, while the latter are labeled *ex ante* controls.

39. Epstein and O'Halloran, *Delegating Powers*, 280.

40. Charles R. Shipan, "Regulatory Regimes, Agency Actions, and the Conditional Nature of Political Influence," *American Political Science Review* 98, no. 3 (2004): 467–480.

41. Barry R. Weingast and Mark J. Moran, "Bureaucratic Discretion or Congressional Control: Regulatory Policymaking by the FTC," *Journal of Political Economy* 91 (1983): 765–800; John Ferejohn and Charles Shipan, "Congressional Influence on Bureaucracy," *Journal of Law Economics, and Organization* 6 (1990): 120; Mary K. Olson, "Explaining Regulatory Behavior in the FDA: Political Control vs. Agency Discretion," *Advances in the Study of Entrepreneurship, Innovation, and Growth* 7 (1996): 71–108; Wood and Waterman, *Bureaucratic Dynamics*.

42. Ferejohn and Shipan, "Congressional Influence"; Shipan, "Regulatory Regimes."

43. Kathleen M. Bawn, "Choosing Strategies to Control the Bureaucracy: Statutory Constraints, Oversight, and the Committee System," *Journal of Law Economics, and Organization* 13 (1997): 101–126.

44. As one observer noted, "Senate Commerce Chairman McCain, who favors a limited reversal of the new FCC rules, is at the forefront of efforts to strike the appropriations rider. He argues the media ownership issue should be addressed instead through an up-or-down Senate vote on a broader, stand-alone bill his committee approved in June. . . . 'I don't know what's going to happen on this,' McCain said. 'It's awfully hard to pry it out of an appropriations bill, but I'm going to engage in a spirited debate on the floor.'" See Molly Peterson, "For Media Rules Foes, No Retreat," *CongressDaily*, October 20, 2003, www.congressdaily.com.

45. See Cox and McCubbins, *Legislative Leviathan*; Forrest Maltzman, *Competing Principals: Committees, Parties, and the Organization of Congress* (Ann Arbor: University of Michigan Press, 1997); and other chapters in this volume (e.g., Rohde (ch. 7) and Sinclair (ch. 8)).

46. It was this stance by party leaders, in fact, that led opponents of the rule to pursue change through the appropriations process.

47. Huber and Shipan, *Deliberate Discretion?*

48. Wilson, *Bureaucracy*. Wilson argues that both individuals and committees benefited here, albeit in different ways.

49. MacDonald, "Congressional Oversight Still Overlooked?"

50. Aberbach, *Keeping a Watchful Eye*.
51. Huber and Shipan, *Deliberate Discretion?*

Bibliography

Aberbach, Joel D. *Keeping a Watchful Eye: The Politics of Congressional Oversight.* Washington, D.C.: Brookings Institution, 1990.

Carpenter, Daniel P. *The Forging of Bureaucratic Autonomy: Reputations, Networks, and Policy Innovation in Executive Agencies, 1862–1928.* Princeton, N.J.: Princeton University Press, 2001.

Epstein, David, and Sharyn O'Halloran. *Delegating Powers: A Transaction Cost Politics Approach to Policy Making under Separate Powers.* New York: Cambridge University Press, 1999.

Fiorina, Morris P. "Congressional Control of the Bureaucracy: A Mismatch of Incentives and Capabilities." In *Congress Reconsidered*, edited by Lawrence C. Dodd and Bruce I. Oppenheimer. 2d ed. Washington, D.C.: CQ Press, 1981.

Huber, John D., and Charles R. Shipan. *Deliberate Discretion?: The Institutional Foundations of Bureaucratic Autonomy.* Cambridge, U.K., and New York: Cambridge University Press, 2002.

Kiewiet, D. Roderick, and Mathew D. McCubbins. *The Logic of Delegation: Congressional Parties and the Appropriations Process.* Chicago: University of Chicago Press, 1993.

Moe, Terry M. "The Politics of Bureaucratic Structure." In *Can the Government Govern?* edited by John E. Chubb and Paul E. Peterson. Washington, D.C.: Brookings Institution, 1989.

Shipan, Charles R. *Designing Judicial Review: Interest Groups, Congress, and Communications Policy.* Ann Arbor: University of Michigan Press, 1997.

Wilson, James Q. *Bureaucracy: What Government Agencies Do and Why They Do It.* New York: Basic Books, 1989.

Wood, B. Dan, and Richard W. Waterman. *Bureaucratic Dynamics: The Role of Bureaucracy in a Democracy.* Boulder, Colo.: Westview, 1994.

ASSESSMENTS AND PROSPECTS

16

IMAGES OF CONGRESS

John R. Hibbing

CONGRESS, IN ADDITION TO BEING TWO LEGISLATIVE
bodies with budgets to pass, opinions to represent, bureaucrats to oversee, and laws to make, is also an institution that is perceived by the
American people. It is trusted or not trusted; respected or not respected. In other
words, Congress is not just what it *is* but also what it is *seen to be* by the people
whom it was created to serve. Unlike the other essays in this volume, the present
one is not about Congress per se but rather the way people see and feel about
Congress. Since people's images of Congress cannot be sufficiently understood
outside of the larger institutional context, this analysis frequently compares attitudes toward Congress and attitudes toward government as a whole.

Importance of Image

Does it matter whether Americans view Congress favorably or unfavorably? The
answer to this question is much the same as the answer to whether it matters that
Americans view the federal government favorably or unfavorably, and this latter
issue has been the focus of considerable disagreement—disagreement that is best
illustrated by a published exchange between the political scientists Arthur Miller
and Jack Citrin in 1974.[1] Both scholars acknowledged that from the mid-1960s
and the early 1970s the American people's trust in government dropped precipitously, but they disagreed fundamentally on the implications of this decline. To
Miller it signaled a basic weakening in Americans' support for their system of
government, a shift from unquestioning acceptance to intense yearning for serious institutional modifications. Citrin, on the other hand, believed that the dissatisfaction merely reflected unhappiness with the officials then in office and the
specific decisions they had made. If people disagreed with the Vietnam War, then

all they had to do to make things right was to elect officials who would quit fighting that war. Unlike Miller, Citrin believed that reversing the decline in trust did not require major systemic change, let alone a revolution, but could be accomplished simply by voting out the incumbents.

The difference of opinion between Miller and Citrin with respect to the consequences of dissatisfaction with government continues to draw scholarly attention. Observers inclined to agree with Citrin point out that a certain level of skepticism toward government is healthy, since undue trust could lead to a citizenry unmotivated to demand appropriate levels of governmental accountability. From this perspective, a low level of trust, far from being a matter of concern, is desirable because it keeps government honest. Others take the opposite position—one closer to Miller's—and believe that a lack of trust in government is cause for grave concern. They fear that a political system unable to generate support from its citizens is doomed to failure. Since modern society requires the coordinated action of government, these individuals worry about the potential of mistrust to rend the very fabric of society. Not surprisingly, differences of opinion regarding the consequences of support for government parallel different views of the consequences of negative attitudes toward Congress, with some observers believing that disapproval of Congress constitutes a serious problem and others believing that it does not matter and may even be desirable.

Which side is right: Are low levels of support dangerous or not? Two points are pertinent to this debate. First, the truth seems to rest, as it often does, in the middle. Survey data reinforces Citrin's view that low levels of governmental trust are not a sure sign that the political system is in peril. People can mistrust government without wanting it to go away; people can disapprove of Congress without wanting it to be eliminated. But this does not necessarily mean that the consequences of mistrust are benign, much less cause for celebration. For example, indications are that when Congress is unpopular, qualified individuals are dissuaded from running for reelection or from seeking election in the first place; members' willingness and ability to tackle unpopular but necessary issues are lessened; the appeal of simplistic institutional reforms (e.g., term limits or direct election of U.S. senators) is enhanced; and citizens' tendency to comply with actions of the institution is diminished.[2] In short, mistrust can bring negative consequences even if it does not bring a desire for revolution. The public's attitudes toward government create a context in which government works; if attitudes are decidedly unfavorable, government will not work as well. A lack of trust is a problem for institutions of democratic government but is not necessarily a sign that those institutions' days are numbered. Both sides in the debate are partially correct.

Second, the justification for analyzing the public's images of Congress specifically and of government generally does not hinge on systemic consequences. Students of representative democracy seek to understand people's interaction with governmental institutions simply because variations in public approval provide substantial information about people's preferences for representative government. The desire to understand people's preferences is not indicative of a desire to give the people what they want, so in this particular case the desire to understand the changes that would improve people's image of Congress is not indicative of a belief that Congress must be popular. Arguments on this latter point can continue apace of any attempt to come to grips with the aspects of representative government that people tend to value or, alternatively, to disfavor.

This essay first looks at historical variations in attitudes toward Congress (and other aspects of government). It then examines the features of Congress and of government that people seem to favor more than others. Finally, the discussion turns to an analysis of the type of person who generally is approving of Congress and of government. A special effort has been made herein to debunk common misconceptions about the sources of congressional mistrust. The expectation is that systematic investigation of the periods of time when approval is high, the specific features of Congress engendering favorable popular reactions, and the type of individual likely to favor Congress will allow the most accurate explanation possible of the sources of Congress's image and, therefore, the best strategies for improving that image—should this be the goal.

Variations over Time in Attitudes toward Government and Congress

The most common depiction of longitudinal variations in Americans' perceptions of their government during the last one hundred years goes something like this: Early in the twentieth century, residents of the United States had deep respect for all things governmental. The Constitution and the political institutions it created helped America to become a cultural, military, and economic focal point of the world. Americans were proud of their president, their flag, their Congress, and their governmental landmarks. Subsequent threats to the country such as those faced in both world wars and then the cold war united Americans and made them even less likely to engage in overt criticism of their government. The people were content and in general agreement about the goodness of their country, the wisdom of its political system, and the need to be strong and united in the face of enemies.

Then came the 1960s. The peaceful, perhaps smug, contentment of television's Ozzie and Harriet Nelson gave way to the agitated, impatient demands for change from prominent activists such as Tom Hayden and Jane Fonda. Race riots, Vietnam War protests, urban unrest, women's liberation, and societal crime and violence conspired to reveal a government that was baffled by people's desire for change and seemingly incapable of dealing with new and diverse public preferences. The United States seemed divided where before it had been unified, and politicians seemed to be concerned for themselves where before they had seemed altruistic. Then, on the heels of the divisiveness of the 1960s, came the Watergate scandal and the resignation of President Richard M. Nixon in 1974. Watergate fanned people's distrust of government directly and also indirectly by encouraging an ever more negative and inquisitive press. Predictably, by the mid-1970s trust in government had plummeted to unprecedented levels and, according to conventional wisdom, has mostly remained at those levels ever since. People harbor residual devotion to the Constitution but believe that politicians such as members of Congress and institutions such as Congress have failed the people and no longer merit trust and confidence.

Despite the popularity of this account, major portions of it are in error or at least open to question. The most appropriate, consistently worded, and regularly posed items on attitudes toward government come from the National Election Studies (NES) at the University of Michigan, which conducts a major national survey every two years.[3] With only a few exceptions (1960 and 1962) since 1958, this organization has asked respondents, "How much of the time do you think you can trust the government in Washington to do what is right?" Possible answers are "just about always," "most of the time," "some of the time," and "none of the time," and it has become conventional for scholars to simplify the presentation of results by displaying the percent of all respondents who answered either "just about always" or "most of the time."

In addition, since 1980 researchers at NES have posed a question specifically on congressional approval: "Do you approve or disapprove of the way the U.S. Congress has been handling its job?" Unfortunately, NES does not ask respondents about their approval of the other central political branch of the U.S. government, the executive, but since 1972 the Harris Poll has asked people about their confidence in the presidency. By juxtaposing attitudes toward government, Congress, and the presidency, it is possible to determine the extent to which people's views of these different referents are intertwined and have changed since 1980. The trend lines are presented in Figure 1.

Readers should avoid the temptation to compare average perceptions of the government with average perceptions of Congress and the president. Trust is not the same as job approval and not the same as confidence. Moreover, the trust item asks for an estimation of the amount of time the government in Washington can be trusted, while the congressional-approval item simply asks whether or not the respondent approves of Congress, and the presidency item asks whether confidence is present or absent. In other words, the figure compares apples and oranges. The fact that the line for Congress in Figure 1 is generally above the lines for the presidency and for the federal government does not mean that Congress is more popular. Indeed, research demonstrates that in those individual years for which item wordings are parallel, Congress is consistently labeled the least popular branch of government, falling a little below both the presidency and the overall federal government and well below the Supreme Court.

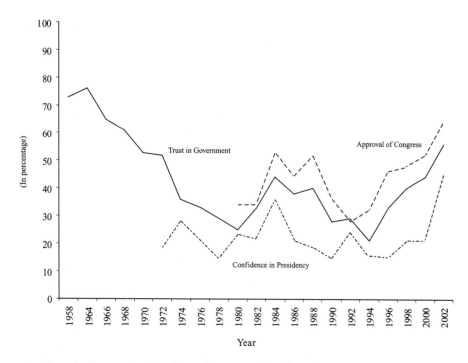

NOTE: "Trust in Government" combines the answers "just about always" and "most of the time" from the following question:"How much of the time do you think you can trust the government in Washington to do what is right—just about always, most of the time or only some of the time?"

SOURCE: National Election Studies (NES) for "Trust in Government" and "Approval of Congress"; Harris Poll for "Confidence in Presidency." Data were unavailable for "Trust in Government" for the years between 1958 and 1964, prior to 1980 for "Approval of Congress," and prior to 1972 for "Confidence in the Presidency."

Figure 1. Attitudes toward Congress, the Presidency, and the Federal Government

Responses derived from the very different questions in Figure 1 are presented together in order to determine the extent to which approval of Congress tracks with attitudes toward other governmental referents over an extended period of time, so the comparison should be to patterns, not to absolute levels.

Evaluations of Congress are somewhat connected to the public's views of the presidency and are even more tightly connected to the federal government in general. In the years when both approval of Congress and trust in government were measured, they appear to move together: low in 1980, higher in the mid-1980s, low again in the early 1990s, and high again in the late 1990s and early 2000s. This assessment is borne out by statistical analysis, which finds that the variation of these two variables correlates at .93, meaning that people's evaluations of Congress and evaluations of government nearly always vary together.

What about Congress and the presidency? Does a favorable public attitude toward one mean a favorable attitude toward the other? Figure 1 again suggests that the answer is yes.[4] Somewhat surprisingly, peaks in favorability in the mid-1980s and early 2000s are shorter lived for the presidency than for Congress, but the general pattern is similar. The correlation between attitudes toward the presidency and attitudes toward Congress are positively correlated but at a lower level (r = .60). The American people almost never feel favorably toward government without feeling favorably toward Congress, whereas when they feel favorably toward the presidency they usually but certainly not always feel favorably toward Congress. Given the strong correlation of evaluations of Congress and of the federal government when measures of both are available, it is probably safe to assume that one follows the other.

And just how have public attitudes changed over time? At first blush, the steep downward movement in trust of the federal government apparent from the mid-1960s to the mid-1970s supports the standard account described above. The early readings—1958, 1964, and 1966—are remarkably high and the Watergate plunge from 1972 to 1974 is the steepest two-year drop on record (seventeen points). But it may be a mistake to assume that just because trust in government was high in 1958 and 1964 it was high in all previous years. In 1958 the Soviet threat was palpable, due largely to the USSR's successful launch of *Sputnik*, the world's first artificial satellite, the year before. President Dwight D. Eisenhower's avuncular demeanor and the relatively bucolic nature of the times could also have been expected to boost trust. In 1964 the country was still reeling from the assassination the year before of a vigorous young president, John F. Kennedy, and was sympathetic toward his successor, Lyndon B. Johnson, who was attempting, along with a strongly supportive Congress, to implement Kennedy's aggressive domestic program. But by the late 1960s, with these circumstances removed and with national problems apparent in abundance, positive attitudes toward government declined.

The question is, did they decline to levels that existed prior to the late 1950s or was the drop unprecedented? Survey questions on people's attitudes toward Congress were actually asked by media pollsters prior to the late 1950s—just not very often—so answers to this question must be tentative.[5] Public opinion of congressional performance was quite negative during World War II; then, after the war, it dropped even further to levels that seem comparable to those registered in the depths of the post-Watergate period (precise comparisons are impossible because the wording of the question was different). By late 1953 public opinion of Congress was much more favorable, perhaps because of the cessation of hostilities in Korea, where American soldiers had been deployed since 1950. Good feelings continued through 1958 and, as already seen from the NES data, were present again in 1964—although the period from 1959 through 1963 is in question because the relevant survey item was not posed. All told, contrary to the conventional account described above, it seems that unwavering positive feelings toward Congress were not present prior to the late-1960s drop. Instead, ups and downs were the norm, with positive perceptions registering very low in the mid- to late 1940s and quite high in the mid- to late 1950s and again in the mid- to late 1960s.

It is likely that vacillation in the public's image of Congress dates to the country's founding. Congress has frequently served as a whipping boy for disgruntled citizens, and sometimes dissatisfaction has been intense. In 1816 members of Congress voted for a change in their individual compensation from a per diem of $6 to an annual salary of $1,500 retroactive to 1815. Public outrage was immediate and dramatic. Sensing the people's anger, many members chose not to seek reelection. Many of those who ran (including the nationally recognized senator Daniel Webster) were defeated.[6] If modern pollsters had been around in 1816 to draw an accurate statistical sample and to administer an item asking people about their approval of Congress, the typical answer would have been as negative as the typical answer after Watergate or the House Bank scandal of 1992 when numerous members were discovered routinely kiting checks. The same could be said for the period subsequent to the great "salary grab" of 1873, when another large and retroactive pay increase sent the public into an anti-Congress frenzy, forced a repeal of the raise, led to the end of many congressional careers, and prevented passage of any new salary increases for the next thirty-four years.

Post–pay raise periods are not the only times that attitudes toward government and especially Congress have been decidedly unfavorable. Controversial policy decisions, such as the Missouri Compromise and Reconstruction, severe economic slumps, such as those in the 1890s and the late 1920s, and scandals, such as the events surrounding the selection by Congress of John Quincy Adams as president in the 1820s and Credit Mobilier in the 1870s, are likely to have had the same effect. In 1906 the magazine *Cosmopolitan*—a different sort of publication then than now—published a series of scathing articles by David Graham Phillips entitled "The Treason of the Senate." These sensationalistic essays reported and often exaggerated instances of robber baron money being given to members of the Senate in order to hasten the passage of pro-business legislation. They were widely read and reprinted and, in fact, public reaction to these articles had much to do with later passage of a constitutional amendment (the Seventeenth) to change the method of electing senators from indirect to direct. Once again, it is difficult to believe that public approval of Congress was anything but rock bottom during this time. In sum, prior to the 1950s, periods of disapproval likely were nearly as common as periods of approval.

If, as alleged here, the public image of government and Congress was not consistently high prior to 1958, the conventional account presented earlier probably owes part of its inaccuracy to the fact that the regularization of measurements of trust happened to occur during a time of positive feelings and just before a sizable diminution in those feelings. If pollsters at the NES had instead begun asking the trust question in the mid- to late 1970s, scholars today might be writing about the tremendous increase in trust and congressional approval.

This is so because just as attitudes in the pre-1960s period were much less favorable (and more variable) than is conveyed by the standard account, the post-Watergate period has been more favorable (and variable). Recent decades have not been characterized by unrelenting hostility toward government and Congress. Trust in government was undeniably low in the late 1970s but both trust in government and approval of Congress moved up sharply in the mid-1980s during the so-called Reagan "feel-good, morning-in-America" period (see Figure 1). Trust and congressional approval returned to low levels in the late 1980s and especially the early 1990s, but then another resurgence began—one that is rarely discussed by congressional observers. Beginning in the late 1990s both trust in government and approval of Congress moved up smartly, so much so that by 2002 NES was reporting the highest levels of trust since 1968 and the highest levels of congressional approval ever (again, see Figure 1).

But was this not merely a predictable reaction to the terrorist attacks of September 11, 2001? Certainly the 2002 reading was driven by fallout from that momentous and horrific event. Just as was the case shortly after Kennedy's assassination, respondents may not have been comfortable voicing negative evaluations of government or any part of it. In times of tragedy and crisis people generally feel that the country needs to come together. Still, 9/11 cannot explain the high levels of approval in the late 1990s and early 2000s. Already by January of 1998 the Gallup polling organization was reporting the highest congressional approval levels since it began asking the question in the early 1970s. Thus the renewal in trust and approval predates 9/11 by nearly four years and is a further indication that the conventional account is flawed. In reality, the post-Watergate period, while more negative than previous eras, gives evidence of periods of reasonably positive feelings.

Another mark against the conventional account is that it does not place attitudes toward government in context. Research by Seymour Martin Lipset and William Schneider demonstrates convincingly that the decline in attitudes toward government from the late 1960s to the early 1970s was actually part of a larger decline in attitudes toward almost every part of society.[7] Relying on Harris Poll data that surveyed respondents about their confidence in the leaders of various institutions, Lipset and Schneider found that confidence in the leaders of Congress dropped twenty-three points from 1966 to 1971, but confidence in the leaders of education dropped twenty-four points and confidence in those running major companies as well as those running the executive branch of government dropped eighteen points. Leaders of the military dropped the most, thirty-five points (understandable in the wake of the Vietnam War), but leaders of organized religion also dropped, by fourteen points, and leaders of the press and of organized labor almost certainly would have had comparable drops except for the fact that they inspired little confidence in 1966 and thus could not drop further.

Something changed in the 1966–1974 period, but it was not limited to the image of Congress or even government. The diversity of American society was suddenly apparent and placed great strain on government. African Americans, other minorities, females, the poor, the young, all spoke up and more than ever made it impossible for people to insist against all evidence that the United States was one big happy homogeneous family. Cynicism flourished and authority was questioned. People were no longer reluctant to report negative feelings toward leaders of any and all institutions. What may have happened was less a loss of trust in government and Congress but the blossoming of a more generalized skepticism of the leaders of virtually all societal institutions. After all, it was during this period that it became somewhat fashionable to mistrust the establishment. Some analysts speculate that the very way respondents approached survey items changed.

Explaining Variations in Attitudes over Time

Having established that attitudes toward government and Congress have swung widely throughout the United States' history, the next task is to explain why people's attitudes are sometimes high and sometimes low. As it turns out, accounting for the pattern is maddeningly difficult. The oft-cited causal agents are unable to account for the variations in approval. For example, a logical expectation is that a prosperous economy will lead to a more popular Congress while a failing economy will lead people to turn against Congress, but scholarly research finds little support for these hypotheses.[8] The economy was booming in the mid-1990s and popular perceptions of government and Congress were extremely low; then, in the early 2000s the economy was slumping badly and perceptions improved.

Similarly, the effects of scandals and international turmoil are uneven at best. Threats to the United States as well as short successful wars tend to boost congressional approval, while costly, drawn-out wars diminish it. Scandals certainly can lower congressional approval but they do not always have this effect. Indeed, a comprehensive 2002 study found that political scandals on average actually increase approval of Congress, though scandals specific to the legislative branch, as expected, tend to decrease approval.[9]

One thing of which we can be certain is that the 9/11 terrorist attack against the United States caused a spike in the approval ratings of Congress and of anybody associated with Congress. From August to October of 2001, approval of

Congress went from 46 to 85 percent, of President George W. Bush from 50 to 86 percent, of then Senate majority leader Tom Daschle from 27 to 60 percent, and of Speaker of the House Dennis Hastert from 29 to 51 percent—even though most respondents at the time probably had no idea who Daschle and Hastert were. After the initial surge, approval of Congress and its leaders moved lower more quickly than did approval of President George W. Bush, but all told, it appears that, like the president, Congress benefits temporarily from rally-around-the-flag effects.

Champions of the conventional account are hard-pressed to provide a theoretical basis for what they believe to be a step-level change in support in the short period of time from the late 1960s to the mid-1970s. They often fall back on an atheoretical assertion that a unique confluence of events led the people to lose trust, but this is vague and unsatisfying. It is probable that the changing nature of media coverage of Congress had some effect. It has been demonstrated that people who watch more television, other things being equal, are more emotionally negative toward Congress.[10] The reason is likely to be the documented tendency of the electronic media to present all political conflicts as horse races or crass contests for political advantage. Almost nothing that members of Congress do is ever interpreted as an honest attempt to solve an important national problem or to make the country better. The results are an increase in the extent to which the public attributes self-interest to members of Congress and a corresponding reduction in congressional approval. Although this line of thinking has the ring of truth, it must also be noted that approval of Congress, like the decline of trust in government, had largely bottomed out by the time of Watergate—and Watergate is often seen to be the beginning of a cynical, negative, and intrusive press. No doubt media outlets were changing before Watergate, but to a certain extent the decline in perceptions of institutions including Congress came before the major changes in media orientation.

One of the more intriguing recent findings is that support for Congress actually goes down when Congress is visibly doing its job.[11] The more Congress is in the news, wrestling with major legislative problems and taking steps to check the president, the more support for Congress diminishes.[12] The explanation is that people do not like to see the debate and conflict that are inevitably part and parcel of representative democracy, especially in a separation-of-powers system. People claim to value the role that Congress plays in checking presidential power, but when Congress performs this role it usually pays the price. Watergate in some respects should have been a high-water mark for Congress. Thanks largely to the brave stance of moderate Republicans, Congress confronted an arrogant, law-breaking executive and showed that the system could rise above partisanship and work. The result? The popularity of the Supreme Court went up but the popularity of Congress, if anything, went down.

When former Speaker of the House Newt Gingrich and his Republican Congress were at loggerheads with the Democratic administration of President Bill Clinton in 1996 over budgetary matters, a stalemate ensued and portions of the government were forced to shut down. A case could be made that the legislative and executive branches were equally intransigent, but public opinion once again delivered a clear verdict. To wit: Clinton's popularity went up and congressional approval declined. And much the same pattern can be seen during and shortly after the impeachment of President Clinton. Despite videotaped evidence that the president had given misleading testimony under oath, the impeachment process increased Clinton's popularity but led to a decline in congressional approval of approximately ten points. The effects of economic and international events on congressional approval may be uncertain, but internal congressional conflict or conflict between Congress and the president always redounds to Congress's distinct disadvantage.

Constituent Likes and Dislikes

Surveys have consistently shown that Americans' knowledge of governmental facts is minimal; their knowledge of congressional facts is no exception. Most people simply do not know much about Congress as an institution, about the political system of which it is a part, and about the role Congress plays within that system. Just to provide a few examples, 65 percent of American adults do not know the purpose of the electoral college; 75 percent do not know the length of a senator's term; 47 percent do not know what a filibuster is; 49 percent erroneously think that Congress can require the president to believe in God; 55 percent do not believe that Congress has the power to declare war; 56 percent can not name even a single branch of government; 45 percent do not know that each state has two senators; 60 percent do not know how presidential candidates are selected; 43 percent do not know that the Republican Party tends to be the more conservative of the two parties; 50 percent erroneously believe the president can suspend the Constitution; at any given time, approximately 40 to 65 percent do not know which party is in control of the House of Representatives; 45 percent can not name either of their state's U.S. senators; 19 percent believe that the Supreme Court is a part of Congress; and 45 percent are convinced that the phrase "from each according to his ability, to each according to his need," is contained in the Constitution.[13] Karl Marx would be amused.

But students of politics should resist the urge to feel superior because ordinary citizens do poorly when forced to play political Trivial Pursuit with a survey researcher. In truth, it is possible to perform adequately in the political system without knowing many of these facts. Still, in some cases lack of knowledge can create problems. The fact that so many people do not know the majority party in Congress (remember, 50 percent should be able to get this answer correct merely by guessing) raises questions about accountability,[14] and even though they are a minority, the fact that nearly one out of five respondents believes that the Supreme Court is a subsection of Congress reflects a fairly basic misconception of the separation-of-powers arrangement that is at the core of the Constitution. Moreover, because politically unknowledgeable people are more likely to refuse to respond to political surveys, the results presented above are in actuality overestimates of people's knowledge about government. If such surveys reflected the knowledge of a true representative sample of all American adults, correct answers would no doubt be diminished even more.

Due in part to people's confusion concerning the various features of Congress and government, it is not helpful to ask them whether they approve or disapprove of these features. For example, since most people do not know that senators serve six-year terms, a question about whether they approve or disapprove of the length of the senatorial term would yield misleading results—unless the factual perception was reported next to the attitude. Even asking people to provide separate evaluations of the House and the Senate is probably a mistake, because most people do not have a well-developed understanding of the two bodies and their differences. As a result, investigation of the aspects of Congress that people favor and disfavor must proceed cautiously.

That Americans love their own member of Congress but hate Congress is one of the most well-known aphorisms in American politics.[15] Americans consistently rate the representatives from their own districts quite highly, as is apparent from the fact that reelection rates for incumbents are in the mid- to high 90-percent range; as previously seen, approval of Congress in general runs lower. Still, the aphorism is incomplete. Just what are people envisioning when they are asked about their approval of "Congress"? People's evaluation of Congress is in actuality their evaluation of the members of Congress *as a group*—535 flawed, machinating, argumentative members wrestling with devilishly difficult national problems while receiving citizens' tax dollars. People understandably prefer their own representatives to that vision. An important addendum, though, is that when people are encouraged to think of Congress as an institution rather than as a collection of politicians, their reaction is even more favorable than their reaction to their own representative, with nearly nine out of ten respondents approving. Just as Citrin found that negative views of government do not equate to a desire to tear it down and build a new one, negativity toward Congress is in fact negativity toward the membership as a whole; support for Congress as an institution remains strong.

What is it about the membership as a whole that people dislike? A national survey in the early 1990s found that 57 percent of American adults believed that Congress did not do a "good job representing the interest of all Americans," 64 percent felt that Congress was not "efficient in addressing issues," 70 percent believed that members "focused too much on events in Washington," 78 percent felt that members were "too far removed from ordinary people," and 86 percent believed that Congress was "too heavily influenced by interest groups."[16] Distance from the people and, relatedly, proximity to special interests are the biggest perceived flaws of members of Congress.

The perceived role of special interests in the legislative process, acting in concert with allegedly self-serving politicians, constitutes the focal point of public dissatisfaction with Congress, a fact confirmed by the results of a nationwide sample of approximately fifteen hundred American adults conducted especially for this volume in late 2004. Responses to three of the most pertinent items are presented below. Note that several of the survey items included were presented only to subsamples of the total.

	Number	Percent
The policy decisions that Congress makes are often negatively influenced by special interest groups.		
Agree	446	73.2
Disagree	125	20.5
Don't know/Refused	38	6.2
Total	609	99.9
When members of Congress make decisions, do you think they act in their own best interests or in the best interests of the people?		
Own best interests	691	46.0
Interests of the people	612	40.8
Don't know/Refused/Depends	198	13.2
Total	1501	100.0
With which of these statements do you agree?		
Interest groups harm the policy-making process and should be weakened	398	51.8
OR		
Interest groups are an essential part of the policy-making process and should be strengthened.	309	40.2
Don't know/Refused	61	7.9
Total	768	99.9

Somewhat surprisingly, political parties, in spite of frequently heard complaints about their divisiveness, were not singled out by this representative sample as being particularly distasteful. In fact, when the last of the three items listed above was repeated in the same 2004 survey, with "political parties" substituted for "interest groups," instead of just 40 percent saying they were essential and should be strengthened, as was the case for interest groups, fully 57.5 percent said that parties were essential and should be strengthened. Political parties are not beloved by Americans, but their value is recognized by a solid majority. The same cannot be said for special interests. In fact, when people were asked to provide a reason for their distrust of Congress, 601 were willing and able to respond to this open-ended item. Many reasons were provided but by far the most common was the influence of special interests (92), member self-interest (65), and corruption (58). By way of contrast, only 23 claimed their distrust was due to generic policy dissatisfaction and just 15 cited a specific policy (the war in Iraq).

Another common source of displeasure is the benefits package that members of Congress receive: 77 percent of respondents in the earlier (1990s) survey thought that congressional salaries were too high and 75 percent believed that members had too many staffers (assistants). No doubt equally high percentages would have registered objection to other aspects of the remuneration package if given the chance. Perhaps the desire to reduce the benefits of congressional service stems from a tendency on the part of the people to overestimate the size of these benefits, but not necessarily. After being asked if the congressional salary was too high, respondents were asked to estimate the salary and the average response worked out to only 76 percent of the real salary at the time. In other words, 77 percent of American adults wanted to lower congressional salaries even though they believed salaries to be much lower than they actually were. What would people have thought if they had known the real salary? And the same pattern applied to perceptions of staff support in Congress. When asked the size of staff available to members of the House, the average response was 7.5, even though the real number at the time, according to the *Congressional Directory*, was 17.4. Three-fourths of Americans believe that members of Congress should have less than 7.5 staff assistants and presumably would be outraged to learn that they actually have 2.3 times that many. The public does misunderstand congressional benefits but at times this misunderstanding serves to insulate members from greater public disfavor.

By and large, people do not take members of Congress to task for particular policy decisions. Political scientists noted in the 1950s that people rarely were aware of even a single policy position taken by their district representatives, and this has not changed since then.[17] Similarly, people do not find fault with representatives who are considered to have insufficiently showered their district with pork barrel projects. When asked to identify the most important tasks performed by a member of Congress, people ranked bringing projects back to the district dead last, and when given the choice, 85 percent of survey respondents claimed to want members to "do what is best for the entire country, not just their district."

Overall, the aspects of Congress that people like and dislike may seem paradoxical. They overwhelmingly (78 percent) want members to come home more often but they rank "passing laws on important national issues" as the most important task of a member. They want members to "help constituents deal with the government bureaucracy" (the second most important task they listed) but

85 percent of them simultaneously want members to "do what is best for the country." Seventy-eight percent think that members are too far removed from ordinary people back in the district, yet most want members to spend their time focusing on national rather than district-level problems. Do people want members to have a local focus, a national focus, or do they just want it all?

People's desires are not as contradictory as they first seem. They just want something different than is typically assumed. People most dislike anything that gives them the sense that they are being ignored in favor of somebody else. Constituents want attention. People dislike political parties and, especially, interest groups because they are seen as unwelcome competitors for the attention of the representative (no amount of cajoling seems capable of persuading people that certain interest groups represent their interests). The confusing element is that people do not want attention because they have policy-based messages they want to communicate to members of Congress; instead, they just want the member to demonstrate a sincere connection with them, to enjoy spending time in the district, and to be there if they ever do have a policy desire. People are fearful that their member will "go Washington," not because policy decisions will then be different but because they want authority figures to understand and to relate to them. Thus, people can fret about their member losing touch with the people back home while still wanting the member to deal with national rather than local issues. The aspects of Congress that people like and dislike only make sense when people are viewed as love-struck teenagers worried about competing suitors (special interests, political parties, and Washington money and glitz). In this view, citizens are not policy-demanding actors; they generally want attention for the sake of attention, not because they seek tangible policy benefits.

It follows from this that citizens are upset with congressional compensation not simply because of the tax burden it places on them, but because they see the benefits package as a contributing factor to their member's psychological departure from the district. Members surrounded by luxury will lose an affinity for the realities back home in the district. People largely acknowledge that members of Congress have a difficult job and need assistance in accomplishing their policy goals. They advocate draconian staff cuts because they do not like the vision of a member insulated from "real people," separated from constituents by an entourage. The reason they frequently support term limits is not that they think this reform will increase accountability or representation but because they distrust members' ability to stay true to them given too much exposure to the artificiality of Washington. People want members to live like them and to like it.

Demographic Profiles of Congressional Approval

Congress is a partisan institution. News accounts are filled with references to the "Republican Congress" or, before 1994, the "Democratic Congress." Stories describe the institution as "supporting" or "opposing" the president and frequently place events in the context of partisan politics. Accordingly, it is not surprising that people who identify with the party that is currently controlling Congress are more likely to approve of the job Congress is doing than are people who identify with the minority party. The truth of this statement is evident from Figure 2, which shows the variations in approval of Congress across the various possible party affiliations of respondents, for the years 1988 and 2000. These years were selected because they were presidential-election years with similar overall levels of congressional approval (52 percent); moreover, the Democrats controlled both houses of Congress in 1988 and the Republicans controlled both houses of Congress in 2000. If partisanship has the expected effect, citizens who self-identify as Democrats should be more approving of Congress when the Democrats are in the majority and those self-identifying as Republicans should be more approving given a Republican majority.

The approval percentages reported in Figure 2 and throughout this section were calculated by dividing the number of respondents approving of Congress by the number either approving or disapproving. This is important, because some respondents either didn't know whether they approved or disapproved or they gave an equivocating response, such as "both" or "neither." Comparisons over time, of the sort reported in Figure 1, usually are calculated by dividing approvers by all eligible respondents, even those that express being unsure. The problem with using this procedure for cross-group comparisons is that members of cer-

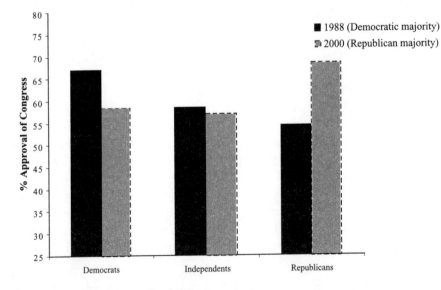

SOURCE: National Election Studies (NES).

Figure 2. Party Control and Congressional Approval

tain groups are much more likely to express uncertainty. In order to minimize variation attributable to differential willingness to give a definite response, only those in the "approve" or "disapprove" camps are included here. This means that the percent approving will appear higher than that in Figure 1, and that the proper interpretation of the results in Figure 2 is as the percent approving of all those with a definite opinion.

Figure 2 shows that partisan approval is indeed an empirical reality. In 1988, when there was a Republican majority, 67.0 percent of Democratic respondents approved of Congress while only 54.3 percent of Republican respondents did. Interestingly, those respondents who reported they were partisan "Independents" were almost as negative as Republicans, with just 58.4 percent approving of Congress, but the main point is that when Congress was controlled by Democrats, the congressional approval rate for Democratic survey respondents was 12.7 percentage points higher than it was for Republican respondents. In 2000, when the Republicans had a (slim) majority in Congress, the pattern, as expected, reversed, with 68.5 percent of Republican respondents approving of Congress compared with just 58.5 percent of Democrats, a difference of 10.0 percentage points in the opposite direction of 1988. Most of the change seems to come from Republicans, as they became 14.2 points more approving between 1988 and 2000, while Democrats became just 8.5 percent less approving. Congressional approval for Independents was largely indifferent to the party controlling Congress, changing just 1.4 points from 1988 to 2000, and tending in both years to be nearly as disapproving as respondents identifying with the party not in power (in 2000, Independents were actually more disapproving than Democrats).

Seeing congressional approval as primarily a function of partisanship is a common practice in the political science community, but like the convention pertaining to changes over time, this bit of cross-sectional traditional wisdom is also incomplete if not misleading. Certainly there are people in the United States whose evaluations of Congress rest heavily on its partisan contours. These are the people responsible for changing the direction of the relationships in Figure 2. But we need to bear in mind that these people are a distinct minority of the population. In 1988, for example, 1,745 NES respondents could be categorized as Democrats, Republicans, or Independents and were asked the question on congressional approval. These individuals fall into the following categories:

Independents	618
Partisans who could not say whether they approved or disapproved of Congress	133
Democrats who disapproved of the Democratic Congress	181
Republicans who approved of the Democratic Congress	242
Potentially influenced by partisanship	571
Total	1745

Independents and those who neither approved nor disapproved could not have based their approval decision on whether their own party affiliation matched the congressional majority. Similarly, those Democrats who disapproved of a Democratic-majority Congress and those Republicans who approved of a Democratic-majority Congress could not be said to have based their approval decision on partisanship. This leaves only 571 respondents, 32.7 percent of the sample, as Democrats who approved of the Democratic Congress or Republicans who disapproved. Even these individuals may have based their decision on some other basis than party affiliation, but at least for them we cannot rule out the possibility that their decision was partisan. The overall point is that in 1988 less than one-third of all respondents reflected a partisan bias in their congressional-approval decision.

It could be that 1988 was unusual in this regard, but this appears not to be the case. When the same procedures were conducted on respondents in 2000, the congressional-approval decision of not more than 28 percent of the sample was influenced by partisanship (Democrats who disapproved of the Republican Congress and Republicans who approved). Partisanship is heavily responsible for the changes in patterns of approval that occur when the partisan majority of Congress switches, but it is not responsible for most people's approval decisions. As is the case with many other features of American politics, a small percentage of the population tends to drive longitudinal change and that small percentage comes in for an inordinate amount of attention from scholars. If the goal is to understand the manner in which ordinary people are deciding whether they approve or disapprove of Congress (and government), the fact remains that for more than two out of three Americans, partisanship is not the deciding factor.

If not partisanship, then what? The usual array of demographic variables can be of assistance in discerning the kind of individual most likely to approve of Congress. In Figure 3 congressional approval is broken down by several of these variables. This breakdown is performed for both of the elections that have been used for illustrative purposes here: 1988 with a Democratic majority and 2000 with a Republican one. Definite patterns are apparent for three of the variables in both of the years analyzed. It can be determined with some confidence that approval of Congress is higher among young people, among females, and among members of racial minorities. The drop in approval from the youngest age bracket, labeled "Y" in Figure 3 (eighteen- to thirty-year-olds) to the oldest, labeled "O" (those over seventy) is 20.5 in 1988 and 15.6 in 2000; the drop from females ("F") to males ("M") is 10.6 in 1988 and 6.7 in 2000; and the drop from African Americans ("B") and from Hispanics ("H") to whites ("W") is modest in 1988 and quite large in 2000 (10.3 for Hispanics and 7.8 for African Americans).[18]

The other three demographic variables yield results that are less clear. Compared to those with less education, respondents with a four-year college

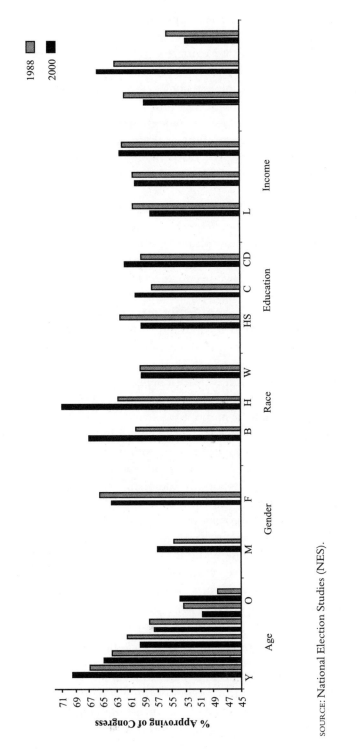

SOURCE: National Election Studies (NES).

Figure 3. Demographic Traits and Approval of Congress in 1988 and 2000

degree ("CD") seemed to be less approving of Congress in 1988 but slightly more approving in 2000. Greater income ("H") seems to be associated with more favorable feelings toward Congress in both years, but the differences are quite small. "Interest in the political race" has a curvilinear relationship in both years, with those in the middle category of "somewhat" interested ("M") being more approving than those with "not much" interest ("L") and especially those "very much" interested ("H"). This demographic analysis thus yields the following profile: the type of person most likely to approve of Congress is a young minority female who is not particularly interested in politics. High income and education levels do not much change the odds that a person will approve of Congress.

What does this mean for interpretations of the public's image of Congress? These findings are in some respects counterintuitive. It might have been expected that the people most pleased with congressional (and governmental) performance would be those benefiting the most from current societal arrangements. Similarly, it might have been expected that people who see individuals most like themselves serving in Congress would be most pleased with the institution. But it is obvious from the results presented in Figure 3 that approval of Congress is not a reflection of the kind of individual occupying positions of advantage in society and it is not a reflection of the kind of individual currently serving in Congress: older, educated, well-to-do, politically interested white males. In fact, this description is close to being an exact match with the description of the kind of person most likely to disapprove of Congress. Why might this be the case, and what does it mean?

Many observers are surprised that educated individuals and those with an interest in politics and campaigns are not more approving of Congress. One reasonable explanation is that those with more education and political interest are likely to have higher expectations for the members, expectations unlikely to be met.[19] Thus, those with substantial interest in the campaign in both 1988 and 2000 were the most disapproving of Congress, and those who likely perceived some distance between themselves and members of Congress—the young, minorities, females, and those without a great deal of interest in politics—were less willing to render negative evaluations.[20] Just as congressional popularity goes down when Congress is in the news a great deal, so congressional popularity is lower among people who claim to pay a great deal of attention to campaigns.

Improving Congress's Image

Whether referring to changes in congressional approval over time, constituent likes and dislikes, or individual profiles of those approving and disapproving of Congress, conventional treatments of the image of Congress frequently miss the mark. Taking into consideration the emerging diversity and associated burgeoning demands on American government as well as the associated general decline in approval of all societal institutions beginning in the late 1960s, it is clear that the images of Congress and the federal government are not all that different at the turn of the twenty-first century than they were long ago. Congress's popularity of late may be down more than it is up, but it is not always down. Further, Congress is not hated, while its individual members are revered. In fact, Congress as an institution is beloved by the American people, even as the membership as a whole, like American politicians in general, are largely reviled. Finally, the kind of person most likely to disapprove of Congress is the very type of person filling the halls of Congress and, relatedly, the kind of person to whom Congress allegedly caters: older, politically interested white males.

The revised and more complete view of the patterns pertaining to congressional approval sheds light on the likely reasons for Congress's image and also provides insights into the manner by which that image could best be improved. For example, since the revised view does not contend that an unprecedented and irreversible decline in Congress's image occurred in the early 1970s, explanations for such a decline are no longer required. More specifically, the notion that growing dissatisfaction with Congress in recent decades is due to a declining quality of behavior on the part of members is called into question. One might wish that congressional debates were conducted with more dignity and decorum, but the claim that the level of exchange was a step level lower in 1975 than it was in 1965—or 1865—is difficult to sustain. Moreover, in order to account for the sharp upturn in congressional approval, proponents of this position would have to argue that beginning in 1998 the nature of these interactions was significantly improved (an end to hostile and overtly partisan debates?), and few observers have made such an assessment. Similarly, the notion that the image of Congress is primarily shaped by the media and that the greater scrutiny and cynicism driving media outlets in the post-Watergate era has tarnished Congress's image seems unlikely. While harsh media treatment unquestionably is a concern for Congress, pre-Watergate press accounts of Congress were often brutal. Congressional reporting in the days of the partisan, and then the muckraking, press was less different from that found in the post-Watergate media than is often imagined. And again, does the upturn in congressional approval beginning in 1998 mean media treatments of Congress became favorable at about that time? The media's tendency to present every elected official's actions as a quest for personal advantage undoubtedly hurts Congress's image. Even so, this tendency did not abate from 1998 to 2003, yet the image of Congress improved markedly during that time. Making member behavior more decorous and media coverage less cynical are both commendable goals, but they would have less effect on the image of Congress than is commonly expected.

Inspection of people's knowledge of and attitudes toward particular aspects of Congress casts doubt on the ability of internal reforms alone to solve any image problem Congress might have. Given the public's minimal understanding of the workings of Congress, rearranging the body (through committee reform and reorganization, strengthening party leadership, changing staff capabilities and responsibilities, modifications of floor procedures) is unlikely to alter its image. Moreover, the data suggests that the institution of Congress itself does not have an image problem. Since negative images are associated with the membership as a whole and not the institution of Congress, institutional reform is unlikely to address the core problem.

Analysis of the type of person most likely to approve of Congress provides additional guidance on the changes that are unlikely to improve Congress's image. Increasing the level of descriptive representation, the degree to which the demographic traits of the overall population match the demographic traits of the members of Congress, though desirable from several points of view, probably will not improve the institution's image. People whose traits are least present among those serving in Congress—females, the young, racial minorities, and those without high interest in politics—are the most likely to approve of Congress, so an absence of descriptive representation does not seem to explain negative perceptions of Congress.

Moreover, findings on the type of person most likely to approve of Congress, as well as findings on the times during which Congress is most approved, cast doubt on the commonly voiced belief that approval of Congress merely indicates satisfaction with policy outputs and outcomes. The conventional argument holds that if times are good and a given individual believes that Congress is enacting desirable policies, then that individual will approve of Congress. Remember, people are largely unaware of congressional actions. The ability of ordinary people to discuss congressional policy activity is difficult to underestimate. It is simply not on most people's radar screens. But even if people do not know whether Congress passed policy A or policy B, perhaps their approval is a response to the conditions of the country. When conditions are good, people approve of Congress; when they are bad, they disapprove. As we have seen, the data does not support this line of argument. People are not necessarily approving of Congress when the economy is good (witness the mid-1990s) and they are not necessarily disapproving when the economy is bad (witness the early 2000s). The relationship of congressional approval to scandals and to international events is also more complicated than expected. In sum, the image of Congress does not automatically improve just because the conditions of the country improve.

But so far the focus has been on explanations that do *not* fit with the revised and more complete presentation of patterns in congressional approval. Is there an explanation that does fit? No single explanation could be expected to account for patterns as complex as congressional approval, but the results do point to one possibility. A significant portion of disaffection with Congress may be attributable to people's lack of appreciation for democratic processes, their unwillingness to admit that disagreement and debate, compromise and conflict, must be part of government. Historical analyses find that congressional disapproval goes up whenever Congress is visible, whenever it is seen debating important divisive legislation, and whenever it is in conflict with the president.

This explanation is also consistent with the aspects of Congress that are liked and disliked. People like Congress when it is presented as an abstract, constitutional, ethereal entity but dislike it when it is presented as a group of human beings. Further, people dislike any part of government that does not try to speak for all people. Specifically, their dislike of political parties, special interests, and self-serving members stems from an unrealistic desire for government to work without conflict between and among these entities. This would also explain why those individuals with the most political interest are the least approving of Congress. Those who do not pay enough attention to be aware of congressional wrangling may be in the best position to return a favorable verdict on the institution's performance.

People believe Americans are in general agreement on societal goals and that members should just quietly and scientifically identify a good, if not the best, way of achieving those goals. The fact that members spend so much time quibbling and bickering indicates to the people that members must be out of touch with mainstream America and are being corrupted by special interests. Thus, people see any interaction between members and special interests or political parties as evidence that members are self-interested and no longer concerned with the common good. Relatedly, the more remuneration members receive, the longer they stay in Washington, the more they rub shoulders with fat cats, and the more they are surrounded by sycophants, the more likely they are to lose touch with the sensible voice of middle America.

Members are baffled by people's perception that they are out of touch, when representatives are back in their districts virtually every weekend, conducting more polls than ever to identify what their constituents (and not just those motivated to contact the member's office) think and desire, and using their staffs to service constituent needs. The explanation may be that people are reacting not to the actual behavior of the members but to the growing diversity and complexity of the country. After all, people tend to believe that their own member is working hard at staying in touch with the district; it is everybody else's representative that they perceive to be deficient. And what is their informational basis for such a claim? Should not the people of a member's district be in the best position to judge the extent to which their member has stayed in touch? People's perception that other people's members are not doing their job is largely unfounded and, to the extent that this perception is more acute now than it was in bygone days (and we do not know that it is), it probably springs from the noise, controversy, and diversity so obviously present in modern society. People's dissatisfaction may actually be a reflection of what representatives as a group must try to represent rather than an honest assessment of member performance. Be this as it may, Congress's image would almost certainly be improved if there were a reduction in people's sense that special interests and partisan hacks were running the institution.

People need to become more realistic, not only about the challenges of representing the views of a diverse country and coming to a resolution in the face of this diversity, but also they must realize that Congress cannot check other institutions of government (something people very much want to happen) without creating conflict. In the abstract, people are strongly supportive of Congress's role as a check on executive power but in practice they do not like it when Congress actually does check presidential power. The very concept of a check demands an adversarial relationship, yet whenever Congress adopts a posture vis-à-vis the president that is remotely adversarial, congressional approval declines.

Americans' confusion regarding their preferred distribution of power in the political system runs even deeper than has been implied to this point. Consider responses to the following three items contained in the 2004 national survey commissioned for this volume.

	Number	Percent
The country would be better off if more decisions were . . .		
made by experts.	357	48.6
made by members of Congress.	302	41.2
Don't know/Refused	74	10.3
Total	733	100.0
If the president believes something should be done about an important national issue, other policy makers should defer to him.		
Agree	871	58.1
Disagree	546	36.4
Don't know/Refused	84	5.6
Total	1501	100.0
When it comes to making important policy decisions, do you think decisions should be made by Congress or by the president?		
Congress	362	59.4
President	125	20.5
Both (volunteered)	85	13.9
Don't know/Refused	38	6.2
Total	610	100.0

The first response indicates a preference for shifting power away from Congress and toward "experts," presumably in the bureaucracy or in the private sector. The second indicates a preference for presidential power, with other policy makers, including members of Congress, deferring to the president. And the third indicates something quite different: that when forced to pick between giving power to the president or to Congress, people overwhelmingly pick Congress. Given the wording of the items, these responses are not necessarily directly contradictory, but they are less than consistent, expressing in short order preference for Congress over the president, for the president over Congress, and for bureaucrats/private individuals over Congress. Rather than attempting to make sense of these desires, it may be best to view the responses as a caution against assuming that Americans have a clear, developed vision of the specific power arrangements that would be present in their preferred political system. Complaining about the flaws of the existing system is easier and infinitely more common than formulating a preferable alternative. This is especially true regarding perceptions of the U.S. Congress.

Although the American people, to say the least, are uncertain regarding their preferred political decision-making structure, people nonetheless are certain that members of Congress are self-serving rather than other-regarding, in all likelihood because they equate debating the common good with not being interested in the common good. The perception that members are self-interested is crucial to the negative image that is frequently associated with Congress. Recent research has shown that people feel much better about a policy decision when it is made for an unselfish reason than when that very same decision is rendered for a selfish reason.[21] The image of Congress would improve if people believed the members were making decisions for non-self-interested reasons. Unfortunately, people are innately suspicious of individuals, including members of Congress, who are desirous of authoritative positions, and they will not be easily convinced that members are sincerely motivated by a desire to help other people. Accordingly, campaign finance reform, limitations on gift giving, and disclosure and ethics requirements have all had minimal impact on the image of Congress. People are unlikely to be aware of reforms in these areas even when they do occur. What percent of the population knows what McCain-Feingold (or BCRA) is, what its provisions are, and whether it passed? Such reforms do little to disabuse people of their belief that members reap huge dividends from congressional service, and it is difficult to imagine what it would take to convince people otherwise. Even a reduction in the congressional salary might not make that much of a difference unless it could be coupled with evidence that members were unable to draw upon their influential position to curry favor with special interests that would respond in turn with gifts, junkets, illicit payments, and cushy post-Congress employment.

One promising though challenging line of attack is to educate schoolchildren and others about the diversity of policy views present across the country and to let them experience the difficulties of making decisions in the context of diverse preferences. Simulations, for example, can be useful in allowing students to see the need for debate and compromise and to recognize that policy debates are not automatically an indication that the common good has been sacrificed for the sake of special interests.[22] Current approaches to civic education seem to focus too exclusively on civic knowledge and civic participation, when civic values and an appreciation of representative democracy need to be encouraged.

Conclusion

It is easy to dislike institutions of representative democracy since they provide a venue for working through disagreements that citizens wish did not exist. The pace is unavoidably slow and the results seldom clean and pleasing. Worse, representative government entails granting authority to selected individuals, thus leaving ordinary people vulnerable to being taken advantage of by those officials. People are habitually suspicious of authority figures even when those authorities are doing their jobs by trying in good faith to promote the common good. Even so, there is good news and it is twofold. First, Congress is not doomed to being disliked. The people like Congress at certain times; they express overwhelming support for the institution of Congress (even when job approval ratings are low); and a slice of the population seems routinely approving of Congress regardless of the situation. Congress may have its work cut out for it if it wants to acquire a favorable image, but the task is not impossible. Second, indications are that Congress can function effectively on those occasions when its public image is unfavorable. This is good, because improving people's vision of the legislature cannot be accomplished by quick and dirty institutional reform; instead, improvement requires convincing a highly skeptical population that self-sacrifice is alive and well in the halls of Congress.

Notes

*The author acknowledges the assistance of Chris Larimer and Eric Whitaker in conducting the data analyses utilized. Data collection was made possible in part by a grant from the National Science Foundation (SES 97-09934), awarded to John Hibbing and Elizabeth Theiss-Morse. Other data utilized herein came from the National Election Studies at the University of Michigan.

1. Arthur H. Miller, "Political Issues and Trust in Government, 1964–1970," *American Political Science Review* 68 (September 1974): 951–972. Jack Citrin, "Comment: The Political Relevance of Trust in Government," *American Political Science Review* 68 (September 1974): 973–988.

2. On members choosing not to seek reelection, see Sean Theriault, "Moving Up or Moving Out: Career Ceilings and Congressional Retirement," *Legislative Studies Quarterly* 23 (August 1998): 419–434. On deciding against running for Congress, see Linda L. Fowler and Robert D. McClure, *Political Ambition: Who Decides to Run for Congress* (New Haven, Conn.: Yale University Press, 1989). On avoiding controversial issues, see David Hess, "Congress Hibernating till Fall," *Houston Chronicle,* March 19, 1998, A8, and also Hetherington, *Why Trust Matters.* On not complying with the law, see Tom Tyler, *Why People Obey the Law* (New Haven, Conn.: Yale University Press, 1990).

3. Consistent soundings of the public's attitudes toward government generally are only available from the very late 1950s to the present, and for Congress specifically only from NES since 1980 (although the Harris Organization began regularly asking people about their "confidence" in Congress in the early 1970s, and Gallup began including in its polling a congressional approval item shortly thereafter).

4. For further evidence on this point, see Davidson, Kovenock, and O'Leary, *Congress in Crisis.* The National Election Studies did not exist prior to 1956.

5. The best summary of these very early survey results is contained in Davidson, Kovenock, and O'Leary, *Congress in Crisis,* chapter 2.

6. Suitably chastened, members promptly reinstated the per diem salary and it was almost forty years before an annual salary was tried again.

7. Lipset and Schneider, *The Confidence Gap.*

8. See, for example, Robert Z. Lawrence, "Is It Really the Economy, Stupid?" in *Why People Don't Trust Government,* edited by Nye, Zelikow, and King.

9. James T. Smith, "The Institutionalization of Politics by Scandal," Ph.D. Diss., University of Nebraska, 2002.

10. John R. Hibbing and Elizabeth Theiss-Morse, "The Media's Role in Public Negativity toward Congress," *American Journal of Political Science* 42 (April 1998): 475–498.

11. Robert H. Durr, John B. Gilmour, and Christina Wolbrecht, "Explaining Congressional Approval," *American Journal of Political Science* 41 (January 1997): 175–207. This finding was generated by correlating survey responses to items such as "How well is Congress doing its job?" with a count of landmark legislation presented in David R. Mayhew, *Divided We Govern: Party Control, Lawmaking and Investigations, 1949–90* (New Haven, Conn.: Yale University Press, 1991). As also discussed in this essay, Congress can be in the news for not doing anything, and these situations also seem to depress the public's approval of Congress. See Sarah A. Binder, *Stalemate: Causes and Consequences of Legislative Gridlock* (Washington, D.C.: Brookings Institution Press, 2003), for evidence that periods of salient gridlock diminish congressional popularity.

12. So the "conspicuous actions" of members, creatively documented in David Mayhew's essay in this volume, may ironically work to the detriment of congressional popularity.

13. These survey results are reported in Delli Carpini and Keeter, *What Americans Know about Politics and Why It Matters;* see especially chapter 2.

14. Some respondents admit that they do not know, but it is also likely that some of those who answered correctly were guessing and (with only two probable answers—Democrats or Republicans) got lucky.

15. Richard F. Fenno Jr., "If, as Ralph Nader Says, Congress Is 'The Broken Branch,' How Come We Love Our Congressmen So Much?" in *Congress in Change: Evolution and Reform*, edited by Norman J. Ornstein, 277–287 (New York: Praeger, 1975).
16. Hibbing and Theiss-Morse, *Congress as Public Enemy*, 64.
17. Warren E. Miller and Donald E. Stokes, "Constituency Influence in Congress," *American Political Science Review* 57 (March 1963): 45–56.
18. It may be surprising to some that a strongly Democratic group like young minority females without high interest in politics is so supportive of the Republican-controlled Congress in 2000. This constitutes additional evidence that partisanship is neither as known nor as important to most people as many pundits anticipate.
19. David C. Kimball and Samuel C. Patterson, "Living Up to Expectations: Public Attitudes toward Congress," *Journal of Politics* 59 (August 1997): 701–728.
20. Part of this difference could be due to some groups being less likely to know which party controls Congress, though given the small percent of people using party to form approval/disapproval judgments, this seems unlikely.
21. John R. Hibbing and John R. Alford, "Accepting Authoritative Decisions: Humans as Wary Cooperators," *American Journal of Political Science* 48 (January 2004): 62–76.
22. For more on this point, see John R. Hibbing and Elizabeth Theiss-Morse, "Civics Is Not Enough: Teaching Barbarics in K–12," *PS: Political Science and Politics* 29 (March 1996): 57–62. State legislative scholar Alan Rosenthal of Rutgers University developed a valuable set of simulations that has produced promising results in selected high school trials.

Bibliography

Cooper, Joseph, ed. *Congress and the Decline of Public Trust.* Boulder, Colo.: Westview Press, 1999. Excellent collection of essays on the topic.

Craig, Stephen C. *The Malevolent Leaders: Popular Discontent in America.* Boulder, Colo.: Westview Press, 1993. Very useful treatment of the reasons people dislike politicians.

Davidson, Roger H., David M. Kovenock, and Michael K. O'Leary. *Congress in Crisis: Politics and Congressional Reform.* Belmont, Calif.: Wadsworth, 1968. The earliest and one of the best treatments of the image of the modern Congress.

Delli Carpini, Michael X., and Scott Keeter. *What Americans Know about Politics and Why It Matters.* New Haven, Conn.: Yale University Press, 1996. Comprehensive analysis of what people know and do not know about government.

Fenno, Richard F., Jr. *Home Style: House Members in Their Districts.* Repr. New York: Longman. 2003. Classic treatment of members of Congress operating among their constituents.

Hetherington, Marc J. *Why Trust Matters: Declining Political Trust and the Demise of American Liberalism.* Princeton, N.J.: Princeton University Press, 2004. Clear-headed account on the manner in which public disapproval of government can have policy consequences.

Hibbing, John R., and Elizabeth Theiss-Morse. *Congress as Public Enemy: Public Attitudes toward American Political Institutions.* New York: Cambridge University Press, 1995. Compares attitudes toward Congress with attitudes toward other political institutions.

Hibbing, John R., and Elizabeth Theiss-Morse. *Stealth Democracy: Americans' Beliefs about How Government Should Work.* New York: Cambridge University Press, 2002. Argues that Americans do not want specific policies so much as they want decision makers who are not selfishly motivated.

Lipset, Seymour Martin, and William Schneider. *The Confidence Gap: Business, Labor, and Government in the Public Mind.* Rev. ed. Baltimore: Johns Hopkins University Press, 1987. Documents the decline in the image of the leaders of virtually all societal institutions in the late 1960s and early 1970s.

Nye, Joseph S., Jr., Philip D. Zelikow, and David C. King, eds. *Why People Don't Trust Government.* Cambridge, Mass.: Harvard University Press, 1997. A strong collection of essays on the causes of Americans' lack of trust of their government.

17

POLITICS OF CONGRESSIONAL REFORM

C. Lawrence Evans

URING THE SUMMER OF 2004, MEMBERS OF THE HOUSE
and Senate repeatedly called for major changes in congressional operations. Frustrated by Democratic obstructionism on a number of Bush
administration judicial nominees, Senate majority leader Bill Frist (R-Tenn.)
proposed significant new restrictions on use of the filibuster in the confirmation
process. In June, a rump group of Senate Republicans met to consider changes to
party rules that would have increased leadership influence over GOP committee
assignments. In the House, minority leader Nancy Pelosi (D-Calif.) proposed a
"minority party bill of rights" for the chamber, including open amendment procedures on the floor; guarantees that the minority party would be able to participate fully in conference committee negotiations with the Senate; and
constraints on the ability of GOP leaders to extend the duration of roll calls, to
whip wavering Republicans into line. In July, the 9/11 Commission recommended reforms of the committee system intended to strengthen oversight of
intelligence and homeland security. "The United States needs a strong, stable,
and capable congressional committee structure," the commission maintained, "to
give America's national intelligence agencies oversight, support, and leadership."[1]

The purpose of this essay is to consider the prospects for meaningful institutional reform on Capitol Hill by addressing several questions about the politics
of congressional reform during the period 1961–2004. What kinds of reform
initiatives have been prominent on the national agenda and what institutional
challenges were they designed to address? What have been the main constituencies supporting and opposing important efforts to revamp congressional operations and how have these cleavages varied by reform area? What are the
conditions associated with successful attempts to alter the institutional and legal

environments of Congress? What are the chances that significant reforms will be adopted in the foreseeable future?

The meaning of *reform* can be ambiguous, because the word typically is interpreted as change for the better and there often is considerable disagreement about the normative consequences of proposed alterations in congressional operations. In this essay, the focus is on institutional reform as an issue area on the national legislative agenda. An initiative is treated as a reform proposal if a significant number of lawmakers and outside observers clearly viewed it as an effort to improve congressional organization, institutions, or operations. The emphasis herein is on the politics of reform across five main areas: campaign finance, institutional integrity (e.g., openness and ethics), the committee system, floor procedure, and congressional resources and interbranch prerogatives.

Reform Imperatives

Under the U.S. Constitution, House members and senators are responsible for determining the internal structures of their respective chambers, and through legislation members of Congress shape the rules that govern the electoral process. These structural and procedural choices matter because they affect who wins and who loses in the electoral and legislative arenas. Many decisions about reform are relatively incremental.[2] At the beginning of a new Congress, for example, members of the House must adopt standing rules for their chamber. The "opening day" rules packages usually are very similar to the procedures utilized during the previous Congress, but also typically include many minor adjustments. Unlike the House, the Senate is a "continuing" body and does not need to adopt standing rules at the beginning of each Congress. But senators regularly pass minor reforms during the normal course of chamber business. In 1995, for example, the passage of a floor amendment offered by Kay Bailey Hutchison (R-Tex.) to an appropriations bill effectively altered Senate rules against adding policy language to spending measures. Four years later, the "Hutchison precedent" was reversed via another midsession floor vote.

Although the process of institutional change in Congress is ongoing and often incremental, over the years lawmakers have adopted major reforms that were substantial departures from the organizational status quo. Table 1 lists the most significant reforms for 1961–2004, categorized by the aspect of the institution targeted for change.[3] It should be emphasized that there are important continuities in the politics of reform across the five areas. For one, significant path dependencies exist in the structural development of Congress, which in turn set parameters on the way that reform issues are framed and on the range of feasible proposals.[4] The landmark budget process reforms of 1974, for instance, were layered on top of existing structures, largely because a "whole cloth" redesign of

TABLE 1
Major Congressional Reforms, 1961–2004

Campaign Finance
Federal Election Campaign Act (1971)
- public disclosure
- expenditure limits
- limits on contributions to own campaign

Federal Election Campaign Amendments (1974)
- contribution limits
- create FEC

Federal Election Campaign Amendments (1976)
- reconstitute FEC

Federal Election Campaign Amendments (1979)
- relax restrictions on party soft money

Disclosure requirements for Section 527 committees (2000)
Bipartisan Campaign Finance Reform Act (2002)
- soft money ban for national parties
- regulate funding of issue-advocacy advertisements
- increase contribution limits

Institutional Integrity
Sunshine reforms (1970, 1973)
Televise floor proceedings in the House (1979) and Senate (1986)
Establish Senate and House Ethics Committees (1964, 1967)
Changes to ethics process (1968, 1977, 1989)
Congressional Accountability Act (1995)
Lobbying disclosure and gift ban (1995)

Committee System
House Democratic Caucus (1971)
- selection of committee chairs

House Democratic Caucus (1973)
- selection of committee chairs
- Subcommittee Bill of Rights

House Democratic Caucus (1974)
- committee assignment process
- multiple referral of legislation
- increase committee staff

House committee reforms (1995)
- term limits for committee chairs
- abolish three committees
- repeal Subcommittee Bill of Rights
- abolish proxy voting
- reduce committee staffs
- "primary" committee when measures multiply-referred

Reorganization of Senate committees (1977)
Term limits for Senate GOP committee chairs (1995)

TABLE 1 (continued)

Floor Procedure
Enlarge House Rules Committee (1961)
Recorded votes on House floor amendments (1970)
House Speaker nominates Democrats to Rules Committee (1974)
Motion to recommit with instructions for House minority party (1995)
Senate cloture reform (1975, 1979, 1986)

Congressional Resources and Interbranch Prerogatives
Increase staff resources in House and Senate (1970s)
Congressional Budget Act (1974)
 • establish Budget Committees
 • budget resolution and reconciliation
 • create CBO
Gramm-Rudman-Hollings (1985, 1987)
Budget Enforcement Act (1990)
 • paygo and discretionary caps
Line Item Veto (1996)
Establish Senate and House Intelligence Committees (1976, 1977)
War Powers Resolution (1973)

---

budgetary procedures would have generated insurmountable political opposition from members who stood to lose power.

In addition, the broader partisan-electoral environment of Congress conditions what is achievable across the entire reform agenda at any point in time. As the table indicates, the decade of the 1970s was a pivotal period in the recent institutional development of Congress. Among other changes, the 1970s reforms include major alterations to campaign finance law, an overhaul of the House and Senate committee systems, and a new congressional budget process.[5] Prior to that decade, congressional decision-making was dominated by a conservative coalition of Republicans and southern Democrats and, at least by contemporary standards, the institution was insulated from outside scrutiny. By the early 1970s, the enfranchisement of black voters in the South, an explosion in the array of interest-group pressures confronting Congress, and changes in candidate-nomination procedures combined to create a significant mismatch between the rules that structured the electoral and legislative arenas and the needs of most members. Several major scandals helped build public support for change. As a result, the House and Senate adopted a series of major reforms over the decade. Since that time, congressional policy making has become increasingly polarized along partisan lines, significantly complicating efforts to build cross-partisan coalitions for reforms that would enhance the institutional capacity of Congress.

Even though there are continuities across reform areas, the pressures for and against organizational change differ substantially depending on the aspect of the institution that is targeted for change. Explored here are five forces, or reform imperatives, that have influenced the decisions members make about congressional organization.[6] First, *public opinion* can create powerful incentives for reform. Although public confidence in Congress rises and falls over time, there is a pervasive skepticism among ordinary citizens about members of Congress and the governing performance of the legislative branch.[7] Polls indicate that the public is highly supportive of reform in the abstract. But the average voter usually lacks the information and the motivation necessary to form coherent views about specific proposals to alter Congress. When public attitudes do become crystallized around specific initiatives, the reason is often the occurrence of a significant focusing event, such as a major scandal. Mass attitudes also tend to be most relevant when a reform initiative can be framed to address core public concerns about Congress—for instance, that members are financially untrustworthy or that they lack empathy for the needs of ordinary Americans.

Second, *interest groups* can influence member decisions about institutional reform. In the 1960s, efforts to lower the threshold for invoking cloture in the Senate were championed by a coalition of liberal advocacy organizations. Over the years, interest groups have been major opponents to proposed alterations of committee jurisdictions.[8] Public interest groups, such as Common Cause and United We Stand, have served as advocates of reform and sources of ideas for institutional change.[9] Third, the reform process in Congress often is shaped by *partisan imperatives*.[10] Party pressures are especially important on matters of floor procedure and campaign finance, which directly touch on the electoral prospects and governing abilities of the two political parties. Especially in recent years, party leaders have used reform issues as campaign fodder, and even traditionally nonpartisan items such as ethics and lobbying reform have sharply divided members along party lines.

Fourth, reform initiatives touch on the *personal power agendas* of individual members.[11] Concerns about personal power are typically a key impediment to major changes in committee jurisdictions. The desire among freshmen lawmakers for a more meaningful policy-making role was an important factor behind the 1970s reforms of the House committee system. And even members of the majority party often oppose restrictions on the filibuster because such changes might reduce their procedural leverage within the Senate. Fifth, although existing theoretical treatments of congressional organization tend to downplay elite-level concerns about the collective performance of Congress, the historical record indicates that members care about the *institutional capacity* of the legislative branch. The 1974 Budget Act, for instance, can only be understood from the perspective of bipartisan concerns that Congress lacked the institutional ability to stave off executive branch encroachments over budget policy making.[12]

How does the relative importance of these imperatives vary across reform areas and over time and what are the implications for ongoing efforts to revamp congressional operations? In the sections that follow, the different areas of reform will be considered in turn, beginning with changes to the laws that govern campaign financing.

Campaign Finance Reform

Proposals to alter the campaign finance system typically are intended to further one or more related goals; to publicize or curtail the influence of special-interest money in political campaigns, hold down campaign costs, and reduce the amount of time and effort that members of Congress allocate to fund-raising rather than legislating. All five reform imperatives are relevant, but the key factors in the enduring fight over campaign finance reform have been significant public concern about the power of special interests, intense lobbying by affected groups, and the divergent interests of the two political parties. The issue is not a priority to the average voter, but members of the public are generally supportive of campaign finance reform. Public opinion is an especially important component in the calculations of legislators following a major scandal, and the passage of major campaign finance legislation is almost always linked to such focusing events.

Although the most significant reforms of the campaign finance system occurred in the early 1970s, the effort to regulate how resources are raised and spent in political campaigns dates to the mid-1800s. Nineteenth-century reformers primarily were concerned about the role played by government workers in the electoral process. The Pendleton Civil Service Act of 1883 prohibited party officials from securing campaign funds from political appointees. The parties, as a result, turned to corporate interests for contributions, raising concerns among progressive reformers that business interests might corrupt the political process. In 1917 Congress passed the Tillman Act, which prohibited direct contributions to campaigns from corporations and banks. Following the Teapot Dome Scandal in the early 1920s, Congress adopted the Federal Corrupt Practices Act of 1925 (FCPA). The FCPA included disclosure requirements and expenditure limits for House and Senate campaigns, but by most accounts was ineffective for regulating campaign finance. The expenditure limits, for instance, applied to individual campaign committees, and candidates routinely circumvented the limits by spinning off multiple committees. During the 1930s and 1940s, the emergence of organized labor as an important source of campaign resources for liberal Democrats led Republicans and conservative Democrats to push through legislation to curtail labor's growing campaign muscle.[13] Still, the basic regulatory structure for campaign finance was largely unaltered from the 1920s to the 1970s.

In the 1960s, several changes in the partisan-electoral environment of Congress created incentives for major reform. Most important, the costs of campaigns increased markedly over the decade, primarily because of greater reliance on television advertising. In addition, several scandals relating to campaign finance helped elevate the issue as a public concern. The first major congressional investigation of the Watergate burglary, for instance, focused on the campaign practices of President Richard Nixon. The result was enactment of two landmark statutes; the Federal Election Campaign Act (FECA 1971) and the Federal Election Campaign Amendments of 1974 (FECA 1974).

FECA 1971 included strict disclosure provisions, ceilings on media expenditures, and limits on how much money candidates (and their family members) could donate to their own campaigns. Although FECA 1971 eventually passed by a large bipartisan majority and few lawmakers were willing to take a public position against the disclosure provisions, the legislation evoked many of the cleavages that still characterize campaign finance issues in the twenty-first century. There were important differences between the parties. Democrats supported the spending limits because they believed that their party was losing the fund-raising war to the GOP. Many Democrats also favored publicly funded campaigns for similar reasons. Republicans, in contrast, feared that limits on contributions and expenditures would mostly advantage incumbents, who at the time were disproportionately Democrats. The advocacy community also was divided over the issue. Common Cause and other public interest groups helped draft proposals and publicize the need for reform. Organized labor was concerned about rising campaign costs, but most unions were adamantly opposed to changes that might clamp down on the activities of political action committees (PACs). Ordinary citizens generally favored reform, but for the most part lacked firm views about particular proposals. In the end, the extensive media coverage of campaign finance abuses made opposing the reform effort politically untenable for members of Congress, leading to passage of the measure.

The Watergate scandal of 1973–1974 created incentives for Congress to further reform the campaign finance system, resulting in FECA 1974, the most important campaign finance statute in American history. Among other provisions, the measure strengthened the disclosure provisions in the 1971 act, placed restrictions on all campaign expenditures, established limits on contributions by individuals and PACs to candidates and parties, provided for partial public funding for presidential campaigns, and created a new regulatory bureaucracy to govern campaign finance (the Federal Election Commission). During congressional consideration of FECA 1974, members continued to divide along partisan and ideological lines and there was considerable skepticism in the interest group community about the new limits on PAC contributions. But widespread public concern about political corruption in the wake of Watergate produced overwhelming momentum for reform and the measure passed by margins of 365–24 in the House and 60–16 in the Senate. In 1976 several key provisions of FECA 1974 were struck by the U.S. Supreme Court in *Buckley v. Valeo*, including the expenditure limitations, the restrictions on contributions by candidates and family members, and the method for appointing members of the Federal Election Commission.[14] The Congress passed legislation in 1976 to bring campaign finance law into line with the Supreme Court's opinion. Perhaps the most significant part of the *Buckley* decision stipulated that Congress may only limit contributions to control corruption or the appearance of corruption. A desire to hold down campaign costs is not enough. Any restrictions on campaign expenditures must be voluntary (perhaps in exchange for receiving some form of governmental subsidy) to pass constitutional muster.

In the years that followed, reformers continued to criticize the campaign finance system, especially the pivotal role played by corporate PACs, which proliferated after passage of FECA 1974. But with the exception of a 1979 statute that relaxed the restrictions on expenditures by political parties, no major campaign finance reform legislation was adopted for twenty years because of disagreements between the parties, the reluctance of reelection-oriented incumbents to change the rules under which they had been elected, and the strict constitutional parameters created by *Buckley v. Valeo.*

During the 1990s, two changes in congressional campaigns transformed the nature of the reform debate. First, the use of soft money grew markedly during the decade. Soft money refers to donations to candidates, parties, or other regulated campaign committees that are not directly used to promote the election of particular candidates to federal office (voter registration drives and other party-building activities are examples of soft-money activities). Second, there was a dramatic increase in issue-advocacy advertising. Over the years, the federal courts have ruled that ads not explicitly calling for the election or defeat of specific candidates are not subject to federal regulation. By avoiding certain key words and phrases (for instance, "vote against" candidate Smith, or "defeat" candidate Smith), parties and interest groups could produce advertisements that obviously were intended to influence voter behavior but were not subject to disclosure or other federal regulations.

In response to the explosion of soft money and issue-advocacy activities, in 1997 Senators John McCain (R- Ariz.) and Russell Feingold (D-Wis.) introduced what eventually became the Bipartisan Campaign Reform Act of 2002 (BCRA). During the late 1990s, the measure twice passed the House but fell victim to filibusters in the Senate led by Mitch McConnell (R-Ky.). Even though Republicans were less reliant on soft money than were Democrats, GOP leaders opposed McCain-Feingold on philosophical grounds (they viewed it as an unconstitutional infringement on free political speech) and because they felt that the measure did not sufficiently clamp down on the role of labor money, which mostly helps Democrats. Republicans also called for increases in the contribution limits that had been in place since passage of FECA 1974. Most Democrats, in contrast, publicly endorsed McCain-Feingold and its House counterpart, a bill introduced by Representatives Christopher Shays (R-Conn.) and Martin Meehan (D-Mass). Although many of them privately expressed reservations about the legislation because of their party's heavy reliance on soft money, the prospect of a successful McConnell filibuster enabled otherwise ambivalent Democrats to cast a costless vote in favor of reform.

In 2000 Congress did enact more targeted reform legislation to require full disclosure of campaign-related activities by so-called "527" organizations. Prior to the 2000 statute, tax-exempt groups that registered under section 527 of the Internal Revenue Code were not required to disclose their political activities to the Federal Election Commission or to regulators at the state level. As with other "disclosure" reforms, the 527 measure was enacted with broad-based support.

The impasse over McCain-Feingold ended during 2001–2002. Turnover in the Senate following the 2000 elections brought supporters of the measure within two votes of the sixty necessary to invoke cloture. McCain's bracing presidential run in 2000 raised the public visibility of campaign finance reform. And the highly publicized corporate scandals of 2001 (especially the bankruptcy of the energy company Enron) increased the potential costs to opposing reform for President George W. Bush and many Republicans on Capitol Hill. Still, the route to final passage was rife with procedural maneuvers, poison-pill amendments, and opposition from key constituencies. Both the AFL-CIO and the National Right to Life Committee, for example, strenuously opposed the restrictions on issue-advocacy activities. Members of the Congressional Black Caucus feared that the soft-money ban would hurt Democratic candidates from impoverished districts. As it became clear that reform advocates had the support to prevail, however, McConnell opted not to filibuster the final agreement and the legislation passed the House (240–189) and Senate (60–40) in early 2002. In both chambers, most Democrats voted yes and most Republicans voted no, but there was sufficient GOP support to ensure final passage. Along with a ban on soft money and restrictions on issue advocacy, the final version of the legislation included subsidies for candidates facing millionaire opponents and a GOP-backed increase in the limits on individual contributions. An obviously ambivalent President Bush quietly signed the legislation into law in March 2002.

There is little consensus among scholars and practitioners about the overall impact of the post-1960s reforms of the campaign finance system. The reforms did make contributions to candidates and campaign expenditures more transparent and open to public scrutiny. But there is little evidence that reform significantly checked the burgeoning costs of running for Congress, and if anything, the amount of time that lawmakers allocate to fund-raising has increased since the 1970s. The funding advantages of incumbents also grew over the period, with the typical House incumbent now spending two or three times as much as the average challenger. Not surprisingly, most congressional races are uncompetitive. The 1970s reforms were intended to reduce the corrupting influence of special interest money, but corporate, labor, and other special interests were able to circumvent the intent of these rules during the 1990s via soft-money donations to the political parties. It remains to be seen whether BCRA will reduce the influence (real and perceived) of wealthy donors and interest groups in the electoral process, or simply shift their contributions toward independent expenditures and other, less-regulated, forms of campaign finance. There was a significant rise in small donations to both parties during the 2004 campaigns, in part because of the increased limits on individual contributions and party efforts to compensate for the ban on soft money. But the soft-money ban also helped fuel an increase in the campaign-related activities of section 527 groups, which are not subject to the same fund-raising and expenditure restrictions confronted by candidates and parties.

Institutional Integrity

As with campaign finance reform, the initiatives in this reform area are intended to curtail corruption in the legislative process, but the emphasis is on causal factors located within the halls of Congress rather than in the electoral arena. All of the "institutional integrity" reforms in Table 1 were strongly conditioned by public distrust of the legislative branch. The changes typically followed a significant scandal that focused the public's distrust of Congress on particular problems within the institution and raised the potential political costs to members from taking positions that could be cast as "antireform." The primary impediments to reform varied from issue to issue, but often were senior lawmakers who viewed the specific initiatives as excessive restrictions on their personal prerogatives and, in any event, unlikely to produce significant improvements in the public image of Congress.

In Table 1, the first set of major reforms in the area of institutional integrity was aimed at opening up the legislative process to greater public scrutiny. Sunshine, so the argument goes, is the best disinfectant. Prior to the 1970s, congressional committees often met in private, behind closed doors, and on the House floor amendments were not subject to recorded votes. This lack of transparency significantly constrained the ability of outside observers to hold individual lawmakers accountable for their actions.

The first wave of sunshine reforms was included in the Legislative Reorganization Act of 1970, which was based on a comprehensive package of reforms that had been proposed by the 1965 Joint Committee on the Organization of Congress. These reforms were pushed by a coalition of liberal reformers seeking to curb the power of conservative committee chairs and by Republicans who wanted to make the traditional power centers of the Democratic majority less insular. Among other provisions, the 1970 act encouraged committees to hold open meetings, required that the records of all roll calls cast in committee be made publicly available, and provided for recorded votes on floor amendments in the House. Three years later, the House adopted a rule requiring that all committee meetings and markups (bill-writing sessions) be open to the public unless a majority of the relevant panel voted otherwise.

The most important of the openness reforms, however, pertained to broadcast coverage of floor proceedings in the House and Senate.[15] During the 1970s, a new generation of legislators was elected; politicians who were comfortable using television to communicate with the public. Many members of the House and Senate also believed that broadcasting congressional floor proceedings might help them counter the president's superior ability to secure media coverage. Entrepreneurs within the new cable television industry recognized that developing a significant public affairs component for the industry might enhance its image. Initially, proposals to televise the House were opposed by influential Democrats, such as Speaker Thomas P. ("Tip") O'Neill, because of concerns that members might lose control over how the chamber was portrayed in the media. But there was widespread support for the change among younger Democrats and O'Neill switched positions in 1977. Republicans such as John Anderson of Illinois had been pushing the reform for many years, and GOP members mostly supported televising the House. C-SPAN coverage of the chamber began in 1979.

Interestingly, the more visible Senate did not embrace televised floor proceedings until 1986, largely because of concerns among senior members that television might undermine the quality of deliberation. Filibusters killed proposals to broadcast the Senate floor in 1982 and again in 1984. Following the 1984 elections, Robert C. Byrd (D-W.V.) a leader of the antibroadcast coalition, switched sides because he feared that the Senate was losing public visibility relative to the now-televised House. Final adoption of a resolution to broadcast the Senate was complicated by member differences over a series of proposed changes to floor procedure (intended to make the chamber more television-friendly), but in February 1986 the Senate endorsed televised proceedings for a trial period, and made the practice permanent in July of that year.

The second set of reforms in the area of institutional integrity relates to the procedures that House members and senators use to regulate their official conduct. Prior to the 1960s, allegations of official misconduct by members were referred to temporary ad hoc panels for investigation. Formal codes of ethical conduct for the House and Senate simply did not exist. During the mid-1960s, a scandal involving Robert "Bobby" Baker, formerly secretary of the Senate under Majority Leader Lyndon Johnson (D-Tex.), sparked concerns among lawmakers and observers about the lack of formal procedures for handling allegations of misconduct. Conflict within the House about the censure of Representative Adam Clayton Powell (D-N.Y.) also added to the demands for a more institutionalized ethics process. The Senate established a standing committee with jurisdiction over internal ethics in 1964 and the House followed suit three years later. Both chambers adopted written codes of conduct in 1968. And both ethics codes were significantly altered in 1977, and again in 1989.

The 1977 changes followed a series of highly publicized scandals, including the revelation that Wayne Hays (D-Ohio), the influential chair of the House Administration Committee, had hired his mistress as a committee staffer. "I can't type, I can't file, I can't even answer the phone," she famously told the *Washington Post*.[16] Included among the reforms were requirements for the disclosure of personal financial information by members, limitations on outside income, and a rule against tapping office accounts for personal use. The proposals were viewed by many senior members as an unnecessarily punitive overreaction to the misdeeds of a few legislators. To overcome such opposition, congressional leaders had to tie the package to a pay raise for members. Similar dynamics characterized congressional passage of the Ethics Reform Act of 1989. Earlier that year, the House Ethics Committee found that Speaker James Wright (D-Tex.) had violated the code of conduct in sixty-nine instances. Wright stepped down as Speaker and soon resigned from the House. In November 1989, both chambers cleared the most sweeping alterations in the congressional code of conduct since the 1977 changes. The package included tougher restrictions on the lobbying activities of former members, tighter rules for gifts and foreign travel, limitations on the use of campaign funds for personal use, and significant changes to the procedures for conducting ethics investigations. As with the 1977 changes, many members (especially senior Democrats) viewed the 1989 reforms as excessively punitive. And once again, passage of the package was facilitated when Democratic leaders linked it to a significant salary increase for members of Congress.

During the early 1990s, the public's distrust of Congress was fueled by highly publicized allegations that members were somehow above the law and awash in a sea of special privileges. In September 1991 the General Accounting Office reported that House members had written over eight thousand checks that were not fully covered by their personal accounts in the House bank. The national media quickly picked up on the GAO report, creating an outcry among the public about congressional perks. In fall 1991, the proportion of Americans who approved of the way that Congress was handling its job plummeted to just 17 percent, an all-time low. The House bank scandal directly resulted in the defeat of a number of lawmakers in the 1992 elections and in the creation of another Joint Committee on the Organization of Congress, charged with formulating comprehensive recommendations for reform. The committee's findings were released in the fall of 1993. Included was a proposal to apply to the legislative branch a range of workplace laws from which it had been exempted (the Occupational Safety and Health Administration regulations and the Fair Labor Standards Act were examples) because of constitutional concerns about subjecting the internal operations of the legislative branch to regulation by the executive branch. In the wake of the bank scandal, members were highly vulnerable to charges that they were not subject to the same laws that were applied to ordinary citizens. As a result, the joint committee proposed adoption of the Congressional Accountability Act, which aimed to end the exemptions by placing enforcement authority in an independent agency of the legislative branch. The proposal fell victim to a parliamentary objection in the Senate during the fall of 1994, but passed both chambers by wide margins the following year when Republicans assumed majority control.[17]

As part of the broader reform efforts of 1995, the House and Senate also adopted tighter restrictions on accepting gifts from lobbyists, as well as a requirement that lobbyists publicly disclose the identities of their clients.[18] Efforts to pass the gift ban and lobby-disclosure legislation were spearheaded by a bipartisan coalition of junior members, and were initially opposed by Republican leaders and other senior members who viewed the measures as unworkable. It became apparent, however, that an overwhelming majority of members supported both reform initiatives and they were adopted by wide margins.

What has been the long-term impact of the institutional integrity reforms of Table 1? The effects of the openness initiatives are difficult to gauge with precision. There is no evidence that these changes have increased public knowledge about the national legislature. The main beneficiaries of open meetings may be lobbyists, who are much more likely than ordinary citizens to consume information about the legislative process. Many participants and observers argue that members are more likely to engage in position taking and grandstanding now that television cameras cover the floor and many committee meetings. But television clearly provides individual lawmakers, especially junior legislators and members of the minority party, with a useful tool for reaching the general public. During the early 1980s, for example, Newt Gingrich (R–Ga.) and other members of the Conservative Opportunity Society, a group of junior GOP conservatives, made regular use of televised "special orders" speeches to publicize their agenda and criticize Democratic leaders. Television coverage of the House and Senate chambers also enables members and staff to better follow floor developments, improving access to information about parliamentary maneuvering and impending roll calls. Finally, C-SPAN coverage provides network and local news organizations with abundant footage, facilitating media coverage of Congress.

The changes to the ethics process, tighter restrictions on lobbying, and passage of the Congressional Accountability Act have not significantly improved the public reputation of Congress. Still, the ethics reforms have provided both chambers with higher and more precise standards for official conduct, as well as procedures for curtailing improper conduct within the legislative branch. By most accounts, the incidence of real corruption among members has declined significantly over the past three decades because of the institutional reforms and enhanced scrutiny by the media and the public.[19] And since the adoption of the

Congressional Accountability Act, the issue of congressional compliance with the laws that govern the private sector has largely disappeared from the national political agenda.

It also is instructive to consider an initiative in the area of institutional integrity that often dominated the reform agenda of the 1990s, but was not adopted—term limitations for members of Congress. Term limits supporters claimed that their reform would result in a Congress comprised of citizen legislators more in touch with the needs of ordinary Americans. Their "movement" gained significant momentum during the late 1980s and early 1990s, primarily because of burgeoning public dissatisfaction with Congress, widespread perceptions that Democrats had a virtual lock on majority control of the House, and the coalition-building efforts of outside advocacy groups such as U.S. Term Limits Inc. Opinion polls consistently indicated that 75 percent or more of Americans supported limits on the duration of congressional service. By 1995, twenty-two states had adopted provisions limiting the terms of members of Congress.[20] The movement was delivered a major blow in May of that year, however, when the U.S. Supreme Court (*U.S. Term Limits Inc. v. Thornton*) ruled that state-imposed term limits on the national legislature were unconstitutional. As a result, supporters changed strategies and focused instead on passing a constitutional amendment limiting congressional service, inducing individual candidates to voluntarily limit their terms, and promoting the adoption of limits on the duration of state legislative service.

A proposed constitutional amendment to limit congressional terms was included in the "Contract with America," the House Republican campaign manifesto of 1994. But even with the backing of GOP leaders, efforts to pass a term limits amendment failed repeatedly in Congress because of opposition from most Democrats and many Republicans. These proposals clearly ran afoul of the personal power agendas of incumbent members. Opponents also argued that term limits would reduce the level of expertise in Congress and shift power to unelected staffers, lobbyists, and the executive branch. Moreover, the watershed elections of 1994 demonstrated that the ballot alone can be sufficient to limit congressional service and transfer majority status to a different party. The sizes of the partisan majorities on Capitol Hill also have been relatively small since 1994, further reducing concerns about one-party dominance. Although some candidates for Congress (especially Republicans) continue to embrace voluntary term limits (and a number of them have followed through on the pledge), the issue was not a major factor in the 2002 or 2004 elections.[21]

Committee System

While campaign finance reform and institutional integrity address the occurrence or appearance of corruption in the electoral and legislative arenas, reforms of the committee system shape the distribution of responsibility and power during the crucial prefloor stage of the legislative process. Committee reform efforts are mostly shaped by partisan imperatives, the personal power agendas of individual members, and interest-group lobbying. Concerns about the membership as a whole or the governing capacity of Congress are generally of secondary importance. The public usually pays little attention. When the majority party is unified on policy, partisan imperatives can lead to centralizing reforms aimed at making the committee system more accountable to the majority-party leadership and rank and file. Party leadership effectiveness, however, is much less dependent on jurisdictional boundaries: Personal power agendas and interest-group lobbying take center stage here. As a result, major shifts in committee jurisdictions are very difficult to achieve.

On Capitol Hill, the period extending from the 1920s to the 1960s is generally viewed as an era of "committee government." Most legislative decisions were made in committee and committee recommendations were seldom overturned by the full chamber. Chairmanships were allocated almost entirely by seniority and southern Democrats were disproportionately represented among the ranks of committee leaders because of their longer careers. A conservative coalition of Republicans and southern Democrats often dominated policy making within the committees of Congress. During the 1960s, as the Democratic Caucus became increasingly homogeneous and liberal, reformers within the party took aim at the committee system, which they viewed as the last bastion of the conservative coalition. Outside groups, especially organized labor, also helped build support for reforms that would end conservative domination of the committee system.

The first wave of reform took place in 1971, when House Democrats adopted major changes in the procedures their caucus used for selecting committee chairs. For the first time, nominations for chairmanships would be presented to the Democratic Caucus one panel at a time, rather than as a single slate, and at the request of ten or more members, debate and a separate vote would be conducted on individual nominees. In 1973, the Democratic Caucus further opened up the process of chair selection and also adopted the "Subcommittee Bill of Rights," which institutionalized the role of subcommittees within the House committee system and further limited the autonomy of full committee chairs. The following year, House Democrats transferred the authority to make committee assignments from the conservative-leaning Committee on Ways and Means to the Steering and Policy Committee, a party panel that was more responsive to the liberal caucus majority. The Speaker was given the authority to nominate all Democratic members of the House Rules Committee, and also to refer measures to multiple committees when panel jurisdictions overlap.[22] In December 1974, to drive home the transformation of the Democratic Caucus, the large class of freshmen Democrats (referred to as the "Watergate Babies") used the new procedures to depose three sitting committee chairs.

Taken together, these reforms eroded the seniority norm, made the committee system more responsive to the liberal majority within the Democratic Caucus, and substantially increased the formal prerogatives of the majority leadership. Throughout, liberal Democrats were the primary constituency for reform and the main opponents were senior members concerned about their personal power prerogatives. But many of the changes also had substantial support among the minority Republicans.[23]

It also should be emphasized that the broader committee reform effort was not uniformly successful. In 1973 the Select Committee on Committees, a temporary panel comprised of Democrats and Republicans and chaired by Richard Bolling (D-Mo.), proposed a plan to comprehensively realign committee jurisdictions and implement other changes in the House committee system. Bolling's goal was to enhance the legislative capacity of the chamber by reducing jurisdictional overlaps, consolidating control over key policy areas within single panels, and spreading the workload more equitably across different committees. The realignment plan sparked a political firestorm within the Democratic Caucus. Senior members of the panels targeted to lose jurisdiction staunchly opposed it. The interest groups associated with the targeted committees likewise fought the Bolling proposal. As a result, Democratic leaders referred the plan to a committee of the Democratic Caucus, which in turn recommended a substantially watered-down reform package that did not include a major jurisdictional overhaul. In October 1974, the House endorsed the caucus proposals over the Bolling plan by a 203–165 vote. The members most likely to vote for the more comprehensive reforms tended to be liberals and junior legislators. But Republicans also supported the failed Bolling proposal by a margin of two to one.

Unlike the House, the Senate did adopt major jurisdictional reforms during the 1970s. In March 1976, the chamber established a bipartisan panel to study the Senate committee system and provide recommendations for reform. Chaired by Illinois Democrat Adlai Stevenson, the committee recommended significant jurisdictional changes, a reduction in the number of panels, and limits on the number of assignments per member. The Senate adopted the Stevenson plan by an 89–1 vote in February 1977. Why was the Senate able to significantly reform committee jurisdictions while the Bolling effort failed in the House? There are fewer senators than there are House members and individual senators have a larger "per capita" workload, reducing their reliance on particular committee assignments to pursue their reelection, policy, and power goals. Moreover, since implementation of the "Johnson rule" in 1953, all Senate Democrats have been guaranteed membership on at least one major committee. The lack of a general germaneness requirement in Senate rules and the chamber's reliance on unanimous-consent agreements guarantee that all senators will have ample opportunity to shape legislation on the floor. The bottom line? Jurisdictional reform in the Senate is much less threatening to the personal power prerogatives of senior lawmakers.

Although members of the House and Senate periodically proposed changes to the committee system during the late 1970s and 1980s, the next serious round of reform did not occur until the 1994 takeover by Republicans. Immediately after their astonishing electoral victory, incoming Speaker Newt Gingrich worked with other Republican leaders to craft a package of reforms to be adopted on the opening day of the 104th Congress in January 1995. Many of the reforms were drawn from the preamble to the Contract with America. The proposals were partially intended to foster public perceptions that a Republican majority would be reformist. But the opening day reforms also were crafted to make the committee system and other aspects of chamber operations more accountable to GOP leaders and the Republican Conference as a whole. As was the case with many of the 1970s changes, partisan imperatives were the key motivation behind the Gingrich reforms of 1995.

First, Gingrich informally assumed the power to appoint committee chairs: He bypassed the most senior Republican on three important panels and instead selected more reliable conservatives to wield the gavel. In addition, significant changes were made to party and chamber rules. First, the GOP fulfilled a Contract pledge by abolishing three committees with jurisdictions that primarily were of interest to Democrats. Second, the House Republicans chose not to maintain the 1970s "Subcommittee Bills of Rights" and instead empowered committee chairs to appoint subcommittee chairs and staffs. Third, Republicans abolished proxy voting, a practice by which committee leaders could cast roll calls during markups on behalf of absent colleagues. According to Republican reformers, Democratic chairs had used proxies to increase their leverage over committee decision making at the expense of quality deliberation. Fourth, Republicans significantly reduced the sizes of committee staffs, which in the short-run primarily affected chamber Democrats. Fifth, to reduce infighting between panels over turf, the chamber adopted a rule requiring that the Speaker designate a "primary" committee to take the lead when legislative is multiply referred. Most important, the House adopted six-year limits on the terms of committee and subcommittee chairs. The rule change would have a lasting impact on the balance of power between the majority leadership and the chairs of standing committees. Unlike certain of their Democratic predecessors, Republican chairs would not be able to turn their positions into semi-autonomous fiefdoms by holding the position for a decade or more. As the first round of GOP chairs reached the six-year ceiling in 2002, campaigns broke out between their would-be replacements, who basically auditioned for the role of chair before Republican leaders. Although Speaker Dennis Hastert (R-Ill.) exhibited a much lower public profile than Gingrich, he was able to exert considerably more control over the committee system than had recent Democratic Speakers.

The House Republican reform effort of 1994–95 is also instructive because of what was not accomplished. The morning after the 1994 elections, Gingrich instructed Representative David Dreier (R- Calif.) to develop a plan for realigning jurisdictions that would restructure the House committee system around the policy priorities of the new Republican majority. The plan that Dreier favored would have reduced the number of House panels from 22 to 17, created new committees to reflect the Republican agenda, and dismantled panels that had become power centers for key Democratic constituencies. His proposal was leaked to the press, and it generated strong opposition from senior Republicans on the committees that stood to lose turf. After a brief but intense struggle within the Republican Conference, Gingrich and other GOP leaders backed away from major jurisdictional change and instead endorsed the more modest provisions that the chamber adopted in January 1995. Senate Republicans considered several committee reforms after the November 1994 elections, but the only consequential change was the adoption of six-year term limits for Republican committee leaders. These limits became binding in 2003 and directly led to chairmanship changes on several major panels. The impact of the reform appears to have been less significant in the Senate, however, because decision making within the chamber is much less committee-centered than is the case in the House.

Overall, then, most of the committee reforms that have been adopted in the House since the 1970s were intended to make committee chairs and members more responsive to the policy agenda of the majority leadership and the majority caucus. Indeed, the insular and autonomous panels that comprised the pre-1970s era of committee government are largely absent from the contemporary Congress. Certain of the reforms have had unintended consequences. Granting the Speaker the authority to refer bills to multiple committees, for instance, did give the leadership enhanced flexibility for managing the committee process. But the change also sparked intense competition between panels over turf, which helped complicate the job of Speaker during the 1980s and early 1990s. Still, the committee reforms of the 1970s and 1990s did restrict the ability of individual chairs and panels to derail the policy priorities of the House majority party.

The jurisdictional makeup of the two committee systems continues to be characterized by overlapping responsibilities in key policy areas and dramatically different workloads across panels. Critical issues such as health care, the environment, and international security fall within the jurisdictions of multiple committees. Indeed, the 9/11 Commission reported that fourteen different House committees shared jurisdictional responsibility for the antiterrorism effort. Overlapping jurisdictions create multiple points of access into the legislative process, potentially promoting innovation and openness. But integrating the legislative initiatives of divergent panels into a single, coherent policy can be difficult and the diffuse lines of authority created by murky committee boundaries also complicate efforts to hold individual members and panels responsible for policy failures. The current committee system also fails to tap fully the talents and energies of all members of the House and Senate. High-visibility committees such as Ways and Means have significantly larger workloads than do less prestigious panels like the Committees on Science or Small Business. The Stevenson Committee reforms of the 1970s were a noteworthy step toward streamlining the committee system and consolidating jurisdictions in the Senate. In the House, though, the jurisdictional reforms adopted in recent decades mostly targeted minor committees and fell substantially short of comprehensive change.

Floor Procedure

Floor procedural reforms matter because they affect the distribution of parliamentary rights in the full House and Senate, and thus touch on the vexing normative tradeoff that exists in any legislature between the ability of a majority to advance its agenda and the rights of a determined minority to present alternatives and perhaps influence policy. Here, the politics of reform is primarily driven by partisan imperatives and the personal power agendas of individual members. When the majority party is cohesive and large, members are most likely to adopt floor procedural reforms that rein in the prerogatives of the minority party. When there is a strong cross-partisan coalition of minority-party members and disaffected members of the majority party, on the other hand, changes that increase minority-party rights are especially likely.[24]

Since the 1970s, reforms of House floor procedure often have focused on the role of the Rules Committee, which devises the special rules that structure floor decision-making on bills and resolutions. During the era of committee government, the Committee on Rules was relatively independent of the majority leadership and decision making within the panel often was dominated by members of the conservative coalition. The obstructive potential of the Rules panel became particularly problematic for the Democratic majority with the election of John Kennedy as president in 1960. The new administration hoped to bring a number of progressive initiatives to the floor and feared that the Rules Committee would be obstructionist. As a result, Speaker Sam Rayburn (D-Tex.) facilitated a successful effort in early 1961 to temporarily enlarge the membership of the committee and provide Democratic leaders with an ideological majority. The change was narrowly adopted by a 217–212 margin. Interestingly, support from twenty-two northern Republicans was pivotal to passage, suggesting that the change derived in part from ideological, as well as partisan, motivations. The expansion of the panel was made permanent at the beginning of the next Congress.

As mentioned, one of the most important of the sunshine reforms was the establishment in 1970 of recorded voting during the floor amendment process in the House. In addition to being a major step toward transparency in decision making, the change had significant implications for floor procedure. Following the change, the number of floor amendments increased substantially, rising from 877 in 1969–70 to almost 1,700 in 1977–78.[25] Many of these amendments were proposed by Republicans and were aimed at forcing Democratic members to cast politically difficult votes. In response, Democrats urged their leaders to limit access to the floor via increasingly restrictive amendment rules. The emergence of the Rules Committee as a vehicle for advancing the interests of the majority party was possible because of the 1974 decision in the Democratic Caucus to allow the Speaker to nominate all majority-party members of the panel. (GOP members would later provide their own leaders with similar control over the Republican contingent on the committee.) In 1975–76, 84.3 percent of the special rules recommended by the Rules panel and adopted by the full chamber were essentially open: Any germane amendment was permissible. By 1985–86, however, the proportion of open rules had dropped to 55.4 percent. And by the late 1990s, it was rare for major legislation to be brought to the floor under open amendment procedures. The standard approach was to employ a "structured" rule in which all permissible amendments were identified and debate time strictly controlled. These rules help the majority leadership protect vulnerable coalitions from strategically crafted floor amendments.

As indicated in Table 1, another significant change to House floor procedure was the 1995 reform guaranteeing the right to offer a motion to recommit with instructions to the minority party. House minorities had exercised the right to offer recommital motions (essentially a motion to send a measure back to committee) for about a century, but in the 1980s and 1990s Rules Committee Democrats occasionally blocked the minority from including amendatory instructions in the motion to recommit. While the adoption of a straight motion to recommit effectively kills the underlying measure, the passage of a motion to recommit with instructions results in the measure being modified to incorporate the instructions. Recommital instructions, in other words, provide the minority party with an amending opportunity immediately prior to the vote on final passage. During the early 1990s, House Republicans made a guaranteed right to offer the motion to recommit with instructions one of their central reform demands, and they placed such a guarantee in House rules in January 1995. Why did a cohesive new majority extend an important floor prerogative to the minority party, rather than clamp down on minority rights? For one, the GOP had championed the change for years and would have had difficulties explaining a change of positions. In addition, many Republicans wanted the change in case they returned to minority status in the near future. The GOP was also sufficiently united on policy grounds that there was little chance that Democrats could regularly use amendatory instructions to divide the majority party.

The reforms of Senate floor procedure in Table 1 all relate to the filibuster. There were no limitations on the filibuster (beyond physical endurance) until 1917, when the Senate adopted Rule 22, which enables members to invoke cloture and bring debate to a close. Over time, the number of votes necessary to adopt cloture has been altered from two-thirds of those present and voting (the 1917 level) to two-thirds of the full membership (in 1949) and back to two-thirds of senators present and voting (in 1959). In 1975, the Senate reformed Rule 22 to require that sixty votes are necessary to pass a cloture motion.

The 1975 changes are instructive about the forces that structure efforts to reform floor procedure in the Senate. Rule 22 stipulates that a two-thirds super-majority is necessary to reform the cloture process. As a result, even large and cohesive majority parties will be unable to reform the process without support from the minority side of the aisle. Consequential reform will only occur when the policy priorities of a supermajority of the chamber (including some minority-party members) are impeded by a determined minority *and* the obstructionism is so problematic that the supermajority is willing to alter the procedural rights enjoyed by all senators. In the early 1970s conservative senators used dilatory tactics to block a consumer protection measure and other legislation important to most Democrats and to liberal Republicans, fueling demands for a lower threshold for cloture. Still, the adoption of the 1975 reform only became possible after the presiding officer temporarily ruled that (as with the House) a simple majority of the membership could adopt new standing rules at the beginning of a Congress. A majority of the Senate refused to overturn the ruling, which raised the prospect that significant rule changes—perhaps even an end to the filibuster—might be adopted by fifty-one votes. As a result, the opponents of reform allowed the chamber to vote on a resolution changing the cloture requirement to sixty votes, and it passed by a margin of 56–27. In return, the Senate voted to reverse the ruling permitting a simple majority to rewrite Rule 22.

Rule 22 was amended again in 1979 and in 1986 to restrict the ability of members to engage in dilatory tactics after cloture has been invoked. Both resolutions passed with seventy-eight votes, with opposition primarily coming from conservative Republicans. In recent decades, proposals to alter the cloture rule have sharply divided senators by party, and members of the minority have strongly opposed tighter debate restrictions. Even members of the majority party, however, have been reluctant to significantly clamp down on the right to extended debate. In a 1993 survey, 77.8 percent of Republican senators disagreed with the assertion that "there are too few limitations on debate on the Senate floor." As members of the minority party, we would expect them to oppose further debate limitations. But over one-third of the majority Democrats who responded to the survey agreed with them.[26] Along with partisan imperatives, then, the power prerogatives of individual members are critical for understanding the politics of floor procedural reform in the Senate.

Although the reforms of floor procedure in Table 1 have not fundamentally altered the decision-making process in either chamber, the changes have somewhat reduced the potential for obstructionism on Capitol Hill. Taken together, they have made the legislative process more responsive to the full membership, especially to policy views within the majority party. In the House, the Rules Committee now provides the majority leadership with its most consequential procedural prerogative for advancing the party agenda. In the Senate, the reduction of the threshold for cloture and tighter restrictions on post-cloture dilatory tactics lowered the hurdles for proponents of a bill or nomination to end a filibuster. The benefits from procedural reform have come at a cost on the House side. The increased reliance of House majorities on restrictive amendment procedures reduces the opportunity for partisan minorities (and some members of the majority party) to secure full consideration of their legislative priorities on the floor, which in turn can undermine the quality of deliberation. In the Senate, however, the sixty-vote requirement for invoking cloture still provides political minorities with ample leverage for obstructing the flow of chamber business. Indeed, the incidence of actual obstructionism in the Senate has increased markedly since the cloture reforms of the 1970s and early 1980s.[27]

Congressional Resources and Interbranch Prerogatives

The final category of reform concerns the resources and prerogatives of Congress, especially in relation to the executive branch. Here, our focus is on member access to policy and political expertise and the ability of the legislative branch to participate as a full partner in the formulation of budgetary and foreign policy. During the 1970s, the shared interest among Democrats and Republicans in enhancing congressional capacity produced major reforms aimed at empowering the legislative branch relative to the executive branch. Since that decade, however, such concerns have become a far less significant feature of reform politics, and reform politics in this area has been dominated by public distrust of the legislative branch and the competing agendas of the two political parties.

Consider first the level of staff assistance provided to members and committees. Although congressional staff resources have increased incrementally over time, rather than in spurts due to the adoption of particular reforms, the 1970s was an important period in the growth of legislative branch resources. In 1968 total staff employment within the House and Senate was just under ten thousand individuals. By 1983, the number had almost doubled.[28] Since that year, total House and Senate employment has been stable, with the exception of a decline in the number of House committee aides as a result of the GOP reforms of 1995. The 1970s expansion of staff resources was intended to promote the reelection and policy goals of members and to counter the informational advantages of the executive branch. Beginning in the 1980s, however, the internal resources of the House and Senate became the subject of intense partisan strife. By the end of the decade, the Republicans were regularly offering amendments to the legislative branch appropriations bill and the annual committee funding resolutions aimed at slashing congressional budgets and eliminating member perks. Such efforts were particularly pronounced after the 1991 House bank scandal, which sparked intense public anger about special privileges and waste within the budget for the legislative branch.

In addition to increasing staff resources during the 1970s, the House and Senate transformed the congressional budget process, arguably the most important structural reform of the decade. Prior to the landmark Budget and Impoundment Control Act of 1974, the legislative branch lacked the capacity to effectively engage the executive branch on budget policy. Decisions about spending were made by the appropriations committees, while other panels (Ways and Means in the House and Finance in the Senate) had jurisdiction over taxation. The 1974 Budget Act established mechanisms for coordination across the two jurisdictions. Among other changes, the Budget Act created the House and Senate Budget Committees, the budget resolution and reconciliation procedures, and the Congressional Budget Office, which provides staff expertise to the legislative branch on budgetary matters.

A range of political interests came together to push through the 1974 Budget Act. During the early 1970s, Democrats and many Republicans believed that President Richard Nixon had made improper use of the impoundment prerogative, a tool by which the chief executive can withhold appropriations to avoid unnecessary spending. They backed the 1974 Budget Act in part because it included major restrictions on the president's discretion to impound funds. Democrats also supported budget process reform because they wanted to empower Congress to compete with the Nixon White House for influence over fiscal policy. Conservative Republicans, on the other hand, viewed the new budgetary procedures as a potential tool for fiscal discipline. The Budget Act also was carefully crafted to avoid disturbing the distribution of power within Congress. Existing committee jurisdictions were left intact, and, in the House, the Appropriations and Ways and Means panels were each guaranteed five seats on the Budget Committee. The Budget Act was adopted by lopsided margins of 401–6 in the House and 75–0 in the Senate. The reforms certainly did not put an end to member frustrations over budgetary procedures in Congress. Still, the 1974 changes did provide the legislative branch with the basic mechanisms for coordination and information gathering that are necessary for consequential participation in the formulation of budgetary policy.

The next wave of budget process reform began in 1985 when Congress adopted the Gramm-Rudman-Hollings Act (GRH). That year, the projections were for $200 billion deficits well into the future unless significant changes were made to spending and revenue. The two parties were unable to coalesce around a program for substantially reducing the deficit, and members began looking for procedural fixes. GRH stipulated that, unless Congress met certain targets for deficit reduction through the normal legislative process, automatic spending reductions would be implemented via a process called sequestration. Interest groups did not heavily lobby the measure and the public was not paying much attention. Still, members perceived that a vote against GRH would be difficult to explain in the 1996 elections. Commented Representative Philip Sharp (D-Ind.), "It's the rule of anticipated reactions. The grassroots will be consulted next fall. We all know that."[29] In July 1986 the U.S. Supreme Court ruled that the enforcement provisions in GRH were unconstitutional. In 1987 Congress adopted an amended version of the measure that was consistent with the Court's decision.

The basic concept behind GRH was fundamentally flawed. Large portions of the budget, including Social Security, were exempt from the automatic cuts, and the sequestration process was filled with loopholes that enabled lawmakers to circumvent the intent of the law. In spring 1990 it became apparent that the deficit would soon exceed the GRH targets by almost $100 billion. The Bush administration and congressional leaders commenced "summit" negotiations over the budget, producing what eventually became the Budget Enforcement Act of 1990 (the BEA). In addition to major changes in spending and revenue, the BEA included two key reforms to budgetary procedures; caps on discretionary expenditures and a pay-as-you-go (paygo) requirement in which deficit-increasing changes to entitlements or taxation would have to be offset with spending cuts or tax hikes elsewhere in the budget. Although the broader debate over the BEA created deep fissures between the parties and within the Republican Conference (Newt Gingrich launched an unsuccessful revolt by party conservatives), the procedural reforms were relatively uncontroversial at the time. By most accounts, the BEA reforms turned out to be more effective than was GRH. While GRH attempted to use procedure to force members to cut spending, the BEA rules were intended to lock in and enforce agreements on budget policy that already had been forged.[30] Throughout the 1990s, paygo and the discretionary caps helped promote fiscal discipline in Congress.

Among the reforms included in the 1994 Contract with America was a proposal to provide the president with the authority to veto portions of the appropriations bills passed by Congress. Although the proposal was regularly referred to as the "line item veto," it was actually a form of enhanced rescission. Under the proposal, the president would be able to target aspects of spending bills for reduction or elimination and a two-thirds vote in both the House and Senate would be required to block the proposed cut. The initiative was adopted in March 1996 after a protracted partisan fight. In 1998 the Supreme Court upheld a lower court ruling that the measure was unconstitutional. Although the reform was short lived, it illustrates a remarkable evolution in member attitudes about budget process reform. Whereas the purpose of the 1974 Budget Act had been to strengthen congressional capacity, the item veto was intended to significantly redistribute power over spending from Congress to the president and to play to public perceptions that members of Congress are fiscally irresponsible.

During the 1970s, the House and Senate also took noteworthy steps to shore up their policy-making roles in national security and foreign affairs. Prior to the decade, oversight responsibility over the Central Intelligence Agency fell within the jurisdictions of the House and Senate Committees on Armed Services, as well as the two Appropriations subcommittees on defense. The chairs of these committees were supportive of the U.S. intelligence community and did not believe that extensive oversight in this area was necessary or desirable. As a result of the Watergate affair, however, the inclination of members, the media, and the public to defer to executive branch authority declined sharply. In 1973 the media reported that the CIA had been involved in a military coup against Chilean president Salvadore Allende. And the following year, the *New York Times* revealed that the agency had conducted spying operations against domestic opponents of the Vietnam War.[31] The ensuing outcry among the public and members of Congress led to the creation of temporary investigative committees in both chambers. Among other proposals, the investigatory panel in the Senate recommended the creation of a permanent committee on intelligence to enhance the chamber's ability to monitor U.S. intelligence agencies. The Senate established a permanent "select" committee on intelligence in May 1976 and the House followed suit in July 1977. Although the creation of the intelligence committees consolidated somewhat responsibilities over the issue area on Capitol Hill, the two panels still shared jurisdiction with other committees (e.g., Foreign Relations, Armed Services, and Appropriations) and there continued to be precious little coordination over intelligence matters between the chambers—shortcomings that would be emphasized in the 2004 report of the 9/11 Commission.

The last reform in Table 1 relates to the constitutional responsibilities of Congress over war making. Since December 1941, the Congress has not chosen to make a formal declaration of war prior to U.S. involvement in hostilities abroad, raising concerns that the national legislature has abdicated a core constitutional prerogative to the executive branch. Such concerns were particularly pronounced during the Vietnam era. In November 1973 the Congress passed the War Powers Resolution (WPR) over the veto of President Nixon. The WPR stipulates that, in the absence of a formal declaration of war, the president is expected to (1) consult with Congress prior to placing U.S. troops in harm's way, and (2) submit a report to Congress shortly after military forces have been placed in a hostile situation (or one in which hostilities are imminent). Although the WPR is not primarily a reform of the internal operations of Congress, it clearly was intended to alter the formal procedures through which the legislative branch fulfills a critical function.

The debate over the WPR occurred during a period of intense conflict between the branches over United States' involvement in Southeast Asia. Without seeking congressional consent, Nixon ordered a massive aerial bombardment of Cambodia in December 1972. His actions produced a bipartisan groundswell in the House and Senate for major restrictions on the president's ability to wage war independently of the legislative branch, leading to the adoption of the WPR. Nixon vetoed the measure but was overridden by votes of 75–18 in the Senate and 284–135 in the House. On Capitol Hill, opposition to the WPR came from hawkish supporters of the president and from liberals who believed that the resolution did not go far enough in constraining the executive branch. But for a time, member concerns about the institutional capacity of Congress dominated ideological or partisan differences over the content of foreign policy.

According to most observers, the new procedures have not had their intended effect in the long term. From Nixon onward, presidents have argued that the WPR is an unconstitutional infringement on their prerogatives as commander in chief. In times of international danger, the general inclination among ordinary citizens and legislators in Washington is to support the president, and Congress has been reluctant to use the WPR to restrict or end the many U.S. military interventions that have occurred since 1973 (U.S. involvement in Lebanon in 1983 is an important exception). President George W. Bush requested formal authorization from Congress to use force prior to the U.S. invasion of Iraq in 2003, but his signing statement on the resolution speaks volumes about the efficacy of the WPR: "My request for [the authorization] did not, and my signing of this resolution does not, constitute any change in the long-term position of the executive branch on either the president's constitutional authority to use force to deter, prevent, or respond to aggression or other threats to U.S. interests or the constitutionality of the War Powers Resolution."[32] In other words, Bush requested formal authorization from Congress because of the strategic leverage that it brought him at home and abroad, rather than because of the procedural requirements of the WPR.

Prospects for Reform

The forces for and against congressional reform vary, depending on the broader political context and on the aspect of the national legislature that is targeted for change. Ordinary citizens are deeply skeptical about Congress and public attitudes can be a strong impetus for institutional change. But the potential public constituency for reform is most important in the areas of campaign finance and institutional integrity, which directly relate to popular perceptions that legislators are mostly concerned with personal gain and are out of touch with the needs of average Americans. The reluctance of members to cast votes that might be framed as "antireform" is particularly strong when the inchoate skepticism of citizens has been crystallized and channeled by a scandal or other focusing event.

Advocacy organizations are activated by reform initiatives that directly affect the ability of individual groups to achieve their political and policy goals—especially campaign finance reform and efforts to alter the congressional committee system, but also (to some extent) in the area of institutional integrity. Public interest groups often formulate reform proposals and build outside momentum for reform, and organized labor and other liberal groups helped push through the 1970s changes that curtailed the power of Democratic committee chairs. For the most part, however, the interest group community has been an impediment to the adoption of major changes in congressional operations, especially comprehensive jurisdictional reform.

Partisan imperatives are significant across all areas of reform, and the importance of party has increased markedly since the 1970s. There are sharp disagreements between the parties on campaign finance reform, and although partisan divisions are less pronounced in the area of institutional integrity, linkages between these issues and the public's distrust of Congress make them potential fodder for party position-taking. The House committee reforms of the 1970s and 1990s were intended to make committee chairs more accountable to the majority party, and member preferences about reforms of floor procedure directly relate to whether a legislator is a member of the majority or minority party. Especially since the 1980s, reforms aimed at altering congressional resources or interbranch prerogatives also have divided members along partisan lines.

The personal power agendas of individual members are consequential across the entire reform agenda, but especially matter for campaign finance reform, the committee system, and floor procedure. Efforts to alter the campaign finance system are complicated by the fund-raising and reelection interests of incumbent members, who may support increased competitiveness in general but seldom for themselves. In any effort to reform committee jurisdictions, the primary opponents will be current committee leaders and members of the panels likely to lose turf. In the Senate, even members of the majority party have been reluctant to place further restrictions on the ability of individual lawmakers to use extended debate to promote their personal agendas.

The recent history of congressional reform indicates that the collective interests of the legislative branch usually play second fiddle to more parochial goals, that is, to partisanship or the narrow interests of particular members and constituencies. But the political entrepreneurs who take the lead in reform are motivated (at least in part) by a desire to strengthen the legislative branch. It is difficult to explain the perseverance of a Richard Bolling, David Dreier, or John

McCain without considering such motivations. During the 1970s, staff increases, the Budget Act, the creation of the intelligence committees, and the War Powers Resolution all were intended to strengthen the institution as a whole. In the contemporary era, however, concerns about the institutional capacity of Congress tend to be drowned out by parochialism, partisan infighting, and a public that is highly skeptical about the exercise of congressional power.

What, then, are the prospects for meaningful reform in the foreseeable future? Briefly consider each reform area, beginning with campaign finance. The passage of McCain-Feingold required three Congresses, complex procedural maneuvering, and the construction of a fragile coalition of divergent interests. Simply getting the measure to the floor was a major struggle in both chambers, and the success of the reform effort in 2002 was greatly facilitated by some conveniently timed corporate scandals. It is unlikely that another coalition for major change in the campaign finance system will emerge anytime soon. There is little support among lawmakers or the public for publicly financing congressional campaigns or for other varieties of comprehensive reform. Certain incremental changes aimed at enhancing competitiveness might be achievable. It might be possible to increase the relative importance of small donations by reinstating tax credits for them.[33] Perhaps further subsidies for broadcast time and other campaign activities could be implemented. Such proposals, however, will almost certainly divide members by party and are contrary to the interests of incumbents. During the 2004 campaign, there was a heightened reliance on the Internet for purposes of fund-raising and advertising. The early indications are that use of the Internet facilitates efforts to raise campaign funds from small donors and provides a relatively inexpensive way for candidates to reach voters with their campaign messages. In the end, technical innovations such as Internet campaigning may do more to level the campaign playing field than the most carefully crafted of institutional reforms.[34]

In the area of institutional integrity, it is difficult to imagine how committee meetings and floor proceedings could be opened up any further to sunshine. There also appears to be little momentum for major changes in the laws that regulate the lobbying process. Indeed, in early 2003 Speaker Hastert pushed through a rules change enabling lobbyists to cater meals in member offices, and Majority Leader DeLay endorsed a relaxation of the 1996 gift ban.[35] Incentives may emerge in the next few years for members to make major changes in the congressional ethics process. During the 1980s and 1990s, politically charged ethics investigations were conducted against Speakers James Wright and Newt Gingrich, ending Wright's career and significantly weakening Gingrich. Following dispensation of the Gingrich case, an informal truce emerged between the parties on ethics charges. For a time, members stopped using the code of conduct as a weapon for partisan infighting. But the truce also may have impeded more appropriate applications of the ethics process. Indeed, no ethics cases at all were filed by individual members until June 2004, when retiring Democrat Chris Bell of Texas submitted a 187-page complaint against Tom DeLay.[36] Bell's action may signal a renewal of the partisan use of congressional ethics procedures, potentially creating an opportunity for reforms that would depoliticize the process. In 1993 the Joint Committee on the Organization of Congress proposed that a committee of nonmembers (outside experts to be appointed by the bipartisan congressional leadership) be given responsibility for conducting ethics investigations, rather than continue to rely on sitting members of the House and Senate.[37] Such a change has been endorsed by prominent scholars of the congressional ethics process and might help avert a return to dueling ethics charges by the congressional parties.[38] In 2004 and 2005, however, the House appeared more inclined to weaken, rather than strength, its internal ethics process. Republicans temporarily adopted a party rule change that would have allowed indicted members to maintain their leadership positions in the chamber. The move was intended to benefit Majority Leader DeLay, who was the subject of a financial probe in Texas. Although the change was quickly reversed because of GOP concerns about adverse public perceptions, in February 2005 Speaker Hastert chose not to reappoint Ethics chairman Joel Hefley (R–Colo.), and removed him from the panel altogether, reportedly because of Hefley's aggressive posture toward DeLay on ethics matters.[39]

In the area of floor procedure, there is limited prospect for the adoption of major reforms. Through its control over the Rules Committee, the House majority party already has the procedural leverage it needs to promote the party's policy agenda, and there are no indications of an emergent cross-partisan coalition that could push through reforms to enhance minority-party rights. In the Senate, on the other hand, there is some chance that calls by Republicans for further limitations on floor obstructionism might lead to significant change. With high party polarization and narrow partisan majorities, it is all but certain that the Senate majority party (whether Republican or Democratic) will not be able to secure the two-thirds support necessary to reform Rule 22. But during 2004, Majority Leader Frist threatened to break precedent and employ the "nuclear option," that is, use obscure chamber precedents to implement cloture reform via a majority vote. Early in 2005, it was not clear that a sufficient number of moderate Republicans would support such a move for Frist to garner the fifty votes necessary to prevail (Vice President Cheney could break a tie in favor of the Republicans). Moreover, the nuclear option would almost certainly destroy the working relationships that exist between the two parties, bringing legislative work in the chamber to a standstill. Some senators have endorsed the abolition of anonymous "holds," a practice by which senators can signal to their party leaders that they may filibuster a pending bill or nomination. But the hold is an informal bargaining tactic that is not even referenced in Senate rules. It is unlikely that a rule change would significantly alter how members choose to communicate with their leaders, and proposed reforms of the hold probably will not curb obstructionism in the chamber.

Recent history also suggests that the prospects for reforms to enhance congressional resources and prerogatives are not very good. There is no apparent constituency on Capitol Hill for increasing congressional staff resources. Members of Congress remain deeply divided about budget procedures. Throughout the spring of 2004, action on the year's budget resolution was stymied in both chambers by a dispute over whether to implement paygo procedures à la the BEA. Conservative Republicans opposed the use of paygo on revenue matters, fearing that the rule would jeopardize efforts to make permanent the Bush tax cuts of 2001. Although paygo helped promote budgetary discipline throughout the 1990s, partisan differences over spending and taxation will complicate efforts to implement the procedure or make other significant alterations in the budget process. Similarly, partisan disputes about foreign and defense policy probably will preclude reforms that would clarify interbranch prerogatives over war making.

Finally, consider the committee system, which remains the primary locus for policy work in Congress. The balance of power between committee chairs and party leaders is shaped by the distribution of preferences within the majority caucus and the degree of polarization between the parties. For now, the congressional parties remain internally homogeneous and there is significant polarization between them on the major issues of the day. Absent fundamental changes in the partisan distribution of preferences, there will be little incentive to adopt reforms that would substantially alter committee-party relations.

For a time, the 9/11 terror attacks appeared to create significant momentum to make some important changes to committee jurisdictions. In July 2004 the bipartisan 9/11 Commission unanimously endorsed a wide range of reforms aimed at enhancing the federal government's ability to combat terrorism. Among other proposals, the commission recommended the creation of a joint panel of House members and senators with jurisdiction over intelligence issues, or, alternatively, the establishment of a committee within each chamber with combined authorizations and appropriations authority in the area. The commission also proposed that jurisdiction over homeland security be concentrated in a single committee in the House and Senate and that the two panels be assisted by a bipartisan staff. Restructuring the executive bureaucracy "will not work," the 9/11 report maintained, "if congressional oversight does not change too. Unity of effort in executive management can be lost if it is fractured by divided congressional oversight."[40]

Not surprisingly, the commission's recommendations quickly ran afoul of personal power agendas on Capitol Hill.[41] After joining with Senator Joseph Lieberman (D-Conn.) to introduce legislation embodying the commission recommendations, John McCain predicted that the package "is going to meet with significant institutional resistance because you're going to be removing somebody's turf."[42] As the public's interest in the 9/11 report became apparent and members of the commission pledged to travel the country mobilizing support for reform, President Bush and congressional leaders promised that they would quickly follow up on the recommendations. After overcoming opposition from two committee chairs and conservative elements within the House Republican Conference, the Congress enacted a sweeping overhaul of the intelligence community in December 2004 that included key recommendations of the 9/11 Commission.

The group's recommendations for reforming Congress, however, were largely ignored. The Senate adopted a few minor alterations to the jurisdiction of its Committee on Governmental Affairs in October 2004 and then changed the name of the panel to Homeland Security and Governmental Affairs. In January 2005 the House did create a permanent committee on homeland security, as the 9/11 Commission urged, but the chairs of ten other panels secured commitments from House leaders that they would retain jurisdiction over major elements of homeland security policy. The leaders of the 9/11 Commission expressed disappointment at the meager adjustments in congressional organization: "Until meaningful reform of congressional oversight occurs," they again argued, "our national security will suffer."[43] It remains to be seen, then, whether the most tragic of focusing events, profound concern about the capacity of American governing institutions, and a national consensus favoring change is enough to overcome the more parochial imperatives that so often impede structural reform in Congress.

Notes

1. *The 9/11 Commission Report: Final Report of the National Commission on Terrorist Attacks on the United States* (New York: Norton, 2004), 419.
2. For an argument that changes in committee jurisdictions primarily occur incrementally through the referral decisions of chamber parliamentarians, consult David C. King, *Turf Wars: How Congressional Committees Claim Jurisdiction* (Chicago: University of Chicago Press, 1997). King's assertions about the primacy of precedent for understanding the organizational development of Congress are much less appropriate for other aspects of the institution and for other time periods.
3. Table 1 is far from comprehensive and many noteworthy reforms are not included. But based on the existing scholarly literature and the author's observations as a staff person to a congressional reform panel (Joint Committee on the Organization of Congress, 1992–1993), these changes were particularly consequential.
4. Sarah A. Binder, *Minority Rights, Majority Rule: Partisanship and the Development of Congress* (Cambridge, U.K., and New York: Cambridge University Press, 1997).
5. For arguments that the broader political environment was primarily responsible for the congressional reforms of the 1970s, see Zelizer, *On Capitol Hill;* and Nelson W.

Polsby, *How Congress Evolves: Social Bases of Institutional Change* (New York: Oxford University Press, 2004).

6. The typology of reform imperatives is adapted from Evans and Oleszek, *Congress under Fire.* See also Eric Schickler, *Disjointed Pluralism: Institutional Innovation and the Development of the U.S. Congress* (Princeton, N.J.: Princeton University Press, 2001), 5–12.

7. The best treatment of public attitudes about Congress is John R. Hibbing and Elizabeth Theiss-Morse, *Congress as Public Enemy: Public Attitudes toward American Political Institutions* (Cambridge, U.K., and New York: Cambridge University Press, 1995).

8. For example, see Adler, *Why Congressional Reforms Fail.*

9. One view is that the 1970s wave of institutional change primarily derived from the activities of a broad-based reform coalition that included ideological liberals, organized labor, and public interest groups such as Common Cause and the League of Women Voters. See Zelizer, *On Capitol Hill.* The author's focus here is more on the goals of legislators and the important differences that exist between reform issues.

10. The partisan perspective on congressional organization is closely associated with the research of Rohde, in *Parties and Leaders in the Postreform House;* and Gary Cox and Mathew D. McCubbins, *Legislative Leviathan: Party Government in the House* (Berkeley: University of California Press, 1994).

11. See Lawrence C. Dodd, "Congress and the Quest for Power," in *Congress Reconsidered,* edited by Lawrence C. Dodd and Bruce I. Oppenheimer (New York: Praeger, 1977).

12. See James L. Sundquist, *The Decline and Resurgence of Congress* (Washington, D.C.: Brookings Institution, 1981).

13. The Taft-Hartley Act of 1947, for example, prohibited the direct use of funds from union treasuries for campaign purposes.

14. *Buckley v. Valeo,* 424 U.S. 1 (1976).

15. For a discussion of the effort to bring broadcast coverage to Congress, see Stephen Frantzich and John Sullivan, *The C-SPAN Revolution* (Norman: University of Oklahoma Press, 1996).

16. Marion Clark and Rudy Maxa, "Closed-Session Romance on the Hill," *Washington Post,* May 23, 1976.

17. The Congressional Accountability Act was first adopted as a House Rule in 1994 and then enacted into statute the following year.

18. Prior to passage of the 1995 statute, most lobbyists were able to use loopholes in existing regulations to avoid formally registering with the clerk of the House or the secretary of the Senate.

19. Consult, for example, Norman J. Ornstein, "Prosecutors Must End Their Big Game Hunt of Politicians," *Roll Call,* April 26, 1993, 16.

20. For an overview of the 1990s movement to limit congressional terms, see Evans and Oleszek, *Congress under Fire,* 144–146.

21. The term limits movement has achieved considerable success at the state legislative level. According to U.S. Term Limits, Inc., legislatures in sixteen states were subject to mandatory term limits in 2002 (www.termlimits.org).

22. While the other changes were Democratic Caucus reforms, the multiple-referral authority was adopted by the full chamber and placed in the chamber's standing rules.

23. On the importance of the minority party as a constituency for reform during this period, see Eric Schickler, Eric McGhee, and John Sides, "Remaking the House and Senate: Personal Power, Ideology, and the 1970s Reforms," *Legislative Studies Quarterly* 28, no. 3 (August 2003): 297–332. The most significant committee reforms of the 1970s, however, were accomplished within the House Democratic Caucus, where Republicans obviously had no vote.

24. There is some disagreement among scholars about the factors associated with reforms that alter minority-party rights. For the twentieth century, intraparty preference homogeneity and majority-party size were not as strong a predictor of such changes as was the distance between the median position within the majority party and the median viewpoint within the full chamber, suggesting that ideological concerns rather than partisan imperatives may be primarily responsible for changes in the balance of procedural power between the parties. Overall, the narrative history of the floor procedural reforms in Table 1 is most consistent with the partisan explanation. For background, see Binder, *Minority Rights, Majority Rule;* and Eric Schickler, "Institutional Change in the House of Representatives, 1867–1998," *American Political Science Review* 94 (2000): 267–288.

25. Steven S. Smith, *Call to Order: Floor Politics in the House and Senate* (Washington, D.C.: Brookings Institution, 1989), 15–48. In 1973 the House also provided for electronic voting on the floor, which reduced the time necessary to take a roll call and probably contributed to the 1970s rise in floor amendments.

26. *Organization of the Congress*, Final Report of the Joint Committee on the Organization of Congress, 103rd Congress, 1st sess., 1993, H.Rept. No. 103–413, vol. II, 274.

27. C. Lawrence Evans and Daniel Lipinski, "Obstruction and Leadership in the U.S. Senate," in *Congress Reconsidered,* edited by Lawrence C. Dodd and Bruce I. Oppenheimer, 8th ed. (Washington, D.C.: Congressional Quarterly, 2005).

28. "Background Materials: Supplemental Information Provided to Members of the Joint Committee on the Organization of Congress," 103rd Cong., 2nd sess., 1993, S. Prt. 103–155, 1391–1395.

29. Ibid.

30. Testimony of Robert D. Reischauer before the Joint Committee on the Organization of Congress, 103rd Cong., 1st sess., March 4, 1993, S. Hrg. 103–30, 30–63.

31. Seymour Hersh, "Huge CIA Operation Reported in U.S. against Antiwar Forces," *New York Times,* December 22, 1974, 1.

32. Statement by the President, The White House, October 16, 2002.

33. A tax incentive for small donations was in place prior to passage of the Tax Reform Act of 1986.

34. For an insightful review of the campaign finance reform agenda post–BCRA, including the potential effects of the Internet, see Thomas E. Mann, "Reform Agenda," in *The New Campaign Finance Sourcebook,* edited by Anthony Corrado et al. (Washington, D.C.: Brookings Institute, 2004).

35. Alexander Bolton, "House Ethics Task Force Looking to Tighten Rule on Members' Gifts," *Hill*, October 22, 2003, 3.
36. Sheryl Gay Stolberg, "Complaint against DeLay Ruptures Seven-Year Truce in House," *New York Times*, June 16, 2004, A13. Bell's complaints were later dismissed by the House Ethics Committee.
37. As required by the U.S. Constitution, members of the House and Senate would be responsible for voting on the recommendations of the outside ethics panel, but political calculations likely would make them reluctant to overturn such recommendations.
38. For examples, see Dennis F. Thompson, *Ethics in Congress: From Individual to Institutional Corruption* (Washington, D.C.: Brookings Institution, 1995); and Thomas Mann and Norman Ornstein, *A First Report of the Renewing Congress Project* (Washington, D.C.: American Enterprise Institute and the Brookings Institution, 1992).
39. Mike Allen, "House GOP Leaders Name Loyalist to Replace Ethics Chief," *Washington Post*, February 3, 2005, A1. In January 2005 Republicans also pushed through several rules changes (by a party-line vote) that many observers viewed as weakening the ethics process. One provided that an ethics complaint would be dropped after forty-five days unless the chair and ranking minority member of the Ethics Committee, or the full membership of the panel, agreed that the case should be continued: Alan K. Ota, "No Pat on the Back for GOP as Intraparty Issues Dominate," *Congressional Quarterly Weekly Report*, January 10, 2005, 69–70.
40. *The 9/11 Commission Report*, 420.
41. After the establishment of the Department of Homeland Security in 2002, House Republican leaders created a temporary select panel, gave it authorizing jurisdiction over the department, and charged it with investigating how congressional rules and procedures (as they relate to homeland security) should be altered in the long run. Members of the panel conducted hearings about whether homeland security juris-diction in the House should be consolidated in a new standing committee. There was intense opposition to creating such a panel from the legislators who would lose jurisdiction.
42. Dan Morgan, "Overhaul of Congressional Panels Urged," *Washington Post*, July 23, 2004, A21.
43. Martin Kady, "House Package of Rules for 109th Muddies Homeland Panel's Turf," *Congressional Quarterly Weekly Report*, January 10, 2005, 68–69.

Bibliography

Adler, E. Scott. *Why Congressional Reforms Fail: Reelection and the House Committee System.* Chicago: University of Chicago Press, 2002.

Evans, C. Lawrence, and Walter J. Oleszek. *Congress under Fire: Reform Politics and the Republican Majority.* Boston: Houghton Mifflin, 1997.

Mann, Thomas, and Norman Ornstein. *A First Report of the Renewing Congress Project.* Washington, D.C.: American Enterprise Institute and Brookings Institution, 1992.

Rohde, David W. *Parties and Leaders in the Postreform House.* Chicago: University of Chicago Press, 1991.

Thompson, Dennis F. *Ethics in Congress: From Individual to Institutional Corruption.* Washington, D.C.: Brookings Institution Press.

Zelizer, Julian E. *On Capitol Hill: The Struggle to Reform Congress and Its Consequences, 1948–2000.* New York: Cambridge University Press.

18

CONGRESS AND AMERICAN DEMOCRACY: ASSESSING INSTITUTIONAL PERFORMANCE

Paul J. Quirk and Sarah A. Binder

MERICAN CITIZENS HOLD EXTRAVAGANTLY CONTRA-
dictory views about Congress. They revere the constitutional design of
the federal government and thus strongly and automatically support the
basic structure of Congress. Consistent with that position, they also want
Congress to exercise considerable power; they oppose arrangements that would
call for congressional subordination or deference to the president. But these
same citizens chronically take a dim view of the actual performance of the current Congress, and they emphatically do not trust it to act in the best interests of
the country. They embrace an additional contradiction in their collective opinions of the senators and representatives. They see members of Congress, in general, as self-serving and often corrupt. Yet they hold their own senators and
representatives in high esteem—and eagerly reelect them time after time.[1]

One reason for the contradictory views, we suspect, is that political leaders
and news commentators—absorbed in day-to-day events—rarely take stock of
Congress as an institution of democracy. Regrettably, neither do scholars. But the
essays in this book have done so. In this concluding essay, therefore, we ask: How
and how well does Congress performs its tasks in the constitutional system?
How do its institutional arrangements—laws, rules, structures—shape that performance? And to the extent that Congress itself determines those arrangements, how does it do so? In particular, does Congress devise laws, rules, and
structures with a view toward improving its performance? From a practical
standpoint, we also ask what reforms, if any, would help overcome any deficien-

cies—and whether such reforms are also feasible. We ask, in other words, if a thoughtful citizen were to take an informed, clear-eyed, and consistent view of Congress, what would it be?

Assessing Congressional Performance

Any evaluation of performance needs to make explicit its premises about values and trade-offs. There are to be sure often partisan, ideological, and philosophical disagreements about how Congress should work. For the most part, partisan and ideological differences are extremely instrumental. When Democrats controlled the Senate in the late twentieth century, they advocated reforms that would limit the right to filibuster. When Democrats found themselves in the minority, they strenuously objected to similar proposals by the Republicans. Such situational ethics are not the sole province of the Democrats. Republicans called for significant expansion in the rights of the minority during the forty years of Democratic House rule. Upon gaining the majority in the 1994 elections, Republicans were quick to adopt as their own Democrats' procedural innovations that severely limited the rights of the House minority party.

There are also broader, philosophical disagreements about the ways in which Congress should work, although they play a far smaller role in most controversies about institutional issues. Some people believe in majority rule, and see any restraint as undemocratic. Others place a high value on building broad consensus. Among legislators, however, such dedication to high-minded principles of procedure is exceedingly rare. Between 1917 and 1994, only 6 percent of all senators exercised "procedural purism"—voting consistently either for cloture or against throughout their Senate careers.[2]

In assessing performance, we steer away from short-term partisan perspectives. We try to use premises that, over a long period, have shown broad support. In terms of parliamentary principles, we believe that Congress should strike reasonable balances on certain long-term trade-offs, such as that between minority rights and majority rule. Both chambers should remain open to the possibility of change, meaning that the House and Senate should not eschew major change, even if it moves the Congress in a new direction. We believe Congress should perform well on ideologically neutral grounds: intelligent deliberation of competing policy alternatives, avoidance of extreme disharmony and of obvious manipulation or violation of important rules and traditional practices.

In policy terms, we believe Congress's decisions should promote a reasonable degree of fiscal responsibility. And we also accept the basic premises of the American constitutional system: that it is important to have an active and responsive Congress, and that it must play an independent role. Congress should not allow the nation to go headfirst into war or make large changes in policy simply at the president's discretion. Given an intensely polarized political environment, we cannot claim that our judgments are completely free of political influence. Our aim is at least to avoid any narrow partisanship.

Performance as a Democratic Institution

In this section, we offer an assessment of Congress's performance as a democratic institution, emphasizing the eventful period from the late 1960s to the present. We note that Congress has been successful and effective in many ways. But we also point out what we argue are, from the perspective of most citizens' likely preferences, significant failures. To a great extent, Congress's performance has depended on conditions in other institutions or the political environment—the political parties, the president, interest groups, the media, campaign politics, and various aspects of election outcomes—as well as basic constitutional provisions. But it also reflects Congress's own decisions about institutions and policies.

Constitutional Stability

To begin with, we look at Congress's performance in upholding constitutional stability and widely shared democratic values. The relevant criteria for evaluation are of course often controversial. We thus try to employ relatively broad and tolerant criteria that most citizens would find reasonable.

With respect to constitutional stability, we cannot expect that Congress's structures, practices, and policies should always conform to the language of the Constitution or to the framers' original intent. The framers did not anticipate all the circumstances that American government would face, or the changes that would occur in Americans' values and preferences about public policy. We assume, however, that changes in constitutional interpretation should occur in an orderly manner, with appropriate judicial sanction. Congressional practice should have the benefit of agreement and certainty about the rules of the game.

Apart from constitutional stability, Congress should strike reasonable balances, reflecting national preferences, on various issues of democratic values. It should strike such balances between acting on majority preferences and seeking broader consensus; between individual members' representing their own constituencies and political parties' representing national interests; and between deliberating thoroughly and acting decisively, among other things.

Assessed in these terms, Congress has had major successes and yet also considerable failures. In undoubtedly the single most important success, Congress, along with the rest of the constitutional system, has survived. And the United States has enjoyed more than two hundred years of stable constitutional republican government. In fact, there has never been an important dissident movement whose complaints were directed largely against the structure of Congress, the separation of powers, or other constitutional arrangements. During the Civil War, the Confederate States of America, though sufficiently disaffected to secede from the Union, established a Congress and a presidency similar to those of the United States.

Admirers of the Constitution, however, often make too much of this accomplishment. It has been enormously beneficial. But although the founders had not dared to hope that the Constitution would last longer than a generation or so, such longevity is in fact fairly routine: Most representative democracies in developed societies have also endured, or have changed peacefully, preserving democracy. The transformation of the German Weimar Republic into a Nazi dictatorship was an extraordinary and horrendous exception to the rule.

In any case, the stability achieved has been fairly limited; only certain features of the constitutional plan for Congress have remained operative. Most important among the stable features, the president, the judiciary, and Congress continue to share power and possess "checks and balances" to protect their respective shares; and the president and Congress are still elected independently—even though the specific arrangements for election have changed considerably.

But as Charles Stewart points out in Chapter 1, some of the framers' other expectations for Congress have not worked out. The deviations have produced considerable conflicts and ambiguities. Most dramatic, Congress and the federal government, instead of remaining confined to narrowly drawn "enumerated powers," have become the dominant force in the nation's domestic affairs. There remain disputes about the legitimacy and the limits of this arrangement. In particular, critics challenge its central constitutional basis: that almost everything that happens is somehow related to interstate commerce. Prior to his nomination to the Supreme Court, Judge John G. Roberts Jr. ridiculed a federal environmental action as claiming that "a hapless toad that, for reasons of its own, lives its entire life in California" was part of interstate commerce. Residual uncertainty about congressional authority has induced Congress to favor grants and other intergovernmental approaches rather than direct federal administration in most areas of federal activity. The intergovernmental approach has made domestic programs hard to administer and even harder to change.[3]

The framers' plans were also upended by the rise of political parties and the development of activist presidential leadership. Party interests compromise the framers' intended separation between the branches. And presidential activism shifts the focus of initiative from its intended location in Congress. For the most part, constitutional qualms about these changes were resolved during the nineteenth century. Through most of the twentieth century a stable and legitimate constitutional system obtained with respect to the basic roles of parties and presidents. As we will discuss below, however, issues of constitutional legitimacy have arisen during George W. Bush's administration. A combination of unified party control of government, extremely assertive presidential leadership, and extraordinary ideological coherence and discipline in the congressional Republican Party has raised the specter of Congress becoming a rubber stamp for presidential decisions. Such a development would undermine the rationale for the separation of powers system without necessarily violating any actual provisions of the Constitution.

The framers' notions were upset, even more flagrantly, by mid-twentieth century developments in presidential and congressional practice regarding war.[4] The Constitutional provision that "Congress shall have the power . . . to declare war" was unceremoniously abandoned. Congress stopped making such declarations, while presidents initiated and Congress implicitly supported many armed conflicts. In the aftermath of the Vietnam War, Congress in the War Powers Resolution attempted to restore a substantial portion of its constitutional role. The resolution stipulated an awkward system for timely congressional approval of military action. But no president has recognized the resolution's constitutional validity. As Christopher Deering points out in Chapter 12, since the early 1990s, presidents have sought prior congressional support for planned military action as a matter of political prudence, without acknowledging their obligation to do so. Members of Congress have been in a bind: Even if a majority voted down a proposed action, the president might decide to go ahead with it—and those who voted against it, in the predictable wartime enthusiasm, might be made to look cowardly or "unpatriotic." In short, the country does not have a legitimate and widely accepted constitutional system for fighting wars.

Democratic Procedural Values

Over the long run, Congress has not provided much certainty or stability with regard to balancing democratic procedural values—majoritarianism versus consensualism, individual versus collective representation, or deliberation versus decisive action. In the *Federalist Papers*, Alexander Hamilton, James Madison, and John Jay outlined a relatively concrete vision of how the constitutional system was supposed to work—a vision that generally emphasized consensualism, individual representation, and deliberation.[5] The lesson of congressional history, however, is that the actual functioning of Congress and the legislative process is subject to fundamental transformations. From deferential Whig presidents to imperial ones; and from patronage-wielding party bosses, to baronial committee chairs, to rank-and-file activists, to well-oiled party machines—Congress can have a wide range of central actors.

As Gary Jacobson shows in Chapter 4, the trade-offs Congress makes between individual and collective representation vary with the dominant issues in politics, trends in financing and organizing campaigns, and the technology of campaigning, among other forces. When party labels, programs, and organizations become central to congressional election campaigns, members cleave to their parties in office, and both the concerns of particular states or districts and the judgment of individual members fade in significance. So too do the degree of consensualism and the nature of deliberation in both the House and Senate vary with electoral and partisan circumstances. As we will discuss below, variation in procedural practices have been on display in the contemporary Congress. The current arrangements combine historically unusual degrees of majority domination in the House and minority resistance in the Senate, with sharp conflict over the legitimacy of the practices in each chamber.

In sum, therefore, Congress has not implemented any coherent or even fixed notion of an appropriate legislative process. In the long run, the matter of which procedural values are served, and how effectively, is up for grabs. Indeed, in purporting that anyone could either predict the motivations that would determine decisions or define the specific functional properties of the system, the *Federalist Papers* were essentially misleading.

This indeterminacy of Congress and the constitutional system does not constitute a profound indictment. One could hope for institutions that would provide a more precise and reliable translation of the nation's political values into the design of a legislative process. But an apparent lesson of this experience—and of the experience of other developed democracies—is that a wide range of systems of representative democracy can work reasonably well.

Policymaking

Beyond questions of structure and procedure, the proof of the pudding for a democratic legislature is in public policy. How has Congress performed as a policymaking institution? If anything, public policy is even harder to assess than institutional structures. We settle for making a few broad observations.

The outstanding fact about American public policy is that government plays a significantly smaller role in the economy and society in the United States than in most other developed democracies. It is tempting to explain this difference as the intended effect of the constitutional separation of powers, the fulfillment of the framers' plan. But that explanation is dubious. For a quarter-century, presidents and congressional leaders have been trying to reduce the size of government as much as to expand its role. The separation of powers has probably blocked cutbacks in government at least as much as growth. Congress blocked or constrained presidential cuts in spending and taxes during the administrations of Ronald Reagan, George H. W. Bush, and George W. Bush. The relatively small size of government in the United States probably reflects the country's political values, interest-group structure, and other influences, more than its policymaking institutions.[6]

Whatever the cause, the relatively small role of government has had mixed and controversial effects. By some accounts, it has given the United States an important advantage in international economic competition.[7] For the past several decades, the United States has generally enjoyed more rapid gains in economic productivity and national income than Europe or Japan. This economic strength may reflect the comparatively modest burdens of taxation and regulation in the American economy.

Such advantage has not come without cost. By comparison to the same countries, the United States has more poverty, inferior performance in public schools, larger numbers without health care, and a dramatically larger prison population. One source of poor results in social policy is that the United States bears a far larger burden of national defense than other developed countries—a cost of its dominant role in international affairs. Military expenditures reduce the resources available for domestic needs. Another source may be the constitutional inhibitions on direct federal administration, and the complexities of intergovernmental administration. In the end, we cannot draw pointed conclusions about congressional policymaking from sweeping assessments of national conditions.

It is more helpful to look at performance in relation to particular problems in policymaking. Clearly, the structure of Congress promotes wasteful spending on geographically based programs—so-called pork-barrel spending on items ranging from post offices, to military bases, to certain forms of university research. Congress is the only national legislature in the world whose members are elected both separately from the executive branch and entirely from single-member districts. The distinct interests of states and districts are, therefore, extremely salient in the legislative process. Senators demand allocation formulas that favor their states; representatives, targeted projects for their districts.[8] As Frances Lee shows in Chapter 10, however, members of Congress also have incentives to control such spending, including their desire to make good policy. Congress uses institutional methods, such as barring floor amendments on vulnerable bills or delegating project decisions to administrative agencies, to help do so.[9] To some degree, these methods work. The total of geographic expenditures amounts to a fairly modest percentage of the federal budget. Not all geographic spending is wasted, of course. The wasted portion may be considered a relatively small "cost of doing business" in the American system.

Congress is often accused of catering to narrowly based organized interests —industries, professional groups, labor unions, farm organizations, veterans groups, and so on.[10] Such interests often contribute heavily to political campaigns and are effectively represented by lobbyists. They sometimes mount issue advertising campaigns, targeted to the states and districts of potentially undecided Congress members. In truth, however, the influence of such groups varies considerably.[11] The American tax system is riddled with exemptions, deductions, and credits. The extraordinary numbers and size of such provisions are the distinguishing feature of U.S. tax policy; and many of them represent Congress's doing favors for narrow groups. Special tax provisions are costly to implement and they induce investment in otherwise unproductive efforts to avoid taxes. This abysmal record is not matched, however, in other areas. Federal agriculture programs subsidize farmers heavily and inefficiently. In 1996 a Republican Congress abolished the sixty-year-old subsidies, only to restore them almost immediately. But government subsidies for the volatile agriculture sector are often more generous in other countries.

In other areas, Congress has resisted special interests. Since the 1970s, Congress and federal regulatory agencies have sharply cut back regulatory programs that were designed explicitly to restrain competition in potentially competitive industries, such as banking, airlines, trucking, and telecommunications.[12] These programs were vigorously defended by the protected industries and their labor unions. But Congress has largely vanquished the opposition. Over the long run, Congress has mostly cooperated with the president in resisting industry groups' demands for protection from imports, although even a robust free-trader like George W. Bush advocated protective tariffs for the steel industry in 2002. It appears that political culture and ideology play a role in these outcomes. Congress more readily defers to narrow groups when they ask for smaller government—as with special tax provisions—than when they ask for larger government—as with regulatory protection from competition.

More important than the distortions of geographic spending or interest-group capture, Congress has great difficulty resisting the pressures it faces on issues that are highly salient to the general public or that energize the ideological constituencies of the political parties. As Gary Mucciaroni and Paul Quirk show in a study of congressional debate, Congress is prone to deal with such issues on the basis of inaccurate information, baseless fears, and unrealistic claims.[13] For example, in debating welfare reform in the mid-1990s, members persisted in claiming that welfare encouraged out-of-wedlock births, and cuts in welfare would therefore reduce them. Extensive research had found no relation between welfare policies and such births.[14] Congress passed a welfare reform that even many conservative welfare experts considered reckless. Over the years, Congress has made widely criticized policy choices under pressure from mass constituencies on a range of salient issues—from the environment, to crime, to health care for the aged.

In particular, pressures from mass constituencies have made it difficult for Congress to balance the budget. Since the Reagan tax cut of 1981, the federal budget has been deeply in deficit most years, with substantial improvements in some years and a short-lived surplus in the late 1990s. Although the effects of large, persistent deficits are somewhat controversial, most economists hold that they crowd out private investment and thus reduce long-term economic growth. But reducing deficits requires either raising taxes; cutting spending from popular entitlements and other programs; or both—any of which elicits disfavor from broad constituencies.

Congress, unfortunately, lacks any fixed disposition toward budget deficits. Despite sharp criticism by informed commentators, Congress enacted the deficit-producing Reagan tax cut in 1981. It enacted major deficit-reduction packages in 1983, 1990, 1993, and 1997—when Republicans pushed President Bill Clinton to agree to the first balanced federal budget in three decades. Four years later, at the urging of President George W. Bush, the same congressional party began a tax-cutting binge that soon helped to contribute to projected ten-year deficits of more than $1 trillion.

Although critics sometimes lay the blame for deficits on Congress—presuming the president to be more responsible—in fact Congress generally has stayed close to the president's fiscal recommendations. Massive budget deficits in the United States have been a story of party politics and presidential leadership, rather than institutional deficiencies of Congress. Congress has tried a series of innovations in budgeting rules—from budget cuts that are triggered automatically to a pay-as-you-go rule for tax and spending proposals. But as Eric Patashnik explains in Chapter 13, any such rule can only have a marginal impact. If members of Congress want to enact a noncompliant tax cut, for example, they can override the rule as easily as passing the measure. Laws trump congressional rules. To impose binding constraints on congressional budgeting would require a constitutional amendment.

More broadly, we can evaluate Congress's performance in terms of the frequency with which it reaches agreement with the president on major matters of public concern. As Sarah Binder shows in Chapter 5, such measures of legislative "stalemate" exhibit a good degree of variability over time. During the heady years of the Great Society and its Democratic Congresses, nearly three-quarters of salient issues were addressed with the enactment of major legislation. During the bitter partisanship of the late 1990s when divided government prevailed, over two-thirds of the agenda remained mired in gridlock. As Binder shows, Congress's performance is shaped largely by electoral change: Congress is more prone to deadlock in periods of divided party control, but also in periods of strong ideological polarization. Ideological disagreement between the chambers matters as well, suggesting that assessments of Congressional performance need to consider how bicameral differences affect Congress's capacity for democratic governance.

From this broad and relatively long-term perspective, then, we can neither praise Congress as a policymaking institution, without major qualification, nor bury it. It performs fairly well in some areas, and less well in others. It is hard to say whether the country would be better or worse governed if the framers had opted for, say, a parliamentary system of the kind then emerging in Great Britain. As we will see below, however, developments in the contemporary Congress arguably change the balance.

Policymaking for Elections

No requirement of democratic government is more central than maintaining a free, fair, and competitive electoral process. Another test of Congress's performance as an institution of democracy occurs, therefore, in policymaking for the conduct of national elections. To be sure, Congress has limited leverage over electoral processes—which are run by state governments, contested by candidates and parties, and represented to voters by the media: none of them readily subject to congressional control. In any case, a pertinent bottom line is that few observers in recent years have had much enthusiasm for the conduct of American national elections—and certainly not many Americans.

By and large, Congress has made modest responses to widespread criticisms of the electoral process.[15] Although it has enacted major laws dealing with the financing of election campaigns—including landmark reforms in 1974 and again in 2002—Congress has not put a dent in private financing of political campaigns. Indeed, the Bipartisan Campaign Reform Act (BCRA) of 2002 has only channeled more funds into advertising by private groups. With their lack of accountability, moreover, the groups often outdo the candidates in dishonest and irresponsible appeals.

Congress also has not directly addressed widespread dissatisfaction with the content of campaigns and with their coverage in the media. It obviously cannot, for example, prohibit misrepresentations by candidates or require news organizations to cover issues in depth. But it probably could have a marginal impact on the quality of campaigns by measures such as providing public funds for more useful forms of candidate advertising.

Congress has prompted improvement in one area, election administration. Responding to the vote-counting fiasco in Florida and other states in the 2000 presidential election, Congress in 2002 set federal standards for election administration. It also offered the states modest funds to help meet the standards, and encouraged states to replace punch-card balloting with more reliable electronic voting systems. Despite pre-election alarms about the vulnerability of paperless voting systems, the 2004 national elections came off without major controversy about balloting.

Finally, Congress has made no effort to reverse the long-term decline in the number of competitive elections, primarily in the House. In part, the decline reflects Congress's generous provision of its members with electorally useful perquisites of office—staff, mailings, communications facilities, trips to the district, and so on. In the House, it also reflects the effects of decennial state redistricting plans that have proliferated extremely safe districts. Most of these plans drawn by state legislatures have district boundaries that increase seats for the party in control of the redistricting process or protect incumbents of both parties.

Especially in the South, some redistricting plans, responding to demands by civil rights groups or federal courts, have created districts in which African Americans or Latinos constitute a majority of the voters. These "majority-minority" districts generally elect racial minority members, otherwise a rare occurrence. But they also concentrate Democratic voters to even higher levels: A district that is 60 percent black may be 80 percent Democratic. By doing so, they also often create, ironically, a larger number of reliable Republican districts by "bleaching" surrounding areas of Democratic voters. And they reduce the number of competitive districts. As David Canon shows in Chapter 6, liberal Democratic supporters of racial minorities face a strategic dilemma on the matter of majority-minority districts. Conservative Republicans, on the other hand, are entirely eager to preserve them. In any case, districts with close races have dwindled to a small fraction of the total. Re-election rates have soared in recent years well above 95 percent.

If Congress wanted to ensure more competition in House races, it could impose constraints on the redistricting process—for example, by requiring that districts be drawn by nonpartisan redistricting commissions in each state. With most incumbents of both parties benefiting from partisan redistricting, however, it has shown no interest in doing so.

The sources of Congress's limitations in policymaking for elections are not mysterious. There are constitutional obstacles, powerful opposed constituencies, or a skeptical public standing in the way of effective measures on any of the problems of national elections. In addition, any policy affecting the electoral process likely will benefit one party at the expense of the other or—what is worse, from the standpoint of feasibility—will benefit challengers at the expense of incumbents. Congress comprises five hundred thirty-five winners of recent elections.

From some perspectives, American national elections work well. In the aggregate, they have been competitive, with reasonable chances for either party to control the presidency and, at least, the Senate. (Republican-controlled redistricting after the 2000 census likely ensured a Republican majority in the House, in the absence of a strong Democratic electoral tide, at least until the 2010 redistricting.) But the combination of massive private funding, with apparent potential, at least, for corrupt influence or unfair advantage; uninformative and often scurrilous campaigns; and the lack of competition in House races make it hard to consider the electoral system entirely healthy.

Performance in the Contemporary Congress

By comparison with the long-term record, unfortunately, the contemporary Congress presents considerably greater cause for concern. At bottom, many scholars have cast blame toward exceptionally polarized congressional parties—a condition that has deep roots in economic, political, and demographic trends across the country.[16] Rebirth of two-party competition in the South—dormant since the Civil War—has propelled Republicans to the ideological right and Democrats to the left. Old pockets of liberalism in the Republican Party in the Northeast dried up with the south and westward movement of the party. Similarly, the deep conservative southern base of the Democratic Party has all but disappeared, as the party has solidified its base in the urban cities of the east and west coasts.

It may seem odd that many scholars of American politics bemoan the rise of ideologically polarized parties. Strong political parties—cohesive and disciplined across the branches—were after all heralded by party government scholars under the auspices of the American Political Science Association (APSA) in the mid-twentieth century. *Toward a More Responsible Two-Party System*—a 1950 report of the APSA—was the mantra of scholars like E. E. Schattschneider, who had remarked years earlier that "democracy was unthinkable save in terms of parties."[17] Responsible parties were expected to propose programmatic party agendas, enact them under the leadership of a strong president and unified congressional party, and present their collective records to the voters. In short, government would be held accountable to voters through vigorous and contested elections.

The problem is, as Morris Fiorina has observed, today's cohesive and disciplined parties have not ushered in an era of responsible parties.[18] Ideologically polarized parties have more often found themselves mired in gridlock, and have been prone to adopt measures marked by programmatic inefficiencies.[19] Public approval of Congress—never very high—has dipped to record lows, along with the president's standing. In a June 2005 Gallup opinion poll, nearly 60 percent of those polled disapproved of the way Congress was handling its job.[20] Even more troubling is the perception that partisanship so colors elites' views about policy and politics that independent judgment is rare. As the economist Paul Krugman has argued, "we're not living in the America of the past, where even partisans sometimes changed their views when faced with the facts. Instead, we're living in a country in which there is no longer such a thing as nonpolitical truth."[21]

As the chapters in this volume suggest, the contemporary environment has had harmful effects on many dimensions of congressional performance. We briefly review the range of forces that have shaped politics in the contemporary Congress, and then consider the profound effects that heightened partisan competition and polarization have had on Congress's capacity for democratic governance.

The Electoral Context

The rise in polarization stems from numerous sources, many related to the contours of contemporary congressional elections.[22] By far the most prevalent explanation is based on the electoral realignments that have occurred in the South and Northeast since the 1960s. As David Rohde has elaborated, the mobilization of African American voters on the heels of pivotal voting rights acts in 1965 and again in 1982 fundamentally altered the partisan landscape of the South.[23] By the 1990s, the solid Democratic South had been converted into

Republican territory, with the GOP holding a majority of House districts. As conservative Democrats were replaced by conservative Republicans, the Democratic Party became more liberal. The realignment also reinforced the conservatism of the newly Republican South. Population shifts to the south and west furthered bolstered the ranks of conservative Republicans, as GOP majorities in those states picked up additional seats after reapportionment following the 1990 and 2000 Censuses. Redistricting after the Census and in subsequent years in Texas also improved Republican control in these regions.

Electoral change in the South had repercussions elsewhere, most pronounced in the North and East, which had been the decades-long base of moderate, even liberal, Republicans. The conservative turn of the Republican Party meant that Northeastern Republicans felt increasingly out of place in the GOP. The result has been the gradual, but marked, disappearance of the Republican's moderate wing, with just a handful of districts held by moderate Republicans in the Mid-Atlantic and New England and a coterie of moderate Republican senators.

The polarized electoral coalitions we see today extend beyond elites in both parties. Scholars have detected the polarization of the parties' electoral bases in demographic terms as well as policy attitudes.[24] Whether mass polarization drives or is driven by elite polarization is a matter of debate. In Gary Jacobson's view, congressional candidates began to take more extreme positions in the 1990s. In turn, those signals may have moved the electorate to embrace more polarized policy views.[25] As Morris Fiorina has warned, however, when the electorate is given polarized choices, voters may look more polarized even if their views have remained moderate.[26] Indeed, opinion surveys continue to suggest that most Americans hold relatively moderate views on major issues, even on more contentious matters of social policy. Still, Fiorina and others have detected ample evidence that political activists within each party have moved to the right and to the left, ensuring that the bases of the two parties have polarized along with their elected partisans.

The Policy Context

Perhaps most often noted about the contemporary Congress is the pervasiveness of budget issues. As budget deficits grew in the 1980s, almost all aspects of the policy agenda came to be seen through the prism of the budget. Deficits constrained the scope of policy initiatives that could be attempted, forced legislators to consider the impact of new policy proposals on the budget, and more importantly focused attention on the critical issue of whether and how to reduce the size of government. That of course is the central issue defining and dividing the two parties.

The difficulty of resolving budget issues (particularly in periods of divided government in the 1980s and 1990s) brought party leaders to the center of most budget negotiations, moving most committee chairs to the sidelines. As Christopher Deering and Steven Smith have noted, the centrality of budgeting decisions and the difficulty of the votes they required, encouraged leaders to lean more heavily on procedural tactics that would obscure legislators' responsibility for those tough choices.[27] The rise of thousand-page omnibus bills in the contemporary period—legislative packages rarely read by members before they cast their vote—has been driven in large part by the emergence of budget issues to the forefront of the congressional agenda. The involvement of party leaders in budgeting decisions no doubt reinforces the polarizing character of debates over fiscal policy.

Partisan Competition

Most striking about the partisan landscape since the Republican takeover of Congress in 1994 has been the near parity of the two parties.[28] Republican majorities since 1994 have been consistent, but small, holding on average just over half of House seats. In comparison, Democratic majorities between 1954 and 1994 held on average 60 percent of chamber seats. Senate Republican majorities have been equally slim, averaging just fifty-three seats between the elections in 1994 and 2004—well short of the sixty votes needed to defeat Democratic filibusters. President George W. Bush's electoral margin has also been exceedingly narrow, winning 51.4 percent of the two-party vote in 2004. Given the distribution of the vote across the states, analysts have noted that neither party has an electoral base sufficient to guarantee victory in the next presidential election.

What impact do slim congressional and presidential majorities have on the contemporary Congress? The Republicans' slim hold on majority status reinforces divisions between the two parties: Neither party has an interest in giving the other side a break. The electoral stakes are simply too high to give much ground on political or policy debates. The rise of the so-called permanent campaign—blurring the lines of campaigning and governing—has fueled the parties' incentives to disagree and to reject compromises that might in fact be preferred by the moderate middle.[29] Although the parties have tightly contested both branches since the mid 1990s, the resumption of unified Republican control in 2003 likely accelerated the majority party's "win at all costs" strategies, as Democrats found themselves with fewer tools to block the Republicans' agenda. And as John Hibbing argues in Chapter 16, the public's dissatisfaction with Congress stems in part from the media's coverage of the body as an institution mired in gridlock and motivated by purely partisan and electoral concerns, when important public problems remain unsolved.[30]

Institutional Context

Heightened partisanship and polarized parties in both the House and Senate raise questions about the impact of chamber rules and practices on the emergence of this partisan state of affairs. Given how differently the two chambers distribute power across their membership, we typically think that the House's concentration of procedural power in the hands of the majority party and its leadership must account for that chamber's heightened partisanship. But as Eric Schickler points out in this volume, record levels of party voting have occurred in the Senate as well—a chamber in which power is diffused across the membership and the majority leader has few procedural advantages over other senators.

Still, the House and Senate exhibit very different procedural tendencies, and such differences lead them to different policy choices. As Steven Smith observes in Chapter 9, the Senate's cloture rule, the lack of a germaneness rule, and the prevalence of unanimous consent make unlikely the success of purely partisan strategies, unlike in the House, where institutional reforms in the 1970s detailed by Barbara Sinclair in Chapter 8 have provided a reservoir of procedural advantages for the majority party and its leadership. In contrast, House majority leaders can use their party's control of the Rules Committee to manipulate the floor agenda and to raise the bar against adoption of proposals preferred by the minority party or even by cross-party coalitions.[31] As Donald Wolfensberger, a former staff director for the House Rules Committee during Republican-led Congresses, has observed, Republican majorities have used restrictive rules during consideration of major measures at a higher rate than their Democratic predecessors.[32] Democrats, to be sure, perfected the art of limiting the minority party's participation in chamber proceedings, but Republicans appear to be taking advantage of these inherited practices to further limit full deliberation and consideration of competing ideas.

Performance as a Democratic Institution

How has this partisan and polarized state of affairs affected Congress's performance as an institution of democracy? In contrast to our mixed assessment above of Congress's performance over the last decades of the twentieth century, our conclusions about the contemporary Congress are decidedly more negative. Here, we evaluate Congress on the four central criteria of performance.

CONSTITUTIONAL STABILITY. As the framers made clear in explaining how the branches would be prevented from encroaching on the rights of the others, "the interest of the man must be connected with the constitutional rights of the place."[33] This is where Congress falls short in our estimation: A Republican-controlled Congress has shown extraordinary deference to a Republican president. Charles Shipan notes in Chapter 15 increased scrutiny of the administration during the period of divided government in the late 1990s, but such oversight dropped off precipitously with the election of a Republican president.

Such deference was widely evidenced in Congress's decision in 2002 to give preemptive authority to the president to go to war in Iraq, and afterwards when it became clear that the rationale for going to war was based on faulty evidence and argument. It is indeed possible that Congress's acquiescence to the president —at least after the war had begun if not before—is partially responsible for the poor trajectory of the war at this writing. Had Congress more vigorously challenged the administration's preference for war, perhaps the administration might have felt compelled to devise an exit strategy before going to war. Nor has Congress asserted its considerable powers of oversight to investigate scandals over the treatment of prisoners abroad. The performance of the military and the administration elicited some attention by the Senate after the events of Abu Ghraib prison were exposed, but Republican leaders essentially quashed any such inquiries in the House of Representatives.

Equally troubling has been recent administrations' extreme reluctance to share information with the Congress. During the George W. Bush administration, only Democrats—with rare exception—have cared enough to seek to assert their institution's right to such information. Such debates have affected the course of confirmation battles and numerous other disputes, with Congress rarely if ever succeeding in extracting information its members deem essential to performing their legislative and oversight responsibilities. Expert assessment is that the reluctance to share information has "become the default position in the post Sept. 11 world."[34] Such a position challenges and weakens Congress's ability to assert its constitutional independence and responsibilities.

DEMOCRATIC VALUES. The contemporary Congress has had a notable lack of success in striking appropriate balances on certain conflicts of democratic values, especially those between majority and minority rights, or majoritarian and consensual procedures. Many scholars decried the limitations on minority rights that Democrats placed on Republicans over the latter half of their forty year rule of the House. In our view, today's House majorities outdo the restraints imposed by their Democratic forerunners. They have excluded minority party alternatives during floor debate, limited minority participation in some House committees and conference committees, and bent rules on voting procedures to secure victories on the floor.[35]

Meanwhile, the Senate has had a breakdown in consensus over the rules of the game. The Senate in early 2005 came to the brink of parliamentary warfare over both the rules for consideration of judicial appointments and the legitimate means of changing those rules. Given their sharp differences over the nominees, senators' stands were driven by partisan and policy goals. Lacking amid the acrimony over the "nuclear option"—which would have abandoned two centuries of Senate practice in considering rules changes—was any semblance of collective deliberation over the institutional issues at stake. Leadership devolved to an *ad hoc* "Gang of 14"—an informal coalition of moderates and mavericks that came together to pull the Senate back from the brink. Although defusing the immediate crisis, the solution was temporary—shelving for future consideration the constitutional and institutional disputes that led to the cirsis in the first place.[36] In short, the Senate has been unable either to deliberate collectively about these major issues of procedure or even to reach a stable resolution.

As the findings of the Annenberg Survey of Congressional Staff reveal (see the appendix in this volume), Democrats and Republicans are sharply divided in their assessment of the contemporary Congress; Democrats are indeed alienated. Ninety percent of Democratic respondents said that "the majority party makes decisions regardless of the minority's views." Only one-third of Republicans agreed. By the same token, only one-third of Democrats believed that "the decision making process faithfully follows established procedures," a view endorsed by 79 percent of Republicans.

As suggested above and explored in detail by Gary Jacobson in Chapter 4, the contemporary Congress's commitment to ensuring fair and competitive elections is fairly weak. Contested elections have all but disappeared in recent House elections, leaving only two dozen or so truly competitive House elections. Most other districts are reliably Democratic or Republican, raising doubts about the degree to which elections still provide a mechanism for holding legislators accountable for their performance in office. To be sure, the absence of turnover may represent the hypersensitivity of legislators to the views of their constituencies. Competitive elections may still be sending highly responsive representatives to Washington. In our view, highly responsive representation is more likely when legislators must retain their seats in competitive elections. It seems hard to evaluate Congress's performance on democratic values very highly so long as the life-blood of democracy—free and competitive elections—are too often missing.

POLICYMAKING. Above we offered a mixed assessment of Congress's policy making performance in recent decades. Here, we take a brief look at the records of the most recent Congresses. Although we cannot take the space for thorough discussion, expert commentary points to a variety of problematic tendencies in policymaking. Today's highly partisan state of affairs has left moderate, responsible policy choices in short supply and has done little to temper Congress's appetite for catering to parochial and narrow interests. Ideologically driven parties seem to produce extreme policies, with decisions greased by parochial bargains to buy wavering votes.[37]

Tax cuts in 2001 and 2003 were heavily skewed to upper income taxpayers; energy reform in 2005 created additional tax cuts for innumerable industries; and a landmark expansion of Medicare was enacted in 2003, laden with giveaways to the pharmaceutical industry and other special interests. A farm bill was enacted in 2002, reversing reforms enacted in 1996 that had been heralded as a positive step towards reducing inefficient agricultural subsidies. And just as the Clinton administration had bought critical votes for its North American Free Trade Agreement in 1993 by doling out particularized benefits for hard-hit interests, the Bush administration in 2005 rounded up votes for a Central American pact by doling out parochial favors.[38]

On social policy, congressional Republicans proposed and voted on, with the president's support, a constitutional amendment to ban gay marriage—even though it was given little chance of mustering the necessary two-thirds majority. Congress also devoted time to intervening in end of life decisions for an incapacitated Florida woman. On economic and social policy, majority party leaders cater to the activist base of the party, rather than risking a full airing of policy alternatives that might pull public policy back to the center.

Any evaluation of Congress's recent performance must include its degree of fiscal responsibility, and on this dimension the contemporary Congress scores quite poorly.[39] In nominal terms, the fiscal 2005 budget deficit appears at this writing to be the third largest in the history of the United States.[40] Highly charged ideological divisions between the parties have made it harder for Congress to agree on the budgeting tools required to address today's fiscal challenges and those of the future. Add in Republicans' fervent commitment to tax cuts, and the resulting equation portends ill for fiscal solvency in the years to come. Presidents of both political parties likely will continue to exploit earlier centralizing reforms in the budget process to control outcomes at the expense of Congress's power of the purse.

The contemporary Congress's deficiencies in policymaking are apparent to congressional insiders. In response to the Annenberg Survey, only 39 percent of congressional staff members said that Congress performs well in policymaking. Three-quarters judged that congressional policy decisions are distorted by pressure from special interests. And most Democrats and even some Republicans denied that policies are made through careful discussion and deliberation. Unfortunately, in their view, the truncated deliberation is not yielding efficient action: 91 percent of the respondents agreed that significant policy change is very difficult.

ADAPTATION AND REFORM. What can we conclude from recent Congresses about the institution's contemporary capacity to adapt effectively to social and political change, as well as scandal and calls for reform? How, if at all, has the rise of polarized parties affected the institution's capacity to police itself and to respond to external demands? To take just one example, the uproar over the ethics of House leaders at the start of the 109th Congress in 2005 suggests that partisan and electoral pressures continue to hamper Congress's reform capacities.

The debacle over ethics started in the fall of 2004 when the House Republican Caucus agreed—before reversing itself when confronted with internal dissent and public disgust—that indicted party leaders would not have to step down from their leadership posts.[41] When the House convened to organize in January, a standoff over the chamber's ethics panel ensued. Ignoring the practice of involving the minority party when considering changes to the bipartisan panel, Republicans adopted on a party-line vote three changes to the structure of the ethics panel that would have made it easier for the majority party to limit minority party influence over investigations of member misconduct. Stymied by their inability to organize the panel, Republicans eventually gave in to most of the elements of a compromise floated by Democrats. Still, despite reports of alleged violations of the chamber's ethics standards regarding privately funded travel (by both Democrats and Republicans), there has of this writing been little progress in reviewing these charges and standards. Partisan disputes over the procedures for judging the ethical standards of their colleagues do not bode well for the chamber's ability to respond to demands for improving congressional integrity.

As suggested above in discussing the Senate's brush with the nuclear option, neither the House nor Senate seems capable of debating institutional reforms in an open and deliberative manner. That is, legislators rarely consider the broader repercussions for Congress's institutional capacities when arguing over the rules of the game. As C. Lawrence Evans observes in Chapter 17, this is nothing new: partisan, policy, and electoral motives have been central to episodes of institutional change across its history.[42] Unfortunately, the heightened partisan state of affairs has made deliberation over the rules of the game even more contentious, meaning that bipartisan agreement is even less likely. In the case of the nuclear option, Republicans initially proposed a change in Senate rules to deal with judicial filibusters, but quickly shelved their proposal in favor of the nuclear route—an approach that was sure to inflame Democrats given its disregard for Senate precedents. Republicans made little effort to educate the public on why change was good for the institution, moving promptly instead to a partisan strategy of whipping up organized interests for a fight over the rules. Would Democrats have done the same, if the tides were turned? Probably so. We are pessimistic because the Congress has yet to develop the incentive or means to consider reforms in light of their impact on critical democratic values.

The Dynamics of Congressional Change

Over the long run, how Congress performs as an institution of democracy depends crucially on how it changes. The ultimate question is deceptively simple: Does Congress change with a view toward improving performance—judged by criteria generally accepted by members and citizens? Or, on the other hand, is change driven mainly by narrower goals—as with competing efforts by the two parties or by other groups to increase their power? In that case, there is no expectation of improved performance in any broad sense. Or, finally, as in an efficient political market, is change motivated by narrow goals but constrained by competition to serve broader ones? Of course merely stable performance cannot always be taken for granted. So the real issue sometimes is whether Congress seeks to avoid deterioration.

The academic study of the dynamics of congressional change is just getting underway. Students of Congress at the beginning of the twentieth century detailed episodes of change with great nuance, but such accounts were primarily descriptive; they told us much about the ways in which Congress changed, but not much about why things changed. In recent years, a flurry of scholarship on the politics of institutional change has begun to offer several explanations of why and when Congress attempts or succeeds at reform. The growing consensus is that legislators have multiple motivations—personal, electoral, partisan, ideological, and institutional—and that different motivations typically lead to different sorts of change. As David Rohde notes in Chapter 7, for example, the emergence of a more liberal and younger Democratic party in the 1970s encouraged Democrats to limit the autonomy of committees, which had become bastions of conservative strength. Although we are learning much about past episodes of reform, we know relatively little about the conditions under which one set of motivations might be more or less important than others.

What is striking in reviewing Eric Schickler's survey of institutional change in Chapter 2, C. Lawrence Evans's overview of congressional reform in Chapter 17, and Paul Quirk's analysis of congressional deliberation in Chapter 11 is how infrequently institutional change is premised on its consequence for congressional performance. Legislators avail themselves of principled arguments about the institution and its capacities when arguing in favor of change. But reform efforts designed to improve Congress's performance—say its capacity for informed deliberation—are rare. When performance does become a motivating force behind change, reformers often face resistance from members of their own parties concerned about their loss of power. Bipartisan efforts in 1993 and 1994 to realign committee jurisdictions, for example, met with considerable opposition by members who stood to lose institutional clout by reorganizing committee turf. Even if reformers emerged more often and were better received by their colleagues, the reality of institutional change in Congress would still undermine many of those principled efforts. Despite ample evidence of purposive action, congressional change quite often yields unintended consequences. As Steven Smith notes in Chapter 9, Senate rules that empower individuals are not the product of rational design. The Senate's lax limits on debate are the unintended consequence of an innocent change in Senate rules in 1806. Similarly, landmark budget reforms in 1974 limited debate (preventing a filibuster) on a newly created budget "reconciliation" measure, a measure not intended to have much impact on the budget. But innovations in the use of reconciliation by the

Reagan administration in 1981 altered the importance of reconciliation. Now Congress has at its disposal a powerful tool for enacting controversial budget changes that would otherwise likely be filibustered—a consequence, but not intention, of budget reformers' decisions in 1974.

It seems clear to us that Congress does not change often for the sake of any broad conception of performance. Most change is driven by partisan or group goals, and only rarely do the needs of Congress as an institution come to the fore in episodes of reform. Congress has on occasion succeeded in promoting such reforms, for example, in both 1946 and 1970 when congressional reorganization acts were enacted by Congress and signed into law by the president. Streamlining congressional committees to improve their legislative and oversight capacities (1946) and bolstering the power of subcommittees and their chairs to bring a broader array of legislators into the policy making process (1970) are rare, but important, examples. One consequence of the heightened polarization in the contemporary Congress is the improbability of seeing bicameral and bipartisan reform committees appointed to generate ideas and support for institutional reforms aimed at improving Congress's performance. More likely, improvements in performance will come as the byproduct of other motivations, as new ways of doing business incidentally improve Congress's capacity for democratic governance.

The Future and Reform

We have reached several conclusions about Congress. First, Congress has always had considerable weaknesses, as well as strengths, as an institution of democracy. Second, as a result of historically rare levels of partisan and ideological conflict, along with other developments in American politics, its performance has been on a downward trajectory, with important institutional norms and working arrangements in virtual collapse. And third—unfortunately, under the circumstances—it has very limited capabilities for broadly based deliberation about institutional matters or for institutional reform. Congress, in a word, is in trouble. In this section, we briefly discuss what the future of Congress may hold, and what, if anything, congressional leaders, reformers, or others might usefully attempt to do about it.

Although scholars cannot predict the future, nothing visible on the horizon indicates an impending reversal or even an approaching limit of the trend toward increasing ideological polarization. Historically, party conflict is moderated primarily by the arrival of important issues that cut across party lines.[43] In fact, some of this moderating already occurs in contemporary American politics, as both parties seek support from economically conservative but socially liberal suburbanites, on the one hand, and from economically liberal but socially conservative working-class families, on the other. If either economic or social issues subside in importance in coming years, party polarization will probably become even more severe.

One potential result is increasingly conflictual, unproductive bouts of divided party control of government. With the relative strength of the two parties quite comparable, divided control—especially with a Democratic president and a Republican Congress—is highly likely. In the most recent period of divided control, from 1995 to 2000, President Bill Clinton and the Republican Congress fought a vicious battle over health care reform, ending in stalemate; allowed the federal government to be shut down for several days in a budget impasse; and spent a full year contesting a doomed Republican effort to remove Clinton from office through impeachment. The next round of divided party control—which could follow the 2008 elections—could witness even more destructive conflict. Projecting present trends into the future, American government may lurch from periods of ill-deliberated, ideologically extreme policy, with Congress acting as a rubber stamp for the president, to periods of profound disagreement and acrimony between the branches, with severe gridlock in policymaking.

Promising strategies for reducing polarization are in short supply. As a long-shot strategy, political reformers should look for viable ways to reduce political party and incumbent-politician control of state redistricting processes. Redistricting reform will certainly encounter powerful resistance. Moreover, it may not be possible, even through a nonpartisan process, to design House districts that produce large numbers of competitive seats. To a great extent, large party majorities reflect the increasing economic and social segregation of the society.[44] And in any case, polarization in the Senate is not affected by redistricting. But politicians should not be permitted to design districts to prevent competition, and even a small increase in competitive seats would make Congress more responsive to national trends.

Another possible strategy is to encourage state parties to adopt open primaries —with voters allowed to participate in either party primary regardless of their party registration. If some Democrats vote in a Republican primary election for Congress, a moderate Republican has a better chance of winning. Finally, any method of increasing voter turnout in general elections and especially in primaries will likely raise the proportion of moderate voters. In the end, however, the prospect of adopting reforms that significantly increase the number of moderates in Congress is fairly remote.

The alternative, more realistic approach is to accept that Congress will be deeply partisan for the foreseeable future and seek to improve the functioning of party government. Above all, the two parties need to work out viable understandings on the structural and procedural issues that have produced extraordinary rancor in recent Congresses. For example, they should seek some agreement to limit the majority's use of restrictive rules in House floor action and the minority's use of filibusters and holds in the Senate. Reform of judicial selection procedures, along the lines suggested by Forrest Maltzman in Chapter 14, might also improve the Senate. Unfortunately, neither the House majority nor the Senate minority has much incentive to give up their respective advantages. As the parties continue to become more centralized, it might eventually be possible to negotiate a single agreement to moderate the practices in both chambers.

But another sort of accommodation is more likely: Congress may have to simply recognize that bipartisan cooperation will be minimal, and avoid procedural practices and expectations that require much of it. Members would understand that the mainstream of the majority party will pass its bills in the House, without much real discussion; that sixty senators will be required to pass bills in the Senate; and that business can proceed without comity. Such a Congress would need to look for ways to substitute for some of its traditional capabilities. With committee and floor deliberative processes compromised, the parties would need to strengthen their internal deliberative processes. They should develop larger, more specialized and expert staff, and create more formal and elaborate arrangements for deliberation within the party. Ideally they should expose party deliberations to more publicity and external criticism.

In addition, if a thoroughly partisan Congress is to continue to play its central and constitutional role in what David Mayhew in Chapter 3 calls "the public sphere"—shaping the broader political discourse of the nation—it will have to rely increasingly on the types of actions that individual members or the minority party can take outside of formal congressional processes. For example, if a rubber-stamp majority party refuses to investigate the executive branch, the minority party may have to run its own, unofficial investigations—as it has occasionally done in recent years. Unless a highly partisan Congress can develop new capabilities and restore its constitutionally mandated independence through some of these means, American government and the nation will be diminished.

American citizens have good reason to be proud of Congress, notwithstanding its weaknesses. But they should recognize that a transformation of Congress has been underway for at least two decades. Anyone who is proud of Congress's past performance also has good reason to be concerned about its future. In our view, American leaders and citizens should place high priority on finding workable ways to restore Congress's capacity for democratic governance.

Notes

1. See Hibbing, Chapter 16, and the appendix in this volume.
2. Procedural purism in the Senate is discussed and calculated in Sarah A. Binder and Steven A. Smith, *Politics or Principle? Filibustering in the United States Senate* (Washington, D.C.: Brookings Institution Press, 1997).

3. David Brian Robertson and Dennis Judd, *The Development of American Public Policy: The Structure of Policy Restraint* (Glenview, Ill.: Scott, Foresman, 1989).

4. See Joseph Cooper, "From Congressional to Presidential Preeminence: Power and Politics in Late Nineteenth-Century American and Today," in *Congress Reconsidered*, 8th ed., edited by Lawrence C. Dodd and Bruce I. Oppenheimer (Washington, D.C.: CQ Press, 2005).

5. Garry Wills, ed., *The Federalist Papers*. (New York: Bantam Books, 1982).

6. For a broad recent treatment of American public policy in comparative perspective see, Martin A. Levin and Martin Shapiro, eds. *Transatlantic Policymaking in an Age of Austerity: Diversity and Drift* (Washington, D.C.: Georgetown University Press, 2004).

7. Evelyn Huber and John D. Stephens, *The Development and Crisis of the Welfare State: Parties and Policies in Global Markets* (Chicago: University of Chicago Press, 2001).

8. Bicameral differences on the pork-barrel are explored in France E. Lee and Bruce I. Oppenheimer, *Sizing Up the Senate* (Chicago: University of Chicago Press, 1999).

9. How and why coalition leaders attempt to limit the "traceability" of tough votes is discussed in Douglas Arnold, *The Logic of Congressional Action* (New Haven, Conn.: Yale University Press, 1990).

10. John R. Wright, *Interest Groups and Congress* (New York: Longman, 2003).

11. See Gary Mucciaroni, *Reversal of Fortune: Public Policy and Private Interests* (Washington, D.C.: The Brookings Institution Press, 1995).

12. See Martha Derthick and Paul J. Quirk, *The Politics of Deregulation* (Washington, D.C.: The Brookings Institution Press, 1985).

13. Gary Mucciaroni and Paul J. Quirk, *Deliberative Choices: Debating Public Policy in Congress* (Chicago: University of Chicago Press, forthcoming).

14. On the politics of welfare reform and on the role of policy expertise in formulation of welfare reform in 1996, see R. Kent Weaver, *Ending Welfare as We Know It* (Washington, D.C.: The Brookings Institution Press, 2000).

15. Frank J. Sorauf provides a historical analysis of Congress's efforts campaign finance reform efforts in *Money in American Politics* (Glenview, Ill: Scott, Foresman, 1988). For an overview and analysis of recent campaign finance efforts, see Anthony Corrado, Thomas Mann, Daniel Ortiz, and Trevor Potter, *The New Campaign Finance Sourcebook* (Washington, D.C.: The Brookings Institution Press, 2005).

16. For accounts of recent partisan change, see Nelson Polsby, *How Congress Evolves* (New York: Oxford University Press, 2003); David Lublin, *The Republican South: Democratization and Partisan Change* (Princeton, N.J.: Princeton University Press, 2004), and Earle and Merle Black, *The Rise of Southern Republicans* (Cambridge, Mass.: Harvard University Press, 2002).

17. E. E. Schattschneider, *Party Government* (New York: Farrar and Rinehart, 1942).

18. See Morris P. Fiorina, "Parties as Problem Solvers," in *Promoting the General Welfare: American Democracy and the Political Economy of Government Performance*, edited by Alan Gerber and Eric Patashnik (Washington, D.C.: The Brookings Institution Press, forthcoming).

19. The link between polarization and gridlock is explored in Sarah A. Binder, *Stalemate: Causes and Consequences of Legislative Gridlock* (Washington, D.C.:

Brookings Institution Press, 2003); programmatic inefficiencies are noted in Fiorina, "Parties as Problem Solvers."

20. Gallup poll, conducted June 6–8, 2005. "Poll Track." www.nationaljournal.com.

21. Paul Krugman, "Karl Rove's America," *New York Times*, July 15, 2005.

22. The following discussion draws heavily from the comprehensive review appearing in Steven S. Smith and Jason Roberts, "Procedural Contexts, Party Strategy, and Conditional Party Voting in the U. S. House of Representatives," *American Journal of Political Science* 47 (April 2003), 305–317.

23. See David Rohde, *Parties and Leaders in the Postreform House* (Chicago: University of Chicago Press, 1991).

24. On demographic polarization, see Mark D. Brewer, Marck D. Mariani, and Jeffrey Stonecash, "Northern Democrats and Party Polarization in the U.S. House," *Legislative Studies Quarterly* 27 (2002): 423–444. On issue polarization, see Gary Jacobson, "Party Polarization in National Politics: The Electoral Connection." In *Polarized Politics: The President and the Congress in a Partisan Era*, edited by Jon Bond and Richard Fleisher (Washington, D.C.: Congressional Quarterly Press, 2000).

25. On the relationship between elite and mass polarization, see Edward G. Carmines and James A. Stimson, *Race and the Transformation of American Politics* (Princeton, N.J.: Princeton University Press, 1990), and Marc Hetherington, "Resurgent Mass Partisanship: The Role of Elite Polarization," *American Political Science Review* 95 (September 2001), 619–631.

26. See Morris Fiorina, Jeremy Pope, and Samuel Adams, *Culture Wars? The Myth of a Polarized America* (New York: Longman, 2003).

27. Christopher J. Deering and Steven S. Smith, *Committees in Congress*, 3rd ed. (Washington, D.C.: Congressional Quarterly Press, 1997).

28. Trends in the size of Republican majorities are drawn from Sarah A. Binder, "Ten More Years of Republican Rule?" *Perspectives on Politics* 3 (September 2005), 541–542.

29. See Norman J. Ornstein and Thomas E. Mann, eds., *The Permanent Campaign and Its Future* (Washington, D.C.: AEI Press, 2000).

30. See also John Hibbing and Elizabeth Theiss-Morse, *Congress as Public Enemy* (New York: Cambridge University Press, 1995).

31. See Gary Cox and Mathew McCubbins, *Setting the Agenda* (New York: Cambridge University Press, forthcoming). For an alternative perspective on legislative organization in the House, see Keith Krehbiel, *Information and Legislative Organization* (Ann Arbor: University of Michigan Press, 1991).

32. See Donald Wolfensberger, "A Reality Check on the Republican House Reform Revolution at the Decade Mark." Paper presented at the Woodrow Wilson International Center for Scholars, January 24, 2005. Available at: http://wwics.si .edu/news/docs/repub-rev-essay.pdf.

33. Federalist No. 51, in *The Federalist Papers*, edited by Garry Wills (New York: Bantam Books, 1982).

34. David Nather, "A Rise in 'State Secrets,'" *CQ Weekly*, July 18, 2005, 1958.

35. A detailed account of Republicans' exploitation of House rules and practices in recent years appears in Thomas E. Mann and Norman J. Ornstein, *The Broken*

Congress (New York: Oxford University Press, forthcoming). Manipulation of the vote to pass a landmark expansion of Medicare in 2003 (an episode noted in several chapters in this volume) was not an isolated incident. In July of 2005, Republicans held open the vote for a nearly an additional hour when it appeared that the majority party lacked the votes to pass President Bush's Central American Free Trade Act. Twisting arms and doling out parochial favors secured sufficient votes to eek out a 217–215 winning vote for the administration. On the politics of CAFTA, see Edmund L. Andrews, "House Approves Free Trade Pact," *New York Times*, July 28, 2005.

36. See Alan K. Ota, "Deal on Nominations Has Political Impact," *CQ Today*, May 24, 2005.

37. On the use of pork-barreling to secure general interest legislation, see Diana Evans, *Greasing the Wheels* (New York: Cambridge University Press, 2004).

38. See Susan Ferrechio, "Pelosi Raises Eyebrows Over Deal-Making But Offers No Specifics," *CQ Today*, July 28, 2005.

39. For an analysis of the return of budget deficits, see Allen Schick, "The Deficit That Didn't Just Happen: A Sober Perspective on the Budget," *The Brookings Review* 20 (Spring 2002), 45–48.

40. Stan Collender, "A $300 Billion Deficit Is No Cause for Celebration," *National Journal*, July 12, 2005. Available at: http://www.nationaljournal.com.

41. For an overview of the disputes, see Patrick O'Connor, "Speaker: New Rules Now," *The Hill*, July 28, 2005.

42. See for example Sarah A. Binder, *Minority Rights, Majority Rule,* (New York: Cambridge University Press, 1997) and, Eric Schickler, *Disjointed Pluralism* (Princeton, N.J.: Princeton University Press, 2000).

43. James L. Sundquist, *The Dynamics of a Party System,* revised ed. (Washington, D.C.: Brookings Institution Press, 1983).

44. Bruce I. Oppenheimer, "Deep Red and Blue Congressional Districts: The Causes and Consequences of Declining Party Competitiveness, in *Congress Reconsidered*, 8th ed., edited by Lawrence C. Dodd and Bruce I. Oppenheimer (Washington, D.C.: CQ Press, 2005).

APPENDIX:
HOW CITIZENS AND INSIDERS SEE
CONGRESS: THE ANNENBERG SURVEYS

A S PART OF THE INSTITUTIONS OF AMERICAN DEMO-
cracy Project, the Annenberg Foundation Trust at Sunnylands and The
Annenberg Public Policy Center at the University of Pennsylvania
commissioned a series of surveys of institutional elites and ordinary citizens.
Several chapters in this book employ data from two of the surveys, which were
conducted by Princeton Survey Research Associates International (PSRAI). A
survey of 252 congressional staff—employed in members' offices as chief of staff,
legislative director, legislative assistant, or in an equivalent position—was conducted between August and November 2004. For most of the analyses in this
book, there were 251 usable responses, representing staff of 105 House
Democrats, 31 Senate Democrats, 76 House Republicans, and 39 Senate
Republicans.[1] A nationally representative sample of 1,500 adults living in the
continental United States was interviewed from December 18, 2004 to January
18, 2005. All interviews in both surveys were conducted by telephone. Both surveys were designed by Paul Quirk, Joel Aberbach, Mark Peterson, and Kathleen
Hall Jamieson, with assistance from Mary McIntosh of PSRAI. In addition, several authors of chapters in this volume contributed questions.

Findings of the surveys are presented in several of the chapters. A major purpose of the surveys was to compare insiders' (congressional staff) and ordinary
citizens' views of the performance of Congress. Some highlights of the survey
are presented in Table 1.

TABLE 1

Congressional Staff and General Public Perceptions of the Contemporary Congress

	Congressional Staff			General Public		
	Rep	Dem	All	Rep	Dem	All
Overall assessments						
Congress performs well in making policy decisions	66%	18	39	39	20	30
Trusts Congress to operate in best interests of people	90	62	75	71	49	56
Problems of congressional policymaking						
Significant policy change is extremely difficult	89	92	91	71	61	64
Policies are distorted by pressure from special interests	62	86	75	76	72	73
Policies are distorted by pressure from poorly informed citizens	56	53	55	64	47	54
Policies are based on ideological beliefs rather than evidence	42	90	69	79	75	75
Individual and Institutional Behavior						
General Public				Rep	Dem	All
Members act in people's interests, not own interests				45	44	41
Congressional Staff				Rep	Dem	All
The general public has a good deal of influence				42	23	32
Interest groups have a good deal of influence				49	59	55
The two parties agree often on important matters				36	20	27
The majority party makes decisions regardless of the minority's views				34	90	65
Policy decisions are the result of careful discussion and deliberation				86	38	59
The decision making process faithfully follows established procedures				79	33	54
Congress looks at information quite objectively, rather than distorting it				77	21	46
Proper Role of Congress						
General Public				Rep	Dem	All
Important decisions should be made by Congress, rather than the president or both (volunteered)				40	75	59
Congressional Staff				Rep	Dem	All
If the president believes something should be done about an important national issue, other policymakers should defer to him				43	15	29

Table reports percentage of respondents agreeing with each statement. Question wording of parallel items were designed, as far as possible, to convey the same meaning in language appropriate to each sample. Wordings thus differed between surveys for some items.

Appendix

Notes

1. The sample was designed to include staff members from as many congressional offices as possible (up to 535), with a minimum of 250 respondents. Staff were selected within offices in the order of seniority of their positions, among those listed. The resulting sample of 252 staffers represented 190 distinct members' offices. Several comparisons indicated that respondents who were the second or (in six cases) third respondents from a single office closely resembled the 190 initial respondents. The sample included sufficient numbers from each party in each chamber for meaningful tabulations of percentages. Within each party, the distribution of ideological positions is a reasonable reflection of the distributions among members.

INDEX

Note: Political party and state of members are listed, except for historical legislators, who are only identified by state because of early political party fluidity. Affiliations of contemporary office holders who have switched parties is designated with a slash (as in D/R or R/D).